"This book is comprehensive, practical, up-to-date and well explained and illustrated. Difficult topic areas are presented in an understandable way. The book is a sound guide to GAAP. I highly recommend it."

—MICHAEL GOLDSTEIN, CPA, Chairman of the Board, Toys-R-Us

"The Handbook *is written in a clear, concise manner and the illustrations and examples make it a 'must' for every bookshelf. It is great having all this accounting information in one place!"*

—DAVID GORIN, Partner, Arthur Andersen, LLP

"The GAAP Handbook of Policies and Procedures *is a valuable resource for practicing accountants. The many examples from real life annual reports should be especially helpful."*

—SIMON R. PEARLMAN, Retired Partner, Ernst & Young, LLP

"Highly informative, interesting, well-written, and very practical. It is 'must reading' for corporate financial accountants and practicing CPAs. The illustrations and examples are clear. Everyone in financial accounting should have a copy."

—ADRIAN P. FITZSIMONS, Accounting Consultant

"Succeeding as a financial officer in today's complex global markets requires the ability to apply accounting theory to solve business problems. I have found the GAAP Handbook of Policies and Procedures *to be an invaluable aid in providing the building blocks necessary to enable the controller to become a trusted advisor to senior management. It does this through its comprehensive examples of how accounting and reporting issues can be identified and solved within a practical business environment."*

—JEFFREY SATENSTEIN, Senior Vice President & Controller, Chase Manhattan Bank Global Markets

"The GAAP Handbook of Policies and Procedures *is an excellent source of guidance. It is clearly written, current, and highly comprehensive. I found the explanations, illustrations and examples to be practical and most helpful in my day-to-day operations. The authors make the highly complex areas of accounting unambiguous and discernible. Every accounting practitioner should own a copy of this book."*

—NEIL LEVINE, Vice President of Finance, Audiovox Communications Corporation

"This user-friendly reference tool will well serve both the neophyte and the experienced practitioner. Highly complex areas such as derivative products are clearly explained, with understandable examples and with minimal technical jargon."

—LEON LEBENSBAUM, JD, MBA, CPA, Managing Partner of Lebensbaum and Russo, CPAs

"The book is nothing less than a monumental undertaking and is quite impressive in its scope and application. It will serve as an excellent source of reference for practitioners."

—IRFAN A. BORA, CFO, Hackensack Meadowlands Development Commission

"Interesting, well-written, and an essential reference guide for financial officers of any size organization. This book is comprehensive, detailed, and covers the major areas that can confront accountants on a day-to-day basis. I highly recommend it ..."

—ANDREW C. LUNETTA, CFO, Salex Corporation

"With the current complexity of financial reporting, it is critical for financial executives to find the proper tools to assist them. The GAAP Handbook of Policies and Procedures *should enable CFOs and controllers of public and private companies to research key accounting and reporting issues. This handbook should be on the desktops of all financial executives."*

—STEVEN L. OSDOBY, Controller, Kimco Realty Services

"The GAAP Handbook of Policies and Procedures *... is by far the best one on the market. Everything you need to know is in it. It is explained and illustrated extremely well. I recommend it in the highest possible terms."*

—JOSEPH GIMIGLIANO, Executive, The Purdue Frederick Company

"The GAAP Handbook of Policies and Procedures *is an outstanding publication. We found the* Handbook *to be a useful reference which includes comprehensive summaries of each subject, plus applicable standards, illustrations, and examples. In addition, this useful reference presents carefully thought out responses to everyday questions experienced by our staff. The* GAAP Handbook of Policies and Procedures *has become an invaluable addition to our firm's library."*

—LEE E. KLINGER, Partner, Klinger & Klinger, LLP

GAAP HANDBOOK OF POLICIES AND PROCEDURES, 2001

Joel G. Siegel, Ph.D., CPA

Marc H. Levine, Ph.D., CPA

Anique Qureshi, Ph.D., CPA, CIA

Jae K. Shim, Ph.D.

Prentice Hall

ISSN 1529-0751

This publication is designed to provide accurate and authoritative information in regard to the subject matter covered. It is sold with the understanding that the publisher is not engaged in rendering legal, accounting, or other professional service. If legal advice or other expert assistance is required, the services of a competent professional person should be sought.

—From a Declaration of Principles jointly adopted by
a Committee of the American Bar Association and a Committee of Publishers and Associations.

Printed in the United States of America

10 9 8 7 6 5 4 3 2 1

ISBN 0-13-012417-6

ATTENTION: CORPORATIONS AND SCHOOLS

Prentice Hall books are available at quantity discounts with bulk purchase for educational, business, or sales promotional use. For information, please write to: Prentice Hall Special Sales, 240 Frisch Court, Paramus, NJ 07652. Please supply: title of book, ISBN, quantity, how the book will be used, date needed.

PRENTICE HALL
Paramus, New Jersey 07652

http://www.phdirect.com

DEDICATION to

Luis Gonzalez,
an exceptionally outstanding editor
Roberta M. Siegel,
loving wife, colleague, and partner
Carol Levine,
dedicated wife and friend
Reva and Daniel Levine,
loving children
Tessie Levine,
my dear mother
Shaheen Qureshi,
loving and devoted wife
Mohammad Rafique Quereshi and Zakia Qureshi,
loving parents
Aamera N. Ahmed, Uzma Qureshi, and Jawad Qureshi,
wonderful sisters and brother
Chung Shim,
dedicated wife

ABOUT THE AUTHORS

JOEL G. SIEGEL, Ph.D., CPA, is a self-employed certified public accountant and professor of accounting at Queens College of the City University of New York. He was previously employed by Coopers and Lybrand, CPAs, and Arthur Andersen, CPAs. Dr. Siegel has acted as a consultant in accounting to many organizations, including Citicorp, International Telephone and Telegraph, United Technologies, American Institute of CPAs, and Person-Wolinsky Associates. Dr. Siegel is the author of 60 books and 250 articles on accounting topics. His books have been published by Prentice Hall, Richard Irwin, McGraw-Hill, Probus, Macmillan, Harper and Row, John Wiley, International Publishing, Barron's, Glenlake, American Management Association, and the American Institute of CPAs. His articles have been published in many accounting and financial journals, including *Financial Executive, The CPA Journal, Financial Analysts Journal, Practical Accountant, National Public Accountant, The Ohio Public Accountant, Massachusetts CPA Review, Michigan CPA, Virginia Accountant Quarterly, Today's CPA* (Texas Society of CPAs), *Delaware CPA,* and the *Journal of Corporate Accounting and Finance.* Dr. Siegel was the recipient of the Outstanding Educator of America Award. He is listed in *Who's Where Among Writers* and *Who's Who in the World.* He has served as chairperson of the National Oversight Board.

MARC H. LEVINE, Ph.D., CPA, is a financial accounting consultant and professor of accounting at Queens College. Dr. Levine was previously associated with Deloitte and Touche, CPAs. He has authored three books, including one for Warren, Gorham and Lamont. He has authored many professional articles in *The CPA Journal, Practical Accountant, National Public Accountant, Michigan CPA, Journal of Corporate Accounting, Accountants Record, Massachusetts CPA Review, Virginia Accountant Quarterly, Cost and Management, Management Accountant,* and *The Accountant.*

ANIQUE A. QURESHI, Ph.D., CPA, CIA, is a consultant in accounting and associate professor of accounting at Queens College. Dr. Qureshi has contributed chapters to books published by Prentice Hall and McGraw-Hill. His articles have appeared in *The CPA Journal, National Public Accountant, Management Accountant,* and *Internal Auditing.* He has made presentations at the American Accounting Association.

JAE K. SHIM, Ph.D., is an accounting consultant to several companies and professor of accounting at California State University, Long Beach. He received his Ph.D. from the University of California at Berkeley. Dr. Shim has 40 books to his credit and has published over 50 articles in accounting and financial journals, including *The CPA Journal, Advances in Accounting, International Accountant,* and *Financial Management.*

WHAT THIS BOOK WILL DO FOR YOU

The *GAAP Handbook of Policies and Procedures* is a valuable reference in applying generally accepted accounting principles (GAAP) in practice. It can be used by either a certified public accountant (CPA) in the performance of his or her accounting and advisory functions to clients, or by accountants responsible for the accounting policies and procedures of a business entity. It also provides guidance in resolving any issues and problems that the accountant might be faced with day to day in applying GAAP. The book helps the professional accountant in determining what to look for, what to watch out for, what to do, and how to do it.

This volume will become an essential reference in assisting you in dealing with the complex, ever changing world of financial accounting. It provides many rules of thumb to guide you in evaluating and solving the problems of accounting and disclosure that a CPA encounters on the job. This is a practical, real-life, comprehensive, and useful working book. Its content includes informative rules, policies, and procedures applicable to public accountants at any level working for CPA firms and to private accountants working for large, medium, or small businesses. It may also be used as a training medium. The uses of this book are as varied as the topics presented.

This practical reference contains all of the important authoritative pronouncements on GAAP and is the most up-to-date source of such pronouncements. The GAAP pronouncements include Financial Accounting Standards Board (FASB) statements, interpretations, technical bulletins, and concepts as well as the unsuperceded GAAP of the American Institute of CPAs (AICPA). This includes the Accounting Principles Board opinions, accounting research bulletins, and statements of position. Securities and Exchange Financial Reporting Releases are also covered when appropriate. Specialized industry accounting principles are included. Consideration is also given to Emerging Issues Task Force Consensus Summaries and future developments in GAAP, such as FASB exposure drafts and proposed interpretations.

This volume contains accounting principles, financial reporting presentation requirements, required and recommended disclosures, and specialized accounting topics to keep you on the forefront of GAAP. It avails you of instant answers to any accounting application question you may have in the course of your work and allows you to perform your duties correctly, productively, and successfully.

The book is comprehensive and detailed, so each topic is presented thoroughly. It includes examples, tables, exhibits, and practice aids to show how GAAP is practically applied. The book is clear, understandable, concise, current, and user friendly. The material is presented in a logical, sequential order to aid reader comprehension.

The book is a valuable reference tool, with guidelines, checklists, diagrams, illustrations, step-by-step instructions, and practical applications. Complex accounting issues are simplified. In some cases, flowcharts are presented to explain in clearer terms the practitioner's decision process in applying a pronouncement. In some cases, for explanatory purposes, references including footnotes from annual reports are presented. Keep this book handy for easy reference and daily use.

In conclusion, the book explains and evaluates in easy-to-read terms promulgated GAAP. It analyzes how to apply GAAP to everyday business situations. The focus of this book is on the accounting practitioner working for a CPA firm rendering accounting and audit services to clients, the corporate accountant applying accounting rules and standards, and the CPA candidate whose future goals include a career in financial accounting.

Joel G. Siegel, Ph.D., CPA
Marc H. Levine, Ph.D., CPA
Anique Qureshi, Ph.D., CPA, CIA
Jae K. Shim, Ph.D.

ACKNOWLEDGMENTS

We express our deep gratitude and thanks to Luis Gonzalez for his outstanding editorial advice and assistance on this project. We appreciate his valuable contribution. In addition, we thank Roberta M. Siegel for her invaluable input and editorial review.

CONTENTS

xiii

3 BALANCE SHEET REPORTING AND DISCLOSURES: ASSETS   *145*

4 BALANCE SHEET PRESENTATION AND DISCLOSURES: LIABILITIES   *223*

12 CONSOLIDATION   587

13 LEASES   643

14 PENSION PLANS AND OTHER POSTRETIREMENT BENEFIT PLANS *707*

15 INCOME TAX ACCOUNTING   *783*

PART III
FOREIGN OPERATIONS AND DERIVATIVE INSTRUMENTS

16 FOREIGN CURRENCY TRANSLATION AND TRANSACTIONS   *833*

Part

FINANCIAL STATEMENTS

Financial Statement Reporting: Reporting, Presentation, and Disclosures for the Income Statement

This chapter discusses the format of the income statement, major income statement categories, extraordinary and nonrecurring items, discontinued operations, research and development costs, deferred compensation arrangements, compensation expense arising under a stock option plan, insurance costs, and earnings per share calculation.

Authoritative generally accepted accounting principles for preparing the income statement are found in the American Institute of CPAs' Accounting Principles Board Opinion Number 30 (*Reporting the Results of Operations*). The income statement segregates between continuing operations and discontinued operations.

REVENUE, EXPENSES, GAINS, AND LOSSES

The four major components of an income statement, according to Statement of Financial Accounting Concepts (SFAC) No. 6, *Elements of Financial Statements*, are revenues, expenses, gains, and losses.

- *Revenues:* Actual or expected inflows of cash or other assets or reductions in liabilities resulting from producing, delivering, or providing goods or services constituting an entity's major or central operations

- *Expenses:* Actual or expected outflows of cash or other assets or incurrences of liabilities resulting from producing, delivering, or providing goods or services constituting an entity's major or central operations

- *Gains:* Increases in equity or net assets from peripheral or incidental activities of an entity and from all other transactions except those resulting from revenues or investments by shareholders or owners

- *Losses:* Decreases in equity or net assets from peripheral or incidental activities of an entity and from all other transactions except those resulting from expenses or distributions to shareholders or owners

Revenues

Revenue is recognized when

- it is *realized* or *realizable* (goods or services are converted or convertible to cash or claims to cash or receivables), *and*

- it is earned (the earning process is complete or virtually complete when the entity has substantially completed what it must do to receive the benefits represented by the revenues).

Revenue from selling products is usually recognized on the date of delivery of goods to customers. Revenue from services performed is usually recognized when the services have been rendered and are billable. Revenue is usually recognized at point of delivery; however, problems can sometimes occur when trying to implement it.

Sales with Buyback Agreements

No sale is recognized when a company sells a product in one accounting period and agrees to buy it back in the next accounting period at a set price which includes not only the cost of inventory but also related holding costs. While the legal title may transfer in such a transaction, the economic substance of the transaction is to leave the risk with the seller, and hence no sale is recognized.

Sales when Right of Return Exists

When a company experiences a high rate of return, it may be necessary to delay reporting sales until the right of return has substantially expired. The right of return may either be specified in a contract or it may be a customary business practice involving "guaranteed sales" or consignments. Three methods are generally used to record sales when the right of return exists. First, the company may decide not to record any sale until the right of return has substantially expired. Second, the company may record the sale and estimated future returns. Finally, the company may record the sale and accounting for returns as they occur. According to FASB Statement No. 48, *Revenue Recognition When Right of Return Exists,* the company may recognize revenue at the time of sale only if *all* of the following six conditions are satisfied:

1. The price is fixed or determinable at the date of sale.
2. The obligation of the buyer to pay the seller is not contingent on resale of the product, or the buyer has paid the seller.
3. Theft or other damage to the product would not affect the buyer's obligation to the seller.
4. The product being acquired by the buyer for resale has economic substance apart from that provided by the seller.
5. Seller does not have significant future obligations to assist directly in the resale of the product by the buyer.
6. Future returns can be reasonably estimated.

While revenue is generally recognized at the delivery date, under certain circumstances revenue may be recognized before the completion and delivery, such as in long-term construction contracts. Two different methods have been used for recognizing revenues from long-term contracts. Under the *percentage-of-completion method,* revenues are recognized based on the progress of construction. The *completed contract method* recognizes revenue only when the contract is complete.

Expenses

Expenses are generally recognized when incurred. Expenses are "matched" against revenues and should be recorded in the same accounting period. Expenses that benefit several periods, such as depreciation, should be allocated systematically over relevant periods.

Gains and Losses

Gains and losses do not involve an earning process and are typically recognized at the time of sale of assets, at disposition of liabilities, or when the price of certain assets changes. Gains or losses may also result from environmental factors, such as damage by fire, flood, or earthquake.

INCOME STATEMENT PRESENTATION BEFORE INCOME FROM CONTINUING OPERATIONS

There are two generally accepted formats for preparing the income statement: the single-step format and the multistep format. The single-step format contains just two sections: Revenues Minus Expenses Equals Net Income. The revenue section includes sales revenue, interest income, gains, and all other types of revenues. The expense section includes cost of goods sold, selling and administrative expenses, interest expense, losses, and taxes. The single-step format does not emphasize any one type of revenue or expense. Potential problems with classifying revenues and expenses are thus eliminated. An example of a single-step income statement is shown in Figure 1–1.

A multistep income statement is used when one wants to emphasize certain sections and relationships. It contains separate sections for operating and nonoperating activities. Expenses are also classified by functions,

XYZ Company
Income Statement
For the Year Ended December 31, 2001

REVENUES

Net sales	$ 3,000,000	
Interest income	120,000	
Dividend income	45,000	
Rental income	36,000	
Gain on sale	150,500	
Total revenues		$ 3,351,500

EXPENSES

Cost of goods sold	$ 2,000,000	
Selling expenses	700,000	
Administrative expenses	250,000	
Interest expenses	65,000	
Loss on disposal	55,000	
Income tax expense	110,500	
Total expenses		3,180,500
NET INCOME		$ 171,000
EARNINGS PER SHARE (500,000 shares)		$ .34

Figure 1–1: *Example of Single-Step Income Statement*

such as merchandising or manufacturing (cost of goods sold), selling, and administration.

It is acceptable to combine the statement of income with the statement of retained earnings to produce a combined Statement of Income and Retained Earnings. The first part of the statement may be prepared using either the single-step or the multistep approach to derive net income. The beginning balance of retained earnings is added to net income. Dividends declared are deducted to arrive at ending retained earnings. An example of a combined Statement of Income and Retained Earnings using a multistep approach is shown in Figure 1–2.

XYZ Company
Combined Statement of Income and Retained Earnings
For the Year Ended December 31, 2001

REVENUES

Sales		$ 5,000,000
Less: Sales returns and allowances	$ 670,000	
Sales discounts	95,000	
Net sales		4,235,000

COST OF GOODS SOLD

Beginning inventory	$ 620,000	
Plus: Net purchases	1,300,000	
Merchandise available for sale	$1,920,000	
Less: Ending inventory	435,000	
Cost of goods sold		1,485,000
Gross profit		$ 2,750,000

OPERATING EXPENSES

Selling expenses		
Advertising	$ 35,000	
Rent	150,000	
Travel	87,000	
Sales salaries	320,000	
Depreciation	120,000	
Utilities	77,000	
Commissions	150,000	
Total selling expenses		939,000

ADMINISTRATIVE EXPENSES

Legal expenses	$ 215,000	
Professional expenses	125,000	
Insurance	83,000	
Supplies	62,000	
Officers' salaries	250,000	
Miscellaneous office expenses	35,000	
Total administrative expenses		770,000

INCOME FROM OPERATIONS $ 1,041,000

OTHER REVENUES AND GAINS

Interest income	$ 370,000	
Dividend income	425,000	
Rental income	325,000	
Gain on sale	175,000	
Total		1,295,000
		$ 2,336,000

OTHER EXPENSES AND LOSSES

Interest expenses	$ 400,000	
Loss on disposal	395,000	
Total		$ 795,000
INCOME BEFORE TAXES		$ 1,541,000
Income tax expense (30%)		462,300
NET INCOME		$ 1,078,700
Beginning Retained Earnings		800,000
		$ 1,878,700
Less: Cash dividends declared & paid		650,000
Ending Retained Earnings		$ 1,228,700
EARNINGS PER SHARE (500,000 shares)		$ 2.16

Figure 1–2: *Combined Statement of Income and Retained Earnings Using the Multi-step Approach*

INCOME STATEMENT PRESENTATION STARTING WITH INCOME FROM CONTINUING OPERATIONS

The income statement is shown in the following form beginning with income from continuing operations:

Income from continuing operations before tax

Less: Tax provision

Income from continuing operations after tax

Discontinued operations:

  Income from discontinued operations (net of tax)

  Loss or gain on disposal of a division (net of tax)

Income before extraordinary items and cumulative effect

Extraordinary items (net of tax)

Cumulative effect of a change in accounting principle (net of tax)

Net income

Each of the preceding components also presents earnings per share. **Note:** Equity in earnings of investees must be presented separately.

COMPREHENSIVE INCOME

Financial Accounting Standards Board Statement Number 130 (*Reporting Comprehensive Income*) requires companies (including investment companies) to report comprehensive income and its components in a complete set of financial statements. (The pronouncement does not apply to nonprofit entities.) FASB Statement Number 130 retains the present reporting requirements for net income, including its major components (e.g., income from continuing operations, income from discontinued operations, extraordinary items, cumulative effect of a change in accounting principle), but it considers net income a major element of comprehensive income. A restatement of prior years' financial statements is required when presented for comparative purposes.

Comprehensive income refers to the change in equity (net assets) arising from either transactions or other occurrences with nonowners. Excluded are investments and withdrawals by owners. Hence, a synonym for comprehensive income is total nonowner changes in equity. Comprehensive income consists of two components: net income and other comprehensive income. Other comprehensive income applies to all items of comprehensive income excluding net income. Thus, net income plus other comprehensive income equals total comprehensive income. Other comprehensive income includes the following:

- Foreign currency items, including translation gains and losses, and gains and losses on foreign currency transactions designated as hedges of a net investment in a foreign entity
- Holding losses or gains on available-for-sale securities
- Excess of additional pension liability over unamortized (unrecognized) prior service cost
- Changes in market value of a futures contract that is a hedge of an asset reported at fair values

FASB Statement Number 130 provides flexibility on how comprehensive income may be presented in the financial statements. There are three acceptable options of reporting other comprehensive income and its components as follows:

1. Below the net income figure in the income statement, or

2. In a separate statement of comprehensive income starting with net income, or

3. In a statement of changes in equity as long as such statement is presented as a primary financial statement. It cannot just be in the footnotes.

Options 1 and 2 are termed income-statement-type formats, while option 3 is termed a statement-of-changes-in-equity format. FASB Statement Number 130 encourages reporting under options 1 and 2.

A sample presentation under option 1 within the income statement follows:

Statement of Income and Comprehensive Income

Net income		$800,000
Other comprehensive income:		
Foreign currency translation gain	$40,000	
Unrealized loss on available-for-sale securities	(5,000)	
Excess of additional pension liability over unamortized prior service cost	(3,000)	32,000
Total comprehensive income		$832,000

Under option 2, in which a separate statement of comprehensive income is prepared, the reporting follows:

Income Statement

Net income	$800,000

Statement of Comprehensive Income

Net income		$800,000
Other comprehensive income:		
Foreign currency translation gain	$40,000	
Unrealized loss on available-for- sale securities	(5,000)	
Excess of additional pension liability over unamortized prior service cost	(3,000)	32,000
Total comprehensive income		$832,000

Under option 3 comprehensive income and its components are presented in the comprehensive income column as part of the statement of changes in equity. An illustrative format of the comprehensive income column follows:

COMPREHENSIVE INCOME:

Net income		xx
Other comprehensive income:		
Foreign currency translation loss or gain	xx	
Unrealized loss or gain on available-for- sale securities	xx	
Excess of additional pension liability over unamortized prior service cost	(xx)	xx
Total comprehensive income		xx

In the stockholders' equity section, accumulated other comprehensive income is presented as one amount for all items or listed for each component separately.

The elements of other comprehensive income for the year may be presented on either a net of tax basis or on a before tax basis, with one amount for the tax effect of all the items of other comprehensive income.

A reclassification adjustment may be needed so as not to double count items reported in net income for the current year which have also been taken into account as part of other comprehensive income in a prior year. An example is the realized gain on an available-for-sale security sold in the current year when an unrealized (holding) gain was also included in other comprehensive income in a prior year. Besides an available-for-sale security, reclassification adjustments may apply to foreign currency translation. However, reclassification adjustments do not apply to the account "excess of additional pension liability over unamortized prior service cost" (minimum pension liability adjustment). The reclassification adjustment associated with foreign exchange translation only applies to translation gains and losses realized from the sale or liquidation of an investment in a foreign entity.

The presentation of reclassification adjustments may be shown with other comprehensive income or in a footnote. The reclassification adjustment may be presented on a gross or net basis (except the minimum pension liability adjustment must be shown on a net basis).

EXAMPLE

On January 1, 19X1, a company bought 1,000 shares of available-for-sale securities having a market price per share of $100. On December 31, 19X1, the available-for-sale securities had a market price of $150 per share. On January 1, 19X2, the securities were sold at a market price of $130. The tax rate is 30%.

The unrealized gain or loss included in other comprehensive income is computed as follows:

	Before Tax	Tax Effect at 30%	Net of Tax
19X1 (1000 × $50*)	$50,000	$15,000	$35,000
19X2 (1000 × $20**)	(20,000)	(6,000)	(14,000)
Total Gain	$30,000	$9,000	$21,000

*$150 − $100 = $50
**$150 − $130 = $20

The presentation in the income statement for 19X1 and 19X2 follows:

	19X1	19X2
Net income		
Gross realized gains in available-for-sale securities		$30,000
Tax expense		9,000
Net realized gain		$21,000
Other comprehensive income:		
Unrealized gain or loss after tax	$30,000	(9,000)
Reclassification adjustment net of tax		(21,000)
Net gain included in other comprehensive income	$30,000	($30,000)
Total effect on comprehensive income	$30,000	($9,000)

In interim financial statements issued to the public, FASB Statement Number 130 requires a company to present total comprehensive income. However, it is not required for interim reporting to present the individual elements of other comprehensive income.

EXTRAORDINARY GAINS AND LOSSES

Extraordinary items are material in nature and are both infrequent (not expected to occur in the foreseeable future) and unusual (abnormal, not typical) given the environment of the company. The corporate environment considers such factors as industry attributes, geographic locality, regulatory requirements, economic characteristics, lines of business, and nature of operations. **Note:** An occurrence is not deemed unusual just because it is beyond management's control. Extraordinary items are presented net of tax. Earnings per share is shown on them. What is extraordinary for one company may not necessarily be extraordinary for another.

In some cases, amounts reported for extraordinary items are based on estimates and may need adjustment in later years.

Materiality is a concern. In applying materiality, items should be examined individually rather than in the aggregate. However, if the items arise from one particular event, they may be combined.

Examples of extraordinary items follow:

- Gain on troubled debt restructuring
- Gain on certain types of life insurance proceeds
- Catastrophe and casualty losses (e.g., earthquake, fire)
- Loss arising from a prohibition because of a new law or regulation
- Gain or loss on the early extinguishment of debt
- Loss from governmental expropriation of property
- Gain or loss on the disposal of a major part of the assets of the previously separate companies arising from a business combination that are disposed of within two years subsequent to the consummation date
- Receipt of Federal Home Loan Mortgage Corporation participating preferred stock
- Writeoff of interstate operating rights of motor carriers

Note: Losses on inventory and receivables relate to the normal operations of a business and thus are not extraordinary. However, such losses would be extraordinary if they arise from a catastrophe (e.g., hurricane) or government seizure or forced destruction (e.g., government forces a company to destroy its existing inventory of a certain chemical just proven to cause cancer).

The following items are not considered extraordinary:

- Impact of a strike
- Modifications to long-term contracts
- Costs incurred to defend against a takeover attempt as per FASB Technical Bulletin Number 85–6

Disclosures required for extraordinary items include the nature of the transaction and the major considerations in determining the amounts.

NONRECURRING GAINS OR LOSSES

Nonrecurring gains or losses are items that are either unusual or infrequent. They are presented separately before tax prior to income from continuing operations. Examples are a loss on the sale of property, plant, and equipment as well as the cost of closing a warehouse as part of a business line. Disclosure should be made of the nature and effect of nonrecurring items.

DISCONTINUED OPERATIONS

A discontinued operation is one actually discontinued during the accounting period or one which will be discontinued in a short time period after year-end. An example is the sale, abandonment, spinning off, or other disposal of a business segment (e.g., major line of business, subsidiary, division, department, joint venture, customer class, geographic area). (The Accounting Principles Board noted that the closing of the sale or abandonment of a discontinued segment should not be longer than one year after the board of directors decide to terminate the segment's business activities.) After it is decided to discontinue a segment, the entity's income from continuing operations must be reported separately from its income from discontinued operations. (Further, the assets and liabilities of a discontinued operation should also be segregated.) Discontinued operations are segregated as to:

- Income or loss from discontinued operations
- Loss or gain on disposal of a division

Exhibit 1–1 presents an illustrative presentation for discontinued operations within the income statement.

Exhibit 1–1
Presentation of Discontinued Operations

Income from continuing operations before tax		$800,000
Income tax		100,000
Income from continuing operations after tax		$700,000
Discontinued operations (See Note X):		
Income (loss) from discontinued operations of Division A (net of tax)	$80,000	
Loss on disposal of Division A including provision of $20,000 for operating losses during the phase-out period (net of tax)	(35,000)	45,000
Net income		$745,000

Income or loss from discontinued operations is the income from the start of the year up to the measurement date (date which management formally commits itself to a discontinuance plan).

Note: When comparative financial statements are shown including years before the measurement date, a segregation should still be made between discontinued and continuing operations. Further, prior years' financial statements presented for comparative purposes should be restated to reflect the profit or loss (after tax) of the discontinued business segment as a separate line item.

Gain or loss on disposal of a division includes the income or loss from activities after the measurement date up to the disposal date (date of sale, closing, or abandonment). If the date of disposal is in the same year as the measurement date, the gain or loss on disposal is recognized in the year of disposal. However, if the date of disposal is in the accounting period subsequent to the the measurement date then anticipated losses as a result of disposal are recognized in the year of the measurement date, even though realization will not occur until the next year. On the other hand, if a gain on disposal is anticipated (in the subsequent period), it should not be recognized until it is realized.

Loss or gain on disposal includes the costs directly applicable to the disposal decision, such as closing costs, employee and equipment relocation expenses, severance allowances, fringe benefits (e.g., health insurance), and additional pension payments. FASB Interpretation Number 27 states that the estimated cost associated with a disposal decision should include future rental payments on long-term leases less any related amounts to be received from subletting the properties. As per Emerging Issues Task Force Consensus Summary Number 87–24, a company has the option of whether to allocate interest to discontinued operations. However, it is prohibited to allocate general corporate overhead to discontinued operations. Reference may be made to Emerging Issues Task Force Consensus Summary Number 94–3 (*Liability Recognition for Certain Employee Termination Benefits and Other Costs to Exit an Activity Including Certain Costs Incurred in a Restructuring*).

As was noted, if a gain on disposal is anticipated, it should be reported in the period of the disposal date. Further, Emerging Issues Task Force Consensus Summary Issues Number 85–36 (*Discontinued Operations with Expected Gain and Interim Operating Losses*) states that estimated losses from operations during the period between the measurement date and the disposal date should be deferred until the disposal date if reasonable assurance exists that a net gain will occur on disposal. The deferral also applies to the disposal of part of a business line.

Generally, the estimated gain or loss is determined at the measurement date. It takes into account the net realizable value of the segment's assets. The loss or gain on disposal should also take into account the amounts received or receivable from selling assets of the discontinued division as well as any insurance claims.

As a general rule, disposal is expected within one year of the measurement date. If the disposal plan is estimated to be completed within one year but is not, a revision to net realizable value will be required. Such revision is accounted for as a change in estimate. Additionally, if actual amounts realized differ from estimates, the change in estimate should be reported net-of-tax in the year realized in the discontinued operations section of the income statement.

As per Emerging Issues Task Force Consensus Summary Number 90–16 (*Accounting for Discontinued Operations Subsequently Retained*), if a company changes its mind about disposing of a segment it reported as discontinued, it must reverse any accrued losses on the disposal. However, prior year financial statements are *not* restated. Such segment which is no longer considered as discontinued should be reclassified as part of continuing operations.

An offsetting should be made of the gains and losses associated with the disposal of two or more segments if a net gain results and the disposal arises from a formal plan. However, offsetting is prohibited for disposals of a part of a business line rather than an entire business segment. Further, gains or losses cannot be netted if the disposals apply to unrelated assets.

Emerging Issues Task Force Consensus Summary Number 95–18 applies to the accounting and reporting for a discontinued business segment when the measurement date occurs after the balance sheet date but before the issuance of financial statements. Appropriate disclosure is required.

Note: Normal operating and business adjustments (e.g., writing off delinquent accounts receivable) are not an element in the loss on disposal.

Caution: The discontinuance or disposal of an activity or operation may not represent the discontinuance or disposal of an entire business segment. In this situation, the occurrence is reported as part of income from continuing operations, not discontinued operations. Further, the following are not deemed to be events associated with disposing of a business segment:

■ Selling or abandoning two or more unrelated assets that do not represent a business segment

■ Changing the physical location of manufacturing or marketing operations

■ Phasing out a product or service line due to new technology

EXAMPLE

On 8/15/19X5, XYZ Company established a plan to dispose of segment L (measurement date). The company expects the sale to occur on 4/1/19X6 for a selling price of $1,600,000. The disposal costs in 19X5 were $200,000. Segment L's actual and anticipated operating losses were:

1/1/19X5 to 8/14/19X5	$170,000
8/15/19X5 to 12/31/19X5	80,000
1/1/19X6 to 4/1/19X6	25,000

The expected carrying value of the segment on April 1, 19X6 is $1,750,000. The loss from discontinued operations in the 19X5 income statement is

Selling price		$1,600,000
Less:		
Disposal costs	$ 200,000	
Actual and expected operating losses subsequent to the measurement date	105,000	
Carrying value	1,750,000	
Total deduction		2,055,000
Loss on disposal		$ 455,000

Because there is a loss on disposal, it is recognized in 19X5, the year of the measurement date.

EXAMPLE

X Company decides to sell its tractor division on June 1, 1999 (measurement date). It is anticipated that the actual disposal of the division will be on February 1, 2000. It is assumed that such a sale constitutes a disposal of a segment of a business. The following actual and expected gains and losses apply to the sale of the division. It is now December 31, 1999.

Actual net income (realized) from operations of the division June 1, 1999–December 31, 1999	$150,000
Estimated net income from operations of the division January 1, 2000–February 1, 2000	$200,000
Estimated gain on sale of division assets on February 1, 2000	$400,000

GAIN OR LOSS DISPOSAL OF DIVISION:	
Actual net income from operations in 1999	$150,000
Estimated net income from operations in 2000	200,000
Estimated gain on sale of division assets in 2000	400,000
Expected gain on disposal of division	$750,000

There is an expected gain on the disposal of the division. In 1999, $150,000 of the total gain is recognized because it is realized in this period. The remaining portion of the gain will be recognized in 2000, when it is expected to be realized. If the results turn out differently than anticipated, they are treated as a change in accounting estimate and the revised outcome is recognized in the period in which the new facts present themselves and become known.

EXAMPLE

Assume the same preliminary facts in the previous problem. Also assume that the following actual and expected gains and losses apply to the disposal of the division. It is now December 31, 1999.

Actual net income (realized) from operations of the division June 1, 1999–December 31, 1999	$ 150,000
Estimated net income from operations of the division January 1, 2000–February 1, 2000	200,000
Estimated loss on sale of division assets on February 1, 2000	(400,000)
GAIN OR LOSS DISPOSAL OF DIVISION:	
Actual gain from operations in 1999	$ 150,000
Estimated net income from operations in 2000	200,000
Estimated loss on sale of division assets in 2000	(400,000)
Expected loss on disposal of division	$ (50,000)

Because there is an expected loss, it is recognized in 1999, the year of the measurement date.

Emerging Issues Task Force Consensus Summary Number 86–22 deals with the display of business restructuring provisions in the income statement.

Emerging Issues Task Force Consensus Summary Number 93–17 applies to the recognition of deferred tax assets for a parent company's excess tax basis in the stock of a subsidiary that is accounted for as a discontinued operation.

Footnote disclosure should be provided for the discontinued operation, including identifying the affected business segment, manner of disposal, disposal date, revenue earned, income from operations from the measurement date to year-end, description of net assets still remaining at year-end, listing of major assets disposed of, adjustments required to prior years for comparability, and the inability to estimate gain or loss on disposing of a segment. Disclosure includes any revision to estimates regarding the income or loss associated with the disposed segment. A subsequent event disclosure is necessary for the estimated loss on disposal occurring after year-end but before the audit report date.

DISCLOSURES ASSOCIATED WITH OPERATIONS

Disclosure should be provided about the company's primary products and services, including major markets by geographic area. This information enables a proper assessment of an entity's nature of operations. In addition, AICPA Statement of Position (SOP) Number 94–6 requires disclosure of major risks and uncertainties facing the business. The SOP also requires disclosure in the significant accounting policies footnote that the financial information presented is based on management's estimates and assumptions. Reference should also be made that actual results may differ from such estimates.

RESEARCH AND DEVELOPMENT COSTS

Research is defined as testing to search for a new product, service, technique, or process. Research may also be undertaken to improve already existing products or services. Development is defined as translating the research into a design for a new product or process. Development may also encompass improvements made to existing products or processes.

FASB Statement Number 2 (*Accounting for Research and Development Costs*) requires the expensing of research and development costs as incurred. Research and development costs may also be incurred through the purchase of R&D from other companies. R&D costs are presented separately within income from continuing operations.

When research is performed under contract for a fee from a third party, a receivable is charged.

Equipment, facilities, materials, and intangibles (e.g., patents) bought that have alternative future benefit in R&D activities are capitalized. Any resulting depreciation or amortization expense on such assets are presented as an R&D expense. For example, the depreciation on an R&D building is classified as an R&D expense. When there is no future alternative use, the costs must be immediately expensed.

R&D costs include employee salaries directly tied to R&D efforts, and directly allocable indirect costs for R&D efforts.

If a group of assets is bought, proper allocation should be made to those applicable to R&D activities.

As per FASB Interpretation Number 4 (*Applicability of FASB Statement Number 2 to Business Combinations Accounted for by the Purchase Method*), in a business combination accounted for under the purchase method, acquired R&D assets should be based on their fair market value.

If payments are made to others to undertake R&D efforts on the company's behalf, R&D expense is charged.

Exception: FASB Statement Number 2 is not applicable to the extractive (e.g., mining) or regulated industries.

Some examples of R&D activities are as follows:

- Testing of the feasibility of products
- Engineering functions so the new product may satisfy manufacturing requirements
- Models and prototypes before manufacturing
- Formulating and designing of product alternatives
- Laboratory research attempting to uncover new knowledge
- Pilot programs before operations commence

The following are not R&D activities:

- Marketing research
- Legal fees to secure a patent
- Quality control during commercial production
- Rearrangement and startup activities
- Design changes due to changes in the season (e.g., winter to spring)
- Identifying and solving manufacturing problems during commercial production
- Construction engineering
- Routine or periodic alterations to existing products, operations, or production processes
- Commercial applications of the product

FASB Statement Number 86 (*Accounting for the Costs of Computer Software to Be Sold, Leased, or Otherwise Marketed*) and FASB Interpretation Number 6 (*Applicability of FASB Statement Number 2 to Computer Software*) provide special treatment for R&D costs incurred for computer software, whether leased, sold, or otherwise marketed. R&D costs for software development are expensed up until there is a working (program) model (technological feasibility). Technological feasibility is established when the enterprise has completed all planning, designing, coding, and testing activities that are necessary to establish that the product can be produced to meet its design specifications, features, functions, and technical performance requirements. Technological feasibility also involves assuring that all risks have been identified. After a working model, the R&D production software costs are deferred to an asset and reflected at the lower of unamortized cost or net realizable value. If unamortized cost exceeds net realizable value, the write-down is charged against earnings. The write-down is not reversed for any subsequent recovery in value. Examples of these R&D production software costs incurred after the working model are refining subroutines, debugging, and alternative adaptations. After the software is available to the public (marketable), the R&D asset is amortized. The amortization expense is based on the greater of

- Straight-line method amount
- Percent of current year revenue to total expected revenue from the product

Note: The purchase price of software bought from others that has future benefit should be deferred and amortized over the period benefited.

Once the product is ready to be sold or otherwise marketed, the costs incurred for duplicating the computer software, documentation, and training materials from the product masters, and for physically packing the product for distribution, shall be capitalized as inventory. Cost of sales is charged when the related revenue from the sales of those units occurs.

Any costs incurred to maintain or provide customer support for the software once sold to the public are expensed to match against the associated revenue generated. Examples of such costs are costs to correct errors, make updates, and perform routine changes. Any costs to modify software due to the year 2000 must be expensed as incurred.

FASB Statement Number 86 does not cover software costs associated with that developed by the company for others or created to use internally within the company. Further, the costs to develop a computer system that enhances the company's administrative or selling activities is not classified as an R&D cost.

According to FASB Statement Number 68 (*Research and Development Arrangements*), if a company contracts with others to fund R&D efforts, a determination must be made of the nature of the obligation. If the company is obligated to repay the funds regardless of R&D success, the company must first debit cash and credit liabilities at the time of borrowing, and then debt R&D expense and credit cash at the time of R&D incurrence.

However, a liability does not exist if the transfer of financial risk to the party is substantive and real. If the financial risk related to the R&D is transferred because repayment depends only on the R&D having future economic benefit, the company treats its obligation as a contract to engage in R&D for others. In this instance, R&D costs are capitalized and revenue is recognized as earned and becomes billable under the agreement. Footnote disclosure should be made of the terms of the R&D agreement, amount of earned compensation, and costs incurred under the agreement.

In the event in which loans or advances to the entity depend only on R&D results, such amounts are considered R&D costs to be charged to expense.

As per FASB Technical Bulletin Number 84–1 (*Accounting for Stock Issued to Acquire the Results of a Research and Development Arrangement*), if stock is issued for R&D it should be recorded at the fair value of the stock issued or fair value of the R&D acquired, whichever is more clearly evident.

If warrants, options, or other financial instruments are issued in connection with an R&D contract, R&D expense is charged. In addition, the company records part of the proceeds to be provided by the other party as paid-in-capital based on their fair market value on the arrangement date.

Emerging Issues Task Force Consensus Summary Number 86–14 covers purchased research and development projects in a business combination.

Footnote disclosures with regard to research and development follow:

- Terms of R&D arrangements, such as options to buy, licensing, royalty basis, and funding commitments

- Valuation basis

- Fees earned from R&D contracts

- Amortization method and time period

COMPENSATION EXPENSE ARISING FROM THE STOCK ISSUED TO EMPLOYEES

FASB Statement Number 123 (*Accounting for Stock-Based Compensation*) is applicable to stock option plans, nonvested stock, employee stock purchase plans, and stock compensation awards that are to be settled by cash payment.

Stock Option Plans

Employers may account for stock option plans by either the "intrinsic value" method or the "fair value" method. However, FASB Statement Number 123 encourages but does not require that compensation expense for stock option plans be based on the fair value of the stock-based compensation paid to employees for their services.

Intrinsic Method

Under the intrinsic value method, compensation expense for services is measured by the difference between the quoted market price of the shares granted by the option and the exercise price that the employee is required to pay. Total compensation expense is computed on the measurement date. In most cases, that date is the date of grant (fixed plan). At the measurement date, compensation expense is computed as the difference between the market price of the shares and their exercise price. This amount (total compensation expense) is then allocated over the compensatory or service period. After the service period (the period in which the stock options are actually earned by the employees), the stock options may be exercised. Generally, the service period is the vesting period—the time between the date of grant and the vesting date. The intrinsic method is so termed because the computation is not based on data derived from external circumstances.

Note: If treasury stock is used in a stock option plan, its market value, not its cost, should be used in measuring the compensation expense.

If an employee chooses not to exercise a stock option, previously recognized compensation expense is not negated or adjusted. The costs of services remain recorded.

The following illustrations demonstrate the mechanics of the intrinsic method.

EXAMPLE: INTRINSIC METHOD

On January 1, 19X1, ABC Company granted stock options to executives to purchase 100,000 shares of $5 par value common stock at an exercise price of $20 per share. The current market price of the stock is $30. Hence, the total compensation equals $1,000,000 [100,000 × ($30 – $20)]. The options are exercisable any time after December 31, 19X4. Thus, the compensatory (service) period is four years commencing January 1, 19X1, and compensation expense should be recognized evenly over this period (19X1–19X4).

Entries

Date of Grant—January 1, 19X1

No entry

December 31, 19X1

Compensation Expense	250,000 ($1,000,000/4)	
Paid-in-Capital Stock Options		250,000

December 31, 19X2–19X4

Compensation Expense	250,000 ($1,000,000/4)	
Paid-in-Capital Stock Options		250,000

Analysis Compensation expense is always recognized in the year in which services are provided. In this problem, $250,000 of compensation expense is disclosed in each income statement of each year during the service period (19X1–19X4). Correspondingly, paid-in capital stock options are reported in the capital stock section in stockholders' equity of the balance sheet.

On December 31, 19X1, after the first year, the paid-in-capital stock options disclosure would be $250,000 and would be so presented in the capital stock section. The next year (19X2) the balance disclosure would be $500,000. In 19X3, $750,000 would be shown, and in 19X4, the amount disclosed would be $1,000,000.

Assuming that all the stock options are exercised by the employees at the beginning of the exercise period (after December 31, 19X4), the following entries are made:

Cash ($20 [exercise price] × 100,000 shares)	2,000,000	
Paid-in-capital stock options	1,000,000	
Common stock ($ 5 × 100,000 shares)		500,000
Paid-in-capital in excess of par		2,500,000

Paid-in-capital in excess of par is the balancing figure and is, of course, a stockholders' equity account.

If options for only 10,000 shares were exercised, then the entry would be

Cash ($20 [exercise price] × 10,000 shares)	200,000	
Paid-in-capital stock options ($10 × 10,000)	100,000	
Common stock ($5 × 10,000 shares)		50,000
Paid-in-capital in excess of par		250,000

If the remaining 90,000 options expired (because the market price of the stock did not exceed the exercise price by the end of the exercise period), then the following entry would be made:

Paid-in-capital stock options (90,000 × $10)	900,000	
Paid-in-capital from expired stock options		900,000

If total compensation expense cannot be measured at the the date of grant because, for example, the number of shares to be received under the stock option plan is based on some performance variable, then compensation expense should be estimated and amortized over the service period based on the estimated number of shares to be received and the year-end market price of the shares each period. Because both of these variables will probably change each period, the amount of compensation expense recorded should be adjusted each year until the measurement date (change in accounting estimate), when the actual amount of total compensation expense can be ascertained. This plan is known as a variable plan. As was previously noted, when total compensation expense is determinable at the date of grant, the stock option plan is known as a fixed plan.

Note: In the case of options accounted for under the intrinsic value method, pro forma disclosures of net income and earnings per share must be computed as if the fair value method (to be discussed next) had been used in measuring compensation expense.

Fair Value Method

Employers may also account for stock option plans using the fair value method. In fact, the FASB considers this method to be the preferable one. Under this method, fair value is computed by using an option-pricing model that considers several factors. A popular option pricing model is Black-Scholes. It is used to determine the equilibrium value of an option. The model provides insight into the valuation of debt relative to equity. This model may be programmed into computer spreadsheets and some pocket calculators. The Black-Scholes model makes it possible to compute the present value of hypothetical instruments. Some assumptions of this model are that the stock options are freely traded and the total return rate (considering the change in price plus dividends) may be determined based on a continuous compounding over the life of the option. (Under FASB Statement Number 123, the life of the option is the anticipated time period until the option is exercised rather than the contractual term. By reducing the option's life, its value is reduced.) It is a random variable derived from a normal bell curve distribution. The Black-Scholes model was formulated based on European-style options exercisable only at expiration. However, most employee stock options are American-style and are exercisable at any time during the life of the option once vesting has occurred. The Black-Scholes model uses the volatility anticipated for the option's life. **Note:** Difficulties will arise in computing option values when there is early option exercise and fluctuations in stock price and dividends. The Black-Scholes model may also be used in valuing put options by modifying computations.

The formula and implications for the Black-Scholes model follow:

$$\text{Present value of call option} = PN(d_1) - EXe^{-r_f t}N(d_2)$$

where P = price of stock now

$\quad$ N(d) = cumulative normal probability density function

$\quad\quad$ EX = exercise price of option

$\quad\quad\quad$ t = time to exercise date

$\quad\quad\quad$ r_f = (continuously compounded) risk-free rate of interest

$\quad\quad\quad$ e = 2.71828

$$d_1 = \frac{\log(P/EX) + r_f t + \sigma^2 t/2}{\sigma \cdot \sqrt{t}}$$

$$d_1 = \frac{\log(P/EX) + r_f t + \sigma^2 t/2}{\sigma \cdot \sqrt{t}}$$

$\quad$ σ^2 = variance per period of (continuously compounded) rate of return on the stock

The formula, while somewhat imposing, actually uses readily available input data, with the exception of σ, or volatility. P, EX, r_f, and t are easily obtained.

The implication of the option model The value of the option increases with the level of stock price relative to the exercise price (P/EX), the time to expiration times the interest rate ($r_f t$), and the time to expiration times the stock's variability ($\sigma^2 \cdot t$).

- The option price is always less than the stock price.
- The option price never falls below the payoff to immediate exercise (P – EX or zero, whichever is larger).
- If the stock is worthless, the option is worthless.

■ As the stock price becomes very large, the option price approaches the stock price less the present value of the exercise price.

Other models may be used for option pricing such as the more complicated binomial model.

Before the current value of an option may be computed, consideration must be given to its expiration value.

Compensation expense is based on the fair value of the award at the grant date and is recognized over the period between the date of grant and the vesting date, in a manner similar to the intrinsic value method.

Under the fair value method, stock options are accounted for in the same way as the journal entries under the intrinsic value method, except the *fair value of the options* at the date of grant would be amortized as compensation expense over the compensatory period (from the date of grant to the date the options are initially exercisable).

EXAMPLE: FAIR VALUE METHOD

On January 1, 19X1, XYZ Company granted stock options to executives to purchase 100,000 shares of $5 par value common stock at an exercise price of $20 per share. The current market price of the stock is $30. Under the Black-Scholes option price model, it is estimated that the fair value of the option plan is $800,000. The options are exercisable any time after December 31, 19X4. The compensatory period is four years commencing January 1, 19X1, and compensation expense should be recognized evenly over this period (19X1–19X4).

The journal entries relating to the stock option plan based on the fair value method follow:

<u>Date of Grant</u>—January 1, 19X1
No entry
<u>December 31, 19X1</u>

Compensation Expense	200,000 ($800,000/4)	
Paid-in-capital stock options		200,000

<u>December 31, 19X2–19X4</u>

Compensation Expense	200,000 ($800,000/4)	
Paid-in-capital stock options		200,000

Assuming that all the stock options are exercised by the employees at the beginning of the exercise period, the following entries are made:

Cash ($20 [exercise price] × 100,000 shares)	2,000,000	
Paid-in-capital stock options	800,000	
Common stock ($5 × 100,000 shares)		500,000
Paid-in-capital in excess of par		2,300,000

As was noted in the prior illustration, paid-in-capital in excess of par is the balancing figure here and is, of course a stockholders' equity account.

If the stock options were not exercised because the market price did not exceed the exercise price during the exercise period, the entry that would be made is

Paid-in-capital stock options	800,000	
Paid-in-capital from expired stock options		800,000

Notice that from an entry point of view, the only difference between the intrinsic method and fair value methods is way that total compensation expense is computed.

Stock Option Forfeiture

If an employee forfeits a stock option because he or she leaves the employer and fails to satisfy the service requirement, then the recorded compensation expense and paid-in-capital stock option should be adjusted (as a change in accounting estimate) to account for the forfeiture.

EXAMPLE: TERMINATION OF STOCK OPTIONS USING THE FAIR VALUE METHOD

On January 1, 2000, Levsee Company adopted a stock option program to compensate its officers and key employees. These employees were offered a total of 5,000 shares of the company's $5 par value common stock at an exercise price of $10 per share. Assume that the Black-Scholes fair value pricing model is used and the determination of the total compensation expense is $200,000. The stock options that were offered were exercisable for three years after a two-year compensatory (service) period commencing

January 1, 2000. In the middle of the second year of the service period, 2,000 shares were terminated because several of the employees had resigned from the company. Assume that the fair value of the company's stock was $15 at the date of termination. What entries for compensation expense should be made during the service period? What adjusting entry should be made?

Entries

January 1, 2000

No entry made on date of grant

December 31, 2000

Compensation Expense	100,000 (200,000/2)	
Paid-in-capital stock options		100,000

July 1, 2001

Paid-in-capital stock options	80,000*	
Compensation Expense		80,000

*200,000/5,000 × 2000 = $80,000

December 31, 2001

Compensation Expense	100,000	
Paid-in-capital stock options		100,000

Note: Noncompensatory stock option plans may also exist. Such plans are characterized by having stock offered to employees on some basis (e.g., equally, percent of salary), participation by full-time employees, a reasonable time period for the exercise of the options, and a discount to employees to buy the stock that is not better than that afforded to company stockholders. If any of these criteria are not met, then the plan is compensatory in nature. The purpose of a noncompensatory plan is to obtain funds and to have greater widespread ownership in the company among employees. It is not primarily designed to provide compensation for services rendered. Therefore, no compensation expense is recognized.

Nonvested Stock

Nonvested stock is stock that cannot be sold currently because the employee who was granted the shares has not yet met the vesting requirements needed to earn the right to the shares. The fair value of a share of nonvested stock awarded to an employee is measured at the market price per share of nonrestricted stock on the grant date unless a restriction will be imposed after the employee has a vested right to the stock, in which event the fair value is approximated, taking into account the restriction.

Employee Stock Purchase Plans

An employee stock purchase plan permits employees to buy stock at a discount. It is noncompensatory if the discount is minor (5% or less), most full-time employees may participate, and the plan has no option features.

Emerging Issues Task Force Consensus Summary Number 89–11 covers the sponsor's balance sheet classification of capital stock with a put option held by any employee stock ownership plan.

AICPA Statement of Position Number 93–6 covers the employers' accounting for employee stock ownership plans.

Stock Compensation Awards Required to Be Settled by Paying Cash

Some stock-based compensation plans require an employer to pay an employee, either on demand or at a particular date, a cash amount based on the increase in the market price of the employer's stock. A ceiling stock price may be set depending on the plan. The compensation cost associated with the award is the amount of change in stock price.

Disclosures

The following should be disclosed in the footnotes in connection with stock-based compensation plans:

- The number of shares under option at the beginning and end of year
- The number of shares granted, forfeited, expired, and exercised during the year

- The option price
- Weighted-average exercise price
- Weighted-average grant date fair value of options and/or other equity instruments granted during the year
- A description of the method and assumptions used to estimate fair values of options
- Compensation expense recognized for the period
- Major changes in terms of stock-based compensation plans
- Amendments to outstanding awards
- If options are accounted for with the intrinsic value method, pro forma disclosure of net income and earnings per share (EPS), assuming the fair value method was used in measuring compensation cost

Tax Aspects

Compensation expense is deductible for tax purposes when paid but deducted for book purposes when accrued. This results in interperiod income tax allocation involving a deferred income tax credit. If for some reason reversal of the temporary difference does not occur, a permanent difference exists which does not affect profit. The difference should adjust paid-in-capital in the period the accrual takes place.

DEFERRED COMPENSATION ARRANGEMENTS

AICPA Accounting Principles Board Opinion Number 12 covers the accounting and reporting requirements of deferred compensation contracts. Deferred compensation plans typically include such stipulations as continued employment over a predetermined time period, availability, and noncompetitive clauses. In a deferred compensation arrangement, expected benefits to be paid should be accrued as an expense and liability in the current year as the associated services are performed. If the plan is based on current and future employment, the accrued amount is based only on current year services. Once the employee has performed all services required to have a vested right to receive the deferred compensation, the amount accrued should then be the discounted (present) value of future benefits to be paid to the worker. Accrued amounts start with the first day of employment.

If the plan pays benefits over the life of a beneficiary, the total liability depends on the life expectancy of the beneficiary or the estimated cost associated with the annuity contract to provide adequate amounts to pay the benefits.

Deferred compensation plans do not apply to pension or to post-retirement benefit plans.

EXAMPLE

An employee is hired on January 1, 19X5. The deferred compensation agreement stipulates a payment of $30,000 at the end of employment. The contract calls for employee services for at least nine months. It is expected that the employee will work three years. The discount rate is 12%.

At year-end 19X5, the employee is still working. Since the employee has worked nine months, he is eligible to cease employment and receive the deferred compensation. The accrual at year-end 19X5 is $23,916 ($30,000 × .79719), which represents the present value of the $30,000 payable at the end of two years at 12%. The two years is the initially expected service of three years less the one year (19X5) already elapsed. The entire amount of accrual is recorded as a deferred compensation cost in 19X5 because the worker is fully eligible by year-end.

Assuming the employee continues working to year-end 19X6, the accrued liability at December 31, 19X6 will be $26,786 ($30,000 × .89286), representing the discounted value of $30,000 at the end of one year at a 12% discount rate.

Thus, the cost to be recorded for 19X6 is $2,870 computed as follows:

Accrual at year-end 19X6	$26,786
Accrual at year-end 19X5	(23,916)
Compensation expense for 19X6	$ 2,870

ADVERTISING COSTS

American Institute of CPAs' Statement of Position 93–7 (*Reporting on Advertising Costs*) requires the expensing of advertising as incurred when the advertising program first occurs. However, the cost of direct-response advertising may be deferred if the major purpose of the promotion is to elicit sales to customers who respond specifically to the advertising and for which future benefit exists. For example, the former condition is met if the response card is specially coded. The latter condition is satisfied if the resulting future revenues exceed the future costs to be incurred. The deferred advertising is amortized over the expected period of benefit using the revenue method (current year revenue to total revenue). The cost of a billboard should also be deferred and amortized. Advertising expenditures incurred after revenue is recognized should be accrued. These advertising costs should be expensed when the related revenues are recognized.

INSURANCE COSTS

The accounting for insurance costs relate to life insurance and casualty insurance.

Life Insurance

FASB Technical Bulletin 85–4 deals with the accounting for purchases of life insurance. As premiums are paid for a life insurance policy, the premiums may consist of two portions—one for insurance expense for the period applicable to the insurer's assumption of risk and the other for cash surrender value.

Cash surrender value of life insurance is the amount payable when the insured cancels the policy. The insured will obviously receive less than the premium paid. The amount to be received upon cancellation by the insured equals the cash value less borrowings against the policy less any fees associated with surrendering the policy. A change in the cash surrender value during the year is treated as an adjustment to the insurance premiums paid. The cash surrender value may also be used as collateral for a loan from the insurer. As per FASB Interpretation Number 39 (*Offsetting of Amounts Related to Certain Contracts*), the cash value should be directly offset against the loans payable account in the balance sheet. Cash surrender value is usually presented under long-term investments. However, if the policy will be cashed in within the next year, the cash surrender value will be reported under current assets.

EXAMPLE

The difference between the premium paid and the amount attributable to the cash surrender value represents insurance expense. If the premium paid is $20,000 and $4,000 of that amount is attributable to the increase in cash surrender value, the journal entry is

Life Insurance Expense	16,000	
Cash Surrender Value	4,000	
Cash		20,000

When the insured dies, the insurer pays the beneficiary the face value of the policy less any associated borrowings against the policy less any redemption fees.

If insurance premium payments are made in a policy that does not transfer risk to the insurer, the payments are considered deposits receivable and presented as an asset.

Casualty Insurance

Casualty insurance is taken out for fire or flood losses. This insurance reimburses the policy holder for the fair market value of destroyed property. Insurance companies usually have a coinsurance provision so the insured is responsible for a portion of the loss. The insurance reimbursement formula assuming an 80% coinsurance provision follows:

$$\frac{\text{Face of Policy}}{.80 \times \text{Fair Market Value of Insured Property}} \times \begin{array}{c}\text{Fair Value} \\ \text{of Loss}\end{array} = \begin{array}{c}\text{Possible} \\ \text{Reimbursement}\end{array}$$

The insurance recovery is based on the lower of the face of the policy, fair market value of the loss, or possible reimbursement.

EXAMPLE

Case	Face of Policy	Fair Market Value of Property	Fair Market Value of Loss
1	$8,000	$20,000	$12,000
2	3,000	5,000	5,000
3	30,000	30,000	12,000

Insurance reimbursement follows:

Case A: $\dfrac{\$8,000}{.8 \times \$20,000} \times \$12,000 = \$6,000$

Answer = $6,000

Case B: $\dfrac{\$3,000}{.8 \times \$5,000} \times \$5,000 = \$3,750$

Answer = $3,000

Case C: $\dfrac{\$30,000}{.8 \times \$30,000} \times \$12,000 = \$15,000$

Answer = $12,000

EXAMPLE

A blanket policy of $22,000 relates to machinery A and B. The fair values of the machinery are $45,000 and $25,000, respectively. Machinery B is partly destroyed, causing a fire loss of $5,000.

The policy allocated to machinery B is determined as follows:

	Fair Market Value	Policy
Machinery A	$45,000	$14,143
Machinery B	25,000	7,857
Total	$70,000	$22,000

Insurance reimbursement equals

$$\frac{\$7,857}{.8 \times \$25,000} \times \$5,000 = \$1,964$$

Answer = $1,964

When there is fire damage, the destroyed asset must be removed from the accounts, with the ensuring fire loss recorded based on book value. The insurance reimbursement reduces the fire loss. The fire loss is presented as an extraordinary item (net of tax).

EXAMPLE

XYZ Company experienced a fire. Inventory costing $10,000 was completely destroyed. The inventory was not insured. Equipment costing $20,000 with accumulated depreciation of $2,000 and having a fair market value of $14,000 is fully destroyed. The policy is for $20,000. A building costing $60,000 with accumulated depreciation of $6,000 and having a fair market value of $40,000 is half destroyed. The face of the policy is $30,000. The journal entries to record the book loss are

Fire Loss	10,000	
Inventory		10,000
Fire Loss	18,000	
Accumulated Depreciation	2,000	
Equipment		20,000
Fire Loss	27,000	
Accumulated Depreciation	3,000	
Building		30,000

Insurance reimbursement totals $32,750, calculated as follows:

Equipment: $\dfrac{\$20,000}{.8 \times \$14,000}$ × $14,000 = $25,000

Answer = $14,000

Building: $\dfrac{\$30,000}{.8 \times \$40,000}$ × $20,000 = $18,750

The journal entry for the insurance reimbursement is

Cash	32,750	
Fire Loss		32,750

The net fire loss is $22,250 ($55,000 – $32,750).

RESTRUCTURING CHARGES

Securities and Exchange Commission Staff Accounting Bulletin Number 67 requires restructuring charges to be expensed and presented as an element in computing income from operations.

In general, an expense and liability should be accrued for employee termination benefits in a restructuring. Disclosure should be made of the group and the number of workers laid off.

An exit plan requires the recognition of a liability for the restructuring charges incurred if there is no future benefit to continuing operations. The expense for the estimated costs should be made on the commitment date of the exit plan. Expected gains from assets to be sold in connection with the exit plan should be recorded in the year realized. These gains are *not* allowed to offset the accrued liability for exit costs. Exit costs incurred are presented as a separate item as part of income from continuing operations. Disclosures associated with an exit plan include the terms of the exit plan, description and amount of exit costs incurred, activities to be exited from, method of disposition, expected completion date, and liability adjustments.

EARNINGS PER SHARE

FASB Statement Number 128 (*Earnings Per Share*) covers the computation, reporting, and disclosures associated with earnings per share. It requires public companies to present earnings per share on the face of the income statement. (Nonpublic entities are not required to present earnings per share.) If the entity's capital structure is simple—that is, it has no potentially dilutive securities—then only basic earnings per share needs to be disclosed. However, if the capital structure is complex (it includes potentially dilutive securities), then presentation of both basic and diluted earnings per share is mandated.

Basic earnings per share takes into account only the actual number of outstanding common shares during the period (and those contingently issuable in certain cases).

Diluted earnings per share includes the effect of common shares actually outstanding and the impact of convertible securities, stock options, stock warrants, and their equivalents. Diluted earnings per share should not assume the conversion, exercise, or contingent issuance of securities having an antidilutive effect (increasing earnings per share or decreasing loss per share) because it violates conservatism.

Basic Earnings Per Share

Basic earnings per share equals net income available to common stockholders divided by the weighted average number of common shares outstanding. Net income available to common stockholders is net income less declared preferred dividends for the current year. If the preferred stock is noncumulative, then preferred stock dividends are subtracted only if they are declared during the period. On the other hand, if the preferred stock is cumulative, then the dividends are subtracted even if they are not declared in the current year. The weighted-average number of common shares outstanding is determined by multiplying the number of shares issued and outstanding for any time period by a fraction, the numerator being the number of months the shares have been outstanding and the denominator being the number of months in the period (e.g., 12 months for annual reporting).

EXAMPLE

On January 1, 19X5, 100,000 shares were issued. On October 1, 19X5, 10,000 of those shares were reacquired. The weighted-average common shares outstanding equals 97,500 shares, computed as follows:

1/1/19X5–9/30/19X5	(100,000 × 9/12)	75,000
10/1/19X5–12/31/19X5	(90,000 × 3/12)	22,500
Weighted outstanding common shares		97,500

EXAMPLE

On January 1, 19X1, 10,000 shares were issued. On April 1, 19X1, 2,000 of those shares were bought back. The weighted-average common stock outstanding is 8,500 shares computed as follows:

1/1/19X1–3/31/19X1	(10,000 × 3/12)	2,500
4/1/19X1–12/31/19X1	(8,000 × 9/12)	6,000
Weighted outstanding common shares		8,500

If a stock dividend or stock split has been issued for the period, it is presumed that such stock dividend or split was issued at the beginning of the period. Thus, stock dividends or stock splits are weighted for the entire period regardless of the fact that they were issued during the period. Further, when comparative financial statements are prepared, the issuance of a stock dividend or stock split requires retroactive restatement of each previous year's earnings per share to give effect to the dividend or split for those prior years.

EXAMPLE

The following occurred during the year regarding common stock:

Shares outstanding—1/1	30,000
2 for 1 stock split—4/1	30,000
Shares issued—8/1	5,000

   The common shares to be used in the denominator of basic EPS is 62,083 shares, computed as follows:

1/1–3/31	$30,000 \times 3/12 \times 2$	15,000
4/1–8/1	$60,000 \times 4/12$	20,000
8/1–12/31	$65,000 \times 5/12$	27,083
Total		62,083

EXAMPLE

On December 1, 19X4, a company declared and issued an 8% stock dividend on its 200,000 outstanding common shares. The number of common shares to be used in determining basic EPS is $216,000 (200,000 shares × 108%).

EXAMPLE

Assume that in 19X4 a 15% stock dividend occurs. The weighted-average shares used for previous years' computations has to be increased by 15% to make basic EPS comparable.

EXAMPLE

The following information is presented for a company:

Preferred stock, $10 par, 6% cumulative, 30,000 shares issued and outstanding	$300,000
Common stock, $5 par, 100,000 shares issued and outstanding	500,000
Net income	400,000

   The company paid a cash dividend on preferred stock. The preferred dividend would therefore equal $18,000 (6% × $300,000).
   Basic EPS equals $3.82, computed as follows:

EARNINGS AVAILABLE TO COMMON STOCKHOLDERS

Net income	$400,000
Less: Preferred dividends	(18,000)
Earnings available to common stockholders	$382,000

Basic EPS = $382,000/100,000 shares = $3.82

EXAMPLE

On January 1, 19X3, Dauber Company had the following shares outstanding:

6% Cumulative preferred stock, $100 par value	150,000 shares
Common stock, $5 par value	500,000 shares

During the year, the following occurred:

- On April 1, 19X3, the company issued 100,000 shares of common stock

- On September 1, 19X3, the company declared and issued a 10% stock dividend

- For the year ended December 31, 19X3, the net income was $2,200,000

Basic earnings per share for 19X3 equals $2.06 ($1,300,000/632,500 shares), calculated as follows:

EARNINGS AVAILABLE TO COMMON STOCKHOLDERS

Net income		$2,200,000
Less: Preferred dividend	(150,000 shares × $6)	(900,000)
Earnings available to common stockholders		$1,300,000

WEIGHTED AVERAGE NUMBER OF OUTSTANDING COMMON SHARES

1/1/19X3–3/31/19X3	(500,000 × 3/12 × 110%)	137,500
4/1/19X3–8/31/19X3	(600,000 × 5/12 × 110%)	275,000
9/1/19X3–12/31/19X3	(660,000 × 4/12)	220,000
Weighted-average outstanding common shares		632,500

Diluted Earnings Per Share

If potentially dilutive securities exist that are outstanding, such as convertible bonds, convertible preferred stock, stock options, or stock warrants, then both basic and diluted earnings per share must be presented.

In the case of convertible securities, the if-converted method must be used. Under this approach, it is assumed that the dilutive convertible security is converted into common stock at the beginning of the period or date of issue, if later. If we assume conversion, then the interest expense (net of tax) that would have been incurred on the convertible bonds must be added back to net income in the numerator. Any dividend on convertible preferred stock would also be added back (dividend savings) to net income in the numerator. The add back of interest expense (net of tax) on convertible bonds and preferred dividends on convertible preferred stock results in an adjusted net income figure for earnings per share determination purposes. Correspondingly, the number of common shares the convertible securities are convertible into (or their weighted-average effect if conversion to common stock actually took place during the year) must also be added to the weighted-average outstanding common shares in the denominator.

In the case of dilutive stock options, stock warrants, or their equivalent, the treasury stock method is used. Under this approach, there is a presumption that the option or warrant was exercised at the beginning of the period, or date of grant, if later. The assumed proceeds received from the exercise of the option or warrant are assumed to be used to buy treasury stock at the average market price for the period. However, exercise is presumed to occur only if the average market price of the underlying shares during the period is greater than the exercise price of the option or warrant. This presumption ensures that the assumed exercise of a stock option or warrant will have a dilutive effect on the earning per share computation. Correspondingly, the denominator of diluted earnings per share increases by the number of shares assumed issued due to the exercise of options or warrants reduced by the assumed treasury shares purchased.

EXAMPLE

One hundred shares are under a stock option plan at an exercise price of $10. The average market price of stock during the period is $25. The assumed issuance of common shares because of the assumed exercise of the stock options is 60, computed as follows:

Issued shares from option	100 shares	×	$10	=	$1,000
Less: Treasury shares	40 shares*	×	$25	=	$1,000
Additional shares that must be issued to satisfy option holders	60 shares			

*It is assumed that $1,000/$25 = 40 shares were acquired.

If options are granted as part of a stock-based compensation arrangement, the assumed proceeds from the exercise of the options under the treasury stock method include deferred compensation and the resulting tax benefit that would be credited to paid-in-capital arising from the exercise of the options.

As a result of the if-converted method for convertible dilutive securities and the treasury stock method for stock option plans and warrants, the denominator of diluted earnings per share computation equals the weighted-average outstanding common shares for the period plus the assumed issue of common shares arising from convertible securities plus the assumed shares issued because of the exercise of stock options or stock warrants, or their equivalent.

Table 1–1 shows in summary form the earnings per share fractions.

Table 1–1
Earnings per Share Fractions

BASIC EARNINGS PER SHARE =

$$\frac{\text{Net income available to common stockholders}}{\text{Weighted average number of common shares outstanding}}$$

DILUTED EARNINGS PER SHARE =

$$\frac{\text{Net income available to common stockholders} + \text{net of tax interest and/or dividend savings on convertible securities}}{\text{Weighted-average number of common shares outstanding} + \text{effect of convertible securities} + \text{net effect of stock options}}$$

EXAMPLE

Assume the same information as in the example dealing with basic earnings per share for Dauber Company. Assume further that potentially dilutive securities outstanding include 5% convertible bonds (each $1,000 bond is convertible into 25 shares of common stock) having a face value of $5,000,000. There are options to buy 50,000 shares of common stock at $10 per share. The average market price for common shares is $25 per share for 19X3. The tax rate is 30%.

Basic Earnings per Share

$$\frac{\text{Net income available to common stockholders}}{\text{Weighted-average number of common shares outstanding}} =$$

$$\frac{\$1,300,000}{632,500} = \$2.06$$

Diluted Earnings per Share

Income for diluted earnings per share:		
Earnings available to common stockholders		$1,300,000
Interest expense on convertible bonds		
($5,000,000 × .05)	$250,000	
Less: Tax savings ($250,000 × .30)	(75,000)	
Interest expense (net of tax)		$ 175,000
Income for diluted earnings per share		$1,475,000
Shares outstanding for diluted earnings per share:		
Weighted-average outstanding common shares		632,500
Assumed issued common shares for convertible bonds (5,000 bonds × 25 shares)		125,000
Assumed issued common shares from exercise of option	50,000	
Less: Assumed repurchase of treasury shares (50,000 × $10 = $500,000/$25)	(20,000)	30,000
Shares outstanding for diluted earnings per share		787,500

Diluted earnings per share for 19X3 is $1.87 ($1,475,000/787,500 shares). Diluted earnings per share must be disclosed because the two securities (the 5% convertible bond and the stock options) had an aggregately dilutive effect on earnings per share. That is, earnings per share decreased from $2.06 to $1.87. The required disclosures are indicated as follows:

EARNINGS PER SHARE DISCLOSURE

Basic Earnings per Share: $2.06

Diluted Earnings per Share: $1.87

Antidilutive Securities

In computing earnings per share, all antidilutive securities should be ignored. A security is considered to be antidilutive if its inclusion does not cause earnings per share to go down. In computing earnings per share, the aggregate of all dilutive securities must be considered. However, in order to exclude the ones that should not be used in the computation, it is necessary to ascertain which securities are individually dilutive and which ones are antidilutive. As was previously noted, a stock option will be antidilutive if the underlying market price of the stock that can be purchased is less than the exercise price of the option. A convertible security is antidilutive if the exercise of the convertible bond or preferred stock causes an increase in the earnings per share computation compared to that derived before the assumed conversion. In this situation, the additive effect to the numerator and denominator as a result of the conversion causes earnings per share to increase. In both of these situations, the antidilutive securities should be ignored in the calculation.

EXAMPLE

Assume a company's net income for the year of $100,000. A 10% $2,000,000 convertible bond was outstanding all year that was convertible into 2,000 shares of common stock. The weighted-average number of shares of common stock outstanding all year was 200,000. The income tax rate was 30%.

BASIC EARNINGS PER SHARE

$$\frac{\$100,000}{200,000} = \$.50$$

$$DILUTED\ EARNINGS\ PER\ SHARE$$

$$\frac{\$100,000 + 200,000\ (1-30\%)}{200,000 + 2,000} = \frac{\$240,000}{202,000} = 1.19$$

Since earnings per share increased as a result of the inclusion of the convertible bond, the bond is antidilutive and should be excluded from the calculation. Only basic earnings per share should be disclosed here.

EXAMPLE

Davis Company has basic earnings per share of $14 for 19X5. There were no conversions or exercises of convertible securities during the year. However, possible conversion of convertible bonds would have reduced earnings per share by $2. The impact of possible exercise of stock options would have increased earnings per share by $.38. Diluted earnings per share for 19X5 equals $12 ($14–$2). **Note:** The dilutive convertible bonds are considered in deriving diluted earnings per share, but the stock options are ignored because they have an antidilutive effect.

EPS and Specialized Disclosures on the Income Statement

When net income of a given period includes specialized activities disclosures, including income or loss from discontinued operations, extraordinary items, and the cumulative effect of change of accounting principle, earnings per share disclosure is required for each of these categories. GAAP requires that per share amounts for each of these amounts be shown either on the face of the income statement or in the notes to the financial statements.

Business Combinations

If a subsidiary has been acquired under the purchase method during the year, the weighted-average shares outstanding for the year are used from the purchase date. If a pooling of interests occurred, the weighted-average shares outstanding are from the beginning of the year.

Disclosures

Basic earnings per share and diluted earnings per share (if required) for income from continuing operations and net income must be disclosed on the face of the income statement. In addition, the earnings per share effects associated with the disposal of a business segment, extraordinary gains or losses, and the cumulative effect of a change in accounting principle must be presented either on the face of the income statement or notes thereto.

A reconciliation is required of the numerators and denominators for basic and diluted earnings per share. Disclosure is also mandated for the impact of preferred dividends in arriving at income available to common stockholders.

Other disclosures include

- Information on the capital structure
- Assumptions made
- Number of shares converted
- Rights and privileges of securities, such as dividend and participation rights, call prices, and conversion ratios

Annual Report References

TECHNITROL
1997 ANNUAL REPORT

5. Research, Development and Engineering Expenses

Research, development and engineering expenses ("RD&E") are included in selling, general and administrative expenses and were $16.4 million, $9.0 million, and $4.4 million in 1997, 1996, and 1995, respectively, for continuing operations. RD&E includes costs associated with new product development, product and process improvement, engineering follow-through during early stages of production, design of tools and dies, and the adaptation of existing technology to specific situations and customer requirements. The research and development component of RD&E, which generally includes only those costs associated with new technology, new products or significant changes to current products or processes, amounted to $7.2 million, $5.6 million, and $3.3 million in 1997, 1996, and 1995, respectively.

LIMITED
1997 ANNUAL REPORT

2. Special and Nonrecurring Items

As a result of an ongoing review of the Company's retail businesses and investments as well as implementation of initiatives intended to promote and strengthen the Company's various retail brands (including closing businesses, identification and disposal of non-core assets and identification of store locations not consistent with a particular brand), the Company recognized special and nonrecurring charges of $276 million during the fourth quarter of 1997 comprised of: 1) a $68 million charge for the closing of the 118 store Cacique lingerie business effective January 31, 1998. The amount includes noncash charges of $30 million comprised principally of write-offs and liquidations of store assets and accruals of $38 million related to cancellations of merchandise on order and other exit costs such as severance, service contract termination fees and lease termination costs. Other than contractual obligations of $5 million, the accrued costs are expected to be paid in fiscal year 1998; 2) an $82 million charge related to streamlining the Henri Bendel business from six stores to one store by September 1, 1998. The amount includes $26 million of noncash charges related primarily to write-offs of store assets, and accruals of $56 million related primarily to contract cancellations and lease termination costs. Other than contractual obligations of $18 million, the accrued costs are expected to be paid in 1998. Termination costs related to Henri Bendel closings will be recognized in first quarter 1998 when the associates are notified; 3) $86 million of impaired asset charges, related principally to the women's businesses, covering certain store locations where the carrying values are permanently impaired; and 4) a $28 million provision for closing and downsizing approximately 80 oversized stores, primarily within the Limited, Lerner New York, Lane Bryant, and Express women's businesses and a $12 million write-down to net realizable value of a real estate investment previously acquired in connection with closing and downsizing certain stores. The $28 million charge includes $13 million of noncash charges related to write-offs of store assets and accruals of $15 million related to lease termination costs. Other than contractual obligations of $7 million, the accrued costs are expected to be paid within 18 months. Additionally, the Company recognized a $13 million cost of sales charge in the fourth quarter for investment liquidation at Henri Bendel. The after-tax cash impact of these charges is estimated to be approximately $30 million. The Company will recognize charges for severance and other associate termination costs for Henri Bendel in the first quarter of 1998 (at the time the associates are notified).

Additionally, the Company recognized a $75.3 million pretax gain during the third quarter of 1997 in connection with the sale of 2.4 million shares of Brylane, which is carried on the equity method, for $46 per share generating cash proceeds of $108 million. This sale represented approximately one-half of its investment in Brylane. This gain was partially offset by valuation adjustments of $12.5 million on certain assets where the carrying values were permanently impaired. On February 20, 1998, the Company entered into an agreement with Pinault Printemps-Radoute to sell its remaining 2.6 million shares of Brylane for $51 per share, or cash proceeds of $131 million. The transaction was expected to close in April 1998.

The $86 million impaired asset charge was in accordance with SFAS No. 121, "Accounting for the Impairment of Long-Lived Assets and for Long-Lived Assets to be Disposed Of." As a result of the Company's strategic review process, including the implementation of brand initiatives within individual businesses, updated analyses were prepared to determine if there was impairment of any long-lived assets. The revised carrying values of these assets were calculated on the basis of discounted cash flows. The impaired asset charge had no impact on the Company's 1997 or future cash flows. As a result of this charge, depreciation and amortization expense related to these assets will decrease in future periods.

In 1996, the Company recorded a $12 million pretax, special and nonrecurring charge in connection with the April 1997 sale of Penhaligon's, a U.K.–based subsidiary of IBI.

In the fourth quarter of 1995, the Company recognized a $73.2 million pretax gain from the sale of a 60% interest in the Company's wholly-owned credit card bank, WFN. Along with the sale of the 60% interest in WFN, the Company recognized a special and non-recurring charge during the fourth quarter of 1995 of approximately $71.9 million. Of this amount, $25.8 million was provided for the closing of 26 stores and $19.8 million was provided for the downsizing of 33 stores, primarily at Limited and Lerner New York. The remaining charge of approximately $26.3 million represented the write-down to market or net realizable value of certain assets arising from nonoperating activities. The net pretax gain from these special and nonrecurring items was $1.3 million.

REGIS
1998 ANNUAL REPORT

112. Nonrecurring ITEMs

The following table summarized nonrecurring tents recorded by the Company:

	(Dollars in Thousands)		
	1998	1997	1996
Salon closures and dispositions, primarily Supercuts		1,500	7,000
Resolution of Supercuts officer litigation		2,004	5,823
Merger and transaction costs (Note 3)		14,322	
Loss on divestiture of Anasazi business attd assets	$1,979		
	$1,979	$18,731	12,823

Anasazi Exclusive Salon Products, LLC., a salon products manufacturing company, was sold to Curtis Acquisition LLC, which is controlled by two members of the Company's Board of Directors, one of whom is the Chairman.

Approximately $2.0 million, $.3 million and $4.4 million of the nonrecurring items in 1998, 1997 attd 1996, respectively, are non-cash in nature.

DUPONT
1998 ANNUAL REPORT

2. Discontinued Operations

On September 28, 1998, the company announced that the Board of Directors had approved a plan to divest the company's 100 percent-owned petroleum business (Conoco Inc.). On October 21, 1998, Conoco sold, in an initial public offering (IPO), 191,456,427 shares of Conoco Class A common stock at $23 per share for net proceeds of $4,228, which were remitted to DuPont to repay a portion of Conoco's intercompany indebtedness to DuPont. In addition, $22 in other costs directly related to the IPO were incurred. The company intends to complete the divestiture with a tax-free split off by exchanging its remaining Conoco shares (69.5 percent) for DuPont shares no later than third quarter 1999. The company has not recognized a deferred tax liability for the difference between the book basis and tax basis of its investment in Conoco's common stock because the company does not expect this basis difference to become subject to tax. The company's consolidated financial statements and notes report its petroleum business as discontinued operations. Prior periods have been restated. Results reported separately by Conoco are reported on a stand-alone basis and may differ from results based on discontinued operations reporting as discussed below. In addition, beginning October 22, 1998, the company's results from discontinued operations reflect minority interests of 30.5 percent.

Income from operations of discontinued business reflects Conoco's operations through September 30, 1998. Effective October 1, 1998, Conoco's results are reported as part of gain on disposal of discontinued business, and include the gain realized by the company from the IP0. For the three months and year ended December 31, 1998, such gain is $2,439. This includes a loss from Conoco's operations of $147 (after a tax benefit of $116) and reflects nonrecurring charges of $164; principally $127 for compensation expense for options granted by Conoco in substitution for DuPont options held by Conoco employees, $69 for employee separation costs and property impairments, partially offset by $32 of asset sales. In addition, net gain from sale of stock by subsidiary includes charges of $40 that are a direct result of the decision to divest Conoco. Also, 1998 results of income from operations of discontinued business includes a $31 tax benefit related to the sale of an international subsidiary, partly offset by a $28 litigation accrual in the United States. The year ended December 31, 1997, includes charges of $112 for impairment of nonrevenue producing properties and $55 for a write-down of an office building held for sale, substantially offset by a $161 gain on the sale of certain North Sea producing and exploration properties. The year ended December 31, 1996, includes charges of $63 for write-down of investment in an European natural gas marketing joint venture and $22 principally for employee separation costs in the United States, partly offset by a net benefit of $44 related to environmental insurance recoveries.

The cumulative translation adjustment reflected in the Consolidated Balance Sheet and Consolidated Statement of Stockholders' Equity pertains to Conoco's operations. Effective January 1, 1996, local currency was designated as the functional currency for Conoco's integrated European petroleum operations to properly reflect changed circumstances in the primary economic environment in which these subsidiaries operate. For Conoco subsidiaries whose functional currency is local currency, assets and liabilities denominated in local currency are translated into U.S. dollars at end-of-period exchange rates, and resultant translation adjustments are reported as a separate component of stockholders' equity.

Income from Operations of Discontinued Business[1]

1998	1997	1996	
Net Sales	$14,446	$20,990	$20,166
In come Before Income Taxes and Minority Interests[2]	921	1,918	1,654
Provision for Income Taxes	311	921	930
Minority Interests	16	24	19
Income from Operations, Net of Income Taxes	$ 594	$ 973	$ 705

[1] 1998 results are nine months ended September 30, 1998.

[2] Includes net interest expense allocations (based on the ratio of net assets of discontinued operations to consolidated net assets plus debt) of $240 through September 30, 1998, $248 for 1997, and $285 for 1996.

Gain on Disposal of Discontinued Business[1]

	1998
Net Sales	$4,737
(Loss) Before Income Taxes and Minority Interests[2]	(308)
Provision for Income Taxes	(116)
Minority Interests	(45)
(Loss) from Operations, Net of Income Taxes	(147)
Net Gain from Sale of Stock by Subsidiary	2,586
Gain on Disposal of Discontinued Business, Net of Income Taxes	$2,439

[1] Three months ended December 31, 1998

[2] Includes interest expense allocation (based on specific debt to be assumed) of $93.

The 1998 effective income tax rate (EITR) of 31.8 percent on Conoco's operations is significantly lower than the 1997 EITR of 48.0 percent and the 1996 EITR of 56.2 percent due to a larger U.S. alternative fuels tax credit, realization of a tax benefit on the sale of a subsidiary and a greater percentage of earnings in countries with lower effective tax rates.

It is expected that there will be a gain on ultimate disposal of Conoco, taking into account its estimated results in 1999.

Net Assets of Discontinued Operations

	1998	1997
December 31		
Cash and Cash Equivalents	$ 375	$ ó
Other Current Assets	2,864	2,938
Property, Plant and Equipment–Net	11,438	10,982
Other Assets	2,011	1,490
Current Liabilities	(2,473)	(3,023)
Other Liabilities	(4,115)	(3,680)
Minority Interests	(1,683)	(309)
Net Assets of Discontinued Operations	$ 8,417	$ 8,398

As of December 31, 1998, DuPont and Conoco had an intercompany receivable and payable, respectively, for $4,596 that has been eliminated for purposes of presenting net assets of discontinued operations. As described in the Restructuring, Transfer and Separation Agreement, Conoco is obligated to repay all outstanding debt owed to DuPont at such time as DuPont's voting power becomes less than 50 percent of Conoco.

CBS CORPORATION
1998 ANNUAL REPORT

10. Discontinued Operations

In recent years, the Corporation adopted various disposal plans that, in the aggregate, provide for the disposal of all of its industrial businesses and its financial services business. The assets and liabilities and the results of operations for all of these businesses are classified as Discontinued Operations for all periods presented except for certain liabilities expected to be retained by the Corporation. See note 11 to the financial statements.

In connection with the adoption of a plan in 1997 to divest all of the industrial businesses remaining at that time, the Corporation recognized a net gain of $871 million. The adoption of two separate disposal plans in 1996 combined with realization of a gain from a 1995 disposal plan resulted in the recognition of a net gain of $1,018 million in 1996.

In connection with these disposal plans, during 1998, the Corporation sold several businesses as well as certain securities and other assets. The most significant of these divestitures was the August 1998 sale of the Power Generation business for $1.2 billion in cash. At December 31, 1998, the remaining assets and liabilities of Discontinued Operations generally consist of (a) the Energy Systems and Government Operations businesses, (b) portfolio investments and related debt, and (c) other miscellaneous assets, including surplus properties, that are expected to be divested. In addition, Discontinued Operations includes a liability for estimated loss on disposal that covers transaction related costs, results of operations through the estimated date of disposal, and other obligations associated with the disposal of the industrial businesses.

The Energy Systems and Government Operations businesses are currently under agreement to be sold for $200 million in cash, subject to certain adjustments, plus the assumption of liabilities, commitments, and obligations of approximately $950 million, all in accordance with the terms of the divestiture agreement. The transaction is expected to be completed in early 1999 and is expected to result in a gain, which will be recognized upon realization.

The assets and liabilities of Discontinued Operations have been separately classified on the consolidated balance sheet as net assets of Discontinued Operations. A summary of these assets and liabilities follows:

Net Assets of Discontinued Operations
(in millions)

At December 31,	1998	1997
Assets:		
Cash and cash equivalents	$ 27	$ 59
Customer receivables	224	537
Inventories	94	560
Costs and estimated earnings over		
billings on uncompleted contracts	87	437
Portfolio investments	642	791
Plant and equipment, net	269	681
Deferred income taxes (note 5)	414	491
Other assets	162	545
Total assets	$ 1,919	$4,101
Liabilities:		
Accounts payable	$ 190	$ 384
Billings over costs and estimated earnings		
on uncompleted contracts	137	377
Short-term debt	—	7
Current maturities of long-term debt	46	96
Long-term debt	382	440
Settlements and environmental liabilities	569	625
Liability for estimated Loss on disposal	1,309	989
Other liabilities	570	971
Total liabilities	3,203	3,889
Net Assets (liabilities) of Discontinued		
Operations	$(1,284)	$ 212

PORTFOLIO INVESTMENTS

Portfolio investments, which remain from the financial services business,
consist of direct financing and leveraged lease receivables of $615 million
and $761 million at December 31, 1998 and 1997, respectively. Generally,

these leases are expected to liquidate in accordance with their contractual terms, which extend to 2015. At December 31, 1998 and 1997, 81 percent and 83 percent of the leases, respectively, related to aircraft while the remainder primarily related to cogeneration facilities. Other portfolio investments, totaled $27 million and $30 million at December 31, 1998 and 1997, respectively. The Corporation has provided for all of the estimated costs associated with liquidation of this portfolio. Cash inflows from contractual liquidation of the leasing portfolio are expected to be sufficient to repay the principal amount of the debt as well as interest and other costs associated with the portfolio.

The following table presents the Corporation's net investment in leases:

Net Investment in Leases
(in millions)

At December 31,	1998	1997
Rental payments receivable (net of principal and interest on non-recourse loans)	$ 465	$ 689
Estimated residual value of leased assets	324	366
Unearned and deferred income	(174)	(294)
Investment in leases (leasing receivables)	615	761
Deferred taxes and deferred investment tax credits arising from leases	(526)	(572)
Investment in leases, net	$ 89	$ 189

At December 31, 1998 and 1997, deferred investment tax credits totaled $19 million and $20 million, respectively. These deferred investment tax credits are amortized over the contractual terms of the respective leases.

Contractual maturities for the Corporation's leasing rental payments receivable at December 31, 1998 are as follows:

Contractual Maturities for Leasing Rental
Payments Receivable at December 31, 1998 (in millions)

			Year of Maturity			
Total	1999	2000	2001	2002	2003	After 2003
$465	$26	$33	$42	$36	$40	$288

SETTLEMENTS AND ENVIRONMENTAL LIABILITIES

Certain environmental and litigation-related liabilities are expected to be assumed by buyers pursuant to divestiture agreements or relate directly to surplus properties and are included in the net assets (liabilities) of Discontinued Operations. Those obligations that are expected to be retained by the Corporation are separately presented in Continuing Operations as retained liabilities of discontinued businesses. See note 11 to the financial statements.

The Corporation has been defending various lawsuits brought by utilities claiming a substantial amount of damages in connection with alleged tube degradation in steam generators sold by the Energy Systems business as components of nuclear steam supply systems.

Since 1993, settlement agreements have been entered resolving ten litigation claims. These agreements generally require the Corporation to provide certain products and services at prices discounted at varying rates. Two eases were resolved in favor of the Corporation after trial or arbitration. In the one remaining steam generator lawsuit, the Corporation's motion for summary judgment was recently granted, in significant part. The plaintiffs have appealed this decision.

The Corporation is also a party to three tolling agreements with utilities or utility plant owners groups that have asserted steam generator claims. The toiling agreements delay initiation of any litigation for various specified periods of time and permit the parties time to engage in discussions.

The Corporation has provided for estimated costs for previous and potential settlement agreements that provide for costs in excess of discounted prices. These obligations will be assumed by the buyer of the Energy Systems business in accordance with the terms of the divestiture agreement.

LIABILITY FOR ESTIMATED LOSS ON DISPOSAL

The liability for estimated loss on disposal of $1,309 million at December 31, 1998, includes estimated losses and disposal costs associated with each divestiture transaction, including estimated results of operations through the expected date of disposition and certain contingencies related to the industrial businesses, as well as interest and other costs associated with the liquidation of portfolio investments. Satisfaction of these liabilities is expected to occur over the next several years. Management believes that the liability for estimated loss on disposal at December 31, 1998, is adequate to cover divestiture or liquidation of the remaining assets and liabilities of Discontinued Operations.

RESULTS OF OPERATIONS

In accordance with APE 30, the consolidated financial statements reflect the operating results of Discontinued Operations separately from Continuing Operations.

Summarized in the following table are the operating results of Discontinued Operations:

Operating Results of Discontinued Operations
(in millions)

Year Ended December 31,	Sale of Products or Services		
	1998	1997	1996
Industrial businesses	$2,235	$4,237	$5,389
Financial services	21	12	26
Total Discontinued Operations	$2,256	$4,269	$5,415

Year Ended December 31	Net Income (Loss) Before Measurement Date		
	1998	1997	1996
Industrial businesses	$—	(191)	$ (609)
Financial services	—	—	—
Total Discontinued Operations	$ —	$ (191)	$ (609)

Net Income (Loss) After Measurement Date Year Ended December 31,	1998	1997	1996
Industrial businesses	$ (100)	$ (43)	$ (134)
Financial services	(12)	(18)	(9)
Other	(3)	(23)	(36)
Total Discontinued Operations	$ (115)	$ (88)	$ (179)

All operating results after the measurement date are charged to the liability for estimated loss on disposal.

In connection with the presentation of various businesses as Discontinued Operations, interest expense on Continuing Operations debt totaling $5 million, $42 million and $60 million was reclassified to Discontinued Operations for the years ended December 31, 1998, 1997, and 1996, respectively. This allocation is based on the quarterly ratio of the net assets of Discontinued Operations to the sum of total consolidated net assets plus consolidated debt.

CASH FLOWS

Cash proceeds from the sale or liquidation of all assets of Discontinued Operations except for portfolio investments, as well as cash requirements to satisfy non-debt obligations of Discontinued Operations will affect cash flows of Continuing Operations. Operating cash flows of Discontinued Operations, which include cash flows from the operations of the businesses as well as payments for disposition-related costs, are presented separately from Continuing Operations in the consolidated financial statements and consist of the following:

Cash Flows from Operating Activities of
Discontinued Operations (in millions)

Year Ended December 31,	1998	1997	1996
Industrial businesses	$(286)	$(382)	$(279)
Financial services	(42)	(30)	3
Other	(3)	(25)	(36)
Cash used by operating activities	$(331)	$(437)	$(312)

DUPONT
1999 ANNUAL REPORT

7. Discontinued Operations

On September 28, 1998, the company announced that the Board of Directors had approved a plan to divest the company's 100 percent-owned petroleum business (Conoco Inc.). On October 21, 1998, the company's interest in Conoco was reduced to 69.5 percent following an initial public offering of Conoco Class A common stock. On August 6, 1999, the company completed the planned divestiture through a tax-free split off whereby the company exchanged its 436,543,573 shares of Conoco Class B common stock for 147,980,872 shares of DuPont common stock. The company's consolidated financial statements and notes report its former petroleum business as discontinued operations. Prior periods have been restated.

Income from operations of discontinued business reflects Conoco's operations through September 30, 1998. Effective October 1, 1998, through August 6, 1999, Conoco's results are reported as part of gain on discontinued business, and include gains recognized by the company from completion of the Conoco exchange offer in 1999 and the IPO in 1998. For 1999, gain on disposal of discontinued business is $7,471 and includes income from Conoco's operations of $165. The gain on the exchange offer of $7,306 results from the difference between the market value and the carrying value of the Conoco Class B common shares, less direct expenses. The company did not recognize a deferred tax liability for the difference between the book basis and tax basis of its investment in Conoco's common stock because this basis difference was not subject to tax. For 1998 gain on disposal of discontinued business is $2,439. This includes a loss from Conoco's operations of $147 (after a tax benefit of $116) and reflects nonrecurring charges of $164; principally $127 for compensation expense for options granted by Conoco in substitution for DuPont options held by Conoco employees, $69 for employee separation costs and property impairments, partially offset by $32 of asset sales. In addition, net gain from sale of stock by subsidiary includes charges of $40 that are a direct result of the decision to divest Conoco. Also, 1998 results of income from operations of discontinued business includes a $31 tax benefit related to the sale of an international subsidiary, partly offset by a $28 litigation accrual in the

United States. The year ended December 31, 1997, includes charges of $112 for impairment of nonrevenue producing properties and $55 for a write-down of an office building held for sale, substantially offset by a $161 gain on the sale of certain North Sea producing and exploration properties.

Income from operations of discontinued business	1999	1998[1]	1997
Net sales	—	$14,446	$20,990
Income before income taxes and minority interests[2]	—	921	1,918
Provision for income taxes	—	311	921
Minority interests	—	16	24
Income from operations, net of income taxes	—	$ 594	$ 973

[1] 1998 results are nine months ended September 30, 1998.

[2] Includes net interest expense allocations (based on the ratio of net assets plus debt) of $240 through September 30, 1998, and $248 for 1997.

Gain on disposal of discontinued business	1999[1]	1998[2]
Net sales	$12,015	$4,737
Income (loss) before income taxes and minority interests[3]	453	(308)
Provision (benefit) for income taxes	164	(116)
Minority interests	124	(45)
Income (loss) from operations, net of income taxes	165	(147)
Net gain from exchange offer	7,306	—
Net gain from sale of stock by subsidiary	—	2,586
Gain on disposal of discontinued business, net of income taxes	$ 7,471	$2,439

[1] Through August 6, 1999.

[2] Three months ended December 31, 1998

[3] Includes interest expense allocation (based on specific debt to be assumed) of $93 for both 1999 and 1998. Conoco repaid this debt in second quarter 1999.

Net assets of discontinued operations	1999	1998
December 31		
Cash and cash equivalents	—	$ 375
Other current assets	—	2,864
Property, plant and equipment—net	—	11,438
Other assets	—	2,011
Current liabilities	—	(2,473)
Other liabilities	—	(4,115)
Minority interests	—	(1,683)
Net assets of discontinued operations	—	$ 8,417

Net assets of discontinued operations reflects divestiture of Conoco Inc. in the third quarter 1999. See Note 26 regarding contingent tax liabilities.

MERCK
1998 ANNUAL REPORT

A reconciliation of the plans' funded status to the net asset (liability) recognized at December 31 is as follows:

	Pension Benefits		Other Postretirement Benefits	
	1998	*1997*	*1998*	*1997*
Funded status (benefit obligation in excess of plan assets)	$ (65.0)	$ (39.2)	$(131.5)	$ (87.5)
Unrecognized net loss (gain). .	380.6	269.1	(95.7)	(171.8)
Unrecognized plan changes. . .	78.8	60.9	(130.3)	(128.3)
Unrecognized transitional net asset	(39.4)	(55.2)		
Net asset (liability)	$ 355.0	$ 235.6	$(357.5)	$(387.6)
Recognized as:				
Other assets	$513.4	$ 387.8	$ —	$ —
Accounts payable and accrued liabilities	(7.9)	(11.0)	(24.8)	(25.6)
Deferred income taxes and noncurrent liabilities	(284.3)	(217.2)	(332.7)	(362.0)
Accumulated other comprehensive loss	133.8	76.0		

For pension plans with benefit obligations in excess of plan assets at December 31, 1998 and 1997, the fair value of plan assets was $402.6 million and $472.6 million, respectively, and the benefit obligation was $871.1 million and $836.4 million, respectively. For those plans with accumulated benefit obligations in excess of plan assets at December 31, 1998 and 1997, the fair value of plan assets was $332.2 million and $197.3 million, respectively, and the accumulated benefit obligation was $551 .0 million and $360.8 million, respectively.

Assumptions used in determining U.S. plan information are as follows:

December 31	Pension Benefits			Other Postretirement Benefits		
	1998	1997	1996	1998	1997	1996
Discount rate	6.75%	7.0%	7.5%	6.75%	7.0%	7.5%
Expected rate of return on plan assets	10.0	10.0	10.0	10.0	10.0	10.0
Salary growth rate	4.5	4.5	4.5	4.5	4.5	4.5

For the three years presented, international pension plan assumptions ranged from 4.0% to 8.0% for the discount rate, 5.5% to 10.0% for the expected rate of return on plan assets and 2.0% to 6.0% for the salary growth rate.

The health care cost trend rate for other postretirement benefit plans was 7.5% at December 31, 1998. The rate will gradually decline to 5.0% over a 5-year period. A one percentage point change in the health care cost trend rate would have had the following effects:

	One Percentage Point	
	Increase	Decrease
Effect on total service and interest cost components	$ 16.7	$ (13.9)
Effect on benefit obligation	138.3	(119.2)

14. Other (Income) Expense, Net

Years Ended December 31	1998	1997	1996
Interest income	$(307.7)	$ (221.4)	$(205.4)
Interest expense	205.6	129.5	138.6
Exchange gains	(44.7	(18.0)	(27.8)
Minority interests	162.4	131.8	144.2
Amortization of goodwill and other intangibles	264.3	197.2	196.2
Other, net	219.8	123.6	(5.0)
	$ 499.7	$ 342.7	$ 240.8

Minority interests include third parties' share of exchange gains and losses arising from translation of the financial statements into U.S. dollars. Minority interests reflect dividends paid to Astra on $2.4 billion par value preferred stock of a subsidiary beginning in July 1998 and, in 1997 and

1996, dividends on the PEGs, which were issued in December 1995 and redeemed in September 1997. (See Note 10.)

Increased amortization of goodwill and other intangibles in 1998 reflects amortization of goodwill and other intangibles associated with the restructuring of AMI in July 1998. (See Note 4.)

In 1998, other, net, includes $338.6 million of nonrecurring charges, primarily for environmental remediation costs and asset write-offs, principally deferred start-up costs.

In 1997, other, net, includes $207.3 million of nonrecurring charges primarily for the loss on sale of assets, endowment of The Merck Company Foundation and environmental remediation costs.

Interest paid was $192.3 million in 1998. $130.5 million in 1997 and $117.4 million in 1996.

15. Taxes on Income

A reconciliation between the Company's the U.S. statutory rate is as follows:

	1998 Amount	Tax Rate 1998	Tax Rate 1997	1996
U.S. statutory rate applied to pretax income	$2,846.6	35.0%	35.0%	35.0%
Differential arising from:				
Acquired research	363.8	4.5		
Foreign earnings	141.4	1.7		
State taxes	129.4	1.6	1.0	.1
Tax exemption for Puerto Rico operations	(133.1)	(1.6)	(1.9)	(1.9)
Equity income from affiliates.	(135.6)	(1.7)	(2.4)	(1.9)
Other	(327.6)	(4.0)	(2.8)	.1
	$2,884.9	35.5%	28.6%	30.0%

The increase in the effective tax rate in 1998 primarily reflects the nondeductibility of the charge for acquired research in connection with the restructuring of AMI and the state tax impact of the gain on the sale of the Company's one-half interest in DMPC.

The differential arising from equity income from affiliates represents the favorable impact of accounting for joint venture taxes as a reduction of equity income, offset in part by significantly higher effective tax rates within the joint ventures. The reduced benefit in 1998 reflects the impact of the AMI restructuring, resulting in pretax partnership returns recorded in equity income.

17. Comprehensive Income

Effective January 1, 1998, the Company adopted the provisions of Statement No. 130, Reporting Comprehensive Income. which modifies the financial statement presentation of comprehensive income and its components. In accordance with this Statement, a Consolidated Statement of Comprehensive Income is included in the consolidated financial statements to present all changes in Stockholders' equity in the periods presented other than changes resulting from transactions relating to the Company's stock. Upon adoption, accumulated other comprehensive income of $9.0 million at December 31, 1997 was reclassified from Retained earnings to a separate component of Stockholders' equity.

The components of Other comprehensive loss are as follows:

	Pretax[1]	Tax	After Tax
Year Ended December 31, 1998			
Net unrealized gain on investments	$ 20.6	$ (4.8)	$ 15.8
Net income realization	(41.9)	20.5	(21.4)
Subtotal	$ (21.3)	$ 15.7	$ (5.6)
Minimum pension liability	(47.2)	22.5	24.7
	$ (68.5)	$ 38.2	$ (30.3)
Year Ended December 31, 1997			
Net unrealized loss on investments	$ (74.6)	$ 57.0	$ (17.6)
Minimum pension liability	(37.8)	25.4	12.4)
	$(112.4)	$ 82.4	$ (30.0)
Year Ended December, 31, 1996			
Net unrealized loss on investments	$ (36.1)	$ 25.3	$ (10.8)
Minimum pension liability	(19.9)	13.4	(6.5)
	$ (56.0)	$ 38.7	$ (17.3)

[1]Net of minority interest

The components of Accumulated other comprehensive (loss) income are as follows:

December 31	1998	1997
Net unrealized gain on investments	$ 22.3	$ 27.9
Minimum pension liability	(43.6)	(18.9)
	$(21.3)	$ 9.0

UNION CARBIDE
1998 ANNUAL REPORT

4. Other Comprehensive Income (Loss)

Comprehensive income is defined as any change in the corporation's equity from transactions and other events originating from non-owner sources. For the corporation, those changes are comprised of reported net income, changes in the unrealized appreciation or depreciation of the corporation's available for-sale securities and changes in unrealized foreign currency translation adjustments. The following summary presents the components of comprehensive income, other than net income:

Millions of Dollars	Pre-Tax	Income Tax Effect	After-Tax
Balance at December 31, 1995	$ (10)	$ —	$ (10)
Foreign currency translation adjustments	(11)	—	(11)
Unrealized gains (losses) on securities:			
Unrealized holding gains (losses) arising during period	(5)	(1)	(4)
Reclassification adjustment for (gains) losses realized in net income	—	—	—
Net unrealized losses	(16)	(1)	(15)
Balance at December 31, 1996	$ (26)	$ (1)	$ (25)
Foreign currency translation adjustments	(81)	—	(81)
Unrealized gains (losses) on securities:			
Unrealized holding gains (losses) arising during period	8	3	5
Reclassification adjustment for (gains) losses realized in net income	—	—	5
Net unrealized losses	(73)	3	(76)
Balance at December 31, 1997	$ (99)	$ 2	$(101)
Foreign currency translation adjustments	(8)	—	(8)
Unrealized gains (losses) on securities:			
Unrealized holding gains (losses) arising during period	—	—	—
Reclassification adjustment for (gains) losses realized in net income	7	2	5
Net unrealized losses	(1)	2	5
Balance at December 31, 1998	$(100)	$ 4	$(104)

O'SULLIVAN
1998 ANNUAL REPORT

3. Restructuring Charge

In March 1996, the Company adopted a business restructuring plan to cut costs and better utilize working capital. The plan included the discontinuance of certain product lines which had received marginal acceptance in the marketplace, costs associated with the initial training of terminated employees at the Company's Utah facility and the modification of the business structure of an international division. A pre-tax charge of $5.2 million was recognized in the third quarter of fiscal 1996 related to the restructuring plan. The components of the restructuring charge and an analysis of the amounts charged against the reserve are outlined in the table below:

Restructuring Charges (in thousands)	Original Reserve	Charges through June 30, 1996	Balance June 30, 1996	Charges through June 30, 1997	Balance June 30, 1997
Discontinued product lines[1]	$4,155	$(4,117)	$ 38	$ (38)	$ —
Initial training costs of terminated employees[2]	387	(387)	—	—	—
Impairment of fixed assets[3]	274	(274)	—	—	—
Modification costs of international division[4]	396	(121)	275	(275)	
Total	$5,212	$(4,899)	$ 313	$ (313)	$

[1]Relates to certain product lines that were discontinued and the remaining inventory was written down to net realizable value.

[2]Certain manufacturing employees were terminated at the Utah facility and the costs associated with the initial training of these employees was written off.

[3]Represents the write off of certain machinery that was used to manufacture the discontinued product lines.

[4]Represents the cost to modify the business structure of an international division.

Proceeds from the disposal of discontinued inventory approximated $1.5 million and was received in fiscal 1997. The restructuring charge has been included as a separate line item in the accompanying consolidated statement of operations and consolidated statement of cash flows.

GOODYEAR
1998 ANNUAL REPORT

2. Rationalizations

(in millions)	1998	1997	1996
Rationalizations and other provisions	$ (29.7)	$265.2	$148.5
Asset sales	(123.81	—	(32.1)
	$(153.5)	$265.2	$116.4

1998

Rationalizations and other provisions—The Company recorded a benefit totaling $22 million ($14.7 million after tax or $.09 per share) in the second quarter resulting from the favorable settlement of obligations related to the Company's withdrawal of support for the worldwide Formula 1 racing series. Additionally, the Company reversed certain reserves totaling $7.7 million ($4.9 million after tax or $03 per share) related to plant downsizing and closure activities in North America, due to a change in the 1997 rationalization plan.

Asset sales—The Company recorded gains totaling $123.8 million ($76.4 million after tax or $.48 per share) on the disposition of a latex processing facility in Georgia, six distribution facilities in North America and certain other real estate.

1997

Rationalizations and other provisions—As a result of continued competitive conditions in the markets served by the Company, a number of rationalization actions were approved in 1997 to reduce costs and focus on core businesses. These actions,the timing of which resulted in part from the finalization of labor contract negotiations in the United States, included the optimization, downsizing or consolidation of certain production facilities, consolidation of distribution operations and withdrawal of support from the worldwide Formula 1 racing series. In connection with these actions, obligations under certain leases and other contracts were accrued, other assets were written off and over 3,000 associates have been or will be released. A charge of $265.2 million ($176.3 million after tax or $1.12 per share) was recorded, of which $52.5 million related to non-cash writeoffs and $212.7 million related to future cash outflows, primarily for associate severance costs. The remaining balance of these provisions totaled $88.2 million and $201.9 million at December 31, 1998 and 1997, respectively.

The Company recorded a charge of $146.1 million for the release of more than 3,000 associates around the world. Of this amount, $31.7 million, resulting from related pension curtailments, was recorded as a pension liability. Approximately 60 percent of the associates to be released under the plan are or were hourly associates at manufacturing and distribution locations, primarily in the United States. The balance of the associates to be released relates to salaried associates in various managerial, sales, supervisory and staff positions scheduled for elimination under the plan, primarily at operations in Europe and the United States. At December 31, 1997, approximately 450 associates, primarily salaried associates in Europe, had been released at a total cost of $25.3 million. During 1998, approximately 1,200 associates, primarily hourly associates, were released at a cost of approximately $30 million. The Company plans to release approximately 1,400 more associates, employed primarily at manufacturing and distribution operations in North America, and had reserved $59.3 million for that cost at December 31, 1998.

Optimization, downsizing, consolidation and withdrawal costs, other than associate-related costs, were recorded, and were incurred through December 31, 1998 as follows:

(In millions)	Recorded	Incurred
Withdrawal of support for the Formula 1 racing series	$ 63.4	$ 43.2
Plant downsizing and closure activities	23.0	3.5
Kelly-Springfield consolidation	12.9	.3
Consolidation of North American distribution facilities	12.3	7.6
Commercial tire outlet consolidation	4.7	3.1
Production realignments	2.8	2.8
	$119.1	$ 60.5

Withdrawal costs associated with Formula 1 racing resulted from the fulfillment of contracts with various racing teams, the writeoff of equipment and other assets no longer needed and estimated operating costs for the 1998 racing season. Plant downsizing and closure activities relate to four production facilities in the United States. Costs associated with downsizing and closure were for the writeoff of buildings and equipment and for lease cancellation costs. The Kelly-Springfield consolidation involves the integration of the Kelly-Springfield tire division located in Cumberland, Maryland, into the Company's Akron, Ohio, world headquarters, the cost of which relates to noncancellable leases and the writeoff of equipment. The consolidation of distribution facilities in North America from 40 to 18 resulted in lease cancellation costs associated with the anticipated closure of these facilities. The commercial tire outlet consolidation involves the writeoff of equipment and lease cancellation costs relating to the planned closing of approximately 30 locations. The cost associated with production realignments involves the writeoff of equipment due to consolidation of production. At December 31, 1998 and 1997, the remaining balance of these provisions totaled $28.9 million and $112.8 million, respectively. During 1998, approximately $54.2 million was charged to the reserve and $29.7 million was reversed ($22 million in respect of withdrawal of support for Formula 1 racing and $7.7 million for plant downsizing and closure activities that were changed). The Company expects that the major portion of the actions will be completed during 1999 with the balance to be completed in 2000.

1996

Rationalizations and other provisions—As part of a rationalization plan the Company recorded charges totaling $148.5 million ($95.3 million after tax or $.61 per share) related to worldwide workforce reductions, consolidation of operations and the closing of manufacturing facilities. The remaining balance of these provisions totaled $9.1 million and $49.6 million at December 31, 1998 and 1997, respectively.

The Company recorded $113.3 million for the release of approximately 2,800 associates around the world. Approximately 50 percent of the associates to be released in accordance with the plan are or were hourly associates at manufacturing and warehouse locations, primarily in Latin America and the United States. The balance of the associates to be released relates to salaried associates in various managerial, sales, supervisory and staff positions planned to be eliminated primarily at locations in Europe and the United States. At December 31, 1997, approximately 2,300 associates, primarily hourly associates in the United States, Latin America and Europe, had been released at a cost of approximately $85.8 million. During 1998, approximately 150 associates, primarily salaried associates in the United States, were released at a cost of $13.1 million. As a result of higher than expected retirements, in 1998 the Company reduced the number of associates it expected to release under the 1996 program by 270 and reduced the 1996 reserve by approximately $8.7 million. A comparable amount was recorded as part of the Company's 1997 rationalization program related to personnel reductions. The Company plans to release approximately 120 associates whose positions will be eliminated under the 1996 plan and had $5.7 million reserved at December 31, 1998 for that cost. These are primarily hourly associates employed at distribution and manufacturing operations in the United States scheduled for closure or consolidation.

Rationalization costs, other than associate-related costs, were recorded, and were incurred through December 31, 1998, as follows:

(In millions)	*Recorded*	*Incurred*
Discontinuance of PVC production	$10.6	$10.6
Canadian retail store closures	9.0	5.9
International production rationalization	8.5	7.7
North American Tire production rationalization	7.1	7.6
	$35.2	$31.8

The costs related to discontinuing the production of polyvinylchloride (PVC) at the Niagara Falls chemical manufacturing facility was for the writeoff of equipment. The costs relating to the closure of certain Canadian retail stores relate primarily to noncancellable leases. Production rationalization plans at international locations, primarily the closure of the

Greece tire manufacturing facility, relate to the writeoff and disposal of equipment. The North American Tire business unit rationalized production at various tire plants in the United States. The costs recorded and incurred related primarily to the writeoff of equipment and noncancellable leases. The remaining balance of these provisions at December 31, 1998 and 1997 totaled $3.4 million and $22.1 million, respectively and, at December 31, 1998, related primarily to lease cancellation costs from the Canadian retail store closings. The Company expects to substantially complete these plans in 1999.

Asset sales—The Company recorded net gains totaling $32.1 million ($21.6 million after tax or $14 per share) related to the sale of business property in Asia, a portion of an investment in an Asian plantation and the loss on the anticipated sale of a U.S. manufacturing facility.

3. DISCONTINUED OPERATIONS

On July 30, 1998, the Company sold substantially all of the assets and liabilities of its oil transportation business to Plains All American Inc., a subsidiary of Plains Resources Inc. Proceeds from the sale were $422.3 million, which included distributions to the Company prior to closing of $25.1 million. The principal assets of the oil transportation business included the All American Pipeline System, a heated crude oil pipeline system consisting of a 1,225 mile mainline segment extending from Las Flores and Gaviota, California, to McCarney, Texas, a crude oil gathering system located in California's San Joaquin Valley and related terminal and storage facilities.

The transaction has been accounted for as a sale of discontinued operations, and accordingly, the accompanying financial information has been restated where required.

Operating results and the loss on sale of discontinued operations follow:

(In millions, except per share)	1998	1997	1996
Net Sales	$ 22.4	$89.8	$ 127.1
Income (Loss) before Income Taxes	$ 12.9	$56.7	$(689.21)
United States Taxes on Income	4.7	20.4	(232.4)
Income (Loss) from Discontinued Operations	8.2	36.3	(456.8)

Loss on Sale of Discontinued Operations, including income from operations during the disposal period (3/21/98-7/30/981 of $10.0 (net of tax of $24.1)	(42.9)		
Discontinued Operations	$(34.7)	$ 36.3	$(456.8)
Income (Loss) Per Share—Basic:			
Income (Loss) from Discontinued Operations$ .05	$ .24	$ (2.94)	
Loss on Sale of Discontinued Operations	(.27)	—	—
Discontinued Operations	$ (.22)	$ .24	$ (2.94)
Income (Loss) Per Share—Diluted:			
Income (Loss) from Discontinued Operations	$ .05	$ .23	$ (2.91)
Loss on Sale of Discontinued Operations	(.27)	—	—
Discontinued Operations	$ (.22)	$ .23	$ (2.91)

In December 1996, industry developments occurred indicating that the quantities of offshore California, onshore California and Alaska North Slope crude oil expected to be tendered in the future to the All American Pipeline System and related assets (the System) for transportation would be below prior estimates and that volumes of crude oil expected to be tendered to the System for transportation to markets outside of California in the future would be significantly lower than previously anticipated. As a result management determined that the future cash flows expected to be generated by the System would be less than its carrying value. In accordance with Statement of Financial Accounting Standards No. 121, "Accounting for the Impairment of Long-Lived Assets and for Long-Lived Assets to Be Disposed Of," the Company reduced the carrying value of the System to $420 million, determined using the present value of expected future cash flows from the System, and recorded a charge of $755.6 million ($499.3 million after tax or $3.18 per share).

4. STRATEGIC ALLIANCE AND NONCASH INVESTING ACTIVITIES

Strategic Alliance

On February 3, 1999, the Company signed a memorandum of understanding (MOU) with Sumitomo Rubber Industries, Ltd. (SRI), under which the

Company and SRI would enter into a strategic alliance for the manufacture and sale of tires. The MOU provides for the creation of jointly held tire companies in Europe, North America and Japan, jointly held companies for global technology exchange and for global purchasing, and the investment by the Company and SRI in the common stock of the other. Definitive agreements are expected to be signed later this year.

Under the terms of the MOU, the Company would acquire 75% ownership of the tire company in Europe, which would hold substantially all of each party's tire manufacturing and sales operations in that region. The Company's businesses in Poland, Slovenia, South Africa, Turkey and Morocco (all of which are managed as part of the Company's European tire business unit) would not be a part of the European tire company. The Company would also acquire 75% ownership of the tire company in North America, which would hold substantially all of SRI's tire manufacturing operations in North America and certain of SRI's sales and distribution operations in that region. The remainder of SRI's North American sales and distribution operations would be acquired in their entirety by the Company.

LOCKHEED MARTIN 1999 ANNUAL REPORT

5. Earnings Per Share

Basic and diluted earnings per share for 1999 and 1998 are computed based on net earnings. For these years, the weighted average number of common shares outstanding during each year was used in the calculation of basic earnings per share, and this number of shares was increased by the effects of dilutive stock options based on the treasury stock method in the calculation of diluted earnings per share. Basic loss per share for 1997 was computed based on net earnings, less the dividend requirement for preferred stock to the date of redemption, and less the deemed preferred stock dividend resulting from the November 1997 GE Transaction representing the excess of the fair value of the consideration transferred to GE (approximately $2.8 billion) over the carrying value of the Lockheed Martin preferred stock redeemed ($1.0 billion). The weighted average number of common shares outstanding during the year was used in this calculation. The diluted loss per share for 1997 was computed in the same manner as basic loss per share, as adjustments related to the assumed conversion of the preferred stock (50.6 million common shares) and the date of redemption ($53 million), and the dilutive effect of stock options (5.8 million common shares), were not made since they would have had antidilutive effects.

The following table sets forth the computations of basic and diluted earnings (loss) per share:

(In millions, except per share data)	*1999*	*1998*	*1997*
Net earnings (loss) applicable to common stock:			
Earnings before cumulative effect of change in accounting	**$737**	$1,001	$1,300
Cumulative effect of change in accounting	**(355)**	—	—
Net earnings	**382**	1,001	1,300
Dividends on preferred stock	—	—	(53)
Deemed preferred stock dividend	—	—	(1,826)

(In millions, except per share data)	*1999*	*1998*	*1997*
Net earnings (loss) applicable to common stock for basic and diluted computations	**$382**	**$1,001**	**$(579)**
Average common shares outstanding:			
Average number of common shares outstanding for basic computations	**382.3**	376.5	370.6
Dilutive stock options—based on the treasury stock method	**1.8**	4.6	—
Average number of common shares outstanding for diluted computations	**384.1**	381.1	370.6
Earnings (loss) per share			
Basic:			
Before cumulative effect of change in accounting	**$1.93**	$2.66	$(1.56)
Cumulative effect of change in accounting	**(.93)**	—	—
	$1.00	$2.66	$(1.56)
Diluted:			
Before cumulative effect of change in accounting	**$1.92**	$2.63	$(1.56)
Cumulative effect of change in accounting	**(.93)**	—	—
	$.99	$2.63	$(1.56)

UNION CARBIDE
1998 ANNUAL REPORT

Basic and diluted earnings per share (EPS) are calculated as follows:

Millions of dollars (except share and per share amounts), for the year ended December 31,	*1998*	*1997*	*1996*
Basic—			
Income before cumulative effect of change in accounting principle	$ 403	$ 676	$ 593
Less: Dividends on ESOP shares, pre-tax	—	(9)	(13)
Appreciation on ESOP shares redeemed for cash	—	(23)	—
Income before cumulative effect of change in accounting principle, adjusted for basic calculation	403	644	580
Cumulative effect of change in accounting principle	—	(17)	—
Net income—common stockholders, adjusted for basic calculation	$ 403	$ 627	$ 580
Weighted average shares outstanding for basic calculation	135,028,100	128,185,093	131,029,621
Earnings per share—			
Income before cumulative effect of change in accounting principle	$ 2.98	$ 5.02	$ 4.43
Cumulative effect of change in accounting principle		—(0.13)	—
Net income—common stockholders	$ 2.98	$ 4.89	$ 4.43
Diluted—			
Income before cumulative effect of change in accounting principle, adjusted for basic calculation	$ 403	$ 644	$ 580
Plus: Dividends on ESOP shares, pre-Tax	—	9	13
Less: Additional ESOP contribution resulting from assumed conversion of ESOP shares	—	(1)	(1)
Income before cumulative effect of change in accounting principle, adjusted for diluted calculation	403	652	592
Cumulative effect of change in accounting principle	—	(17)	—
Net income—common stockholders, adjusted for diluted calculation	$ 403	$ 635	$ 592
Weighted average shares outstanding for basic calculation	138,028,100	128,184,093	131,029,621

Add: Effect of stock options	**3,381,795**	4,034,969	4,495,656
Effect of equity Put options	—	—	403
Shares issuable upon conversion of the corporation's convertible ESOP shares	—	11,739,036	16,120,754
Weighted average shares outstanding, adjusted for diluted calculation	**138,409,895**	143,959,098	151,646,434

Earnings per share—

Income before cumulative effect of change in accounting principle, adjusted for diluted calculation	**$ 2.91**	$ 4.53	$ 3.90
Cumulative effect of change in accounting principle	—	(0.12)	—
Net income—common stockholders, adjusted for diluted calculation	**$ 2.91**	$ 4.41	$ 3.906

CHEVRON
1997 ANNUAL REPORT

19. Earnings per Share

In February 1997, the Financial Accounting Standards Board issued SFAS No. 128, "Earnings Per Share," which became effective for reporting periods ending after December 15, 1997. Under the previous standard, APB No. 15, the company presented a single earnings per share (EPS) amount that was calculated by dividing net income by the weighted-average number of shares outstanding for the period. Under the provisions of SFAS No. 128, the company will present basic and diluted EPS. Basic EPS includes the effects of award and salary deferrals that are invested in Chevron stock units by certain officers and employees of the company. Diluted EPS includes the effects of these deferrals as well as the dilutive effects of outstanding stock options awarded under the LTIP and Broad-based Employee Stock Option Program (See Note 18. Stock Options). For purposes of comparability, all prior-period earnings-per-share data have been restated to conform with SFAS No. 128. The following table sets forth the computation of basic and diluted EPS:

Options to purchase 1,731,750 shares of common stock at $80.9375 per share were outstanding at year-end but were not included in the computation of diluted EPS because the options' exercise price was greater than the average market price of the common shares. These options expire October 29, 2007.

BOWATER
1999 ANNUAL REPORT

19. Stock Options Plans

Bowater has three stock options plans—1988, 1992 and 1997. These plans authorized the grant of up to 6.0 million shares of our common stock in the form of incentive stock options, non-qualified stock options, stock appreciation rights, performance stock and restricted stock awards. The option granted under the 1988 and 1992 plans was based on the fair market value of our common stock on the date of grant, or the average fair market value of our common stock for the 20 business days immediately preceding the date of grant. The option price for options granted under the 1997 plan was based on the fair market value of our common stock on the date of grant.

All options granted through December 31, 1997, were exercisable at December 31, 1999. Options granted in 1999 and 1998 generally become exercisable over a period of two years. Unless terminated earlier in accordance with their terms, all options expire 10 years from the date of grant. The plans provide that any outstanding options will become immediately exercisable upon a change in control of Bowater. In such event, grantees of options have the right to require us to purchase such options for cash in lieu of the insurance of common stock. We received $10.7 million in 1999, $6.8 million in 1998 and $24.5 million in 1997 from the exercise of stock options. The exercise of stock options also generated tax benefits for us of $4.7 million in 1999, $2.6 million in 1998 and $7.9 million in 1997.

We record compensation expense resulting from stock option grants based on intrinsic value in accordance with APB Opinion No. 25. In accordance with SFAS No. 123, the following pro forma disclosures present the effects on income had the fair value-based method been chosen. These disclosures are shown below for 1999, 1998 and 1997 and have no impact on our reported financial position or results of operations.

(In millions, except per-share amounts)	*1999*	*1998*	*1997*
Net income (loss):			
As reported	$78.7	$(18.5)	$53.7
Pro forma	75.9	(22.0)	50.8
Earnings (loss) per share—basic			
As reported	1.43	1.43	1.26
Pro forma	1.38	(0.51)	1.19
Earnings (loss) per share—diluted:			
As reported	1.41	(0.44)	1.25
Pro forma	$1.36	$(0.51)	$1.17

The pro forma net income effects of SFAS No. 123 in 1999, 1998 and 1997 may not be representative of the pro forma net income effects in future years due to changes in assumptions and the number of options granted in future years.

The fair value of each option granted was estimated on the date of grant using the Black-Scholes option-pricing model with the following weighted average assumptions:

	1999	*1998*	*1997*
Assumptions:			
Dividend yield	2.0%	1.6%	1.9%
Expected volatility	30.0%	29.1%	29.5%
Risk-free interest rate	4.8%	5.6%	6.4%
Expected option lives	5.6 years	5.6 years	5.5 years
Weighted average fair value of each option	$12.34	$15.68	$13.65

Information with respect to options granted under the stock option plans is as follows:

	1999		1998		1997	
	Number of Shares (000's)	Weighted Average Exercise Price	Number of shares (000's)	Weighted Average Exercise Price	Number of Shares (000's)	Weighted Average Exercise Price
Outstanding at beginning of year	2,040	$35	1,907	$31	2,477	$27
Granted during the year	245	$41	388	$49	404	$42
Exercised during the year	(387)	$28	(250)	$27	(934)	$26
Canceled during the year	(14)	$24	(5)	$42	(40)	$35
Outstanding at end of year	1,884	$37	2,040	$35	1,907	$31
Exercisable at end of year	1,455	$35	1,470	$30	1,371	$26

	Options Outstanding at December 31,1999			Options Exercisable at December 31, 1999	
Range of Exercise Prices	Number of Shares (000's)	Weighted Average Exercise Price	Weighted Average Remaining Contractual Life (years)	Number of Shares (000's)	Weighted Average Exercise Price
$21 to $30	609	$26	4.1	609	$26
$30 to $40	329	$35	5.9	329	$35
$40 to $50	946	$44	7.9	517	$44
	1,884	$37	6.3	1,455	$35

STRIDE RITE
1998 ANNUAL REPORT

10. Stock Purchase and Option Plans

The Company's Employee Stock Purchase Plan, as amended, permits eligible associates to elect to subscribe for an aggregate of 5,640,000 shares of common stock of the Company. Under the Plan, participating associates may authorize the Company to withhold either 2.5% or 5% of their earnings for a one- or two-year payment period for the purchase of shares. At the conclusion of the period, associates may purchase shares at the lesser of 85% of the market value of the Company's common stock on either their entry date into the Plan or ten days prior to the end of the payment period. The Board of Directors may set a minimum price for the stock. For the payment period which ended in fiscal 1997, 118,050 shares were issued under the Plan for an aggregate amount of $1,083,000. Funds are currently being withheld from participating associates during a payment period ending October 31, 1999. As of November 27, 1998, $809,000 has been withheld from associates' earnings and, if all participants had been allowed to exercise their stock purchase rights at that date, approximately 107,300 shares could have been purchased at a price of $7.54 per share. At November 27, 1998, a total of 5,063,331 shares had been purchased under the Plan and 576,669 shares were available for purchase by participating associates.

In April 1998, the Company's shareholders approved The Stride Rite Corporation 1998 Non-Employee Director Stock Ownership Plan (the "1998 Director's Plan"). This Plan replaced a similar plan, the 1994 Non-Employee Director Stock Ownership Plan. Under the 1998 Director's Plan, awards of common stock and options to purchase common stock are granted to any director who is not an employee of the Company in accordance with the provisions of the Plan. An aggregate of 300,000 shares is authorized for issuance under the Plan. Options to purchase common stock are granted at a price equal to the closing price of the Company's common stock on the date the option is granted. Each non-employee director annually receives an award of 500 shares of common stock and an option to purchase 5,000 shares of common stock. Non-employee directors may elect to defer receipt of the annual stock award in connection with their participation in the Company's Deferred Compensation Plan for Directors. Options have a term of ten years and are non-transferable. Under the Plan, options become exercisable over a three-year period and must be paid for in full at the time of exercise. Under the terms of the Plan, the Company awarded 1,000 shares of common stock during 1998. Under the 1994 Director's Plan, which was terminated in April 1998, each non-employee director was granted an option to purchase 5,000 shares of common stock upon his or her initial appointment or election to the Board and an annual award of 500 shares of common stock. Under the terms of the 1994 Director's Plan, the Company awarded 3,500 and 3,000 shares of common stock during 1997 and 1996, respectively.

In April 1998, the Company's shareholders approved The Stride Rite Corporation 1998 Long-Term Growth Incentive Plan (the 1998 Incentive Plan). The 1998 Incentive Plan replaced a similar long-term incentive plan which had been approved by the shareholders in 1995. Under the 1998 Incentive Plan, which expires in April 2001, options to purchase common stock and stock awards of up to an aggregate of 2,400,000 shares of the Company's common stock may be granted to officers and other key associates. The option price of the shares may not be less than the fair market value of the Company's common stock at the date of grant. Options under the 1998 Incentive Plan will generally vest over a three-year period and the rights to purchase common shares expire ten years following the date of grant. Stock awards, which are limited to 200,000 shares in the Plan, generally vest over a five-year period. During fiscal 1998, no stock awards were made under the Plan. The 1995 Incentive Plan had replaced the 1975 Executive Incentive Stock Purchase Plan, which was terminated in April 1995. Rights under the 1975 Plan vested over a five-year period with a minimum option price established at the then par value of the Company's common stock, which is $.25 per share. During fiscal 1997 and 1996, stock awards of 5,000 and 20,779 shares, respectively, were made under the 1995 Incentive Plan.

A summary of the activity in stock options with respect to all plans for the three years in the period ended November 27, 1998 is as follows:

	Number of Options	Weighted Average Exercise Price
Outstanding at December 1, 1995	1,267,916	$ 8.90
Granted	1,072,800	8.14
Exercised	(112,801)	0.25
Canceled	(418,553)	8.16
Outstanding at November 29, 1996	1,809,362	9.16
Granted	1,023,250	11.44
Exercised	(89,807)	6.36
Canceled	(160,105)	10.04
Outstanding at November 28, 1997	2,582,700	10.11
Granted	1,054,650	11.11
Exercised	(297,074)	5.98
Canceled	(533,246)	10.23
Outstanding at November 27, 1998	2,807,030	$10.90

The following table summarizes information about stock options outstanding at November 27, 1998:

Range of Exercise Prices	Number Outstanding	Weighted Average Remaining Contractual Life	Weighted Average Exercise Price	Number Exercisable	Weighted Average Exercise Price
		Life	Price		Price
$ 0.25–$10.875	669,298	7.2 years	$ 7.64	414,957	$ 7.20
$11.00–$11.875	1,460,832	8.3 years	11.12	223,982	11.25
$12.00–$15.875	676,900	6.5 years	13.63	539,732	13.84
	2,807,030	7.6 years	$10.90	1,178,671	$11.01

At November 28, 1997, options to purchase 911,093 shares at an average price of $9.42 per share were exercisable (549,197 shares at $8.81 per share at November 29, 1996). At November 27, 1998, stock awards and options to purchase a total 6,852,473 shares had been granted under all plans and rights to purchase an additional 2,025,250 shares (250,775 shares at November 28, 1997) could be granted.

ROHM HAAS
1999 ANNUAL REPORT

3. Purchased In-process Research and Development

In acquisitions accounted for by the purchase method, purchased in-process research and development (IPR&D) represents the value assigned to research and development projects of an acquired company where technological feasibility had not yet been established at the date of the acquisition, and which, if unsuccessful, have no alternative future use. Amounts assigned to IPR&D are charged to expense at the date of acquisition. Accordingly, the company has charged $105 million to expense in 1999 related to the Morton acquisition. (See Note 1.)

Eight IPR&D projects were identified based upon discussions with Morton personnel, analyses of the acquisition agreements, and analyses of data provided by Morton. The two most significant research and development projects are Passive Materials and Lamineer coating which together represent more than 90% of the overall in-process research and development value. The remaining value was assigned to six other in-process projects.

The Passive Materials project is being developed by the Electronic Materials product group, which principally manufactures dry film photoresists sold to printed circuit board manufacturers. Passive Materials will be, if successfully developed, a new form of film materials. As of the date of acquisition, this project had been in development since July 1996; however, it had not yet reached technological feasibility and will not achieve technological feasibility until all of the component technologies are each successfully developed. The nature of the efforts necessary to complete the project relate to completing the design and building of machinery and processes required to manufacture the passive material and developing full-scale production capabilities that can meet desired customer specifications. Management estimates that this technology will be developed and technological feasibility will be reached in 2000.

Lamineer coating is a new and innovative product for Morton's Powder Coatings business and will be, if successfully developed, a family of powder coatings used for a variety of wood applications. The technology will provide manufacturers an alternative method for applying coatings to wood at increased operating and manufacturing efficiencies. Lamineer coating had been in development since early 1996. During this time, a material portion of the Lamineer technology, the base resins, was completely developed. This portion of technology was identified as having an alternative future use and, therefore, was not classified as IPR&D. The curing technologies, however, have been identified as IPR&D. Related products are in the testing and trial stage of development. The efforts required to complete the Lamineer coating project are developing the necessary curing technologies and meeting customer specifications. Management estimates that Lamineer product efforts will be generally completed and will reach technological feasibility in 2000. The estimated cost to complete both the Passive Materials and Lamineer coatings projects is under $6 million.

The fair values of the in-process completed portion of these research and development projects are as follows:

(Millions of dollars)	Fair Value
Passive Materials	$ 50
Lamineer Coating	48
All Others	7
Total	$105

The valuation analysis of these was performed just prior to the date of acquisition and was based on information available at that time. The projects identified in the analysis were analyzed based primarily on an evaluation of their status in the product development process, the expected release dates, and the percentage completed.

The technique used in valuing each purchased research and development project was the income approach, which includes an analysis of the markets, cash flows, and risks associated with achieving these cash flows. Significant appraisal assumptions include: The period in which material net cash inflows from significant projects are expected to commence; material anticipated changes from historical pricing, margins and expense levels; and the risk adjusted discount rate applied to the project's cash flows.

Material net cash inflows that are attributable to the completed IPR&D are expected to begin in 2001 and expected to last through 2015 for both Passive Materials and Lamineer coating. The forecast for both of these in-process projects relied on sales estimates derived from targeted market share, pricing estimates and expected product life cycles. Both Passive Materials and Lamineer coating are expected to generate higher profit margins, two to three times the margins of historical products in their respective product groups. This is due to their new and innovative characteristics, which allow pricing commensurate with their performance. The discount rate used for the acquired in-process technologies was estimated at 20% for Passive Materials and 25% for Lamineer based upon Morton's weighted average cost of capital of 12%. The discount rate used for the in-process technology was determined to be higher than Morton's weighted average cost of capital because the technology had not yet reached technological feasibility as of valuation. In using a discount rate greater than Morton's weighted average cost of capital, management has reflected the risk premium associated with achieving the forecasted cash flows associated with these projects, and because the in-process technology had not yet reached technological feasibility as of the date of valuation.

The nature of the efforts required to develop the acquired in-process technologically feasible and commercially viable products principally related to the completion of all planning, designing and testing activities that are necessary to establish a product or service that can be produced to meet its design requirements, including functions, features and technical performance requirements. The company currently expects that the acquired in-process technology will be successfully developed, but there can be no assurance that the technological feasibility or commercial viability of these products will be achieved.

During 1995, the Financial Accounting Standards Board issued Statement of Financial Accounting Standards No. 123, "Accounting for Stock-Based Compensation" (SFAS 123). SFAS 123 defines a fair-value method of accounting for employee stock options or similar equity instruments and encourages companies to adopt that method of accounting beginning in the Company's 1997 fiscal year. However, SFAS 123 also allows companies to continue to use the intrinsic value method of accounting prescribed by Accounting Principles Board Opinion No. 25, "Accounting for Stock Issued to Employees" (APB 25) and to make pro forma disclosures of the impact on net income and earnings per share of applying SFAS 123. The Company has elected to continue to account for stock options in accordance with APB 25 and related interpretations. Accordingly, no compensation expense has been recorded in connection with fair market value stock option grants under the Company's stock option plans and its employee stock purchase plan.

Pro forma net income and earnings per share information included in the table below has been calculated as if the Company had accounted for employee stock options and other stock-based compensation under the fair value method. The fair value was estimated as of the date of grant using the Black-Scholes option pricing model with the following weighted average assumptions: risk-free interest rates of 5.76% for 1998, 5.95% for 1997 and 5.59% for 1996; a dividend yield of 1.5% for each year; a volatility factor of the Company's common stock of 37% for 1998 and 35% for 1997 and 1996; and a weighted average expected life of the stock options of 4.5 years in each year. The weighted average grant date fair values of stock options granted during 1998, 1997 and 1996 were $3.75, $3.95 and $2.88, respectively. For purposes of pro forma disclosure, the estimated fair value is amortized to expense on a straight-line basis over the options vesting periods.

in thousands, except: for per share data		1998	1997	1996
Net income	As reported	$21,052	$19,780	$2,499
	Pro forma	19,412	19,058	1,958
Net income per diluted				
share of common stock	As reported	.44	.40	.05
	Pro forma	.41	.39	04

The Black-Scholes option pricing model was developed for use in estimating the fair value of traded options that have no vesting restrictions and are fully transferable. In addition, option pricing models require the use of highly subjective assumptions, including the expected stock price volatility. Because the Company's employee stock options have characteristics significantly different from those of traded options, and because changes in the subjective assumptions can materially affect the fair value estimates, in management's opinion, the existing models do not necessarily provide a reliable single measure of the fair value of its employee stock options and other stock-based compensation.

PITNEY BOWES
1999 ANNUAL REPORT

2. Inventories

Inventories consist of the following:

December 31	1999	1998
Raw materials and work in process	$ 41,149	$ 54,001
Supplies and service parts	122,726	106,864
Finished products	93,577	105,869
Total	$257,452	$266,734

If all inventories valued at LIFO had been stated at current costs, inventories would have been $22.4 million and $24.9 million higher than reported at December 31, 1999 and 1998, respectively.

Chapter 2

Revenue Recognition

This chapter covers the accounting, reporting, and disclosures associated with revenue recognition for the sale of products or rendering of services. Revenue involves a gross increase in assets or decrease in liabilities. Revenue may be recognized at the time of sale or service, during production, at the completion of production, and at the time of cash receipt. Long-term construction contracts may be accounted for under the percentage of completion method or the completed contract method. When a right of return exists, revenue may or may not be recognized depending on the circumstances. The recording of revenue in the case of warranty and maintenance contracts is also included. The accounting treatment of contributions is also discussed.

SERVICE SALES REVENUE

The AICPA and FASB have attempted to provide guidance on establishing accounting standards through the issuance of *Accounting for Certain Service Transactions,* FASB Invitation to Comment. A draft of the AICPA's Statement of Position is included in the Invitation to Comment. While no progress has been made on this issue, the draft Statement of Position still provides guidance about recognizing revenue from such service sales transactions.

Frequently, a transaction involves both the sale of a product and a service. It is therefore necessary to determine whether the transaction should be classified as primarily a service transaction or primarily a product transaction or a transaction which is both a service transaction and a product transaction.

For transactions that have a product and service component, the following applies:

- A transaction should be classified as primarily a service transaction if the inclusion or exclusion of the product would not change the total price of the transaction.

- If the inclusion or exclusion of the service would not change the total transaction price, then the transaction should be classified as primarily a product transaction.

- If the inclusion or exclusion of the service or product would change the total transaction price, then that transaction should be split and the product component should be accounted for separately from the service component.

According to SFAC Number 5, revenue is generally recognized when

- it is realized or realizable, and
- it has been earned.

Revenue from service transactions is recognized based upon performance. Performance may either be based upon the passing of time or may involve a single action or a series of actions. The following four methods should be used to recognize revenue from service transactions:

- *The specific performance method* should be used when performance involves a single action and revenue is recognized when that action is completed. For example, a CPA is retained to prepare a tax return. Revenue is recognized when the single action of preparing the tax return is completed.

- *The proportional performance method* is used when performance involves a series of actions. If the transaction involves an *unspecified number* of actions over a given period of time, an equal amount of revenue should be recognized at fixed intervals. The use of the straight-line method is recommended unless another method is deemed to be more appropriate. If the transaction involves a *specified number* of *similar* or *essentially similar* actions, an equal amount of revenue should be recognized when each action is performed. If the transaction involves a *specified number* of *dissimilar* or *unique* actions, revenue should be recognized based upon the following:

$$\frac{\text{Direct costs involved in a single action}}{\text{Total estimated direct costs of the transaction}} \times \text{Total revenues from the entire transaction}$$

- *The completed performance method* should be used to recognize revenue when completing the final action which is so critical that the entire transaction would be considered incomplete without it.

- *The collection method* is used to recognize revenue when there is significant uncertainty regarding the collection of revenue. Revenue should not be recognized until cash is collected.

The matching principle requires that expenses be matched to revenues. In other words, revenues should be recognized in the same period as their associated expenses. If expenses are expected to be recovered from future revenues, then those expenses should be deferred. Three major categories of costs result from service transactions:

- *Initial direct costs* are incurred to negotiate and obtain a service agreement. They include costs such as commissions, credit investigation, processing fees, legal fees, etc. They do not include indirect costs such as rent and other administrative costs.

- *Direct costs* result from performing the service. A strong correlation exists between performing the service and incurring of direct costs.

- *Indirect costs* are all costs that are necessary to performing the service but cannot be classified as either initial direct costs or direct costs. Indirect costs include selling and administrative expenses, rent, depreciation, allowance for bad debts, and costs associated with negotiating transactions that are not consummated.

Indirect costs should always be expensed in the period in which they are incurred. No attempt should be made to match these costs with service revenue. The accounting treatment for initial direct costs and direct costs depends upon the method used for revenue recognition.

Initial direct costs and direct costs should be expensed at the time related revenue is recognized when using the specific performance or completed performance methods. In other words, initial direct costs and direct costs should be recorded as prepaid assets and expensed once the service has been performed. The same accounting treatment is used to expense initial direct costs under the proportional performance method; that is, initial direct costs are recorded as prepaid assets and expensed when the revenue is recognized. In contrast, direct costs should be expensed as incurred when using the proportional performance method. This is done because a strong relationship exists between the direct costs incurred and the completion of service. When the collection method is used to recognize revenue, both initial direct costs and direct costs should be expensed as incurred.

Sometimes a loss is incurred in a service transaction. A loss should be recognized when initial direct costs and estimated total direct costs are greater than estimated revenues. This loss should first be used to reduce any prepaid assets (deferred costs), and if any loss remains, then it should be charged to an estimated liability account.

Frequently service transactions involve initiation fees and/or installation fees. These fees are generally nonrefundable. If it is possible to determine objectively the value of the right or privilege granted by the initiation fees, then the fees should be recognized as revenue and the related direct costs should be expensed on the initiation day. On the other hand, if the value cannot be objectively determined, the fees should initially be considered unearned revenue and recorded as a liability. Revenue should be recognized from such initiation fees using one of the service revenue recognition methods.

The accounting treatment for equipment installation fees depends upon whether the customer can purchase the equipment independent of installation. If equipment may be purchased independent of installation, then the transaction should be considered a product transaction and installation fees accounted for as part of a product transaction. On the other hand, if both the equipment and its installation are essential for service and the customer cannot purchase the equipment separately, then the installation fees should be considered unearned revenue. Unearned revenue should be recognized, and the cost of installation and equipment should be amortized over the estimated service period.

REVENUE RECOGNITION METHODS

There are four major methods of revenue recognition:

- Realization (at time of sale of merchandise or rendering of service)
- At the completion of production
- During production
- On a cash basis

Realization

Revenue is recognized when goods are sold or when services are performed. This method is used in most cases. When a sale is made, the earnings process is complete. There is an exchange that can be objectively measured. Revenue is being recognized as accrued (earned). Realization is appropriate when

- Selling price is ascertainable.
- Future costs are estimable.

EXAMPLE

In the year 2000, J&M Corp. sold a magazine to Magazines-R-Us Inc. The contract between the parties specified that J&M would receive royalties of 30% of all future revenues derived from the magazine. At December 31, 2001, J&M reported royalties receivable of $100,000. During 2002, J&M received royalty payments of $250,000. Magazines-R-Us reported revenues of $2,500,000 in 2002 from the magazine. What amount should J&M report as royalty revenue from the magazine in its 2002 income statement?

In this problem we assume that an accrual basis is being used because an alternative basis is not specified (e.g., cash; see subsequent discussion). Therefore, J&M Corp. should make the following accrual in 2002 for royalty revenue expected to be collected from Magazines-R-Us:

$$30\% \times \$2,500,000 \quad = \quad \underline{\$750,000}$$

The other three methods of revenue recognition are used when special circumstances exist. They are discussed next.

At the Completion of Production

Revenue is recognized at the completion of production (before sale or exchange) only if all of the following exist:

- Stable selling price
- Interchangeable units
- Absence of significant marketing costs to consummate the final transfer

This method might be appropriate in the following cases:

- Accounting for construction contracts using the completed contract method (Construction contracts are discussed in a separate section.)
- Agricultural products, byproducts, and precious metals

During Production

Revenue may be recognized during production when

- There exists an assured price for the product such as arising from a written contract.

- The degree of completion can be accurately determined with each stage of the manufacturing process.

An example of the use of this approach is the percentage of completion method for long-term construction contracts. This is discussed in a later section.

On a Cash Basis

Under the cash basis, revenue is recognized when cash is received.

A service business does not have inventory and therefore may use either the accrual basis or the cash basis. A company selling merchandise must use accrual accounting. However, there are exceptions when the cash basis would be used for a company manufacturing or selling inventory. These exceptions are as follows:

- Uncertain or extended collection period
- Failure to estimate accurately expenses at the time of sale
- Risk of noncollection
- Inability to determine reliably the selling price at time of sale

If any of these exceptions exist, revenue is recorded only as cash is received under either the installment sales method or the cost recovery method, discussed next. There exists uncertainty of cash collection, forcing revenue recognition to be deferred until the actual receipt of money.

Installment Sales Method

An installment transaction takes place when a seller sells a product or conducts a service and the purchaser is to remit periodic payments over an extended time period. Installment sales should be segregated from regular sales. A seller will typically protect itself when making installment sales by keeping title to the product such as through a conditional sales agreement, mortgage, etc.

If the installment method is appropriate, income recognition is deferred (delayed) until the period of cash collection. The seller recognizes both revenues and cost of goods sold at the time of sale, but the related unrealized gross profit is deferred to later years based on cash collection. Selling and administrative costs are immediately expensed.

Each payment received consists of both a recovery of cost and gross profit based on the same proportion as those components were in for the original sale. The gross profit rate equals installment sales revenue less cost of installment sales divided by installment sales revenue. Since gross profit ratios differ by product and department as well as by year, the company must maintain separate records of sales by year, product line, and department. Therefore, care must be taken to identify the year in which the receivable arose when accounting for cash collections.

Revenue recognition equals the cash received multiplied by the gross profit percentage. When collections are received, deferred gross profit is debited and revenue is credited. Any gross profit not collected is deferred in the balance sheet. Deferred gross profit equals the installment accounts receivable balance at year-end multiplied by the gross profit rate.

The interest charged to customers on installment sales is credited to interest income when cash is received. This is in addition to the gross profit recognized.

The current asset section of the balance sheet shows the following:

Installment accounts receivable (cost + profit)
Less: deferred gross profit (profit)
Net accounts receivable (cost)

Note: Deferred gross profit is a contra asset account.

The accounts receivable is a current asset because it is based on the normal operating cycle of the business (which may, of course, be more than one year in the case of installment sales).

EXAMPLE

Zieden Corp. began its business operations in the year 2002. It accounts for revenue recognition using the installment method. Zieden's sales and collections for the year were $160,000 and $135,000, respectively. In addition, uncollectible accounts receivable of $15,000 were written off during 2002. Zieden's gross profit rate is 40%. What amount should Zieden report as deferred revenue in its December 31, 2002 balance sheet?

The installment method is primarily utilized when there is a high degree of uncertainty regarding cash collections. Under this method of accounting for revenue recognition, revenue is recognized by determining the product of cash collected times the gross profit percentage for the period in which the sale was made. Any gross profit not collected is "deferred" on the balance sheet pending collection. When collections are subsequently made, realized gross profit is increased by debiting the deferred gross profit account.

Installment Sales		$160,000
Less: Collections	$135,000	
Uncollectible Accounts Written Off	15,000	150,000
Installment Receivables, December 31, 2002		$ 10,000
Deferred Revenue, December 31, 2002: $10,000 × 40% =		$ 4,000

EXAMPLE

A Company sells a product for $500 that costs $350. The gross profit percentage is 25%. Therefore, the company recognizes each collection as 75% recovery of cost and 25% as realized gross profit.

The journal entry for the sale follows:

Accounts receivable	500	
Installment sales		500
Cost of installment sales	350	
Inventory		350

At the end of the first year, the closing journal entry follows:

Installment sales	500	
Cost of installment sales		350
Unrealized gross profit		150

Assuming a collection of $200 is received, the journal entries are

Cash	200	
Accounts receivable		200
Unrealized gross profit	50	
Realized gross profit		50
$200 \times 25\% = \$50$		

The balance owed ($300) was defaulted upon and the merchandise was repossessed, having an inventory value of $180. The journal entry is

Unrealized gross profit (25% × $300)	75	
Loss	45	
Inventory	180	
Accounts receivable		300

EXAMPLE

On January 2, 19X5, a company sold a product for $3,000,000. The cost of the product was $2,000,000. Collections received in 19X5 were $1,200,000. The installment method of revenue recognition is used. The amount of realized gross profit to be reported is

Installment sales	$3,000,000
Less: Cost of installment sales	2,000,000
Gross profit	$1,000,000
Gross profit percentage $1,000,000/$3,000,000 = 33.3%	
19X5 collections	$1,200,000
Realized gross profit, 12/31/19X5 $1,200,000 × 33.3% =	$ 400,000

EXAMPLE

Blake Company uses the installment sales method. The following information applies for 19X3:

Installment accounts receivable, 12/31/19X3	$450,000
Deferred gross profit, 12/31/19X3 (prior to recognizing realized gross profit for 19X3)	280,000
Gross profit on sales	35%

For 19X3, cash collections is computed as follows:

Installment sales for 19X3 $280,000/35%	$800,000
Installment accounts receivable, 12/31/19X3	450,000
Cash collections	$350,000

For 19X3, realized gross profit equals

$350,000 × 35%	$122,500

EXAMPLE

On January 3, 19X5, a company sold equipment for $2,700,000, resulting in a gain of $1,900,000. Collections received during the year were $700,000. Deferred gross profit at year-end 19X5 is computed as follows:

Installment sales	$2,700,000
Cost of installment sales ($2,700,000 – $1,900,000)	800,000
Gross profit	$1,900,000

$$\text{Gross profit percent} = \frac{\text{Gross profit}}{\text{Sales}} = \frac{\$1,900,000}{\$2,700,000} = 70.4\%$$

Installment receivables $2,700,000 – $700,000	$2,000,000
Deferred gross profit, 12/31/19X5 $2,000,000 × 70.4%	$1,408,000

EXAMPLE

Mavis Company uses the installment sales method to recognize revenue. The following information applies to installment sales for the year-end 19X8 and 19X9:

	19X8	19X9
Installment receivables at year-end on 19X8 sales	$300,000	$150,000
Installment receivables at year-end on 19X9 sales	—	350,000
Installment sales	400,000	450,000
Cost of sales	200,000	300,000

The deferred gross profit on the December 31, 19X9 balance sheet is computed as follows:

Installment receivables at 12/31/19X9 on 19X8 sales	$150,000
19X8 gross profit rate ($400,000 – $200,000/$400,000)	× 50%
	$ 75,000
Installment receivables at 12/31/19X9 on 19X9 sales	$350,000
19X9 gross profit rate ($450,000 – $300,000/$450,000)	× 33.3%
	$116,667
Total deferred gross profit, 12/31/19X9	$191,667

Disclosure should be made of amounts to be collected within the next year by type of installment receivable.

When using the installment sales method, bad debts are based on the direct writeoff method. Bad debts are recognized when the account becomes uncollectible. Because of the default on an installment sales contract, the merchandise will likely be repossessed. There must be a writeoff of the accounts receivable and unrealized gross profit. The repossession loss or gain on the default of the contract is calculated as follows:

Loss (gain) = accounts receivable balance less unrealized gross profit less carrying value of repossessed goods

Any reconditioning costs for repossessed merchandise increase the loss or decrease the gain.

The value of the repossessed merchandise is based on its net realizable value and is presented in the inventory section of the balance sheet.

Cost Recovery Method

The cost recovery method should be used when extreme uncertainty exists as to cash collections from installment sales. Under the cost recovery method, both sales and cost of sales are recorded at the time of sale. However, the related gross profit is not recognized until all costs have first been recovered. After all the costs have been recovered, the additional cash receipts are included as profit. The only remaining expenses are those applicable to the collection process. Obviously, the cost recovery method is much more conservative than the installment sales method.

The installment sales method is commonly used for tax purposes.

LONG-TERM CONSTRUCTION CONTRACTS

The accounting, reporting, and disclosures for long-term construction contracts are provided in Accounting Research Bulletin Number 45 (*Long-Term Construction-Type Contracts*), the AICPA Industry Audit and Accounting Guide entitled *Construction Contractors,* and AICPA Statement of Position Number 81–1 (*Accounting for Performance of Construction-Type and Certain Production-Type Contracts*). If there are any revisions in revenue, cost, and profit estimates on contracts or in measuring the progress toward completion, they are considered changes in accounting estimates.

Contract Costs

The accounting for contract costs is similar to the reporting for inventory. As costs are incurred, they are charged to the construction-in-progress (CIP) account, which is an inventory account for a construction company presented under current assets. It is a current asset because the construction period represents the operating cycle of the business. CIP is charged for both direct and indirect construction costs on specific contracts. However, general and administrative expenses as well as selling expenses are expensed as incurred because they are not attributable to specific construction contracts. **Exception:** General and administrative costs may be included in CIP under the completed contract method, at the option of the company, if costs are being allocated, particularly in years when no contracts have been finished.

Contract costs include subcontractor charges billed to the contractor for work performed. The CIP account is charged for costs directly attributable to projects.

Costs incurred to date include precontract costs and costs incurred after the contract date. Precontract costs include design fees, learning costs for a new process, and any other expenditures likely to be recouped after the contract is signed. After the contract, the precontract costs are considered contract costs to date.

Some precontract costs, such as for materials and supplies, may be deferred to an asset called Deferred Contract Costs in expectation of a specific contract as long as recoverability is probable. If recoverability is not probable, the precontract costs must be immediately expensed. If excess goods are manufactured in expectation of future orders, related costs may be deferred to inventory if the costs are deemed recoverable.

After the status of a contract bid has been determined (accepted or rejected), a review should be made of the precontract costs associated with the contract. If the contract has been approved, the deferred precontract costs become included in contract costs. If the contract is rejected, the precontract costs are immediately expensed unless there are other related contracts pending that might recoup these costs.

Back charges are billable costs for work conducted by one party that should have been done by the party billed. Such an arrangement is typically provided for in the contract between the parties. Back charges are accounted for by the contractor as a receivable from the subcontractor with a corresponding reduction in contract costs. The subcontractor accounts for the back charge as contract costs and as a payable.

In the event the back charge is disputed by the subcontractor, the contractor treats the cost as a claim. The claim is the amount exceeding the agreed upon price. The contractor records a receivable and the subcontractor records a payable for the likely amount to be paid under the dispute.

A change order is an amendment to the initial contract that alters its terms. As per Statement of Position Number 81–1, if the price change is mutually agreeable by the contractor and customer, the contractor appropriately adjusts the applicable costs and revenue. However, under the completed contract method, costs applicable to unpriced change orders are deferred if it is probable that the total contract costs (including those subject to the charge order) will be recovered from contract revenues. Under the percentage-of-completion method, if it is probable that the unpriced change order costs will be recoverable, such costs are either deferred until the changed price has been agreed upon or immediately expensed, at the option of the company. However, if it is not probable that the unpriced change order costs will be recoverable, such costs are immediately expensed.

Contract Types

There are various types of construction contracts, including time and materials, unit price, fixed price, and cost type. A contract may also have a provision awarding a bonus for excellent performance or early completion.

Time-and-materials contracts reimburse the contractor for direct labor and direct material costs.

Unit-price contracts provide payment to the contractor based on the amount of units worked.

Fixed-price contracts usually have a constant price associated with them. They are not typically subject to adjustment such as because of increasing construction costs.

Cost-type contracts may be either cost without fee or cost plus fee. In the first type, the contractor recoups its costs. In the second type, the contractor receives payment for its costs plus a fixed fee. The fee is usually based on a profit margin. The fee may be based on variables such as total expected costs, uncertainty in estimating costs, risk of the project, economic conditions, etc. The costs of a contract should never exceed its net realizable value because in that case the contract is not financially feasible. If accumulated costs exceed net realizable value during the term of the contract, a loss should be recognized immediately.

Aggregating and Segmenting Contracts

Highly similar contracts may be combined for accounting purposes. As specified in Statement of Position Number 81–1, similarity in contracts may be indicated by a single customer or similar project management and be performed sequentially or concurrently, interrelated, or negotiated as a package deal.

The segmenting of a contract involves segregating the larger unit into smaller ones for accounting purposes. By breaking up a unit, revenues can be associated with different components or phases. As a result, different profitability margins may apply to each different unit or phase. As per Statement of Position Number 81–1, segmenting of a project may be indicated when all of the following conditions are met: (1) The entire project can be explained by all of the components added together, (2) a contract bid price is made for the whole project and for its major elements, and (3) customer approval is received. Even though all of these criteria are not satisfied, the project may still be segmented if all of the following exist: (1) similarity in services and prices, (2) cost savings, (3) stability, (4) contractor with a track record, (5) explainable risk differences, (6) negotiation of each segment, and (7) logical and consistent segregation.

Contract Options

An addition or modification made to an existing contract arising from an option clause is accounted for as a separate contract if any of the following conditions exist: (1) product or service contracted for is substantially different from the product or service stipulated in the initial agreement, (2) product or service to be provided for is similar to that in the original contract but explainable differences exist in contract price and costing, or (3) price of the new product or service is distinct.

Claims

A claim is an amount exceeding the contract price that a contractor wants customers to pay because of customer delays, customer mistakes in specifications, sudden changes requested by the customer, or other unexpected causes resulting in higher costs to the contractor. The contractor may recognize additional revenue arising from these claims if justification exists and the amount can be reliably estimated. The revenue is recorded only to the degree that contract costs applicable to the claim have been incurred. Statement of Position Number 81–1 provides the following guidelines to establish the ability to record the additional revenue: (1) The claim is objective and verifiable, (2) costs are identifiable or determinable, (3) additional costs incurred were not initially anticipated at the time of contract, and (4) the claim is legally justifiable. If these criteria are not satisfied, a contingent asset should be disclosed.

COMMON CONSTRUCTION CONTRACT METHODS

The two popular methods to account for construction contracts are the percentage-of-completion method and the completed contract method.

Percentage-of-Completion Method

When the percentage-of-completion method is used, a construction company records revenue as production activity takes place. The progress toward a construction project's completion may be based on costs, efforts expended, units of work, units of delivery, or some other reasonable measure of activity (e.g., engineering estimates). (However, the degree of completion should never be based on cash received or interim billings.) The gradual recognition of revenue acts to level out earnings over the years and is more realistic because revenue is occurring as performance occurs. It results in matching of expenses against revenue each period. The major disadvantage of this method is the reliance on estimates. According to Statement of Position Number 81–1, the percentage-of-completion method should be used when the following conditions exist: (1) Reliable estimates of the degree of completion are possible, (2) the contractor is capable of meeting its contractual responsibilities, (3) the customer is expected to meet his or her contractual obligations, and (4) contractual terms are clear regarding the rights of the parties and the terms of payment. If these criteria are not satisfied, the completed contract method would be used (discussed in the next section).

Revenue is recognized under the percentage-of-completion method based on the following cost-to-cost approach:

$$\frac{\text{Actual costs to date}}{\text{Total estimated costs}} \times \frac{\text{Contract}}{\text{price}} = \text{Cumulative revenue}$$

Estimates of costs to complete should be analyzed periodically in light of current data. Such estimates may need revision because of increasing raw material costs, new union labor agreements, political strife with foreign suppliers, and delays.

Revenue recognized in previous years is subtracted from cumulative revenue to compute the revenue for the current year as follows:

Cumulative Revenue (1–3 years)
Less: Revenue Recognized (1–2 years)
Revenue (Year 3–current year)

The expenses for the current year are subtracted from the revenue for the current year to determine the current year's profit as follows:

$$\text{Revenue} - \text{Expenses} = \text{Profit}$$

EXAMPLE

In year 3 of a contract, the actual costs to date were $100,000. Total estimated costs are $400,000. The contract price is $2,000,000. Revenues recognized in previous years (years 1–2) are $300,000.

$$\text{Cumulative Revenue} = \frac{\$100,000}{\$400,000} \times \$2,000,000 = \$500,000$$

Cumulative Revenue	$500,000
Prior Years' Revenue	$300,000
Current Year Revenue	$200,000

In the early years of a contract, costs may occur that distort the degree of completion. An example is materials bought shortly after the contract was signed but not to be used until later years. In this case, these types of costs may be excluded in calculating the percentage of completion based on the cost-to-cost approach.

Under the percentage-of-completion method, realized gross profit recognized each year is determined as follows:

Realized gross profit = (percentage of completion × total anticipated gross profit) – gross profit recognized to date

Journal entries under the percentage-of-completion method using hypothetical figures follow:

Construction-in-Progress (CIP)	60,000	
Cash		60,000
For construction costs incurred		
Progress Billings Receivable	90,000	
Progress Billings on Construction-in-Progress (CIP)		90,000
For periodic billings		
Cash	20,000	
Progress Billings Receivable		20,000
For collections		
Construction-in-Progress	15,000	
Profit		15,000
Annual profit recognition based on percentage of completion during the year		

In the final year of the project, the following additional entry is required to record the profit in the last year:

> Progress Billings on Construction-in-Progress (for total billings)
> Construction-in-Progress (for total cost plus profit)
> Profit (for incremental profit for last year only)

If a loss on a construction contract is evident, it must be recognized immediately based on the conservatism principle. A loss account is charged and a current liability is credited for such expected loss. **Note:** Under the percentage-of-completion method, any gross profit (loss) reported in previous years must be added (deducted) from the total estimated loss. If a loss is expected on a contract that is part of a group of contracts, the group is treated as the accounting unit to determine the need, if any, of a loss provision. For example, a loss on one contract in the group may be offset by profits on other contracts in the group so a loss need not be accrued.

If construction-in-progress (CIP) minus progress billings on construction-in-progress is a debit, it is presented as a current asset, as previously stated, because the balance represents an inventory account for a construction company. In this case, costs exceed billings. If the net balance is a credit, the credit balance is reported as a current liability because billings exceed costs.

Assets cannot be offset against liabilities unless a right of offset is present. Hence, the net debit balances on construction contracts should not offset any net credit balances on other contracts.

EXAMPLE

The Levita Company is a construction entity with the following data relating to two particular jobs, which began during 2002:

	Job X	*Job Y*
Contract Price	$210,000	$150,000
Cost Incurred during 2002	120,000	140,000
Estimated Cost to Complete	60,000	20,000
Billed to Customers during 2002	75,000	135,000
Received from Customers during 2002	45,000	125,000

Assuming Levita uses the percentage-of-completion method of accounting for long-term contracts, what amount of gross profit (loss) should Levita report in its 2002 income statement?

As was previously noted, under the percentage-of-completion method of accounting for long-term contracts, the amount of revenue that would be recognized in a given period during construction equals

$$\frac{\text{Actual costs to date}}{\text{Total estimated costs}} \times \text{Contract price} = \text{Cumulative revenue}$$

With respect to Job X, since the total actual costs incurred during 2002 are $120,000 and estimated costs to complete are $60,000, the total estimated costs to complete the project as this time are $180,000. Therefore, the amount of revenue that would be recognized on this project would be:

$$\frac{\$120,000}{180,000} \times \$210,000 = \$140,000$$

Therefore, the amount of gross profit that would be recognized for Project X would be

Project X

Revenue	$140,000
Less: Construction Costs Actually Incurred in 2002	120,000
Gross Profit for 2002 for Project X	$ 20,000

With respect to Job Y, since the total actual costs incurred during 2002 are $140,000 and estimated costs to complete are $20,000, the total estimated costs to complete the project at this time are $160,000. Given a contract price of $150,000, it appears, based on current data, that a loss will be recognized on the project overall. Therefore, the loss must be recognized immediately regardless of whether the contract is completed or not. The loss that would be recognized would be

Project Y

Revenue – Contract Price		$150,000
Less: Construction Costs Actually Incurred in 2002	$140,000	
Estimated Costs to Complete	20,000	160,000
Loss for Project Y in 2002		$(10,000)

In total, assuming that Levita Construction Corp. utilizes the percentage-of-completion method of recognizing revenue, then gross profit of $10,000 [Project X: $20,000 + Project Y: $(10,000)] would be recognized from both jobs in year 2002.

Completed Contract Method

Under the completed contract method for construction contracts, a construction company does not recognize revenue until the completion of the job. A contract is deemed substantially complete when remaining completion costs are insignificant. The completed contract method should be used only when it is inappropriate to use the percentage-of-completion method.

The major benefit of this method is its basis on final results instead of on estimates. The major drawback is its failure to reflect current activity on a multiyear contract.

Under this method, construction costs (including direct costs and overhead) are charged to construction-in-progress. In the year the contract is completed, gross profit (loss) is recognized equal to the difference between the contract price and total costs.

If a loss on a construction contract is evident, it must be recognized immediately. Under the completed contract method, the total expected loss on the contract equals the total estimated contract costs less the total estimated contract revenue.

EXAMPLE

Hercules Construction Company has a debit balance in its construction-in-progress account of $400,000 for the costs incurred on this project. Although the company originally expected to make a profit on the contract, it now apparent that there will be an estimated loss of $100,000 on the project at its completion. The appropriate journal entry for this loss is

Estimated Loss on Construction Project	100,000	
Construction-in-Progress		100,000

This entry reduces the construction-in-progress (inventory) account by $100,000. The loss is recognized in full immediately in the current year. If the estimated loss is accurate, future costs will be charged to the CIP account as incurred and the balance in that account will equal contract revenue.

Journal entries under the completed contract method using assumed figures follow:

Construction-in-Progress	60,000	
Cash		60,000
For construction costs		
Progress Billings Receivable	90,000	
Progress Billings on Construction-in-Progress		90,000
For periodic billings		
Cash	20,000	
Progress Billings Receivable		20,000
For collections		

In the final year of the project, the following additional entry is required to record the profit in the last (completion) year:

Progress Billings on Construction-in-Progress (for total billings)	
Construction-in-Progress (for total costs)	
Profit (profit for all the years)	

EXAMPLE

Let's use the same data for the Levita Construction Company that was used before. However, now let us assume that the long-term construction jobs will be accounted for using the completed contract method. You may recall the following data relating to the two different construction jobs for Levita Construction during 2002:

	Job X	Job Y
Contract Price	$210,000	$150,000
Cost Incurred during 2002	120,000	140,000
Estimated Cost to Complete	60,000	20,000
Billed to Customers during 2002	75,000	135,000
Received from Customers during 2002	45,000	125,000

Assuming Levita now uses the completed contract method of accounting for long-term contracts, what amount of gross profit (loss) should Levita report in its 2002 income statement?

 The completed contract method strictly follows the revenue recognition principle, requiring that revenue should not be recognized until the earning process is fully completed. Therefore, the following computations for each project must be made.

Job X

For Job X, costs were incurred of $120,000 in 2002 with an estimate of additional costs needed to complete the project of $60,000 in the future. Assuming that the contract price is $210,000, it appears that the gross profit that should be recognized would be $30,000 [210,000 − (120,000 + $60,000)]. However, since we are accounting for revenue recognition under the completed contract method, no gross profit is recognized at all. Zero gross profit is recognized since the contract was not completed this period.

Job Y

In Job Y, actual costs were incurred of $140,000, with an estimate of $20,000 needed to complete the project in the future. Thus, at this point, it is estimated that $160,000 of costs will be required to complete the job in total. Based on this current data, it appears that Levita will generate a loss of $10,000 on the overall contract. As was previously noted, if a loss on a construction contract is evident, it must be recognized immediately. Thus, this loss must be disclosed and recognized in the company's income statement for 2002 even though construction has not been completed. The disclosure that should be made is the same as that disclosed for the completed contract previously shown under the same circumstances. It is replicated here for the reader's convenience:

Job Y

Revenue – Contract Price		$150,000
Less: Construction Costs Actually Incurred in 2002	$140,000	
Estimated Costs to Complete	20,000	160,000
Loss for Project Y in 2002		$(10,000)

Therefore, overall, the amount of gross profit that should be recognized in the Levita's income statement based on both jobs is a loss of $10,000 [Job X: $0 + Job Y: $(10,000)].

Long-term construction contracts require certain disclosures in the financial statements, including

- Accounting method used and any change therein
- Nature of claims and associated amounts
- Significant commitments made
- Changes in estimates and their impact on the financial statements
- Approach in determining the percentage of completion when the percentage-of-completion method is used
- Criteria used to ascertain when substantial completion has occurred

GOVERNMENT CONTRACT ACCOUNTING

The percentage method to account for contracts should be used when the buyer is financially sound to pay its obligations and the contractor is expected to complete all of its work.

On cost-plus-fixed-fee government contracts, fees should usually be accrued as billable. If an advance payment is received from the government, it should *not* offset receivables unless the payment is work-in-process. If any amounts are offset, proper disclosure is required.

If a government contract is subject to renegotiation, a renegotiation claim to which the contractor is responsible should be debited to sales and credited to a current liability account. Disclosure should be made of the basis to compute the expected refund.

If the government terminates a contract, contract costs included in inventory should be transferred to receivables. The claim against the government should be presented under current assets except if a long delay in receipt of payment is expected. A termination claim should be treated as a sale. A subcontractor's claim because of the termination should be included in the contractor's claim against the government. Assume a contractor has a termination claim receivable of $500,000, of which $100,000 arises from the contractor's obligation to the subcontractor. In this case, a liability of $100,000 should be accrued. The termination claim is reduced by any inventory related to the contract that the contractor is retaining. Disclosure should be made of the particulars of terminated contracts.

All direct costs are included in contract costs, such as material, labor, and subcontracting. Indirect costs should be allocated to contracts on a rational basis. Allocable costs include contract supervision, tools, quality control, inspection, insurance, and repairs and maintenance. Learning and startup costs should be charged to existing contracts. The entry for an expected loss on a contract is to debit a loss provision and credit a liability account.

REVENUE RECOGNITION WHEN A RIGHT OF RETURN EXISTS

FASB Statement Number 48 deals with the accounting and disclosures when there is a right of return. However, the pronouncement is not applicable to real estate transactions, dealer leases, or service industries. Returns do not include exchanges for similar items in type, quality, and price. In some cases, the return privilege expires shortly after sale, such as with perishable food. In other situations, the return privilege has a longer time period, such as in textbook publishing.

If a buyer has the right to return a product, the seller cannot recognize revenue when sold unless all of the following exist:

- The buyer is obligated to pay for the product even if he or she loses it or the item becomes damaged.

- The acquisition of the product makes economic sense to the buyer.

- The seller is not obligated to provide future services in order for the buyer to resell the item.

- Selling price is known or determinable.

- The buyer must pay for merchandise even if he or she is not able to resell it. For example, a wholesaler buying goods from a manufacturer does not have the right to return the goods if he or she cannot find a retailer.

- There is a reasonable basis to estimate returns.

If all of these conditions are satisfied, the seller must make an appropriate provision (accrual) for expenses and losses related to possible returns of products by buyers. Further, sales and cost of sales should be reduced for estimated returns.

The provisions for estimated returns and cost of receiving these returns are contra accounts to accounts receivable. The deferred cost of sales is the inventory cost of items expected to be returned. The deferred cost of reacquiring returns may increase either deferred charges or inventory.

If any one of the foregoing is not satisfied, revenue must be deferred along with the deferral of related costs until either all the criteria are met or the right of return stipulation has expired or changed from agreement. An alternative treatment to the deferral of revenue is just to have a memo entry of the sale. Another acceptable alternative treatment is to consider the transaction as a consignment.

EXAMPLE

On January 1, 19X6, a sale of $100,000 is made with a right of return. The related costs associated with this sale are $60,000. On May 4, 19X7, the right of return no longer applied. The journal entries are

1/1/19X6

Cash	100,000	
Deferred Revenue		100,000
Deferred Expenses	60,000	
Cash		60,000

Alternatively, instead of a journal entry, a memo entry may have been made

5/4/19X7

Deferred Revenue	100,000	
Revenue		100,000
Expenses	60,000	
Deferred Expenses		60,000

EXAMPLE

Davis Corporation expects that sales of $400,000 will be returned and the related cost of goods sold will be $250,000. It is anticipated that costs of $16,000 will be incurred to process the returns. The journal entry required to accrue sales returns follows:

Sales returns	400,000	
Inventory	250,000	
Processing expense for sales returns	16,000	
Allowance for expected returns		400,000
Cost of goods sold		250,000
Accrued expense to process sales returns		16,000

In predicting returns, consider

- Time period awarded to return merchandise
- Experience with the product in estimating returns
- Obsolescence risk of goods
- Transaction volume
- Type of customer and relationship

- Type of product
- Product demand
- Marketing policies

A reasonable estimate of returned merchandise may be impaired if the products are not homogeneous, there is a lack of prior experience in estimating returns because the product is relatively new or circumstances have changed, a lengthy time period exists for returns, and the product has a high degree of obsolescence.

EXAMPLE

On February 6, 19X2, product sales of $500,000 were made. The cost of goods is $300,000. A 60-day return privilege exists. The expected return rate of merchandise is 10%. On March 17, 19X2, a customer returns goods having a selling price of $40,000. The criteria to recognize revenue when the right of return exists have been met. The journal entries follow:

2/2/19X2		
Accounts Receivable	500,000	
Sales		500,000
Cost of Sales	300,000	
Inventory		300,000
Sales Returns	50,000	
Allowance for Sales Returns		50,000
$500,000 \times 10\% = \$50,000$		
Inventory	20,000	
Cost of Sales		20,000
$\$50,000 \times 40\%$ (gross profit rate)$= \$20,000$		
3/17/19X2		
Allowance for Sales Returns	40,000	
Accounts Receivable		40,000
Cost of Sales	4,000	
Inventory		4,000*

*Inventory Assumed Returned ($50,000 \times 40\%$)	$20,000
Less: Amount Returned ($40,000 \times 40\%$)	16,000
Adjustment to Inventory	$ 4,000

SOFTWARE REVENUE RECOGNITION

According to AICPA Statement of Position (SOP) Number 97–2 (*Software Revenue Recognition*), revenue should be recognized when the contract for software does not involve major production, alteration, or customization provided the following conditions are satisfied:

1. Receipt of payment is probable.
2. The selling price is fixed or known.
3. The software has been delivered.
4. The contract is enforceable.

Separate accounting is required for the service aspect of a software transaction if the following conditions exist:

1. A separate provision exists in the contract covering services so a price for such services is stipulated.
2. The services are not mandatory for the software transactions.

A software contract may include more than one component, such as add-on software, upgrades, customer support after sale, and exchange or return privileges. The total selling price of the software transaction should be allocated to the contractual components based on fair value. If fair value is not determinable, revenue should be deferred until it is determinable or when all components of the transaction have been delivered. **Note:** The four preceding revenue criteria must be satisfied before any allocation of the fee to the contractual elements may be made. Further, the fee for a contractual component is determinable if the element is sold separately.

AICPA SOP No. 98-9 modifies SOP 97-2 regarding software revenue recognition. The modification requires revenue recognition under the "residual method" if (1) fair market values are determinable for undelivered items in a multiple-element agreement that is not recorded using long-term contract accounting, (2) objective evidence of fair value does not exist for one or more of the delivered elements in the arrangement, and (3) all other revenue recognition criteria are met. Using the residual method, the arrangement fee is recorded as follows:

- Deferral is made of the total fair value of undelivered elements

■ The difference between the total arrangement fee and the deferred amount for the undelivered items is recognized as revenue applicable to the delivered elements.

CONTRIBUTIONS

FASB Number 116, *Accounting for Contributions Received and Contributions Made,* and FASB Interpretation Number 42, *Accounting for Transfer of Assets in which a Not-for-Profit Organization Is Granted Variance Power,* are the primary authoritative sources for accounting for contributions.

Contributions are a voluntary and unconditional conveyance of assets or cancellation of liabilities by one entity to another entity, in a nonreciprocal relationship, where one entity does not have an ownership interest in the other entity. These entities may be either for profit or not for profit. Cash as well as other monetary and nonmonetary assets, services, or unconditional promises to give those assets or services qualify as contributions.

FASB Number 116 distinguishes between donor-imposed restrictions and donor-imposed conditions. If a donor limits the way a contribution is to be used (such as to build a hospital building), it is considered a *restriction,* and the revenue from such a contribution and any related expenses should be recognized immediately. In contrast, if the donor imposes a condition, such as that the donee-entity must raise matching funds, then that *condition* must be satisfied before revenue may be recorded.

A promise by a donor may be either unconditional or conditional. A promise is considered unconditional if the donor has no right to take back the donated asset and the contribution would be available after some time or on demand. Unconditional promises to give contributions should be recognized immediately. A conditional promise is contingent upon the occurrence of a future event. If that event does not occur, the donor is not bound by the promise. A vague promise is deemed conditional. Conditional promises should be recorded only when their conditions have been fulfilled. A conditional promise may be treated as an unconditional promise if the possibility that the condition will not be met is remote.

A promise to give may be either written or oral. Of course, evidence of the promise must exist before any amount is recorded. Such evidence may consist of information about the donor, such as the donor's name and address, the amount that the donor promised to give, when the amount will be given (e.g., payment schedule), when the promise was made, and to whom was the promise to give made. A public announcement by the donor may be made. The donor may make partial payments. The donee may have taken actions relying on the promise. If a promise to give is recorded, it should be recorded at fair value. If the promised amount is not expected to be collected within a year, the use of discounted cash flow may be appropriate. If discounted cash flow is used, the interest should be treated as a contribution income rather than as interest income.

Contributions received should be recorded at fair value by debiting the asset and crediting revenue. Quoted market prices or market prices for similar assets, appraisal by an independent expert, or valuation techniques such as discounted cash flows should be used to determine fair value. The value of contributed services should also be based on quoted market prices for those services. An increase in the fair value of nonmonetary assets resulting from the performance services may alternatively be used to measure the fair value of services.

Both skilled and unskilled contributed services should be recognized if nonmonetary assets are created or enhanced. Contributed services should also be recognized if specialized skills are provided by the donor and those skills would have to be purchased by the donee if they were not donated.

FASB Number 116 requires certain disclosures in the financial statements of recipients of contributions. For unconditional promises to give, the amount of receivables due within one year, in one to five years, and in more than five years should be disclosed along with the amount for allowance for uncollectible unconditional promises receivable. For conditional promises to give, disclosure is required of the promised amounts and a description of the promise. Promises with similar characteristics may be grouped together. Disclosure should also be made in the financial statements that describes the nature and extent of contributed services, restrictions or conditions set, and the programs or activities which utilized contributed services. Entities are encouraged to disclose the fair value of services received but not recorded as revenues.

When donations are made of works of art, historical items, and other such valuable assets, the recording of such assets is optional if the following conditions are satisfied:

- The assets added to collections are held for public exhibition, education, or research

- The assets are protected, preserved, and kept unencumbered

- The proceeds from the sale of such assets are used to obtain other items for the collection

Contributed collection items should be recorded as revenues or gains and as assets if collections are capitalized. Certain disclosures are required if collections are not capitalized, including the cost of collection items purchased, the proceeds from the sale of collection items, and the proceeds from insurance recoveries of lost or destroyed collection items.

The donor should recognize an expense and a corresponding decrease in assets, or an increase in liabilities, at fair value, in the period in which the contribution is made. If the fair value differs from the book value, a gain or loss on disposition should be recognized, as appropriate.

WARRANTY AND MAINTENANCE CONTRACTS

Extended warranty and product maintenance contracts are frequently offered by retailers as separately priced items in addition to their products. Accounting for *separately priced* extended warranty and maintenance contracts is given by FASB Technical Bulletin 90–1. Warranty and maintenance contracts that are *not* separately priced should be accounted for as *contingencies.*

Extended warranty contracts provide protection beyond the scope of the manufacturer's warranty or beyond the period of the original warranty. Product maintenance contracts provide services to maintain a product for a specified duration. Service may be provided at fixed intervals, or a specified number of times, or as required to keep the product operational.

Revenues and incremental direct costs from separately priced extended warranty and product maintenance contracts should be initially deferred. Revenue should be recognized on a straight-line basis over the contract period. Related incremental direct costs should be expensed in proportion to revenue recognized. Incremental direct costs result from obtaining the contract; these costs would not otherwise have been incurred. Other costs, such as the cost of services performed, general and administrative expenses, and costs of contracts not consummated, should be expensed when incurred.

Losses from such contracts should be recognized when the estimated costs of providing the service plus the unamortized portion of acquisition costs exceed corresponding unearned revenue. To determine loss, contracts should be grouped in a consistent manner, similar to the pool of risk concept from FASB Statement Number 60, *Accounting and Reporting by Insurance Enterprises;* that is, losses are not recognized on individual contracts but rather on a group of similar contracts. Loss is recognized by first reducing unamortized acquisition costs, and if this is not adequate, then a liability should be recorded.

Annual Report References

VIACOM
1997 ANNUAL REPORT
Footnote Recognition

Revenue Recognition

Subscriber fees for Networks are recognized in the period the service is provided. Advertising revenues for Networks and Broadcasting are recognized in the period during which the spots are aired. Revenues from the video and music stores are recognized at the time of rental or sale. The publishing segment recognizes revenue when merchandise is shipped.

Theatrical and Television Revenues—On average, the length of the initial revenue cycle for feature films approximates four to seven years. Theatrical revenues from domestic and foreign markets are recognized as films are exhibited; revenues from the sale of videocassettes and discs are recognized upon delivery of the merchandise; and revenues from all television sources are recognized upon availability of the film for telecast.

Television series initially produced for the networks and first-run syndication are generally licensed to domestic and foreign markets concurrently. The more successful series are later syndicated in domestic markets and in certain foreign markets. The length of the revenue cycle for television series will vary depending on the number of seasons a series remains in active production. Revenues arising from television license agreements are recognized in the period that the films or television series are available for telecast and therefore may cause fluctuation in operating results.

GENERAL MOTORS
1997 ANNUAL REPORT
Footnote Reference

Revenue Reference

Sales are generally recorded when products are shipped or when services are rendered to independent dealers or other third parties. Provisions for normal dealer sales incentives, returns and allowances, and GM Card rebates are made at the time of vehicle sale. Costs related to special sales incentive programs are recognized as reductions to sales when determinable.

To conform to the consensus reached by the Emerging Issues Task Force of the Financial Accounting Standards Board on Issue No. 95–1, Revenue Recognition on Sales with a Guaranteed Minimum Resale Value, the Corporation modified its revenue recognition policy on sales to daily rental car companies, effective January 1, 1995, which resulted in an unfavorable cumulative effect of $52 million after-tax or $0.07 per share of $1-2/3 par value common stock.

Financing revenue is recorded over the terms of the receivables using the interest method. Certain loan origination costs are deferred and amortized to financing revenue over the lives of the related loans using the interest method.

Income from operating lease assets is recognized on a straight-line basis over the scheduled lease term. Certain operating lease origination costs are deferred and amortized to financing revenue over the lives of the related operating leases using the straight-line method.

Insurance premiums are earned on a basis related to coverage provided over the terms of the policies. Commission, premium taxes, and other costs incurred in acquiring new business are deferred and amortized over the terms of the related policies on the same basis as premiums are earned. The liability for losses and loss expenses includes a provision for unreported losses, based on past experience, net of the estimate salvage and subrogation recoverable.

MINNESOTA MINING AND MANUFACTURING 1997 ANNUAL REPORT
Footnote Reference

Revenue Recognition

Revenue is recognized upon shipment of goods to customers and upon performance of services. The company sells a wide range of products to a diversified base of customers around the world and, therefore, believes there is no material concentration of credit risk.

EASTMAN KODAK
1997 ANNUAL REPORT
Footnote Reference

Revenue

Revenue is recognized from the sale of film, paper, supplies and equipment (including sales-type leases for equipment) when the product is shipped; from maintenance and service contracts over the contractual period, or as the services are performed; from rentals under operating leases in the month in which they are earned; and from financing transactions at level rates of return over the term of the lease or receivable.

CBS
1997 ANNUAL REPORT
Footnote Reference

Revenue Recognition

Revenues are primarily derived from the sale of advertising spots and are recognized when the spots are broadcast. The Corporation also receives syndication revenues on sales of owned programming, cable license fees from distribution of its cable networks, and advertising revenues on the sale of outdoor advertising space. Syndication revenues are recognized when the programming is available to telecast and certain other conditions are met. Revenues from cable license fees are recorded in the period that service is provided. Revenues on outdoor advertising space are recognized proportionately over the contract term.

UNIGENE
1997 ANNUAL REPORT
Footnote Reference

11. Research and Licensing Revenue

In June 1995, the Company entered into a joint venture agreement effective as of March 1996, with the Qingdao General Pharmaceutical Company and its Huanghai factory for the production and marketing of calcitonin in China. Under the agreement, the Chinese partners will finance the project, including the construction and operation of a dedicated manufacturing facility in China which will utilize the non-proprietary aspects of the Company's production technology. Unigene will provide the joint venture with technology and training as well as the Company's proprietary enzyme at a discounted price. Unigene will receive a combination of fixed fees and annual royalties based upon sales of the end product. This joint venture contributed $300,000 to 1996 revenues. It is uncertain whether any additional revenues will be recognized or received in connection with this joint venture.

In July 1997, the Company entered into an agreement under which it granted to the Parke-Davis division of Warner-Lambert Company a worldwide license to use the Company's oral calcitonin technology. Upon execution of the agreement, the Company received $6 million in payments from Warner-Lambert, consisting of a $3 million licensing fee and a $3 million equity investment by Warner-Lambert (695,066 shares of Common Stock were purchased at a price of approximately $4.32 per share). In addition, the Company is eligible to receive up to an additional $48.5 million in milestone payments during the course of the development program if specified milestones are achieved, of which $15.5 million would be received prior to the commencement of Phase I clinical studies in the U.S. The first of these milestones was achieved in February 1998, resulting in a payment to the Company of $2 million. If the product is successfully commercialized, the Company also would receive revenue from the sale of raw material to Warner-Lambert and royalties on product sales by Warner-Lambert and its affiliates. The Company has retained the right to license the use of its technologies for injectable and nasal formulations of calcitonin on a worldwide bases.

RAYTHEON
1998 ANNUAL REPORT

Note D: Contracts in Process

(In millions)

Contracts in process consisted of the following at December 31, 1998:

	Cost Type	Fixed Price Type	Total
U.S. government end-use contracts			
Billed	$ 374	$ 555	$ 929
Unbilled	928	4,150	5,078
Less progress payments	—	(2,753)	(2,753)
Total	1,302	1,952	3,254
Other customers			
Billed	300	498	798
Unbilled	418	864	1,282
Less progress payments	—	(492)	(492)
Total	718	870	1,588
	$2,020	$2,822	$4,842

(In millions)

Contracts in process consisted of the following at December 31, 1997:

	Cost Type	Fixed Price Type	Total
U.S. government end-use contracts:			
Billed	$ 534	$ 400	$ 934
Unbilled	404	3,658	4,062
Less progress payments	—	(1,968)	(1,968)
Total	938	2,090	3,028
Other customers			
Billed	70	321	391
Unbilled	210	1,308	1,518
Less progress payments	—	(276)	(276)
Total	280	1,353	1,633
	$1,218	$3,443	$4,661

The U.S. government has a security title to unbilled amounts associated with contracts that provide for progress payments.

Unbilled amounts are primarily recorded on the percentage of completion method and are recoverable from the customer upon shipment of the product, presentation of billings, or completion of the contract.

Billed and unbilled contracts in process include retentions arising from contractual provisions. At December 31, 1998, retentions amounted to $279 million and are anticipated to be collected as follows: 1999—$132 million, 2000—$90 million, and the balance thereafter.

3

Balance Sheet Reporting and Disclosures: Assets

This chapter discusses GAAP for assets. It includes a discussion of accounts and loans receivable, inventory, prepaid expenses, fixed assets, capitalized interest, exchange of assets, impairment of assets, involuntary conversion, intangibles, and transfer of financial assets. Promulgated GAAP for current assets is provided in the American Institute of CPA's Accounting Principles Board's Accounting Research Bulletin Number 43, chapter 3A. Current assets have a life of one year or the normal operating cycle of the business, whichever is greater. The accounting policies and any restrictions on current assets must be disclosed.

Assets are recorded at the price paid plus normal incidental costs necessary to bring that asset into existing use and location. Examples of incidental costs include installation, freight, insurance, tooling, testing, instruction, flooring, and taxes. As a general rule, costs incurred before an asset is put into use for the first time is capitalized to the asset. If an asset is bought in exchange for the issuance of stock, the asset is recorded at the fair value of the stock issued. If the fair value is not known, such as in the case of a closely held company, the asset is presented at its appraised value. If an asset is acquired because of the incurrence of long-term debt, the asset is recorded at the present (discounted) value of future payments.

This chapter was co-authored by Roberta M. Siegel, an accounting consultant.

EXAMPLE

Equipment is bought in exchange for making ten $30,000 payments at an interest rate of 10%. The asset should be recorded at

$$\$30,000 \times 6.145* = \$61,450$$

The asset is recorded at the principal amount excluding the interest payments.

Some assets are recorded at net realizable value, which equals the amount of cash expected to be obtained for them in the ordinary course of business less any direct costs associated with their conversion to cash.

FASB Statement Number 125 (*Accounting for Transfers and Servicing of Financial Assets and Extinguishment of Liabilities*) provides the GAAP for the transfer and servicing of financial assets. Derivatives and liabilities arising from the transfer of financial assets are recorded at fair market value.

CASH

Cash includes money, available cash funds on deposit, and bank drafts. Petty cash is typically presented with other cash accounts.

Note: Bank overdrafts are presented under current liabilities, typically accounts payable. Bank overdrafts are usually not offset against the cash account. However, offsetting is allowed for two or more accounts at the same bank.

Note: Certificates of deposit and similar types of deposit are classified as temporary investments rather than cash because they contain restrictions or penalties if cashed in before maturity. However, cash restricted as to withdrawal or use for other than current operations will not be presented as a current asset.

Cash *restricted* for specified purposes may be segregated and may be presented as a current asset if it is the basis to pay a current liability. If not, the restricted cash will be presented under noncurrent assets. Further, cash

---

*Factor using the present value of an ordinary annuity table for $n = 10$, $i = 10\%$.

may be presented as a noncurrent asset if it is to be used to pay long-term debt, or if the cash is to be used to buy or construct a noncurrent asset.

The amount of cash constituting a compensating balance has to be segregated and presented under noncurrent assets if the related debt is noncurrent. If, however, the debt is current, the compensating balance may be shown separately as a current asset.

The cash surrender value of life insurance policies is classified under noncurrent investments unless the policy will be cashed in within one year from the balance sheet date.

Any restrictions or commitments on cash must be disclosed. Compensating balance requirements must be noted.

As per FASB Statement Number 105 (*Disclosures of Information About Financial Instruments*), footnote disclosure is required of off-balance-sheet risk of loss as applied to cash, such as possible theft because cash is at an unsecured location or high crime area. An example of a disclosure is when the company keeps more than $100,000 in a bank account and therefore has off-balance-sheet risk because amounts on deposits exceeding $100,000 are not insured by the Federal Deposit Insurance Corporation.

RECEIVABLES

Receivables may consist of accounts receivable, notes receivable, trade acceptances, travel advances and loans receivable. Postdated checks and IOUs are classified as receivables.

Nontrade receivables include advances to officers and employees, advances to subsidiaries or affiliated companies, receivable from stockholders, third-party instruments, deposits owed the company (e.g., deposits to cover product damages or guarantees of performance), interest and dividends receivable, and claims against others (e.g., insurance recoveries, tax refunds, returned items, damaged goods in transit by carrier). Nontrade receivables should be segregated from trade receivables in the balance sheet. **Note:** Accounting Research Bulletin Number 43, chapter 1A, covers receivables from officers, employees, or affiliated companies.

Unearned discounts (excluding for cost or volume), finance charges, and interest included in the face of receivables should be subtracted therefrom to determine net receivables.

Accounts Receivable

Accounts receivable are presented in the balance sheet at net realizable value. Net realizable value equals the gross receivable less the allowance for bad debts. Bad debts may be recognized under the allowance method or direct writeoff method. The *allowance method* recognizes bad debts expense in the year of sale. The bad debt provision may be based on either a percentage of credit sales or an aging of the ending accounts receivable balance. A company may estimate bad debt percent based on several factors, such as past experience, the experience of other companies in the industry, or current economic conditions. The allowance method is the only one required in financial reporting. The *direct writeoff method* records bad debt expense only when a customer's balance is uncollectible. This method is not allowed for financial reporting purposes because it does not match expenses against sales in the year of sale. However, the direct writeoff method is required for tax reporting purposes.

An accrual should also be made in the year of sale for estimated returns and allowances due to product deficiency. Collection expenses may be accrued by debiting collection expenses and crediting allowance for collection expenses. An allowance for trade discounts should also be provided. The allowance account is a contra to gross accounts receivable to determine net accounts receivable.

EXAMPLE

If a company sells on terms of 4/15, net 30, and 30% of its customers take advantage of the discount on sales of $90,000, the allowance for discounts will be $1,080 ($90,000 × .30 × .04).

EXAMPLE

Harris Company presents the following data related to its accounts receivable for 19X5:

Accounts receivable, 1/1/19X5	$ 325,000
Credit sales	1,350,000
Sales returns	37,500
Accounts written off	20,000
Collections from customers	1,075,000

Gross accounts receivable equals $542,500, computed as follows:

Accounts receivable—1/1/19X5	$ 325,000
Credit sales	1,350,000
Sales returns	(37,500)
Accounts written off	(20,000)
Customer collections	(1,075,000)
Total	$ 542,500

EXAMPLE

Mavis Company's allowance for bad debts has a credit balance of $48,000 at December 31, 19X3. During 19X4, the company wrote off customer accounts of $192,000. The aging of accounts receivable shows that a $200,000 allowance account is needed at December 31, 19X4.

Bad debts for 19X4 should be $344,000, computed as follows:

Allowance—12/31/19X3	$ 48,000
Accounts written off in 19X4	(192,000)
Debit balance before year-end adjustment	$(144,000)
Desired credit balance (based on aging)	200,000
Year-end adjustment (increase in expense)	$ 344,000

EXAMPLE

Erlach Company computed its net value of accounts receivable at December 31, 19X6 as $162,500 based on aging the receivable. Additional information for 19X6 follows:

Allowance for bad debts—1/1/19X6	$ 15,000
Uncollectible accounts written	9,000
Uncollectible accounts recovered	1,000
Accounts receivable—12/31/19X6	175,000

Bad debts for 19X6 will be $5,500, computed as follows:

Allowance—1/1/19X6	$15,000
Accounts written off	(9,000)
Recovery of accounts written off	1,000
Balance before adjustment	7,000
Desired allowance balance ($175,000 – $162,500)	12,500
Bad debts	$ 5,500

The *pledging* of accounts receivable involves using accounts receivable as *security* for a loan. The company retains title to the receivable but must disclose the pledging agreement in the footnotes. The agreement usually stipulates that as collections are received they must be used to reduce the loan. The pledged accounts receivable must be identified as such in the current asset section. The related debt must be identified as being collateralized by the pledged receivable. Customers whose accounts have been pledged are usually not informed of it. They continue to mail their payments to the company.

An *assignment* of account receivable involves using the receivable as collateral for a loan. Typically, less than the face value of the receivable (e.g., 80%) will be advanced to the borrower by the lender, depending on the credit worthiness of the borrower and the quality of the customer base. Accounts receivable that are assigned are presented in the current asset section and are required to be disclosed as such. The assignment of accounts receivable usually involves both a finance charge and interest on the note. Prepaid finance charges are deferred and amortized over the period of the agreement.

EXAMPLE

Levsee Company assigns $1,000,000 of its accounts receivable to Levine Bank as collateral for a loan of $800,000 made by the bank on January 1. The loan agreement provides that Leesee's credit customers will not be notified of the arrangement and the company will continue to collect payments on account as usual. Levine Bank charges a finance charge of 2% of the accounts receivable assigned and is required to pay 10% interest on the amount borrowed. The bank requires that collections on the accounts receivable that were assigned and interest payments on the outstanding debt be remitted monthly.

The following are the entries made by Levsee Company:

Issuance of the note for the loan of $800,000

Cash	600,000	
Finance expense (2% × $1,000,000)	200,000	
Notes payable		800,000

Sales discounts and sales returns for the month of January were $1,000 and $2,000, respectively.

Sales discounts	1,000	
Sales returns	2,000	
Accounts receivable		3,000

Collections of accounts receivable net of discounts and returns for the month of January amounted to $500,000.

Cash	500,000	
Accounts receivable		500,000

Remitted collections on accounts receivable plus interest owed on note to Levine Bank for the month of January are as follows:

Notes payable	500,000	
Interest expense	6,667 (800,000 × 10% × 1/12)	
Cash		506,667

During February, $25,000 was written off as uncollectible.

Allowance for doubtful accounts	25,000	
Accounts receivable		25,000

Remaining collections of receivables net of uncollectible accounts amounted to $472,000 for February. The balance of the note payable plus accrued interest for the month was remitted to Levine Bank by Levsee Company.

Cash		472,000	
Accounts receivable			472,000
Note payable	300,000		
Interest expense	2,500 (300,000 × 10% × 1/12)		
Cash			302,500

In a *factoring* arrangement, accounts receivable are, in effect, sold to a financial institution (factor). Title is transferred. Notification is usually made to customers, and remissions are made directly to the factor. Factoring is accomplished usually without recourse, meaning the risk of uncollectibility of the customer's account resides in the lender (factor). Interest is based on how long it is expected to take the factor to collect on customer balances. A fee is also assessed based on expected bad debts. The factor usually does the billing and collection. The difference between the factored receivable and the amount received constitutes a gain or loss as follows:

Cash
Loss (or gain)
   Accounts receivable

EXAMPLE

ABC Company sells its receivable without recourse to a factor. The total face value of the accounts receivable is $100,000. There is a 4% allowance provided. The interest rate is 12% and is to apply to a 60-day period before collection is expected. A 2% fee is provided for expected uncollectible balances. An 8% holdback is stipulated for expected customer returns of merchandise. The amount of merchandise actually returned was $3,000. The remaining holdback will be paid by the factor after the return privilege period expires. The journal entries for this factoring arrangement follow:

Cash	88,000	
Allowance for bad debts ($100,000 × .04)	4,000	
Interest expense ($100,000 × .12 × 60/360)	2,000	
Factoring fee ($100,000 × .02)	2,000	
Factor's holdback receivable ($100,000 × .08)	8,000	
Bad debts expense		4,000
Accounts receivable		100,000

Note: As an alternative, $4,000 may be charged to a loss on sale of receivable account based on the total interest and factoring charges.

Sales returns and allowances	3,000	
Factor's holdback receivable		3,000
Cash*	5,000	
Factor's holdback receivable		5,000

*When the return privilege period expires, the remaining holdback is due the borrower amounting to $5,000 ($8,000 − $3,000).

FASB Statement Number 125, *Accounting for Transfers and Servicing of Financial Assets,* superseded FASB Number 77, *Reporting by Transferors for Transfers of Receivables With Recourse,* after December 31, 1996. Statement 125 provides new GAAP guidelines concerning the transfer of financial assets with continuing involvement on the part of the transferor to either the assets transferred or to the transferee. Examples of continuing involvement are recourse and pledges of collateral. Transfers of financial assets with continuing involvement raise questions as to whether the transfers should be considered a sale of all or part of the assets or a secured borrowing. Guidelines regarding these issues follow.

Sale of Financial Assets

A transfer of financial assets in which the seller surrenders control over the financial assets should be accounted for as a *sale.* A seller is considered to have surrendered control over the transferred assets if and only if all of the following conditions are met:

1. The transferred assets have been isolated from the seller. That is, they have been put beyond the reach of the seller and its creditors, even in bankruptcy or other receiverships.

2. Each buyer obtains the right to pledge or exchange the transferred assets.

3. The seller does not maintain effective control over the transferred asset(s) through

   a. an agreement that both entitles and obligates the seller to purchase or redeem the assets before their maturity or

   b. an agreement that entitles the seller to repurchase or redeem the transferred assets that are not readily obtainable.

Upon completion of a transfer of financial assets that is considered a sale, Statement 125 requires that the seller should

1. Derecognize all assets that were sold.

2. Recognize all assets that were obtained and liabilities that were incurred as proceeds of the sale (e.g., cash, put, or call options held or written; for example, guarantee or recourse obligations).

3. Initially measure the assets obtained and liabilities incurred in a sale at their fair values.

4. Recognize any gain or loss on the sale.

If the transfer of financial assets in exchange for cash or other consideration does not meet the aforementioned requirements, then the transferee should account for the transfer as a secured borrowing with the pledge of collateral.

Emerging Issues Task Force Consensus Summary Number 92–2 (*Measuring Loss Accruals by Transferors for Transfers of Receivable With Recourse*) requires that probable credit losses associated with transferred receivables should be included in the obligation recorded at date of sale. The recourse obligation may be based on a present value determination of future cash flows, if reliability exists in estimation.

Footnote disclosure for accounts receivable includes

- Receivables arising from major sources such as trade, officers, and employees

- Year-end receivable balance and amounts received by the transferor during the period

- Receivables that have been billed or unbilled
- Loss contingencies on receivables
- Collateralized or pledged receivables
- Significant concentration of credit risk arising from receivables
- Related party receivables
- Losses on receivables after year-end but before the financial statements are issued

Notes Receivable

A note receivable may be discounted at the bank to obtain the proceeds before the maturity date. The amount of cash (proceeds) received by the holder when the note is discounted equals the face value of the note plus interest income to maturity to obtain the maturity value less the discount based on the maturity value. The bank discount equals the maturity value of the note multiplied by the discount rate for the time period the note will be held by the bank. If the note is discounted with recourse, the company is contingently liable if the note is not paid. The discounted notes receivable account is a contra to notes receivable.

EXAMPLE

A $10,000, six-month note having a 12% interest rate is discounted at the bank after being held for two months. The bank discount rate is 15%. The cash received is

Principal	$10,000
Interest ($10,000 × 6/12 × .12)	600
Maturity value	$10,600
Bank discount ($10,600 × 4/12 × .15)	530
Proceeds	$10,070

The journal entry is as follows:

Cash	10,000	
Notes receivable discounted		10,000
Interest income		70

EXAMPLE

Blake Company bought from David Company a $10,000, 8%, five-year note involving five equal annual year-end payments of $2,505. The note was discounted at 9% to Blake. At the purchase date, the note's present value was $9,743. Interest income earned over the life of the note will be $2,783, computed as follows:

Total cash receipts $2505 × 5	$12,525
Less: Acquisition cost of note	9,743
Interest revenue over life of note	$ 2,782

An installment note receivable should *not* be offset against a related bank debt in a note monetization situation.

A note received in payment for common stock issued should usually be deducted in the stockholders' equity section of the balance sheet.

Footnote disclosure for notes receivable include the amount of notes receivable discounted, description of the notes, face amount of the notes, and interest rate on the notes.

Loans Receivable

FASB Statement Number 91 (*Accounting for Nonrefundable Fees and Costs Associated With Originating or Acquiring Loans and Initial Direct Costs of Leases*) is applicable to both the incremental direct costs incurred in originating a loan and internally incurred costs that are directly related to loan or loan commitment activity. Loan origination fees are netted with the related loan origination costs and are accounted for as follows:

- For loans held for resale, the net cost is deferred and recognized at the time the loan is sold.

- For loans held for investment purposes, the net cost is deferred and amortized over the term of the loan by the interest method.

Loan commitment fees are initially deferred and recognized in earnings as follows:

- If the commitment is exercised, the fee is recognized over the term of the loan by the interest method.

- If the commitment expires without exercise, the fee is recognized at the expiration date.

- If, based upon past experience, exercise of the commitment is remote, amortize the fee over the term of the commitment by the straight-line method.

IMPAIRMENT OF LOANS

FASB Statement Number 114, *Accounting by Creditors for Impairment of a Loan,* is the primary authoritative guideline for recognizing impaired loans. A loan is a contractual right to receive cash either on demand or at a fixed or determinable date. Loans include accounts receivable and notes only if their term is longer than one year. If it is probable (likely to occur) that some or all of the principal or interest will not be collected, then the loan is considered impaired. Any loss on an impaired loan should be recognized immediately by debiting bad debt expense and crediting the valuation allowance. Creditors may exercise their judgment and use their normal review procedures in determining the probability of collection.

Determining the Value of an Impaired Loan

If a loan is considered impaired, the loss is the difference between the investment in loan and the present value of the future cash flows discounted at the loan's effective interest rate. The investment in loan will generally be the principal and the accrued interest. Future cash flows should be determined using reasonable and supportable assumptions and projections. The discount rate will generally be the effective interest used at the time the loan was originally made. As a practical matter, the loan's value may be determined using the market price of the loan, if available. The loan's value may also be determined using the fair value of the collateral, less estimated costs to sell, if the loan is collateralized and the collateral is expected to be the sole source of repayment.

EXAMPLE

On December 31, 2000, Debtor Inc. issues a five-year, $100,000 note bearing a 10% interest, payable annually, to Creditor Inc. The market interest rate for such loans is 12%. The present value of the principal, $100,000 discounted at 12% for five years, is $56,742. The present value of the interest payments of $10,000 (10% of $100,000) per year for five years discounted at 12% is $36,048. Therefore, the present value of the loan is $92,790. Discount on notes receivable is $7,210, and it will be amortized using the effective interest method. Creditor Inc. will record the note as follows:

Notes receivable	100,000	
Discount on notes receivable		7,210
Cash		92,790

The following table shows the amortization of the discount and the increase in the carrying amount of the note:

Year	Interest Income	Cash Received	Discount Amortization	Discount Remaining	Carrying Amount
12/31/00				7,210	92,790
12/31/01	11,135	10,000	1,135	6,075	93,925
12/31/02	11,271	10,000	1,271	4,804	95,196
12/31/03	11,424	10,000	1,424	3,380	96,620
12/31/04	11,594	10,000	1,594	1,786	92,214
12/31/05	11,786	10,000	1,786	0	100,000

On December 31, 2002, Creditor Inc. determines that it is probable that Debtor Inc. will only be able to repay interest of $8,000 per year (instead of $10,000 per year) and $70,000 (instead of $100,000) of the principal at maturity. This constitutes a loan impairment, and a loss should be recorded immediately. The present value of future cash flows should be discounted for three years at the historical effective interest rate of 12%. The present value of $70,000 discounted at 12% for three years is $49,824, and the present value of interest payments of $8,000 discounted at 12% for three years is $19,215. The total present value of future cash flows is $69,039.

Carrying amount of investment in loan on 12/31/02	$95,196
Present value of future cash flows from loan	69,039
Loss due to impairment	$26,157

The entry to record the loss is as follows:

Bad debt expense	26,157	
Allowance for doubtful accounts		26,157

Evaluating Loan Collectibility

A loan is considered impaired if it is probable that the creditor will be unable to collect the entire principal and interest. The definition of *probable* is consistent with the definition given in FASB Statement Number 5, *Accounting for Contingencies. Probable* does not mean certainty or virtual certainty; it only means that the impairment is likely to occur.

GAAP does not provide any specific guidance on how to determine collectibility of loans. Normal loan review procedures utilized by the creditor may be used to determine the collectibility of loans. The following items may be considered in making such judgments:

- The materiality of the loan amount
- Previous loss experience
- Reports of total loan amounts by borrower
- Regulatory reports
- Internal reports, such as "watch list," past due reports, loans to insiders, listing of overdrafts, etc.
- Borrower experiencing financial problems, such as operating losses, insufficient working capital or inadequate cash flows, etc.
- Borrower in unstable industry or country

- Loans secured by collateral that is not readily marketable or is subject to decline in value

- Compliance exception reports

- Loan files containing missing or inadequate current financial data on borrowers or guarantors

  A loan is *not* considered impaired if

- There is an insignificant delay or shortfall in collecting payments.

- The creditor expects, despite a delay, to collect the full amount plus accrued interest.

Income Recognition

Interest income from an impaired loan may be recognized using several methods, such as the cash basis method, the cost recovery method, or some combination. GAAP does not specifically recommend or prescribe a method for measuring, recording, or disclosing interest income from impaired loans (FASB Statement Number 118 amends FASB Statement Number 114). Use of some accounting methods, or the creditor charging off some part of the loan, may lead to recording an investment in an impaired loan at less than the present value of expected future cash flows, and hence no additional impairment would need to be recognized.

Disclosure Requirements

The following information should be disclosed either in the body of the financial statements or in the notes that accompany them:

- The total investment in impaired loans as of the balance sheet date, including (1) the amount of investments for which there is a related valuation allowance, and (2) the amount of investments for which there is no valuation allowance

- The creditor's policy for recognizing interest revenue on impaired loans, including the recording of cash receipts

- For each period that is presented, the average recorded investment in impaired loans, the related interest income recognized while the loans were impaired, and, if possible, the amount of interest income recognized using the cash basis while the loans were impaired

According to FASB Statement Number 118 (paragraph 6), the total allowance for credit losses related to impaired loans should be disclosed, including the beginning and ending valuation allowance account balance, additions charged to operations, direct write-downs charged against the valuation allowance, and recoveries of amounts previously charged off, if any.

INVENTORY

The accounting, reporting, and disclosures associated with inventory are provided by various authoritative pronouncements, including Accounting Research Bulletin Number 43, chapter 4 (*Inventory Pricing*), FASB Interpretation Number 1 (*Accounting Changes Related to the Cost of Inventory*), and Emerging Issues Task Force Consensus Summary Number 86–46 (*Uniform Capitalization Rules for Inventory under The Tax Reform Act of 1986*).

Inventories consist of merchandise to be sold for a retailer. Inventories for a manufacturing company include raw materials, work-in-process (partially completed goods), finished goods, operating supplies, and ordinary maintenance parts.

Inventories are presented under current assets. However, if inventory consists of slow-moving items or excessive amounts that will not be sold within the normal operating cycle of the business, such excess amounts should be classified as noncurrent assets.

Inventory includes direct and indirect costs associated with preparing inventory for sale or use. Therefore, the cost of inventory to a retail store includes the purchase price, taxes paid, delivery charges, storage, and insurance. A manufacturer includes in its cost of inventory the direct materials (including the purchase price and freight-in), direct labor, and factory overhead (including factory utilities, rent, and insurance).

Inventory may be valued at the lower of cost or market value. The value of inventory may decrease because of being out-of-date, deteriorated, or damanged or because of price-level changes. Specialized inventory methods also exist including retail, retail lower of cost or market, retail Last-in, First-out (LIFO), and dollar value LIFO.

Footnote disclosure for inventory includes the valuation basis method, inventory categorization by major type, unusual lossess, and inventory pledged or collateralized.

Purchases may be recorded gross or net of any cash discount, whether or not taken. If the discount is not taken, purchase discount lost is charged and is considered a financial expense.

Purchase Contract Commitments

If a loss occurs on a purchase contract commitment, it should be recorded in the current year.

EXAMPLE

In 19X5, XYZ Company entered into a purchase contract to buy 10,000 units of product X at $2 per foot. At year-end, the price of the product declined to $1.50 per foot. The loss of $.50 per foot must be immediately recognized. The journal entry is

Loss on purchase commitment	5,000	
Allowance for purchase commitment loss		5,000
10,000 units × $.50 = $5,000		

Freight Terms

If items are bought on terms of freight-on-board (FOB) shipping point, title passes to the buyer when the goods are shipped by the seller. If items are bought on terms of FOB destination, title passes to the purchaser when the merchandise is received by the buyer.

EXAMPLE

Akel Company's inventory at December 31, 19X7, was $2,000,000 based on a physical count priced at cost and before any adjustments due to the following:

- Merchandise costing $60,000 was shipped FOB shipping point from the vendor on December 30, 19X7 but was received on January 4, 19X8

- Goods in the shipping area were excluded from inventory even though shipment was not made until January 6, 19X8. The merchandise was billed to the customer FOB shipping point on December 29, 19X7. It had a cost of $140,000

The amount of inventory to be reported on the December 31, 19X7 balance sheet is $2,200,000 ($2,000,000 + $60,000 + $140,000).

Consigned Goods

Consigned goods are included in the consignor's inventory in the balance sheet. The consignee holds the inventory as an agent to sell it on behalf of the consignor. When the consigned goods are sold, the sale is credited by the consignor. The consignee records commission revenue.

EXAMPLE

The following items were included in Travis Company's inventory account at December 31, 19X4:

Goods held on consignment by Travis	$10,000
Goods bought, in transit, shipped FOB shipping point	24,000
Goods out on consignment at sales price, including 30% markup on selling price	30,000

Travis Company's inventory account at December 31, 19X4 should be reduced by $40,000, computed as follows:

Goods held on consignment belonging to consignor	$10,000
Goods out on consignment $30,000 × .30	9,000*
Total reduction	$19,000

*The goods out on consignment are appropriately considered the property of Travis. However, they must be included in ending inventory at cost. Therefore, inventory should be reduced by the 30% markup on selling price.

The goods in transit bought FOB shipping point are correctly included in inventory.

Financing Product Arrangements

FASB Statement Number 49 (*Accounting for Product Financing Arrangements*) states that a financing arrangement may be entered into for the sale and repurchase of inventory. Such an arrangement is reported as a borrowing, not a sale. In many situations, the product is kept on the company's (sponsor's) premises. In addition, a sponsor may guarantee the debt of the other company.

Typically, most of the financed product is ultimately used or sold by the sponsor. However, in some instances, minimal amounts of the product may be sold by the financing entity to other parties.

The company that provides financing to the sponsor is typically a creditor, nonbusiness entity, or trust. In a few cases, the financing entity may have been set up solely to furnish financing to the sponsor.

The sponsor should footnote the terms of the product financing arrangement.

Examples of the different forms of financing arrangements are as follows:

- Sponsor has another entity purchase the good on its behalf and agrees to repurchase the product from the other entity, usually over a specified time period at predetermined prices. The repurchase price includes the original selling price plus carrying and financing costs

- Sponsor sells the product to another business and agrees to reacquire the product or one identical to it
- Sponsor controls the distribution of the product that has been purchased by another company
- A financing entity procures the funds remitted to the sponsor by borrowing from a financial institution, using the newly bought merchandise as collateral

Regardless of the arrangement, the company (sponsor) either commits to repurchase the product at established prices over a designed time period or commits to resale prices to third parties.

Note: Although a financing institution may sell small amounts of the product, FASB Statement Number 49 requires that most of the product be used or sold by the sponsor.

When the sponsor sells the good to the other company and in a related transaction commits to rebuy it, the sponsor records a liability when the proceeds are received.

Caution: A sale should not be recorded and the product should be retained as inventory on the sponsor's books. It is important to note that the substance of a product financing arrangement, irrespective of its legal form, is a financing deal instead of a sale or purchase by the sponsor.

When another company purchases the merchandise for the sponsor, inventory is debited and a liability is credited at the date of acquisition. The sponsor accrues the carrying and financing costs.

EXAMPLE

On January 1, 19X3, a sponsor borrows $50,000 from another and gives the inventory as collateral for the loan. The entry is

Cash	50,000	
Liability		50,000

On December 31, 19X3, the sponsor pays back the other company. The collateralized inventory is returned. Assume a 10% interest rate and storage charges of $600. The entry is

Liability	50,000	
Interest expense	500	
Holding charges	600	
Cash		51,100

EXAMPLE

A sponsor sells goods costing $5,000 to a purchaser for $6,000 and commits to repurchase the same goods for $6,200 in 60 days. The sponsor's journal entries are as follows:

Cash (or receivable)	6,000	
Liability		6,000
Inventory under PFA*	5,000	
Inventory		5,000

*PFA = product financing arrangement.

EXAMPLE

A sponsor arranged for the purchaser to buy goods costing $6,000 from a third party and commits to purchase that inventory from the purchaser for $6,200 in 60 days. The sponsor's journal entry is

Inventory under PFA	6,000	
Liability		6,000

EXAMPLE

A sponsor sells goods costing $900 to a purchaser for $1,000 and commits to a resale price of $1,200 to outside parties. The sponsor's journal entries are

Cash (or receivable)	1,000	
Liability		1,000
Inventory under PFA	900	
Inventory		900

EXAMPLE

A sponsor arranges for a purchaser to buy inventory from an outside party for $850 and guarantees the resale price to outside parties for $1,000. The sponsor's journal entry is

Inventory under PFA	850	
Liability		850

Financing Product Arrangements— Other Considerations

Product financing arrangements require the sponsor to purchase the product at specified prices which are not subject to change except for fluctuations due to finance and holding costs. The payments that the other company will receive are established by the financing arrangement. These costs (which will be paid by sponsor) are required to be adjusted to cover all fluctuations in costs incurred by the other entity in purchasing and holding the product. This includes interest costs as well.

The requirement that the sponsor purchase the inventory at predetermined prices may be met if any of the following circumstances exist:

1. The specified prices in the financing arrangement are in the form of resale price guarantees under which the sponsor agrees to make up any difference between the specified price and resale price for products sold to third parties.

2. The sponsor is not required to purchase the product but has an option to purchase the product, which has the effect of compelling the sponsor to purchase the product (e.g., the sponsor is penalized if it does not exercise the option to purchase the product).

3. The sponsor is not required to purchase the product, but the other entity has an option whereby it can require the sponsor to purchase the product.

Lower of Cost or Market Value

Inventory is valued at the lower of cost or market value applied on either an aggregate basis, category basis, or individual basis. Whatever approach is chosen, it must be applied on a consistent basis.

If cost is less than market value (replacement cost), cost is selected. If market value is less than cost, we start with market value.

- Market value cannot be more than the "upper limit" of net realizable value. Net realizable value equals selling price less costs to complete and dispose. If it does, the upper ceiling is selected.

- Market value cannot be less than the "lower limit" equal to net realizable value less a normal profit margin. If market value is below the lower limit, the lower limit is selected.

- Market value is selected when it lies between the upper and lower limits. A useful diagram follows:

Diagram of Lower of Cost or Market Value

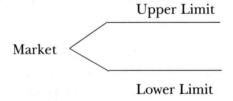

Upper Limit

Market

Lower Limit

EXAMPLE

Company ABC uses the lower of cost or market value method on an item-by-item basis. The valuation of each product follows:

Product	Cost	Market	Upper Limit	Lower Limit	Answer
M	$10	$14	$18	$12	$10
N	28	24	22	14	22
O	36	30	32	24	30
P	40	24	36	32	32
Q	12	10	24	14	12

With respect to Q, market value of $10 was initially selected. However, the market value of $10 exceeds the lower limit of $14, so the lower limit would be used. However, if after applying the lower of cost or market value rule the valuation derived ($14) is more than the cost ($12), the cost figure is used because of conservatism.

The write-down of inventory to market is charged to cost of goods sold if the amount is insignificant or to a separate loss account if the amount is significant. This loss account is called "loss to reduce inventory to lower of cost or market." The inventory account is credited.

Note: If market value (replacement cost) is less than the original cost but the selling price has not similarly declined, no loss can be recognized. To do so would result in an abnormal profit in a later year.

The lower of cost or market value method is not used with LIFO because under LIFO current costs are matched against current revenue. Further, as a general rule, once a company uses LIFO for tax return preparation, it must use LIFO for book purposes.

Note: Inventories may be stated at market value when it is above cost in exceptional cases, such as when

- Immediate marketability exists at quoted prices and units are interchangeable (e.g., certain agricultural and mineral products, and precious metals).
- No basis exists for cost apportionment (e.g., meat packing industry) or there is some other inability to determine approximate costs.

In these cases, inventory is stated at market price less disposal costs. When inventory is valued above cost, revenue is recognized before sale. Appropriate disclosure should be made when inventory is carried above cost.

Retail Method

The *retail method* is followed by department stores and other large retail businesses that stock merchandise at retail selling price. The retail method is used to estimate period-end inventory at cost by using a cost to retail (selling price) ratio. Initially, the ending inventory is determined at selling price and then converted to cost. Markups and markdowns are taken into account in calculating the cost to retail ratio, resulting in a higher ending inventory than the retail lower of cost or market value method. In using the retail method, separate calculations may be made for departments within the business that experience substantially lower or higher profit margins. The retail method may be used based on First-in, First-out (FIFO), LIFO, or average cost methods.

Retail Lower of Average Cost or Market Value (Conventional Retail) Method

The *retail lower of cost or market value method* is a variation of the retail method and is preferable to it because it results in a lower (conservative) inventory balance. In deriving the cost or retail ratio, markups are taken into account but not markdowns.

The following example shows the difference in calculation between the retail method and the retail lower of cost or market value method.

EXAMPLE

Retail Lower of Cost or Market Value Method

		Cost	Retail	
Inventory—1/1		$ 32,000	$ 60,000	
Purchases		60,000	120,000	
Purchase Returns		(10,000)	(20,000)	
Purchase Discount		(4,000)		
Freight In		2,000		
Markups	$ 50,000			
Markup Cancellations	(10,000)			
Net Markups			40,000	
Total		$80,000	$200,000	40%
Markdowns	$44,000			
Markdown Cancellations	(4,000)			

(continued)

	Cost	Retail	
Net Markdowns		40,000	
Cost of Goods Available	$80,000	$160,000	50%
Deduct:			

	$ 80,000	
Sales	$ 80,000	
Less: Sales Returns	(10,000)	
Net Sales		70,000
Inventory—Retail		$90,000
Retail Method:		
At cost 50% × $90,000		$45,000
Retail Lower of Cost or Market Method:		
At cost 40% × $90,000		$36,000

Retail LIFO

In determining ending inventory, the approach of the retail method is basically practiced. Markups and markdowns are both considered in computing the cost to retail ratio. However, this ratio excludes beginning inventory. A decline in inventory during the period is subtracted from the most recently added layers in the inverse order of addition. Inventory is restated based on a retail price index.

EXAMPLE: RETAIL LIFO

Retail price indices follow: 19X7 100, 19X8 104, and 19X9 110

19X8	Cost	Retail	
Inventory—Jan. 1 (Base Inv.)	$ 80,000	$130,000	
Purchases	$240,000	$410,000	
Markups		10,000	
Markdowns		(20,000)	
Total (excluding Beginning Inventory)	$240,000	$400,000	60%

(continued)

19X8	Cost	Retail		
Total (including Beginning Inventory)	$320,000	$530,000		
Sales		389,600		
19X8 Inventory—End at Retail		$140,400		
Cost Basis				
19X8 Inventory in terms of 19X7 Prices				
$140,400 ÷ 1.04		$135,000		
19X7 Base	$ 80,000	130,000	$130,000 × 1.04	$135,200
19X8 Layer in 19X7 prices		$ 5,000		
19X8 Layer in 19X8 prices		$ 5,200	$5,000 × 1.04	5,200
				$140,400
19X8 LIFO Cost 60% × $5200	3,120			
19X9	$ 83,120	$140,400		
Inventory—Jan. 1	$ 83,120	$140,400		
Purchases	$260,400	$430,000		
Markups		20,000		
Markdowns		(30,000)		
Total (excluding Beginning Inventory)	$260,400	$420,000	62%	
Total (incuding Beginning Inventory)	$343,520	$560,400		
Sales		408,600		
19X9 Inventory—End at Retail		$151,800		
Cost Basis				
19X9 Inventory in 19X7 prices $151,800 ÷ 1.10		$138,000		
19X7 Base	$ 80,000	130,000	$130,000 × 1.10	$143,000
Excess over base year		$ 8000		
19X8 Layer in 19X8 prices	3,120	5,000	$5,000 × 1.10	5,500
19X9 Layer in 19X7 prices		$ 3,000		
19X9 Layer in 19X9 prices		3,300	$3,000 × 1.10	3,300
19X9 Increase in 19X9 Prices				
LIFO Cost 62% × $3,300	2,046			
	$85,166	$151,800		$151,800

Dollar Value LIFO

Dollar value LIFO extends the historical cost principle. This method groups (pools) dollars rather than units. Any decrease in inventory is subtracted from the last year.

Dollar value LIFO has the following steps:

- Restate ending inventory in the current year into base dollars via a price index.

- Deduct the year 0 inventory in base dollars from the current year's inventory in base dollars.

- Multiply the incremental inventory in the current year in base dollars by the price index to derive the incremental inventory in current dollars.

- Derive the reportable inventory for the current year by adding to the year 0 inventory in base dollars the incremental inventory for the current year in current dollars.

EXAMPLE

At December 31, 19X4, Company ABC had a year-end inventory of $150,000, and the price index is 1.20. On January 1, 19X4, the base inventory was $110,000. The December 31, 19X4 inventory is calculated as follows:

12/31/19X4 inventory in base dollars ($150,000/1.2)	$125,000
1/1/19X4 beginning base inventory	110,000
19X4 increment in base dollars	$ 15,000
× Price index	× 1.2
Increment in current year dollars	$ 18,000
Inventory in base dollars	$110,000
Increment in current year dollars	18,000
Reportable inventory	$128,000

Base Stock Method

The base stock method presumes there will be a minimum base stock of inventory each year. Amounts over the base are costed under FIFO, LIFO, average cost, etc. A decrease in inventory is charged against earnings based on current cost. This method is not allowed on the tax return.

Costs Excluded from Inventory

Idle capacity costs, abnormal spoilage costs, double freight charges, and rehandling costs may require writeoff immediately in the current year rather than being allocated as a component of inventory valuation. Inventory cost does not include selling expenses. Selling expenses and interest incurred to finance inventory are period costs (charged directly against earnings as incurred). However, general and administrative expenses are inventoriable when they apply to manufacturing operations. It is a violation of GAAP to exclude all overhead from inventory costing. Thus, the direct costing method for inventory valuation is not accepted for financial reporting purposes.

Standard Costing

Inventory may be valued based on standard cost as long as it is adjusted at the end of the accounting period to actual cost for financial reporting purposes. Proper disclosure is required. Insignificant variances between standard cost and actual cost are adjusted to cost of goods sold. Significant variances must be adjusted to a loss or gain account.

Relative Sales Value Method

Relative sales (or net realizable) values may be used as a basis to assign costs to inventory that is bought or produced in groups. This is because costs cannot be determined individually. The method is appropriate for allocating costs to joint products, real estate lots, and lump-sum purchases.

EXAMPLE

Joint products X and Y arise from the same manufacturing process up to the split-off point. The units produced for X and Y are 10,000 and 50,000, respectively. The selling prices per unit for X and Y are $3 and $1.20, respectively. The joint cost is $63,000. Allocated cost based on relative sales value follows:

Joint Product	Units Produced	Selling Price	Sales Value	Allocated Cost
X	10,000	$3.00	$30,000	$21,000
Y	50,000	1.20	60,000	42,000
Total				$63,000

EXAMPLE

XYZ Company bought inventory comprising of four items of product for $115,000. At the time of purchase the appraised values and relative percents were as follows:

		Percent
Product A	$ 11,000	.09
Product B	30,000	.25
Product C	50,000	.42
Product D	29,000	.24
Appraised value	$120,000	1.00

The costs of each type of product allocated based on relative appraisal value percentages were

Product A .09 × $115,000	$ 10,350
Product B .25 × $115,000	28,750
Product C .42 × $115,000	48,300
Product D .24 × 115,000	27,600
Total cost allocation	$115,000

Research and Development

According to FASB Statement Number 2 (*Accounting for Research and Development Costs*), supplies inventory used in R&D activities should be expensed unless there is an alternative future use or benefit. If the company uses its supplies or materials for R&D efforts, such inventory is charged as an R&D

expense. On the other hand, if R&D activities result in salable inventory, inventory would be debited and R&D expense credited.

Terminated Contracts

If inventory was bought for a particular customer who has since canceled the order or the contract has been terminated for some other reason, the inventory should be written down to recognize a loss in value, if any.

Discontinued Operations

Inventories used in discontinued operations of a business must be written down to net realizable value. The write-down is included as an element of the gain or loss on disposal of the discontinued activity.

Taxes

For tax return preparation purposes, the tax law requires manufacturers to defer the following costs related to inventory: warehousing costs, accounting and data service costs, and personnel costs such as recruiting and hiring. The tax law requires large retailers and wholesalers (having gross receipts of $10 million or more) to defer the following costs related to inventory: handling and unloading charges, incidental purchasing costs, assembling and processing costs, and storage costs.

Deferred taxes arising from temporary differences result when inventory is accounted for differently on the books and the tax return.

Disclosures

The following should be footnoted with regard to inventory:

- The cost basis to determine inventory valuation
- Inventory method used
- Nature of any accounting changes (e.g., change in method) and their effect upon earnings

- Inventory classification and categorization
- Unusual losses associated with inventory such as in applying the lower of cost or market value rule and losses on purchase commitments
- Excessive exposure to risk (e.g., health hazards, safety concerns, limited supply availability, labor strife)

PREPAID EXPENSES

Prepaid expenses result from prepaying cash or incurring a liability. Prepaid expenses are presented under current assets even though they are not expected to be converted into cash because the prepaid items would have required the use of current assets if they were not paid in advance. Prepaid expenses include insurance, rent, advertising, taxes, interest, and office supplies. However, prepayments that will not be charged to operations within one year or the normal operating cycle of the business, whichever is greater, are classified under deferred charges or other assets. Prepaid expenses expire and become expenses because of usage, events, or the passing of time. Prepaid expenses should be amortized on a ratable basis over their life.

LONG-TERM INVESTMENTS

Long-term investments include amounts held within special funds, such as sinking funds and the cash surrender value of life insurance that will not be cashed in within the next year. Long-term investments are discussed in detail in Chapter 10.

FIXED ASSETS

GAAP for the accounting, reporting, and disclosures associated with fixed assets are included in the American Institute of CPAs' Accounting Principles Board Opinion Number 6 dealing with depreciation, Accounting Principles Board Opinion Number 12, paragraphs 4 and 5 (*Disclosure of Depreciable Assets and Depreciation*), American Institute of CPAs' Accounting Research Bulletin Number 43, chapter 9A (*Depreciation and High Costs*), and Emerging Issues Task Force Consensus Summary Number 89–11 (*Allocation of Purchase Price to Assets to be Sold*).

When bought, a fixed asset is recorded at its fair market value or the fair market value of the consideration given, whichever is more clearly evident. The basis of accounting for a fixed asset is its cost, which includes normal incidental costs necessary to put it into location or initially use it (e.g., delivery, installation, sales taxes, testing, breaking in, setup, assembling, trial runs, foundation). However, abnormal costs are not charged to the asset but rather expensed, such as repairs of a fixed asset which was damaged during shipment because of mishandling.

If a fixed asset is to be disposed of, it should not be depreciated. Further, it should be recorded at the lower of its book value or net realizable value. Net realizable value equals fair value less costs to sell. Expected costs to sell beyond one year should be discounted. Idle or obsolete fixed assets should be written down and reclassified as other assets. The loss on the write-down is presented in the income statement.

Expenditures incurred that increase the capacity, life, or operating efficiency of a fixed asset are capitalized. However, insignificant expenditures are usually expensed as incurred.

Additions to an existing asset are deferred and depreciated over the shorter of the life of the addition or the life of the building. Rearrangement and reinstallation costs should be deferred if future benefit exists. Otherwise, they should be expensed. If fixed assets are obsolete, they should be written down to salvage value, recognizing a loss, and reclassified from property, plant, and equipment to other assets.

If two or more assets are purchased at a lump-sum price, cost is allocated to the assets based on their fair market values.

A liability secured by a fixed asset should not be offset.

Self-Constructed Assets

Self-constructed assets are recorded at the *incremental or direct costs* to build (material, labor, and variable overhead) assuming idle capacity. Fixed overhead is excluded unless it increases because of the construction effort. However, self-constructed assets should not be recorded at an amount in excess of the outside cost.

EXAMPLE

Incremental costs to self-construct equipment are $80,000. The equipment could be bought from outside for $76,000. The journal entry is

Equipment	76,000	
Loss	4,000	
Cash		80,000

EXAMPLE

Mavis Company uses its excess capacity to build its own machinery. The associated costs are direct material of $80,000, direct labor of $20,000, variable overhead of $10,000, and fixed overhead of $5,000. The cost of the self-constructed machine is $110,000. The fixed overhead is excluded because it is not affected by the construction effort.

Donation of Fixed Assets

As per FASB Statement Number 116 (*Accounting for Contributions Received and Contributions Made*), a donated fixed asset should be recorded at its fair market value by debiting fixed assets and crediting contribution revenue.

FASB Statement Number 116 states that the company donating a nonmonetary asset recognizes an expense for the fair market value of the donated asset. The difference between the book value and fair market value of the donated asset represents a gain or loss.

EXAMPLE

Harris Company donates land costing $50,000 with a fair market value of $70,000. The journal entry is

Contribution expense	70,000	
Land		50,000
Gain on disposal of land		20,000

If a company pledges unconditionally to give an asset in the future, accrue contribution expense and a payable. This includes a conditional promise which has satisfied all conditions and, in effect, is now unconditional. However, if the pledge is conditional, an entry is not made until the asset is, in fact, transferred. If it is unclear whether the promise is conditional or unconditional, the former is presumed.

Writing Up Fixed Assets

It is prohibited to write up fixed assets except for a discovery on a natural resource, in a business combination accounted for under the purchase method, or in a quasi-reorganization. If a natural resource is discovered on land, such as oil or coal, the appraised value is charged to the land account and then depleted using the units of production method.

Land and Land Improvements

The cost of land includes closing costs (e.g., attorney fees, recording fees), costs to get land in condition for intended use (e.g., grading, draining, filling), assumption of any liens or encumbrances on the property, and costs to remove an old structure to build on the property. For example, if an old building is torn down to make way for the construction of a new building, the demolition costs are charged to land.

Land held for investment, speculation, or a future plant site should be classified under investments rather than fixed assets.

Land held for resale by a real estate company is considered inventory.

Land improvements such as fences, driveways, sidewalks, and parking lots are deferred and depreciated over their useful lives.

Repairs

Ordinary repairs such as a tune-up for a delivery truck are expensed because they only benefit less than one year.

Extraordinary repairs are deferred to the fixed asset because they benefit more than one year. An example is a new motor for a salesperson's automobile. Extraordinary repairs either increase the asset's life or make the asset more useful. Capital expenditures enhance the quality or quantity of services to be obtained from the asset.

Environmental

As per Emerging Issues Task Force Consensus Summary Number 90–8 (*Capitalization of Costs to Treat Environmental Contamination*), the costs to prevent, contain, or remove environmental contamination should be expensed. **Exception:** These costs can be deferred to the fixed asset in the following cases:

- The costs increase the asset's life or capacity or improve its efficiency or safety.
- The costs are incurred to prepare the property for sale.

According to Emerging Issues Task Force Consensus Summary Number 89–13 (*Accounting for the Cost of Asbestos Removal*), the cost to treat property bought having an asbestos problem should be deferred to the asset. Disclosure should be made of the asbestos problems amd related costs to correct.

Depreciation

If a fixed asset is bought during the year, there will be fractional year depreciation requiring proration.

EXAMPLE

On April 1, 19X4, a fixed asset costing $30,000 with a salvage value of $2,000 and a life of 10 years is bought.

Depreciation for 19X5 using the sum-of-the-years' digits method is

1/1/19X5–3/31/19X5 10/55 × $28,000 × 3/12	$1,273
4/1/19X5–12/31/19X5 9/55 × $28,000 × 9/12	3,436
	$4,709

Depreciation expense for 19X5 under the double declining balance method is

Year	Computation	Depreciation	Book Value
0			$30,000
4/1/19X4–12/31/19X4	9/12 × $30,000 × 20%	$4,500	25,500
19X5	$25,500 × 20%	5,100	20,400

It is also an acceptable GAAP to provide depreciation based on the *group and composite methods*. While the group method is used for similar assets, the composite method is used for dissimilar assets. Both methods are usually accepted. One accumulated depreciation account applies for the whole group.

$$\text{Depreciation rate} = \text{depreciation/gross cost}$$

For the accounting period

$$\text{Depreciation expense} = \text{Depreciation rate} \times \text{gross cost}$$
$$\text{Depreciable life} = \text{Depreciable cost/depreciation}$$

When one asset in the group is sold, the entry is

Cash (proceeds received)
Accumulated depreciation (balancing figure)
Fixed asset (cost)

No gain or loss is recorded on the sale. The only occurrence in which a gain or loss would be recorded is when all of the assets are sold.

EXAMPLE

Computations under the composite depreciation method follow:

Asset	Cost –	Salvage =	Depreciable cost/life =		Depreciation
X	$ 50,000	$10,000	$ 40,000	10	$ 4,000
Y	80,000	4,000	76,000	5	15,200
Z	104,000	8,000	96,000	6	16,000
	$234,000	$22,000	$212,000		$35,200

Composite rate = Depreciation/Cost = $35,200/$234,000 = 15%
Composite life = Depreciable cost/Depreciation
= $212,000/$35,200 = 6 years

The entry to record depreciation is

Depreciation expense   35,200
    Accumulated depreciation   35,200

The journal entry to sell asset X for $43,000 is

Cash   43,000
Accumulated depreciation   7,000
    Fixed asset   50,000

Capitalized Interest

In almost all cases interest on borrowed funds is expensed. However, there is one exception in that interest on borrowings is deferred to the asset account and amortized when the following exist:

- Self-made assets for the company's own use
- Assets for sale or lease built as discrete, individual projects. An example is real estate development. **Note:** If land is being prepared for a specific use in the company, the cost of buying the land meets the test for capitalized interest.
- Assets bought for the entity's own use by agreements requiring a down payment and/or process payments
- Assets received due to gift or grant in which donor restrictions exist

Interest is not capitalized for

- Assets in use or ready for use
- Assets manufactured in large quantity or on a continual basis
- Assets not in use and not being prepared for use

Interest capitalization is based on the average accumulated expenditures for that asset. The interest rate used is generally based on the:

- Interest rate on the specific borrowing
- Weighted-average interest rate for corporate debt

Interest capitalization begins when the following commences:

- Interest is being incurred.
- Expenditures are being incurred.
- The asset is being made ready for use in terms of construction or when administrative and technical activities before construction are taking place. Consideration should also be given to costs related to labor problems and litigation.

The capitalization period ends when the asset is substantially finished and ready for use. When an asset has individual components such as cooperative units, the capitalization period of interest costs related to one of the separate units ends when the particular unit is significantly complete and usable. Interest capitalization does not continue when construction ends, except for temporary and unexpected delays.

When the total asset must be completed to be useful, interest capitalization continues until the total asset is substantially complete. An example is a production facility where sequential manufacturing activities must occur.

Foreign currency losses on gains associated with debt funds denominated in a foreign currency may *not* be capitalized.

FASB Statement Number 34 (*Capitalization of Interest Cost*) requires disclosure of both the interest capitalized and expensed.

The following are hints in solving interest capitalization problems under SFAS 34. They are fully demonstrated in a comprehensive problem following the enumeration.

- The amount of interest that is required to be capitalzed under SFAS 34 is the amount of interest that could have been avoided if the qualifying assets upon which the interest is based had not been constructed. This amount of interest is sometimes referred to as avoidable interest. However, the amount of interest that is actually capitalized may never exceed the actual interest cost incurred by the entity for the period.

- To calculate the amount of interest cost that should be capitalized for a given accounting period, the average accumulated expenditures (AAE) for the period must be computed. These expenditures are weighed based on the time that they were incurred.

- In computing the amount of interest that should be capitalized, the following interest rates should be utilized in weighing the AAE:

  a. For the portion of the AAE represented by the specific borrowings incurred to acquire qualifying assets, use the interest rates on those borrowings to determine the amount of interest to be capitalized.

b. For the remaining portion of the AAE of the period (excess of AAE over the amount of specific borrowings), use the average interest rate incurred on other borrowings of the entity that are outstanding during the period. The averge rate incurred on the other borrowings of the period are weighed based on the magnitude of the specific debt outstanding and their respective interest rates.

EXAMPLE

Assume X Company begins construction on a new building on January 1, 1999. In addition, X obtained a $100,000 loan to finance the construction of the building on January 1, 1999 at an annual interest rate of 10%. The company's other outstanding debt during 1999 consists of two notes of $600,000 and $800,000 with interest rates of 11% and 13%, respectively. Expenditures that were made on the building project follow:

Expenditures	
January 1	$200,000
April 1	300,000
July 1	400,000
December 1	120,000

Step 1

Compute the AAE:

AAE		
$ 200,000 × 12/12 (January–December)	=	$200,000
300,000 × 9/12 (April–December)	=	225,000
400,000 × 6/12 (July–December)	=	200,000
120,000 × 1/12 (December)	=	10,000
$1,020,000	AAE =	$635,000

Step 2

Compute the average interest rate based on the other outstanding debt of the entity other than specific borrowings:

$$
\begin{array}{rcll}
\$ \ 600,000 & \times & 11\% & = & \$ \ 66,000 \\
\underline{\ \ \ \ 800,000} & \times & 15\% & = & \underline{\ \ \ 120,000} \\
\underline{\underline{\$1,400,000}} & & & & \underline{\underline{\$186,000}}
\end{array}
$$

$$\text{Average interest rate:} = \$186,000/\$1,400,000$$
$$= 13\%$$

Step 3

Compute the interest that could be avoided based on the AAE:

AAE	Interest That Should Be Capitalized (Based on AAE)
$100,000 (Specific borrowing) × 10% =	$10,000
535,000 ($635,000 − 100,000) × 13% =	69,550
$635,000	$79,550

Step 4

Compute actual interest costs incurred during the year:

$$
\begin{array}{rcl}
\$100,000 \times 10\% = & \$ \ 10,000 \\
600,000 \times 11\% = & 66,000 \\
800,000 \times 15\% = & \underline{120,000} \\
\text{Total} & \underline{\underline{\$196,000}}
\end{array}
$$

Since the interest that could have been avoided if the building was not constucted (based on the AAE) is *more* than X's actual interest cost, the actual interest cost should be capitalized. Otherwise, the avoidable interest would be capitalized.

The journal entry is as follows:

Building ($200,000 + 300,000 + 400,000 + 120,000 + (196,000) 1,216,000
    Cash   1,216,000

Nonmonetary Transactions

Accounting Principles Board (APB) Opinion Number 29 (*Accounting for Nonmonetary Transactions*) deals with nonmonetary transactions and covers the accounting for exchanges or distributions of fixed assets. Nonmonetary transactions involve the exchange of nonmonetary assets such as inventories, plant and equipment, property, etc. In general, the accounting for nonmonetary transactions is predicated on the fair values of the assets exchanged. APB 29 requires the determination of fair value to be used based on the fair value of the asset given up or the fair value of asset received, whichever is more clearly determinable. In addition, GAAP requires recognition of any gain and loss on the exchange transaction. However, there are several caveats to this rule that require further analysis. The following analysis discusses the exceptions to the general guidelines. The discussion is divided into two parts: (1) dissimilar assets exchanges and (2) similar assets exchanges.

Dissimilar Assets

Exchanges of dissimilar nonmonetary assets consist of exchanging one non-monetary asset for another that has a dissimilar function (for example, exchanging automobiles for land or buildings for machinery). The transaction should be recorded at its fair value, with any gains and losses that may be incurred fully recognized. That is, the cost basis of the new asset received should be accounted for based on the fair value of the asset given up (or received, if that is more clearly determinable) plus or minus any cash paid or received, respectively, on the transaction. Fair value may be derived from appraisal, quoted market price, or cash transaction for comparable items. It should also be noted that the new asset can never be recorded at more than its fair market value.

EXAMPLE

An old fixed asset costing $30,000 with accumulated depreciation of $6,000 is traded in for a dissimilar, new fixed asset having a fair market value of $27,000. Cash paid on the exchange is $12,000. The fair market value of the old asset is $15,000.

Compute the gain or loss on the exchange:

Fair value of the asset exchanged	$15,000
Less: Book value of asset exchanged ($30,000 – $6,000)	24,000
Loss on Exchange	$ 9,000

The journal entry is as follows:

Fixed asset ($15,000 + $12,000)	27,000 (fair value given up)	
Accumulated depreciation	6,000	
Loss	9,000	
Fixed asset		30,000
Cash		12,000

Similar Assets

When *similar assets* are exchanged (e.g., machine for a machine, land for land, etc.), any gain realized on the transactions should be deferred and not recognized because there is continuity of function and the owner of the exchanged assets is in the same economic position as it was before the exchange. That is, the company has the same asset performing the same function as before, and therefore consummation of the earnings process (exchange process) has not taken place. Therefore, if a gain is realized, it should not be recognized and the new asset should be recorded without gain recognition. That is, the asset received should be recorded at the book value of the asset given up. If cash is received, however, then a part of the gain (proportionate to the amount of cash received relative to the total amount received—see formula in examples that follow) is recognized because the transaction is viewed in part as a sale of an asset for cash. On the other hand, if a loss is realized, it should be recognized fully because of the conservative convention. Remember, if there is a gain on the exchange, the cost basis of the new asset received should be accounted for at the fair value of the asset given up adjusted for the gain deferred plus or minus any cash paid or received, respectively, on the transaction. If there is a loss on the exchange, the cost of the new asset received should be accounted for the fair value of the asset given up plus or minus any cash paid or received, respectively, on the transaction.

Note: A nonmonetary exchange that includes cash (boot) of 25% or more of the fair market value of the total value exchanged should recognize all gains or losses generated in their entirety.

EXAMPLE: LOSS ON EXCHANGE

An old fixed asset costing $30,000 with accumulated depreciation of $6,000 is traded in for a similar, new fixed asset having a fair market value of $27,000. *Cash paid* on the exchange is $12,000. The fair market value of the old asset is $15,000.

Compute the loss on the exchange:

Fair value of the asset exchanged	$15,000
Less: Book value of asset exchanged ($30,000 − $6,000)	24,000
Loss on exchange—recognize fully	$ 9,000

The journal entry assuming a similar exchange follows:

Fixed Asset (15,000 + $12,000)	27,000 (fair value given up)	
Accumulated depreciation	6,000	
Loss	9,000	
Fixed asset		30,000
Cash		12,000

EXAMPLE: GAIN ON EXCHANGE WITH NO CASH RECEIVED

An old fixed asset costing $30,000 with accumulated depreciation of $16,000 is traded in for a similar, new fixed asset having a fair market value of $15,000. The fair market value of the old asset is $15,000.

Compute the gain on the exchange:

Fair value of the asset exchanged	$15,000
Less: Book value of asset exchanged ($30,000 − $16,000)	14,000
Gain on exchange—not recognized	$ 1,000

The journal entry follows:

Fixed asset ($15,000 – $1,000)	14,000 (fair value given up)	
Accumulated depreciation	16,000	
Fixed asset		30,000

EXAMPLE: GAIN ON TRANSACTION WITH AN AMOUNT OF CASH *RECEIVED* EQUALING LESS THAN 25% OF THE FAIR VALUE OF THE EXCHANGE

An old fixed asset costing $30,000 with accumulated depreciation of $16,000 is traded in for a similar, new fixed asset having a fair market value of $14,000. Cash received on the exchange is $1,000. The fair market value of the old asset is $15,000.

Compute the gain on the exchange:

Fair value of the asset exchanged	$15,000
Less: Book value of asset exchanged ($30,000 – $16,000)	14,000
Gain on exchange	$ 1,000

Since cash is received, a proportionate part of the gain must be recognized. The asset is viewed as being partly sold for cash. The formula for gain recognition follows:

$$
\begin{aligned}
\text{Gain recognized} \;&=\; \text{Cash received/Total value of assets received} \times \text{Total gain} \\
&=\; \$1{,}000/\ \$1{,}000 + \$14{,}000 \times \$1{,}000 \\
&=\; 6.67\% \times \$1{,}000 \\
&=\; \$67
\end{aligned}
$$

Therefore, the portion of the gain not recognized is $1,000 – 67 = $933.

Compute the gain on the exchange:

Fair value of the asset exchanged	$15,000
Less: Book value of asset exchanged ($30,000 – $16,000)	14,000
Gain on exchange	$ 1,000

Since cash is received, a proportionate part of the gain must be recognized since we view the asset as being partly sold for cash. Again, the formula for gain recognition requires the following computation:

Gain recognized = Cash received/Total value of assets received × Total gain

= $5,000/ $5,000 + $10,000 × $1,000

= 33.34% × $1,000

= $333

However, since the percentage (33.34%) in this illustration equals or exceeds 25% of the fair value of the exchange, the entire gain (not a proportionate part) must be recognized since GAAP requires that such a transaction be considered monetary (because of the size of the cash receipt; 25% or more).

The journal entry follows:

Cash	5,000	
Fixed asset ($15,000 − $5,000)	10,000 (fair value given up)	
Accumulated depreciation	16,000	
Fixed asset		30,000
Gain		1,000

Note: Full disclosure should be made of the nature and description of nonmonetray transactions and the accounting basis of the transferred assets.

FASB Emerging Issues Task Force (EITF) Issue No. 93-11 "Accounting for Barter Transactions Involving Barter Credits"

A barter transaction may relate to an exchange of goods or services or barter credits. With respect to the latter, for example, the asset inventory may be exchanged for barter credits.

EITF Issue No. 93-11 stipulates that APB Opinion No. 29 (Accounting for Nonmonetary Transactions) should be applied to an exchange of a nonmonetary asset for barter credits. With respect to barter credits, it is assumed that the fair market value of the asset exchanged is more clearly evident than the fair market value of the barter credits received. As a result, the barter credits received should be recorded at the fair market value of the asset exchanged. In ascertaining the fair market value asset surrendered, it is assumed that the market value of the asset does not exceed its book value.

In the event the fair market value of the asset surrendered is below its book value, an impairment should be recorded before making the entry for the exchange. As an example, inventory being exchanged in a barter transaction should be reflected at the lower cost or market value before recording the barter transaction.

At year-end, the recorded amount of barter credits should be appraised for impairment. We recognize an impairment loss when the fair market value of any remaining barter credits is below its book value, or in the event it is probable that what is left of the barter credits will not be used.

Impairment of Fixed Assets

According to FASB Statement Number 121 (*Accounting for the Impairment of Long-Lived Assets and for Long-Lived Assets to Be Disposed Of*), a long-lived asset is deemed impaired if the total (undiscounted) estimated cash flows from using it are less than the book value of the asset. **Note:** Future cash flows applicable to environmental exist costs that have been accrued for the asset should not be included in determining the undiscounted anticipated future cash flows in applying the asset impairment test. (In determining if asset impairment exists, the asset's book value should include any associated goodwill.) If this recoverability test for asset impairment is met, an impairment loss must be calculated as the excess of the asset's book value over its fair market value. Fair value is the amount at which the asset could be bought or sold between willing parties; fair value is not determined by the value of an asset in a forced or liquidation sale. FASB Number 121 (pararagraph 7) identifies three methods for determining an asset's fair value:

- Market price quoted in an active market
- Estimate based on prices of similar assets
- Estimate based on valuation techniques, including discounted cash flows and other asset-specific models, such as options pricing model, fundamental analysis, etc.

If fair market value is not determinable and the present value (discounted) of expected future cash flows is used, then the assets should be grouped at the lowest level at which the cash flows are separately identifiable. Reasonable and supportable assumptions and projections should be used to make the best estimate. All evidence pertinent to impairment of assets should be considered. Evidence which is objectively verifiable should be given more weight.

An impairment loss is charged against earnings with a similar reduction in the recorded value of the impaired fixed asset. (If there is any related goodwill, it should be eliminated before reducing the carrying value of the fixed asset.) After impairment, the reduced carrying value becomes the new cost basis for the fixed asset. Thus, the fixed asset cannot be written up for a later recovery in market value. In other words, the impairment loss cannot be restored. Depreciation is based on the new cost basis.

If an impaired asset is intended to be disposed of rather than kept in service, the impaired asset should be recorded at the lower of cost or net realizable value.

An impairment may be due to such reasons as

- A major change in how the asset is used
- A decline in the market value of the fixed asset
- Excess construction costs relative to estimated amounts
- Adverse business climate or legal factors
- Continued expected losses from the asset

EXAMPLE

A company has a fixed asset with a cost of $500,000 and accumulated depreciation of $100,000. In applying the recoverability to determine if an impairment has occurred, it is determined that the total (undiscounted) expected future net cash flows is $420,000. No impairment has occurred because the undiscounted future net cash flows ($420,000) exceed the carrying value ($400,000) of the fixed asset.

EXAMPLE

Assume the same information as in the previous example except that the total (undiscounted) future net cash flows is $350,000. The recoverability test now indicates that an impairment has occurred because the total (undiscounted) cash flows ($350,000) are less than the carrying value ($400,000) of the fixed asset. Assuming the fixed asset has a fair market value of $340,000, the impairment loss to be recognized equals $60,000 (book value of $400,000 less fair market value of $340,000). The journal entry to record the impairment is

Loss on impairment of fixed asset	60,000	
Accumulated depreciation		60,000

EXAMPLE

An asset impairment has occurred. The book value of a fixed asset is $700,000 (cost $950,000 less accumulated depreciation of $250,000). Projected future net cash flows are $60,000 per year for the remaining 10 years of the expected remaining life of the asset. Th discount rate is 10%.

To test the recoverability of the book value of the asset,

Book value	$700,000
Less: Total undiscounted net cash inflows $60,000 × 10 years	600,000
Excess of book value over undiscounted future cash flows	$100,000

An impairment exists because of the excess of the carrying value over the undiscounted csah flows. The impairment loss is computed as follows:

Fair value of asset based on the discounted net cash inflows	
$60,000 × 6.145*	$368,700
Less: Book value	700,000
Impairment loss	$331,300

*Present value of an ordinary annuity factor for $n = 10$, $i = 10\%$ equals 6.145.

The journal entry to record the impairment loss follows:

Loss on impairment	331,300	
Accumulated depreciation	250,000	
Fixed asset		581,300

The new value of the fixed asset equals $368,700 ($950,000 − $581,300). Depreciation will be based on the new cost basis.

While FASB Statement Number 121 applies to all entities, it does not apply to

- Financial instruments
- Long-term customer relationships, such as core deposit intangibles and credit cardholder intangibles, of financial institutions
- Servicing rights, including those for mortgages
- Deferred tax assets
- Deferred policy acquisition costs
- Certain assets whose accounting is prescribed by FASB Statement Numbers 50, 53, 63, 86, or 90

Loss due to impairment of assets held for use is recognized as a component of income from continuing operations before taxes (1) in the income statement of for-profit entities, and (2) in the statement of activities for nonprofit entities. The disclosure requirements for impaired assets held for use are as follows:

- Complete description of the impaired assets, including the events that resulted in the impairment
- The amount of loss due to impairment and how the fair value of impaired asset was determined
- The location in the income statement or statement of activities where the impairment loss is situated (e.g., an individual caption, parenthetical disclosure, or caption where the loss is aggregated)
- The business segments, if any, that were affected by loss impairments

If an impaired asset is to be disposed rather than held for use, the impaired asset is reported at the lower of cost or net realizable value (fair value less cost to sell). The costs to sell an impaired asset include such costs as broker's commission and transfer fees. Insurance, security services, utility expenses, and other costs to protect or maintain the asset are generally not considered costs to sell for determining the net realizable value. The present value of costs to sell may be used when the fair value of the asset is determined using discounted cash flows and the sale is expected to occur after one year.

When the asset will be disposed shortly, the net realizable value is a better indicator of the cash flows that one can expect to receive from the impaired asset. Assets held for disposal are not depreciated. Conceptually, these assets are more like inventory, since they are expected to be sold shortly.

Assets held for disposal are revalued at the lower of cost or net realizable value during each period that they are reported. These assets may be written up or down in future periods as long as the write-up is not greater than the carrying amount of the asset before the impairment. Such losses or gains are reported as a component of income from continuing operations.

The following items should be disclosed either in the body of the financial statements or in the related notes:

- Description of assets to be disposed, including the events that led to the impairment, expected disposal date, and the carrying amount of the assets

- The amount of loss, if any, due to impairment

- The amount of loss or gain, if any, due to changes in the carrying value of assets that occurs after initial recognition of impairment

- The place in the income statement or the statement of activities where the loss from impairment, and the loss or gain from changes in value of asset subsequent to impairment, is disclosed

- The business segment, if any, affected by the assets to be disposed

Emerging Issues Task Force Consensus Summary Number 84–28 covers the impairment of long-lived assets. An FASB Exposure Draft titled *Accounting for Certain Liabilities Related to Closure and Removal of Long-Lived Assets* would, if adopted in its present form, set forth rules on the recognition of liabilities associated with the closure or removal of long-lived assets. It applies to such issues as site reclamation, decontamination, and dismantlement.

Involuntary Conversion

An involuntary conversion of nonmonetary assets to monetary assets may arise because of fire, flood, theft, or condemnation. The destruction is followed by replacement of the involuntarily converted assets. An example is a building destroyed by a fire and the insurance proceeds received used to buy a similar building.

An *extraordinary gain or loss* is usually recorded for the difference between the insurance proceeds and the book value of the demolished asset. The new building is recorded at its purchase price.

Caution: A contingency arises if the old fixed asset is damaged in one year, but the insurance recovery is not received until a later year. A contingent gain or loss is recognized in the period the old fixed asset was damaged. The gain or loss may be reflected for book and tax reporting in different years, resulting in a temporary difference mandating interperiod income tax allocation.

Disclosure

The following should be footnoted in connection with fixed assets:

- Fixed assets by major category. Category may be in terms of nature or function
- Description of depreciation method and estimates used
- Fixed assets subject to pledges, liens, or other commitments
- Fixed assets held to be disposed of and any anticipated losses. The reasons why such assets are to be disposed of should be provided. Disclosure includes expected disposal dates, carrying amounts of such assets, and business segments affected.
- Contracts to buy new fixed assets
- Fixed assets that are fully depreciated but still in use
- Idle fixed assets
- Amount of capitalized interest

NATURAL RESOURCES

Natural resources are wasting assets such as petroleum, timber, and minerals. They are characterized as being subject to complete removal and being replaced only by an act of nature. Natural resources are subject to depletion. Depletion is the physical exhaustion of a natural resource from usage. It is a process of allocating the cost of the natural resource over its anticipated life and is similar to depreciation except that it relates to a natural resource instead of a fixed asset. Depletion is based on the units of production method. An estimate is required of how much of the natural resource will be extracted in terms of tons, barrels, units, etc. The cost of the natural resource is divided by the total recoverable units to arrive at the depletion per unit. Depletion expense equals the units extracted for the year multiplied by the depletion per unit. A change in estimate requires the use of a new depletion rate per unit. Depletion expense is presented in the income statement, while accumulated depletion reduces the cost of the natural resource in the noncurrent asset section of the balance sheet. In some cases, depletion is charged to inventory (or cost of sales). For example, if depletion on a coal mine equals $20,000, the entry would be to debit coal inventory (or cost of sales) for $20,000 and credit accumulated depletion (or land rights) for $20,000.

The basis upon which depletion is computed is called the depletion base. The depletion base is generally made up of three components, consisting of the following:

1. **Acquisition cost of the depletable property:** Property may be acquired in hope of finding natural resources or may already have been determined to have proved resources on it. Alternatively, the property may also be leased, with subsequent royalties being paid to the owner if resources are found on it.

2. **Exploration costs:** When the rights to explore the property are secured (through acquisition or lease), exploration costs are incurred to determine the existence of natural resources. For most natural resources, the costs of exploration are expensed in the period in which they are incurred. However, for certain industries, such as oil- and gas-producing enterprises, certain specialized guidelines prevail (see Chapter 18 for greater detail). For example, oil and gas entities may choose between the successful efforts method or full cost method of accounting for exploration costs. In the successful efforts approach, only those exploratory costs related to successful wells are capitalized. Exploratory costs related to unsuccessful

wells are expensed. In the full cost method, exploratory costs related to both successful wells and unsuccessful wells are capitalized as part of the depletion base.

3. Development costs: These are the costs incurred in extracting the natural resource from the ground, making it ready for production or sale. Costs incurred on machinery and equipment that can be used for different wells or mines are generally not considered part of the depletable base and should be separately depreciated as they are utilized. On the other hand, intangible costs incurred on specific wells or mines which cannot be of benefit to any other should be considered part of that resource's depletion base. Such costs primarily include the costs incurred to dig, physically secure, and utilize the wells, mines, tunnels, shafts, etc.

In summary, the components of the depletion base of a natural resource upon which depletion should be computed include (1) acquisition costs, (2) capitalized exploratory costs, and (3) development costs.

Note: After a depletable asset has been fully consumed, local, state, and federal laws may require that the company pay for any restoration costs that may be required so that the residual property that remains does not represent a detriment to the local area in which it is situationed. Estimated restoration costs represent a negative salvage value that should be added to the components of the depletion base of the natural resource. The property's estimated salvage value should, of course, be subtracted from the depletion base in computing depletion expense.

EXAMPLE

In January 1999, LevSe Co. incurred costs of $3,500,000 in connection with the acquisition of a mineral mine. In addition, $200,000 of development costs were incurred in preparing the mine for production. It is estimated that 1,200,000 tons of ore will be removed from the mine over its useful life, at which point it is estimated that the company can sell the property for $250,000. After all the ore has been extracted, it is estimated that it will cost the company $100,000 to restore it to an acceptable level as required by law. During 1999, 30,000 tons of ore were extracted and sold. On its 1999 income statement, what amount should LevSe report as depletion?

DEPLETION BASE

Acquisition cost	$3,500,000
Development costs	200,000
Restoration costs—negative salvage value	100,000
Estimated salvage value	(250,000)
Depletion base	$3,550,000
1999 production	30,000 tons
Depletion Rate: $3,550,000/1,200,000 tons	$2.96/ton
Depletion—1999 $2.96 × 30,000 tons	$ 88,800

INTANGIBLE ASSETS

Intangible assets have a life of one year or more and lack physical substance (e.g., goodwill) or reflect a right granted by the government (e.g., trademarks, copyrights) or by another company (e.g., license fee, franchise). Intangibles generally have a high degree of uncertainty concerning future benefits. APB Opinion Number 17 deals with the accounting and reporting of intangible assets. Intangibles should be recorded at cost. Intangibles may be internally generated or they may be purchased. Intangibles acquired from others should be separately reported.

The cost at which intangibles are recorded depends upon whether the intangible was developed internally or acquired from others. In general, expenses incurred to develop an identifiable intangible asset, such as patents, trademarks, and copyrights, should be capitalized. Research and development costs, however, should not be capitalized and expensed when incurred. Unidentifiable internally developed intangibles, such as goodwill, should not be recorded. Such an asset is recognized only if it is purchased from another entity.

When an intangible is purchased from another entity, its value equals the cash or fair market value of the consideration given. The present value of payments on the liability incurred or the fair value of the stock issued may also be used to value externally acquired intangibles. When a group of assets is acquired, the identifiable intangible assets are allocated a part of the total cost based on the fair values of the individual assets in the group. The unidentifiable intangible assets, acquired as part of a group of assets, are valued at the excess of costs assigned to identifiable tangible and intangible assets, net of liabilities assumed.

EXAMPLE

Purchase price		$150,000
Fair value of assets acquired:		
Tangible assets		
Equipment	$ 20,000	
Land	80,000	
Identifiable intangible assets		
Copyrights	35,000	
Patents	40,000	
Total assets	175,000	
Less: Liabilities assumed	(65,000)	110,000
Unidentifiable intangible assets		$ 40,000

Any costs to develop and maintain intangibles should generally be charged against earnings. For example, the costs incurred to develop a name are expensed (e.g., McDonald's) even though the name represents internally developed goodwill. Some costs, such as legal costs associated with registering or successfully defending a patent, may be capitalized. The costs of purchasing an externally developed patent should also be capitalized.

All intangibles, except those on the books before 1970, are amortized over the period benefited under the straight-line method (unless another method is demonstrated to be more appropriate) not exceeding 40 years. There is no minimum amortization period according to GAAP. A company should periodically evaluate the useful life of the intangibles and, if necessary, reassess the amortization period. Such revisions should be recorded prospectively, and the asset should be amortized over the remaining useful life. Even with reevaluation, the intangible asset's total life should not exceed 40 years. Disclosure must be made of the valuation basis, description, amortization period, and method. In estimating useful life, consideration should be given to

- Legal, regulatory, or contractual terms
- Renewal or extension provisions
- Product demand
- Service lives of key employees
- Competition
- Obsolescence

Patents, for example, give the holder exclusive rights for a period of 20 years. It would, therefore, be inappropriate to amortize a patent for a period greater than 20 years. Copyrights are granted for the life of the creator plus 50 years. The useful life of copyrights is typically much shorter. In any event, the amortization period on copyrights should not exceed 40 years. Trademarks and trade names have legal protection for a period of 20 years and may be renewed for an indefinite number of times. Franchises and licenses with a limited life should be amortized over their useful life. If franchises and licenses have an indefinite or unlimited life, they should be amortized over a period not exceeding 40 years. Organization costs, which include initial corporation, legal, and accounting fees that are incurred in connection with establishing an entity, are required to be expensed as incurred.

Intangibles on the books before October 31, 1970 do not have to be amortized. Such intangibles are classified into one of two categories under ARB Number 43: (1) intangible assets with a life limited by law, regulation, agreement, or by nature, such as patents, copyrights, leases, franchises, licenses, etc.; and (2) intangibles with an unlimited or indeterminate life, such as trade name, organization costs, goodwill, etc. Intangible assets with a limited life should be amortized over their useful life without exceeding 40 years. However, intangibles with an unlimited or indeterminate life do not have to be amortized unless their life becomes limited, or the asset may not continue to have value to the company, or the asset becomes worthless.

A permanent difference in taxes arises when an amortization expense (e.g., amortization of goodwill) is not deductible for tax purposes.

GOODWILL

Goodwill is theoretically equal to the discounted value (present value) of future excess earnings of a company over other companies in the industry.

In purchasing a new business, a determination is needed of the estimated value of the goodwill. Two possible methods are

- Capitalization of earnings
- Capitalization of excess earnings

EXAMPLE

The following data are provided for a company we are thinking of buying:

Expected average annual earnings	$ 25,000
Expected fair value of net assets excluding goodwill	$180,000
Normal rate of return	10%

Goodwill is estimated as follows under the capitalization of earnings method:

Total asset value implied ($25,000/10%)	$250,000
Estimated fair value of assets	180,000
Estimated goodwill	$ 70,000

Assuming the same information, except that the capitalization of excess earnings method is used with a capitalization rate of 20%, goodwill is estimated at

Expected average annual earnings	$25,000
Return on expected average assets ($180,000 × 10%)	18,000
Excess earnings	$ 7,000
Goodwill ($7,000/.20)	$35,000

EXAMPLE

The net worth of XYZ Company excluding goodwill is $600,000, and total profits for the last five years were $550,000. Included in the latter figure are extraordinary gains of $40,000 and nonrecurring losses of $30,000. A 15% return on net worth is considered normal for the industry. The capitalization of excess earnings is 30%. What is the estimated goodwill?

Profits for 5 years	$550,000
Less: Extraordinary gains	(40,000)
Add: Nonrecurring losses	30,000
Adjusted 5-year earnings	$540,000
Average earnings ($540,000/5 years)	$108,000
Normal earnings ($600,000 × .15)	90,000
Excess annual earnings	$ 18,000
Excess earnings capitalized at 30%: $18,000/.30 =	$ 60,000

Goodwill can only be recorded in a business combination accounted for under the purchase method. It occurs when the acquirer's cost exceeds the fair market value of the net assets acquired. Goodwill is amortized using the straight-line method over the period benefited not exceeding 40 years. On the other hand, if the acquirer's cost is below the fair market value of the net assets acquired, a credit results. This reduces the noncurrent assets bought on a pro rata basis (excluding long-term investments). If a credit still remains, it is accounted for as a deferred credit not to be amortized over more than 40 years using the straight-line method.

Internally generated costs to derive a patented product are expensed (e.g., research and development incurred in developing a new product). The patent account is charged for registration fees, legal fees in successfully defending the patent in court, and the cost of buying competing products. The patent account is amortized over its useful life not exceeding 17 years.

When an intangible asset is worthless, it should be written off as either a nonrecurring loss or extraordinary loss, depending on its nature and recurrence.

Leaseholds are rentals paid in advance and are amortized over the life of the lease.

Leasehold improvements are improvements to leased property and are amortized over the life of the property or of the lease, whichever is shorter. If a lease contains a renewal option, it is included in the life of the lease unless exercise of the option is uncertain, in which case it is ignored.

OTHER ASSETS

The "other assets" section is the last classification of assets presented on the balance sheet. It is sometimes labeled "deferred charges" instead of other assets. Other assets is an all-inclusive heading representing those assets that do not fit into other asset categories. Other assets include long-term prepaid expenses (e.g., advertising, rent, insurance), deferred startup costs, deferred moving costs, deferred taxes, noncurrent receivable, and possibly restricted cash. Long-term prepaid expenses and deferred charges are amortized over the period benefited. Some deferred charges usually have no cash realizability in the event of corporate bankruptcy because they represent past expenditures of cash and cannot be sold to satisfy a bankruptcy judgment. Examples are deferred startup and moving costs.

Annual Report References

LSI LOGIC
1997 ANNUAL REPORT

4. Balance Sheet Detail

(in thousands)	December 31st 1997	1996
Inventories:		
Raw materials	$ 19,892	$ 19,540
Work-in-process	58,621	53,785
Finished goods	23,754	17,085
	$ 102,267	$ 90,410
Property and equipment:		
Land	$ 39,885	$ 42,861
Buildings and improvements	145,297	166,862
Equipment	856,745	817,144
Leasehold improvements	46,839	54,573
Preproduction engineering	58,972	27,222
Furniture and fixtures	35,460	32,512
Construction in progress	557,350	208,203
	1,740,548	1,349,377
Accumulated depreciation and amortization	(616,639)	(537,718)
	$1,123,909	$ 811,659

The Company had $34 million and $1 million of unamortized preproduction engineering costs at December 31, 1997 and 1996, respectively, associated with the construction of a new manufacturing facility in Gresham, Oregon. This new facility is expected to become operational during the third quarter of 1998, at which time capitalized preproduction will be amortized over the expected useful life of the manufacturing technology of approximately four years.

Accumulated amortization for preproduction engineering was $25 million and $20 million at December 31, 1997 and 1996, respectively. Capitalized interest included within property and equipment totaled $17 million and $12 million at December 31, 1997 and 1996, respectively. Accumulated amortization of capitalized interest was $7 million and $5 million at December 31, 1997 and 1996, respectively.

During 1996, the Company completed the shutdown of its Milpitas wafer manufacturing facility and determined that the majority of the equipment for that facility was no longer needed for current or future capacity requirements. Accordingly, the equipment was made available for sale and was written down by $15 million to its estimated net realizable value. The Company utilized $15 million of its restructuring reserves, which became available as a result of a favorable court decision (see Notes 6 and 11), and therefore, the writedown did not necessitate a charge to the income statement.

During 1997, the Company dispositioned assets held for sale with a carrying amount of $15 million that were associated with the 1996 shutdown of the Milpitas wafer manufacturing facility. In August 1997, approximately $5.6 million of the Milpitas equipment held for sale was transferred to another facility within the Company as it was determined that the equipment could be used to meet current capacity requirements. In October 1997, approximately $9.4 million of the Milpitas equipment held for sale was sold for $6.7 million. The loss on the sale of $2.7 million was included in other expense.

Assets held for sale at December 31, 1997 are fully reserved. Assets held for sale were $15.6 million at December 31, 1996.

PEPSICO
1997 ANNUAL REPORT

3. Impairment of Long-Lived Assets

Impairment charges included in unusual items:	1997	1996	1995
Held and used in the business			
Investments in unconsolidated affiliates	$ —	$ 190	$ —
Concentrate-related assets	5	116	—
Disposal of assets			
Investments in unconsolidated affiliates	21	20	—
Other business/assets	174	47	—
Initial adoption of SFAS 121	—	—	66
Total	$ 200	$ 373	$ 66
After-tax	$ 169	$ 356	$ 64
Per share	$0.11	$0.22	$0.04
By segment			
Beverages	$ 162	$373	$ 62
Snack Foods	38	—	$ 4
	$ 200	$373	$ 66

The charges associated with assets to be held and used in the business reflect a reduction in forecasted cash flows attributable to increased competitive activity and weakened macroeconomic factors in various geographic regions. The net charges for disposal of assets primarily reflect strategic decisions to realign the international bottling system, restructure certain Snack Foods operations and exit certain businesses. We anticipate the disposal of assets to be completed in 1998.

PepsiCo early adopted SFAS 121 as of the beginning of the fourth quarter of 1995. The initial, noncash charge resulted from PepsiCo grouping assets at a lower level than under its previous accounting policy for evaluating and measuring impairment.

WOOLWORTH
1997 ANNUAL REPORT

3. Impairment of Long-Lived Assets

In 1995, the Company adopted SFAS No. 121 and recorded a non-cash pre-tax charge of $241 million ($165 million after-tax) of which $211 million related to continuing operations. Of the total impairment loss recognized upon adoption, $209 million represented impairment of long-lived assets such as properties, store fixtures and leasehold improvements, $24 million related to goodwill and $8 million pertained to other intangibles. For continuing operations, pre-tax impairment of $3 million and $6 million for 1997 and 1996, respectively, is included in selling, general and administrative expenses.

MILLENNIUM CHEMICALS
1997 ANNUAL REPORT

5. Impairment of Long-Lived Assets

During 1996, the Company recorded a $75 non-recurring charge ($48 after tax), to reduce the carrying value of certain facilities employed in sulfate-process manufacturing of TiO_2 and to provide for the cost associated with the closure of certain of these facilities. During the first half of 1996, intense price competition was experienced, as customers of the anatase products associated with the sulfate-process operations sought more cost-efficient manufacturing inputs to their applications. As a result of the deterioration of market conditions in the TiO_2 industry, the Company decided to implement programs which included a reduction of its sulfate-process manufacturing capacity both in the United Kingdom and the United States. The 10,000 metric tons per annum ("tpa") sulfate-process plant in Stallingborough, United Kingdom, has been closed, and production at the 66,000 tpa sulfate-process facility in Baltimore, Maryland, has been reduced by approximately one-third. The carrying value of plant and equipment associated with sulfate-process manufacturing was reduced by $60 as a result of evaluating the recoverability of such assets under the unfavorable market conditions existing at that time. The amount of the write-down was determined by comparison to the fair value of the related assets, as determined based on the projected discounted cash flows associated with such assets.

During 1996, the Company also recorded an initial non-cash charge resulting from adopting the evaluation methodology provided by SFAS 121 of $4,497 ($3,206 after tax), related to one of the Discontinued Businesses. Prior to the adoption of SFAS 121, asset impairment was evaluated at an operating company level based on the contribution of operating profits and undiscounted cash flows being generated from those operations. Under this policy, assets used in one of the Discontinued Businesses, comprised of approximately 20 separate operating companies, were evaluated for impairment based on gross margins and cash flows generated by each separate operating company in a given business cycle. Evaluation of the businesses' assets at this level did not result in any impairment.

SFAS 121 requires the impairment review to be performed at the lowest level of asset grouping for which there are identifiable cash flows, which represents a change from the level at which the previous accounting policy measured impairment. In this case, economic groupings of assets were made based on local marketplaces. Evaluation of assets at this lower grouping level indicated an impairment of certain of those assets. The impairment loss was measured based on the difference between estimated discounted cash flows and the carrying value of such assets.

NOVELL
1998 ANNUAL REPORT

(Dollars in thousands)	Cost at Oct. 31 1998	Gross Unrealized Gains	Gross Unrealized Losses	Fair Market Value at Oct. 31 1998
Cash and cash equivalents				
Cash	$ 98,44	$ —	$ —	$ 98,444
Repurchase agreements	8,092	—	—	8,092
Money market fund	55,957	—	—	55,957
Municipal securities	14,590	—	—	14,590
Cash and cash equivalents	$ 177,083	$ —	$ —	$ 177,803
Short-term investments				
Municipal securities	$ 448,195	$ 8,027	$ —	$ 456,222
Money market mutual funds	95,631	—	—	95,631
Money market preferreds	181,179	—	(19)	95,631
Mutual funds	15,340	—	—	15,340
Equity securities	128,837	30,159	(77,805)	81,191
Short-term investments	$ 869,722	$38,186	(77,824)	$ 830,084
Cash and short-term investments	$1,046,805	$38,186	$(77,824)	$1,007,167

(Dollars in thousands)	Cost at Oct. 31 1997	Gross Unrealized Gains	Gross Unrealized Losses	Fair Market Value at Oct. 31 1997
Cash and cash equivalents				
Cash	$ 84,151	$ —	$ —	$ 84,151
Repurchase agreements	4,932	—	—	4,932
Money market fund	42,581	—	—	42,581
Municipal securities	76,879	—	—	76,879
Cash and cash equivalents	$ 208,543	$ —	$ —	$ 208,543
Short-term investments				
Municipal securities	$ 463,443	$ 4,551	$ (84)	$ 467,910
Money market mutual funds	88,999	—	—	88,999
Money market preferreds	150,817	—	(17)	150,800
Mutual funds	14,621	33	(1)	14,753
Equity securities	153,785	25,829	(77,146)	102,468
Short-term investments	$ 871,765	$30,413	$(77,248)	$ 824,930
Cash and short-term investents	$1,080,308	$30,413	$(77,248)	$1,033,473

The Company had unrealized losses of $24 million and $29 million at the end of fiscal 1998 and 1997, respectively, and unrealized gains of $7 million, net of deferred taxes, at the end of fiscal 1996. The Company realized gains on the sales of securities of $14 million, $28 million, and $20 million in fiscal 1998, 1997, and 1996, respectively, while realizing losses on sales of securities of $16 million in fiscal 1998 and $11 million in fiscal 1997.

SPIEGEL
1997 ANNUAL REPORT

2. Receivables

Receivables consist primarily of proprietary credit card receivables generated in connection with the sale of the Company's merchandise as well as receivable balances generated on the MasterCard credit cards offered by the Company's bank subsidiary. At January 3, 1998, customer receivables serviced were $1,683,783, of which 83% related to the Company's proprietary credit card. The Company's customer base is diverse in terms of both geographic and demographic coverage. Due to the revolving nature of the credit card portfolio, management believes that the current carrying value of credit card receivables approximates fair value. The average interest rate collected on the receivables approximates the current market rates on new accounts. The allowance for credit card losses is based upon management's evaluation of the collectability of credit card receivables after giving consideration to current delinquency data, historical loss experience and general economic conditions. This allowance is continually reviewed by management; however, the actual losses incurred may differ from these estimates.

Receivables at January 3, 1998 and December 28, 1996 consist of the following:

Composition of Customer Receivable Portfolio	1997	1996
Receivables serviced	$ 1,683,783	$ 1,865,040
Receivables sold	(1,292,713)	(1,463,730)
Receivables owned	391,070	401,310
COMPOSITION OF RECEIVABLES OWNED		
Retained certificates	145,732	188,299
Receivables with no certificates issued	245,338	213,011
Receivables owned	391,070	401,310
Less allowance for returns on proprietary credit card sales	(21,247)	(32,243)
Less allowance for doubtful accounts	(11,757)	(12,270)
Other trade receivables, net	205,310	148,445
Receivables, net	$ 563,376	$ 505,242

The Company routinely transfers portions of its customer receivables to trusts which, in turn, sell certificates representing undivided interests in the trusts to investors. The receivables are sold without recourse, and accordingly, no bad debt reserve related to the net receivables sold is maintained. Cash flows generated from the receivables in the trusts are, to the extent allocable to the investor percentage, applied to payment of interest on the certificates, reinvestment in additional receivables to maintain the investors' percentage, and payment of servicing fees to the Company. Excess cash flows revert to the Company. The Company owns the remaining undivided interest in the trusts not represented by the certificates and will continue to service all receivables for the trusts.

In addition to the certificates sold, an additional class of investor certificates, currently held by the Company, was issued by the trust in certain transactions. The aggregate principle balances for these retained certificates were $145,732 and $188,299 as of January 3, 1998 and December 28, 1996, respectively. These retained certificates, classified as trading and stated at market value, are included in the Company's balance sheet under "Receivables, net." Cash flows generated from the receivables in the trust are expected to be adequate to cover any loses which may be incurred on uncollectible amounts associated with the receivables supporting these retained certificates. Therefore, no bad debt reserve is maintained on these balances as of January 3, 1998. The Company also held a total of $59,592 at January 3, 1998 and $55,670 at December 28, 1996 in reserve funds used as credit enhancement for related receivables sold. Restricted cash accounts have been maintained for these reserve funds, none of which has been utilized as of January 3, 1998. The value of these funds is included in the Company's balance sheet under "Other assets."

As a result of these transactions, finance revenue increased by $18,637 in 1995. In 1997, the Company adopted SFAS Number 125, which requires gain recognition based on the revolving nature of sold customer receivables. Incremental gains of $75,141 were recorded as finance revenue in 1997 pursuant to SFAS Number 125.

DUPONT
1998 ANNUAL REPORT

11. Accounts and Notes Receivable

December 31	1998	1997
Trade—net of allowances of $101 in 1998 and $66 in 1997	$3,591	$3,438
Miscellaneous	610	871
	$4,201	$4,309

Accounts and notes receivable are carried at amounts that approximate fair value and include $70 for 1998 and $74 for 1997 due from equity affiliates.

See Note 28 for a description of business segment markets and associated concentrations of credit risk.

12. Inventories

December 31	1998	1997
Finished products	$2,209	$2,115
Semifinished products	836	827
Raw materials and supplies	749	659
Total	3,794	3,601
Less: Adjustment of inventories to a last-in, first-out (LIFO) basis	665	809
	$3,129	$2,792

Inventory values before LIFO adjustment are generally determined by the average cost method, which approximates current cost. Inventories valued under the LIFO method comprised 85 percent of consolidated inventories before LIED adjustment at December 31, 1998 and 1997.

13. Property, Plant and Equipment

December 31	1998	1997
Buildings	$ 3,889	$ 3,464
Equipment	28,485	27,326
Land	288	260
Construction	2,066	1,861
	$34,728	$32,911

Property, plant and equipment includes gross assets acquired under capital leases of $115 and $130 at December 31, 1998 and 1997, respectively; related amounts included in accumulated depreciation and amortization were $54 and $57 at December 31, 1998 and 1997, respectively.

HORMEL
1998 ANNUAL REPORT

B. Cash and Cash Equivalents and Short-term Marketable Securities

The company considers all investments with an original maturity of three months or less on their acquisition date to be cash equivalents. The company classifies investments with an original maturity of more than three months on their acquisition date as short-term marketable securities. The company's cash and cash equivalents and short-term marketable securities at October 31, 1998, and October 25, 1997, consisted of the following (cost approximates fair value):

(In Thousands)	October 31, 1998 Cash and Cash Equivalents	October 31, 1998 Short-term Marketable Securities	October 25, 1997 Cash and Cash Equivalents	October 25, 1997 Short-term Marketable Securities
Held-to-maturity securities:				
Commercial paper	$ 29,808	$ 27,198	$ 15,780	$ 5,533
Municipal securities	33,791		80,064	
Preferred securities	60,647	4,400	10,000	
Taxable securities	31,609	2,500	4,700	
Cash	48,079		36,309	
Total	**$203,934**	**$ 34,098**	$146,853	$ 5,533

C. Inventories

Principal components of inventories are:

(In Thousands)	October 31, 1998	October 25, 1997
Finished products	$137,444	$145,897
Raw materials and work-in-process	68,653	86,762
Materials and supplies	60,820	59,846
LIFO reserve	(27,369)	(27,159)
Total	**$ 239,548**	$265,346

Inventoriable expenses, packages and supplies and turkey products amounting to approximately $82.6 million at October 31,1998, and $84.5 million at October 25, 1997, are stated at cost determined by the last-in, first-out method and are $27.4 million and $27.2 million lower in the respective years than such inventories determined under the first-in, first-out method.

REEBOK
1999 ANNUAL REPORT

4. Intangibles

Intangibles consist of the following:

| | December 31 | |
	1999	1998
Excess of purchase price over fair value of assets acquired	$ 39,600	$ 38,900
Other intangible assets:		
Purchased technology	52,827	52,827
Company tradename and trademarks	51,384	47,678
Other	12,969	12,969
	156,780	152,374
Less accumulated amortization	87,888	83,726
	$ 68,892	$ 68,648

LIMITED
1999 ANNUAL REPORT

3. Property and Equipment

(Thousands)

Property and Equipment, at Cost	1999	1998
Land, buildings and improvements	$ 390,121	$ 411,483
Furniture, fixtures and equipment	2,016,237	1,930,906
Leaseholds and improvements	498,232	563,217
Construction in progress	40,237	108,478
Total	2,944,827	3,014,084
Less: accumulated depreciation and amortization	1,715,215	1,652,323
Property and equipment, net	$1,229,612	$1,361,761

CENTOCOR
1997 ANNUAL REPORT

7. Intangible and Other Assets

Intangible and other assets consist of the following, net of accumulated amortization of $16,311,000 and $10,804,000 at December 31, 1997 and 1996, respectively, (in thousands):

| | December 31, | |
	1997	1996
Licenses	$ 5,339	$ 5,378
Goodwill	—	5,158
Prepaid royalties related to CPIII	29,398	—
Debt issuance costs	598	755
Deferred charges	23,084	23,026
Other	2,869	1,017
	$61,288	$35,334

Prepaid royalties related to CPIII at December 31, 1997 represent an advance of payment of approximately $13,600,000 in cash paid to the former limited partners of CPIII in connection with the purchase of the limited partnership interests in CPIII and an additional $15,800,000 payable to the former limited partners of CPIII in connection with the revision of future royalties. See Note 3—Commitments and Contingencies.

Deferred charges at December 31, 1997 and 1996 include a prepayment of certain future royalties and a prepayment associated with the commercialization and market development of ReoPro.

In June 1997, the Company sold its U.K. diagnostic manufacturing facility and its related infectious disease product line. In connection with the transaction the Company recorded a one-time charge to earnings of $4,565,000 in the second quarter of 1997, a component of which was the write-off of goodwill on the facility and related business.

Licensing agreements and other assets are reviewed for impairment whenever events or circumstances provide evidence that suggest that the carrying amount of the asset may not be recoverable. Impairment is evaluated by using identified or expected cash flows.

Chapter 4

Balance Sheet Presentation and Disclosures: Liabilities

The American Institute of CPAs' Accounting Research Bulletin Number 43, Chapter 3, provides coverage of liabilities.

This chapter discusses the accounting, reporting, and disclosures associated with liabilities. The topics include loss contingencies, compensated absences, termination benefits, troubled debt restructuring, refinancing of current to noncurrent debt, callable obligations by creditors, issuance of bonds, calling debt, imputing interest on noninterest notes payable, environmental liabilities, and offsetting of liabilities.

INTRODUCTION TO LIABILITIES

A liability is liquidated from either the use of an asset or the incurrence of another liability. Liabilities may arise from a contract, by law, by a judicial decision, etc.

Current liabilities are those to be paid or liquidated from current assets or created from other current liabilities. Current liabilities are due on demand or within one year or the normal operating cycle of the business, whichever is greater. Current liabilities may arise in the following situations:

■ The payee and amount are known.

- The payee is not known but the amount may be reasonably estimated.
- The payable is known but the amount must be estimated.
- The liability arises from a loss contingency.

The current portion of long-term debt to be paid within the next year or that amount which is due on demand is classified as a current liability.

Refundable deposits are classified as current liabilities if the company intends to refund the money within the next year.

Agency liabilities are amounts withheld by the company from employees or customers for tax purposes owed to either federal, state, or local taxing agencies. They are listed as current liabilities.

A company may offer potential customers premiums (something free or for a minimal charge such as samples) to stimulate product sales. The customer may be required to return evidence of purchase of something else (e.g., box top) to get the premium. A nominal cash payment may be necessary. A current liability arises for the amount of anticipated redemptions in the next year. If the premium and redemption period is for more than one year, an estimated liability must be allocated to the current and noncurrent portions.

EXAMPLE

XYZ Company offers its customers a camera in exchange for 20 boxtops and $3. The camera costs the company $18. It is expected that 60% of the boxtops will be redeemed. The following journal entries are required.

1. To record the purchase of 10,000 cameras at $18 each.

Inventory of Premium Cameras	180,000	
Cash		180,000

2. To record the sale of 400,000 boxes of the company's major product at $3 each.

Cash	1,200,000	
Sales		1,200,000

3. To record the actual redemption of 120,000 boxtops, the receipt of $3 per 20 boxtops, and the delivery of the cameras.

Cash [(120,000/20 × $3)]	18,000	
Premium expense	90,000	
Inventory of Premium Cameras [(120,000/20) × $18]	108,000	

4. To record end-of-year adjusting entry for estimated liability for outstanding offers (boxtops).

Premium expense	90,000	
Estimated liability		90,000

Computation:

Total boxtops sold	400,000
Total estimated redemptions (60%)	240,000
Boxtops redeemed	120,000
Estimated future redemptions	120,000

Cost of estimated claims outstanding
  (120,000/20) × ($18 − 3) = $90,000

Note: The Premium Expense account is presented as a selling expense. The inventory of premium cameras account balance is presented as a current asset, while the estimated liability account is reported as a current liability.

EXAMPLE

On November 30, 20X6, a consignee received 1,000 units on consignment. The cost and selling price per unit were $60 and $85, respectively. The commission rate is 8%. At December 31, 20X6, the units in inventory were 200. The amount to be presented as a payable for consigned goods at year-end 20X6 is computed as follows:

Units sold (1,000 − 200)	$800
× Amount to be remitted per unit ($85 − $6.80)	78.20
Payable	$62,560

Emerging Issues Task Force Consensus Summary Number 86–5 covers the classification of demand notes with repayment terms. Obligations due on demand or within one year are classified as current debt even if liquidation is not anticipated within that period.

Emerging Issues Task Force Consensus Summary Number 95–22 deals with the balance sheet classification of borrowings outstanding under revolving credit agreements that include both a subjective acceleration clause and a lock-box agreement. If the borrowings reduce the debt outstanding, the borrowings are classified as current liabilities.

EXAMPLE

Shapiro Company presented the following liabilities at year-end 19X7:

Accounts payable	$100,000
Notes payable, 10%, due 7/1/19X8	600,000
Contingent liability	150,000
Accrued expenses	20,000
Deferred income tax credit	25,000
Bonds payable, 9%, due 5/1/19X8	500,000

The contingent liability represents a reasonably possible loss arising from a $400,000 lawsuit against Shapiro. In the opinion of legal counsel, the lawsuit is expected to be resolved in 19X9. The range of loss is $200,000 to $600,000. The deferred income tax credit is expected to reverse in 19X9.

At year-end 19X7, current liabilities equal $1,220,000, computed as follows:

Accounts payable	$ 100,000
Notes payable, due 5/1/19X8	600,000
Accrued expenses	20,000
Bonds payable, due 5/1/19X8	500,000
Total	$1,220,000

EXAMPLE

Morgan Company requires nonrefundable advance payments with special orders for equipment built to customer specifications. The following data were provided for 20X5:

Customer advances 1/1/20X5	$300,000
Advances related to canceled orders during the year	80,000
Advances for orders shipped during the year	160,000
Advances received with orders during the year	200,000

The amount to be presented as a current liability for customer advances at year-end 20X5 is computed as follows:

Balance—1/1/20X5	$300,000
Add: Advances received with orders	200,000
Less: Advances related to orders canceled	(80,000)
Advances for orders shipped	(160,000)
Balance—12/31/20X5	$260,000

EXAMPLE

Schwartz Company requires an advance payment for orders specially designed for particular customers. Such advances are not refundable. Relevant information for 19X6 follows:

Customer advances—1/1/19X6	$69,000
Advances associated with canceled orders	30,000
Advances received with orders	90,000
Advances applied to orders shipped	85,000

On December 31, 19X6, the current liabilities associated with customer advances was $44,000, computed as follows:

Balance—1/1/19X6	$69,000
Add: Advances received with orders	90,000
Less: Advances applicable to orders shipped	(85,000)
Advances related to canceled orders	(30,000)
Balance—12/31/19X6	$44,000

EXAMPLE

On December 31, 19X1, Fox Company received 200 units of a product on consignment from Jacoff Company. The cost of the product is $50 each, and the selling price per unit is $75. Fox's commission is 8%. At 12/31/19X1, 10 units were in stock. The payable for consigned goods to be shown under current liabilities is $13,110, computed as follows:

Units sold (200 – 10)	190
Per unit owed ($75 selling price less $6 commission)	× $69
Total	$13,110

EXAMPLE

As of December 31, 20X3 before adjustment for the following items, accounts payable had a balance of $700,000:

- A check to a supplier amounting to $40,000 was recorded on December 30, 20X3. The check was mailed on January 3, 20X4.

- At December 31, 20X3, the company has a $30,000 debit balance in its accounts payable to a supplier due to an advance payment for a product to be produced.

The accounts payable to be presented on the December 31, 20X3 balance sheet is computed as follows:

Unadjusted balance	$700,000
Unmailed check	40,000
Customer with debit balance	30,000
Adjusted balance	$770,000

Debt is classified as noncurrent if it is to be refinanced with another long-term issue or extinguished from noncurrent assets (e.g., sinking fund). It is not to be paid from current assets or the incurrence of current liabilities.

Long-term debt should be recorded at the present value discounted of future payments using the market rate of interest.

Derivatives and liabilities arising from the transfer of financial assets are recorded at fair market value.

In a deferred interest-rate-setting agreement that is an important element in the original issuance, amounts paid or received because of such agreement should be treated as a premium or discount on the initial debt and amortized over the term of the debt. A deferred interest rate arrangement means the issuing company sells its debt at a fixed rate but also contracts to set an interest rate at a later date based on some index. As a result, the set interest rate will differ from the fixed interest rate during the designated period.

If a borrowing arrangement permits the debtor to redeem the debt instrument within one year, it is presented under current liabilities. However, the debt is classified as noncurrent if the letter of credit agreement satisfies the following criteria:

- The financing agreement does not terminate within one year.
- The refinancing is on a long-term basis.
- The lender cannot cancel the agreement unless there is a clearly ascertainable violation.

If debt is tied to a certain index or market value of a commodity so that a contingent payment will be due at maturity, a liability must be recorded for the amount by which the contingent payment exceeds the amount initially assigned to the contingent payment feature.

In a joint venture, there may be take-or-pay or through-put contracts to construct capital facilities (e.g., factory building). The debt is incurred by the joint venture, but the individual companies buy the goods (take-or-pay contract) or services (through-put contract) arising from the project. The goods or services are paid for periodically irrespective of whether the items are delivered or not. A minimum amount of goods or services is usually provided for. Such agreements require disclosure.

An indirect guarantee of indebtedness of others is an assurance obligating one company (the first company) to transfer money to a second company upon the occurrence of some happening whereby the funds are available to creditors of the second company, and those same creditors have a legal right to collect from the first company debt owed by it to the second company.

Emerging Issues Task Force Consensus Summary Number 86–15 (*Increasing-Rate Debt*) stipulates that notes maturing in three months having a continual extension option for up to five years may be classified after taking into account the intentions of the parties and the issuer's ability to pay the debt. If the source of repayment is current, the debt should be classified as current. However, if the source of repayment is noncurrent, then the debt is noncurrent in nature. Interest should be computed based on the interest method. Debt interest costs should be deferred and amortized over the outstanding period of the debt. If excess accrued interest arises from paying the debt before maturity, it should be used to adjust interest expense. **Note:** The classification of the debt need not be the same as the period used to compute periodic interest cost.

EXAMPLE

A company has an escrow account from which it pays property taxes on behalf of customers. Interest less a 5% service fee is credited to the mortgagee's account and is used to reduce future escrow payments. Additional data are as follows:

ESCROW ACCOUNTS LIABILITY—BEGINNING OF YEAR	$500,000
Receipt of escrow payments	800,000
Payment of property taxes	450,000
Interest earned on escrow funds	65,000

At year-end, the escrow accounts liability equals $911,750, determined as follows:

Balance—1/1	$500,000
Receipt of escrow payments	800,000
Payment of property taxes	(450,000)
Interest earned net of service fee ($65,000 × 95%)	61,750
Balance—12/31	$911,750

Disclosures for debt include

- Type of debt (e.g., debentures, secured)
- Major classes of debt
- Pledging or collateral requirements
- Stated interest rate
- Restrictive covenants (e.g., dividends limitations, working capital requirements)
- Maturity value, maturity period, and maturity date
- Open lines of credit
- Conversion options
- Unused letters of credit
- Sinking fund requirements
- Amounts due to related parties
- Amounts due to officers

ESTIMATED LIABILITIES AND CONTINGENCIES

According to FASB Statement Number 5 (*Accounting for Contingencies*), a loss contingency is accrued if both of the following conditions are satisfied:

- At year-end, it is probable (likely to occur) that an asset was impaired or a liability was incurred.
- The amount of loss may be reasonably estimated.

Examples of loss contingencies are pending or threatened lawsuits, warranties or defects, assessments and claims, expropriation of property by a foreign government, environmental remediation guarantees of indebtedness, and agreement to repurchase receivables that have been sold. The accrual is required because of the conservatism principle.

The journal entry to record a probable loss contingency is

Expense (loss)
　　Estimated liability

EXAMPLE

On December 31, 19X3, warranty expenses are estimated at $30,000. On March 2, 19X4, actual warranty costs paid were $27,000. The journal entries are

12/31/19X3	Warranty expense	30,000	
	Estimated liability		30,000
3/2/19X4	Estimated liability	27,000	
	Cash		27,000

If a probable loss cannot be estimated, it should be footnoted.

If there is a loss contingency at year-end but no asset impairment or liability incurrence exists (e.g., uninsured equipment), footnote disclosure should be made.

If there is a loss contingency occurring after year-end but before the audit report date, subsequent event disclosure should be made. An explanatory paragraph should be provided regarding the contingency.

If the loss amount is within a range, the accrual should be based on the best estimate within that range. If no amount within the range is better than any other amount, the minimum amount (not maximum amount) of the range should be accrued. There should be disclosure of the maximum loss. If later events indicate that the minimum loss initially accrued is insufficient, an additional loss must be accrued in the year this becomes evident. This accrual is treated as a change in estimate.

EXAMPLE

XYZ is involved in a tax dispute with the Internal Revenue Service (IRS). As of December 31, 2001, XYZ Company believed that an unfavorable outcome is probable and the amount of loss may be in the range of $2.5 million to $3.5 million. After year-end, when the 2001 financial statements had been issued, XYZ Company settled with the IRS and accepted an offer of $3 million. Since a range of loss is involved, it is appropriate to accrue the minimum amount or $2.5 million for 2001 year-end.

If there exists a reasonably possible loss (more than remote but less than likely), no accrual should be made. However, footnote disclosure is required. The disclosure includes the nature of the contingency and the estimated probable loss or range of loss. In the event an estimate of loss cannot be made, that fact should be stated.

A remote contingency (slight chance of occurring) is typically ignored with no disclosure required. **Exceptions:** Disclosure is made of agreements to repurchase receivables, indebtedness guarantees (direct or indirect), and standby letters of credit.

EXAMPLE

A company cosigned a loan guaranteeing the indebtedness if the mortgagee defaults on it. The likelihood of default is remote. This is an exception to the rule that remote contingencies need not be disclosed because it represents a guarantee of indebtedness and thus requires disclosure.

No accrual is made for general (unspecified) contingencies such as for self-insurance and hurricane losses. However, footnote disclosure and/or appropriation of retained earnings can be made for such contingencies. To be accrued, the future loss must be specific and measurable, such as freight or parcel post losses.

Gain contingencies can never be booked because doing so violates conservatism. However, footnote disclosure should be made.

Warranty obligations are contingencies and estimates. They may be based upon prior experience, experience of other firms in same industry, or estimates by specialists, such as engineers. If the warranty liability cannot be reasonably estimated, then significant uncertainty exists as to whether a sale should be reported, and another method, such as the installment sales method, cost recovery method, or some other method of revenue recognition used.

Unasserted claims exist when the claimant has elected not to assert the claim or because the claimant lacks knowledge of the existence of the claim. If it is probable that the claimant will assert the unasserted claim, and it is either probable or reasonably possible that the outcome will be unfavorable, the unasserted claim should be disclosed in the financial statements.

Estimated liability needs to be recorded when a company offers customers something free or for a minimal charge to increase product sales. The customer may be required to provide proof of purchase to get the free product. Sometimes a nominal cash payment is also required.

EXAMPLE

XYZ Company includes a coupon in each cereal box that it sells. Customers may redeem 10 coupons and $5.00 in exchange for a toy that costs XYZ Company $10.00. Approximately 70% of the coupons are expected to be redeemed. This promotion began on December 1, 2001 and the company sold 200,000 boxes of cereal. As of December 31, 2001, no coupons had been redeemed. The estimated liability for coupons is calculated as follows:

Total coupons issued	200,000
Percentage expected to be redeemed	70%
Coupons expected to be redeemed	140,000
Number of coupons per toy	10
Number of toys to be distributed	14,000
Liability per toy	$5
Total liability for coupons	$70,000

EXAMPLE

In December 20X1, Mavis Company started to include one coupon in each box of popcorn. A customer will receive as a promotion a toy if 10 coupons and $1 is received. The toy costs $2.50. It is expected that 80% of the coupons will be exchanged. During December, 200,000 boxes of popcorn were sold, with no coupons being redeemed yet since the promotion just started. At year-end 20X1, the estimated liability for coupons is computed as follows:

Total coupons issued	200,000
Percentage of coupons expected to be redeemed	× 80%
To be redeemed	160,000
Number of toys to be distributed: 160,000/10 coupons =	16,000
Estimated liability for coupons—12/31/20X1: 16,000 × $1.50*=	$24,000

*The liability is $2.50 cost per each toy less $1 to be received, or $1.50 per toy.

RISKS AND UNCERTAINTIES

The American Institute of CPAs' Accounting Standard Executive Committee issued Statement of Position 94-6 (*Disclosure of Certain Significant Risks and Uncertainties*). It requires disclosure of risks involving the nature of operations, use of estimates, and business vulnerability. With regard to the nature of operations, disclosure should be made of the company's major products and services, including by geographic locations. The relative importance of operations in multiple markets should also be discussed. Disclosure should be made of estimated accounts on which estimates are sensitive to near-term changes, such as technological obsolescence. Disclosure of corporate vulnerability to concentrations includes lack of diversification (e.g., customer base, suppliers, lenders, geographic areas, government contracts). An entity whose revenue is concentrated in certain products or services must make disclosure. Disclosure of information about significant concentrations of credit risk is also required for all financial instruments. Disclosure is mandated when concentrations exist for labor, supplies, materials, or other services which are necessary for an enterprise's operations. Overreliance on licenses and other rights should be noted.

Disclosure is required when a change in estimate would have a material effect on the financial statements. Examples of items requiring disclosure according to SOP 94–6 include

- Rapid technological obsolescence of assets
- Inventory subject to perishability, changing fashions, and styles
- Capitalization of certain costs, such as for computer software or motion picture production
- Insurance companies' deferred policy acquisition costs
- Litigation-related liabilities and contingencies due to obligations of other enterprises
- Valuation allowances for commercial and real estate loans, and allowances for deferred tax assets

- Amounts of long-term obligations, such as for pension obligations and other benefits

- Amounts of long-term contracts

- Proceeds or expected loss on disposition of assets

- Nature and amount of guarantees

If an entity is vulnerable to concentration-related risks, disclosure is required if the concentration existed at the date of financial statements, the entity may suffer significantly due to the concentration risk, and it is reasonably possible that concentration risk-related events will occur in the near future.

Uncertainties with labor unions should be noted. For organizations with significant concentrations of labor subject to collective bargaining agreements, the disclosure should include

- The percentage of the labor force covered by a collective bargaining agreement

- The percentage of the labor force covered by a collective bargaining agreement where the agreement will expire within one year

COMPENSATED ABSENCES

FASB Statement Number 43 (*Accounting for Compensated Absences*) states that compensated absences include sick leave, vacation time, and holidays. The pronouncement also applies to sabbatical leaves related to past services rendered. The pronouncement does not apply to deferred compensation, postretirement benefits, severance (termination) pay, stock option plans, and other long-term fringe benefits (e.g., disability, insurance).

An estimated liability based on current salary rates should be accrued for compensated absences when all of the following criteria are satisfied:

- Employee services have been rendered.

- Employee rights have vested, meaning the employer is obligated to pay the employee even though he or she leaves the employment voluntarily or involuntarily.
- Probable payment exists.
- The amount of estimated liability can be reasonably determined.

If the conditions are met but the amount cannot be determined, no accrual can be made. However, there should be footnote disclosure.

Accrual for sick leave is required only when the employer allows employees to take accumulated sick leave days off regardless of actual illness. No accrual is made if workers may only take accumulated days off for actual illness, because losses for these are usually insignificant in amount. An employer should not accrue a liability for nonvesting rights for compensated absences expiring at the end of the year they are earned since no accumulation is involved. However, if unused rights do accumulate, a liability should be accrued.

EXAMPLE

Estimated compensation for future absences is $40,000. The journal entry is

Expense	40,000	
Estimated liability		40,000

If, at a later date, a payment of $35,000 is required, the journal entry is

Estimated liability	35,000	
Cash		35,000

EXAMPLE

Blumenfrucht Corporation has a plan for compensated absences providing workers with 8 and 12 paid vacation and sick days, respectively, that may be carried over to future years. Instead of taking their vacation pay, the workers may select payment. However, no payment is allowed for sick days not taken. At year-end 19X5, the unadjusted balance of the liability for compensated absences was $34,000. At year-end 19X5, it is estimated that there are 110 vacation days and 80 sick leave days available. The average per day pay is $125. On December 31, 19X5, the liability for compensated absences is $13,750 ($125 per day × 110 days). There is no accrual for unpaid sick days because payment of the compensation is not probable.

DEFERRED COMPENSATION AGREEMENT

An accrual should be made over the service years of active employees for deferred compensation starting with the agreement date. Examples of deferred compensation agreements are a covenant not to compete, continued employment for a specified period, and availability to render services after retirement. The total amount accrued at the end of the employee's service years should at least equal the discounted value of future payments to be made. The annual journal entry to record deferred compensation is

Deferred compensation expense	XXX	
Deferred compensation liability		XXX

ACCOUNTING FOR SPECIAL TERMINATION BENEFITS (EARLY RETIREMENT)

An accrual of a liability for employee termination benefits in the period that management approves the termination benefit package is required if the following circumstances are met:

1. The benefits that terminated employees will receive have been agreed on and have been accepted by management prior to the financial statement date.

2. Employees are made aware of the termination agreement prior to the issuance of the financial statements.

3. The termination benefit plan provides the following data: (a) the number of employees to be terminated, (b) their job categories, and (c) the location of their jobs.

4. Significant changes to the plan are not likely so that completion of the plan may be expected in a short time.

The termination plan may include both individuals who have been involuntarily terminated and those who have voluntarily decided to leave their current employ. The latter may have been coaxed into leaving with the promise of higher termination benefits. The accrued liability should be based on the number of employees who will be terminated and the benefits that will be paid to both involuntary and voluntary terminated employees. The amount of the accrual equals the down payment plus the present value discounted of future payments.

When it can be objectively measured, the impact of changes on the employer's previously accrued expenses related to other employee benefits directly associated with employee termination should be included in measuring termination expense.

EXAMPLE

On January 1, 19X3, an incentive is offered for early retirement. Employees are to receive a payment of $100,000 today, plus payments of $20,000 for each of the next 10 years. Assume a discount rate of 10%. The journal entry is

Expense	222,900	
Estimated liability		222,900
Down payment		$100,000
Present value of future payments ($20,000 × 6.145)*		122,900
Total		$222,900

*Present value factor for $n = 10$, $i = 10\%$ is 6.145.

TROUBLED DEBT

Frequently, during depressed economic times, debtors may be unable to pay their creditors. Because of the debtors' financial difficulties, it may be necessary for a creditor to grant a concession that otherwise would not have been considered. The accounting of debtors and creditors for troubled debt is based on the guidance of two FASB statements, including

- FASB Statement Number 15, *Accounting by Debtors and Creditors for Troubled Debt Restructuring*
- FASB Statement Number 114, *Accounting by Creditors for Impairment of a Loan*

The latter statement modifies the former with respect to accounting by a creditor for modification of loan terms. When a troubled loan materializes, the creditor is required first to recognize a loss on impairment of the debt. After this, either the terms of the loan are modified or the loan is settled on terms that are not favorable to the creditor.

The concept of impairment of loans will be discussed first, followed by the restructuring of troubled debt.

Accounting by Creditors for Impairment of a Loan

FASB 114 requires that impairment of a loan by a creditor be recognized when it is probable that a creditor will be unable to collect all that is contractually owed, including both principal and interest. A loan, for example, that is modified in a troubled debt restructuring is considered impaired. A temporary delay of payment, however, is not considered an impairment. In addition, a loan should not be considered impaired if the creditor expects to collect all amounts that are due including any accrued interest for any delay in payment that may have occurred.

When a loan is classified as being impaired, measurement of the impairment is based on the expected new future cash flows discounted using the original historical contractual rate, not the rate specified in the restructuring agreement. If, on the other hand, the loan is collateralized or has a market price, the amount of impairment may be measured with the assistance of those amounts. For example, if foreclosure is probable, the impairment of the loan may be based on the fair market value of the collateral. The difference between the book value of the impaired loan and the amount of impairment should be recorded by debiting the bad debts expense account with a corresponding credit to a valuation allowance account. If a change occurs in the amount or timing of the new expected cash flow subsequent to the measurement of impairment, the creditor should recalculate the amount of impairment and adjust the valuation account in the period in which this change becomes known.

When the impairment is recognized using the present value of new expected cash flows, the creditor should recognize interest income using the effective interest method. Any changes in the initial impairment resulting from changes in the amount or timing of cash flows should be recorded as an entry in the bad debt expense, and allowance valuation accounts. This includes any changes that are based on the modifications of the market value of the loan or its collateral.

Disclosure should be made, as of the balance sheet date, of the recorded investment in loans for which impairment has been recognized less the allowance for related loan losses. In addition, each period for which an income statement is presented, an analysis should be disclosed of any changes in the valuation allowance account. The creditor's income recognition policy with respect to loan impairment should also be shown.

EXAMPLE

On January 1, 2000, X Financing Company loaned $1,000,000 to Y Company. The loan was issued in the form of a six-year zero-interest-bearing note due on December 31, 2005, generating an effective yield of 8%. As a result, Y Company was paid proceeds of $630,170. This amount was computed in the following way:

$1,000,000 \times$ present value of $1 discounted for 6 years at 8%
$$= \$1,000,000 \times .63017$$
$$= \$630,170$$

The following entry would be made on January 1, 2000 by the creditor, X Financing Company, when the note was accepted and the proceeds issued to the Y Company, the debtor:

Notes receivable	1,000,000	
Discount on notes receivable		369,830
Cash		630,170

The following table shows the amortization of the discount on the note by X Financing Company over the life of the note.

Date	Interest Revenue (8%)	Discount Amortized	Carrying Value of the Note
1/1/2000			$ 630,170
12/30/2000	$50,414*	$50,414	680,584
12/31/2001	54,447	54,447	735,031
12/31/2002	58,802	58,802	793,833
12/31/2003	63,507	63,507	857,340
12/31/2004	68,587	68,587	925,927
12/31/2005	74,073**	74,073	1,000,000

* $630,170 \times 8\%$
** Understated by $1 due to rounding.

On December 31, 2003 because of a downturn in the economy and depression in the industry of Y Company, X Financing Company, after a comprehensive review of all available evidence at its disposal, determined that it was probable that Y Company would pay back only $400,000 of the loan at maturity. These facts indicated to X Financing Company that the loan was impaired and that a loss should be recorded immediately.

FASB 114 requires that X Financing Company compute the present value of the new expected cash flows at the original contractual effective rate of interest. Based on present value calculations, this amount is $342,936, computed in the following way:

$$\$400,000 \times \text{present value of \$1 discounted for 2 years at 8\%}$$
$$= \$400,000 \times .85734$$
$$= \$342,936$$

The impairment loss is the difference between the recorded value of the loan and the new expected present value of future cash flows from it. The impairment loss to X Financing Company is calculated as follows:

Carrying value of loan to creditor at Dec. 31, 2003	$857,340
Less: present value of new expected cash flows of $400,000 discounted for 2 years at 8%	342,936
Impairment loss to X Financing Company	$514,404

The entry to record the impairment of the loan on the accounting records of X Financing is

Bad debts expense	514,404	
Allowance for impairment of note		514,404

No entry is made on the accounting records of the debtor entity, Y Company, for the impairment of the loan.

Troubled Debt Restructuring

FASB 15 states that in a troubled debt situation the debtor is having significant financial problems and receives partial or full relief of the debt by the creditor. The relief may be in the form of any of the following:

- Creditor/debtor agreement
- Repossession or foreclosure
- Relief dictated by law

The types of troubled debt restructuring include

- Debtor transfers to creditor receivables from third parties or other assets in part or in full satisfaction of the obligation
- Debtor transfers to creditor stock to satisfy the debt
- Modification of debt terms such as through extending the maturity date, reducing the balance due, or reducing the interest rate

In restructuring, an extraordinary gain is recognized by the debtor, but either an ordinary or extraordinary loss is recognized by the creditor depending on how unusual or infrequent the occurrence is. In most cases, it is an ordinary loss.

The extraordinary gain of the debtor equals the difference between the fair market value of the assets exchanged and the book value of the debt, including accrued interest. In addition, there may arise a gain on the disposal of the assets exchanged equal to the difference between the fair market value and the book value of the transferred assets. This gain or loss is not from the restructuring but instead an ordinary gain or loss arising from asset disposal.

EXAMPLE

A debtor transferred assets having a fair market value of $7,000 and a book value of $5,000 to satisfy a debt with a carrying value of $8,000. The gain on restructuring is $1,000 ($8,000 – $7,000), while the ordinary gain is $2,000 ($7,000 – $5,000).

If a debtor transfers an equity interest to the creditor, the debtor records the stock issued at its fair market value, not the recorded value of the debt relieved. The difference between these values is recorded as an extraordinary gain.

Any adjustment in the terms of the initial obligation is accounted for prospectively. A new interest rate is computed based on the new terms. The interest rate is then used to allocate future payments as a reduction in principal and interest. When the new terms of the agreement result in the total future payments being less than the book value of the debt, the debt is reduced, with a restructuring gain being recorded for the difference. FASB Statement 15 requires that the gain on restructuring be based on the undiscounted restructured cash flows. Future payments are considered a reduction of principal only. Interest expense is not recognized.

There may be a mix of concessions offered to the debtor. This may arise when assets or equity are transferred for part satisfaction of the debt, with the balance subject to the modification of the terms. The two steps are as follows:

1. Reduce the debt by the fair market value of the asset or equity transferred.

2. The balance of the debt is treated as an adjustment of the terms for accounting purposes.

Any direct costs (e.g., attorney fees) incurred by the debtor in the equity transfer reduce the fair market value of the equity interest. Any other costs reduce the gain on restructuring. If no gain is involved, direct costs are expensed.

Footnote disclosure by the debtor should be made of the terms surrounding the restructuring, gain on restructuring in aggregate and per share amounts, and contingently payable amounts and terms.

The creditor's loss is the difference between the fair market value of assets received and the carrying value of the investment. When credit terms are modified, the following occurs:

- FASB Statement 114 requires that the creditor's loss be based upon the new expected cash flows discounted at the original contractual effective interest rate. The FASB believes that since loans are recorded initially at discounted amounts, the ongoing assessment for impairment should be made in a similar manner. (The debtor's gain on restructuring, as was previously noted, should be based upon undiscounted amounts as required by FASB Statement 15.)

- Direct costs are immediately expensed.

- Assets are recorded at fair market value.

- Interest revenue is recorded for the excess of total future payments over the carrying value of the receivable. Interest revenue is determined using the effective interest method.

- An ordinary loss is recognized for the difference between the carrying value of the receivable and the total payments.

- Any cash received in the future is treated as investment recovery.

The creditor does not recognize contingent interest until the contingency no longer exists and interest has been earned.

Any change in interest rates is treated as a change in estimate.

The following should be footnoted:

- Description of restructuring provisions (e.g., time period, interest rate)

- Outstanding commitments

- Receivables by major category

EXAMPLE

The debtor owes the creditor $80,000 and due to financial difficulties may be unable to make future payments. Footnote disclosure is required.

EXAMPLE

The debtor owes the creditor $70,000. The creditor relieves the debtor of $10,000, with the balance payable at a future date. The journal entries follow:

Debtor		
Accounts payable	10,000	
Extraordinary gain		10,000
Creditor		
Ordinary loss	10,000	
Accounts receivable		10,000

EXAMPLE

The debtor owes the creditor $90,000. The creditor commits to accept a 30% payment in full satisfaction of the obligation. The journal entries are

Debtor		
Accounts payable	27,000	
Extraordinary gain		27,000
Creditor		
Ordinary loss	27,000	
Accounts receivable		27,000

EXAMPLE

The following information applies to the transfer of property arising from a troubled debt restructuring:

Book value of liability liquidated	$300,000
Fair market value of property transferred	170,000
Book value of property transferred	210,000

The extraordinary gain on restructuring equals

Book value of liability liquidated	$300,000
Less: Fair market value of property transferred	170,000
Extraordinary gain	$130,000

The ordinary gain (loss) on the transfer of the property equals

Book value of property transferred	$210,000
Fair market value of property transferred	170,000
Ordinary loss	$ 40,000

Impairment of Loans

Financial Accounting Standards Board Statements Numbers 114 (*Accounting by Creditors for Impairment of a Loan*) and 118 (*Accounting by Creditors for Impairment of a Loan—Income Recognition and Disclosures*) apply to the accounting, reporting, and disclosures by a creditor for the impairment of a loan. They require creditors to determine the impaired value of a loan typically based on the discounted value of expected net cash flows associated with the loan. In addition to accounting for ensuing losses, appropriate footnote disclosure should be made. A number of methods may be used to determine how much impairment has occurred, including

- Present value of anticipated future cash flows discounted at the loan's effective interest rate
- The loan's market price
- The face value of the collateral (assuming probable foreclosure)

The creditor records the impaired value of the loan as a debit to bad debts expense and a credit to the valuation allowance.

The creditor may recognize income on an impaired loan using the cost recovery method, cash basis method, or a combination.

The creditor should disclose, either in the body or footnotes to the financial statements, the following:

- Total investment in impaired loans along with valuation allowances
- Method used and interest revenue recorded on impaired loans
- Credit losses incurred

REFINANCING SHORT-TERM DEBT TO LONG-TERM DEBT

According to Financial Accounting Standards Board Statement Number 6 (*Classification of Short-Term Obligations Expected to be Refinanced*), a short-term debt should be reclassified as a long-term debt when either of the following conditions apply:

1. After year-end but before the audit report date, the short-term debt is rolled over into a long-term debt, or an equity security is issued in substitution.

2. Before the audit report date, the company contracts to refinance the current debt on a long-term basis and all of the following conditions are satisfied:

— Agreement is for a period of one year or more.

— No provision of the agreement has been violated.

— The parties are financially sound and therefore able to satisfy all of the requirements of the agreement.

When debt is reclassified from short term to long term, it should be classified under long-term liabilities, not stockholders' equity, even if equity securities were issued in substitution of the debt.

If short-term debt is excluded from current liabilities, the amount of short-term debt excluded from current liabilities should be the minimum amount expected to be refinanced based on conservatism.

Caution: The exclusion from current liabilities cannot exceed the net proceeds of debt or security issuances, or amounts available under the refinancing agreement. The latter amount must be adjusted for any restrictions in the contract that limit the amount available to pay off the short-term debt. If a reasonable estimate is not ascertainable from the agreement, the full amount must be classified as current debt. Further, a refinancing intent may be absent if the contractual provisions permit the lender or investor to establish unrealistic interest rates, security, or other related terms.

The refinancing of one short-term obligation with another is not sufficient to demonstrate the ability to refinance on a long-term basis.

FASB Interpretation Number 8 (*Classification of Short-Term Obligation Repaid Prior to Being Replaced by a Long-Term Security*) stipulates that if cash is paid for the short-term debt, even if long-term debt of a similar amount is issued the next day, the short-term debt should be presented under current liabilities because cash was paid.

Footnote disclosure is required of the amount excluded for current liabilities. Disclosure is also mandated of the contractual terms and any noncurrent debt or equity securities issued or expected to be issued in substitution of the short-term debt.

CALLABLE OBLIGATIONS BY THE CREDITOR

Financial Accounting Standards Board Statement Number 78 (*Classification of Obligations That Are Callable by the Creditor*) deals with long-term debt callable or payable on demand by the creditor. If the debtor violates the debt agreement, and the long-term obligation therefore becomes callable, include the debt as a current liability, except if one of the following conditions exists:

- The creditor waives or loses his or her right to require repayment for a period exceeding one year from the balance sheet date. Refer to Emerging Issues Task Force Consensus Summary Number 86–30 (*Classification of Obligations When a Violation Is Waived by the Creditor*).
- There exists a grace period under which it is probable that the debtor will cure the violation.

FASB Technical Bulletin Number 79–3 (*Subjective Acceleration Clauses in Long-Term Debt Agreements*) defines a subjective acceleration clause as one allowing the lender unilaterally to accelerate all or part of a noncurrent debt. For example, the lender in its sole discretion may accelerate repayment of the debt if it is believed that the borrower is experiencing significant profitability or cash difficulties. If it is probable that the acceleration provision will be enforced by the lender, the amount of the noncurrent debt likely to be accelerated should be classified as a current liability by the debtor. However, if acceleration by the lender is only reasonably possible, footnote disclosure is sufficient. If a remote possibility exists as to acceleration, no disclosure is needed.

An objective acceleration clause in a long-term debt agreement includes objective criteria to assess calling all or part of the debt. Examples are setting forth a minimum cash position or a minimum current ratio. If there is a violation of an objective acceleration provision, most noncurrent debts become callable immediately by the lender, or are callable after some predetermined grace period. In such cases, the creditor may demand repayment of all or part of the debt due as per the contract.

Footnote disclosure is required for the reasons and circumstances surrounding callable obligations and their balance sheet classification. Subsequent event disclosure is required when the violation occurs after year-end but before the audit report date.

Other reference sources are Emerging Issues Task Force Consensus Summaries Numbers 86–5 (*Classifying Demand Notes with Repayment Terms*) and 95–22 (*Balance Sheet Classification of Borrowings Outstanding Under Revolving Credit Agreements That Include Both a Subjective Acceleration Clause and a Lock-Box Arrangement*).

INDUCEMENT OFFER TO CONVERT DEBT TO EQUITY

Financial Accounting Standards Board Statement Number 84 (*Induced Conversions of Convertible Debt*) states that if convertible debt is converted to stock because of an inducement offer where the debtor changes the conversion privileges (e.g., conversion price, issuance of warrants), the debtor records an expense. Convertible debt is not an extraordinary item. The amount of expense equals the fair market value of the securities transferred in excess of the fair market value of the securities issuable based on the original conversion terms. The fair market value is measured at the earlier of the conversion date or agreement date. If the additional inducement is comprised of stock, the market value of the stock is credited to common stock at par value, with the excess over par credited to paid-in-capital and with the offsetting debit to debt conversion expense. If the additional inducement is assets, then the market value of the assets is credited with an offsetting charge to debt conversion expense. For example, the inducement may be in the form of cash or property.

FASB Statement Number 84 applies only to induced conversions that may be exercised for a limited time period and involve the issuance of at least or more than the equity securities required under the original conversion terms.

An inducement offer may be achieved by giving debtholders

■ Payment of additional consideration

■ A higher conversion ratio

■ Other favorable changes in terms

EXAMPLE

On April 1, 19X1, a company issued $500,000 8% bonds. Each $1,000 bond is convertible into 15 shares of common stock having a par value of $30. On July 1, 19X3, the company offers to increase the conversion rate to 18 shares per $1,000 bond to induce conversion through this "sweetener." The debtholders accept this offer. At this date, the market value of the stock is $50 per share. Therefore, the additional consideration given as an inducement to the holders of the $500,000 bonds will be $75,000, computed as follows:

$$(\$500,000/\$1,000) = 500 \text{ bonds}$$
$$500 \text{ bonds} \times 3 \text{ shares per } \$1,000 \text{ bond} = 1500 \text{ shares}$$

Fair market value of additional consideration equals

$$1500 \text{ shares} \times \$50 = \$75,000$$

The journal entry for the conversion is:

Bonds payable	500,000	
Debt conversion expense	75,000	
Common stock (9,000 shares* × $30)		270,000
Paid-in-capital		305,000

*500 bonds × 18 shares per bond = 9,000 bonds

EXAMPLE

A company has outstanding $400,000 of convertible bonds issued at par value. Each $1,000 bond is convertible into 12 shares of $20 par value common stock. To induce bondholders to convert, the company increased the conversion rate from 12 shares per $1,000 bond to 16 shares per $1,000 bond. When the market price of the stock was $25, one bondholder converted his $1,000 bond. The amount of incremental consideration is $100 (4 additional shares × $25). The journal entry is

Bonds payable	1,000	
Debt conversion expense	100	
Common stock (16 shares × $20)		320
Paid-in-capital		780

EXAMPLE

Convertible bonds with a face value of $100,000 were the subject of an induced conversion by giving in exchange no par common stock having a fair value of $103,000. The journal entry is

Bonds payable	100,000	
Debt conversion expense	3,000	
Common stock—no par		103,000

EXAMPLE

A bondholder is holding a $10,000 face value convertible bond. Each $1,000 bond is convertible into 50 shares of stock having a par value of $12. To induce conversion, the company offers the bondholder land having a fair market value of $1,500. The cost of the land is $1,200. The journal entries associated with the induced conversion are

Land	300	
Gain		300

To increase land to fair value to use as inducement

Bonds payable	10,000	
Debt conversion expense	1,500	
Land		1,500
Common stock (500* shares × $12)		6,000
Paid-in-capital		4,000

*$10,000/$1,000 = 10 bonds.

$$10 \text{ bonds} \times 50 \text{ shares} = 500 \text{ shares.}$$

If the debtor places cash or other assets in an irrevocable trust to be used only to pay interest and principal on the obligation, disclosure is required of the particulars concerning the transaction and the amount of debt considered extinguished.

ACCOUNTING FOR BONDS PAYABLE

The yield on a bond may be calculated based on either the simple yield or yield to maturity (effective interest) methods.

$$\text{Simple yield} = \text{Nominal interest/Present value of bond}$$

$$\text{Yield to maturity} = \frac{\text{Nominal interest} + \text{Discount/Years (or} - \text{Premium/Years)}}{(\text{Present value} + \text{Maturity value})/2}$$

Simple yield is less accurate than yield to maturity.

EXAMPLE

A $300,000, 8%, 10-year bond is issued at 98%.

$$\text{Simple yield} = \frac{\text{Nominal interest}}{\text{Present value of bond}}$$

$$\frac{\$24,000}{\$294,000} = 8.16\%$$

$$\text{Yield to maturity} =$$

$$\frac{\text{Nominal interest} + \text{Discount/Years}}{(\text{Present value} + \text{Maturity value/2})}$$

$$\frac{\$24,000 + \$6,000/10}{(\$294,000 + \$300,000)/2} = 8.28\%$$

If a bond is sold at a discount, yield will exceed the nominal interest rate. However, if a bond is sold at a premium, yield will be less than the nominal interest rate.

A bond discount or premium may be amortized using either the straight-line method or the effective interest method (scientific amortization). The latter method is preferred because it results in a better matching of periodic expense with revenue. Under the straight-line method, the amortization per period results in a fixed dollar amount but at a varying effective rate. Under the effective interest method, the amortization per period results in a constant rate of interest but a varying dollar amount.

The amortization entry under the effective interest method is

Interest expense (Yield × Carrying value of bond at the beginning of the year)

   Discount (for balance)

      Cash (nominal interest rate × face value of bond)

In the early years, using the effective interest method results in a lower amortization amount relative to the straight-line method (either for discount or premium).

EXAMPLE

On January 1, 19X3, a $200,000 bond is issued at 98%. The yield rate is 5% and the nominal interest rate is 4%. The effective interest method is used. A schedule for the first two years follows.

Date	Debit Interest Expense	Credit Cash	Credit Discount	Book Value
1/1/19X3				$196,000
12/31/19X3	$9,800	$8,000	$1,800	194,200
12/31/19X4	9,710	8,000	1,710	192,490

Note: Interest expense is decreasing because the carrying value of the bond is decreasing.

On 12/31/19X3, the journal entry is

Interest expense	9,800	
Cash		8,000
Discount		1,800

EXAMPLE

On January 1, 19X8, a company issued 10% bonds with a face value of $600,000 for $560,000 to yield 11%. Interest is payable semiannually on January 1 and July 1. The effective interest method of amortization is used. The journal entries for 19X8 are

1/1/19X8		
Cash	560,000	
Discount on bonds payable	40,000	
Bonds payable		600,000
7/1/19X8		
Interest expense (11% × $560,000 × 6/12)	30,800	
Cash (10% × $600,000 × 6/12)		30,000
Discount on bonds payable		800

The book value of the bonds on July 1, 19X8 after the preceding entry is as follows:

Bonds payable	$600,000	
Less: Discount on bonds payable ($40,000 – $800)	39,200	
Book value	$560,800	
12/31/19X8		
Interest expense (11% × $560,800 × 6/12)	30,844	
Cash (10% × $600,000 × 6/12)		30,000
Discount on bonds payable		844

EXAMPLE

Cohen Company has outstanding an 8%, 10-year, $200,000 bond. The bond was initially issued to yield 7%. Amortization is based on the effective interest method. On July 1, 19X5, the carrying value of the bond was $225,000. The unamortized premium on the bond on July 1, 19X6 was $24,750, computed as follows:

Unamortized premium—7/1/19X5 ($225,000 – $200,000)		$25,000
Less: Amortized premium for the year-ended 7/1/19X6:		
Nominal interest ($200,000 × 8%)	$16,000	
Effective interest ($225,000 × 7%)	15,750	250
Unamortized premium—7/1/19X6		$24,750

Bonds payable may be issued between interest dates at a premium or discount. If a bond is issued between interest dates, the journal entry is

Cash
Discount (or credit premium)
Bonds payable
Interest expense

EXAMPLE

On April 1, 19X3, a $500,000, 8% bond with a five-year life is issued at 106%. Interest is payable on 1/1 and 7/1. The company uses the straight-line amortization method. The journal entries are

4/1/19X3

Cash ($530,000 + $10,000)	540,000	
Bonds payable		500,000
Premium on bonds payable ($500,000 × 6%)		30,000
Interest expense ($500,000 × 8% x 3/12)		10,000

7/1/19X3

Interest expense	20,000	
Cash		20,000
Premium on bonds payable	1,578	
Interest expense		1,578

4/1/19X3 – 7/1/19X8 = 4 years, 9 months = 57 months

$30,000/57 = $526 per month (rounded)

4/1/19X3 – 7/1/19X3 = 3 months

3 months x $526 – $1,578

12/31/19X3

Interest expense	20,000	
Interest payable		20,000
Premium on bonds payable	3,156	
Interest expense		3,156

6 months × $526 = $3,156

1/1/19X4

Interest payable	20,000	
Cash		20,000

Bonds Payable is presented in the balance sheet at its book value in the following manner:

Bonds payable

Add: Premium on bonds payable

Less: Discount on bonds payable

Carrying Value

Bond issue costs are the expenditures incurred in issuing bonds, such as legal, accounting, underwriting, commissions, registration, engraving, and printing fees. Bond issue costs should preferably be deferred and amortized over the life of the bond. They are presented as a deferred charge. However, two alternative acceptable methods exist to account for bond issue costs: to expense such costs immediately or to treat them as a reduction of bonds payable.

Serial bonds (bonds maturing in installments) may be issued as if each series were a separate bond issue or as one issue having varying maturity dates. In most cases, each series has the same interest rate and yield but different issue prices, depending upon their maturity period. One discount or premium account exists for all the bonds in the series. The effective interest method is used in determining amortization of the discount or premium.

The price of a bond is calculated as follows:

■ The face value is discounted using the present value of $1 table.

■ Interest payments are discounted using the present value of ordinary annuity of $1 table.

■ Yield is used as the discount rate.

EXAMPLE

A $100,000 10-year bond is issued at an 8% nominal interest rate. Interest is payable semiannually. The yield rate is 10%. The present value of $1 table factor for $n = 20$, $i = 5\%$ is 12.46221. The price of the bond is

Present value of principal $100,000 × .37689	$37,689
Present value of interest payments $4,000 × 12.46221	49,849
Present value	$87,538

The issuance of convertible bonds usually allows the company to issue the securities at a lower interest rate with less restrictions compared to a straight bond. When issued, the face value of the convertible bond will be more than the market value of the stock that it is convertible into. Further, at issuance no value is assigned to the conversion feature. The sale is only recorded as the issuance of debt. The conversion price is typically set at about 15% more than the market price of the stock when the convertible bond is issued. Unless due to antidilution, the conversion price remains the same. There may be a call feature allowing the issuer to call the bonds back before maturity. As the value of the stock increases, so does the value of the convertible bond. When the market value of the shares associated with the convertible bond exceeds the face value of the debt, the holder will benefit by converting the debt into shares. Alternatively, in such a situation the issuer may force conversion. If the market price of the stock remains the same or goes down, the holder of the convertible bond will not convert it into the stock. This is referred to as an overhanging bond. In other words, a holder will not convert if the market value of the common stock is less than the face value of the convertible bond. When this occurs, the issuer has a number of options such as either exercising the call feature and paying the bondholders the face amount of the bond, or providing an inducement in the form of additional consideration to convert, or waiting until maturity to pay the principal of the debt. In bankruptcy, the convertible bond is subordinate to nonconvertible debt.

The strongly preferred and widely used method to account for the conversion of a bond into stock is the book value of bond method. A drawback to the book value method is that it fails to recognize in the accounting for the conversion the total value of the equity security issued. Although much less desirable, in a few exceptional cases when justified, the market value of bond or market value of stock method might be used. **Special Note:** The market value method is rarely used in practice and may be precluded under Accounting Interpretation Number 1 of APB Opinion Number 26 (*Early Extinguishment of Debt*).

Under the book value of bond method, there is no gain or loss reported on bond conversion because the book value of the bond is the basis to credit equity. The entry to record the conversion using this method follows:

Bonds payable: At face value

Premium on bonds payable: Unamortized amount

Discount on bonds payable: Unamortized amount

Common stock: At par value of shares issued

> *Paid-in-capital:* For the difference between the book value of the
> bonds and the par value of common stock

Under the market value methods, gain or loss arises because the book value of the bond differs from the market value of the bond or market value of the stock, which is the basis to credit the equity account.

EXAMPLE

A $200,000 bond with an unamortized premium of $17,000 is converted to common stock. There are 200 bonds ($200,000/$1,000). Each bond is convertible into 100 shares of stock. Therefore, there are 20,000 shares of common stock to be issued. Par value per share is $8. The market value of the stock is $12 per share. The market value of the bond is 115.

Using the book value of bond method, the journal entry for the conversion is

Bonds payable	200,000	
Premium on bonds payable	17,000	
Common stock (20,000 × $8)		160,000
Premium on common stock		57,000

Using the market value of stock method, the journal entry is

Bonds payable	200,000	
Premium on bonds payable	17,000	
Loss on bond conversion	23,000	
Common stock (20,000 × $8)		160,000
Premium on common stock (20,000 × $4)		80,000
20,000 shares × $12 = $240,000		

Using the market value of bond method, the journal entry is

Bonds payable	200,000	
Premium on bonds payable	17,000	
Loss on bond conversion	13,000	
Common stock (20,000 × $8)		160,000
Premium on common stock		70,000
$200,000 × 115% = $230,000		

EXAMPLE

On July 1, 19X6, Klemer Company converted $1,000,000 of its 10% convertible bonds into 25,000 shares of $3 par value common stock. On the date of the conversion the book value of the bonds was $1,200,000, while the market value of the bonds was $1,250,000 and the market price of the stock was $54 per share. Using the preferred book value of bond method, the journal entry would be

Bonds payable	1,000,000	
Premium on bonds payable	200,000	
Common Stock (25,000 × $3)		75,000
Paid-in-capital		1,125,000

EXAMPLE

A convertible bond having a face value of $80,000 with an unamortized discount of $5,000 is converted into 10,000 shares of $6 par value stock. Under the book value method, the journal entry for the conversion is

Bonds payable	80,000	
Discount on bonds payable	5,000	
Common stock (10,000 × $6)		60,000
Paid-in-capital		25,000

Emerging Issues Task Force Consensus Summary Number 85–17 (*Accrued Interest upon Conversion of Convertible Debt*) states that if the debt agreement specifies that accrued interest at the conversion date is forfeited by the bondholder, such accrued interest (net of tax) since the last interest date to the date of conversion should be treated as interest expense, with a corresponding credit to capital, because it is considered an element of the cost of the securities issued.

Other authoritative sources of GAAP with regard to convertible debt are Emerging Issues Task Force Consensus Summaries Numbers 87–25 (*Sale of Convertible, Adjustable-Rate Mortgages with Contingent Repayment Agreement*) and 90–19 (*Convertible Bonds with Issuer Option to Settle for Cash upon Conversion*).

EARLY EXTINGUISHMENT OF DEBT

The American Institute of CPAs' Accounting Principles Board Opinion Number 26 (*Early Extinguishment of Debt*), Accounting Interpretations of APB Opinion Number 26, Financial Accounting Standards Board Statement Number 4 (*Reporting Gains and Losses from Extinguishment of Debt*), FASB Statement Number 76 (*Extinguishment of Debt*), and FASB Statement Number 125 (*Accounting for Transfers and Servicing of Financial Assets and Extinguishments of Liabilities*) cover the accounting, reporting, and disclosures associated with retiring debt early. Long-term debt may be called before its maturity date and new debt issued instead at a lower interest rate. On the other hand, the company may just retire the long-term debt early because it has excess funds and wants to avoid paying interest charges and having debt on its balance sheet. (A call provision allows the issuer the right to retire all or part of the debt prior to the maturity date, typically at a premium price.)

If a defeasance clause exists instead of a call provision, the issuer may satisfy the obligation and receive a lien release without retiring the debt. In a defeasance arrangement, the old debt is satisfied under law with a gain or loss being recognized.

Special Note: FASB Statement Number 125 supersedes FASB Statement Number 76 and FASB Technical Bulletin Number 84–4 (*In-Substance Defeasance of Debt*). FASB Statement Number 125 no longer permits in-substance defeasance as an option to extinguish debt.

According to FASB Statement Number 125, when financial assets are transferred, any resulting debt or derivatives must be measured initially at fair value. The amortization of a servicing liability is proportionate based on the time period associated with the net servicing loss or gain. A change in fair value must be also considered. Disclosure is required of the nature of any limitations placed on assets set aside to pay debt payments.

FASB Statement Number 125 also addresses the issue of a debtor becoming secondarily liable, such as because of a third-party assumption and a creditor's release. In this case, the original party is considered a guarantor. It is necessary to recognize a guarantee obligation based on the likelihood that the third party will pay. The guarantee obligation must initially be recognized at fair value. The guarantee obligation serves either to reduce the gain or increase the loss on debt extinguishment.

In an advance refunding arrangement, new debt is issued to replace the old debt issue that cannot be called. The amount received from issuing the new debt is used to buy high-quality investments, which are retained in an escrow account. The income earned on the investments in the escrow account is used to pay the interest and/or principal on the existing debt for a period ending on the date the existing debt is callable. When the call of the existing date occurs, the balance in the escrow account is used to pay the call premium. Any residual remaining is used to pay any interest due on the existing debt as well as the principal balance.

The reacquisition price for debt includes the call premium and any other associated costs (e.g., prepayment penalties, reacquisition costs) to buy back the debt. If the extinguishment is based on the issuance of securities, the reacquisition price is the fair value of the securities issued. The net carrying amount of the debt extinguished is its book value (including any associated unamortized discount or premium) and any other issuance costs (e.g., accounting, underwriter's commissions, legal). Any unamortized bond issue costs reduce the carrying value. FASB Technical Bulletin Number 80–1 (*Early Extinguishment of Debt through Exchange for Common or Preferred Stock*) stipulates that the gain or loss on extinguishment is based on either the fair value of the stock issued in exchange for the debt or the value of the debt extinguished, whichever is more clearly evident.

The gain or loss on the retirement of debt equals the difference between the retirement price and the carrying value of the bonds. The gain or loss on an early extinguishment of debt is an extraordinary item. It is presented net of tax. Extraordinary classification is given whether the extinguishment is early, at maturity, or later. **Exception:** According to FASB Statement Number 64 (*Extinguishments of Debt Made to Satisfy Sinking Fund Requirements*), the gain or loss is ordinary if it is due to meeting a sinking fund requirement that has to be paid within one year of the date of extinguishment. This also applies to debt having characteristics comparable to sinking fund requirements such as an agreement to extinguish debt annu-ally based on a predetermined ratio. **Note:** As per FASB Statement Number 4, serial bonds do not have characteristics of sinking fund requirements. As such, any associated gains or losses associated with serial bond extin-guishment are extraordinary.

Debt is considered extinguished when the debtor is relieved of the principal liability and will most likely not need to make future payments. This occurs when either the debtor pays the debt or reacquires the debt in the securities market, or the debtor is legally discharged and it is probable that the debtor will not need to make future payments as guarantor of the obligation. The latter occurs when the debtor is legally discharged as the primary obligor but is secondarily liable for the debt.

EXAMPLE

A $300,000 bond payable with an unamortized bond discount of $7,000 is called at 90%. The journal entry is

Bonds payable	300,000	
Discount on bonds payable		7,000
Cash (90% × $300,000)		270,000
Extraordinary gain		23,000

EXAMPLE

On January 1, 19X8, a company called 500 outstanding, 8%, $1,000 face value bonds at 108%. The unamortized bond premium on this date was $25,000. The journal entry is

Bonds payable	500,000	
Premium on bonds payable	25,000	
Extraordinary loss	15,000	
Cash ($500,000 × 108%)		540,000

EXAMPLE

A bond having a face value of $300,000 and an unamortized discount of $8,000 is called at 102%. Unamortized deferred issue costs representing legal and accounting fees are $12,000. The journal entry for the extinguishment is

Bonds payable	300,000	
Extraordinary loss	26,000	
Cash ($300,000 × 102%)		306,000
Discount on bonds payable		8,000
Deferred issue costs		12,000

If an early extinguishment of debt is achieved via an exchange of securities, the acquisition price equals the total par value of the new securities.

No gain or loss arises from an early extinguishment of a fully owned subsidiary's mandatory preferred stock by the parent company. It should be accounted for as a capital transaction.

There should be footnote disclosure in one footnote or cross-referenced footnotes concerning the extinguishment as follows:

- Description of the extinguishment transaction including the funding used for it
- Income tax effects
- Per share gain or loss (net of tax)
- Direct and indirect guarantees of indebtedness of others (this includes a situation in which the debtor is released as the primary obligor but is contingently liable).

Emerging Issues Task Force Consensus Summary Number 95–15 (*Recognition of Gain or Loss When a Binding Contract Requires a Debt Extinguishment to Occur at a Future Date for a Specified Amount*) stipulates that when a debtor contracts with a holder of its debt to redeem the obligation within one year for a predetermined amount, it is classified as a current liability. The debtor recognizes an extraordinary loss when the contract becomes legally binding on the parties. However, a gain is not recognized until the redemption actually occurs.

Emerging Issues Task Force Consensus Summary Number 84–19 relates to modifications in mortgage loan payments.

EXTINGUISHMENT OF TAX-EXEMPT DEBT

FASB Statement Number 22 (*Changes in the Provisions of Lease Agreements Resulting from Refundings of Tax-Exempt Debt*) stipulates that if a modification is made to a rental because of a lessor's refunding of tax-exempt debt and the lessee receives the ensuing advantages and the modified lease qualifies as a capital lessee to the lessee or a direct financing lease to the lessor, the change in the lease may qualify as a debt extinguishment. If so, the lessee adjusts the lease debt to its discounted value of future minimum lease payments based on the modified (new) arrangement. The discount rate used is the interest rate associated with the new lease contract. An ensuing gain or loss is considered as being associated with an early debt extinguishment resulting in an extraordinary gain or loss. Meanwhile, the lessor adjusts its lease receivable account for the difference between the discounted value of payments associated with the old and modified (new) agreement. The ensuing gain or loss is recognized in the current year's income statement.

IMPUTING INTEREST ON NONINTEREST NOTES PAYABLE

APB Opinion Number 21 (*Interest on Receivables and Payables*) covers noninterest notes. If the face value of a note differs from the present value of the consideration transacted, interest imputation is required to avoid profit misstatement. Interest is imputed on noninterest notes, on notes with unreasonably low interest rates relative to market rates, and when a note's face value is substantially different from the prevailing selling price of the property or market value of the note.

If a note is issued just for cash, the note is recorded at the cash exchanged regardless of whether the interest rate is realistic or of the amount of the face value of the note. The present value of the note at the issue date is presumed to be the cash transacted.

If a note is exchanged for property, goods, or services, it is assumed that the interest rate is fair and appropriate. However, if the interest rate is not reasonable and adequate, the note must be recorded at the fair market value of the goods or services or at an amount approximating fair value. If fair value is nonascertainable for the product or service, the discounted present value of the note must be used.

The imputed interest rate is the one in which an independent borrower or lender would have engaged in a similar transaction. In determining the imputed interest rate, consideration should be given to such factors as credit rating, tax effect, collateral requirements, and restrictions.

EXAMPLE

It is the "going" interest rate the borrower would have paid for financing in an "arms-length" transaction. There are several considerations involved in determining an appropriate interest rate, such as prevailing market interest rates, the prime interest rate, security pledged, loan restrictions, issuer's financial position, tax rate, and tax planning issues.

EXAMPLE

ABC Company sells equipment to XYZ Company on January 1, 2001 in exchange for a $50,000 non-interest-bearing note due December 31, 2002. Assume that there is no established price for this equipment, and the prevailing interest rate for this type of note is 10%. The present value of $1 at 10% for 2 years is 0.826446. Interest income will be recognized by ABC Company each year and the discount amortized.

Date	Interest Income	Discount Amortized	Carrying Amount
1/1/2001			$41,322
12/31/2001	$4,132	4,132	45,454
12/31/2002	4,546*	4,546	50,000

*$1 adjustment for rounding

APB Opinion Number 21 applies to long-term payables and receivables. Short-term payables and receivables are usually recorded at face value because the additional work of amortizing a discount or premium on a short-term note does not justify the information benefit derived.

APB Opinion Number 21 is not applicable to receivables or payables in the ordinary course of business, amounts not requiring repayment, security deposits, parent/subsidiary transactions, and customary lending of banks and other similar financial institutions.

The difference between the face value of a note and its present value constitutes a discount or premium, which is to be treated as interest over the life of the note. The present value of the payments of the note depends on the imputed interest rate.

Discount or premium is amortized using the interest method, which results in a constant interest rate. Amortization equals the interest rate multiplied by the present value of the note payable at the beginning of the year.

The borrower recognizes interest expense while the lender recognizes interest revenue. Issuance costs are accounted for as a deferred charge.

The presentation of the note payable or note receivable in the balance sheet follows:

> Notes payable (principal and interest)
> Less: Discount (interest)
> Present value (principal)

> Notes receivable (principal and interest)
> Less: Premium (interest)
> Present value (principal)

EXAMPLE

On January 1, 19X3, a fixed asset is purchased for $40,000 cash and the incurrence of a $60,000, five-year, non-interest-bearing note payable. Assume an imputed interest rate of 10%. The present value factor for $n = 5$, $i = 10\%$ is .62. The journal entries follow:

1/1/19X3

Fixed asset ($40,000 + $37,200)	77,200	
Discount	22,800	
Notes payable		60,000
Cash		40,000

Present value of note = $60,000 × .62 = $37,200

On 1/1/19X3, the balance sheet presents

Notes payable	$60,000	
Less: Discount	22,800	
Present value	$37,200	
12/31/19X3		
Interest expense	3,720	
Discount		3,720

10% × $37,200 = $3,720

On 1/1/19X4, the balance sheet presents

Notes payable	$60,000	
Less: Discount ($22,800 − $3,720)	19,080	
Present value	$40,920	
12/31/19X4		
Interest expense	4,092	
Discount		4,092

10% × $40,920 = $4,092

ENVIRONMENTAL LIABILITIES

In determining a loss contingency to accrue for environmental liabilities, the following should be taken into account:

- Type and degree of hazardous waste at a site
- Remediation approaches available and remedial action plan
- Level of acceptable remediation
- Other responsible parties and their extent of liability

Securities and Exchange Commission Staff Accounting Bulletin Number 92 requires full disclosure of environmental problems, how environmental liabilities are determined, "key" factors associated with the environment as it affects the business, and future contingencies. Depending on the circumstances, a liability and/or footnote disclosure would be required. Examples of environmental importance requiring accounting or disclosure recognition based on the facts follow:

- Information on site remediation projects, such as current and future costs, and remediation trends (Site remediation may include hazard waste sites.)
- Contamination due to environmental health and safety problems
- Legal and regulatory compliance issues, such as with regard to cleanup responsibility
- Water or air pollution

Emerging Issues Task Force Consensus Summary Number 93–5 (*Accounting for Environmental Liabilities*) stipulates that if a liability for environmental losses is required, it should only be reduced when there is probable realization of recovery from a third party. However, both the liability and probable recovery must be shown separately. The present value of payments associated with a liability may be recognized only when the future cash flows are reliably determinable in amount and timing. If the liability is discounted, so must be the anticipated recovery. Disclosure is required of the gross cash flows and the discount rate used to determine present value.

Other authoritative guidance for the accrual and disclosure of environmental liabilities include FASB Interpretation Number 14 (*Reasonable Estimation of the Amount of a Loss*), FASB Interpretation Number 39 (*Offsetting Amounts Relating to Certain Contracts*), and Emerging Issues Task Force Consensus Summaries Numbers 89–13 (*Accounting for the Cost of Asbestos Removal*) and 90–8 (*Capitalization of Costs to Treat Environmental Contamination*).

Environmental costs should be allocated across departments, products, and services.

DISCLOSURE OF LONG-TERM OBLIGATIONS

According to Financial Accounting Standards Board Statement Number 47 (*Disclosure of Long-term Obligations*), the following must be disclosed with respect to long-term obligations for each of the five years following the balance sheet date:

- The total payments for unconditional purchase obligations which have been recognized on the purchaser's balance sheet. An unconditional purchase obligation is a duty to transfer a fixed or minimum amount of funds at a later date or to transfer products or services at constant or minimum prices.

- The combined aggregate amount of maturities and sinking fund requirements for all long-term borrowings.

- The amount of redemption requirements for all issues of capital stock that are redeemable at fixed or determinable prices on fixed or determinable dates.

COMMITMENTS

Footnote disclosure may be required of commitments, including their description and amount. Examples of such commitments are those associated with forward exchange contracts; employment agreements; agreements not to acquire another company, to reduce debt by a certain amount, not to issue debt, and not to issue debt exceeding a specified amount; agreements to maintain a minimum ratio (e.g., current ratio); and agreements to purchase a specified amount of assets.

EXAMPLE

On January 1, 20X5, Walter Company entered into a three-year noncancelable contract to buy up to 600,000 units of a product each year at $.15 per unit with a minimum annual guarantee purchase of 150,000. At year-end 20X5, 280,000 units of inventory were in stock. It is expected that each unit can be sold as scrap for $.04 per unit. The probable loss on the purchase commitment to be recorded in 20X5 is

(150,000 units × 2 years remaining on contract × $.11 unit cost) = $33,000

OFFSETTING ASSETS AND LIABILITIES

In most cases, debts owed between two parties, a debtor and creditor, may be offset. However, a right to set off may be prohibited or restricted under federal or state bankruptcy law if the debtor is filing for bankruptcy. When related assets and liabilities are offset because of a right of setoff, they are shown in the balance sheet as a net amount.

FASB Technical Bulletin Number 88–2 (*Definition of a Right of Setoff*) applies to Accounting Principles Board Opinion Number 10 (*Omnibus Opinion*). An asset may be used to offset a liability if all of the following conditions are satisfied:

1. The reporting entity intends to set off.
2. A contractual right of setoff exists.
3. The setoff is legal.
4. Each of the two parties owes a determinable amount.

Note: A setoff right is a debtor's legal right to discharge an obligation owed another by applying against the obligation funds the other party owes the debtor.

An asset and liability may still be offset if they are in different currencies or have different interest rates associated with them. However, if the maturities of the asset and liability differ, only the company with the earlier maturity may offset.

A government security can only be used to offset a tax obligation if the security can be used as a direct offset of taxes due.

FASB Interpretation Number 39 (*Offsetting of Amounts Related to Certain Contracts*) may allow for the offsetting of fair value amounts associated with forward, multiple swap, option, and conditional or exchange contracts in a master netting arrangement. In other words, the fair value of contracts with a loss may offset the fair value of contracts with a gain. Reference may be made to Emerging Issues Task Force Consensus Summary Number 86–25 (*Offsetting Foreign Currency Swaps*).

FASB Interpretation Number 41 (*Offsetting of Amounts Related to Certain Repurchase and Reverse Repurchase Agreements*) discusses when amounts recognized as payables in repurchase contracts may be used to offset the amounts attributable to receivables in reverse repurchase agreements. Once a decision is made to offset or not to offset, it must be applied consistently. An offset of the payables and receivables is allowed if all of the following conditions are satisfied:

1. The reporting company will use the same account at the clearing financial institution at the settlement date to transact the cash inflows and cash outflows associated with the contracts.

2. There are adequate funds available at the settlement date for each party.

3. The agreements are executed with the same counterparty.

4. A master netting arrangement is involved.

5. The settlement dates are the same for both agreements.

6. The underlying securities are in "book entry" form.

An insurance recovery cannot be used to offset the associated litigation liability since they do not involve the same two parties. **Recall:** A condition for setoff is that the two parties have a receivable and payable of determinable amounts.

Emerging Issues Task Force Consensus Summary Number 84–11 (*Offsetting Installment Notes Receivables and Bank Debt*) stipulates that a seller is not allowed to offset an installment note receivable against a bank debt with recourse irrespective of whether the debt has a put option associated with it, making the debt a secured nonrecourse obligation.

Other sources of reference related to offsetting are Emerging Issues Task Force Consensus Summaries Numbers 84–25 (*Offsetting Nonrecourse Debt with Sales-Type or Direct Financing Lease Receivables*) and 87–20 (*Offsetting Certificates of Deposit Against High-Coupon Debt*).

Annual Report References

GENERAL SEMICONDUCTOR
1998 ANNUAL REPORT

6. Accrued Expenses

Accrued expenses consist of:

	December 31, 1998	December 31, 1997
Salaries and compensation liabilities	$14,355	$14,849
Distribution and reorganization liabilities	—	1 8,734
Restructuring liabilities	7,809	—
Benefit plan liabilities	7,709	4,916
Other	15,211	19,853
Total	$45,084	$58,352

In connection with the Distribution, the Company recorded in income (loss) from continuing operations a pre-tax charge of $32.7 million to cost of sales and $1.1 million to selling, general and administrative expenses during the year ended December 31, 1997. These costs relate to employees of General Semiconductor and were incurred in connection with the separation of the Taiwan operations between General Semiconductor and General Instrument.

On November 6, 1998 the Company announced a restructuring plan designed to enhance the interface of operations and customers, to improve its cost structure, efficiency and its competitive position and to accelerate growth. The restructuring included reducing the workforce by decentralizing certain purchasing, marketing, finance and research and development functions and providing early retirement to a group of employees, closing two sales offices and writing off assets related to an unprofitable product that will no longer be manufactured. Restructuring charges recorded in the fourth quarter included approximately $8.4 million in charges primarily related to severance and early retirement costs and $3.9 million in non-cash charges for asset write-offs.

JC PENNEY
1999 ANNUAL REPORT

6. Short-Term Debt

($ in millions)	1999	1998
Commercial paper	$330	$1,924
Average interest rate at year-end	6.3%	5.1%

The decline in short-term debt as of the end of 1999 is the result of paying down commercial paper balances with the proceeds from the sale of the Company's proprietary credit card receivables in December 1999. Committed bank credit facilities available to the Company as of January 29, 2000 totaled $3.0 billion. The facilities, as amended and restated in 1999, support the Company's short-term borrowing program and are comprised of a $1.5 billion, 364-day revolver (expires September 29, 2000) and a $1.5 billion, five-year revolver (expires November 21, 2002). None of the borrowing facilities was in use as of January 29, 2000.

The Company also has $1 billion uncommitted credit lines in the form of letters of credit with seven banks to support its direct import merchandise program. As of January 29, 2000, $404 million of letters of credit issued by the Company were outstanding.

COCA-COLA
1998 ANNUAL REPORT

6. Long-Term Debt

Long-term debt consists of the following (in millions):

December 31,	1998	1997
5 3/4% German mark notes due 1998	$ —	$ 141
7 7/8% U.S. dollar notes due 1998	—	250
6% U.S. dollar notes due 2000	251	251
6 5/8% U.S. dollar notes due 2002	150	150
6% U.S. dollar notes due 2003	150	150
7 3/8% U.S. dollar notes due 2093	116	116
Other, due 1999 to 2013	23	140
	690	1,198
Less current portion	3	397
	$687	$ 801

After giving effect to interest rate management instruments (see Note 9), the principal amount of our long-term debt that had fixed and variable interest rates, respectively, was $190 million and $500 million on December 31, 1998, and $480 million and $718 million on December 31, 1997. The weighted-average interest rate on our Company's long-term debt was 6.2 percent for the years ended December 31, 1998 and 1997. Total interest paid was approximately $298 million, $264 million and $31 5 million in 1998, 1997 and 1996, respectively.

Maturities of long-term debt for the five years succeeding December 31, 1998, are as follows (in millions):

1999	2000	2001	2002	2003
$3	$254	$17	$150	$150

The above notes include various restrictions, none of which is presently significant to our Company.

POLAROID
1999 ANNUAL REPORT

Long-term debt outstanding as of December 31 was as follows:

(In millions)	1998	1999
$6^3/_4\%$ Notes	$149.0	**$149.3**
$7^1/_4\%$ Notes	148.4	**148.7**
8% Notes	200.0	—
$11^1/_2\%$ Notes	—	**275.0**
Total	$497.4	**$573.0**

On January 14, 1997, the Company issued $300.0 million in debt securities consisting of $150 million $7^1/_4\%$ Notes due January 15, 2007 (the "2007 Notes") and $150 million $6^3/_4\%$ Notes due January 15, 2002 (the "2002 Notes") to refinance existing debt. The 2007 Notes were placed with a discount at a price of 99.43% of par with a yield of 7.33%. The 2002 Notes were placed with a discount, at a price of 99.53% of par with a yield of 6.86%. The net proceeds from the sale of the Notes were used primarily for the payment of $150.0 million principal amount of the Company's $7^1/_4\%$ Notes due January 15, 1997 and to exercise the Company's right to repurchase the remaining principal amount of its $139.5 million 8% Subordinated Convertible Debentures due 2001. The balance of the net proceeds were used for general corporate purposes.

In February 1999, the Company issued $275 million of $11^1/_2\%$ Notes due February 15, 2006 (the "2006 Notes"). The 2006 Notes were placed at par value. The net proceeds of $268 million from the sale of the 2006 Notes were used primarily for the payment of $200 million aggregate principal amount of the Company's 8% Notes which were due on March 15, 1999 and for general corporate purposes, including reducing amounts outstanding under the Amended Credit Agreement and short-term lines of credit. Because the Company intended to refinance the 8% Notes, the principal amount of these notes were classified as a long-term note payable on December 31, 1998. The indenture, pursuant to which the 2006 Notes were issued, contains certain covenants that restrict, among other things: the Company and its subsidiaries from making certain restricted payments, including dividends on and the purchase of the Company's common stock and certain other payments; incurring additional debt and issuing preferred stock; incurring certain liens; entering into sale leaseback transactions; entering into certain transactions with affiliates and entering into certain mergers and consolidations or selling all or substantially all of the properties or assets of the Company.

The $200 million 8% Notes due March 15, 1999 (the "8% Notes") were issued with a discount and were not redeemable prior to maturity.

In February 2000, the Company filed a shelf registration statement with the Securities and Exchange Commission to issue securities of up to $275.0 million. When combined with $225.0 million of securities that remain unissued under an existing shelf registration statement, the Company can issue up to an additional $500.0 million of debt securities, preferred stock, depository shares, common stock, preferred stock rights, stock purchase contracts, stock purchase units, warrants and warrant units.

The aggregate scheduled repayments on long-term debt outstanding at December 31, 1999 were $150.0 million in 2002 and $425.0 million in 2005 and thereafter.

RAYTHEON
1997 ANNUAL REPORT

I. Notes Payable

(In millions)	Notes payable consisted of the following at December 31: 1997	1996
Notes payable	$3,641	$ 63
Commercial paper	2,010	2,156
Weighted average interest rate		
Average notes payable	6.37%	6.51%
Average commercial paper	6.11%	5.40%
Notes payable at December 31	6.30%	5.11%
Commercial paper at December 31	6.46%	5.53%
Aggregate borrowings outstanding		
Maximum month-end balance	$5,744	$3,136
Average during the year	$3,472	$2,890

Credit lines or commitments with banks were maintained by subsidiary companies amounting to $252 million and $188 million in 1997 and 1996, respectively. Compensating balance arrangements are not material. In addition, lines of credit with certain commercial banks exist as sources of direct borrowing and/or as a standby facility to support the issuance of commercial paper by the company. The lines of credit were $9.0 billion and $3.5 billion at December 31, 1997 and 1996, respectively. At December 31, 1997, $3.5 billion had been borrowed under the lines of credit. Total interest payments were $295 million, $257 million, and $160 million for 1997, 1996, and 1995, respectively.

J. Long-term Debt

(In millions)	Long-term debt consisted of the following at December 31: 1997	1996
3 year 6.3% notes due 2000, not redeemable prior to maturity	$ 498	$ —
5 year 6.45% notes due 2002, not redeemable prior to maturity	975	—
10 year 6.5% notes due 2005, not redeemable prior to maturity	733	730
10 year 6.75% notes due 2007, not redeemable prior to maturity	957	—
30 year 7.375% debentures due 2025, redeemable after July 15, 2005	362	362
30 year 7.2% debentures due 2027, not redeemable prior to maturity	464	—
Commercial paper backed by 5 year fixed for variable interest rate swap at 6.40%	375	375
Notes (including $16 million and $19 million at December 31, 1997 and 1996, respectively, of mortgage notes and industrial revenue bonds) interest in the range of .1% to 11.01% in installments, maturing at various dates from 1999 and 2006	47	41
Less installments due within one year	5	8
	$4,406	$1,500

The aggregate amounts of installments due for the next five years are:		
(In millions)	1998	$ 5
	1999	11
	2000	880
	2001	5
	2002	1,005

Interest expense on long-term debt was $190 million, $103 million, and $52 million for 1997, 1996, and 1995, respectively.

Commercial paper in the amount of $375 million has been classified as long-term due to company borrowings of that amount which are supported by a 5 year Syndicated Bank Credit Agreement combined with a 5 year fixed for variable interest rate swap.

In 1997, the company issued $500 million of 7.2% debentures due in 2027, $1,000 million of 6.75% notes due in 2007, $1,000 million of 6.45% notes due in 2002, and $500 million of 6.3% notes, due in 2000. The proceeds from these issues were used for acquisition financing.

In 1995, the company issued $375 million of 7.375% debentures due in 2025, redeemable after ten years, and $750 million of 6.5% notes due in 2005. The proceeds from these issues were used for acquisition financing. The principal amounts of debt were reduced by debt issue discounts and interest rate hedging costs of $42 million and $105 million, respectively, on the date of issuance, and are reflected as follows at:

(In millions)	December 31, 1997	December 31, 1996
Principal	$4,125	$1,125
Unamortized issue discounts	(38)	(17)
Unamortized interest rate hedging costs	(98)	(16)
Net debt	$3,989	$1,092

The company has bank agreement covenants. The most restrictive requires that the ratio of total debt to total capitalization not exceed 65%. The company was in compliance with this covenant during 1997 and 1996.

BOEING
1998 ANNUAL REPORT

12. Accounts Payable and Other Liabilities

Accounts payable and other liabilities at December 31 consisted of the following:

	1998	1997
Accounts payable	$5,263	$ 5,609
Accrued compensation and employee benefit costs	2,326	2,154
Lease and other deposits	539	819
Other	2,605	2,966
	$10,733	$11,548

Chapter 5

Balance Sheet Reporting: Stockholders' Equity*

Stockholders' equity in a corporation is composed of three fundamental sources: capital stock, additional paid-in-capital, and retained earnings. Treasury stock is a reduction of stockholders' equity.

Capital stock represents monies paid or to be paid into the corporation by investors who purchase shares of stock. Each share of stock represents a unit of ownership in the corporation. Capital stock also includes shares to be issued at a later date, such as stock options and warrants, and stock dividends distributable. *Additional paid-in-capital* represents additional monies paid into the corporation by investors above the par value of shares issued, gifts received by the corporation, and a variety of other sources that will be discussed in this chapter. (If stock is issued below par value, paid-in-capital is reduced.) *Retained earnings* represents income that the corporation has accumulated as a result of its day-to-day operating activities. *Legal capital* is typically defined by state law. Legal capital is how much capital the company must have in order to protect the creditors. Legal capital usually includes common and preferred stock.

Stockholders' equity represents the cumulative net contributions by stockholders plus accumulated earnings less dividends. Stockholders' equity

---

*This chapter was co-authored by David Erlach, Ph.D., J.D., M.B.A., Instructor of Accounting at Queens College, CUNY.

285

is synonymous with net worth, or net assets (assets less liabilities). This chapter discusses the accounting, financial statement presentation, and disclosures associated with preferred and common stock, stock retirement, treasury stock, dividends, appropriation of retained earnings, stock splits, stock warrants (including fractional share warrants), and quasi-reorganization.

PREFERRED STOCK

The capital stock component of stockholders' equity consists of two types of stock: preferred and common. Common stock has one major characteristic that preferred stock does not. *Common stock* has voting rights. Preferred stockholders usually do not have voting rights, but they enjoy other characteristics. *Preferred stock* may have a "participation" feature. *Participating* preferred stock is entitled to partake in dividend payments in excess of its predetermined dividend rate, on a proportionate basis using the total par values of the preferred and common shares outstanding. *Nonparticipating* preferred stock does *not* partake in excess dividends.

Preferred stock may be *cumulative*. If dividends are not declared by the board of directors in a particular year, the dividends accumulate. These "backlogged" dividends are termed dividends in arrears. Dividends in arrears must be paid before any dividends are paid to noncumulative preferred stock or to common stock. If preferred stock is *noncumulative*, the bypassed dividends do *not* accumulate.

Preferred stock has *preference* over common stock in the event of corporate liquidation. Preferred stockholders will receive the "liquidation value," sometimes stated as par value, before any monies are disbursed to common stockholders.

Convertible preferred stock may be exchanged for common stock based on a stipulated conversion ratio. (As the market price of the common stock changes, so does the related convertible preferred stock.) When preferred stock is converted to common stock, any excess of preferred contributed capital over the par value is credited to paid-in-capital; any deficit is debited to retained earnings.

EXAMPLE

Siegel Company issued 10,000 shares of $100 par value convertible preferred stock for $120 per share. The conversion is based on one share of preferred stock for four shares of common stock. The par value of the common stock is $18 per share. All preferred shares were converted into common shares. The journal entry for the conversion is

Convertible preferred stock (10,000 × $100)	1,000,000	
Premium on preferred stock (10,000 × $20)	200,000	
Common stock (40,000 × $18)		720,000
Paid-in-capital (balance)		480,000

Preferred stock usually has no maturity date. However, there may be a call feature. *Callable preferred stock* may be redeemed at the stipulated call price at a predetermined date by the issuing company. The call (redemption) price is typically slightly more than the initial issue price. Emerging Issues Task Force Consensus Summary Number 86–32 deals with the early extinguishment of a subsidiary's mandatorily redeemable preferred stock.

Preferred stock issued for services or property should be recorded at the market price of the stock issued. If market price of the stock is not known, the services or property should then be reported at their fair market value.

EXAMPLE

Erlach Company issued 2,000 shares of $10 par value preferred stock as compensation for 1,500 hours of legal services performed billable at $100 per hour. The market price of the stock is $60 per share. The journal entry is

Compensation expense (2,000 shares × $60)	120,000	
Common stock (2,000 shares × $10)		20,000
Paid-in-capital (2,000 shares × $50)		100,000

The *costs to issue* stock include accounting and legal fees, printing charges, underwriting commissions, Securities and Exchange Commission (SEC) filing fees, and promoting costs for the issue. The prevalent accounting treatment is to charge such costs against paid-in-capital as incurred. However, costs incurred to defend against a takeover attempt of the company are expensed. Payments made to stockholders to induce them *not* to buy additional shares are also expensed.

When increasing rate preferred stock is issued, it should be recorded at its fair value, including the periodic increases in value in the early years due to dividends not being paid or paid at below market rates.

As per GAAP, full disclosure must be made of

1. Par, stated, or assigned value of preferred stock.
2. Number of shares authorized, issued and outstanding.
3. The amount of dividends in arrears, per share and in the aggregate.
4. Liquidation values in the aggregate for preferred stock.
5. The amounts of dividends in arrears, per share and in the aggregate.
6. Call and conversion features (FASB Statement Number 47, *Disclosures of Long-Term Obligations*, mandates footnote disclosure of call features and a five-year redemption schedule associated with preferred stock).
7. Restrictions placed on issuance of stock.
8. Participation rights.

Emerging Issues Task Force Consensus Summary Number 85–25 covers the sale of preferred stock with a put option in which the buyer may later transfer the securities back to the issuer at a fixed price. If the exercise of the put option is *probable*, the transaction is accounted for as a borrowing. In such a case, the difference between the selling price and the price of the put is amortized from the issue date to the first permissible put date. If the exercise of the put option is *not* probable, the transaction is accounted for as a straight sale.

Emerging Issues Task Force Consensus Summary Number 96–1 applies to the sale of put options on the issuer's stock that require or permit cash settlement. This transaction is accounted for as a liability marked to fair value, with any resulting gain or loss included in the income statement.

COMMON STOCK

Common stock is the residual corporate interest that bears the ultimate risk of loss and receives the benefits of success; it is guaranteed neither dividends nor assets upon dissolution; common stockholders generally control the management of the corporation and tend to profit the most if the company is successful (Kieso & Weygandt, 1998, p. 760). The accounting to record the issuance of common shares is as follows:

> Cash   (full amount of proceeds)
> > Common stock   (par value of shares issued)
> > Additional paid-in-capital   (excess, if any)

If common and preferred shares are issued as a *unit* (e.g., three shares of common and one share of preferred), the proceeds received are allocated based on the relative market values of the securities.

Disclosure for common stock should include unusual voting rights, dividend rates, restrictions on dividends, rights and privileges of stockholders, shares authorized and issued, outstanding shares, and commitments to issue additional shares.

Emerging Issues Task Force Consensus Summary Number 85–1 applies to the classification of a contribution to an entity's equity in the form of a note receivable. Such a note should usually be presented as a reduction of equity. However, if the note is to be paid within the near term, it may be reported as an asset.

Emerging Issues Task Force Consensus Summary Number 87–31 covers the sale of put options on the issuer's common stock. The proceeds received from issuing the puts should be reported as equity. Disclosure should also be made of the fair value of the put.

Emerging Issues Task Force Consensus Summary Number 84–40 applies to long-term debt repayable by a capital stock transaction.

Emerging Issues Task Force Consensus Summary Number 94–7 deals with the accounting for financial instruments indexed to, and potentially settled in, a company's own stock.

Emerging Issues Task Force Consensus Summary Number 87–17 covers spinoffs or other distributions of loans receivable to shareholders.

STOCK RETIREMENTS

When capital stock is outstanding, the corporation has fiduciary and financial obligations to the shareholders. In order to reduce these obligations, the corporation could decide to retire some of the outstanding shares. If capital stock is retired at par value, the accounting is as follows:

Capital stock	(par value)	
Cash		(par value)

If capital stock is retired for less than par value, the entry is

Capital stock	(par value)	
Cash		(full amount paid)
Paid-in-capital		(difference)

If capital stock is retired for more than par value, the entry is

Capital stock	(par value)	
Paid-in-capital	(original premium per share)	
Retained earnings	(excess over original premium)	
Cash		(full amount paid)

Note: In accounting for the retirement of stock, retained earnings can only be reduced, not increased.

EXAMPLE

In 19X2, Levine Company issued $20 par value stock for $32 per share. In 19X4, the company bought some of these issued shares for $30 per share and retired them. In this case, paid-in-capital should be reduced by $10 per share.

TREASURY STOCK

Treasury stock is a term used to refer to shares of stock that have been issued and then reacquired by the issuing corporation. These shares are in shareholders' hands, and the corporation buys them in the market. The corporation holds the shares temporarily and then reissues them. Treasury stock may be kept on a FIFO or average cost basis. While the corporation is holding on to these shares, the shares are said to be "in the treasury." Treasury shares lose all their rights and characteristics while in the treasury. For example, treasury stock does not have the right to vote or to partake in dividends.

The reasons for acquiring treasury stock are diverse. The acquisition may be an effort to thwart a takeover attempt. It may be to support the market value of the shares. When the firm reacquires its own shares, the supply in the market is naturally reduced. With a sufficient demand, market price will then increase. Earnings per share will also become more attractive, because while treasury shares are considered issued shares, they are not considered to be outstanding while they are in the treasury. Another common reason for purchasing treasury shares is to reallocate ownership without issuing additional shares.

An appropriation of retained earnings equal to the cost of treasury stock on hand is required.

There are two methods to account for treasury stock: the cost method and the par value method. The former method is more commonly used.

Under the *cost method*, the acquisition of treasury stock is recorded at the cost of the acquired shares. The journal entry is

Treasury stock	(shares × price per share)
Cash	(shares × price per share)

Treasury stock is the last deduction in arriving at total stockholders' equity. Under certain circumstances, treasury stock can be reported as an asset, with proper disclosure (ARB 43, Ch. 1A, par. 4, and APB–6, par. 12b). For example, some corporations present treasury stock as an asset if the shares were bought to pay off specific obligation. The entry to record the reissuance of treasury shares would take a credit to treasury stock in an amount equal to the cost of the shares, and a debit to cash for the full amount received. If the reissuance is for an amount greater than the original purchase price, there would be a credit for the excess to an account titled Additional Paid-in-Capital: Treasury Stock. If the reissuance is for less than the original issue price, there would be a debit to this Additional Paid-in-Capital account for the difference.

The Additional Paid-in-Capital: Treasury Stock account, like any other equity account, has a normal credit balance. Consequently, it can only have a credit balance or a zero balance. It cannot have a debit balance. If a corporation "falls behind" more than it "comes out ahead" on treasury stock reissuance, the amount to complete the entry would be debited to retained earnings.

EXAMPLE

A partial chart of accounts for ABC, Inc. indicates

Treasury stock	$8,000
Additional paid-in-capital:	
Treasury Stock	3,000

All of these shares are reissued for $4,000. This would be recorded as follows:

Cash	4,000	
Additional paid-in-capital	3,000	
Retained earnings	1,000	
Treasury stock		8,000

If treasury stock is *donated*, only a memo entry is required. When the donated treasury shares are subsequently sold, the entry is based on the market price at that time. The journal entry is

Cash	xxx	
Paid-in-capital (donation)		xxx

FASB Technical Bulletin 85–6 deals with the accounting for a purchase of treasury shares at a price significantly in excess of the current market price of the shares and the income statement classification of costs incurred in defending against a takeover attempt.

Footnote disclosures associated with treasury stock include the circumstances when it is presented as an asset, and amounts of treasury stock associated with rights and privileges.

The second method for recording treasury stock transactions is the *par value method.* Under this method, the treasury stock account is charged with the par (or stated) value of the shares involved. Other paid-in-capital accounts are proportionately reduced based on amounts recorded in the issuance of the shares. The balance in the common or preferred stock account remains the same.

Under the par value method, if treasury stock is purchased at more than the par value, the entry is

Treasury stock	(par value)	
Paid-in-capital	(original premium per share)	
Retained earnings	(if necessary)	
Cash		(full amount paid)

If treasury stock is purchased at less than the par value, the entry is

Treasury stock	(par value)	
Cash		(full amount paid)
Paid-in-capital		(difference)

If treasury stock is sold above par value, the entry is

Cash	(full proceeds)	
Treasury stock		(par value)
Paid-in-capital		(difference)

If treasury stock is sold under par value, the entry is

Cash	(full proceeds)
Paid-in-capital	(amount available)
Retained earnings	(if necessary)
Treasury stock	(par value)

Under the par value method, treasury stock is presented as a contra account to the common stock it applies to under the capital stock section of stockholders' equity.

Some state laws prohibit the purchase of treasury stock unless earnings available for dividends exist; consequently, the retained earnings account must be restricted in an amount equal to the cost of treasury stock being held. This restriction must be disclosed by a note to the financial statements (Kieso & Weygandt, 1998, pp. 812–813). The underlying theory here is that when a corporation purchases treasury stock, it is paying money to its own shareholders. This is viewed as being tantamount to a dividend. Consequently, the amount otherwise available for the distribution of dividends is restricted.

DIVIDENDS

There are a variety of dividends that a corporation can distribute. This section will discuss cash dividends, stock dividends, property dividends, scrip dividends, and liquidating dividends.

A cash dividend is based on the number of outstanding shares (issued shares less treasury shares). As an example, a corporation has 7,000 shares of $50 par value, 8% preferred stock outstanding. Eight hundred shares are in the treasury. Dividends will be declared and paid only on the 6,200 shares that are actually in shareholders' hands. The dividend per share is $4, computed as 8% of the $50 par value. The total amount of dividends is $24,800 (6,200 shares × $4 per share). The following entry would be recorded on the date of declaration:

Retained earnings	24,800	
Cash dividends payable		24,800

No entry is made at the date of record. On the date of distribution, the following entry would be made:

Cash dividends payable	24,800	
Cash		24,800

An alternative treatment is to debit a dividends account in lieu of retained earnings. The dividends account would be closed out at the end of the accounting period against the retained earnings account. With this treatment, everything nets out the same as the treatment in the illustration, but by utilizing a dividends account, there is a specific record of dividends declared that can be utilized during the accounting period.

Cumulative preferred stockholders have priority in receiving first any dividends in arrears, and then any current year dividend. If preferred stock is fully participating, the first dividend payment (after arrearages) goes to preferred stockholders in the amount stipulated, stated either as a dollar amount per share or as a percentage of par value. Next, common stockholders receive a total amount to the extent available based on the same per share percentage that the participating preferred stockholders got. Thereafter, the amounts to be paid are on a pro rata basis to each class of stock based on the par value of the shares outstanding. Partially participating preferred stockholders share in the manner specified.

EXAMPLE

At December 31, 19X4 and 19X5, Simon Corp. had outstanding 2,000 shares of $100 par value 7% cumulative preferred stock and 10,000 shares of $10 par value common stock. At December 31, 19X4, preferred dividends in arrears were $6,000. The cash dividends declared in 19X5 were $22,000. The amount of dividends for 19X5 associated with the preferred and common stock is calculated as follows:

Total cash dividends declared		$22,000
Preferred stockholders receive:		
19X4 dividends in arrears	$ 6,000	
19X5 dividends (2,000 × $7)	14,000	20,000
Balance to common stockholders		$ 2,000

A *stock dividend* arises when the corporation distributes additional shares of its own stock to its current stockholders. The number of shares to be distributed is phrased in terms of a percentage of the number of shares outstanding at the declaration date. For example, if a corporation has 120,000 shares outstanding when it declares a 10% stock dividend, the dividend will consist of 12,000 shares, and there will be 132,000 shares outstanding once the dividend shares are distributed. If the stock dividend is less than 20 to 25% of the outstanding shares at the date of declaration, retained earnings will be reduced in an amount equal to the market price of the shares at the date of declaration. This is referred to as a small stock dividend. If the stock dividend is greater than 20 to 25% of the outstanding shares at the date of declaration, retained earnings will be reduced in an amount equal to the par or stated value of the shares at the date of declaration. This is referred to as a large stock dividend. The area between 20 and 25% is considered a gray area. Accounting for stock dividends entails the use of an account called stock dividend distributable. This is not a liability account. It is shown in the paid-in-capital section of stockholders' equity.

EXAMPLE

A 5% stock dividend is declared on 6,000 shares of $6 par value common stock. The market price is $8 per share on the date of declaration. On the date of declaration, the following entry is made:

Retained earnings (300 shares × $8)	2,400	
Stock dividend distributable		
(300 shares × $6)		1,800
Paid-in-capital		600

The following entry would be made on the date of distribution:

Stock dividend distributable	1,800	
Common stock		1,800

Assume that the dividend was 30%. On the date of declaration, the following entry would be made:

Retained earnings (1,800 shares × $6)	10,800	
Stock dividend distributable		10,800

The following entry would be made to record the distribution of the shares:

Stock dividend distributable	10,800	
Common stock		10,800

A *property dividend,* also called a "dividend in kind," is payable in assets of the corporation other than cash (e.g., inventory, securities). Property dividends are formally defined as a nonreciprocal transfer of nonmonetary assets between an enterprise and its owners; they should be recorded at the fair value of the asset transferred, and a gain or loss should be recognized on the disposition of the asset (APB 29, par. 18). Disclosure should be made of the nature of the distribution and the accounting basis for the transferred assets.

The accounting for a property dividend entails a journal entry that will adjust the asset to be distributed to its market value at the date of declaration. For example, if the fair value of the asset is higher than the book value, the following would be the format for this entry:

Asset	xxx	
Gain on appreciation of asset		xxx

The following entry would record the declaration of the property dividend:

Retained earnings	xxx	
Property dividends payable		xxx

When the asset is distributed, the following entry is made:

Property dividends payable	xxx	
Asset		xxx

Exception: Property distributions in a reorganization or liquidation should be based on recorded amounts less any required reduction for impairment in value.

A *scrip (liability) dividend* is payable in the form of a liability such as a note payable. This type of dividend may occur when a business has financial difficulties. Interest expense is accrued. However, the interest is *not* part of the dividend.

EXAMPLE

On January 1, 19X4, a liability dividend of $100,000 is declared in the form of a one-year, 10% note. The journal entry at the declaration date is

Retained earnings	100,000	
Scrip dividends payable		100,000

When the scrip dividend is paid, the entry is

Scrip dividends payable	100,000	
Interest expense	10,000	
Cash		110,000

A *liquidating dividend* is any dividend that is not based on earnings but instead is a reduction of paid-in-capital. A liquidating dividend is a return of paid-in-capital and requires full disclosure. Paid-in-capital is debited and dividends payable is credited. The existence of a liquidating dividend does not necessarily mean that the company is going out of business. However, a company which decides to halt operations may declare a final, liquidating dividend. The accounting for a liquidating dividend is based on the state laws where the business is incorporated. A liquidating dividend is *not* taxable to the recipient.

APPROPRIATION OF RETAINED EARNINGS

An appropriation of retained earnings is the setting aside of retained earnings and making that portion unavailable for the declaration of dividends. It indicates the need to stockholders to restrict asset disbursements because of unexpected major uses or contingencies. Examples include appropriations for a bond sinking fund, for plant expansion, or for general contingencies. The appropriation may be prompted by legal constraints, contractual terms, or reasonably possible losses. An appropriation of retained earnings does not involve the setting aside of cash. Appropriate footnote disclosure should be made of the nature of the restriction. The following journal entry records the appropriation of retained earnings:

Retained earnings	xxx	
Appropriation of retained earnings		xxx

If the appropriation of retained earnings is no longer needed because the loss has taken place or the particular purpose achieved, the previous entry would be reversed as follows:

Appropriation of retained earnings	xxx	
Retained earnings		xxx

Appropriation of retained earnings is part of total retained earnings.

EXAMPLE

On December 31, 19X4, Qureshi Corporation had appropriated retained earnings of $437,500 for plant expansion. The plant was completed in 19X5 at a cost of $375,000. In 19X5, the company appropriated $300,000 for general contingencies. Cash of $500,000 was restricted for bond retirement due in 19X8. At December 31, 19X5, appropriated retained earnings will equal $300,000.

STOCK SPLITS

A corporation may have a superlative history of performance. The financial statements show a positive trend, and retained earnings are sizable. This will cause a high demand for this corporation's stock in the market. A share of stock with a $50 par value could attain a market value of $150 or more. On the surface, a corporation whose stock is performing so well in the market seems attractive. In reality, a market value that is too high will prove debilitating to the issuing company. The phenomenon that results is that there will actually be a chill on trading in that company's shares because the investment is not affordable. The corporation would like the market price to be lower, so that trading in its shares becomes more affordable and new investors are attracted. Further, the brokerage commission and/or dealer spread per share for a round lot (100 shares) is typically lower than for an odd lot (less than 100 shares).

In this situation, the corporation may engage in an accounting mechanism called a *stock split*. The size of a stock split is stated in the form of a ratio. The following illustration will demonstrate the effect of a 2 : 1 stock split. The corporation will call in all of the outstanding shares of $50 par value stock and reissue to each shareholder double the number of shares initially held, but with half of the original par value—in this example, $25. This will cause the presplit market value of $150 to drop to approximately $75. Now the corporation's shares will become a lot more affordable than before the split. The corporation will have achieved its aim of increasing trading in its shares and attracting new investors.

A stock split does not affect the balance in any account. The total par value of the shares outstanding is the same after the stock split as it was before. The stock split requires a memorandum entry in the general journal and in the relevant stock account. For example,

April 30   Memorandum: Issued additional 5,000 shares of Capital Stock
in a 2 : 1 stock split. There are now 10,000 shares of Capital Stock
outstanding with a par value of $25 per share.

A stock split has no impact on the financial statements except for a description of the stock shown on the balance sheet and disclosure of the cause.

EXAMPLE

A company had 200,000 shares outstanding at the beginning of the year. On March 1 it issued a 15% stock dividend. On May 1, the company purchased 40,000 of its shares. On November 1, a 2-for-1 stock split was issued. On December 31, there will be 380,000 shares outstanding, computed as follows:

	Shares
Balance—1/1	200,000
3/1—Stock dividend (200,000 × 15%)	30,000
5/1—Purchased treasury stock	(40,000)
Subtotal	190,000
10/1—Stock split	190,000
Balance—12/31	380,000

A reverse stock split achieves the opposite effects of a stock split by increasing the par value per share.

STOCK WARRANTS

Stock warrants are certificates entitling the holder to acquire shares of stock at a predetermined price for a predetermined period of time. A corporation may decide to sell stock warrants as part of a bond sale to make the securities more attractive to the potential investor and to justify a lower interest rate. A *nondetachable* warrant is one that must be traded with the related security as a package. In other words, the issue is accounted for as convertible debt. A *detachable* warrant is one that can be traded separately from the bond. Consequently, the warrant has its own market value separate from that of the attached security. An allocation must be engaged in to account for the valuation of these warrants apart from the related bonds, and they are accounted for as additional paid-in-capital (APB Opinion 14, paragraph 16). The method of first resort for this allocation is the *proportional* method. If the market value of the bonds or their detachable warrants cannot be determined, then the *incremental* method is used for this allocation.

EXAMPLE

A $10,000 convertible bond is issued at $12,000 with $2,000 applicable to nondetachable stock warrants. The entry is as follows:

Cash	12,000	
Bonds payable		10,000
Premium on bonds payable		2,000

Now let us assume that the warrants are detachable. The fair market value of the bonds without the warrants is determined to be $9,500, and the fair market value (FMV) of the warrants is $3,000. The proportional method would produce the following allocation:

1. FMV of bonds $ 9,500

     FMV of warrants   3,000

     Total FMV $12,500

2. $\dfrac{\$9,500}{\$12,500} \times \$12000 = \$9,120$ allocated to bonds

    $\dfrac{\$3,000}{\$12,500} \times \$12,000 = \$2,880$ allocated to warrants

The following journal entries would be necessary:

Cash	9,120	
Discount on bonds payable	880	
Bonds payable		10,000
Cash	2,880	
Paid-in capital: stock warrants		2,880

Now assume that the fair market value of the stock warrants was $1,500, but the fair market value of the bonds could not be determined. The incremental method would be used for the allocation. If the proceeds for the entire sale were $12,000, and $1,500 is the fair market value of the warrants, then the difference of $10,500 will be accounted for as the fair market value of the bonds. The following journal entries would be necessary:

Cash	10,500	
Bonds payable		10,000
Premium on bonds payable		500
Cash	1,500	
Paid-in-capital: stock warrants		1,500

If stock warrants expire or lapse, the entry is to debit paid-in-capital: stock warrants and to credit additional paid-in-capital.

EXAMPLE

On December 31, 19X4, a company issued 2,000 of its 12%, 8-year, $1,000 face value bonds with detachable stock warrants, at par. Each bond has a detachable warrant for one common share at an option price of $40 per share. After issuance, the bonds had a market value of $2,100,000, and their warrants had a market value of $200,000. At year end 19X4, the bonds payable will be reported at $1,826,087, computed as follows:

Proceeds of issuance ($1,000 × 2,000)		$2,000,000
Allocated to warrants:		
Market value of bonds	$2,100,000	
Market value of warrants	200,000	
Total market value	$2,300,000	

To warrants:	$\dfrac{\$200,000}{\$2,300,000} \times \$2,000,000$	173,913
Bonds payable—12/31/19X4		$1,826,087

Note: A holder may become a stockholder by exercising the warrant and continue as a bondholder.

Disclosures associated with stock warrants include conversion terms and exercise prices.

Emerging Issues Task Force Consensus Summary 86-35 relates to debentures with detachable stock purchase warrants.

FRACTIONAL SHARE WARRANTS

A fractional share warrant is a warrant that is redeemable for a fractional share of stock. Consequently, more than one fractional warrant is required in order for the holder to acquire one full share.

EXAMPLE

A corporation has 2,000 shares of $10 par value stock outstanding. Each share has a market value of $18. A 15% stock dividend is declared. The number of dividend shares is 300 (2,000 × 15%). Included in the 300 shares are 200 fractional share warrants, each equaling one fourth of a share of stock. Thus, the dividend consists of 50 fractional shares and 250 regular shares. The journal entry at the date of declaration would be

Retained earnings		
(300 shares × $18)	5,400	
Stock dividends distributable		
(250 shares × $10)		2,500
Fractional share warrants		
(50 shares × $10)		500
Paid-in-capital		2,400

The journal entries at the date of issuance are

Stock dividends distributable	2,500	
Common stock		2,500
Fractional share warrants	500	
Common stock		500

If only 60% of the fractional share warrants were turned in, the journal entry would be

Fractional share warrants	300	
Common stock		300

STOCK RIGHTS

Stock rights allow current stockholders to buy additional shares of the company's stock to maintain their proportionate interest in the company. This is usually referred to as the preemptive right. In some cases, existing stockholders can purchase the newly issued shares at a discount and at either no or reduced fees.

No entry is made upon the issuance of stock rights. There is only a memorandum notation. When stock rights are exercised, common stock increases by the par value of the shares issued, and additional paid-in-capital increases for the excess of the issue price over the par value of the shares issued. If stock rights are redeemed by the issuing company, the effect is the same as if a cash dividend had been paid. For example, if 10,000 rights were redeemed at $.20 per right, stockholders' equity would be reduced by $2,000.

QUASI-REORGANIZATION

A quasi-reorganization gives a "new start" to a company with a deficit in retained earnings. It is undertaken to avoid a bankruptcy. The assets and liabilities are revalued, and the deficit in retained earnings is eliminated via a reduction of paid-in-capital. The date of the quasi-reorganization should be disclosed.

As per ARB 43, Ch. 7A, in a quasi-reorganization

1. The approval of the stockholders and creditors is required.
2. Net assets are almost always written down (a write-up is possible) to fair market value. If this is not available, then a conservative estimate must be made. Significant subsequent adjustments to such estimates should be charged or credited to paid-in-capital.
3. Paid-in-capital is debited to reduce the deficit in retained earnings. If paid-in-capital is not sufficient, then the capital stock account will be debited.
4. Retained earnings will acquire a zero balance and will bear the date of the quasi-reorganization for 10 years subsequent to the reorganization (ARB 46, par. 2). This puts readers on notice that the company's retained earnings have undergone a readjustment and are not representative of historic earnings and dividends.

The basic entry for a quasi-reorganization is

Paid-in-capital
Capital stock (if required)

Assets
Retained Earnings

Caution: If potential losses exist at the readjustment date but the amounts of losses cannot be determined, there should be a provision for the maximum probable loss. If estimates used are subsequently shown to be incorrect, the difference goes to the paid-in-capital account.

Note: New or additional common stock or preferred stock may be issued in exchange for existing indebtedness. Thus the current liability account would be debited for the indebtedness and the capital account credited.

A parent with subsidiaries must not wind up with a credit balance in retained earnings when losses and deficits have been charged to paid-in-capital.

Any deferred tax liabilities as well as any tax loss carryforwards should be reported as an adjustment to paid-in-capital when they are recognized in a year after the quasi-reorganization.

EXAMPLE

A business shows the following balances before a quasi-reorganization:

Current assets	$200,000	Capital stock	$1,600,000
Fixed assets	600,000	Paid-in-capital	300,000
		Retained earnings	(1,100,000)
	$800,000		$ 800,000

Current assets are overvalued by $40,000, and fixed assets are overvalued by $150,000. The entries for a quasi-reorganization are

Quasi-reorganization	190,000	
Current assets		40,000
Fixed assets		150,000
Quasi-reorganization	1,100,000	
Retained earnings		1,100,000
Paid-in-capital	300,000	
Quasi-reorganization		300,000
Common stock	990,000	
Quasi-reorganization		990,000

DISCLOSURE

Disclosure should be made of the following regarding stockholders' equity: dividend and liquidation preferences, unusual voting rights, conversion features (e.g., dates, rates), participation rights, sinking fund provisions, agreements to issue additional shares, dividends in arrears, call features associated with redeemable stock, and any other relevant rights or privileges of stockholders.

SUMMARY

An illustrative stockholders' equity section of the balance sheet appears as follows:

Capital stock:		
Preferred stock	$1,000,000	
Common stock	3,000,000	
Stock subscribed	300,000	
Stock options	100,000	
Stock dividends	50,000	
Total capital stock		$4,450,000
Paid-in-capital		
Issue price in excess of par		
value: common stock	$ 120,000	
From treasury stock transactions	80,000	
Total paid-in-capital		200,000
Retained earnings		
Appropriated	$ 100,000	
Unappropriated	600,000	
Total retained earnings		700,000
Subtotal		$5,350,000
Less: Treasury stock		(300,000)
Total Stockholders' equity		$5,050,000

An illustrative statement of retained earnings follows:

	Balance—1/1/19X8	$ 400,000
Less:	Correction of error	
	(prior period adjustment)	(100,000)
	Balance—restated—1/1/19X8	$ 300,000
Add:	Net income	550,000
Less:	Dividends	(150,000)
	Balance—12/31/19X8	$ 700,000

REFERENCE

Kieso, D. E., & Weygandt, J. J. (1998). *Intermediate Accounting* (9th ed.). New York: John Wiley & Sons.

Annual Report References

SIGMA DESIGNS
1998 ANNUAL REPORT

Preferred Stock

In July 1997, the Company issued 45,000 shares of Series A nonvoting convertible preferred stock and warrants to purchase 64,285 shares of the Company's common stock for net proceeds of approximately $4,176,000 (net of issuance costs of approximately $324,000). The warrants are exercisable at $9.425 per share beginning in January 1998 and expire in January 2001. Subsequent to January 31, 1998, the Company issued 5,000 shares of Series B nonvoting convertible preferred stock for $1,000 per share and warrants to purchase 50,000 shares of the Company's common stock for proceeds of approximately $5,000,000. The warrants are exercisable at 130% of the average closing bid prices of the Company's common stock for the five trading days ending April 30, 1998 and expire on April 30, 2001.

The significant terms of the Series A and Series B convertible preferred stock are as follows:

- Beginning 120 days from the date of issuance, each share of Series A preferred stock is convertible into common stock at a 10% discount from the low reported market price of the Company's common stock for the five days preceding the date of conversion (subject to certain limitations as defined). Under certain conditions, the Company may elect to repurchase the Series A preferred stock for a cash amount equivalent to the value of the converted common stock that would have been obtained upon conversion as described above. Any

311

shares of Series A preferred stock outstanding on the second anniversary of their original issuance date will automatically convert into shares of the Company's common stock at the conversion rate described above.

■ Beginning 180 days from the date of issuance, each share of Series B preferred stock is convertible into common stock based on the average of the lowest six daily market prices of the Company's common stock during the twenty day trading period preceding the date of conversion (subject to certain limitations as defined). Under certain conditions, the Company may elect to repurchase the Series B preferred stock. Any shares of Series B preferred stock outstanding on January 30, 2000 will automatically convert into shares of the Company's common stock at the conversion rate described above.

■ The holders of Series A preferred stock are entitled to receive quarterly dividends in cash or common stock of the Company at a rate of 3% per annum of the original issuance price. Series B preferred stock does not bear dividends.

■ In the event of any liquidation, dissolution, or winding up of the Company ("an Event"), either voluntarily or involuntarily:

— the holders of the Series A preferred stock shall be entitled to receive, prior and in preference to any distribution of assets and surplus funds of the Company to the holders of the common stock an amount equal to the original purchase price of the Series A preferred stock, plus an amount equal to accrued and unpaid dividends to the date of liquidation. After payment has been made to the holders of the Series A preferred stock, the holders of the Company's common stock shall be entitled to receive the remaining assets of the Company.

— the holders of Series B preferred stock shall be entitled to an amount equal to the original purchase price of the Series B preferred stock plus three percent per annum of the original issuance price. However, in the case that there are no shares of Series A preferred stock outstanding at the time of an Event, Series B preferred stockholders will be entitled to an amount equal to 115% of the amount described in the preceding sentence.

The 10% discount on conversion of Series A preferred stock into common stock as described above is considered a deemed preferential dividend to the holders of Series A preferred stock and, accordingly, a $500,000 deemed dividend has been accreted which, for purposes of computing earnings per share, reduces income available to common stockholders over the minimum conversion period of seven months.

During fiscal 1998, holders of Series A preferred stock converted 18,450 shares of preferred stock into 445,745 shares of common stock.

Each share of common stock incorporates a purchase right which entitles the shareholder to buy, under certain circumstances, one newly issued share of the Company's common stock at an exercise price per share of $75. The rights become exercisable if a person or group acquires 20% or more of the Company's common stock or announces a tender or exchange offer for 30% or more of the Company's common stock under certain circumstances. In the event of certain merger or sale transactions, each Right will then entitle the holder to acquire shares having a value of twice the Right's exercise price. The Company may redeem the Rights at $.01 per Right prior to the earlier of the expiration of the Rights on November 27, 1999 or at the time that 20% or more of the Company's common stock has been acquired by a person or group. Until the Rights become exercisable, they have no dilutive effect on the earnings of the Company.

Stock Option Plan

The Company's 1994 stock option plan provides for the granting of options to purchase up to 3,400,000 shares of common stock at the fair market value on the date of grant. Of this amount, 1,000,000 shares were authorized for grant by the Board of Directors in both fiscal year 1997 and fiscal year 1998. Generally, options granted under the 1994 plan become exercisable over a five-year period and expire no more than ten years from the date of grant (all options outstanding at January 31, 1998 expire six to ten years from date of grant). On April 22, 1997, the Company repriced 1,167,779 options to purchase common stock to $2.31, the market price on that date. The repriced options are treated as cancelled and regranted; however, they retain their original vesting terms.

Stock option activity and balances are summarized as follows:

	Number of Shares	Weighted Average Exercise Price Per Share
Balances, February 1, 1995		
(470,514 exercisable at a weighted-average price of $3.86)	1,643,341	$ 4.28
Granted *(weighted-average fair value of $2.60)*	1,046,295	3.55
Cancelled	(366,222)	4.50
Exercised	(98,990)	2.78
Balances, January 31, 1996		
(701,938 exercisable at a weighted-average price of $4.17)	2,224,424	3.97
Granted *(weighted -average fair value of $4.22)*	326,000	7.71
Cancelled	(144,509)	4.78
Exercised	(813,536)	4.21
Balances, January 31, 1997		
(441,362 exercisable at a weighted-average price of $4.17)	1,592,379	4.57
Granted *(weighted-average fair value of $1.37)*	2,235,779	2.38
Cancelled	(1,441,776)	5.01
Exercised	(111,554)	0.98
Balances, January 31, 1998		
(Includes repricing of 1,167,779 options)	2,274,848	$ 2.34

At January 31, 1998, options to purchase 663,709 shares were exercisable and 987,580 shares were available for future grant.

Options Outstanding

Range of Exercise Prices	Number of Shares Outstanding at January 31, 1998	Weighted Average Remaining Life	Weighted Average Exercise Price
$0.0875—0.2272	110,382	7.81	$ 0.21
2.31—3.06	2,092,603	9.26	2.34
3.50—5.02	69,363	7.60	4.56
6.38	2,500	7.42	6.38
$0.0875—6.38	2,274,848	9.14	$ 2.31

Options Exercisable

Number Exercisable at January 31, 1998	Weighted Average Exercise Price
15,892	$ 0.10
624,954	2.32
21,613	4.48
1,250	6.38
663,709	$ 2.34

The Company uses the intrinsic value method specified by Accounting Principles Board Opinion No. 25 to calculate compensation expense associated with issuing stock options and, accordingly, has recorded no such expense through January 31, 1998 as such issuances have been at the fair value of the Company's common stock at the date of grant.

Statement of Financial Accounting Standards No. 123, Accounting for Stock-Based Compensation, (SFAS 123) requires the disclosure of pro forma net income and earnings per share had the Company adopted the fair value method as of the beginning of fiscal 1996. Under SFAS 123, the fair value of stock-based awards to employees is calculated through the use of option pricing models, even though such models were developed to estimate the fair value of freely tradable, fully transferable options without vesting restrictions, which significantly differ from the Company's stock option awards. These models also require subjective assumptions, including future stock price volatility and expected time to exercise, which greatly affect the calculated values. The Company's calculations were made using the Black-Scholes option pricing model with the following weighted average assumptions for the years ended January 31, 1998 and 1997, respectively: expected life, 14 and 13 months following vesting; stock volatility, 89% and 87%; risk free interest rates, 5.6% and 5.6%; and no dividends during the expected term. The Company's calculations are based on a multiple option valuation approach and forfeitures are recognized as they occur. If the computed fair values of awards in fiscal 1998 and 1997 had been amortized to expense over the vesting period of the awards, pro forma net income (loss) would have been ($7,283,000) (a loss of $0.66 per share) and $347,000 (income of $0.03 per share). However, the impact of outstanding non-vested stock options granted prior to February 1, 1995 has been excluded from the pro forma calculation; accordingly, the pro forma adjustments for the years ended January 31, 1998 and 1997 are not indicative of future period pro forma adjustments, when the calculation will apply to all applicable stock options.

Employee Stock Purchase Plan

The Company's 1986 Employee Stock Purchase Plan provides for the sale of up to 100,000 shares of common stock. Eligible employees may authorize payroll deductions of up to 10% of their regular base salaries to purchase common stock at 85% of the fair market value at the beginning or end of each six-month offering period. During fiscal 1998, 1997 and 1996, 38,666, 13,685 and 10,905 shares were purchased at an average price of $3.35, $7.63 and $5.15 per share, respectively.

Issuance of Common Stock and Warrants

On December 15, 1995, the Company issued convertible debt and warrants to purchase 415,921 shares of common stock at an exercise price of $7.62 per share for proceeds of $6,276,000 (net of issuance costs of $374,000). All such debt was converted to 1,134,323 shares of common stock on the same day. In addition, the warrants were fully exercised in the year ended January 31, 1997 for total proceeds of $3,170,000 which have been shown in the statement of shareholders' equity for the year ended January 31, 1997 net of $159,000 of additional costs related to the original issuance of the convertible debt and the warrant.

CORNING
1998 ANNUAL REPORT

12. Convertible Preferred Stock

Corning has 10 million authorized shares of Series Preferred Stock, par value $100 per share. Of the authorized shares, 2.4 million shares have been designated Series A Junior Participating Preferred Stock of which 110 shares have been issued.

At year end 1998, 1997 and 1996, 178,700. 198,100 and 222,000 shares of Series B Convertible Preferred Stock were outstanding, respectively. Each Series B share is convertible into 4.79 shares of Corning common stock and has voting rights equivalent to four common shares. The Series B shares were sold exclusively to tile trustee of Corning's existing employee investment plans. based upon directions from plan participants. Participants may cause Corning to redeem the shares at 100% of par upon reaching age 55 or later, retirement termination of employment or in certain cases of financial hardship. The Series B shares are redeemable by Corning at 5100 per share.

13. Common Shareholders' Equity

Corning has established the Corning Stock Ownership Trust (CSOT) to fund future employee purchases of common stock through its contributions to Corning's Investment and Employee Stock Purchase Plans (tile Plans). Corning sold 4 million treasury shares to the CSOT. At December 31, 1998. 1.9 million shares remained in the CSOT. Shares held by the CSOT are not considered outstanding for earnings per common share calculations until released to the Plans. Corning and the trustee of the CSOT reached an agreement whereby the trustee waived its right to receive the Distribution of Quest Diagnostics and Covance and, in lieu thereof. received 400,000 additional shares of Corning common stock.

Corning repurchased approximately 2.0 million, 1.1 million and 2.2 million shares of its common stock in 1998. 1997 and 1996, respectively. All of the 1998, 1997 and approximately 1.3 million of the 1996 shares were repurchased pursuant to a systematic plan authorized by the Board of Directors. Corning's systematic plan is designed to provide shares for Corning's various employee benefit programs. The remainder of the 1996 stock repurchases were from employees to satisfy tax withholding requirements on shares issued under employee benefit plans.

In June 1996, the Board of Directors approved the renewal of the Preferred Share Purchase Right Plan which entitles shareholders to purchase one-hundredth of a share of Series A Junior Participating Preferred Stock upon the occurrence of certain events. In addition, the rights entitle shareholders to purchase shares of common stock at a 50% discount in the event a person or group acquires 20% or more of Corning's outstanding common stock. The preferred share purchase rights became effective July 15, 1996 and expire July 15, 2006.

Accumulated other comprehensive income at December 31, 1998 included unrealized losses on marketable securities of $1.0 million, net of tax of $0.6 million, and foreign currency translation adjustments of $8.9 million. At December 31, 1996 and 1997, accumulated other comprehensive income included foreign currency translation adjustments of $43.6 million and $32.2 million respectively.

CBS CORPORATION
1998 ANNUAL REPORT

13. Shareholders' Equity

In 1998, the Corporation's Board of Directors authorized a $3 billion multi-year stock repurchase program. During the year, the Corporation purchased 28,342,000 shares of common stock under the program at a cost of $859 million. At December 31, 1998 and 1997, 43,204,000 shares and 21,673,000 shares, respectively, of the Corporation's common stock were held in treasury. Of the common stock held in treasury on these dates, 16 million and 18 million shares, respectively, were held by the Corporation's rabbi trusts for the payment of benefits under executive benefit plans.

On May 30, 1997, the Corporation redeemed all outstanding shares of its Series C Conversion Preferred Stock (Series C Preferred) and, in connection with the redemption, issued 32 million shares of common stock. All accrued and unpaid dividends on the redeemed shares of Series C Preferred were paid on May 30, 1997.

Common Shares
(shares in thousands)

	Issued	In Treasury	Outstanding
Balance at January 1, 1996	425,970	29,952	396,018
Shares issued for dividend reinvestment plan		(1,071)	1,071
Shares issued for employee plans		(6,254)	6,254
Shares issued for Infinity acquisition	183,002		183,002
Balance at December 31, 1996	608,972	22,627	586,345
Shares issued for dividend reinvestment plan	384	(29)	413
Shares issued for employee plans	17,245	(925)	18,170
Shares issued for TNN and CMT acquisition	59,058		59,058
Shares issued for conversion of Series C Preferred	31,859	—	31,859

Balance at December 31, 1997	717,518	21,673	695,845
Shares used for dividend reinvestment plan	1 32	—	1 32
Shares issued for employee plans	15,881	(6,811)	22,692
Shares repurchased		28,342	(28,342)
Balance at December 31, 1998	733,531	43,204	690,327

On December 29, 1995, the Board of Directors adopted a shareholder rights plan providing for the distribution of one right for each share of common stock outstanding on January 9, 1996 or issued thereafter until the occurrence of certain events. The rights become exercisable only in the event, with certain exceptions, that an acquiring party accumulates 15 percent or more of the Corporation's voting stock or a party announces an offer to acquire 30 percent or more of the voting stock. The rights have an exercise price of $64 per share and expire on January 9, 2006. The Board of Directors has adopted a resolution affirming its intention to redeem the rights in January 2001 (if still outstanding). Upon the occurrence of certain events, holders of the rights will be entitled to purchase either CBS Corporation preferred shares or shares in an acquiring entity at half of market value. The Corporation is entitled to redeem the rights at a value of $.01 per right at any time until the tenth day following the acquisition of a 15 percent position in its voting stock.

Other Comprehensive Income

At March 31, 1998, the Corporation adopted the provisions of SFAS 130 which establishes standards for reporting and disclosing comprehensive income in the financial statement Comprehensive income is used to describe all changes in equity from transactions and other events and circumstances, including net income, from nonowner sources. The following table presents the accumulated components of comprehensive income other than net income reflected within shareholders' equity at December 31, 1998 and December 31, 1997:

Accumulated Other Comprehensive
Income (Loss)
(in millions)

At December 31,	1998	1997
Unrealized gains on securities	$ 1	$ —
Minimum pension liability adjustment	(808)	(771)
Total accumulated other comprehensive loss	$(807)	$(771)

SNAP-ON
1999 ANNUAL REPORT

12. Capital Stock

Since 1995, the Corporation has undertaken stock repurchases from time to time to prevent dilution created by shares issued for employee and dealer stock purchase plans, stock options and other corporate purposes, as well as to repurchase shares when market conditions are favorable. At its January 1999 meeting, the board of directors authorized the repurchase of up to $50.0 million of the Corporation's common stock. This action followed the board's authorization in 1998 to purchase up to $100.0 million of common stock and its authorization in 1997 for up to $100.0 million of common stock. At the end of 1999, all of the 1999 authorization and substantially all of the 1998 authorization remained available. The Corporation repurchased 492,800 shares of its common stock in 1999, 2,279,400 shares in 1998 and 986,333 shares in 1997. Since 1995, the Corporation has repurchased 8,570,083 shares.

The board of directors declared on August 22, 1997, a dividend distribution of one preferred stock purchase right for each share of the Corporation's outstanding common stock. The rights are exercisable only if a person or group acquires 15% or more of the Corporation's common stock ("Acquiring Person") or publicly announces a tender offer to become an Acquiring Person. Each right may then be exercised to purchase one one-hundred-and-fiftieth of a share of Series A Junior Preferred Stock for $190, but if a person or group becomes an Acquiring Person, then each right entitles the holder (other than an Acquiring Person) to acquire common stock of the Corporation having a market value equivalent to two times the current purchase price. If the Corporation is acquired in a merger or other business combination not approved by the board of directors, then each holder of a right will be entitled to purchase common stock of the surviving company having a market value equivalent to two times the current purchase price. The effect of the rights is to cause ownership dilution to a person or group attempting to acquire the Corporation without approval of the Corporation's board of directors. The rights expire on November 3, 2007, and may be redeemed by the Corporation at a price of $.01 per right under certain circumstances.

The Corporation created a Grantor Stock Trust ("GST") in 1998 that was subsequently amended. In conjunction with the formation of the GST, the Corporation sold 7.1 million shares of treasury stock to the GST. The sale of these shares had no net impact on shareholders' equity or on the Corporation's Consolidated Statements of Earnings. The GST is a funding mechanism for certain benefit programs and compensation arrangements, including the incentive stock program and employee and franchised dealer stock purchase plans. The Northern Trust Company, as trustee of the GST, will vote the common stock held by the GST based on the terms set forth in the GST Agreement as amended. The GST is recorded as Grantor Stock Trust at Fair Market Value on the accompanying Consolidated Balance Sheets. Shares owned by the GST are accounted for as a reduction to shareholders' equity until used in connection with employee benefits. Each period, the shares owned by the GST are valued at the closing market price, with corresponding changes in the GST balance reflected in additional paid-in capital. At January 1, 2000, the GST held 6,677,450 shares of common stock.

REYNOLDS METALS COMPANY
1997 ANNUAL REPORT

7. Stockholders' Equity

Preferred Stock   The Company has 21,000,000 shares of preferred stock authorized. Two million shares have been designated Series A Junior Participating Preferred.

On December 31, 1996, the Company called for redemption of all of its outstanding PRIDES. As a result of the call, the Company issued a total of 9,019,990 shares of common stock upon the redemption or conversion of all of the PRIDES. A total of 4,673,800 shares of common stock were issued in redemption of 5,699,756 shares of PRIDES. The redemption rate of .82 of a share of common stock for each share of PRIDES was based on a call price of $48.077 per share and a common stock market price of $58.79 per share (determined as provided in the PRIDES governing documents). In lieu of redemption, holders of 5,300,244 shares of PRIDES elected to convert their shares of PRIDES (on or before the redemption date) into 4,346,190 shares of common stock (at a conversion rate of .82 of a share of common stock for each share of PRIDES). Dividends declared on each share of PRIDES were $3.31 in 1996 (1995 — $3.31).

Common Stock   The Company has 200,000,000 shares of common stock (without par value) authorized.

The Company has authorization to repurchase up to five million shares of common stock. In early 1998, the Company repurchased one million shares at market prices. The cost of the repurchase was $63 million.

Stock Options   The Company has a non-qualified stock option plan under which key employees may be granted stock options at a price equal to the fair market value at the date of grant. Other than the performance-based options discussed below, the stock options currently outstanding vest in one year and are exercisable between one year and ten years from the date of grant. A summary of stock option activity and related information follows (options are in thousands):

	1997	*1996*	*1995*
Outstanding at January 1	**5,318**	4,680	4,404
Granted	**711**	750	755
Exercised	**(1,190)**	(103)	(453)
Canceled	**(11)**	(9)	(26)
Outstanding at December 31	**4,828**	5,318	4,680
Exercisable at December 31	**4,121**	4,569	3,931
Available for grant (increased on January 1, 1996 by 2 million shares)	**923**	1,630	520
Weighted-average prices:			
Outstanding at January 1	**$52**	$52	$51
Granted	**64**	55	52
Exercised	**50**	39	43
Canceled	**56**	52	53
Outstanding at December 31	**55**	52	52
Exercisable at December 31	**53**	52	52

The following table summarizes information about stock options outstanding at December 31, 1997 (options are in thousands and remaining contractual life and exercise prices are weighted averages):

Range of Exercise Prices	*Options Outstanding*			*Options Exercisable*	
	Options	*Remaining Contractual Life*	*Exercise Price*	*Options*	*Exercise Price*
$35 to $49	1,003	6 Years	$45	1,003	$45
52 to 64	3,825	6 Years	57	3,118	56
$35 to $64	4,828	6 Years	$55	4,121	$53

In 1996, the Company also granted 150,000 performance-based stock options at an exercise price of $53.50 per share. The stock options will not be exercisable unless, on or before September 30, 1999, the closing price of the common stock equals or exceeds $80.25 per share for 30 consecutive days. If this condition is satisfied, the options may be exercised any time before March 31, 2000.

Pro forma net income and earnings per share have been prepared based on expensing (after tax) the estimated fair value of stock options granted during 1997, 1996 and 1995. The estimated fair value of the stock options was determined by using a Black-Scholes option-pricing model. The estimated fair values and the weighted-average assumptions used to estimate those values follow:

	Stock Options			Performance-Based Options
	1997	*1996*	*1995*	*1996*
Risk-free interest rate	**6.4%**	6.9%	6.5%	6.5%
Dividend yield	**2.2%**	2.6%	3.0%	2.1%
Volatility factor of the expected market price of the Company's common stock	**.265**	.278	.270	.262
Expected life of the option	**6 years**	6 years	6 years	3 years
Estimated fair value of each stock option granted	**$19.53**	$16.97	$14.30	$11.73

The Black-Scholes option-pricing model was not developed for use in valuing employee stock options. This model was developed for use in estimating the fair value of traded options that have no vesting restrictions and are fully transferable. In addition, it requires the input of highly subjective assumptions including expectations of future dividends and stock price volatility. The assumptions are only used for making the required fair value estimate and should not be considered as indicators of future dividend policy or stock price appreciation. Because changes in the subjective input assumptions can materially affect the fair value estimate and because the employee stock options have characteristics significantly different from those of traded options, the use of the Black-Scholes option-pricing model may not provide a reliable single measure of the employee stock options.

The pro forma information follows:

	1997	*1996*	*1995*
Pro forma net income	**$ 127**	$ 79	$ 382
Pro forma earnings per share: Basic	**$1.73**	$0.67	$5.48
Diluted	**$1.72**	$0.67	$5.15

Shareholder Rights Plan In November 1997, the Company adopted a new shareholder rights plan that replaced an existing, similar plan that was adopted in 1987 and expired on December 1, 1997, in accordance with its terms. Under the new plan, each share of common stock has one right attached and the rights trade with the common stock. The rights are exercisable only if a person or group buys 20% or more of the Company's common stock, or announces a tender offer for 20% or more of the outstanding common stock. Each right will entitle a holder to buy one-hundredth of a share of the Company's Series A Junior Participating Preferred Stock at an exercise price of $300.

If at any time after the rights become exercisable, the Company is acquired in a merger, or if there is a sale or transfer of 50% or more of its assets or earning power, each right would permit its holder to buy common stock of the acquiring company having a market value equal to two times the exercise price of the right. In addition, if a person or group acquires 25% or more of the common stock of the Company, or if certain other events occur, each right would permit its holder to buy common stock of the Company having a market value equal to two times the exercise price of the right.

The rights, which do not have voting privileges, expire in 2007. The Board of Directors may redeem the rights before expiration, under certain circumstances, for $0.01 per right. Until the rights become exercisable, they have no effect on earnings per share.

These rights should not interfere with a business combination approved by the Board of Directors. However, they will cause substantial dilution to a person or group that attempts to acquire the Company without conditioning the offer on redemption of the rights or acquiring a substantial number of the rights.

AMERICAN HOME PRODUCTS 1999 ANNUAL REPORT

7. Capital Stock

There were 2,400,000,000 shares of common stock and 5,000,000 shares of preferred stock authorized at December 31, 1999 and 1998, respectively. Of the authorized preferred shares, there is a series of shares (24,241 and 25,480 outstanding at December 31, 1999 and 1998, respectively) which is designated as $2 convertible preferred stock. Each share of the $2 series is convertible at the option of the holder into 36 shares of common stock. This series may be called for redemption at $60 per share plus accrued dividends.

On October 7, 1999 the Company's Board of Directors declared a dividend of one preferred share purchase right for each share of common stock outstanding on October 18, 1999. The rights also will apply to all future stock issuances. Each right permits the holder, under certain circumstances and upon the occurrence of certain events, to purchase from the Company one-thousandth of a share of Series A Junior Participating Preferred Stock of the Company (the Series A Preferred Stock) at an exercise price of $225 per one one-thousandth of a share of Series A Preferred Stock under a Rights Plan relating to such Series A Preferred Stock. The 5,000,000 shares of preferred stock authorized will be used for the exercise of any preferred share purchase rights. The Rights Plan has provisions that are triggered if any person or group acquires beneficial ownership of 15% or more of the outstanding common stock or acquires the Company in a merger or other business combination (an Acquiring Person). In such event, shareholders (other than the Acquiring Person) would receive stock of the Company or the Acquiring Person, as the case may be, having a market value of twice the exercise price along with substantially increased voting and dividend rights, among other things. The rights expire on October 7, 2009, and prior to there being an Acquiring Person, the Company may redeem the rights issued under the Rights Plan for $0.01 per right. The Board can, except with respect to the redemption price, amend the Rights Plan in any manner without the consent of the holders of the rights, provided that such amendment does not adversely affect the rights of the holder at any time after there is an Acquiring Person.

Changes in outstanding common shares during 1999, 1998 and 1997 were as follows:

(In thousands except shares of preferred stock)	*1999*	*1998*	*1997*
Balance at January 1	**1,312,399**	1,300,755	1,279,966
Issued for stock options	**10,589**	19,811	20,723
Purchases of common shares for treasury	**(19,226)**	(8,284)	(419)
Conversion of preferred stock (1,239, 3,365 and 2,588 shares in 1999, 1998 and 1997, respectively) and other exchanges	**154**	177	485
Balance at December 31	**1,303,916**	1,312,399	1,300,755

The Company has a common stock repurchase program under which the Company is authorized to repurchase shares. At December 31, 1999, 13,906,960 shares were authorized for future repurchases.

K MART
1997 ANNUAL REPORT

12. Common and Treasury Stock

Shares (000's)	1997	1996	1995
Common Shares:			
Beginning of the year	486,996	486,511	464,550
Sold under stock option plan	1,469	49	171
Issued under performance restricted stock plan	1,220	420	504
Issued under directors stock plan	5	21	9
Issued from redemption of Series C and D convertible preferred	—	—	21,314
Forfeited or withheld under performance restricted stock plan	(879)	(5)	(37)
End of the year	488,811	486,996	486,511
Treasury Shares:			
Beginning of the year	2,261	5,883	5,883
Reissued shares for the retirement savings plan	(1,635)	(3,622)	—
End of the year	626	2,261	5,883

As of the end of 1997, the Board of Directors has approved the repurchase of 2,000,000 shares of K mart common stock to be used to fund the Retirement Savings Plan and other employee benefit plans or trusts.

TELEPHONE AND DATA SYSTEMS, INC. 1997 NOTES TO CONSOLIDATED FINANCIAL STATEMENTS

1. Proposed Corporate Restructuring

The Board of Directors of Telephone and Data Systems, Inc. (the "Board") has adopted a proposal which, if approved by shareholders and implemented by the Board, would authorize the Board to issue three new classes of common stock and change the state of incorporation of Telephone and Data Systems, Inc. ("TDS" or "the Company") from Iowa to Delaware (the "Tracking Stock Proposal"). The three new classes of stock are intended to separately reflect the performance of the Company's cellular telephone, landline telephone and personal communications services businesses ("Tracking Stocks").

The Tracking Stocks are intended to result in greater market recognition of the value (individually and collectively) of the Company and of the Company's three principal business groups ("Tracking Groups"), thereby enhancing shareholder value over the long term, while at the same time enabling the Company's businesses to preserve the benefits of being part of a consolidated enterprise. The Tracking Stock Proposal is expected to:

- provide the Company with greater flexibility in raising capital and making acquisitions, using equity securities specifically related to the Tracking Groups,

- enable the Company to more effectively tailor employee benefit plans to provide incentives to employees of the Tracking Groups,

- provide shareholders with the opportunity to invest in separate securities that specifically reflect the underlying businesses, depending upon their investment objectives, and

- permit shareholders to continue to invest in all of the TDS businesses through the Common Shares and the Series A Common Shares.

The Cellular Group Shares, when issued, are intended to reflect the separate performance of the Cellular Group, which consists of the Company's interest in United States Cellular Corporation, a subsidiary of the Company. The Telecom Group Shares, when issued, are intended to reflect the separate performance of the Telecom Group, which primarily consists of the Company's interest in TDS Telecommunications Corporation, a subsidiary of the Company. The Aerial Group Shares, when issued, are intended to reflect the separate performance of the Aerial Group, which consists of the Company's interest in Aerial Communications, Inc., a subsidiary of the Company.

Subject to approval of the Tracking Stock Proposal by shareholders, the Company intends to:

- offer and sell Telecom Group Shares in a public offering for cash, subject to prevailing market and other conditions (the "Telecom Public Offering"), and allocate the net proceeds thereof to the Telecom Group,

- issue Cellular Group Shares in exchange for all of the Common Shares of U.S. Cellular which are not owned by the Company, subject to approval by the board of directors and the shareholders of U.S. Cellular (the "U.S. Cellular Merger"),

- issue Aerial Group Shares in exchange for all of the Common Shares of Aerial which are not owned by the Company, subject to approval by the board of directors and the shareholders of Aerial (the "Aerial Merger"), and

- distribute one Cellular Group Share, two-thirds of a Telecom Group share and two-thirds of an Aerial Group Share in the form of a stock dividend with respect to each outstanding Series A Common Share and Common Share of the Company (the "Distribution").

It is currently expected that the Distribution would take place in July 1998 or later, after the completion of the Telecom Public Offering, the U.S. Cellular Merger and the Aerial Merger.

The TDS Series A Common Shares and Common Shares will continue to be outstanding and are intended to reflect the performance of the Cellular Group, the Telecom Group and the Aerial Group to the extent of the Retained Interest in the respective groups, and to reflect the performance of the other assets and businesses attributed to the TDS Group.

Subject to the completion of the U.S. Cellular Merger and the Aerial Merger, the Company intends to terminate certain intercompany agreements between the Company and U.S. Cellular and Aerial, respectively. Thereafter, some or all of the policies between the Company and such subsidiaries would be determined solely by methods that management of the Company believes to be reasonable. Many of such policies would continue the arrangements which presently exist between the Company and U.S. Cellular or Aerial pursuant to the intercompany agreements, but the Company would have no contractual obligation to continue such policies after the intercompany agreements have been terminated.

If the Tracking Stock Proposal is approved by the shareholders and implemented by the Board, following the issuance of the Tracking Stocks, the Company will prepare and file with the Securities and Exchange Commission, consolidated financial statements of the Company and financial statements of the Cellular Group, the Telecom Group and the Aerial Group for so long as the respective Tracking Stock is outstanding and the TDS Group for as long as any Tracking Stock is outstanding.

For additional information regarding the Tracking Stock Proposal, see "Proposed Corporate Restructuring" in Management's Discussion and Analysis of Results of Operations and Financial Condition.

Chapter 6

Statement of Cash Flows

A statement of cash flows is required as part of a full set of financial statements. It must be prepared in conformity with GAAP. The statement is not required if the financial statements are prepared on a basis of accounting other than GAAP. The statement must be included in both annual and interim financial statements.

This chapter discusses the requirements of FASB Statement Number 95 (*Statement of Cash Flows*), FASB Statement Number 102 (*Statement of Cash Flows—Exemption of Certain Enterprises and Classification of Cash Flows from Certain Securities Acquired for Resale*), and FASB Statement Number 104 (*Statement of Cash Flows—Net Reporting of Certain Cash Receipts and Cash Payments and Classification of Cash Flows from Hedging Transactions*). FASB Statement Number 117 (*Financial Statements of Not-for-Profit Organizations*) requires the statement of cash flows for not-for-profit entities.

The statement presents the net effect of cash flows on the company's *cash and cash equivalents*. It includes a reconciliation of beginning and ending cash and cash equivalents. The total amount of cash and cash equivalents at the beginning and end of year presented in the statement of cash flows should match the totals presented in the balance sheet. The statement presents cash flows from operating, investing, and financing activities. Separate disclosure must be made of noncash investing and financing transactions.

The statement of cash flows provides many benefits to the preparers and users of the statement, such as the following:

- Enables the assessment of the amounts, timing, and uncertainty surrounding future cash flows
- Furnishes a reconciliation between net income and cash flow from operations
- Provides the net effects of operating transactions on profit and cash flow
- Indicates the impact on the company's financial status of its investing and financing transactions
- Shows the company's ability to obtain financing
- Provides important information about the entity's cash receipts and cash payments for the period
- Shows the company's ability to generate recurring cash earnings
- Evaluates the company's ability to pay debt when due
- Allows for the evaluation of the company's ability to pay its expenses and conduct normal operations
- Shows the entity's ability to pay dividends
- Provides the reasons for the change in cash and cash equivalents for the period

It is prohibited to present cash flow per share because doing so will give the false impression that such a statistic is as important as earnings per share. Further, the use of the term *funds* should not be used because of its ambiguity and misinterpretation.

CASH AND CASH EQUIVALENTS

Cash consists of currency on hand and demand deposits. Cash also includes other accounts having demand deposit characteristics and allowing for customer deposit or withdrawal at will without penalty, such as unrestricted certificates of deposit and unrestricted repurchase agreements.

SEC Regulation S-X, Rule 5-02(1), provides that amounts held in bank accounts that are unavailable for immediate withdrawal (e.g., compensating balances) should be considered as cash for the purposes of preparing the statement of cash flows. Any restrictions on withdrawal should be disclosed.

A *cash equivalent* is a short-term, highly liquid investment that is easily convertible into cash and has an original maturity of three months or less. There will be very little change in market price, if any, arising from a change in interest rate because of the short maturity. Examples are treasury bills, money market funds, and commercial paper.

The company must disclose its policy of classifying assets as cash equivalents. If a change in such policy is made, it must be accounted for as a change in principle, requiring the restatement of prior years' financial statements for comparability purposes.

RECONCILIATION OF NET INCOME TO CASH FLOW FROM OPERATIONS

A reconciliation of net income to cash flow from operations is required whether the direct method or indirect method is used. The reconciliation presents the various adjustments required to net income. Under the direct method, the operating section presents gross cash receipts and gross cash payments from operating activities, with a reconciliation of net income to cash flow from operations in a separate schedule accompanying the statement of cash flows. The cash flow from operations derived in this separate schedule must agree with the cash flow from operations in the operating section of the statement of cash flows.

Under the indirect method, gross cash receipts and gross cash payments from operating activities are not presented. Instead, only the reconciliation of net income to cash flow from operations may be presented either in the body of the operating section or in a separate schedule. If presented in a separate schedule, the net cash flow from operating activities is presented as a single line item in the operating section. The reconciling adjustments to derive cash flow from operations include adding back non-cash expenses to and deducting noncash revenues from net income. Examples of these adjustments include adding back depreciation and depletion expense, adding back amortization expense on intangibles, adding back pension expense arising from a deferred pension liability, adding back bad debts, adding back accrued warranty expense, adding back tax expense arising from a deferred tax liability, adding back the loss on a fixed asset, adding back compensation expense arising from an employee stock option plan, deducting the amortization of deferred revenue, deducting the amortization of bond premium, subtracting tax expense arising from a deferred tax asset, subtracting the gain on a fixed asset, subtracting pension expense associated with a deferred pension asset, subtracting unrealized gains on trading securities, and subtracting income from investments under the equity method. Irrespective of whether the direct method or the indirect method is used, there must be separate disclosure of income taxes and interest paid during the year.

Figure 6–1 presents an illustrative reconciliation of net income to cash flow from operations. It shows the adjustment process for the various reconciling items.

Net income

Adjustments required to convert net income to the cash basis:

Add: Noncash expenses (depreciation, depletion, amortization expense, loss on sale of fixed assets)

Less: Noncash revenues (amortization of deferred revenue, amortization of bond premium, gain on sale of fixed assets)

Add (deduct) changes in current assets

    Add: Decrease in current asset accounts

    Less: Increase in current asset accounts

Add (deduct) changes in current liabilities

    Add: Increase in current liability accounts

    Less: Decrease in current liability accounts

Cash provided by operations

Figure 6–1: *Illustrative Reconciliation of Net Income to Cash Flow from Operations*

Note: A decrease in a current asset account results in an increase in cash flow. An example is a collection on accounts receivable. An increase in a current asset account results in a cash payment, such as the purchase of inventory. An increase in a current liability results in a cash receipt, such as the receipt of a short-term advance. A decrease in a current liability account results in a cash payment, such as a payment on an account payable.

EXAMPLE

XYZ Company reports net income of $50,000, depreciation expense of $4,000, amortization of goodwill of $500, amortization of deferred revenue of $3,000, loss of the sale of a fixed asset of $2,000, a decrease in accounts receivable of $8,000, a decrease in prepaid expenses of $1,000, a decrease in accounts payable of $6,000, and an increase in accrued liabilities of $4,000. Based on this information, we prepare a reconciliation of net income to cash flow from operations.

Reconciliation	
Net income	$50,000
Add: Noncash expenses	
Depreciation expense	4,000
Amortization expense	500
Loss on sale of fixed asset	2,000
Less: Noncash revenue	
Amortization of deferred revenue	(3,000)
Decrease in accounts receivable	8,000
Decrease in prepaid expenses	1,000
Decrease in accounts payable	(6,000)
Increase in accrued liabilities	4,000
Cash provided by operations	$60,500

The topic of reconciliation is discussed more fully in the following sections on the direct and indirect methods.

DIRECT METHOD

The *direct method* is preferred by FASB Statement Number 95. Under this method, companies present cash flows from operating activities by major categories of gross receipts and gross payments and the resulting net amount. A company using the direct method should report separately operating cash receipts and operating cash payments. These cash flows from operations are discussed in the section of this chapter titled "Operating Activities."

Note: The only difference between the direct method and the indirect method is the presentation in the operating activities section of the statement of cash flows. The investing and financing sections are identical under both methods.

The direct method enables the user to comprehend better the relationship between the company's profit and its cash earnings. The direct method shows that the amount of net cash received or used in operating activities during the year equals the difference between the total amount of gross cash receipts and total gross cash payments applying to operating activities.

It would be helpful to show how to convert income statement amounts for the direct method presentation from the accrual to cash basis. Some typical conversion formulas are presented next.

To go from the accrual basis to cash basis, do the following:

1. Net sales + beginning accounts receivable – ending accounts receivable – writeoffs of accounts receivable = cash received from customers.

2. Cost of sales + ending inventory + beginning accounts payable – beginning inventory – ending accounts payable = cash paid to suppliers.

3. Operating expenses + ending prepaid expenses + beginning accrued expenses – beginning prepaid expenses – depreciation and amortization – ending accrued expenses payable – bad debt expense = cash paid for operating expenses.

EXAMPLE

A company's cost of sales for the year 20X3 was $300,000. During the year, the inventory increased by $60,000 and accounts payable to suppliers decreased by $50,000. The amount paid to suppliers to be reported in the statement of cash flows under the direct method is $410,000, computed as follows:

Cost of sales	$300,000
Add: Increase in inventory	60,000
Add: Decrease in accounts payable	50,000
Cash paid to suppliers	$410,000

INDIRECT (RECONCILIATION) METHOD

The *indirect method* is commonly used by companies in financial reporting because of its simplicity, although it is a less preferred approach. The company presents net cash flow from operating activities indirectly, by adjusting earnings to reconcile net income to net cash flow from operations. The indirect method emphasizes changes in most current asset and current liability accounts as they apply to operating activities. This was discussed in the reconciliation section of this chapter. **Caution:** Changes in current assets and current liabilities relating to investing or financing activities (e.g., short-term loans or short-term notes payable not involving sales of goods or services) should be presented as investing or financing activities, as applicable.

The amounts paid for interest and income taxes must be disclosed either on the face of the statement of cash flows or in the notes. If explained in the footnotes, they may appear in the relevant footnote on long-term debt or income taxes or may be discussed in a separate footnote dealing with supplemental cash flow disclosures.

A disadvantage of the indirect method is possible user confusion as to where the cash was received or paid to. The indirect method only shows adjustments to accrual basis net income to cash flow from operations in the operating activities section.

An illustrative format of the statement of cash flows under the indirect method is presented in Figure 6–2.

Operating activities:
  Net income
  Adjustments
  Cash flow provided from operating activities
Investing activities:
  Cash received from investing activities
  Cash paid for investing activities
  Net cash flow provided (used) by investing activities
Financing activities:
  Cash received from financing activities
  Cash paid for financing activities
  Net cash flow provided (used) by financing activities
Net increase (decrease) in cash
Schedule of noncash investing and financing activities

Figure 6–2: *Illustrative Indirect Method Presentation*

EXAMPLE

Levine Company used the following data in its preparation of it 2002 Statement of Cash Flows:

	December 31	January 1
Accounts receivable, net	$14,000	$11,100
Prepaid rent expense	4,100	6,200
Accounts payable	11,200	9,700

Levine's 2002 net income is $75,000. In ascertaining the amount that Levine should include as net cash provided by operating activities in the statement of cash flows, the following rule should be adhered to when the indirect method is used: In converting net income to net cash flow from operating activities, the following additions and subtractions must be made: net income + decreases in current assets accounts (other than cash) –

increases in current assets accounts (other than cash) + increases in current liability accounts – decreases in current liability accounts + noncash expenses (e.g., depreciation, bond discount amortization) – noncash revenues (e.g., gain on sale of plant assets, bond premium amortization.

COMPUTATION	
Net income	$75,000
Add (subtract)	
Increase in net accounts receivable $14,000 – $11,100	(2,900)
Decrease in prepaid rent expense: $6,200 – $4,100	2,100
Increase in accounts payable: $11,200 – $9,700	1,500
Net cash provided by operating activities, 2002	$75,700

GROSS VERSUS NET CASH FLOWS

In the investing and financing sections, gross cash inflows should be shown separately from gross cash outflows for similar items. In general, you cannot net the cash inflows and cash outflows for similar items. (**Note:** There are a few exceptions in which netting is permitted, such as when the items involve fast turnover, are significant in amount, and have short maturities, such as transactions involving long-term investments, loans, and debts having a maturity of three months or less.) For example, in the investing section, the acquisition of a fixed asset would be a use of cash (say $100,000) while the sale of a fixed asset (say $60,000) would be a source of cash. Separate presentation of both the cash inflow and cash outflow aids reader comprehension and realism of the financial statements. The netting of the two (net cash outflow of $40,000) distorts what is really happening. In the financing section, the issuance of long-term debt (say $80,000) would be a source of cash, but paying back the debt principal (say $50,000) would be an application of cash. Both the cash inflows and cash outflows must be presented separately. You are not allowed to present the net effect as a net source of cash of $30,000.

EXAMPLE

Carol Company reported net income of $150,000 for 2002. The following changes occurred in several of the company's balance sheet accounts:

Equipment	$12,500 increase
Accumulated depreciation	$20,000 increase
Note payable	$15,000 increase

In addition, the following pertinent activities took place:

1. Depreciation expense for the year was $26,000.

2. In December 2002, Carol purchased equipment costing $25,000, with $10,000 down and the issuance of a 12% note payable of $15,000.

3. During 2002, Carol sold equipment costing $12,500, with accumulated depreciation of $6,000 for a gain of $2,500.

What is the net cash used in investing activities that should be reported by Carol?

In general, the cash flows from investing activities of an enterprise include transactions involving long-term assets and include the acquisition and disposal of investments and long-lived assets and the extension and collection of loans. Therefore, in Carol Company's 2002 statement of cash flows, the net cash used in investing activities should be computed in the following way:

Sale of equipment (cash inflow) ($12,500 − $6,000 + $2,500)	$ 9,000
Acquisition of equipment (cash outflow)	(10,000)
Net cash used in investing activities, 2002	$(1,000)

In Carol's 2002 statement of cash flows, net cash flow provided by operating activities would be computed as follows:

Net income	$150,000
Add(subtract):	
Depreciation expense	26,000
Gain on sale of equipment	(2,500)
Net cash provided by operating activities	$173,500

EXAMPLE

During 2002, Dran Inc. had the following transactions related to its financial operations:

- Proceeds from the sale of stock of treasury stock (carrying amount at cost, $21,500) $25,000

- Carrying amount of convertible preferred stock in Dran Inc., converted in common shares   30,000

- Distribution in 2002 of cash dividend declared in 2001 to preferred stockholders   15,500

- Payment for the early retirement of long-term bonds payable (carrying amount $185,000)   187,500

What is the net cash flow used in Dran's financing operations?

In general, the financing activities of an entity relate to liability and stockholder equity items and include obtaining cash from creditors and repaying these amounts and obtaining capital from owners and providing them in return with dividends as well returning their investments (reacquisition of capital stock).

In Dran's statement of cash flows for 2002, therefore, the net cash flow used in its financing operations should be computed as follows:

Proceeds from the sale of treasury stock (cash inflow)	$ 25,000
Cash dividend distributed in 2002 (cash outflow)	(15,500)
Payment for the early retirement of bonds payable	(187,500)
Net cash used in investing activities, 2002	$(178,000)

OPERATING ACTIVITIES

Operating activities apply to producing or selling merchandise or performing services. Under the direct method, items applying to the income statement are presented in the operating activities section.

Cash inflows from operating activities include

- Cash receipts from sales or servicing, such as from customers, licensees, and lessees
- Interest and dividend receipts
- Proceeds received from an insurance policy
- Refunds from suppliers
- Sale of trading securities
- Award received from a lawsuit
- Other operating receipts

Cash outflows from operating activities include

- Cash paid to buy materials and merchandise purchases
- Cash paid for services
- Payment of general and administrative expenses
- Employee salary payments
- Payments to suppliers
- Insurance payments
- Advertising and promotion payments
- Payment for lawsuit damages
- Cash refunds such as to customers for inferior goods
- Interest payments
- Income tax payments
- Cash purchase of trading securities
- Payment of duties, fines, and penalties

- Charitable contribution payments
- Other operating cash payments

There may be further breakdowns of operating cash receipts and cash payments to improve financial reporting. For example, a producer may divide cash paid to vendors into payments to buy merchandise and payments for selling expenses.

Figure 6–3 illustrates the presentation of cash flows from operating activities using the direct method.

Cash inflows:		
Cash received from customers	$600,000	
Dividend and interest receipts	100,000	
Award received from a lawsuit	200,000	
Cash inflows from operating activities		$900,000
Cash outlays:		
Cash paid to vendors	$300,000	
Cash paid to employees	50,000	
Interest paid	20,000	
Income taxes paid	80,000	
Payment of insurance	30,000	
Advertising outlays	70,000	
Purchase of trading securities	150,000	
Cash outlays from operating activities		700,000
Net cash flow from operations		$200,000

Figure 6–3: *Cash Flows from Operating Activities Section Under the Direct Method*

As stated before, with the direct method, the reconciliation of earnings to cash flow from operations is presented in a separate schedule.

Under the indirect method, as previously noted, the operating section just presents the reconciliation of net income to cash flow from operations based on adjustments for noncash revenue and noncash expense items as well as changes in current asset and current liability accounts affecting operating activities.

INVESTING ACTIVITIES

Investing activities include making and collecting loans; purchasing and selling property, plant, and equipment; and buying or selling available-for-sale or held-to-maturity securities in other companies. **Note:** Trading securities are considered operating activities.

Cash inflows from investing activities include

■ Proceeds received from selling fixed assets (**Note:** Gains or losses on sales of fixed assets are included as investing activities along with the assets they relate to. These gains or losses are not included in net cash flow from operating items. Thus, they are an adjustment to net income in obtaining cash flow from operations.)

■ Selling available-for-sale or held-to-maturity securities in other companies

■ Collecting on loans made to debtors

Cash outlays for investing activities include

■ Acquiring fixed assets

■ Buying available-for-sale or held-to-maturity securities of other companies

■ Granting loans to borrowers

Note: Cash flows for investing activities should only include advance payments, the down payment, or other payments at the date when fixed assets are bought, or shortly before or after. If there are principal payments on an installment loan at later dates, such payments are included in financing activities. Any noncash element of a transaction to buy a fixed asset such as through debt incurrence is disclosed in a supplementary schedule titled "Noncash Investment and Financing Activities."

Tip: If a company is bought or sold under the purchase method to account for a business combination, any cash paid or received is considered an investing activity. The fair market value of any assets acquired or liabilities incurred in such a transaction would be presented in the schedule of noncash investing and financing activities.

FINANCING ACTIVITIES

Financing activities include issuing or repurchasing a company's own stock (common stock or preferred stock), paying cash dividends to stockholders, and issuing or paying back short-term or long-term debt.

Cash inflows from financing activities include

- Funds received from issuing the company's own short-term or long-term debt (e.g., bonds payable, notes payable, mortgage payable)
- Funds received from selling the company's own equity securities (**Note:** This also includes the subsequent reissuance of treasury stock.)

Cash outflows for financing activities include

- Purchase of treasury stock
- Cash dividend payments (**Note:** Dividends declared but unpaid and stock dividends are noncash transactions and are presented in a supplementary schedule titled "Noncash Investing and Financing Activities.")
- Retiring or paying off the principal on short-term or long-term debt (This includes payments of principal on capital lease obligations.)
- Other principal payments to long-term creditors
- Payment of debt issue costs

Caution: Gains or losses from the early extinguishment of debt are part of the cash flow related to the repayment of the amount borrowed as a financing activity. Such gains or losses are not an element of net cash flow from operating activities.

MULTICLASSIFICATION

If a cash receipt or cash payment relates to more than one classification (operating, investing, and financing), classification is based on the major activity involving the cash flow. For example, the acquisition and sale of machinery is usually deemed an investing outlay. Further, the purchase and sale of equipment used by the business or rented out typically is considered an investing activity. However, if the business intends to use or rent the equipment for a short time period and then sell it, this would be considered an operating activity.

NONCASH INVESTING AND FINANCING ACTIVITIES

There must be separate supplementary disclosure in a section (schedule) following the statement of cash flows or in the notes in narrative form presenting investing and financing activities that affect assets and liabilities but do not impact cash flow. In addition, while a transaction having cash and noncash components should be discussed, only the cash aspect should be presented in the statement of cash flows. In other words, if a transaction is part cash and part noncash, the cash part is reported in the cash flow statement while the noncash portion is disclosed in narrative form or in a schedule of noncash activities. Examples of noncash investing and financing activities are buying property in exchange for a mortgage payable and/or common stock, purchasing an intangible asset with the issuance of preferred stock, converting long-term debt into common stock, converting preferred stock to common stock, converting long-term notes receivable to held-to-maturity securities, conducting nonmonetary exchange of assets, and acquiring an asset though a capital lease. The following are also noncash investing and financing activities: stock issue costs not paid in cash, third-party financing, stock dividends, and property dividends. An illustrative presentation follows:

NONCASH INVESTING AND FINANCING ACTIVITIES:

Purchase of land by issuing a mortgage payable	$100,000
Conversion of a bond payable to common stock	$400,000

SPECIAL ITEMS IN THE INCOME STATEMENT

Extraordinary items, cumulative effect of a change in principle, and income from discontinued operations do not have to be broken out separately in the statement of cash flows. These items may be classified under operating, investing, or financing activities as appropriate. For example, an extraordinary loss due to a lawsuit would be presented under operating activities. An extraordinary gain on the early extinguishment of debt would be shown under financing activities. An extraordinary loss on equipment due to a fire would be presented as an investing activity.

AGENCY ARRANGEMENTS

Some changes in certain current assets and liabilities do not affect net income or cash earnings. An example is a company that collects sales taxes from customers that it must remit to the government. This type of agency transaction is an operating activity and results in cash inflow and then cash outflow. Although the company does not receive any benefit for tax collection and remittance, it must still present the transaction in the operating section of the statement of cash flows.

HEDGING TRANSACTIONS

Cash inflow and outflow may relate to futures contracts, swap agreements, or option contracts designed to hedge specific transactions, such as the purchase or sale of goods. The cash flow arising from the hedge transaction should be classified in the same manner as the cash flow associated with the hedge item (e.g., inventory). Disclosure should be made of the company's accounting treatment for hedged events and transactions.

FOREIGN CURRENCY CASH FLOWS

A company may have foreign operations and foreign currency translations. For accounting purposes in treating foreign currency cash flows, use the exchange rate at the time of the cash flow in reporting the currency equivalent. Alternatively, the weighted-average exchange rate may be used if there is an immaterial difference relative to using the actual currency exchange rate. The weighted-average exchange rate may be suitable for revenues and expenses. The effect of changes in the exchange rate on cash balances held in foreign currencies is presented as a separate item when reconciling the change in cash and cash equivalents for the year. Further, noncash exchange gains and losses presented in the income statement should be shown as a separate item when reconciling net income to cash flow from operations. Footnote disclosure should be made of the exchange rate to convert cash flows.

CASE STUDIES

Case Study

X Company provides the following financial statements:

X Company
Comparative Balance Sheets
December 31
(in millions)

	19X8	*19X9*
ASSETS		
Cash	$ 47	$ 40
Accounts receivable	35	30
Prepaid expenses	2	4
Land	35	50
Building	80	100
Accumulated depreciation	(6)	(9)

Equipment	42	50
Accumulated depreciation	(7)	(11)
Total assets	$228	$254
LIABILITIES AND STOCKHOLDERS' EQUITY		
Accounts payable	$ 16	$ 20
Long-term notes payable	20	30
Common stock	100	100
Retained earnings	92	104
Total liabilities and stockholders' equity	$228	$254

X Company
Income Statement
For the Year Ended December 31, 19X9
(in millions)

Revenue		$300
Operating expenses (excluding depreciation)	$200	
Depreciation	7	207
Income from operations		$ 93
Income tax expense		32
Net income		$ 61

Additional information is as follows:

1. Cash dividends paid totaled $49.

2. The company issued long-term notes payable for cash.

3. Land, building, and equipment were acquired for cash.

We can now prepare the statement of cash flows under the indirect method as follows:

X Company
Statement of Cash Flows
For the Year Ended December 31, 19X9
(in millions)

Cash flow from operating activities:		
Net income		$61
Add (deduct) items not affecting cash:		
Depreciation expense	$ 7	
Decrease in accounts receivable	5	
Increase in prepaid expenses	(2)	
Increase in accounts payable	4	14
Net cash flow from operating activities		$75
Cash flow from investing activities:		
Purchase of land	$(15)	
Purchase of building	(20)	
Purchase of equipment	(8)	(43)
Cash flow from financing activities:		
Issuance of long-term notes payable	$ 10	
Payment of cash dividends	(49)	(39)
Net decrease in cash		$ 7

A financial analysis of the statement of cash flows reveals that the profitability and operating cash flow of X Company improved. This indicates good earnings performance as well as the fact that earnings are backed up by cash. The decrease in accounts receivable may reveal better collection efforts. The increase in accounts payable is a sign that suppliers are confident in the company and willing to give interest-free financing. The acquisition of land, building, and equipment points to a growing business undertaking capital expansion. The issuance of long-term notes payable indicates that part of the financing of assets is through debt. Stockholders will be happy with the significant dividend payout of 80.3% (dividends divided by net income, or $49/$61). Overall, there was a decrease in cash of $7, but this should not cause alarm because of the company's profitability and the fact that the cash was used for capital expansion and dividend payments. We recommend that the dividend payout be reduced from its high level and the funds be reinvested in the profitable business. Also, the curtailment of dividends by more than $7 would result in a positive net cash flow for the year. Cash flow is needed for immediate liquidity needs.

Case Study

Y Company presents the following statement of cash flows:

Cash flows from operating activities:		
Net income		$134,000
Add (deduct) items not affecting cash		
Depreciation expense	$ 21,000	
Decrease in accounts receivable	10,000	
Increase in prepaid expenses	(6,000)	
Increase in accounts payable	35,000	60,000
Net cash flow from operating activities		$194,000
Cash flows from investing activities:		
Purchase of land	$ (70,000)	
Purchase of building	(200,000)	
Purchase of equipment	(68,000)	
Cash used by investing activities		(338,000)
Cash flows from financing activities:		
Issuance of bonds	$ 150,000	
Payment of cash dividends	(18,000)	
Cash provided by financing activities		132,000
Net decrease in cash		$ (12,000)

An analysis of the statement of cash flows reveals that the company is profitable. Also, cash flow from operating activities exceeds net income, which indicates good internal cash generation. The ratio of cash flow from operating activities to net income is a solid 1:45 ($194,000/$134,000). A high ratio is desirable because it shows that earnings are backed up by cash. The decline in accounts receivable could indicate better collection efforts. The increase in accounts payable shows that the company can obtain interest-free financing. The company is definitely in the process of expanding for future growth, as evidenced by the purchase of land, building, and equipment. The debt position of the company has increased, indicating greater risk. The dividend payout was 13.4% ($18,000/$134,000). Stockholders look positively on a firm which pays dividends. The decrease in cash flow for the year of $12,000 is a negative sign.

COMPREHENSIVE EXAMPLES

The Cash Flow Statement Using the Direct Method

Cherry Inc.
Balance Sheets
December 31

	2002	2001
ASSETS		
Current Assets		
Cash	$16,225	$28,125
Accounts receivable	56,400	60,800
Notes receivable—Lou Company	13,900	5,700
Interest receivable	725	400
Inventory	74,750	91,650
Total current assets	$162,000	$186,675
Property and Equipment		
Land	30,000	30,000
Building	160,000	160,000
Machinery	27,500	20,000
Fixtures	9,250	9,250
Autos	5,500	11,750
	$232,250	$231,000
Accumulated depreciation	97,975	92,500
	$134,325	$138,500

(continued)

Other Assets

Cash surrender value of insurance policy	11,475	9,675
Organization costs	675	1,350
	12,150	11,025
Total assets	$308,475	$336,200

LIABILITIES AND STOCKHOLDERS' EQUITY

Current Liabilities

Notes payable	$20,000	$25,000
Current portion of serial bonds	36,000	33,750
Accounts payable	85,425	89,700
Accrued liabilities		
Wages	5,500	4,075
Interest	925	700
Payroll taxes	650	475
Income taxes	2,175	1125
Total current liabilities	$150,675	$154,825
Serial long term debt, less current portion	90,250	121,250

Stockholders' Equity

Common Stock	10,000	10,000
Retained Earnings	57,550	50,125
TOTAL STOCKHOLDERS' EQUITY	$ 67,550	$ 60,125
TOTAL LIABILITIES AND STOCKHOLDERS' EQUITY	$308,475	$336,200

Cherry Inc.
Statement of Income
Year Ended December 31, 2002

REVENUES

Sales	$368,600
Gain on sale of auto	125
Interest income	1200
	$369,925

(continued)

COST OF SALES

Raw materials	157,600
Labor	16,450
Transportation-in	8,350
	$182,400

GROSS PROFIT	$187,525

SELLING AND ADMINISTRATIVE EXPENSES

Administrator's salaries	44,800
Sales employees salaries	24,200
Office salaries	25,800
Payroll taxes	9,325
Rent expense	12,925
Office expenses	5,400
Life insurance of administrators	2,100
Fees to outside professionals	2,950
Telephone expenses	2,350
Utilities expenses	4,675
Maintenance expense	3,350
Insurance expense	7,150
Uncollectible accounts expense	10,000
Amortization expense	675
Depreciation expense	9,425
Miscellaneous taxes	1,600
Interest expense	7,325
	$174,050
Income before income taxes	$ 13,475
Income taxes	4,050
NET INCOME	$ 9,425
RETAINED EARNINGS—BEGINNING OF THE YEAR	50,125
DIVIDENDS PAID	(2,000)
RETAINED EARNINGS—END OF THE YEAR	$ 57,550

Additional Data for Cherry Inc.

1. Lou Company repaid $1,800 of its $5,700 receivable during the year. At December 31, 2002, the Lou Company borrowed an additional $10,000.

2. Cherry Company purchased machinery in exchange for a $2,500 down payment on a $5,000 note. The first payment on the machinery note is due in 2003.

3. An auto with an original cost of $6,250 and accumulated depreciation of $4,000 was sold for $2,375.

4. The notes payable indicated in the current liabilities section have original maturities of less than three months.

Statement of Cash Flows—Direct Method

CASH FLOWS FROM OPERATING ACTIVITIES		
Collections from customers	$363,000	(1)
Interest received	875	(2)
Cash paid to suppliers and employees	(316,600)	(3)
Interest paid	(7,100)	(4)
Income taxes paid	(3,000)	(5)
Net cash provided by operating activities	$37,175	
NET FLOWS FROM INVESTING ACTIVITIES		
Purchase of machinery	(2,500)	
Proceeds from sale of auto	2,375	
Loans made to Lou Company	(10,000)	
Collections of loans	1,800	
Net cash used by investing activities	(8,325)	
CASH FLOWS FROM FINANCING ACTIVITIES		
Short-term payment of debt	(5,000)	
Long-term payment of debt	(33,750)	
Dividends paid	(2,000)	
Net cash used by financing activities	(40,750)	
Net decrease in cash	(11,900)	
Cash at the beginning of year	28,125	
Cash at end of year	$16,225	

Supplemental Disclosures

Noncash investing and financing activities

Purchase of $7,500 of machinery paid for
in part with a $5,000 note $5,000

Analysis of Captions in the Statement
of Cash Flows—Direct Method

(1) Collections from customers

Sales from the income statement	$368,600
Increase in accounts receivable	(5,600)
Total	$363,000

(2) Interest received

Interest income	$ 1,200
Increase in interest receivable	(325)
Total	$ 875

(3) Cash paid to suppliers and employees

Cost of sales	$182,400
Selling and administrative cost	174,050
Deduct for interest—separately disclosed	(7,325)
Deduct noncash expenditures	
Depreciation	(9,425)
Amortization	(675)
Increase in cash surrender value of insurance policy	1800
Uncollectible accounts expense	(10,000)
Decrease in inventory	(16,900)
Decrease in payables	4,275
Increase in compensation and payroll taxes	(1,600)
Total	$316,600

(4) Interest paid

Interest expense on income statement	$7,325
Increase in interest payable	(225)
Total	$7,100

(continued)

(5) Income taxes paid

Income taxes per income statement	$ 4,050
Increase in income taxes payable	(1,050)
Total	$ 3,000

FASB Statement 95 requires that if an enterprise uses the direct method to present cash flow from operating activities, it also must provide in a separate schedule the reconciliation of net income to net cash flow provided by operating activities. This reconciliation represents the identical form and content of the indirect method. The reconciliation shown next should be presented at the bottom of the statement of cash flows when the direct method is used or in a separate schedule.

Reconciliation

Net income	$ 9,425
Adjustment to reconcile net income to net cash provided by operating activities	
Depreciation	9,425
Amortization	675
Gain on sale of auto	(125)
Cash surrender value of insurance	(1800)
Uncollectible accounts expense	10,000
Increase in accounts receivable	(5,600)
Increase in interest receivable	(325)
Decrease in inventories	16,900
Decrease in accounts payable	(4,275)
Increase in accrued liabilities	2875
Net cash provided by operating activities	$37,175

FASB Statement Number 95

This example illustrates the direct and indirect methods of preparing the statement of cash flows.

Assume that the comparative balance sheet of CF Inc. is as follows:

CF Inc.
Comparative Balance Sheet
As of 12/31/02 and 12/31/01

	12/31/02	12/31/01
ASSETS		
Cash	268,120	10,000
Accounts receivable	20,000	17,000
Short-term investments	15,000	25,000
Inventory	85,000	75,000
Prepaid rent	5,000	17,000
Prepaid insurance	4,500	3,000
Office supplies	2,500	500
Land	100,000	250,000
Building	800,000	800,000
Less: Accumulated depreciation	(220,000)	(150,000)
Equipment	750,000	500,000
Less: Accumulated depreciation	(180,000)	(160,000)
Patent	30,000	50,000
Total assets	1,680,120	1,437,500
LIABILITIES AND EQUITY		
Accounts payable	350,000	400,000
Taxes payable	8,000	3,000
Wages payable	25,000	15,000
Short-term notes payable	75,000	75,000
Long-term notes payable	65,000	85,000
Bonds payable	500,000	500,000
Premium on bonds payable	80,000	90,000
Common stock	260,000	170,000
Paid-in-capital in excess of par	80,000	60,000
Retained earnings	292,620	95,000
Total liabilities and equity	1,735,620	1,493,000

Assume that the income statement of CF Inc. is as follows:

CF Inc.
Income Statement
For Year Ended 12/31/02

Sales revenue		1,350,000
Cost of goods sold		(800,000)
Gross margin		550,000
Operating expenses		
Selling expenses	(120,000)	
Administrative expenses	(195,000)	
Depreciation/amortization	(110,000)	
Total operating expenses		(425,000)
Income from operations		125,000
Other revenues and expenses		
Gain on sale of land	60,000	
Gain on sale of short-term investments	35,000	
Dividends revenue	6,600	
Interest expense	(80,000)	
Total other revenues and expenses		21,600
Income before taxes		146,600
Income taxes (30%)		(43,980)
Net income		102,620
Dividends—common stock		95,000
Addition to retained earnings		197,620

The first step in preparing the statement of cash flows is to analyze the changes in the balance sheet accounts.

Change in:	
Cash	258,120
Accounts receivable	3,000
Short-term investments	(10,000)
Inventory	10,000
Prepaid rent	(12,000)
Prepaid insurance	1,500
Office supplies	2,000
Land	(150,000)
Building	—
Less: Accumulated depreciation	(70,000)
Equipment	250,000
Less: Accumulated depreciation	(20,000)
Patent	(20,000)
Accounts payable	(50,000)
Taxes payable	5,000
Wages payable	10,000
Short-term notes payable	—
Long-term notes payable	(20,000)
Bonds payable	—
Premium on bonds payable	(10,000)
Common stock	90,000
Paid-in-capital in excess of par	20,000
Retained earnings	197,620

The statement of cash flows using the direct method may now be prepared as follows:

CF Inc.
Statement of Cash Flows—Direct Method
For Year Ended 12/31/02

CASH FLOWS FROM OPERATING ACTIVITIES

Cash received from customers	1,347,000	(1)
Dividends received	6,600	
Cash paid to suppliers	(860,000)	(2)
Cash paid for operating expenses	(296,500)	(3)
Taxes paid	(38,980)	(4)
Interest paid	(90,000)	(5)
Net cash from operating activities	68,120	

CASH FLOWS FROM INVESTING ACTIVITIES

Sale of short-term investment	45,000	
Sale of land	210,000	
Purchase of equipment	(250,000)	
Net cash from investing activities	5,000	

CASH FLOWS FROM FINANCING ACTIVITIES

Issuance of common stock	110,000	
Payment of principal on long-term debt	(20,000)	
Payment of dividends	95,000	
Net cash from financing activities	185,000	
Net change in cash	258,120	
Beginning cash balance	10,000	
Ending cash balance	268,120	

The supporting computations are as follows:

(1)	Sales revenue	1,350,000	
	– Increase in accounts receivable	(3,000)	
	Cash received from customers		1,347,000
(2)	Cost of goods sold	800,000	
	+ Increase in inventory	10,000	
	+ Decrease in accounts payable	50,000	
	Cash paid to suppliers		860,000
(3)	Operating expenses	425,000	
	– Depreciation/amortization expense	(110,000)	
	– Decrease in prepaid rent	(12,000)	
	+ Increase in prepaid insurance	1,500	
	+ Increase in office supplies	2,000	
	– Increase in wages payable	(10,000)	
	Cash paid for operating expenses		296,500
(4)	Income taxes (30%)	43,980	
	– Increase in tax payable	(5,000)	
	Taxes paid		38,980
(5)	Interest Expense	80,000	
	+ Decrease in bond premium	10,000	
	Interest paid		90,000

Whenever the direct method is used, FASB Statement Number 95 requires reconciliation of net income to net cash from operating activities.

Reconciliation

Net income		102,620
Adjustments		
+ Depreciation/amortization expense	110,000	
– Amortization of bond premium	(10,000)	
– Gain on sale of land	(60,000)	
– Gain on sale of investment	(35,000)	
– Increase in accounts receivable	(3,000)	
– Increase in inventory	(10,000)	
+ Decrease in prepaid rent	12,000	
– Increase prepaid insurance	(1,500)	
– Increase in office supplies	(2,000)	
– Decrease in accounts payable	(50,000)	
+ Increase in taxes payable	5,000	
+ Increase in wages payable	10,000	
Total adjustments		(34,500)
Net cash from operating activities		68,120

Alternatively, the statement of cash flows using the indirect method may be prepared as follows:

CF Inc.
Statement of Cash Flows—Indirect Method
For Year Ended 12/31/02

CASH FLOWS FROM OPERATING ACTIVITIES

Net income		102,620
Adjustments		
+ Depreciation/amortization expense	110,000	
– Amortization of bond premium	(10,000)	
– Gain on sale of land	(60,000)	
– Gain on sale of investment	(35,000)	
– Increase in accounts receivable	(3,000)	
– Increase in inventory	(10,000)	
+ Decrease in prepaid rent	12,000	
– Increase prepaid insurance	(1,500)	
– Increase in office supplies	(2,000)	
– Decrease in accounts payable	(50,000)	
+ Increase in taxes payable	5,000	
+ Increase in wages payable	10,000	
Total adjustments		(34,500)
Net cash from operating activities		68,120

CASH FLOWS FROM INVESTING ACTIVITIES

Sale of short-term investment	45,000	
Sale of land	210,000	
Purchase of equipment	(250,000)	
Net cash from investing activities		5,000

CASH FLOWS FROM FINANCING ACTIVITIES

Issuance of common stock	110,000	
Payment of principal on long-term debt	(20,000)	
Payment of dividends	95,000	
Net cash from financing activities		185,000
Net change in cash		258,120
Beginning cash balance		10,000
Ending cash balance		268,120

FASB Statement Number 102:
Statement of Cash Flows—Exemption
of Certain Enterprises and Classification
of Cash Flows from Certain Securities Acquired
for Resale

As per FASB 102, cash inflows and cash outflows for transactions in securities, and other assets bought only for *resale* and carried at market value in a *trading account* of banks, dealers, and brokers must be classified in the operating section of the statement of cash flows. A similar treatment is afforded for loans acquired for resale and carried at market value. They are also presented in the operating section.

Exception: Securities, other assets, or loans bought solely for investment purposes are presented in the investing section.

A statement of cash flows need not be prepared for a defined pension plan that is reporting under FASB Statement Number 35 (*Accounting and Reporting by Defined Benefit Pension Plans*).

A statement of cash flows in not required for investment companies or for a common collective investment trust fund provided that the following conditions are satisfied:

1. The entity prepared a statement of changes in net assets.
2. The investments held are very liquid and expressed at market value.
3. The entity's debt position is either minimal or none.

FASB Statement Number 104:
Statement of Cash Flows—Net Reporting
of Certain Cash Receipts and Cash Payments and
Classification of Cash
Flow from Hedging Transactions

According to FASB 104, financial institutions may present *net* cash inflows and outflows for collections of loans, principal, deposit repayments, withdrawal of deposits, deposits with other financial institutions (e.g., credit unions, banks, savings institutions), time deposits, and client loans.

FASB 104 permits an entity that satisfies certain criteria to classify the cash flow arising from a hedging transaction in the same section of the cash flow statement as the hedged item (e.g., investing activity, financing activity). Appropriate disclosure should also be made of the accounting policy.

Annual Report References

PHILLIPS PETROLEUM
1999 ANNUAL REPORT

17. Cash Flow Information

	1999	Millions of Dollars *1998*	*1997*
Non-Cash Investing and Financing Activities			
Issuance of seller-financed promissory notes to purchase property, plant and equipment	$ 27	8	—
Company stock issued (canceled) under compensation and benefit plans	20	(2)	(1)
Change in fair value of securities	15	28	13
Fair market value of property, plant and equipment exchanged in monetary transactions	3	8	49
Investment in joint ventures in exchange for non-cash assets	8	14	—
Net book value of property, plant and equipment involved in oil and gas property non-monetary exchanges	120	4	—
Investment in equity affiliate through direct guarantee of debt	—	13	—
Accrued repurchase of company common stock	—	13	—
Investment sold in exchange for a receivable	—	9	—
Cash Payments			
Interest			
Debt	$256	170	166
Taxes and other	19	7	22
	$275	177	188
Income taxes	$184	436	770

369

FORD MOTOR
1999 ANNUAL REPORT

17. Cash Flows

The reconciliation of net income to cash flows from operating activities follows (in millions):

	1999		1998		1997	
	Automotive	Financial Services	Automotive	Financial Services	Automotive	Financial Services
Net income	**$5,721**	**$1,516**	$4,752	$17,319	$4,714	$2,206
Adjustments to reconcile net income to cash flows from operating activities:						
Depreciation and amortization	**5,895**	**9,298**	5,844	8,624	6,020	7,764
Losses/(earnings) of affiliated companies in excess of dividends remitted	**(37)**	**25**	82	(2)	127	(1)
Provision for credit and insurance losses	—	**1,465**	—	1,798	—	3,230
Foreign currency adjustments	**316**	—	(208)	—	(27)	—
Net (purchases)/sales of trading securities	**2,316**	**(157)**	(5,434)	(205)	(2,307)	67
Provision for deferred income tax	**278**	**1,565**	421	1,307	908	(102)
Gain on spin-off of The Associates (Note 16)	—	—	—	(15,955)	—	—
Gain on sale of Common Stock of a subsidiary (Note 16)	—	—	—	—	—	(269)
Changes in assets and liabilities:						
Decrease/(increase) in accounts receivable and other current assets	**(1,107)**	**(331)**	1,027	(1,189)	(179)	256
(Increase)/decrease in inventory	**893**	—	(254)	—	1,234	—
Increase/(decrease) in accounts payable and accrued and other liabilities	**2,648**	**(1,213)**	2,915	890	3,772	(240)
Other	**348**	**372**	477	891	(278)	739
Cash flows from operating activities	**$17,271**	**$12,540**	$9,622	$13,478	$13,984	$13,650

The company considers all highly liquid investments purchased with maturity of three months or less, including short-term time deposits and government, agency and corporate obligations, to be cash equivalents.

Automotive sector cash equivalents at December 31, 1999 and 1998 were $3.1 billion and $3.4 billion, respectively; Financial Services sector cash equivalents at December 31, 1999 and 1998 were $1.1 billion and $500 million, respectively. Cash flows resulting from futures contracts, forward contracts and options that are accounted for as hedges of identifiable transactions are classified in the same category as the item being hedged. Purchases, sales and maturities of trading securities are included in cash flows from operating activities. Purchases, sales and maturities of available-for-sale and held-to-maturity securities are included in cash flows from investing activities.

Cash paid for interest and income taxes was as follows (in millions):

	1999	1998	1997
Interest	$8,524	$9,120	$10,430
Income taxes	1,125	1,764	1,289

Chapter 7

Other Financial Statement Types and Related Items

Interim financial statements are issued during the year, usually quarterly, to gauge periodically the entity's financial health and operating performance. Personal financial statements are discussed in this chapter; they reveal the net worth of an individual or family and may be used in loan applications. The accounting procedures for incorporating a business and for contemplating a startup venture are also covered. Finally, the accounting and disclosure requirements for divestitures are presented.

INTERIM FINANCIAL REPORTS

APB Opinion Number 28 covers interim financial reporting. Interim reporting is presenting financial information for a period less than one year. Each interim period is viewed as an integral part of the annual period. Interim financial reports may be issued semiannually, quarterly, or monthly. Complete financial statements or summarized information may be presented. Typically, interim reports include the operating results of the current interim period and the cumulative year-to-date figures, or last 12 months to date. Comparisons are usually made to results of comparable interim periods for the previous year. The authors recommend the following format:

ABC Company
Interim Financial Information
For Quarter Ending March 31, 19X7 and Comparable Periods

	Current Quarter		*Twelve Months to Date*	
	Three Months Ending	*Three Months Ending*	*One Year Ending*	*One Year Ending*
Accounts Listed	*3/31/19X7*	*3/31/19X6*	*3/31/19X7*	*3/31/19X6*

Quarterly reports are much less detailed than annual reports. They often just present condensed information. Interim statements do not have to be audited. Each page should be labeled "Unaudited."

Interim results should be based on those accounting principles used in the last year's annual report unless a change in accounting has been made subsequently. Further, accounting policies do not have to be disclosed in interim reports unless there has been a change in an accounting policy (principle or estimate).

Income statement information is required in interim reports. However, it is recommended but not required to present a balance sheet and cash flow statement at interim dates. If these statements are not reported, the company must disclose significant changes in liquid assets, working capital, noncurrent liabilities, and stockholders' equity.

Extraordinary items, nonrecurring items, and gain or loss on the disposal of a business segment are recognized in the interim period in which they occur.

Earnings per share determination for interim purposes is handled in a fashion similar to annual reporting.

Materiality should be related to the full fiscal year. However, an item not disclosed in the annual financial statement due to immateriality would still be presented in the interim report if it is material to that interim period.

Revenue and Expense Recognition

Sales or service revenue should be recorded as earned in the interim period. If an advance is received in the first quarter that benefits the whole year, it should be proportionately allocated over all quarters affected.

Expenses should be deducted in the interim period as incurred. Expenses are matched to related revenue in the same interim period. Matching expenses to revenue includes cost of material used, salaries and fringe benefits, rent, utilities, and warranty expense. Yearly expenses (e.g., insurance, pension, year-end bonuses) should be proportionately allocated to the interim periods affected on some rational basis (e.g., time, activity, benefit derived). For example, insurance premiums and property taxes should be allocated among the interim periods based on time expired. Some expenses (e.g., bad debts) are subject to year-end adjustment.

Gains or losses that would not be deferred at year-end should be reflected in the interim period in which they arise. It is prohibited to defer a gain or loss to a later interim period unless the deferral would have been allowed in annual reporting.

Inventory

In estimating interim inventory, the gross profit method may be used when interim physical inventory counts do not take place (or in the case of a fire). The method, assumptions, and reconciling adjustments must be disclosed.

Emerging Issues Task Force Issue Number 86–13 covers recognition of inventory market declines at interim reporting dates. If a permanent loss occurs in inventory value in the interim period, it should be recognized immediately. A recovery in a later interim period is recognized as a gain. The gain from price recovery in a later interim period cannot exceed the previously recognized loss. Temporary losses in inventory value are not recognized because no loss is anticipated for the annual period. In other words, temporary losses are viewed as seasonal price fluctuations.

If a temporary liquidation occurs in the LIFO base with replacement anticipated by year-end, the cost of sales should be based on replacement cost.

EXAMPLE

The historical cost of an inventory item is $30,000 with an anticipated replacement cost of $36,000. The entry is

Cost of Sales	36,000	
Inventory		30,000
Reserve for Liquidation of LIFO Base		6,000

The reserve for liquidation of LIFO base is a current liability.

At the time of inventory replenishment at year-end, the journal entry is

Reserve for Liquidation of LIFO Base	6,000	
Inventory	30,000	
Cash		36,000

Disclosure should be made of unusual accounting methods for computing interim inventories such as LIFO estimations.

If quantity (volume) discounts are granted to buyers that depend on expected annual purchases, an apportionment is required to the interim period based on the following ratio:

Purchases in the interim period/Total estimated annual purchases

If a standard cost system is used, variances that are expected to reverse by year-end may be deferred to a liability or asset account. However, if variances are not expected to reverse by year-end, they should be recognized in the interim period in which they arose.

Taxes

FASB Interpretation 18 and FASB Technical Bulletin 79-9 cover the accounting for income taxes in interim statements, including the accounting for changes in tax rates.

The federal and local income tax provision for an interim period includes current and deferred taxes and should be cumulative for year-to-date. For example, the total tax expense for the first half of the year should be shown in the second quarter. Further, the second quarter's tax expense may also be presented for the three-month period of the second quarter.

Tax expense is based on income using the anticipated annual effective tax rate. The tax rate should take into account annual earnings, tax rates, tax credits, and alternative tax treatments. The tax rate should be based on continuing operations. A modification may be required to the anticipated annual effective tax rate at the end of each interim period based on new information.

$$\text{Effective tax rate} = \frac{\text{Expected annual income tax expense/}}{\text{Expected annual before-tax income}}$$

Extraordinary items and prior period adjustments should be shown net of tax in the interim period in which they occur.

The effect of a change in tax law should be recognized in the interim periods affected only after the effective date of the law.

Accounting Changes

FASB Statement Number 3 deals with the reporting of accounting changes in interim financial statements. If a change in method occurs in the first interim period, the cumulative effect account should be presented net of tax in the first interim period. If a change in method takes place in a quarter other than the first (e.g., third quarter), it is presumed that the change occurred at the start of the first quarter, showing the cumulative effect in the first quarter. A restatement of the interim periods will be needed using the new method (e.g., first and second quarters).

If interim information is presented for comparative reasons, data will need to be restated to conform with the new accounting policy. Alternatively, disclosure can be presented of the impact on previous data, if the new practice was used in that period.

When accounting principles are changed, a footnote is required of the nature and justification in the interim period of change. The impact of the change on per share amounts should be stated.

Prior Period Adjustments

FASB Statement Number 16 covers prior period adjustments. Prior period adjustments in interim reports are presented as follows:

- Net income of the current period should include the part of the effect applicable to current operations.

- Earnings of the affected interim periods of the current year should be restated to include the portion related thereto.

- If the prior period adjustment impacts previous years, it should be included in the profit of the first interim period of the current year.

Criteria to be satisfied for prior period adjustments in interim periods are identifiable to a previous interim period, subject to estimate, and material.

Prior period adjustments for interim reporting include correction of errors, renegotiation proceedings, settlement of a lawsuit or claim, and utility revenue in connection with rate-making issues.

Disclosures

Minimum disclosure in interim reports is as follows:

- Revenue, tax expense, extraordinary items, cumulative effect of a change in accounting principle, and net income
- Earnings per share
- Seasonal revenue and costs
- Material changes in tax expense, including reasons for significant differences between tax expense and income subject to tax
- Information on disposal of a business segment
- Commitments, contingencies, and uncertainties
- Significant changes in financial position and cash flows

Other disclosures peculiar to interim reporting are as follows:

- Seasonal factors bearing upon interim results. Seasonal companies should present supplementary information for the current and preceding 12-month periods ending at the interim date so that proper evaluation of the seasonal impact on interim results may be revealed.

- Significant items affecting the interim period.

- Whether a purchase or pooling-of-interests transaction took place, and the financial effects thereto.

- Material adjustments to the fourth quarter if such quarter is not presented in the annual report.

- A change in the anticipated effective tax rate.

PERSONAL FINANCIAL STATEMENTS

Personal financial statements may be prepared for an individual or family to reveal financial position. Personal financial statements show both business and personal interests. Accrual accounting must be followed. Such statements may be used in financial planning, in loan applications, and for governmental compliance mandates.

The statement of financial condition is prepared as follows:

- No segregation is made between current and noncurrent classifications.

- Assets are presented at estimated current values and are listed in liquidity (maturity) order. Current values may be based on appraisals, present value of future cash flows, and inflation adjusted historical cost. If assets are jointly owned, the person's beneficial interest should be presented. Receivables should be presented at the discounted amounts expected to be collected using the appropriate interest rate. The investment in life insurance is at the cash value of the policy less the amount of any loans against it. Option prices may not be available to value options. In such a case, the estimated current value may be based on the asset values subject to option, taking into account exercise prices and option periods. Intangible assets are presented at the present value of future net cash flows to be derived from them. Nonforfeitable rights to receive future sums should be presented at their discounted amounts.

- Liabilities are presented at current amounts in maturity order. Liabilities are typically shown at principal plus accrued interest due.

- Estimated taxes payable are presented as a liability, including provision for unpaid taxes of prior years. The tax obligation is reduced by withholding and estimated tax payments.

EXAMPLE

An illustrative Statement of Financial Condition follows:

Mr. and Mrs. Paul Jones
Statement of Financial Condition
December 31, 19X7

ASSETS	
Cash	$ 7,000
Interest and dividend receivable	1,000
Trading securities	12,000
Equity interest in a closely held business	5,000
Cash surrender value of life insurance	2,000
Real estate	185,000
Personal property	40,000
Total assets	$252,000
LIABILITIES	
Credit cards	$ 13,000
Income taxes payable	14,000
Loans payable	20,000
Mortgage payable	50,000
Total liabilities	$ 97,000
Estimated taxes on the differences between estimated current values of assets and liabilities	28,000
Net worth	$127,000
Total liabilities and net worth	$252,000

Preparation of a statement of changes in net worth is optional. Items increasing net worth include income, increases in the current value of assets, decreases in the current amounts of liabilities, and decreases in estimated taxes on the difference between estimated current asset values and liability amounts and their tax bases. Of course, items decreasing net worth are the opposite.

Comparative financial statements are optional.

The following should be footnoted:

- Individuals or family involved
- Nature of joint ownership of assets
- Information about receivables and payables, including collateral, maturities, and interest rates
- Noncancellable commitments, such as particulars of leasing arrangements
- Major investments by type
- Listing of intangibles with anticipated lives
- Approach followed in computing current values
- Method and assumptions used in determining income taxes
- Nonforfeitable rights (e.g., pension rights)
- Face amount of life insurance
- Names of companies/industries and estimated current values of any significant investments relative to other assets
- Percentage equity in a closely held company, including the type of business activities, summarized financial information, and accounting basis used

INCORPORATION OF A BUSINESS

If an unincorporated business incorporates and issues equity and debt securities in exchange for the assets of the unincorporated entity, the following accounting procedures are followed:

- Assets are brought forth at fair market value.

- Current liabilities are recognized at face value while noncurrent liabilities are recorded at present value.

- Stock issued is recorded at par value.

- The gain or loss is not recorded on the issuance of stock in exchange for the unincorporated entity's assets.

The journal entry follows:

> Current assets
> Noncurrent assets
> > Current liabilities
> > Noncurrent liabilities
> > Common stock
> > Paid-in-capital

DIVESTITURES

As per APB Opinion Number 29 (*Accounting for Nonmonetary Transactions*), a gain or loss cannot be recognized on a corporate divestiture. However, disclosure should be made of the nature and terms of the divestiture.

If there is an exchange of stock held by a parent in a subsidiary for stock of the parent company itself held by stockholders in the parent, there is a non-pro rata splitoff of the business segment because a reorganization is recorded at fair value. However, if there is a splitoff of a targeted company distributed on a pro rata basis to the one holding the applicable targeted stock, it should be recorded at historical cost as long as the targeted stock did not arise in contemplation of the later splitoff. If the contemplated situation did in fact exist, then the transaction is recorded at fair value. In a splitoff, there is a distribution of shares in the business segment, with the investor's shares being exchanged on a pro rata basis for the shares of the new company. In a splitoff, the transaction is, in effect, the purchase of treasury stock. Retained earnings is not changed.

In a spinoff, there is a distribution of the segment's shares to the investor's shareholders without the holders surrendering their shares.

In some cases, a splitoff or spinoff may be treated as a discontinued operation of a business segment.

EXAMPLE

X Company declares and pays a dividend to stockholders of 200,000 shares of common stock of Y Company. The investment in Y Company at the date of spinoff under the equity method was $900,000.

The journal entries follow:

Retained earnings	900,000	
Property dividends payable		900,000
To record the declaration of the property dividend.		
Property dividends payable	900,000	
Investment in Y Company		900,000
To record the payment of the property dividend.		

Note that in a spinoff no gain or loss is recorded.

Assume the same information except that in exchange for the 200,000 shares of Y Company, X Company's stockholders give up 50,000 shares of X Company's common stock. The journal entry at the splitoff date is

Treasury stock	900,000	
Investment in Y Company		900,000

To reflect the purchase of treasury stock in exchange for the investment in Y Company.

In a splitup, there is a transfer of the operations of the original entity to at least two *new* entities.

EXAMPLE

L Company transfers Division A to M Company (a newly formed company) and its Division B to N Company (a newly formed company). L Company only had divisions A and B, so it terminates in existence. L Company shareholders receive a half share in M Company and a half share in N Company for each one share of L Company.

Divisions A and B have the same book value of net assets.

Prior to the transfer, L Company's assets were $1,000,000, liabilities were $600,000, and equity was $400,000.

The liquidation entry to record the termination of L Company is

Liabilities	600,000	
Stockholder's equity	400,000	
Assets		1,000,000

The entry to record M Company and N Company (the newly formed companies) would be identical based on the information given in this example. The entry is

Assets	500,000	
Liabilities		300,000
Paid-in-capital		200,000

Annual Report References

COLGATE-PALMOLIVE 1999 ANNUAL REPORT

15. Quarterly Financial Data (Unaudited)

	First Quarter	Second Quarter	Third Quarter	Fourth Quarter
1999				
Net sales	**$2,175.3**	**$2,285.0**	**2,314.0**	**2,343.9**
Gross profit	**1,165.9**	**1,221.3**	**1,253.6**	**1,253.4**
Net income	**208.9**	**228.1**	**239.7**	**260.6**
Earnings per common share				
Basic	**.35**	**.38**	**.40**	**,44**
Diluted	**.32**	**.36**	**.38**	**.41**
1998				
Net sales	$2,159.5	$2,256.5	$2,265.4	$2,290.2
Gross profit	1,123.5	1,172.6	1,192.6	1,192.6
Net income	196.0	203.5	214.9	234.2
Earnings per common share				
Basic	.32	.34	.35	.39
Diluted	.30	.31	.33	.36

Market and Dividend Information

The Company's common stock and $4.25 Preferred Stock are listed on the New York Stock Exchange. The trading symbol for the common stock is CL. Dividends on the common stock have been paid every year since 1895, and the amount of dividends paid per share has increased for 37 consecutive years.

	Common Stock				$4.25 Preferred Stock			
Market Price	1999		1998		1999		1998	
Quarter Ended	**High**	**Low**	High	Low	**High**	**Low**	High	Low
March 31	$47.06	$37.53	$43.90	$33.94	$89.50	$86.75	$79.50	$72.50
June 30	52.41	45.78	45.72	41.22	87.50	85.50	81.00	76.50
September 30	58.38	45.75	48.47	32.78	88.00	86.00	87.00	80.50
December 31	65.00	47.81	47.37	34.00	91.00	87.00	88.00	85.00
Closing Price	$65.00		$46.44		$87.00		$88.00	

Dividends Paid Per Share				
Quarter Ended	1999	1998	1999	1998
March 31	$.1375	$.1375	$1.0625	$1.0625
June 30	.1375	.1375	1.0625	$1.0625
September 30	.1575	.1375	1.0625	1.0625
December 31	.1525	.1375	1.0625	1.0625
	$.59	$.55	$4.25	$4.25

CATERPILLAR
1998 ANNUAL REPORT

2. Selected Quarterly Financial Results (Unaudited)

Financial information for interim periods was as follows:

Quarters	1998			
(Dollars in millions except per share data)	1st	2nd	3rd	4th
Sales and revenues	$ 4,794	$ 5,604	$ 5,173	$ 5,406
Less: Revenues	221	247	267	270
Sales	4,573	5,357	4,906	5,136
Cost of goods sold	3,334	3,978	3,748	3,971
Gross margin	1,239	1,379	1,158	1,165
Profit	$ 430	$ 446	$ 336	$ 301
Profit per share of common stock	$ 1.17	$ 1.22	$ .93	$ .84
Profit per share of common stock— assuming dilution	$ 1.15	$ 1.20	$ .92	$ 83

Quarters	1997			
(Dollars in millions except per share data)	1st	2nd	3rd	4th
Sales and revenues	$ 4,262	$ 4,870	$ 4,600	$ 5,193
Less: Revenues	190	194	215	216
Sales	4,072	4,676	4,385	4,977
Cost of goods sold	2,981	3,450	3,278	3,665
Gross margin	1,091	1,226	1,107	1,312
Profit	$ 394	$ 435	$ 385	$ 451
Profit per share of common stock	$ 1.04	$ 1.15	$ 1.03	$ 1.22
Profit per share of common stock— assuming dilution	$ 1.03	$ 1.13	$ 1.01	$ 1.20

Fourth-Quarter 1998 Results

Fourth-quarter sales and revenues were a fourth-quarter record and were up 4 percent from the comparable period in 1997. Profit of $301 million was down 33 percent from the fourth-quarter record set in 1997 and profit per share of $.83 was down 31 percent. Profits were lower as the benefit from higher sales and revenues was more than offset by lower margin rates and continued spending for growth initiatives. Revenues were a record $270 million, up $54 million or 25 percent from the fourth quarter of 1997, principally due to Cat Financial's continued portfolio growth.

PEPSI
1998 ANNUAL REPORT

17. Selected Quarterly Financial Data

[See next page.]

	First Quarter (12 Weeks)		Second Quarter (12 Weeks)		Third Quarter (12 Weeks)		Fourth Quarter(a) (12 Weeks)		Full Year (52 Weeks)	
	1998	1997	1998	1997	1998	1997	1998	1997	1998	1997
Net sales	$ 4,353	4,213	$ 5,258	5,086	$ 5,544	5,362	$ 7,193	6,256	$22,348	20,917
Gross profit	$ 2,603	2,492	$ 3,110	3,017	$ 3,261	3,183	$ 4,044	3,700	$13,018	12,392
Unusual impairment and other items—loss/(gain)(b)	$ —	(22)	$ —	326	$ —	—	$ 288	(14)	$ 288	290
Operating profit	$ 590	581	$ 778	436	$ 889	929	$ 327	716	$ 2,584	2,662
Income from continuing operations(c)	$ 377	318	$ 494	176	$ 761	551	$ 361	446	$ 1,993	1,491
Income (loss) from discontinued operations(d)	$ —	109	$ —	480	$ —	107	$ —	(45)	$ —	651
Net income	$ 377	427	$ 494	656	$ 761	658	$ 361	401	$ 1,993	2,142
Net income (loss) per share—basic										
Continuing operations	$ 0.25	0.21	$ 0.33	0.11	$ 0.50	0.36	$ 0.25	0.30	$ 1.35	0.98
Discontinued operations	$ —	0.07	$ —	0.31	$ —	0.07	$ —	(0.03)	$ —	0.42
Net income	$ 0.25	0.28	$ 0.33	0.42	$ 0.52	0.43	$ 0.25	0.27	$ 1.35	1.40
Net income (loss) per share—assuming dilution										
Continuing operations	$ 0.24	0.20	$ 0.33	0.11	$ 0.50	0.35	$ 0.24	0.29	$ 1.31	0.95
Discontinued operations	$ —	0.07	$ —	0.31	$ —	0.07	$ —	(0.04)	$ —	0.41
Net income	$ 0.24	0.27	$ 0.33	0.42	$ 0.50	0.42	$ 0.24	0.25	$ 1.31	1.36
Cash dividends declared per share	$ 0.125	0.115	$ 0.13	0.125	$ 0.13	0.125	$ 0.13	0.125	$ 0.515	0.49
Stock price per share(e)										
High	$ 43 9/16	34 55/64	$ 44 11/16	39	$ 43 5/8	39 11/16	$ 41 1/16	40	$ 44 11/16	40
Low	$ 34 7/8	29 1/8	$ 37 5/8	31 1/4	$ 27 11/16	35 1/2	$ 28 11/16	34 1/4	$ 27 11/16	29 1/8
Close	$ 43	32 1/2	$ 40 11/16	39	$ 30 5/16	37 5/8	$ 40 7/16	34 11/16	$ 40 7/16	34 11/16

(a)Fourth quarter 1998 includes the operating results of Tropicana which was acquired in August of 1998. (b) unusual impairment and other items—loss/(gain) (see Note 3):

	1998			1997		
	Pre-Tax	After-Tax	Per Share	Pre-Tax	After-Tax	Per Share
First quarter	$ —	$ —	$ —	$ (22)	$ 2	$ —
Second quarter				326	238	0.15
Fourth quarter	288	261	0.17	(14)	(1)	—
Full year	$288	$261	$0.17	$290	$239	$ 0.15

(c)Includes in 1998 a tax benefit of $200 million (or $0.13 per share) in the third quarter and $294 million (or $0.19 per share) in the fourth quarter. See Note 12.

(d)See Note 4.

(e)Represents the high, low and closing prices for one share of Pepsico's capital stock on the New York Stock Exchange. Stock prices on or before October 6, 1997 are not adjusted to reflect the IRICON spin-off. See Note 4.

LOCKHEED MARTIN
1999 ANNUAL REPORT

The Statement of Position requires that, at the effective date of adoption, costs of start-up activities previously capitalized be expensed and reported as a cumulative effect of a change in accounting principle, and further requires that such costs subsequent to adoption be expensed as incurred. The adoption of SOP No. 98-5 resulted in the recognition of a cumulative effect adjustment which reduced net earnings for the year ended December 31, 1999 by $355 million, or $.93 per diluted share. The cumulative effect adjustment was recorded net of income tax benefits of $227 million, and was primarily composed of approximately $560 million of costs which were included in inventories as of December 31, 1998.

Effective January 1, 1999, the Corporation adopted the AICPA's SOP No. 98-1, "Accounting for the Costs of Computer Software Developed or Obtained for Internal Use." This SOP, which requires the capitalization of certain costs incurred in connection with developing or obtaining software for internal use, affects the future cash flows under contracts with the U.S. Government. However, the impact of the adoption of SOP No. 98-1 was not material to the Corporation's consolidation results of operations, cash flows or financial position.

New accounting pronouncement to be adopted—On June 1, 1998, the Financial Accounting Standards Board (FASB) issued SFAS No. 133 "Accounting for Derivative Instruments and Hedging Activities." SFAS No. 133 requires the recognition of all derivatives as either assets or liabilities in the Consolidated Balance Sheet, and the periodic measurement of those instruments at fair value. The classification of gains and losses resulting from changes in the fair values of derivatives is dependent on the intended use of the derivative and its resulting designation. In general, these provisions of the Statement could result in a greater degree of income statement volatility than current accounting practice. At adoption, existing hedging relationships must be designated anew and documented pursuant to the provisions of the Statement. The Corporation does not   intend to adopt SFAS No. 133, as amended, prior to the required date of January 1, 2001. The Corporation is continuing its process of analyzing and assessing the impact that the adoption of SFAS No. 133 is expected to have on its consolidated results of operations, cash flows and financial position, but has not yet reached any conclusions.

2. Traction Agreement with COMSAT Corporation

In September 1998, the Corporation and COMSAT Corporation (COMSAT) announced that they had entered into an Agreement and Plan of Merger (the Merger Agreement) to combine the companies in a two-phase traction with a total estimated value of approximately $2.7 billion at the date of the announcement (the Merger). The Merger Agreement was approved by the respective Board of Directors of the Corporation and COMSAT.

In connection with the first phase of this transaction, subsequent to obtaining all necessary regulatory approvals and approval of the Merger by the stockholders of COMSAT, the Corporation completed a cash tender offer (the Tender Offer) on September 18, 1999. On that date, the Corporation accepted for payment approximately 26 million shares of COMSAT common stock, representing approximately 49 percent of the outstanding common stock of COMSAT, for $45.50 a share pursuant to the terms of the Merger Agreement. The total value of this phase of the transaction was $1.2 billion, and such amount is included in investments in equity securities in the December 31, 1999 Consolidated Balance Sheet. The Corporation accounts for its 49 percent investment in COMSAT under the equity method of accounting.

The second phase of the transaction, which will result in consummation of the Merger, is to be accomplished by an exchange of one share of Lockheed Martin common stock for each remaining share of COMSAT common stock. Consummation of the Merger remains contingent upon the satisfaction of certain conditions, including the enactment of federal legislation necessary to remove existing restrictions. ...

3. Divestiture Activities

The Corporation executed a definitive agreement in March 1997 to reposition 10 of its non-core business units as a new independent company, L-3, in which the Corporation retained an approximate 35 percent ownership interest at closing. The transaction did not have a material impact on the Corporation's 1997 earnings. During May 1998, L-3 completed an initial public offering resulting in the issuance of an additional 6.9 million shares of its common stock to the public. This transaction resulted in a reduction in the Corporation's ownership to approximately 25 percent and the recognition of a pretax gain of $18 million. The gain increased net earnings by $12 million, or $.03 per diluted share. In February 1999, the Corporation sold 4.5 million of its shares in L-3 as part of a secondary public offering by L-3. This transaction resulted in a reduction in the Corporation's ownership to approximately seven percent and the recognition of a pretax gain of $114 million. The gain increased net earnings by $74 million, or $.19 per diluted share. After this transaction was consummated, the Corporation began accounting for its remaining investment in L-3 as an available-for-sale investment. In October 1999, the Corporation sold its remaining interest in L-3. This transaction resulted in the recognition of a pretax gain of $41 million which increased net earnings by $27 million, or $.07 per diluted share.

In September 1999, the Corporation sold its interest in Airport Group International Holdings, LLC which resulted in a pretax gain of $33 million. In October 1999, the Corporation exited its commercial 3D graphics business through consummation of a series of transactions which resulted in the sale of its interest in Real 3D, Inc., a majority-owned subsidiary, and a pretax gain of $33 million. On a combined basis, these transactions increased net earnings by $43 million, or $.11 per diluted share.

In November 1997, the Corporation exchanged all of the outstanding capital stock of a wholly-owned subsidiary, LMT Sub, for all of the outstanding Series A preferred stock held by General Electric Company (the GE Transaction). LMT Sub was composed of two non-core commercial business units which contributed approximately five percent of the Corporation's 1997 net sales, Lockheed Martin's investment in a telecommunications partnership, and approximately $1.6 billion in cash, of which $1.4 billion was subsequently refinanced with a 6.04% note, due November 17, 2002, from Lockheed Martin to LMT Sub. The fair value of the non-cash net assets exchanged was approximately $1.2 billion. During the second quarter of 1998, the final determination of the closing net worth of the business exchanged was completed, resulting in a payment of $51 million from the Corporation to MRA Systems, Inc. (formerly LMT Sub). Subsequently, the remainder of the cash included in the transaction was refinanced with a

5.73% note for $210 million, due November 17, 2002, from Lockheed Martin to MTA Systems, Inc.

The GE Transaction was accounted for at fair value, and resulted in the reduction of the Corporation's stockholders' equity by $2.8 billion and the recognition of a tax-free gain of approximately $311 million during the fourth quarter of 1997. The final settlement payment in 1998 did not impact the gain previously recorded on the transaction. For purposes of determining net loss applicable to common stock used in the computation of loss per share for 1997, the excess of the fair value consideration transferred to GE (approximately $2.8 billion) over the carrying value of the Series A preferred stock ($1.0 billion) was treated as a deemed preferred stock dividend and deducted from 1997 net earnings in accordance with the requirements of the Emerging Issues Task Force's Issue D-42. This deemed dividend had a significant impact on the loss per share calculations, but did not impact reported 1997 net earnings. The effect of this deemed dividend was to reduce the basic and diluted loss per share amounts by $4.93.

PHILIP MORRIS
1998 ANNUAL REPORT

2. Divestitures

During 1997, the Company sold several domestic and international food businesses, including its Brazilian ice cream businesses and its North American maple-flavored syrup businesses, for total proceeds of $1.5 billion and net pre-tax gains of $958 million. In addition, the Company sold its equity interest in a Canadian beer operation and sold a minority interest in a beer import operation for proceeds of $306 million and a pre-tax gain of $12 million. The Company also sold its real estate operations for total proceeds of $424 million and a pre-tax gain of $103 million.

During 1996, the Company sold several domestic and international food businesses, including its North American bagel business, for total proceeds of $612 million and net pre-tax gains of $320 million.

The operating results of these businesses were not material to the Company's consolidated operating results in any of the periods presented. Pre-tax gains on these divestitures were included in marketing, administration and research costs on the Company's consolidated statements of earnings.

FIRST DATA
1997 ANNUAL REPORT

4. Dispositions

Business Sold (in millions)	Period	Cash Proceeds	Pretax Gain (Loss) on Sale		
			1997	1996	1995
Nationwide Credit	December 1997	$155.2	**$(51.0)**	$ —	$ —
FIRST HEALTH Strategies and Services	July 1997	200.0	**(93.8)**		
GENEX	February 1997	70.0	**50.5**		
MoneyGram	December 1996	199.5		46.0	
Health Systems	June 1995	231.1			93.0
Cable Services	November 1994	143.4			12.0

Revenues from these businesses were approximately 5% of the Company's consolidated revenues in 1997, compared with 13% in 1996 and 17% in 1995.

A description of 1997 divestitures is contained in Note 2.

In December 1996, the Company divested its MoneyGram operation through an initial public offering of 100% of its common stock. Since the merger with FFMC required the divestiture of MoneyGram pursuant to an order by the Federal Trade Commission, the gain on the divestiture has been reflected as a component of the 1996 restructuring, loss on business divestitures and impairment amount.

The pretax gains on the 1995 dispositions have been included in "Product sales and other" in the Company's consolidated statements of operations. The aggregate pretax gain in 1995 on the sale of the health systems business (which included a $24.0 million pretax gain on the September 1995 sale of the buyer's stock received as consideration in the sale) was substantially offset by income taxes related to the sale totaling $76.9 million. The Company also recorded pretax gains in 1995 resulting from the favorable resolution of certain indemnification issues related to the 1994 sale of the cable services business.

CHESAPEAKE
1999 ANNUAL REPORT

2. Acquisitions and Divestures
1999

On October 22, 1999, the Company completed the acquisition of Consumer Promotions International, Inc. ("CPI"), a designer and manufacturer of point-of-sale displays. CPI, based in Mount Vernon, New York, has operations in the United States, the United Kingdom and France, and has annual sales of approximately $50.0 million.

Effective October 3, 1999, Wisconsin Tissue Mills Inc., renamed WTM 1 Company ("WT"), a wholly-owned subsidiary of Chesapeake, completed the formation of a joint venture with Georgia-Pacific Corporation ("GP") through which the companies combined their commercial businesses. WT contributed substantially all of the assets and liabilities of the Company's tissue business to the joint venture, known as Georgia-Pacific Tissue LLC (the "Tissue JV") and received a 5% equity interest in the Tissue JV and tax-deferred cash distribution of approximately $755.0 million (the "Special Distribution"). G-P contributed certain of its commercial tissue assets and related liabilities to the Tissue JV return for a 95% equity interest. The respective net values of WT's and G-P's contributed businesses were based on a multiple of each businesses' 1998 earnings before interest, income taxes, depreciation and amortization ("EBITDA"), which valuation principle was negotiated on an arm's length basis. Chesapeake used a portion of the proceeds to reduce debt and repurchase its common stock.

In connection with the receipt of the Special Distribution, WT entered into an Indemnity Agreement pursuant to which it agreed to indemnify G-P, under certain circumstances, against principal payments G-P may make under a guaranty of the Tissue JV's debt that was incurred to finance the Special Distribution (the "Tissue JV Debt"). G-P will control and manage the Tissue JV, subject to obtaining WT's consent connection with certain actions. As a result of WT's continued interest in the Tissue JV, the remaining 5% interest has been recorded using the equity method of accounting. During 1999, the results of operations included an after-tax gain of approximately $194.1 million, or $9.51 diluted share, related to the formation of the Tissue JV.

The WT assets contributed to the Tissue JV include production facilities located in Bellemont and Flagstaff, Arizona; Alsip, Illinois; Greenwich, New York; Menasha and Neenah, Wisconsin; and Toluca, Mexico. The Tissue JV has assumed substantially all of WT's liabilities that relate primarily to its contributed business, including any liabilities associated with certain alleged violations of antitrust laws, but specifically excluding most tax liabilities related to the contributed assets for periods prior to formation of the Tissue JV and certain liabilities associated with the discharge of polychlorinated-biphenyls ("PCB's") and other hazardous materials in the Fox River and Green Bay System (see Note 13).

At any time on or after the third anniversary of the October 4, 1999 closing date, WT will have up to three "put" rights to sell to G-P, or cause the Tissue JV to redeem, all or any portion of WT's equity interest in the Tissue JV. At any time after the tenth anniversary of the closing date, G-P will have the right to "call" all, but not less than all, of WT's equity interest in the Tissue JV. The purchase and sale price of WT's equity interest for both the put and call will be based on the Tissue JV's EBITDA for the immediately preceding four fiscal quarters and the same multiple used to value WT's and G-P's initial contributions to the Tissue JV.

Certain events, including exercise of a put or call, reduction of the principal amount of the Tissue JV Debt, or the Tissue JV's sale of some or all of the assets contributed to it by WT, may trigger recognition of all or a portion of WT's deferred tax liability related to the transaction. Under certain circumstances, the Tissue JV or G-P may be obligated to fund all or a portin of WT's deferred tax liability.

On Septembet 10, 1999, the Company completed the sale of approximately 278,000 acres of timberland in Virginia, Maryland and Delaware, and on July 30, 1999, the Company completed the sale of its Building Products business (two sawmills, a lumber processing plant, and a wood chip mill) for combined cash proceeds of approximately $185.0 million. The results of operations include a nonrecurring after-tax gain on the sales of these businesses of $47.9 million, or $2.35 per diluted share, net of a revision of $11.7 million after tax for costs associated with the 1997 disposal of the Kraft Products business segment.

On March 18, 1999, Chesapeake completed its acquisition of substantially all of the outstanding capital shares of Field Group PLC ("Field

Group"), a European specialty packaging company headquartered in the United Kingdom. The acquisition was effected through a tender offer by Chesapeake UK Acquisitions PLC, a wholly-owned subsidiary of Chesapeake, for all of the outstanding capital shares of Field Group at purchase price of £3.60 per share. As of April 30, 1999, Chesapeake acquired compulsorily all remaining outstanding shares of Field Group. The purchase price of approximately $373.0 million was funded through a combination of approximately $316.0 million in borrowings under a credit facility, $22.0 million in unsecured loan notes issued to certain Field Group shareholders, and $35.0 million in cash.

During 1999, Field Group acquired Berry's (Holding) Limited, one of Ireland's largest suppliers of printed pharmaceutical leaflets and self-adhesive labels, and formed a joint venture with one of Spain's leading printing groups, Mateu Cromo Artes Graphicas S.A.

1998

On November 20, 1998, Chesapeake Corporation acquired all of the outstanding capital stock of Capitol Packaging Corporation, a specialty packaging company located in Denver, Colorado. On February 2, 1998, Chesapeake Packaging Co. purchased substantially all of the assets, and assumed certain liabilities, of Rock City Box Company, Inc. located in Utica, New York. This operation manufactures corrugated containers, trays, and pallets, as well as wood and foam packaging products.

1997

On May 23, 1997, the Company completed the sale to St. Laurent Paperboard (U.S.) Inc. ("St. Laurent U.S."), a wholly-owned subsidiary of St. Laurent Paperboard, Inc. ("St. Laurent") (Toronto and Montreal: SPI), of: (i) the sole membership interest in Chesapeake Paper Products Company L.L.C. (successor to Cheasapeake Paper Products Company), a wholly-owned subsidiary of the Company which, as of the closing date, owned and operated the Company's kraft products mill located in West Point, Virginia (the "West Point Mill"); (ii) all of the capital stock of Chesapeake Box Company which, as of the closing date, owned and operated directly or through a subsidiary substantially all of the assets of four of the Company's corrugated box plants; and (iii) all of the capital stock of Chesapeake Fiber Company which, as of the closing date, owned and operated, directly or through a subsidiary, certain assets related to the West Point Mill's wood procurement operations. The four box plants involved in the transaction are located in Richmond, Virginia; Roanoke, Virginia; Baltimore, Maryland; and North Tonawanda, New York.

The sales price of approximately $500.0 million was paid in cash at closing, with a post-closing adjustment of approximately $10.0 million paid to the buyer. The transaction resulted in an after-tax gain of $49.1 million, or $2.07 a share, which was recorded in the second quarter of 1997. Chesapeake used approximately $250.0 million of the net after-tax proceeds to reduce debt and $79.0 million of the net after-tax proceeds to repurchase its common stock. Chesapeake has agreed to indemnify St. Laurent and St. Laurent (U.S.) against losses incurred by them which are attributable to certain environmental matters and breaches of representations, warranties or covenants made by Chesapeake in the Purchase Agreement, provided notice is given to Chesapeake or losses are paid or incurred within the applicable survival periods specified therein.

Summary

Each of the acquisitions has been accounted for using the purchase method and is included in the results of operations since the purchase date. The purchase prices have been allocated to the assets acquired and liabilities assumed based on their estimated market values at the respective dates of acquisition. The purchase prices for the acquired companies exceeded the fair value of net assets by approximately $278.3 million in 1999 and $8.8 million in 1998, which is being amortized on a straight line basis over 40 years. The purchase price amounts for acquisitions have been allocated to the acquired net assets as summarized below:

(In millions)	1999	1998	1997
Acquisitions:			
Fair value of assets acquired	$620.8	$24.6	$—
Liabilities assumed or created	(187.3)	(6.5)	—
Cash acquired	(17.4)	—	—
Cash paid for acquisitions, net	$416.1	$18.1	—

(In millions)	*1999*	*1998*	*1997*
Dispositions:			
Fair value of assets sold	**$941.7**	$—	$491.0
Non-cash consideration received	**(1.2)**	—	—
Cash received from sale of businesses	**$940.5**	$—	$491.0

Pro Forma Operating Data

Pro forma financial information reflecting the combined results of the Company and Field Group as if the acquisition occurred on January 1, 1998, is as follows:

(in millions, except per share data)	Year Ended December 31,	
	1999	*1998*
Acquisition of Field Group:		
Net sales	$1,241.4	$1,360.9
Income before cumulative effect of accounting change	$ 247.0	$ 37.1
Net income	$ 247.0	$ 50.4
Earnings per share before cumulative effect of accounting change:		
Basic	$ 12.29	$ 1.75
Diluted	$ 12.11	$ 1.72
Net income per share:		
Basic	$ 12.29	$ 2.38
Diluted	$ 12.11	$ 2.34

Chapter 8

Disclosures

This chapter discusses the disclosures required of companies, including those related to accounting policies, segmental information, related parties, contingencies, long-term purchase contract obligations, inflation, and derivatives. The financial reporting and disclosure requirements of development stage companies are also presented. Changes bearing upon the comparability of financial statements should also be disclosed. Comparative statements aid reader comprehension of the significance of trends and their impact on the business.

DISCLOSURE OF ACCOUNTING POLICIES

APB Opinion Number 22 covers the disclosure of accounting policies. Accounting policies include accounting principles and their methods of application in the preparation of financial statements, including

- Choosing between alternative GAAP
- Unusual or innovative applications of GAAP
- Accounting methods peculiar to a particular industry

A company's major accounting policies should be disclosed in the first footnote or in a section called "Summary of Significant Accounting Policies," which appears before the footnotes. Examples of accounting policies to be disclosed include inventory method, construction contract method, depreciation method, consolidation basis, amortization method and period for intangibles, method to account for bad debts, foreign currency translation process, recognition of franchise revenue, method to amortize deferred revenue, definition of cash equivalents in preparing the cash flow statement, description of how deferred taxes are calculated, method to account for unconsolidated investees, and accounting policies for pension plans.

If more than one accounting method is used (e.g., different depreciation methods), the one disclosed in the footnote should be the primary method. Accounting policy disclosures need not duplicate information presented elsewhere in the financial statements.

Disclosure of accounting policies should not repeat what is stated elsewhere in other footnotes or within the face of the financial statements. However, reference may be made to other footnotes. In most cases, accounting policies are expressed broadly, with specifics disclosed in other notes or in the body of the financial statements.

Nonprofit entities must disclose their significant accounting policies. Financial statements not requiring a description of the accounting policies followed include unaudited interim statements (unless a change in principle was adopted after the preparation of the last year-end financial statement) and financial statements issued only for internal use.

SEGMENTAL REPORTING

Segmental reporting aids in evaluating a company's financial statements by revealing growth prospects, including earning potential, areas of risk, and financial problems. It facilitates the appraisal of both historical performance and expected future performance. FASB Statement Number 131 (*Disclosures About Segments of an Enterprise and Related Information*) requires that the amount reported for each segment item be based on what is used by the "chief operating decision maker" in formulating a determination as to how many resources to assign to a segment and how to appraise the performance of that segment. The term *chief operating decision maker* may apply to the chief executive officer or chief operating officer or to a group of executives. **Note:** The term of *chief operating decision maker* may apply to a function and not necessarily to a specific person(s). This is a management approach rather than an industry approach in identifying segments. The segments are based on the company's organizational structure, revenue sources, nature of activities, existence of responsible managers, and information presented to the Board of Directors.

Revenues, gains, expenses, losses, and assets should only be allocated to a segment if the chief operating decision maker considers doing so in measuring a segment's earnings for purposes of making a financial or operating decision. The same is true with regard to allocating to segments eliminations and adjustments applying to the company's general-purpose financial statements. Any allocation of financial items to a segment should be rationally based.

In measuring a segment's earnings or assets, the following should be disclosed for explanatory purposes:

- Measurement or valuation basis used
- Differences in measurements used for the general-purpose financial statements relative to the financial information of the segment
- A change in measurement method relative to prior years
- A symmetrical allocation, meaning an allocation of depreciation or amortization to a segment without a related allocation to the associated assets

Segmental information is required in annual financial statements. Some segmental disclosures are required in interim financial statements. Segmental information is not required for unconsolidated subsidiaries or investees accounted for under the equity method.

An operating segment is a distinct revenue-producing component of the business for which internal financial data are produced. Expenses are recognized as incurred in that segment. **Note:** A startup operation would qualify as an operating segment even though revenue is not being earned.

An operating segment is periodically reviewed by the chief operating decision maker to evaluate performance and to determine what and how many resources to allocate to the segment.

A reportable segment requiring disclosure is one which is an operating segment and meets certain percentage tests, discussed in the next section. If a segment does not generate revenue or insignificant revenue, it is *not* an operating segment to be reported. An example is corporate headquarters.

An aggregation may be made of operating segments if they are similar in terms of products or services, customer class, manufacturing processes, distribution channels, legal entity, regulatory control, geographical area, and government contract.

The accounting principles used in preparing segmental information should be the same as those used in preparing the financial statements. However, intercompany transactions (which are eliminated in consolidation) are included for segmental reporting purposes, including in applying the 10% and 75% rules discussed later. Segmental information may be provided in the body of the financial statements, in separate schedules, or in footnotes. Most companies report segmental data in separate schedules.

Disclosures should be made of how reporting segments were determined (e.g., customer class, products, services, geographical areas). Disclosure should be given identifying those operating segments that have been aggregated. The following should be disclosed for each reportable segment:

- Nature and identification of products or services
- Sales to unaffiliated customers
- Method used to allocate costs
- Tax effects
- Geographic areas of operations
- Interest revenue and interest expense
- Unusual items included in segmental earnings

- Book values of identifiable assets
- Capital expenditures
- Aggregate depreciation, depletion, and amortization expense
- Effect of a change in method on a segment's operating earnings
- Other profitability measures, such as contribution margin
- Transfer pricing method (Sales or transfers to other industry segments should be noted, including the accounting basis.)
- Equity in unconsolidated subsidiaries or investees

Disclosures should be in both dollars and percentages.

A reportable segment is determined by

- Grouping by industry line
- Identifiable products or services
- Significant segments to the company in the entirety

If any one of the following exist, a segment must be reported upon:

- Revenue, including unaffiliated and intersegment sales or transfers, is 10% or more of total revenue of all operating segments.
- Operating profit or loss is 10% or more of the greater, in absolute amount, of the combined operating profit (or loss) of all industry segments with operating profits (or losses).
- Identifiable assets are 10% or more of total assets of all operating segments.

Operating segments that are not reportable should be combined and disclosed in the "all other" category. Disclosure should be made of the sources of revenue for these segments.

EXAMPLE

A company reports the following information for its reportable segments:

Segment	Total Revenue	Operating Profit	Identifiable Assets
1	$ 500	$ 50	$ 200
2	250	10	150
3	3,500	200	1,950
4	1,500	100	900
	$5,750	$360	$3,200

The revenue test is 10% × $5,750 = $575. Segments 3 and 4 satisfy this test. The operating profit (loss) test is 10% × $360 = $36. Segments 1, 3, and 4 satisfy this test. The identifiable assets test is 10% × $3,200 = $320. Segments 3 and 4 satisfy this test. Therefore, the reportable segments are 1, 3, and 4.

EXAMPLE

Assume a company has six industry segments with operating profits and losses as follows:

Industry Segment	Operating Profit (Loss)	
1	$400,000	
2	100,000	
3	800,000	Total $1,300,000
4	(200,000)	
5	(80,000)	
6	(1,000,000)	Total ($1,280,000)

The absolute amount of the combined operating profits of all profitable industry segments is $1,300,000, and the absolute amount of the combined operating losses of all industry segments with losses is $1,280,000. The greater of these two absolute amounts is $1,300,000. Thus, all industry segments with operating profits or losses having an absolute amount equal to or greater than $130,000 (10% × $1,300,000) satisfy the operating profit or loss test. Therefore, industry segments 1, 3, 4, and 6 are reportable.

If a segment failed the 10% test this year but was significant in previous years and is expected to be significant in the future, it should still be reported upon in the current year. On the other hand, a segment may not be reported this year that satisfies the 10% test due to abnormal profits but was not reportable in previous years nor is expected to be reportable in the future. In other words, if a segment passes the 10% test in the current year because of some unusual or rare occurrence, it should be excluded from reporting in the current year.

In applying the 10% rule, note the following:

- *Revenue.* Revenue to unaffiliated customers and revenue to other businesses should be separated. Transfer prices are set for intersegment transfers. However, intersegment sales should not include the cost of joint facilities or other joint costs. Interest income on intersegment receivables is includable in intersegment sales as long as the receivables are part of identifiable assets. However, interest earned on advances or loans to industry segments is excluded from intersegment revenues. Disclosure should be made of the accounting bases used.

- *Operating Profit or Loss.* Operating earnings excludes general (nonallocable) corporate income and expenses, interest expense (unless its a financial segment), income taxes, extraordinary gain or loss, cumulative effect of a change in accounting principle, minority interest, and income from unconsolidated subsidiaries or investees. Directly traceable and allocable costs should be charged to segments. Examples of allocation bases for common costs are sales, operating income before common costs, or total assets.

- *Identifiable Assets.* Segmental assets include those directly in the segment and reasonably allocable general corporate assets. Allocation methods should be used consistently. Excluded from identifiable assets are advances or loans to other segments, excluding income derived therefrom that is used to compute operating results.

Segments shall represent a significant portion (75% or more) of the entity's total revenue of all operating segments. The 75% test is applied separately each year.

In deriving 75%, no more than 10 segments should be presented because to do otherwise would result in too cumbersome and detailed reporting. If more than 10 are identified, similar segments may be combined. For example, if the reportable segments identified by the materiality tests account for only 70% of all industry segment revenue from unaffiliated customers, one or more additional industry segments must be included among reportable segments so that at least 75% of all industry segment revenue is accounted for by the reported segments.

Disclosures are not mandated for 90% enterprises (a company obtaining 90% or more of its revenues, operating earnings, and total assets from one segment). In essence, the segment is the business. Dominant industry segments should be identified.

The source of segmental revenue should be disclosed with the percent so derived when

- Ten percent or more of revenue is generated from either a foreign government contract or domestic contract (as required by FASB Statement Number 30).

- Ten percent or more of sales is made to one customer. A group of customers under common control (e.g., subsidiaries of a parent, federal or local government) is deemed as one customer (as required by FASB Statement Number 30). **Note:** Departments or agencies within governments are not considered a single customer. The identity of the customer need not be disclosed.

- Ten percent or more of revenue or assets are in a particular foreign country or similar group of countries. Similarity might be indicated by proximity, business environment, interrelationships, and economic and/or political ties. If foreign activities are in more than one geographic area, required disclosures should be made for both—each *significant* individual foreign area and in total for *other insignificant* areas. For revenues from foreign operations, the amount of sales to unaffiliated customers and the amount of intracompany sales between geographic areas should be disclosed. The geographic areas that have been disaggregated should be identified along with the percentages derived.

Information about foreign geographic areas and customers is required even if this information is not used by the business in formulating operating decisions.

In some cases, prior period segmental financial information, such as for industry segments, foreign operations, and major customers, needs to be restated for comparative purposes when

- There has been a change in the grouping of products, services, or geographic areas for segment determination and presentation.
- There has been a change in the grouping of foreign activities.
- There has been a change in accounting principle or reporting entity.
- The pooling-of-interests method is used for the business combination.
- Financial statements of the entire company have been restated.

There should be disclosure of the nature and effect of restatement.

A company does not have to use the same accounting principles for segmental purposes as that used to prepare the consolidated financial statements. There must be a reconciliation between segmental financial data and general-purpose financial statements. The reconciliation is for revenue, operating profit or loss, and assets. Any differences in measurement approaches between the company as a whole and its segments should be explained. If measurement practices have changed over the years regarding the operating segments, that fact should be disclosed and explained. The business must describe its reasoning and methods in deriving the composition of its operating segments.

RELATED PARTIES*

FASB Statement Number 57 covers the accounting for and disclosing of related party transactions. Related party transactions take place when a transacting party has the ability to influence significantly or exercise control of another transacting party due to a financial, common ownership, or familial relationship with that party. Related party transactions may also occur when a nontransacting party can substantially affect the policies of two other transacting parties. Related party transactions include those involving

- Activities between a parent and its subsidiaries
- Activities between affiliates of the same parent company
- Joint ventures
- Relationships between the company and its major owners, management, or their immediate families
- Company and employee trusts established and managed by the company, such as a profit sharing or pension plan

FASB Statement Number 57 notes that related party transactions often take place in the ordinary course of business and may include such activities as sales, purchases, services performed or received, property transfers, rentals, filing consolidated tax returns, guarantees, granting loans or incurring debt, compensating balance requirements, and allocating common costs as the basis for billings.

The pronouncement also indicates that related party transactions are assumed not to be at arm's length. That is, they are not derived under conditions of competitive, free market dealings. Because of this, GAAP requires that material related party transactions be disclosed in the financial statements. Exceptions include compensation arrangements, expense allowances, and similar items in the normal course of business.

AICPA Statement of Position 94-6 requires disclosure of concentrations in the volume of transactions with a particular customer if loss of that customer could result in a significant negative impact on the business.

A transaction between related parties may not have occurred or may have been on different terms if the entities were autonomous and conducted their own best interests. The following examples illustrate this point:

---

*This section is partly based on the authors' article: Marc Levine, Adrian Fitzsimons, and Joel Siegel, "Auditing Related Party Transactions," *CPA Journal,* March 1997, pp. 46–50.

- A lease of property from the parent to subsidiary occurs at a significantly different price than if a related party relationship existed.

- A loan is made at an unusually low interest rate because a bank is associated with the borrower.

- A "shell corporation" (with no economic substance) buys goods at inflated prices.

- A company pays consulting fees for the year ending December 31, 1999 in the amount of $400,000 to an individual who is a director and stockholder of the company.

Examples of events that may suggest that undisclosed related party transactions may be occurring include

- Unusual guarantees or pledging of personal assets
- Low-cost leases
- Sales with a commitment to repurchase that, if known, would preclude recognition of all or part of revenue
- Sales at below market rates
- Interest revenue at above market rates on loans
- Borrowing at below market rates of interest
- Loans to parties that do not possess the ability to repay
- Purchases of assets at prices in excess of fair market value
- Payments for services at inflated prices
- Sales without substance, such as funding the other party to the transaction so that the sales price is fully remitted

Related party disclosures usually include the following:

- Terms and settlements
- Nature and substance of relationship
- Description of the transactions, whether or not dollar amounts are involved

- Dollar figures for the applicable transactions
- Balances due from or owed to the related parties at year-end, including payment terms
- Nature of the control relationship between entities under common ownership or management control
- Significant customers or leases

While related party transactions are not inherently bad, they have proven to be an easy and effective means to perpetrate a misstatement of economic substance and reality of financial transactions. There are inherent measuring problems with related party dealings which, by their nature, may not be comparable to what would have occurred had the transactions taken place between unrelated third parties.

DISCLOSURE OF CONTINGENCIES AND COMMITMENTS

Footnote disclosure is required for reasonably possible losses arising from contingencies. The disclosure includes the type of contingency and estimate of probable loss or range of loss. If the loss cannot be estimated, that fact should be stated. Examples of items to be disclosed are guarantees, renegotiation proceedings on government contracts, tax disputes, and environmental risks. Gain contingencies, such as a possible award from a lawsuit, are also disclosed.

DISCLOSURE OF LONG-TERM PURCHASE CONTRACT OBLIGATIONS

FASB Statement Number 47 covers the disclosure of long-term obligations. An unconditional purchase obligation is any obligation to provide funds from products and services at a specified price at a later date. An example is a take-or-pay contract in which the purchaser must make periodic specified payments for goods or services even if it did not receive them. Another example is a through-put contract in which the shipper contracts to pay another party stipulated sums to deliver or process the product even if it does not provide the minimum amount of goods for transporting or processing.

Unconditional purchase obligations with a term less than one year do not require disclosure. Unconditional purchase obligations must be disclosed in the footnotes if the following criteria exist:

- The term is one year or more.
- The obligation is noncancelable. However, it may be cancelable only due to a remote contingency, with the other party's consent, such as a replacement agreement mutually agreed to or a mutual agreement to pay a penalty.

It is optional whether to disclose the amount of imputed interest required to reduce the unconditional purchase obligation to present value.

For unrecorded unconditional purchase obligations, disclosure should be made of the fixed and variable amounts, description of variable portions, total amount for the current year and for the next five years, total amount due after five years (labeled "subsequent years"), nature and term, and purchases for each year presented.

When unconditional purchase obligations are recorded in the balance sheet, disclosure should be made of any payments made, maturity dates, sinking fund provisions, and redemptions of capital stock at determinable prices. Disclosure must be made of the payments to be made under the obligation for each of the next five years.

Certain types of leases require disclosure if the leases are noncancelable, involve financing facilities to provide merchandise or services, and have a time period of more than one year.

An example of a typical disclosure required under FASB 47 follows:

ABC Company signed a long-term agreement to buy product XYZ from vendor DEF. The contract is for a 10 year period. ABC Company is obligated to make minimum annual payments to DEF regardless of whether ABC is able to accept delivery of the product XYZ. The minimum total payments of each of the five and later years after December 31, 19X1 follows:

Year	Total Payments (in thousands)
19X2	$5,000
19X3	10,000
19X4	12,000
19X5	14,000
19X6	13,000
Later years	20,000
Total	$74,000
Less: Imputed interest	28,000
Present value of payments	$46,000

DEVELOPMENT STAGE COMPANIES

FASB Statement Number 7 and FASB Interpretation Number 7 deal with the accounting, reporting, and disclosure for development stage enterprises. A development stage company is one starting a new business in which either operations have not begun or operations have begun but no significant revenue has been obtained. After the business starts its principal activities and generates substantial revenues, it is no longer in the development stage.

A development stage enterprise usually is involved with such activities as hiring and training workers, obtaining initial financing, beginning production, budgeting and planning, engaging in research, entering markets, testing products, fostering relationships with vendors, and buying operating assets such as machinery.

A development stage company must use the same GAAP and prepare the same required financial statements as an established company. However, the following reporting is required for development stage enterprises:

- In the balance sheet, retained earnings will typically show a deficit. A descriptive caption would be "deficit accumulated in the development stage." For each equity security, the number of shares issued and dollar figures per share must be shown from inception. The dates of issue must also be presented. Besides common stock or preferred stock, the company must provide similar information for stock warrants, stock rights, or other equities. If noncash consideration is received, such consideration must be specified along with the basis of deriving its value.

- In the income statement, the total revenue and expenses from the beginning of the business must be disclosed separately.

- In the statement of cash flows, cumulative cash flows from operating, investing, and financing activities from inception, in addition to current year amounts, must be shown.

The financial statements must be headed "Development Stage Enterprise." Footnote disclosure is required of the development stage activities and the proposed lines of business. In the first year the company is no longer in the development stage, it must disclose that in prior years it was.

If comparative financial statements are issued, the company must disclose that in previous years it was in the development stage.

REPORTING ON THE COSTS OF STARTUP ACTIVITIES

Newly issued SOP 98-5 requires that start-up costs be expensed as incurred. Start-up costs are commonly referred to as preopening expenditures. They are those one-time costs that are incurred, for example, when opening a new facility, introducing a new product or service, conducting business in a new territory, conducting business with a new class of customer, or beginning some new operation. In some industries, it was common to defer some of those costs if it could be shown that future net operating results would be sufficient to recover these costs. They would then be expensed when the business opened or over a period not to exceed one year. Under the new guidance, all such start-up costs, including organization costs, are to be expensed as incurred.

INFLATION INFORMATION

FASB Statement Number 89 (*Financial Reporting and Changing Prices*) allows a company to disclose voluntarily, in its annual report, inflation data so management and financial statement readers can better assess the effect of inflation on the company. The pronouncement recommends that businesses present selected summarized financial data based on current costs and adjusted for inflation (in constant purchasing power) for a five-year period. The Consumer Price Index for All Urban Consumers may be used. Inflation information to be disclosed includes sales and operating revenue expressed in constant purchasing power, income from continuing operations (including per share amounts) on a current cost basis, cash dividends per share in constant purchasing power, market price per share restated in constant purchasing power, purchasing power gain or loss on net monetary items, inflation-adjusted inventory, restated fixed assets, foreign currency translation based on current cost, net assets based on current cost, and the Consumer Price Index used.

DISCLOSURES FOR DERIVATIVES

The Securities and Exchange Commission requires disclosures for derivative financial products, including financial instruments and commodities. Commodities may include futures, options, forwards, and swaps. Disclosures for derivatives include the method of accounting, much like the fair value or accrual method, the presentation of the financial effects of the derivatives in the financial statements, how expired derivative instruments are accounted for, types of derivatives being employed, and risk. A distinction should be made with regard to the accounting for derivatives used for trading versus nontrading purposes.

Annual Report References

PROCTER AND GAMBLE
1998 ANNUAL REPORT

1. Summary of Significant Accounting Policies

Basis of Presentation: The consolidated financial statements include The Procter & Gamble Company and its controlled subsidiaries (the Company). Investments in companies that are at least 20% to 50% owned, and over which the Company exerts significant influence but does not control the financial and operating decisions, are accounted for by the equity method. These investments are managed as integral parts of the Company's segment operations, and the Company's share of their results is included in net sales for the related segments.

Use of Estimates: Preparation of financial statements in conformity with generally accepted accounting principles requires management to make estimates and assumptions that affect the amounts reported in the consolidated financial statements and accompanying disclosures. These estimates are based on management's best knowledge of current events and actions the Company may undertake in the future. Actual results may ultimately differ from estimates.

Accounting Changes: In 1998, the Company adopted several FASB statements. Statement No. 128, "Earnings per Share," which revises the manner in which earnings per share is calculated, did not impact the Company's previously reported earnings per share. Statement No. 130, "Reporting Comprehensive Income," requires the components of comprehensive income to be disclosed in the financial statements. Statement No. 131, "Disclosures about Segments of an Enterprise and Related Information," requires certain information to be reported about operating segments on a basis consistent with the Company's internal organizational structure. Statement No. 132, "Employers' Disclosures about Pensions and Other Postretirement Benefits," revises the disclosures for pensions and other postretirement benefits and standardizes them into a combined format. Required disclosures have been made and prior years' information has been reclassified for the impact of FASB Statements 130, 131 and 132.

New Pronouncements: In June 1998, the FASB issued Statement No. 133, "Accounting for Derivative Instruments and Hedging Activities which revises the accounting for derivative financial instruments. In March 1998, the AICPA issued SOP 98-1, "Accounting for the Costs of Computer Software Developed or Obtained for Internal Use," which revises the accounting for software development costs and will require the capitalization of certain costs which the Company has historically expensed. The Company is currently analyzing the impacts of these statements, which are required to be adopted in 2000, and does not expect either statement to have a material impact on the Company's financial position, results of operations or cash flows.

Currency Translation: Financial statements of subsidiaries outside the U.S. generally are measured using the local currency as the functional currency Adjustments to translate those statements into U.S. dollars are accumulated in a separate component of shareholders' equity For subsidiaries operating in highly inflationary economies, the U.S. dollar is the functional currency. Remeasurement adjustments for highly inflationary economies and other transactional exchange gains (losses) are reflected in earnings and were $0, $1 and $(28) for 1998, 1997 and 1996, respectively.

Cash Equivalents: Highly liquid investments with maturities of three months or less when purchased are considered cash equivalents.

Inventory Valuation: Inventories are valued at cost, which is not in excess of current market price. Cost is primarily determined by either the average cost or the first-in, first-out method. The replacement cost of last-in, first-out inventories exceeds carrying value by approximately $91 and $122 at June 30, 1998 and 1997, respectively.

Goodwill and Other Intangible Assets: The cost of intangible assets is amortized, principally on a straight-line basis, over the estimated periods benefited, generally 40 years for goodwill and periods ranging from 10 to 40 years for other intangible assets. The realizability of goodwill and other intangibles is evaluated periodically when events or circumstances indicate a possible inability to recover the carrying amount. Such evaluation is based on various analyses, including cash flow and profitability projections that incorporate the impact of existing Company businesses. The analyses necessarily involve significant management judgment to evaluate the capacity of an acquired business to perform within projections. Historically, the Company has generated sufficient returns from acquired businesses to recover the cost of the goodwill and other intangible assets.

Property, Plant and Equipment: Property, plant and equipment are recorded at cost reduced by accumulated depreciation. Depreciation expense is provided based on estimated useful lives using the straight-line method.

Selected Operating Expenses: Research and development costs are charged to earnings as incurred and were $1,546 in 1998, $1,469 in 1997 and $1,399 in 1996. Advertising costs are charged to earnings as incurred and were $3,704 in 1998, $3,466 in 1997 and $3,254 in 1996.

Net Earnings Per Common Share: Net earnings less preferred dividends (net of related tax benefits) are divided by the weighted average number of common shares outstanding during the year to calculate basic net earnings per common share. Diluted net earnings per common share are calculated to give effect to stock options and convertible preferred stock.

Basic and diluted net earnings per share are reconciled as follows:

	Years Ended June 30		
	1998	*1997*	*1996*
Net earnings available to common shareholders	$3,676	$3,311	$2,943
Effect of dilutive securities			
Preferred dividends, net of tax benefit	104	104	103
Preferred dividend impact on funding of ESOP	(25)	(32)	(39)
Diluted net earnings	3,755	3,383	3,007

Basic weighted average common shares outstanding	1,343.4	1,360.3	1,372.6
Effect of dilutive securities			
Conversion of preferred shares	99.8	101.9	103.8
Exercise of stock options	22.3	24.8	19.8
Diluted weighted average common shares outstanding	1,465.5	1,487.0	1 496.2

Stock Split: In July 1997, the Company's board of directors approved a two-for-one stock split that was effective for common and preferred shareholders of record as of August 22, 1997. The financial statements, notes and other references to share and per-share data reflect the stock split for all periods presented.

Fair Values of Financial Instruments: Fair values of cash equivalents, short and long-term investments and short-term debt approximate cost. The estimated fair values of other financial instruments, including debt and risk management instruments, have been determined using available market information and valuation methodologies, primarily discounted cash flow analysis. These estimates require considerable judgment in interpreting market data, and changes in assumptions or estimation methods may significantly affect the fair value estimates.

Major Customer: The Company's largest customer, Wal-Mart Stores, Inc. and its affiliates, accounted for 11% and 10% of consolidated net sales in 1998 and 1997, respectively These sales occurred primarily in the North America segment.

Reclassifications: Certain reclassifications of prior years' amounts have been made to conform with the current year presentation, primarily related to certain component parts of research and development costs.

MOTOROLA
1998 ANNUAL REPORT

1. Summary of Significant Accounting Policies

Consolidation and Investments: The consolidated financial statements include the accounts of Motorola, Inc. and all majority-owned subsidiaries (the Company) in which it has control. The Company's investments in noncontrolled entities in which it has the ability to exercise significant influence over operating and financial policies are accounted for by the equity method. The Company's investments in other entities are carried at their historical cost. Certain of these cost-based investments are marked-to-market at the balance sheet date to reflect their fair value with the unrealized gains and losses, net of tax, included in a separate component of stockholders' equity.

Cash Equivalents: The Company considers all highly liquid investments purchased with an original maturity of three months or less to be cash equivalents.

Revenue Recognition: The Company uses the percentage-of-completion method to recognize revenues and costs associated with most long-term contracts. For contracts involving certain new technologies, revenues and profits or parts thereof are deferred until technological feasibility is established, customer acceptance is obtained and other contract-specific factors have been completed. For other product sales, revenue is recognized at the time of shipment, and reserves are established for price protection and cooperative marketing programs with distributors.

Inventories: Inventories are valued at the lower of average cost (which approximates computation on a first-in, first-out basis) or market (net realizable value or replacement cost).

Property, Plant and Equipment: Property, plant and equipment are stated at cost less accumulated depreciation. Depreciation is recorded principally using the declining-balance method, based on the estimated useful lives of the assets (buildings and building equipment, 5-40 years; machinery and equipment, 2-12 years).

Fair Values of Financial Instruments: The fair values of financial instruments are determined based on quoted market prices and market interest rates as of the end of the reporting period.

Foreign Currency Translation: The Company's European and Japanese operations and certain non-consolidated affiliates use the respective local currencies as the functional currency. For all other operations, the Company uses the U.S. dollar as the functional currency. The effects of translating the financial position and results of operations of local functional currency operations into U.S. dollars are included in a separate component of stockholders' equity.

Foreign Currency Transactions: The effects of remeasuring the nonfunctional currency assets or liabilities into the functional currency as well as gains and losses on hedges of existing assets or liabilities are marked-to-market, and the result is recorded within selling, general and administrative expenses in the statement of operations. Gains and losses on financial instruments which hedge firm future commitments are deferred until such time as the underlying transactions are recognized or recorded immediately when the transaction is no longer expected to occur. Foreign exchange financial instruments which hedge investments in foreign subsidiaries are marked-to-market, and the results are included in stockholders' equity. Other gains or losses on financial instruments which do not qualify as hedges are recognized immediately as income or expense.

Use of Estimates: The preparation of financial statements in conformity with generally accepted accounting principles requires management to make certain estimates and assumptions that affect the reported amounts of assets and liabilities and disclosure of contingent assets and liabilities at the date of financial statements and the reported amounts of revenues and expenses during the reporting period. Actual results could differ from those estimates.

Reclassifications: Certain amounts in prior years' financial statements and related notes have been reclassified to conform to the 1998 presentation.

Recent Accounting Pronouncements: As of January 1, 1998, the Company implemented Statement of Financial Accounting Standards (SFAS) No. 130, "Reporting Comprehensive Income"; SFAS No. 131, "Disclosures about Segments of an Enterprise and Related Information"; and SFAS 132, "Employers' Disclosures about Pensions and Other Postretirement Benefits."

SFAS No. 130, which is solely a financial statement presentation standard, requires the Company to disclose non-owner changes included in equity but not included in net earnings or loss. These changes include the fair value adjustment to certain cost-based investments, the foreign currency translation adjustments and the minimum pension liability adjustment.

SFAS No. 131 establishes standards for the way public business enterprises report information about operating segments in annual financial statements and in interim financial reports issued to shareholders. The Company has restated the previously reported annual segment operating results to conform to the Statements management approach.

SFAS No. 132 only modifies the financial statement presentation of the Company's pension and postretirement benefit obligations and does not impact the measurement of such obligations.

During 1998, the Financial Accounting Standards Board issued SFAS No. 133, "Accounting for Derivative Instruments and Hedging Activities," which will be effective for the Company's fiscal year 2000. The Company is currently assessing the impact of this new statement but does not expect any material effect an its consolidated financial position, liquidity or results of operations.

3M
1999 ANNUAL REPORT

Note

In the third quarter of 1999, the company reorganized its management reporting structure into six business segments. Prior year amounts have been retroactively restated to reflect this change in business segment reporting. 3M's businesses are organized, managed and internally reported as six segments based on differences in products, technologies and services. These segments are Industrial; Transportation, Graphics and Safety; Health Care; Consumer and Office; Electro and Communications; and Specialty Material. These segments have worldwide responsibility for virtually all of the company's product lines. 3M is not dependent on any single product or market.

Transactions among reportable segments are recorded at cost. 3M is an integrated enterprise characterized by substantial intersegment cooperation, cost allocations and inventory transfers. Therefore, management does not represent that these segments, if operated independently, would report the operating income and other financial information shown.

Operating income in 1999 includes a non-recurring net gain of $100 million. This relates to divestitures of certain health care businesses and Eastern Heights Bank, litigation expense, an investment valuation adjustment, and a change in estimate that reduced the 1998 restructuring charge. Of this $100 million gain, $62 million was recorded in Health Care and $38 million in Corporate and Unallocated. Operating income in 1998 includes a restructuring charge of $493 million in Corporate and Unallocated.

Business segments	Major products
Industrial	Tapes and coated abrasives
Transportation, Graphics and Safety	Reflective sheeting, commercial graphics systems, films, inks and respirators, automotive products and optical films
Health Care	Medical/surgical supplies, skin health products, pharmaceuticals, dental products, health information systems, microbiology products and closures for disposable diapers
Consumer and Office	Sponges, scour pads, high performance cloths, consumer and office tapes, repositionable notes, carpet and fabric protectors, floor matting, commercial cleaning products and do-it-yourself products

Business segments	Major products
Electro and Communications	Connecting, insulating and splicing solutions for the electronics and telecommunications industries
Specialty Material	Fluorochemicals for automotive, electronics, textile, paper and other industries

Business segment information

(millions)		Net Sales	Operating Income	Assets**	Depreciation and Amortization	Capital Expenditures
Industrial	1999	$3,394	$613	$2,357	$220	$200
	1998	3,360	561	2,394	199	276
	1997	3,419	544	2,366	186	283
Transportation, Graphics and Safety	1999	3,228	679	2,673	140	197
	1998	3,021	532	2,652	170	331
	1997	3,112	585	2,368	191	363
Health Care	1999	3,118	686	2,076	203	187
	1998	3,086	571	2,168	161	221
	1997	3,004	521	2,042	183	217
Consumer and Office	1999	2,688	408	1,589	118	121
	1998	2,613	398	1,614	136	178
	1997	2,616	438	1,561	105	131
Electro and Communications	1999	2,014	406	1,359	130	192
	1998	1,741	263	1,177	111	222
	1997	1,739	327	1,103	114	167
Specialty Material	1999	1,166	188	1,323	79	142
	1998	1,105	194	1,112	66	186
	1997	1,090	192	928	70	200
Corporate and Unallocated*	1999	51	(24)	2,519	10	—
	1998	95	(480)	3,036	23	16
	1997	90	68	2,870	21	45
Total Company	1999	$15,659	$2,956	$13,896	$900	$1,039
	1998	15,021	2,039	14,153	866	1,430
	1997	15,070	2,675	13,238	870	1,406

*Corporate and Unallocated Income principally includes corporate investment gains and losses, derivative gains and losses, insurance-related gains and losses, banking operating results (divested June 30, 1999), certain litigation expenses, restructuring charges and other miscellaneous items. Because this category includes a variety of miscellaneous items, it is subject to fluctuations on a quarterly and annual basis.

**Segment assets primarily include accounts receivable; inventory; property, plant and equipment—net; and other miscellaneous assets. Assets included in Corporate and Unallocated principally are cash and cash equivalents; other securities; insurance receivables; deferred income tax; certain investments and other assets; and certain unallocated property, plant and equipment.

TEXACO
1998 ANNUAL REPORT

1. Segment Information

We are presenting below information about our operating segments for the years 1998, 1997 and 1996, according to Statement of Financial Accounting Standards 131, *Disclosures about Segments of an Enterprise and Related Information,* which we adopted this year.

We determined our operating segments based on differences in the nature of their operations and geographic location. The composition of segments and measure of segment profit is consistent with that used by our Extent Council in making strategic decisions. The Executive Council is headed by the Chairman and Chief Executive Officer and includes, among others, the Senior Vice Presidents having oversight responsibility for our business units.

Operating Segments 1998

(Millions of dollars)	Sales and Services Outside	Inter-segment	Total	After Tax Profit (Loss)	Income Tax Expense (Benefit)	DD&A Expense	Other Non-cash Items	Capital Expen-ditures	Assets at Year-End
Exploration and production									
United States	$ 1,712	$ 1,660	$ 3,372	$ 301	$ 34	$ 892	$ 1	$ 1,200	$ 8,699
International	2,028	1,358	3,386	120	127	513	20	951	4,352
Manufacturing, marketing and distribution									
United States	2,582	107	2,689	223	96	6	228	1	4,095
International	19,835	86	19,921	332	130	204	135	403	8,306
Global gas marketing	4,692	84	4,776	(18)	5	14	50	61	879
Segment totals	$ 30,849	$ 3,295	34,144	958	392	1,629	434	2,616	26,331
Other business units			91	7	4	2	(2)		506
Corporate/Non-operating			4	(362)	(298)	44	(67)	33	1,945
Intersegment eliminations			(3,329)	—	—	—	—	—	(212)
Consolidated, before cumulative effect of accounting change			$30,910	$ 603	$ 98	$ 1,675	$ 365	$ 2,649	$ 28,570

Operating Segments 1997

(Millions of dollars)	Sales and Services			After Tax Profit (Loss)	Income Tax Expense (Benefit)	DD&A Expense	Other Non-cash Items	Capital Expenditures	Assets at Year-End
	Outside	Inter-segment	Total						
Exploration and production									
United States	$ 365	$ 4,156	$ 4,521	$ 990	$ 487	$ 783	$ 281	$ 1,349	$ 8,769
International	2,573	1,751	4,326	807	566	442	105	934	4,036
Manufacturing, marketing and distribution									
United States	16,992	357	17,349	324	172	178	169	262	5,668
International	19,992	235	20,227	508	117	173	(166)	482	8,048
Global gas marketing	5,207	254	5,461	(43)	(9)	14	61	75	1,012
Segment totals	$ 45,131	$ 6,753	51,884	2,586	1,333	1,590	450	3,102	27,533
Other business units			101	5	5	2	4	—	544
Corporate/ Non-operating			6	73	(675)	41	242	57	2,030
Intersegment eliminations			(6,804)	—	—	—	—	(507)	
Consolidated			$ 45,187	$ 2,664	$ 663	$ 1,633	$ 696	$ 3,159	$29,600

Operating Segments 1996

(Millions of dollars)	Sales and Services			After Tax Profit (Loss)	Income Tax Expense (Benefit)	DD&A Expense	Other Non-cash Items	Capital Expenditures	Assets at Year-End
	Outside	Inter-segment	Total						
Exploration and production									
United Stares	$ 204	$4,146	$4,350	$1,074	$ 528	$ 670	$ 109	$ 990	$6,067
International	2,384	1,930	4,314	493	523	393	(21)	755	3,651
Manufacturing, marketing and distribution									
United States	18,424	493	18,917	210	143	176	92	271	6,310
International	18,750	363	19,113	447	127	161	201	356	7,751
Global gas marketing	4,754	342	5,096	34	19	13	(7)	110	1,152
Segment totals	$ 44,516	$ 7,274	51,790	2,258	1,340	1,413	374	2,482	24,931
Other business units			112	10	10	7	3	—	530
Corporate/ Non-operating		5	(250)	(385)	35	332	35	2,216	
Intersegment eliminations		(7,346)	—	—	—	—	—	(714)	
Consolidated			$44,561	$2,018	$ 965	$ 1,455	$ 709	$ 2,517	$26,963

Our exploration and production segments explore for, find, develop and produce crude oil and natural gas. The U.S. segment includes minor operations in Canada. Our manufacturing, marketing and distribution segments process crude oil and other feedstock into refined products and purchase, sell and transport crude oil and refined petroleum products. Global gas marketing purchases natural gas and natural gas products from our exploration and production operations and others for resale, and operates natural gas processing plants and pipelines in the United States. This segment, which operates primarily in the U.S., sold its U.K. wholesale gas business in 1998 and announced its intention to dispose of its U.K. retail gas marketing business as well. Other business units include our insurance, power generation and gasification operations and investments in undeveloped mineral properties. None of these units is individually significant in terms of revenue, income or assets.

You are encouraged to read Note 6–*Investments and Advances*, beginning on page 52, which includes information about our affiliates and the formation of the Equilon and Motiva alliances in 1998.

Corporate and non-operating includes the assets, income and expenses relating to cash management and financing activities, our corporate center and other items nor directly attributable to the operating segments.

We apply the same accounting policies to each of the segments as we do in preparing the consolidated financial statements. Intersegment sales and Services are generally representative of marker prices or arms-length negotiated transactions. Intersegment receivables are representative of normal trade balances. Other non-cash items principally include deferred income taxes, the difference between cash distributions and equity in income of affiliates and non-cash charges and credits associated with asset sales. Capital expenditures are presented on a cash basis, excluding exploratory expenses.

The countries in which we have significant sales and services and long-lived assets are listed below. Sales and services are based on the origin of the sale. Long-lived assets include properties, plant and equipment and investments in foreign producing operations where the host governments own the physical assets under terms of the operating agreements.

(Millions of dollars)	Sales and Services			Long-lived assets at December 31		
	1998	1997	1996	**1998**	1997	1996
United States	**$ 8,184**	$21,657	$22,643	**$8,757**	$11,437	$8,683
International — Total	**22,726**	23,530	21,918	**6,250**	5,876	4,914
Significant countries included above:						
Brazil	**3,175**	3,175	2,670	**301**	266	235
Netherlands	**1,636**	1,901	2,129	**257**	250	212
United Kingdom	**7,529**	6,862	5,846	**2,257**	2,384	1,846

INGERSOLL RAND
1999 ANNUAL REPORT

10. Commitments and Contingencies

The company is involved in various litigations, claims and administrative proceedings, including environmental matters, arising in the normal course of business. In assessing its potential environmental liability, the company bases its estimates on current technologies and does not discount its liability or assume any insurance recoveries. Amounts recorded for identified contingent liabilities are estimates, which are reviewed periodically and adjusted to reflect additional information when it becomes available. Subject to the uncertainties inherent in estimating future costs for contingent liabilities, management believes that recovery or liability with respect to these matters would not have a material effect on the financial condition, results of operations, liquidity or cash flows of the company for any year.

The company has established two wholly-owned special purpose subsidiaries to purchase accounts and notes receivable at a discount from the company on a continuous basis. These special purpose subsidiaries simultaneously sell an undivided interest in these accounts and notes receivable to a financial institution up to a maximum of $170.0 million. The agreements between the special purpose corporations and the financial institution expire annually and will be renewed with either the current or another financial institution. The company is retained as the servicer of the pooled receivables. During 1999, 1998 and 1997, such sales of receivables amounted to $781.8 million, $723.7 million and $614.0 million, respectively. At December 31, 1999, $170.0 million of such sold receivables remained uncollected.

Receivables, excluding the designated pool of accounts and notes receivable, sold during 1999 and 1998 with recourse, amounted to $57.5 million and $55.4 million, respectively. At December 31, 1999 and 1998, $18.7 million and $12.4 million, respectively, of such receivables sold remained uncollected.

As of December 31, 1999, the company had no significant concentrations of credit risk in trade receivables due to the large number of customers which comprised its receivables base and their dispersion across different industries and countries. In the normal course of business, the company has issued several direct and indirect guarantees, including performance letters of credit, totaling approximately $104.0 million at December 31, 1999. The company has also guaranteed the residual value of leased product in the aggregate amount of $39.1 million. Upon the termination of a dealer, a newly selected dealer generally acquires the assets of the prior dealer and assumes any related financial obligation. Accordingly, the risk of loss to the company is minimal, and historically, only immaterial losses have been incurred relating to these arrangements. Management believes these guarantees will not adversely affect the consolidated financial statements.

Certain office and warehouse facilities, transportation vehicles and data processing equipment are leased. Total rental expense was $71.6 million in 1999, $71.2 million in 1998 and $69.5 million in 1997. Minimum lease payments required under noncancellable operating leases with terms in excess of one year for the next five years and thereafter, are as follows: $46.3 million in 2000, $37.2 million in 2001, $27.2 million in 2002, $17.9 million in 2003, $15.7 million in 2004 and $25.7 million thereafter.

COLGATE-PALMOLIVE

16. Commitments and Contingencies

Minimum rental commitments under noncancellable operating leases, primarily for office and warehouse facilities, are $67.3 in 1999, $63.5 in 2000, $56.2 in 2001, $51.0 in 2002, $48.9 in 2003 and $122.6 thereafter. Rental expense amounted to $102.7 in 1998, $94.4 in 1997 and $93.3 in 1996. Contingent rentals, sublease income and capital leases, which are included in fixed assets, are not significant.

The Company has various contractual commitments to purchase raw materials, products and services totaling $60.6 that expire through 2001.

The Company is a party to various superfund and other environmental matters and is contingently liable with respect to lawsuits, taxes and other matters arising out of the normal course of business. Management proactively reviews and manages its exposure to, and the impact of, environmental matters and other contingencies.

On September 8, 1998, one of the Company's Brazilian subsidiaries, Kolynos do Brasil Ltda. ("Kolynos"), received notice of an administrative proceeding from the Central Bank of Brazil. The notice primarily takes issue with certain filings made with the Central Bank in connection with financing arrangements related to the acquisition of Kolynos in January 1995. The Central Bank seeks to impose fines prescribed by statute, and it, in no way, challenges or seeks to unwind the acquisition. Management believes, based on the opinion of its Brazilian legal counsel, that the filings challenged by the Central Bank fully complied with Brazilian law and that the issues raised in the notice are without merit.

While it is possible that the Company's cash flows and results of operations in particular quarterly or annual periods could be affected by the one-time impacts of the resolution of the above contingencies, it is the opinion of management that the ultimate disposition of these matters, to the extent not previously provided for, will not have a material impact on the Company's financial condition or ongoing cash flows and results of operations.

HEWLETT-PACKARD
1998 ANNUAL REPORT

Commitments

The company leases certain real and personal property under noncancelable operating leases. Future minimum lease payments at October 31, 1998 are $216 million for 1999, $175 million for 2000, $129 million for 2001, $94 million for 2002, $73 million for 2003 and $240 million thereafter. Certain leases require the company to pay property taxes, insurance and routine maintenance, and include escalation clauses. Rent expense was $465 million in 1998, $388 million in 1997 and $353 million in 1996.

Contingencies and Factors That Could Affect Future Results

Contingencies. The company is involved in lawsuits, claims, investigations and proceedings, including patent, commercial, and environmental matters, which arise in the ordinary course of business. There are no such matters pending that the company expects to be material in relation to its business, financial condition, or results of operations.

Factors that could affect future results. A substantial portion of the company's revenues each year are generated from the development, manufacture and rapid release to market of high technology products newly introduced during the year. In the extremely competitive industry environment in which the company operates, such product generation, manufacturing and marketing processes are uncertain and complex, requiring accurate prediction of market trends and demand as well as successful management of various manufacturing risks inherent in such products. Additionally, the company's production strategy relies on certain key suppliers' ability to deliver quality components, subassemblies and completed products in time to meet critical manufacturing and distribution schedules, and its sales strategy relies on the ability of certain third-party resellers to support sales channels to the mass market effectively. In light of these dependencies, it is reasonably possible that failure to successfully manage a significant product introduction, failure of certain key suppliers to deliver as needed, or failure of certain resellers to remain customers and channel partners could have a severe near-term impact on the company's order growth, revenue growth, or results of operations.

The Company expects to implement successfully the changes necessary to address its Year 2000 (Y2K) internal readiness, product compliance, and material third-party relationship issues. Based on current estimates, the Company does not believe that the incremental costs associated with such actions will have a material effect on the Company's results of operations or financial condition. There can be no assurance, however, that there will not be a delay in, increased costs associated with, or legal claims related to the implementation of such changes. In addition, failure to achieve Y2K readiness could result in delays in the company's ability to manufacture and ship products and deliver services, disrupt its customer service and technical support facilities, and interrupt customer access to its online products and services. The Company's inability to perform these functions could have an adverse effect on future results of operations or financial condition.

GENEVA STEEL
1998 ANNUAL REPORT

6. Commitments and Contingencies

Capital Projects

The Company has incurred substantial capital expenditures to modernize its steelmaking, casting, rolling and finishing facilities, thereby reducing overall operating costs, broadening the Company's product line, improving product quality and increasing throughput rates. The Company spent $10.9 million (net of the $12.5 million insurance reimbursement for capital expenditures covered by the January 1996 power outage insurance claim settlement described in Note 2) and $47.7 million on capital projects during the fiscal years ended September 30, 1998 and 1997, respectively. These expenditures were made primarily in connection with the Company's ongoing modernization and capital maintenance efforts. Capital expenditures for fiscal year 1999 are estimated at $15 to $20 million, which includes completing the implementation of new business and financial software and completion of other projects that either are already in progress or are believed essential to maintaining ongoing operations. The Company is implementing SAP software, on enterprise-wide business system. The Company expects to benefit significantly from such implementation, including addressing the year 2000 issue inherent in its legacy systems. The implementation is estimated to cost $8 to $10 million with the implementation substantially completed by the fall of 1999. Depending on liquidity needs, market conditions, operational requirements, and other factors, the Company may elect to adjust the design, timing and budgeted expenditures of its capital plan.

The Company is a member of a limited liability company which has entered into a cooperative agreement with the United States Department of Energy ("DOE") for the demonstration of a cokeless ironmaking facility and associated power generation and air separation facilities. As of September 30, 1998, the Company had spent (net of DOE reimbursement) approximately $1.2 million in connection with the project. Expenditures on the project are subject to government cost sharing arrangements. Completion of the project remains subject to several contingencies.

Legal Matters

The Company is subject to various legal matters, which it considers normal for its business activities. Management, after consultation with the Company's legal counsel, believes that these matters will not have a material impact on the financial condition or results of operations of the Company.

Environmental Matters

Compliance with environmental laws and regulations is a significant factor in the Company's business. The Company is subject to federal, state and local environmental laws and regulations concerning, among other things, air emissions, wastewater discharge, and solid and hazardous waste disposal. The Company believes that it is in compliance in all material respects with all currently applicable environmental regulations.

The Company has incurred substantial capital expenditures for environmental control facilities, including the Q-BOP furnaces, the wastewater treatment facility, the benzene mitigation equipment, the coke oven gas desulfurization facility and other projects. The Company has budgeted a total of approximately $2.0 million for environmental capital improvements in fiscal years 1999 and 2000. Environmental legislation and regulations have changed rapidly in recent years and it is likely that the Company will be subject to increasingly stringent environmental standards in the future.

Although the Company has budgeted for capital expenditures for environmental matters, it is not possible at this time to predict the amount of capital expenditures that may ultimately be required to comply with all environmental laws and regulations.

Under the Comprehensive Environmental Response, Compensation and Liability Act of 1980, as amended ("CERCLA"), the EPA and the states have authority to impose liability on waste generators, site owners and operators and others regardless of fault or the legality of the original disposal activity. Other environmental laws and regulations may also impose liability on the Company for conditions existing prior to the Company's acquisition of the steel mill.

At the time of the Company's acquisition of the steel mill, the Company and USX Corporation ("USX") identified certain hazardous and solid waste sites and other environmental conditions which existed prior to the acquisition. USX has agreed to indemnify the Company (subject to the sharing arrangements described below) for any fines, penalties, costs (including costs of clean-up, required studies and reasonable attorneys' fees), or other liabilities for which the Company becomes liable due to any environmental condition existing on the Company's real property as of the acquisition date that is determined to be in violation of any environmental law, is otherwise required by applicable judicial or administrative action, or is determined to trigger civil liability (the "Pre-existing Environmental Liabilities"). The Company has provided a similar indemnity (but without any similar sharing arrangement) to USX for conditions that may arise after the acquisition. Although the Company has not completed a comprehensive analysis of the extent of the Pre-existing Environmental Liabilities, such liabilities could be material.

Under the acquisition agreement between the two parties, the Company and USX agreed to share on an equal basis the first $20 million of costs incurred by either party to satisfy any government demand for studies, closure, monitoring, or remediation at specified waste sites or facilities or for other claims under CERCLA or the Resource Conservation and Recovery Act. The Company is not obligated to contribute more than $10 million for the clean-up of wastes generated prior to the acquisition. The Company believes that it has paid the full $10 million necessary to satisfy its obligations under the cost-sharing arrangement. USX has advised the Company, however, of its position that a portion of the amount paid by the Company may not be properly credited against the Company's obligations. Although the Company believes that USX's position is without merit, there can be no assurance that this matter will be resolved without litigation. The Company and USX has similarly had several disagreements regarding the scope and actual application of USX's indemnification obligations. The Company's ability to obtain indemnification from USX in the future will depend on factors which may be beyond the Company's control and may also be subject to litigation.

Purchase Commitments

On February 10, 1989, the Company entered into an agreement which was subsequently amended on July 1, 1997, to purchase interruptible and firm back-up power through February 28, 2002. For interruptible power, the Company pays an energy charge adjusted annually to reflect changes in the supplier's average energy costs and facilities charge, based on 110,000 kilowatts, adjusted annually to reflect changes in the supplier's per megawatt fixed transmission investment.

Effective July 12, 1990, the Company entered into an agreement, which was subsequently amended in April 1992, to purchase 100% of the oxygen, nitrogen and argon produced at a facility located at the Company's steel mill which is owned and operated by an independent party. The contract expires in September 2006 and specifies that the Company will pay a base monthly charge that is adjusted semiannually each January 1 and July 1 based upon a percentage of the change in PPI.

Effective September 1, 1994, the Company entered into a five year agreement, which was amended on July 25, 1997 and September 30, 1998, to purchase taconite pellets. The Company has commitments to purchase 2,700,000 net tons in the fifth year of the contract, which is defined as a five-quarter period ending December 31, 1999. Prices are adjusted each year based on an index related to the "Cartier Pellets Price." Given current market conditions, the Company may not have a need for the minimum volume requirements under the USX agreement.

Effective June 6, 1995, the Company entered into an agreement to purchase 800 tons a day of oxygen from a new plant constructed at the Company's steel mill which will be owned and operated by an independent party. The new plant was completed June 20, 1997. The Company pays a monthly facility charge which is adjusted semiannually each January 1 and July 1 based on an index. The contract continues through July 2012.

Effective June 10, 1997, the Company entered into an agreement to purchase 100% of the oxygen, nitrogen and argon produced at a facility that is owned and operated by an independent party. The contract expires in September 2002 and specifies that the Company will pay a monthly facility charge that is adjusted semi-annually each January 1 and July 1 based upon a percentage of the change in PPI.

Effective September 1, 1998, the Company entered into an agreement to purchase 26,000 MMBtu per day of firm natural gas to offset other agreements with the expiration dates of August 31, 1998 to October 31, 1998. Effective November 1, 1998 and continuing through June 30, 2000 the commitment increases to 35,000 MMBtu per day of firm natural gas with provisions to offsell any unusable volumes. The price is adjusted monthly based on the index price as reported by "Inside FERC Gas Market Report."

On September 12, 1997, the Company entered into an agreement to purchase natural gas transportation service for 35,000 decatherms per day commencing October 1, 1998 and continuing through September 30, 2003.

REVLON
1998 ANNUAL REPORT

16. Related Party Transactions

Transfer Agreements

In June 1992 Revlon, Inc. and Products Corporation entered into an asset transfer agreement with Holdings and certain of its wholly owned subsidiaries (the "Asset Transfer Agreement"), and Revlon, Inc. and Products Corporation entered into a real property asset transfer agreement with Holdings (the "Real Property Transfer Agreement" and, together with the Asset Transfer Agreement, the "Transfer Agreements"), and pursuant to such agreements, on June 24, 1992 Holdings transferred assets to Products Corporation and Products Corporation assumed all the liabilities of Holdings, other than certain specifically exceeded assets and liabilities (the liabilities excluded are referred to as the "Excluded liabilities"). Holdings retained the Retained Brands. Holdings agreed to indemnify Revlon, Inc. and Products Corporation against losses arising from the Excluded Liabilities, and Revlon, Inc. and Products Corporation agreed to indemnify Holdings against losses arising from the liabilities assumed by Products Corporation. The amounts reimbursed by Holdings to Products Corporation for the Excluded liabilities for 1998, 1997 and 1996 were $0.6, $0.4 and $1.4, respectively.

Operating Services Agreement

In June 1992, Revlon, Inc., Products Corporation and Holdings entered into an operating services agreement (as amended and restarted, and as subsequently amended, the "Operating Services Agreement") pursuant to which Products Corporation has manufactured, marketed, distributed, warehoused and administered, including the collection of accounts receivable, the Retained Brands for Holdings. Pursuant to the Operating Services Agreement, Products Corporation was reimbursed an amount equal to all of its and Revlon, Inc.'s direct and indirect costs incurred in connection with furnishing such services, net of the amounts collected by Products Corporation with respect to the Retained Brands, payable quarterly. The net amounts due from Holdings to Products Corporation for such direct and indirect costs plus a fee equal to 5% of the net sales of the Retained Brands for 1998, 1997 and 1996 were $0.9 (which amount was offset against certain notes payable to Holdings), $1.7 and $5.7, respectively.

Reimbursement Agreements

Revlon, Inc., Products Corporation and MacAndrews Holdings have entered into reimbursement agreements (the "Reimbursement Agreements") pursuant to which (i) MacAndrews Holdings is obligated to prove (directly or through affiliates) certain professional and administrative services, including employees, to Revlon, Inc. and its subsidiaries, including Products Corporation, and purchase services from third party providers, such as insurance and legal and accounting services, on behalf of Revlon, Inc. and its subsidiaries, including Products Corporation, to the extent requested by Products Corporation, and (ii) Products Corporation is obligated to provide certain professional and administrative services, including employees, to MacAndrews Holdings land its affiliates) and purchase services from third party providers, such as insurance and legal and accounting services, on behalf of MacAndrews Holdings and its affiliates) to the extent requested by MacAndrews moldings, provided that in each case the performance of such services does not cause an unreasonable burden to MacAndrews Holdings or Products Corporation, or as the case may be. The Company reimburses MacAndrews Holdings for the allocable costs of the services purchased for or provided to the Company one its subsidiaries and for out-of-pocket expenses incurred in connection with the provision of such services. MacAndrews Holdings (or such affiliates) reimburses the Company for the allocable costs of the services purchased for or provided to MacAndrews Holdings (or such affiliates) and for the reasonable out-of-pocket expenses incurred in connection with the purchase or provision of such services. The net amounts reimbursed by MacAndrews Holdings to the Company for the services provided under the Reimbursement Agreements for 1998, 1997 and 1996 were $3.1 ($0.2 of which was offset against certain notes payable to Holdings), $4.0 and $2.2, respectively. Each of Revlon, Inc. and Products Corporation, on the one hand, and MacAndrews Holdings, on the other, has agreed to indemnify the other party for losses arising out of the provision of services by it under the Reimbursement Agreements other than losses resulting from its willful misconduct or gross negligence. The Reimbursement Agreements may be terminated by either party on 90 days' notice. The Company does not intend to request services under the Reimbursement Agreements unless their costs would be at least as favorable to the Company as could be obtained from unaffiliated third parties.

Tax Sharing Agreement

Holdings, Revlon, Inc., Products Corporation and certain of its subsidiaries and Mafco Holdings are parties to the Tax Sharing Agreement, which is described in Note 13. Since payments to be made under the Tax Sharing Agreement will be determined by the amount of taxes that Revlon, Inc. would otherwise have to pay if it were to file separate federal, state or local income tax returns, the Tax Sharing Agreement will benefit Mafco Holdings to the extent Mafco Holdings can offset the taxable income generated by Revlon, Inc. against losses and tax credits generated by Mafco Holdings and its other subsidiaries.

Financing Reimbursement Agreement

Holdings and Products Corporation entered into a financing reimbursement agreement (the "Financing Reimbursement Agreement") in 1992, which expired on June 30, 1996, pursuant to which Holdings agreed to reimburse Products Corporation for Holdings' allocable portion of (i) the debt issuance cost and advisory fees related to the capital restructuring of Holdings, and (ii) interest expense attributable to the higher cost of funds paid by Products Corporation under the credit agreement in effect at that time as a result of additional borrowings for the benefit of Holdings in connection with the assumption of certain abilities by Products Corporation under the Asset Transfer Agreement and the repurchase of certain subordinated notes from affiliates. In February 1995, the Financing Reimbursement Agreement was amended and extended to provide that Holdings would reimburse Products Corporation for a portion of the debt issuance costs and advisory fees related to the credit agreement then in effect (which portion was approximately $4.7 and was evidenced by a noninterest-bearing promissory note payable on June 30, 1996) and 112% per annum of the average balance outstanding under the credit agreement then in effect and the average balance outstanding under working capital borrowings from affiliates through June 30, 1996 and such amounts were evidenced by a noninterest-bearing promissory note payable on June 30, 1996. As of December 31, 1995 the aggregate amount of notes payable by Holdings under the Financing Reimbursement Agreement was $8.9. In June 1996, $10.9 in notes due to Products Corporation, which included $2.0 of interest reimbursement from Holdings in 1996, under the Financing Reimbursement Agreement was offset against an $11.7 demand note payable by Products Corporation to Holdings.

Registration Rights Agreement

Prior to the consummation of the Revlon IPO, Revlon, Inc. and Revlon Worldwide Corporation (subsequently merged into REV Holdings), the then direct parent of Revlon, Inc., entered into the Registration Rights Agreement pursuant to which REV Holdings one certain transferees of Revlon, Inc.'s Common Stock held by REV Holdings (the "Holders") have the right to require Revlon, Inc. to register all or part of the Class A Common Stock owned by such Holders and the Class A Common Stock issuable upon conversion of Revlon, Inc.'s Class B Common Stock owned by such Holders under the Securities Act of 1933, as amended (a "Demand Registration"); provided that Revlon, Inc. may postpone giving effect to a Demand Registration up to a period of 30 days if Revlon, Inc. believes such registration might have a material adverse effect on any plan or proposal by Revlon, Inc. with respect to any financing, acquisition, recapitalization, reorganization or other material transaction, or if Revlon, Inc. is in possession of material non-public information that, if publicly disclosed, could result in a material disruption of a major corporate development or transaction then pending or in progress or in other material adverse consequences to Revlon, Inc. In addition, the Holders have the right to participate in registrations by Revlon, Inc. of its Class A Common Stock (a "Piggyback Registration"). The Holders will pay all out-of-pocket expenses incurred in connection with any Demand Registration. Revlon, Inc. will pay any expenses incurred in connection with a Piggyback Registration, except for underwriting discounts, commissions and expenses attributable to the shares of Class A Common Stock sold by such Holders.

Other

Pursuant to a lease dated April 2, 1993 (the "Edison Lease"), Holdings leased to Products Corporation the Edison research and development facility for a term of up to 10 years with an annual rent of $1.4 and certain shared operating expenses payable by Products Corporation which, together with the annual rent, were not to exceed $2.0 per year. Pursuant to an assumption agreement dated February 18, 1993, Holdings agreed to assume all costs and expenses of the ownership and operation of the Edison facility as of January 1, 1993, other than (i) the operating expenses for which Products Corporation was responsible under the Edison Lease and (ii) environmental claims and compliance costs relating to matters which occurred prior to January 1, 1993 up to an amount not to exceed $8.0 (the amount of such claims and costs for which Products Corporation is responsible, the "Environmental Limit"). In addition, pursuant to such assumption agreement, Products Corporation agreed to indemnify Holdings for environmental claims and compliance costs relating to matters which occurred prior to January 1, 1993 up to an amount not to exceed the Environmental Limit and Holdings agreed to indemnify Products Corporation for environmental claims and compliance costs relating to matters which occurred prior to January 1, 1993 in excess of the Environmental Limit and all such claims and costs relating to matters occurring on or after January 1, 1993. Pursuant to an occupancy agreement, during 1998, 1997 and 1996 Products Corporation rented from Holdings a portion of the administration building located at the Edison facility and space for a retail store of Products Corporation's now discontinued retail operation. Products Corporation provided certain administrative services, including accounting, for Holdings with respect to the Edison facility pursuant to which Products Corporation paid on behalf of Holdings costs associated with the Edison facility and was reimbursed by Holdings for such costs, less the amount owed by Products Corporation to Holdings pursuant to the Edison ease and the occupancy agreement. In August 1998, Holdings sold the Edison facility to an unrelated third party, which assumed substantially all liability for environmental claims and compliance costs relating to the Edison facility, and in connection with the sale, Products Corporation terminated the Edison Lease and entered into a new lease with the new owner. Holdings agreed to indemnify Products Corporation to the extent rent under the new lease exceeds rent that would have been payable under the terminated Edison Lease had it not been terminated. The net amount reimbursed by Holdings to Products Corporation with respect to the Edison facility for 1998, 1997 and 1996 was $0.5, $07 and $1.1, respectively.

During 1997, a subsidiary of Products Corporation sold an inactive subsidiary to a company that was an affiliate of the Company during 1997 and part of 1998 for approximately $1.0.

Effective July 1, 1997, Holdings contributed to Products Corporation substantially all of the assets and liabilities of the Bill Blass business not already owned by Products Corporation. The contributed assets approximated the contributed liabilities and were accounted for at historical cost in a manner similar to that of a pooling of interests and, accordingly, prior period financial statements were restated as if the contribution took place prior to the beginning of the earliest period presented.

In the fourth quarter of 1996, a subsidiary of Products Corporation purchased an inactive subsidiary from an affiliate for net cash consideration of approximately $3.0 in a series of transactions in which the Company expects to realize foreign tax benefits in future years.

Effective January 1, 1996, Products Corporation acquired from Holdings substantially all of the assets of Tarlow in consideration for the assumption of substantially all of the liabilities and obligations of Tarlow Net liabilities assumed were approximately $3.4. The assets acquired and liabilities assumed were accounted for at historical cost in a manner similar to that of a pooling of interests and, accordingly, prior period financial statements have been restated as if the acquisition took place at the beginning of the earliest period. Products Corporation paid $4.1 to Holdings which was accounted for as an increase in capital deficiency. A nationally recognized investment banking firm rendered its written opinion that the terms of the purchase are fair from a financial standpoint to Products Corporation.

On February 2, 1998, Revlon Escrow Corp., an affiliate of Products Corporation, issued and sold in a private placement $650.0 aggregate principal amount of $8\frac{5}{8}\%$ Notes and $250.0 aggregate principal amount of $8\frac{1}{8}\%$ Notes, with the net proceeds deposited into escrow. The proceeds from the sale of the $8\frac{5}{8}\%$ and $8\frac{1}{8}\%$ Notes were used to finance the redemption of Products Corporation's $555.0 aggregate principal amount of $10\frac{1}{2}\%$ Senior Subordinated Notes due 2003 (the "Senior Subordinated Notes") and $2600 aggregate principal amount of $9\frac{3}{8}\%$ Senior Notes due 2001 (the "Senior Notes" and, together with the Senior Subordinated Notes, the "Old Notes"). Products Corporation delivered a redemption notice to the holders of the Senior Subordinated Notes for the redemption of the Senior Subordinated Notes on March 4, 1998, at which the Products Corporation assumed the allegations under the $8\frac{5}{8}\%$ Notes and the related indenture (the "8⅝% Notes Assumption"), and to the holders of the Senior Notes for the redemption of the Senior Notes on April 1, 1998, at which time Products Corporation assumed the obligations under the 8⅛% Notes and the related indenture (the "8⅛% Notes Assumption" and, together with the 8⅝% Notes Assumption the "Assumption"). A nationally recognized investment banking firm rendered its written opinion that the Assumption, upon consummation of the redemptions of the Old Notes, and the subsequent release from escrow to Products Corporation of any remaining net proceeds from the sale of the 8⅝% and 8⅛% Notes are fair from a financial standpoint to Products Corporation under the 1999 Notes Indenture.

Products Corporation leases certain facilities to MacAndrews & Forces or its affiliates pursuant to occupancy agreements and leases. These induced space at Products Corporation's New York headquarters and at Products Corporation's offices in London during 1998, 1997 and 1996; in Tokyo during 1996 and in Hong Kong during 1997 and the first half of 1998. The rent paid to Products Corporation for 1998, 1997 and 1996 was $2.9, $3.8 and $4.6, respectively.

In June 1997, Products Corporation borrowed from Holdings approximately $0.5, representing certain amounts received by Holdings from the sale of a brand and inventory relating thereto. Such amounts are evidenced by noninterest-bearing promissory notes. Holdings agreed not to demand payment under such notes so long as any indebtedness remains outstanding under the Credit Agreement.

During 1998, approximately $5.7 due to Products Corporation from Holdings was offset against certain notes payable to Holdings.

Products Corporation's Credit Agreement is supported by, among other things, guarantees from Holdings and certain of its subsidiaries. He obligations under such guarantees are secured by, among other things, (i) the capital stock and certain assets of certain subsidiaries of Holdings and (ii) until the disposition of the Edison facility n August 1998, a mortgage on the Edison facility.

Products Corporation borrows funds from its affiliates from time to time to supplement its working capital borrowings. No such borrowings were outstanding as of December 31, 1998, 1997 or 1996. The interest rates for such borrowings are more favorable to Products Corporation than interest rates under the Credit Agreement and, for borrowings occurring prior to the execution of the Credit Agreement, the credit facilities in effect at the time of such borrowing. The amount of interest paid by Products Corporation for such borrowings for 1998, 1997 and 1996 was $0.8, $0.6 and $0.5, respectively.

During 1998, the Company made advances of $0.25 and $0.3 to Mr. Fellows and Ms. Dwyer, respectively. During 1998, the Company made an advance of $0.4 to Mr. Levin, which advance was repaid in January 1999.

In November 1993, Products Corporation assigned to Holdings a lease for warehouse space in New Jersey (the "N.J. Warehouse") between Products Corporation and a trust established for the benefit of certain family members of the Chairman of the Board. The N.J. Warehouse had become vacant as a result of divestitures and restructuring of Products Corporation. The ease has annual lease payments of approximately $2.3 and terminates on June 30, 2005. In consideration for Holdings assuming all abilities and obligations under the lease, Products Corporation paid Holdings $7.5 (for which a liability was previously recorded) in three installments of $2.5 each in January 1994, January 1995 and January 1996. A nationally recognized investment banking firm rendered its written opinion that the terms of the lease transfer were fair from a financial standpoint to Products Corporation. During 1996 Products Corporation paid certain costs associated with the N.J. Warehouse on behalf of Holdings and was reimbursed by Holdings for such amounts. The amounts reimbursed by Holdings to the Company for such costs were $0.2 for 1996.

During 1997 and 1996, Products Corporation used an airplane owned by a corporation of which Messrs. Gittis, Drapkin and, during 1996, Levin, were the sole stockholders, for which Products Corporation paid approximately $0.2 and $0.2 for 1997 and 1996, respectively.

During 1998 and 1997, Products Corporation purchased products from a company that was an affiliate of the Company during part of 1998, for which it paid approximately $0.4 and $0.9, respectively.

During 1997, Products Corporation provided licensing services to a company that was an affiliate of the Company during 1997 and part of 1998, for which Products Corporation was paid approximately $0.7 in 1997.

In connection with the termination of the licensing arrangement and its agreement to provide consulting services during 1998, Products Corporation received payments of $2.0 in 1998 and is entitled to receive an additional $1.0 in 1999.

A company that was an affiliate of the Company during 1996, 1997 and 1998 assembled lipstick cases for Products Corporation. Products Corporation paid approximately $1.1, $0.9 and $1.0 for such services for 1998, 1997 and 1996, respectively.

AMGEN
1999 ANNUAL REPORT

2. Related Party Transactions

The Company owns a 50% interest in Kirin-Amgen, Inc. ("Kirin-Amgen"), a corporation formed in 1984 for the development and commercialization of certain products based on advanced biotechnology. Pursuant to the terms of agreements entered into with Kirin-Amgen, the Company conducts certain research and development activities on behalf of Kirin-Amgen and is paid for such services at negotiated rates. Included in revenues from corporate partners for the years ended December 31, 1999, 1998 and 1997, are $138.5 million, $212 million and $87.9 million, respectively, related to these agreements.

In connection with its various agreements with Kirin-Amgen, the Company has been granted sole and exclusive licenses for the manufacture and sale of certain products in specified geographic areas of the world. In return for such licenses, the Company pays Kirin-Amgen royalties based on sales. During the years ended December 31, 1999, 1998 and 1997, Kirin-Amgen earned royalties from Amgen of $128.1 million, $105 million and $91.4 million, respectively, under such agreements, which are included in "cost of sales" in the accompanying consolidated statements of operations.

At December 31, 1999, Amgen's share of Kirin-Amgen's undistributed retained earnings was approximately $87.1 million.

BAXTER INTERNATIONAL 1999 ANNUAL REPORT

12. Legal Proceedings, Commitments & Contingencies

Baxter International Inc. and certain of its subsidiaries are named as defendants in a number of lawsuits, claims and proceedings, including product liability, claims involving products now or formerly manufactured or sold by the company or companies that were acquired by Baxter. These cases and claims raise difficult and complex factual and legal issues and are subject to many uncertainties and complexities, including, but not limited to, the facts and circumstances of each particular case or claim, the jurisdiction in which each suit is brought, and differences in applicable law. Accordingly, in many cases, the company is not able to estimate the amount of its liabilities with respect to such matters.

Upon resolution of any legal matters, Baxter may incur charges in excess of presently established reserves. While such a future charge could have a material adverse impact on the company's net income and net cash flows in the period in which it is recorded or paid, management believes that no such charge would have a material adverse effect on Baxter's consolidated financial position.

Following is a summary of certain legal matters pending against the company. For a more extensive description of such matters and other lawsuits, claims and proceedings against the company, see Baxter's Annual Report on Form 10-K for the year ended December 31, 1999.

Mammary Implant Litigation

The company, together with certain of its subsidiaries, is currently a defendant in various courts in a number of lawsuits brought by individuals, all seeking damages for injuries of various types allegedly caused by silicone mammary implants formerly manufactured by the Heyer-Schulte division (Heyer-Schulte) of American Hospital Supply Corporation (AHSC). AHSC, which was acquired by the company in 1985, divested its Heyer-Schulte division in 1984.

A class action on behalf of all women with silicone mammary implants was filed in March 1994. The class action was certified for settlement purposes only by the federal court in which it was filed in September 1994, and the settlement terms were subsequently revised and approved in

December 1995. The monetary provisions of the settlement provide compensation for all present and future plaintiffs and claimants through a series of specific funds and a disease-compensation program involving certain specified medical conditions. All appeals directly challenging the settlement have been dismissed in January 1996. Baxter, Bristol-Myers Squibb Company and Minnesota Mining and Manufacturing Company each paid $125 million into the court-established fund as an initial fund to pay claims under the settlement. In addition to the class action, there are a large number of individual suits currently pending against the company primarily consisting of plaintiffs who have opted-out of the class action.

In 1993, Baxter accrued $556 million for its estimated liability resulting from the settlement of the mammary related class action and recorded a receivable for estimated insurance recoveries totaling $426 million resulting in a net charge of $130 million. In 1995, based on a continuing evalution of this litigation, the company accrued an additional $298 million for its estimated liability to litigate or settle cases and claims involving opt-outs and recorded an additional receivable for estimated insurance recoveries totaling $258 million, resulting in an additional net charge of $40 million. In 1998, the company accrued an additional $250 million for its estimated liability resulting from the class action settlement and remaining opt-out cases and claims, and recorded a receivable for related estimated insurance recoveries of $121 million, resulting in an additional net charge of $129 million.

In December 1998, a panel of independent medical experts appointed by a federal judge announced their findings that reported medical studies contained no clear evidence of a connection between silicone mammary implants and traditional or atypical systemic diseases. In June 1999, a similar conclusion was announced by a committee of independent medical experts from the Institute of Medicine, an arm of the National Academy of Sciences. The mammary implant litigation includes issues related to which of Baxter's insurers are responsible for covering each matter and the extent of the company's claims for contribution against third parties. Baxter believes that a substantial portion of its liability and defense costs for mammary implant litigation will be covered by insurance, subject to self-insurance retentions, exclusions, conditions, coverage gaps, policy limits, and insurer solvency.

Plasma-Based Therapies Litigation

Baxter currently is a defendant in a number of claims and lawsuits brought by individuals who have hemophilia, all seeking damages for injuries allegedly caused by antihemophilia factor concentrates VIII or IX derived from human blood plasma (factor concentrates) processed by the company from the late 1970s to the mid-1980s. The typical case or claim alleges that the individual was infected with the HIV virus by factor concentrates, which contained the HIV virus. None of these cases involves factor concentrates currently processed by the company.

In addition, Immuno has settled claims for damages for injuries allegedly caused by its plasma-based therapies. A portion of the liability and defense costs related to these claims will be covered by insurance, subject to exclusions, conditions, policy limits and other factors. In addition, pursuant to the stock purchase agreement between the company and Immuno, approximately 84 million Swiss Francs of the purchase price was withheld to cover these contingent liabilities. In April 1999, the stock purchase agreement between the company and Immuno was amended to revise the holdback amount from 84 million Swiss Francs to 26 million Swiss Francs (or approximately $16 million at December 31, 1999) in consideration for an April 1999 payment by the company of 29 million Swiss Francs to Immuno as additional purchase price. Based on management's estimates, the company has recorded an appropriate liability and related insurance receivable with regard to the matters above.

Baxter is also currently a defendant in a number of claims and lawsuits, including one certified class action in the U.S.D.C. for the Central District of California, brought by individuals who infused the company's Gammagard® IVIG (intravenous immunoglobulin), all of whom are seeking damages for Hepatitis C infections allegedly caused by infusing Gammagard® IVIG. In December 1999, the U.S.D.C. for the Central District of California granted preliminary approval to a proposed settlement of the class action agreed upon by plaintiffs' class counsel and Baxter that would provide financial compensation for U.S. individuals who used Gammagard® IVIG between January 1993 and February 1994.

Baxter believes that a substantial portion of the liability and defense costs related to its plasma-based therapies litigation will be covered by insurance, subject to self-insurance retentions, exclusions, conditions, coverage gaps, policy limits and insurer solvency. In 1993, the company accrued $131 million for its estimated worldwide liability for litigation and settlement expenses involving factor concentrates cases and recorded a receivable for insurance coverage of $83 million, resulting in a net charge of $48 million. In 1995, significant developments occurred, primarily in the United States, Europe and Japan relative to claims and litigation pertaining to Baxter's plasma-based therapies. The company revised its estimated exposure from the $131 million previously recorded for factor concentrates litigation to $378 million for all litigation relating to plasma-based therapies, including the factor concentrates litigation and the Gammagard® IVIG litigation. Related estimated insurance recoveries were revised from $83 million for factor concentrates to $274 million for all plasma-based therapies. This resulted in a net charge of $56 million in 1995. The company further revised its estimate of liabilities and insurance recoveries in 1998, and accrued an additional $180 million for its estimated liability for plasma-based therapies litigation and other litigation and recorded a receivable for related estimated insurance recoveries of $131 million, for a net charge of $49 million.

Other Litigation

As of September 30, 1996, Allegiance Corporation (Allegiance) assumed the defense of litigation involving claims related to Allegiance's businesses, including certain claims of alleged personal injuries as a result of exposure to natural rubber latex gloves. Allegiance has not been named in most of this litigation but will be defending and indemnifying Baxter pursuant to certain contractual obligations for all potential liabilities associated with claims pertaining to latex gloves.

In addition to the cases discussed above, Baxter is a defendant in a number of other claims, investigations and lawsuits, including certain environmental proceedings. Based on the advice of counsel, management does not believe that, individually or in the aggregate, these other claims, investigations and lawsuits will have a material adverse effect on the company's results of operations, cash flows or consolidated financial position.

Commitment

In November 1999, the company and Nexell entered into an agreement whereby Baxter agreed to guarantee certain amounts up to a maximum of $63 million, associated with a private placement by Nexell of preferred stock and other securities.

EASTMAN CHEMICAL COMPANY 1997 ANNUAL REPORT

18. Environmental Matters

Certain Eastman manufacturing sites generate hazardous and nonhazardous wastes, of which the treatment, storage, transportation, and disposal are regulated by various governmental agencies. In connection with the cleanup of various hazardous waste sites, the Company, along with many other entities, has been designated a potentially responsible party ("PRP") by the U.S. Environmental Protection Agency under the Comprehensive Environmental Response, Compensation and Liability Act, which potentially subjects PRPs to joint and several liability for such cleanup costs. In addition, the Company will be required to incur costs for environmental remediation and closure/postclosure under the federal Resource Conservation and Recovery Act. Because of expected sharing of costs, the availability of legal defenses, and the Company's preliminary assessment of actions that may be required, the Company does not believe its liability for these environmental matters, individually or in the aggregate, will be material to Eastman's consolidated financial position, results of operations, or competitive position.

The Company's environmental protection and improvement cash expenditures were approximately $220 million, $175 million, and $150 million in 1997, 1996, and 1995, respectively, including investments in construction, operations, and development.

The Chemical Intermediates segment contains industrial intermediate chemicals that are produced based on the Company's oxo chemistry technology and chemicals-from-coal technology and are sold to customers operating in mature markets in which multiple sources of supply exist. They are sold generally in large volume mostly to North American industries, with increasing focus in Southeast Asia. These products are targeted at markets for industrial additives, agricultural chemicals, esters, pharmaceuticals, and vinyl compounding. Competitive factors include price, reliability of supply, and integrated manufacturing capability. Favorable cost position, proprietary products, and improving standards of living worldwide are key value drivers for this segment.

(Dollars in millions)	1997	1996	1995
Sales			
Specialty and Performance	$2,607	$2,657	$2,647
Core Plastics	1,338	1,409	1,685
Chemical Intermediates	733	716	708
Total	$4,678	$4,782	$5,040
Operating earnings (loss)			
Specialty and Performance	$ 416 [1]	$ 519	$ 433
Core Plastics	(56) [1]	(1)	347
Chemical Intermediates	146 [1]	145	184
Total	$ 506	$ 663	$ 964
Assets			
Specialty and Performance	$3,019	$2,887	$2,776
Core Plastics	2,188	1,854	1,598
Chemical Intermediates	571	525	498
Total	$5,778	$5,266	$4,872
Depreciation expense			
Specialty and Performance	$ 172	$ 174	$ 178
Core Plastics	123	109	96
Chemical Intermediates	32	31	34
Total	$ 327	$ 314	$ 308
Capital expenditures			
Specialty and Performance	$ 227	$ 302	$ 176
Core Plastics	390	388	215
Chemical Intermediates	132	99	55
Total	$ 749	$ 789	$ 446

[1] Operating earnings for 1997 reflect the $62 million ($40 million after tax) charge for partial settlement/curtailment of pension and other postemployment benefit liabilities. The charge was allocated to segments as follows: Specialty and Performance, $34 million; Core Plastics, $18 million; and Chemical Intermediates, $10 million. See note 14 for a discussion of the charge.

Geographic Segments

Sales are reported in the geographic area where they originate. Transfers among geographic areas are made on a basis intended to reflect the market value of the products, recognizing prevailing market prices and distributor discounts. Export sales to unaffiliated customers from the United States were $626 million in 1997, $687 million in 1996, and $698 million in 1995.

(Dollars in millions)	United States	Europe	Other Areas	Eliminations	Consolidated
1997					
Sales	$3,500	$755	$423		$4,678
Transfers among geographic areas	798	18	74	$ (890)	—
Total sales	$4,298	$773	$497	$ (890)	$4,678
Operating earnings (losses)	$ 580	$(51)	$(37)	$ 14	$ 506
Assets at end of year	$5,628	$805	$625	$(1,280)	$5,778
1996					
Sales	$3,674	$735	$373		$4,782
Transfers among geographic areas	785	27	55	$ (867)	—
Total sales	$4,459	$762	$428	$ (867)	$4,782
Operating earnings (losses)	$ 717	$(36)	$(31)	$ 13	$ 663
Assets at end of year	$5,076	$582	$424	$ (816)	$5,266
1995					
Sales	$3,864	$806	$370		$5,040
Transfers among geographic areas	806	50	17	$ (873)	—
Total sales	$4,670	$856	$387	$ (873)	$5,040
Operating earnings	$ 881	$ 47	$ 25	$ 11	$ 964
Assets at end of year	$4,569	$508	$324	$ (529)	$4,872

METRIS COMPANIES
1998 ANNUAL REPORT

11. Related Party Transactions

Prior to September 1998, FCI owned approximately 83% of the outstanding common shares of the Company. In September 1998, FCI distributed the remaining shares of the Company to shareholders of FCI in a tax free distribution.

FCI and its various subsidiaries have historically provided financial and operational support to the Company Direct expenses incurred by FCI and/or its subsidiaries for the Company, and other expenses, have been allocated to the Company using various methods (headcount, actual or estimated usage, etc.). Since the Company has not historically operated as a separate stand-alone entity for all periods presented, these allocations do not necessarily represent the expenses and costs that would have been incurred directly by the Company had it operated on a stand-alone basis. However, management believes such allocations reasonably approximate market rates for the services performed. The direct and allocated expenses represent charges for services such as data processing and information systems, audit, certain accounting and other similar functions, treasury legal, human resources, certain customer service and marketing analysis functions, certain executive time, and space and property usage allocations. In addition, the Company has historically managed the sales of credit insurance products for Fingerhut. In accordance therewith, the Company has allocated back to Fingerhut certain direct and other expenses using methods similar to those mentioned above. The historical expenses and cost allocations have been agreed to by the management of both PCI and the Company, the terms of which are summarized in an ongoing administrative services agreement between PCI and the Company. This agreement provides for similar future services using similar rates and cost allocation methods for various terms.

The financial statements also include an allocation of PCI interest expense for the net borrowings of the Company from PCI, or a net interest credit for the net cash flows of the Company loaned to PCI in 1996. These allocations of interest expense or income for 1996 were based on the net loans made or borrowings received between the Company and PCI, plus or minus the effects of intercompany balances outstanding during 1996.

The interest rate used to calculate such expense or credit during 1996 was based on the average short-term borrowing rates of PCI during 1996.

The Company and Fingerhut have also entered into several other agreements that detail further business arrangements between the companies. The retroactive effects of these additional business arrangements have been reflected in the consolidated financial statements of the Company. The agreements entered into include a co-brand credit card agreement and a data sharing agreement, which provide for payment for every Fingerhut co-branded credit card account booked, as defined, and a payment based on card usage from such accounts. The parties have also entered into a database access agreement, which provides the Company with the exclusive right to access and market financial services products, as defined, to Fingerhut customers, in exchange for a license fee. The agreement also calls for a solicitation fee per product mailed to a Fingerhut customer and a suppress file fee for each consumer name obtained from a third party and matched to the Fingerhut suppress file before its solicitation.

The Company and Fingerhut have also entered into an extended service plan agreement, which provides the company with the exclusive right to provide and coordinate the marketing of extended service plans to the customers of Fingerhut. Revenues are received from Fingerhut from such sales, and the Company reimburses Fingerhut and/or its subsidiaries for certain marketing costs. Additionally, the Company and ECI have entered into a tax sharing agreement (see Note 2) and a card registration agreement.

The following table summarizes the amounts of these direct expense charges and cost allocations (including net interest income or expense), and the costs to the Company of the agreements mentioned above, for each of the years reflected in the financial statements of the Company:

Year ended December 31,	1998	1997	1996
Revenues:			
Fee-based services	$12,937	$7,911	$20,420
Expenses:			
Interest expense			
Credit card account and other product solicitation and marketing expenses	8.274	8,432	9.335
Data processing services and communications	2,344	1,837	1,324
Other	659	1,336	950

In the ordinary course of business, executive officers of the Company or ECI may have credit card loans issued by the Company. Pursuant to the Company's policy, such loans are issued on the same terms as those prevailing at the time for comparable loans with unrelated persons and do not involve more than the informal risk of collectibility.

On November 13, 1998, the Company entered into agreements with the Lee Company to invest $300 million in the Company (see Note 6). The terms of the transaction provided that the Lee Company investment would convert into 0.8 million shares of Series C Preferred upon shareholder approval and receipt of notice that there was no regulatory objection to the transaction. The Company determined that this conversion might result in a "Change of Control" as defined in certain agreements between the Company and Fingerhut, which would permit Fingerhut to terminate any or all of the agreements. Therefore, on December 8, 1998, the Company obtained an agreement (the Waiver Agreement) from Fingerhut to waive its right to terminate the agreements if a Change of Control occurred as a result of the conversion.

Pursuant to the Waiver Agreement, the Company and Fingerhut amended certain of their other agreements. The most significant change was made in the database access agreement. The Company's exclusive license to use Fingerhut's customer database to market financial service products will now become non-exclusive after October 31, 2001.

On March 12, 1999, shareholders approved the conversion into the Series C Preferred. If notice is received that there is no regulatory objection to the conversion to the Series C Preferred, the Lee Company will own approximately 30% of the Company on a diluted basis, assuming conversion of the Series C Preferred into common stock.

MARRIOTT
1998 ANNUAL REPORT

Subsequent Event

On January 6, 1999, we entered into a definitive agreement to acquire Exe-cuStay Corporation (ExecuStay), a provider of leased corporate apartments. The total acquisition cost is estimated to be $115 million, to be paid with approximately $53 million in our Class A Common Stock and $62 million in cash. Holders of more than 55 percent of the voting stock of ExecuStay have agreed to the terms of the acquisition. Completion of the acquisition, which is expected to occur during the 1999 first quarter, is contingent on customary conditions, including the successful completion of a cash tender offer and expiration or termination of the Hart-Scott-Rodino Act waiting period requirements.

FORM 10-K FOR AMERIGON INC
Footnote: Development Stage Company

General

Amerigon Incorporated (the "Company") is a *development stage company* incorporated in California in 1991 to develop, manufacture and market proprietary high technology automotive components and systems for sale to automobile and other original equipment manufacturers. The Company was founded on the premise that technology proven for use in the defense and aerospace industries could be successfully adapted to the automotive and transportation industries. The Company has focused on technologies that it believes can be readily adapted to automotive needs for advanced vehicle electronics and for electric vehicle systems. The Company seeks to avoid direct competition with established automotive suppliers of commodity products by identifying market opportunities where the need for rapid technological change gives an edge to new market entrants with proprietary products. The Company has principally focused on developing proprietary positions in the following technologies: (i) thermoelectric heated and cooled seats; (ii) radar for maneuvering and safety; (iii) voice interactive navigation and entertainment; and (iv) electric vehicle components and production systems.

The Company has recently determined to focus its resources primarily on developing its heated and cooled seat and radar for maneuvering and safety technologies. The Company has adopted this strategy primarily because the Company believes that the markets for these products have greater near-term potential than the markets for its other products, and because these technologies presently afford the Company its best opportunities to exploit competitive advantages over rival companies. The Company also expects continued necessary development and marketing of the Company's voice interactive navigation technologies and electric vehicle systems to entail very high costs, to the point that they are likely to exceed the Company's financial resources. Even if the Company were able to overcome this financial challenge, management also believes that the Company might not be able to develop and successfully market the next generation of IVS-TM-, and might not be able to successfully develop and profitably manufacture electric vehicles or their components, without commercial or technical assistance from one or more strategic partners. Recently, the Company entered into a non-binding letter of intent that contemplates the possible formation of a joint venture to pursue further development and marketing of the IVS-TM- product. See "—Products" herein. If the proposed joint venture (or a similar transaction) is not consummated or the Company is unable to sell the IVS-TM- technology and product line in the near future, the Company plans to discontinue sales and further manufacture and development of the ITV-TM- and related technology. The Company is also presently seeking strategic and financial partners to help support continued development and marketing of the Company's electric vehicle systems. See "—Products" herein. If the Company is unable to arrange such a relationship in the near term, the Company will attempt to sell its proprietary interests and other assets in and relating to its electric vehicle technology or abandon their development.

The Company's heated and cooled seats and radar products are in various stages of development. The Company is presently working with three of the world's largest automotive original equipment manufacturers on pre-production development programs for heated and cooled seats. In addition, the Company has sold multiple prototypes of its heated and cooled seats and radar for maneuvering and safety to potential customers for evaluation and demonstration.

The Company has recently experienced significant cash shortfalls because its expenses have greatly exceeded its revenues. On October 31, 1996, the Company completed a $3,000,000 private placement (the "Bridge Financing") of Units, each consisting of $47,500 principal amount of unsecured promissory notes (the "Bridge Notes") and $2,500 principal amount of subordinated convertible debentures (the "Debentures"), to enable it to continue operations until the completion of a public offering (the "Offering") of Units consisting of Class A Common Stock and Class A Warrants. The sale of 17,000 Units in the Offering was completed on February 18, 1997, and the sale of an additional 2,550 Units pursuant to the underwriter's exercise of an over-allotment option was completed on March 7, 1997. The aggregate proceeds from the Offering, net of underwriting fees and discounts and all expenses, were approximately $17,700,000. Approximately $4,100,000 of the proceeds of the Offering were applied to repayment of the Bridge Notes and other indebtedness, with the balance of the net proceeds to be used to fund future operations.

WEIRTON STEEL
1997 ANNUAL REPORT

17. Formation of Joint Ventures

On October 3, 1997, the Company announced their intent to form a joint venture with Koninklijke Hoogovens for the purpose of constructing and operating a 300,000 ton hot-dipped galvanizing line. The construction of the galvanizing line is expected to be completed in 1999. No investment was made in this joint venture during 1997.

On September 4, 1997, the Company announced the formation of a joint venture with Balli Group, plc, named WeBCo International LLC ("WeBCo"). The primary function of WeBCo will be to market and sell the Company's products globally. In 1997, the Company invested $0.1 million in the joint venture.

NEOR CORPORATION
1997 ANNUAL REPORT

9. Changes in and Disagreements with Accountants on Accounting and Financial Disclosure

In April 1997, the Board of Directors, at the recommendation of the Audit Committee, terminated the engagement of Arthur Andersen LLP as the Company's certifying accountants.

The report of Arthur Andersen LLP on the Company's financial statements for either of the last two fiscal years did not contain any adverse opinion or disclaimer of opinion and was not qualified or modified as to uncertainty, audit scope or accounting principles.

During the Company's two most recent fiscal years and subsequent interim periods preceding the date of termination of the engagement of Arthur Andersen LLP, the Company was not in disagreement with Arthur Andersen LLP on any matter of accounting principles or practices, financial statement disclosure or auditing scope or procedure, which disagreement, if not resolved to the satisfaction of Arthur Andersen LLP, would have caused Arthur Andersen LLP to make reference to the subject matter of the disagreement in connection with its report.

The required letter from Arthur Andersen LLP with respect to the above statements made by the Company is filed as an exhibit hereto.

Also in April 1997, the Board of directors, at the recommendation of the Audit Committee, engaged KPMG Peat Marwick LLP as the Company's certifying accountants. The Company had not consulted with KPMG Peat Marwick LLP during its previous two most recent fiscal years or during any subsequent interim period prior to its engagement regarding the application of accounting principles to a specified transaction, either completed or proposed, or the type of audit option that might be rendered on the Company's financial statements.

Part II

MAJOR ACCOUNTING AREAS AND REPORTING

Chapter 9

Accounting Changes and Error Corrections

This chapter covers the accounting, reporting, and disclosures associated with changes in accounting principles (method), estimates, and reporting entities as stipulated in various pronouncements, such as APB Opinion Number 20 (*Accounting Changes*) and FASB Interpretation Number 20 (*Reporting Accounting Changes under AICPA Statements of Position*). If an accounting change is immaterial in the current year but is expected to be significant in future years, it should be completely disclosed in the year of change. This chapter also discusses how to present and disclose corrections of errors made in a prior year.

In evaluating the appropriateness of accounting changes, consideration should be given to the hierarchy of generally accepted accounting principles (GAAP) as follows:

- Level One (highest level): FASB statements and interpretations, APB opinions, and AICPA accounting research bulletins

- Level Two: FASB technical bulletins, AICPA industry audit and accounting guides, and AICPA statements of position

- Level Three: Consensus positions of the FASB Emerging Issues Task Force and AICPA practice bulletins

- Level Four: AICPA accounting interpretations, FASB implementation guides (questions and answers), and industry practices widely recognized and prevalent

■ Level Five (lowest level): FASB concepts statements, Accounting Principles Board statements, AICPA issues papers and technical practice aids, Governmental Accounting Standards Board pronouncements, International Accounting Standards Committee statements, pronouncements of other professional associations or regulatory bodies, and accounting books and articles

If there is a conflict between accounting principles, the one preferred is that enumerated in the highest level of GAAP hierarchy.

The Securities and Exchange Commission requires in Accounting Series Release 177 that the independent CPA auditing the company must state in writing that the newly selected accounting procedure is preferred in management's judgment. Reference may be made to AICPA statements of position and industry audit guides to determine whether accounting principles are preferred.

CHANGE IN ACCOUNTING PRINCIPLE (METHOD)

There is an underlying presumption that an accounting principle, once adopted, should not be changed for similar events and transactions. A change in principle may be due to new events, changing conditions, and additional information or experience. A change in principle is presented in an account called "cumulative effect of a change in principle" (net of tax). The amount of the cumulative effect equals the difference between retained earnings at the beginning of the year with the old method versus what retained earnings would have been at the beginning of the year if the new method had been used in previous years. The cumulative effect account appears as the last item in the income statement before arriving at net income. Further, earnings per share is shown on the cumulative effect account. In a cumulative effect change in principle, prior years' financial statements remain as previously reported.

EXAMPLE

Levita Corporation decided to change from the FIFO periodic inventory system to the weighed-average periodic inventory system on October 31, 2002. Levita is on a calendar-year basis. For financial accounting purposes, the cumulative effect of the change in accounting principle is determined as of January 1, 2002 and not on October 31, the actual date of the change. A change in inventory method generally constitutes an accounting change that necessitates a cumulative catch-up presentation in the income statement as required by APB 20. All such computations are determined as of the beginning of the fiscal year in which the change is made. The theory supporting this determination is that if a change in accounting principle is made anytime in a given year, then that principle should be used during the whole period of the change (as of beginning of the period, i.e., January 1) as well as future periods. Therefore, in summary, the cumulative effect of a change from the FIFO periodic inventory system to the weighed-average method is determined as of the beginning of the year, January 1, 2002, regardless of the actual date of the change.

If comparative financial statements are not presented, pro forma disclosures (recalculated figures) should be shown after the body of the financial statements but before the footnotes (or in a separate schedule). Pro forma disclosure is disclosure of what earnings would have been in previous years if the new principle was used in those prior years.

If income statements are provided for comparative purposes, they should reflect the change on a pro forma basis as if the change had been in effect in each of such years.

Comparative financial statements for previous years are presented as previously reported. Income before extraordinary items, net income, and earnings per share for past years presented are recalculated and disclosed on the face of the previous years' income statements as if the new principle was used in those years. These data may be shown in a separate schedule presenting both the initial and recomputed figures.

If only the current year's income statement is shown, actual and pro forma amounts for the immediately prior year should be disclosed.

If pro forma amounts are not determinable or reasonably estimated for previous years, the cumulative effect account should be presented on the income statement with disclosure of why the pro forma amounts cannot be presented. In a rare case, both the cumulative effect and pro forma figures cannot be computed. In such a case, the effect of the change on the current year's earnings (year of change) should be disclosed. Further, the reasons for the omission should be disclosed. An example is when a problem arises due to switching from the FIFO to LIFO inventory methods.

As per FASB Interpretation Number 1 (*Accounting for Changes Related to the Cost of Inventory*), a change in the composition of the cost factors in valuing inventory represents an accounting change in principle and must be footnoted as to why it is preferred.

EXAMPLE

In 19X5, ABC Company changed from the double declining balance (DDB) depreciation method to the straight-line (SL) method. Its tax rate is 40%. The following information is presented:

Depreciation

Year	DDB	SL	Difference
19X3	$100,000	$50,000	$50,000
19X4	80,000	50,000	30,000
19X5	70,000	50,000	20,000

The following journal entries are made to account for the change in depreciation method in 19X5:

Depreciation expense	50,000	
Accumulated depreciation		50,000
For straight line depreciation in current year.		
Accumulated depreciation		
(50,000 + 30,000)	80,000	
Deferred tax liability (80,000 × .40)		32,000
Cumulative effect of a change in		
principle (80,000 × .60)		48,000
For previous years' effect.		

The effect of a change in principle for the current year is not included in the cumulative effect account because the new principle is used in determining the net income for the current year.

EXAMPLE

In 2004, D Corporation decided to change from the FIFO method of inventory valuation to the weighted-average method. Inventory balances under each of the methods were as follows:

	FIFO	*Weighted Average*
January 1, 2004	$171,000	$177,000
December 31, 2004	179,000	183,000

D's income tax rate is 40%.

In its 2004 financial statements, what amount should D report as the cumulative effect of this accounting change?

APB Opinion 20 requires that changes in accounting principles be treated as cumulative effect items disclosed net of taxes on the income statement. The required measurement is the difference between the beginning retained earnings and the retained earnings balance had the new inventory method been retroactively applied.

The required computation is as follows:

Weighted-average method as of January 1, 2004, the year in which the change is adopted	$177,000
Less: FIFO method	171,000
Cumulative effect of the change before taxes	6,000
Cumulative effect, net of taxes: $6,000 × (1–40%)	$3,600

EXAMPLE

X Corporation elects to change its method of depreciation (for its equipment) to the units of output method from the straight-line method. The equipment was originally purchased on January 2, 2000 for $10,000 and had an estimated useful life of five years. X Corporation estimates that the equipment will have a useful life of approximately 25,000 hours. The equipment was used for 4,250 hours during 2001 and 1,750 hours during 2000. X Corporation's tax rate is 35%.

How should X Corporation report the accounting change in its 2002 financial statements?

In this situation, the cumulative effect of the change to the units of production method from the straight-line method is the net of tax difference in the retained earnings that would have existed if the units of output method had been used since acquisition. The computation is as follows:

Accumulated depreciation:	
Units of output method ($10,000/25,000) × 6,000 hours	$2,400
Straight-line method ($10,000/5 years) × 2 years	4,000
Cumulative effect before income taxes	($1,600)
Cumulative effect, net of taxes : $1,600 × (1–35%)	$1,040

There are several exceptions to the cumulative effect rule, which requires the restatement of previous years' financial statements as if the new principle had been used in those years rather than the old. These exceptions are as follows:

- Change in accounting for construction contracts (e.g., changing from the percentage of completion method to or from the completed contract method).

- Change from LIFO to another inventory method.

- Change in accounting for exploration costs by companies in the extractive industry (e.g., changing from the full cost method to the successful efforts method). In the extractive industry, companies may either use the successful efforts method, where only successful exploration costs are charged to the asset account and amortized while unsuccessful costs are immediately expensed, or the full cost method, which defers both the successful and unsuccessful exploration costs to the asset and amortizes such costs.

- Change in the composition of the cost components in inventory.

- Change from retirement-replacement-betterment accounting to depreciation accounting for railroad track structures. For a detailed discussion, refer to FASB Statement Number 73 (*Reporting a Change in Accounting for Railroad Track Structures*).

Retroactive restatement may be required for changes due to new authoritative pronouncements.

Retroactive application is permitted (but not required) for a change in principle arising from an initial public offering of equity or debt securities by a closely held business.

In a retroactive restatement, the effect of the change in accounting principle is adjusted directly to the beginning balance of retained earnings in the year of change.

Footnote disclosure should be made if an accounting change in principle is considered immaterial in the current year but is expected to be material in a later year.

The following is not considered a change in principle:

- A principle adopted for the first time on new (e.g., different depreciation method for a new fixed asset) or previously insignificant events or transactions. (**Note:** A change in principle occurs when a new principle is used for a pre-existing asset.)
- A principle adopted or changed because of significantly different occurrences or transactions. However, footnote disclosure should be made of the change in policy.

Changes in classification are not a change in principle but should be disclosed.

Footnote disclosure should be made of the nature and justification for a change in principle, including the reason why the new principle is preferred. Justifiable reasons for a change in principle include the issuance of a new authoritative pronouncement (e.g., FASB statement), a change in tax law, a new AICPA recommended policy (e.g., AICPA statement of position), a change in circumstances of the company, and a change in principle that better conforms to industry practice. However, note that a change in principle solely for income tax purposes is not a change in principle for financial reporting purposes.

CHANGE IN ACCOUNTING ESTIMATE

A change in estimate arises from new events or occurs from additional information or experience. A change in estimate is accounted for only over current and future years. Prior years are not adjusted. Examples of a change in estimate are changing the life or salvage value of a fixed asset, the life of an intangible, and the estimated percent of bad debts or warranties.

Footnote disclosure should be made of the nature and reasons for the change unless it involves changes in the ordinary course of business (e.g., modifying a bad debt percentage). The impact of the change in estimate on net income and per share earnings should be disclosed if the change will affect future year results.

In the case where a change in estimate is coupled with a change in principle and the effects cannot be distinguished, the change should be accounted for as a change in estimate. An example is a change from deferring and amortizing cost to expensing it as incurred because of doubtful future benefit.

A permanent loss on an asset is not a change in accounting estimate but rather a current period loss.

EXAMPLE

In 19X3, ABC Company changed its bad debt estimate based on an aging of accounts receivable, resulting in recording bad debts of $60,000, which is $3,000 less than if a revised estimate was not made. The journal entry is

Bad debts	60,000	
Allowance for bad debts		60,000

The related footnote would state that ABC Company modified its estimate of uncollectible accounts to reflect better the net realizable value of accounts receivable. The impact of the change in estimate was to increase 19X3 net income by $3,000.

EXAMPLE

On January 1, 19X4, a fixed asset was purchased costing $50,000 and having an estimated life of 20 years with a salvage value of $2,000. On January 1, 19X7, the estimated life was revised to 14 additional years with a new salvage value of $2,200. The journal entry on December 31, 19X7 for depreciation expense follows:

Depreciation expense	2,900	
Accumulated depreciation		2,900
Computation:		
Book value on 1/1/19X7:		
Initial cost		$50,000
Less: Accumulated depreciation ($50,000 − $2,000)/20 years		(7,200)
Book value		$42,800
Depreciation for 19X7:		
Book value		$42,800
Less: New salvage value		2,200
Balance		$40,600

$$\frac{\text{Depreciable cost}}{\text{New life}} = \frac{\$40,600}{14 \text{ years}} = \$2,900$$

CHANGE IN REPORTING ENTITY

A change in reporting entity refers to preparing financial statements for an entity different from the one reported in previous years. Examples of a change in reporting entity are

- Change in the subsidiaries making up consolidated financial statements

- A business combination accounted for under the pooling-of-interests method

■ Presentation of consolidated or combined statements rather than individual company statements

A change in reporting entity requires the restatement of previous years' financial statements as if both of the previously separate companies were always combined. No more than five years are restated. The restatement is needed for comparative financial purposes and for meaningful historical trends.

The impact of the change in reporting entity on income before extraordinary items, net income, and earnings per share is presented for all years.

A change in the legal structure of a business is not considered a change in reporting entity. An example is a sole proprietorship becoming a corporation. Further, the purchase or sale of an investee is not a change in reporting entity.

A footnote is required on the nature of and reason for the change in reporting entity in the year it is made.

ERROR CORRECTIONS

FASB Statement Number 16 covers correction of errors made in a previous year. They are treated for accounting purposes as prior period adjustments. Prior period adjustments adjust the beginning balance of retained earnings for the net of tax effect of the error as follows:

> Retained Earnings—1/1 Unadjusted
> Prior Period Adjustments (net of tax)
> Retained Earnings—1/1 Adjusted
> Add: Net Income
> Less: Dividends
> Retained Earnings—12/31

Errors may arise because of mathematical mistakes, erroneous application of GAAP, or misuse of information existing at the time the financial statements were prepared. Additionally, changing a principle which is not GAAP to one that is GAAP represents an error correction.

In ascertaining whether an error is material and therefore reportable, consideration should be given to the significance of each correction on an individual basis and to the aggregate effect of all corrections. An error must be corrected immediately when uncovered.

If comparative financial statements are presented, there should be a retroactive adjustment for the error as it impacts previous years. The retroactive adjustment is presented via disclosure of the impact of the adjustment on prior years' earnings and components of net income.

Footnote disclosure for error corrections in the year found include the nature and description of the error, financial effect on income before extraordinary items, net income, and related earnings per share amounts.

EXAMPLE

At year-end 19X8, a company omitted the accrual of utilities expense of $3,000, which was paid on January 4, 19X9. The correcting entry on December 31, 19X9 is

Retained Earnings	3,000	
Utilities expense		3,000

EXAMPLE

Drake Company bought Travis Company on January 1, 19X5, recording goodwill of $80,000. Goodwill has not been amortized. Assume that amortization is over 20 years. The correcting entry on December 31, 19X7 is

Amortization expense		
($80,000/20 years = $4,000 × 1 year for 19X7)	4,000	
Retained earnings		
($4,000 × 2 years for 19X5 and 19X6)	8,000	
Goodwill		12,000

EXAMPLE

At the beginning of 19X6, a company purchased machinery for $500,000 with a salvage value of $50,000 and an expected life of 20 years. Straight-line depreciation is used. By mistake, salvage value was not subtracted in arriving at depreciation. The calculations on December 31, 19X9 are

	19X6–19X8
Depreciation taken (incorrect):	
$500,000/20 years × 3	$75,000
Depreciation (correct):	
($500,000 – $50,000)/20 years × 3	67,500
Difference	$ 7,500

The correcting journal entries on December 31, 19X9 are

Accumulated depreciation	7,500	
Retained earnings		7,500
To correct for error.		
Depreciation expense	22,500	
Accumulated depreciation		22,500
To record depreciation for 19X9.		

EXAMPLE

Mills Corporation purchased equipment on January 1, 19X3 for $40,000 with a $5,000 salvage value and a 10-year life. Maintenance expense was charged by mistake. On December 31, 19X6 the error was uncovered before the books were closed. The calculations and correcting entry follow:

Depreciation expense equals:		
($40,000 – $5,000)/10 years = $3,500 per year		
Depreciation expense	3,500	
Equipment	40,000	
Accumulated depreciation ($3,500 × 4 years)		14,000
Retained earnings ($40,000 – $10,500*)		29,500

*$3,500 × 3 years (19X3–19X5) = $10,500.

EXAMPLE

On January 1, 19X4, a six-year advance of $120,000 was received. In error, revenue was recorded for the entire amount. The error was found on December 31, 19X5 before the books were closed. The correcting entry is

Retained earnings ($120,000 – $20,000)	100,000	
Revenue (for current year)		20,000
Deferred revenue ($20,000 × 4 years)		80,000

EXAMPLE

If an enterprise changes from the recognition of vacation pay expense from the cash basis to the accrual basis, how should the change be accounted for?

In general, a change from an accounting principle that is not generally accepted (accounting for vacation pay expense on the cash basis) to one that is generally accepted (accounting for it on the accrual basis) should be presented as a correction of an error. The following procedures should be followed in this circumstance:

- The correction should be accounted for as a prior period adjustment (i.e., an adjustment as of the beginning balance of retained earnings, net of taxes) for the earliest year presented.

- There should be a restatement of all comparative prior financial statements presented so that they now reflect the accounting for vacation pay expense on the accrual basis instead of the cash basis.

- Footnote disclosure should be made in the financial statements regarding the prior period adjustment correcting the error, the restatement of the financial statements presented, and the effect of the correction on net income.

EXAMPLE

If an entity changes from the cash basis of accounting for service contracts to the accrual method, how should the change be treated in the financial statements?

This represents another example of a change from an accounting principle that is not generally accepted to one that is generally accepted. It therefore should be accounted for as a correction of an error. As in the previous example, the correction should be handled as a prior period adjustment, net of taxes, for the earliest year presented of the beginning balance of retained earnings. Restatement of all comparative financial statements presented should also be made as well as proper footnote disclosure of the changes and their effects.

EXAMPLE

Tessie Co. had a retained earnings balance of $800,000 at December 31, 2001. In September 2002, Tessie ascertained that insurance premiums of $120,000 covering a four-year period beginning January 1, 2001 had been fully paid and fully expensed in 2001. Tessie has a 40% tax rate. What amount should Tessie report as adjusted beginning retained earnings in its 2002 statement of retained earnings?

The $120,000 of insurance premiums for the four-year period beginning January 1, 2001, which had been fully paid and expensed, clearly should not have been expensed in total. Since the premiums represented coverage for a four-year period and only one (2001) had transpired, net income and retained earnings in 2001 was understated by 3/4 of $120,000 ($90,000), net of taxes. This amount, $90,000, should have been accounted for as an insurance prepayment at the end of 2001. Thus, a correction (an addition) of $90,000 × (1–40%), or $54,000, is needed to correct the beginning balance of retained earnings in 2002. Tessie should report $854,000 ($800,000 + $54,000) as its adjusted beginning retained earnings balance in its 2002 statement of retained earnings.

Classification errors usually do not affect net income. However, prior years' financial statements issued for comparative purposes should be corrected to present the appropriate classification.

Annual Report References

CHEVRON
1998 ANNUAL REPORT

3. Cumulative Effect on Net Income from Accounting Changes

In April 1998, the AICPA released Statement of Position 98-5, "Reporting on the Costs of Start-up Activities" (SOP 98-5), which introduced a broad definition of items to expense as incurred for start-up activities, including new products/services, entering new territories, initiating new processes or commencing new operations. Chevron was substantially in compliance with the pronouncement, and it had no impact on the company's accounting practices. However, Caltex capitalized these types of costs for certain projects. Chevron, accordingly, restated its 1998 quarterly financial statements for its $25 share of the charge associated with Caltex's fourth quarter 1998 implementation of SOP 98-5, effective January 1, 1998.

In the fourth quarter 1998, Chevron changed its method of calculating certain Canadian deferred income taxes, effective January 1, 1998. The benefit from this change was $32 and resulted in the restatement of first quarter 1998 net income.

The net benefit to Chevron's restated first quarter 1998 net income from the cumulative effect of adopting SOP 98-5 by Caltex and the change in Chevron's method of calculating Canadian deferred taxes was immaterial.

Chevron also adopted other new accounting statements and positions during 1998, but these were not material to the company's results of operations or its consolidated balance sheet.

481

4. Information Relating to the Consolidated Statement of Cash Flows

The Consolidated Statement of Cash Flows excludes the following noncash transactions:

During 1997, the company's Venice, Louisiana, natural gas facilities were contributed to a partnership with Dynegy Inc. (Dynegy). An increase in "Investments and advances" from this merger is considered a noncash transaction and resulted primarily from the contribution of properties, plant and equipment.

During 1996, the company merged substantially all of its natural gas liquids and natural gas marketing businesses with Dynegy. The company received cash, a note and shares of Dynegy common stock and participating preferred stock in exchange for its contribution of net assets to Dynegy. Only the cash received is included in the Consolidated Statement of Cash Flows as "Proceeds from asset sales."

The major components of "Capital expenditures" and the reconciliation of this amount to the capital and exploratory expenditures, excluding equity in affiliates, presented in "Management's Discussion and Analysis of Financial Condition and Results of Operations" are presented below:

| | *Year ended December 31* | | |
	1998	*1997*	*1996*
Additions to properties, plant and equipment	**$3,678**	$3,840	$3,250
Additions to investments	**306**	153	195
Payments for other liabilities and assets, net	**(104)**	(94)	(21)
Capital expenditures	**3,880**	3,899	3,424
Expensed exploration expenditures	**438**	462	400
Payments of tong-term debt and other financing obligations	**2**	6	33
Capital and exploratory expenditures, excluding equity affiliates	**$4,320**	$4,367	$3,857

There have been other noncash transactions that have occurred during the years presented. These include the contribution of working capital balances in exchange for an equity interest in a newly formed entity; the acquisition of longterm debt in exchange for the termination of a capital lease obligation; the reissuance of treasury shares for management and employee compensation plans; and changes in assets, liabilities and stockholders' equity resulting from the accounting for the company's Employee Stock Ownership Plan (ESOP), minimum pension liability and market value adjustments on investments. The amounts for these transactions are not material in the aggregate in relation to the company's financial position.

"Other, net" operating activities in 1998 include a noncurrent provision for the Cities Service litigation.

AMERADA HESS
1999 ANNUAL REPORT

3. Accounting Changes

Effective January 1, 1999, the Corporation adopted the last-in, first-out (LIFO) inventory method for valuing its refining and marketing inventories. The Corporation believes that the LIFO method more closely matches current costs and revenues and will improve comparability with other oil companies. The change to LIFO decreased net income by $97,051,000 for the year ended December 31, 1999 ($1.08 per share basic and diluted). There is no cumulative effect adjustment as of the beginning of the year for this type of accounting change.

On January 1, 1998, the Corporation began capitalizing the cost of internal use software in accordance with AICPA Statement of Position 98-1. This accounting change increased net income for 1998 by $13,867,000 ($.15 per share).

In June 1998, the Financial Accounting Standards Board issued FAS No. 133, Accounting for Derivative Instruments and Hedging Activities. The Corporation must adopt FAS No. 133 by January 1, 2001. This statement requires that the Corporation recognize all derivatives on the balance sheet at fair value. For derivatives that are not hedges, the change in fair value must be recognized in income. For derivatives that hedge changes in the fair value of assets, liabilities or firm commitments, the gains or losses are recognized in earnings together with the offsetting losses or gains on the hedged items. For derivatives that hedge cash flows of forecasted transactions, the gains or losses are recognized in other comprehensive income until the hedged items are recognized in income.

The Corporation has not yet determined what the effect of FAS No. 133 will be on its income and financial position.

Chapter 10

Investments in Equity and Debt Securities

FASB Statement Number 115 (*Accounting for Certain Investments in Debt and Equity Securities*) sets forth the accounting and financial reporting requirements for investments in equity securities with determinable fair market value and for all investments in debt securities. FASB 115 applies to preferred stock and common stock (if ownership is below 20% or if ownership exceeds 20% but effective control [significant influence] is lacking). The statement is not applicable to investments under the equity method, consolidated subsidiaries, specialized industries such as brokers and dealers, or not-for-profits. Nonprofit entities are governed by FASB Statement Number 124, which requires fair value reporting for all investment categories, including held-to-maturity. APB Opinion Number 18 (*The Equity Method of Accounting for Investments in Common Stock*) provides the accounting, reporting, and disclosure requirements under the equity method. The equity method generally applies if the investor owns between 20 and 50% of the voting common stock of the investee. The equity method may also apply if ownership is less than 20% but effective control exists.

FASB STATEMENT NUMBER 115 (MARKET VALUE METHOD AND AMORTIZED COST METHOD)

Equity securities are securities representing an ownership interest. They are either ownership in common stock or preferred stock, or rights to buy or sell ownership interests such as warrants, rights, or options (calls, puts). Redeemable preferred stock, however, is not treated as equity securities.

Debt securities are financial instruments evidencing a creditor relationship with a company or government. Examples are redeemable preferred stock, corporate bonds, municipal bonds, U.S. government obligations, convertible debt, collateralized mortgage obligations, strips, and commercial paper. Debt securities do not include futures contracts and option contracts.

Equity and debt securities are broken down into the following categories:

- Trading securities
- Available-for-sale securities
- Held-to-maturity securities

Classification of the securities will be based on factors such as management intent considering past history of investments, subsequent events after the balance sheet date, and the nature and objective of the investment.

Trading Securities

Trading securities may include equity and debt securities. Mortgage-backed securities held for sale related to mortgage banking activities are included in trading securities. Trading securities are purchased and held mainly to sell them in the short term (usually three months or less). There is active buying and selling of the securities to earn short-term profits from price appreciation.

Trading securities are recorded in the balance sheet under *current assets* at *fair market value*. Fair market value is based on stock or bond quotations on listed exchanges or in the over-the-counter market. However, restricted stock (stock restricted by governmental or contractual provisions) does not have a readily available fair value because it is not traded. Foreign securities are based on the market price of the foreign exchange if comparable to U.S. markets. Fair value of investments in a mutual fund is based on the published fair value per share. To determine the fair value of debt securities in which market price is unavailable, other valuation methods may be used, including present value of future cash flows, fundamental analysis, matrix pricing, and option-adjusted spread models. Market value is compared to cost on a total portfolio basis.

The valuation allowance (adjustment) account is a contra (offset) account to trading securities in the balance sheet to present market value. Balance sheet presentation follows:

> Trading securities (cost)
> Add (Less): Valuation allowance
> Net (market value)

Unrealized (holding) gains and losses on trading securities are presented separately in the income statement.

Disclosure should be made of the method on which cost was determined in computing realized gain or loss on sale (e.g., specific identification, first-in, first-out [FIFO], and average cost).

EXAMPLE

On December 31, 19X1, a company had a portfolio of trading securities having a total cost of $200,000 and a total market value of $225,000. The entry is

> Valuation allowance   25,000
>   Unrealized gain   25,000

Recall that the unrealized gain on trading securities is shown as a separate item in the income statement. Also recall that the valuation allowance account is a contra account to trading securities in the balance sheet. As such, the following is presented in the financial statements:

Income Statement
For the Year Ended December 31, 19X1

Unrealized Gain on Trading Securities	$25,000

Balance Sheet
December 31, 19X1

Current Assets	
Trading securities (cost)	$200,000
Add: Valuation allowance	25,000
Net (market value)	$225,000

On February 5, 19X2, trading securities costing $60,000 were bought. The entry is

Trading securities	60,000	
Cash		60,000

On July 1, 19X2, a cash dividend of $15,000 is received. The entry is

Cash	15,000	
Dividend revenue		15,000

On October 8, 19X2, trading securities costing $50,000 were sold for $49,000. The entry is

Cash	49,000	
Realized loss on sale	1,000	
Trading securities		50,000

On December 31, 19X2, the total cost of trading securities remaining equaled $210,000 ($200,000 + $60,000 − $50,000). Assume the total market value of the portfolio is $206,000. Before showing the journal entry at year-end, it is easier to understand by presenting the current asset section of the balance sheet on 12/31/19X2:

CURRENT ASSETS	
Trading securities (cost)	$210,000
Less: Valuation allowance	4,000
Net (market value)	$206,000

The valuation allowance account appears as follows:

Valuation Allowance

12/31/19X1	25,000	Entry	29,000
		12/31/19X2	4,000

This requires a credit for the year to the valuation allowance of $29,000 to balance. Therefore, the journal entry to do this follows:

12/31/19X2	Unrealized loss	29,000	
	Valuation allowance		29,000

The following is presented in the income statement for the year ended December 31, 19X2:

Dividend revenue	$15,000
Realized loss on sale of trading securities	1,000
Unrealized loss on trading securities	29,000

In the case of trading securities, a change in market value of a forward contract or option contract is recognized in the income statement in the year it accrues. Trading securities bought under a forward contract or by exercising an option are recognized at fair value on the settlement date.

Available-for-Sale Securities

Available-for-sale securities may include equity and debt securities. Available-for-sale securities are not held for short-term profits, nor are they to be held to maturity. Therefore, they are in between trading and held-to-maturity classifications. Available-for-sale securities are presented in the balance sheet as either current assets or noncurrent assets at *fair market value.* They are *often* listed as *noncurrent assets.* However, if the intent is to hold for less than one year, they are current assets. Further, available-for-sale securities available for use in current operations should be listed as current assets. For example, if cash is used to buy equity securities for a contingency fund to be used as needed, the securities would be classified as current.

Available-for-sale securities bought when exercising an option are recorded at the option strike price plus the fair value of the option at the exercise date. If the option is worthless and the same security is bought in the market, the security is recorded at the market value plus the remaining carrying amount of the option premium.

Market value is compared to cost on a total portfolio basis. Cumulative unrealized (holding) gains and losses are presented as a separate item in the stockholders' equity section and identified as "accumulated other comprehensive loss or gain." In addition, the holding loss or gain arising during the period is presented in the Statement of Comprehensive Income as Other Comprehensive Income.*

The valuation allowance (adjustment) account is a contra (offset) account to available-for-sale securities in the balance sheet to present market value. Balance sheet presentation follows:

Available-for-sale securities (cost)
Add (Less): Valuation allowance
Net (market value)

EXAMPLE

On April 1, 19X3, the following three available-for-sale securities were bought:

Stock	Shares	Cost per Share	Total Cost
A	1,000	$60	$ 60,000
B	2,000	40	80,000
C	500	90	45,000
			$185,000

---

*Source: FASB Statement Number 130.

The entry is

4/1/19X3	Available-for-sale securities	185,000	
	Cash		185,000

On September 1, 19X3, a cash dividend of $20,000 is received. The entry is

9/1/19X3	Cash	20,000	
	Dividend revenue		20,000

On December 31, 19X3, the market prices per share of the securities were stock A $55, stock B $42, and stock C $83.

An analysis of the year-end portfolio is now possible.

Portfolio of Available-for-Sale Securities
12/31/19X3

Stock	Cost	Market Value	
A	$ 60,000	$ 55,000	(1,000 × $55)
B	80,000	84,000	(2,000 × $42)
C	45,000	41,500	(500 × $83)
Total	$185,000	$180,500	
Unrealized Loss		$ 4,500	

The entry is

12/31/19X3	Unrealized loss	4,500	
	Valuation allowance		4,500

Recall that the unrealized loss on available-for-sale securities for the period is disclosed in the statement of comprehensive income and transferred to the "accumulated other comprehensive loss or gain" section of stockholders' equity on the balance sheet. Also recall that the valuation allowance account is a contra account to available-for-sale securities in the balance sheet. As such, the following is presented in the financial statements:

Combined Statement of Comprehensive Income (Select Items)
For the year ended 12/31/19X3

Dividend revenue	$20,000
Unrealized holding loss (other comprehensive income)	(4,500)

Balance Sheet
12/31/19X3

Noncurrent assets	
Available-for-sale securities (cost)	$185,000
Less: Valuation allowance	4,500
Net (market value)	$180,500
Stockholders' equity:	
Accumulated other comprehensive loss	$ 4,500

On July 8, 19X4, the company sold all of stock A for $62 per share. The journal entry is

7/8/19X4 Cash	62,000	
Available-for-sale securities		60,000
Realized gain on sale		2,000

The computation of the gain follows:

Net proceeds from sale	$62,000
Cost basis	60,000
Gain on sale of stock	$ 2,000

Recall that the realized gain on sale is presented separately in the income statement.

On September 5, 19X4, 4,000 shares of stock D were bought at $10 per share. The entry is

9/5/19X4 Available-for-sale securities	40,000	
Cash		40,000

On December 31, 19X4, the market prices per share of the securities remaining in the portfolio were stock B $36, stock C $78, and stock D $11. An analysis of the year-end portfolio is now possible.

Portfolio of Available-for-Sale Securities
12/31/19X4

Stock	Cost	Market Value	
B	$ 80,000	$ 72,000	(2,000 × $36)
C	45,000	39,000	(500 × $78)
D	40,000	44,000	(4,000 × $11)
Total	$165,000	$155,000	

Before showing the journal entry needed at year-end, it is easier to understand by presenting the asset section of the balance sheet on December 31, 19X4:

NONCURRENT ASSETS

Available-for-sale securities (cost)	$165,000
Less: Valuation allowance	10,000
Net (market value)	$155,000

The valuation allowance account appears as follows:

Valuation Allowance

	12/31/19X3	4,500
	Entry	5,500
	12/31/19X4	10,000

This requires an additional credit for the year to the valuation allowance of $5,500 to balance. Therefore, the journal entry to do this follows:

12/31/19X4	Unrealized loss	5,500	
	Valuation allowance		5,500

The unrealized loss to be presented in the December 31, 19X4 stockholders' equity section of the balance sheet is a cumulative $10,000. This is because as a balance sheet account the unrealized loss is cumulatively carried forward. In the statement of comprehensive income for the year ended

December 31, 19X4, the holding loss arising during the year of $5,500 would be reported as part of comprehensive income as another comprehensive loss item.

EXAMPLE

Assume the same information as in the example above except that the December 31, 19X4 total market value of the portfolio was $163,000 instead of $155,000. In that case, the asset section of the December 31, 19X4 balance sheet would be

Available-for-sale securities (cost)	$165,000
Less: Valuation allowance	2,000
Net (market value)	$163,000

The valuation allowance account would appear as follows:

Valuation Allowance			
Entry	2,500	12/31/19X3	4,500
		12/31/19X4	2,000

This requires a debit of $2,500 to the valuation allowance account to balance. Therefore, the journal entry to do this follows:

12/31/19X4	Valuation allowance	2,500	
	Unrealized gain		2,500

The net unrealized cumulative loss to be presented in the December 31, 19X4 stockholders' equity section (as accumulated other comprehensive income) of the balance sheet is a net $2,000 ($4,500 − $2,500). However, the unrealized gain of $2,500 would be reported as part of comprehensive income as a $2,500 gain item of other comprehensive income.

EXAMPLE

Assume the same information as in the example on page 432 except that the December 31, 19X4 total market value of the portfolio was $170,000. In that case, the asset section of the December 31, 19X4 balance sheet would be

Available-for-sale securities (cost)	$165,000
Add: Valuation allowance	5,000
Net (market value)	$170,000

The valuation allowance account would appear as follows:

Valuation Allowance			
Entry	9,500	12/31/19X3	4,500
12/31/19X4	5,000		

This requires a debit of $9,500 to the valuation allowance account to balance. Therefore, the journal entry to do this follows:

12/31/19X4	Valuation allowance	9,500	
	Unrealized gain		9,500

The net unrealized cumulative gain to be presented in the December 31, 19X4 stockholders' equity section of the balance sheet is a net $5,000 ($9,500 − $4,500). In addition, the unrealized gain is disclosed as other comprehensive income in the comprehensive income statement.

Held-to-Maturity Securities

Held-to-maturity securities can only be debt securities (principally bonds) because they have maturity dates and the intent is to hold to maturity. (Since equity securities do not have a maturity date, they are not in this category.) It is presumed that the company has the ability and is able to hold the securities to maturity. If the company is not financially able to do so, then held-to-maturity classification is not possible. Held-to-maturity securities may be still be classified as such even if they are pledged as collateral for a loan.

Debt securities should not be classified as held to maturity if they may be sold to respond to changing market conditions (e.g., prepayment risk, interest rate risk, foreign currency risk, liquidity requirements), changing fund sources and terms, changing availability and yield on alternative investments, or other asset-liability management reasons. If contractual provisions allow a debt security to be paid off in advance or settled in some other manner before maturity, held-to-maturity classification may not be appropriate. However, certain circumstances of an unusual and nonrecurring nature, which were not expected initially, may force a company to alter its intent to hold the security to the maturity date. In such case, no intent to deceive was present. For example, selling a security classified as held to maturity would not indicate initial incorrect classification if the sale decision was due to such reasons as change in tax law (e.g., interest on the security is no longer tax free) or governmental rules (e.g., SEC requirements), deteriorating financial condition of the issuer, change in credit risk policy due to a business combination, change in regulatory policy concerning the issuer's capital balances, or change in statutory requirements amending what qualifies as an allowable or dollar amount of investment in certain types of securities.

The sale of a debt security classified as held to maturity is deemed to be at maturity if the sale takes place just prior to the maturity date (usually within three months) and as such the security's fair value is not affected (or minimally affected) by changing market interest rates. The sale of a debt security classified as held to maturity is also considered at maturity if the company has already received 85% or more of the principal from the investment.

Held-to-maturity securities in the balance sheet are presented under *noncurrent assets* at *amortized cost.* However, those held-to-maturity securities maturing within one year are presented under current assets. An example is a 30-year bond that is maturing next year (its thirtieth year). **Warning:** If a held-to-maturity security is sold before its maturity date, this may raise questions as to management's "real intent" and may result in reporting problems, such as reclassification.

Held-to-maturity securities are not recorded at fair market value, so there will not be unrealized gains and losses.

Amortization of bond discount or premium is either based on the effective interest method (preferred) or the straight-line method. The effective interest method of amortization results in the following journal entry:

Interest receivable (nominal interest rate × face value of bond)
Held-to-maturity securities (for discount amortization) – for difference
    Interest revenue (yield × carrying value of bond)
      Held-to-maturity securities (for premium amortization) – for difference

Under the effective interest method, yield is based on the yield to maturity formula (not simple yield formula). Yield to maturity equals

$$\frac{\text{Nominal interest} + \text{Discount/Years or } (- \text{Premium/Years})}{(\text{Purchase price} + \text{Maturity value})/2}$$

EXAMPLE

A $10,000, 8% bond is bought at $9,500 having a 10-year life. The yield equals

$$\frac{\$800 + \$500/10}{(\$9,500 + \$10,000)/2} = \frac{\$850}{\$9,750} = 8.7\%$$

The effective interest method results in a constant rate but different dollar amount of amortization each period. The straight-line method of amortization for discount or premium per period equals

Discount or (− Premium)/Number of periods

EXAMPLE

A $10,000, 10% bond bought at $9,000 and having a 10-year life would have an annual amortization of

$1,000/10 years = $100

The straight-line method results in the following journal entry:

Interest receivable (nominal interest × face value of bond)
Held-to-maturity securities (for discount amortization)
　　Held-to-maturity securities (for premium amortization)
Interest revenue (for difference)

The straight-line method results in a constant dollar amount of amortization each period but at a different rate.

EXAMPLE

On January 1, 19X1, ABC Company buys $100,000, 10%, five-year bonds of XYZ Company at 98%. Interest is payable annually on January 1. The effective interest method of amortization is used. The yield to maturity (effective interest rate) equals

$$\text{Nominal (coupon) interest} = \$100,000 \times 10\% = \$10,000$$
$$\text{Purchase price} = \$100,000 \times 98\% = \$98,000$$
$$\text{Discount} = \$100,000 - \$98,000 = \$2,000$$

Yield to maturity equals

$$\frac{\text{Nominal interest} + \text{Discount/Years}}{(\text{Purchasing price} + \text{Maturity value})/2} = \frac{\$10,000 + \$2,000/5}{(\$98,000 + \$100,000)/2} = \frac{\$10,400}{\$99,000} = 10.505\%$$

The yield (10.505%) exceeds the nominal interest rate (10%) because the bond was bought at a discount (below face value). The investor earns the $2,000 discount between the purchase date and maturity date so as to increase the effective rate of return.

The entry for the purchase of the bond is

1/1/19X1	Held-to-maturity securities	98,000	
	Cash		98,000

Table 10–1 is used to compute the cash interest received, interest revenue, amortization of bond discount, and carrying value of the bond.

Table 10–1
10% Bond Bought to Yield 10.505%

Date	Cash Interest Received 10% × $100,000	Interest Revenue 10.505% × Carrying Value	Amortization of Bond Discount	Carrying Value of Bond
1/1/19X1				$98,000
1/1/19X2	$10,000	$10,295	$ 295	98,295
1/1/19X3	10,000	10,326	326	98,621
1/1/19X4	10,000	10,360	360	98,981
1/1/19X5	10,000	10,398	398	99,379
1/1/19X6	10,000	10,440	440	99,819*
Total	$50,000	$51,819	$1,819	

*Difference between $99,819 and $100,000 maturity value is due to rounding.

Note: The carrying value of the bond increases from $98,000 to $100,000 because it was bought at a discount (below face value). At maturity, the bond is worth its face value. Interest revenue increases because the carrying value of the bond increases. Amortization of bond discount increases because of the increasing interest revenue.

Based on Table 10–1, we prepare journal entries for 19X1 and 19X2.

12/31/19X1	Interest receivable	10,000	
	Held-to-maturity securities	295	
	Interest revenue		10,295
1/1/19X2	Cash	10,000	
	Interest receivable		10,000
12/31/19X2	Interest receivable	10,000	
	Held-to-maturity securities	326	
	Interest revenue		10,326

At the end of 19X1 and 19X2, respectively, the following are presented in the balance sheet and income statement:

Balance Sheet

	19X1	19X2
Current assets		
Interest receivable	$10,000	$10,000
Noncurrent assets		
Held-to-maturity securities (amortized cost)	98,295	98,621

Income Statement

	19X1	19X2
Other Revenue		
Interest revenue	$10,295	$10,326

EXAMPLE

Assume the same facts as the previous example except that instead of using the effective interest method of amortization (the preferred method), the straight-line amortization method is used (less preferable under GAAP but accepted). The straight-line amortization per year equals

$$\text{Discount/Years} = \$2,000/5 = \$400$$

The entry on January 1, 19X1 for the purchase of the bond is still the same. However, the other journal entries would be different because the amount of amortization per year is different. The entries would be

12/31/19X1	Interest receivable	10,000	
	Held-to-maturity securities	400	
	Interest revenue		10,400
1/1/19X2	Cash	10,000	
	Interest receivable		10,000
12/31/19X2	Interest receivable	10,000	
	Held-to-maturity securities	400	
	Interest revenue		10,400

At the end of 19X1 and 19X2, respectively, the following are presented in the balance sheet and income statement:

Balance Sheet

	19X1	*19X2*
Current assets		
Interest receivable	$10,000	$10,000
Noncurrent assets		
Held-to-maturity securities (amortized cost)	$98,400	$98,800

Income Statement

	19X1	*19X2*
Other revenue		
Interest revenue	$10,400	$10,400

With regard to held-to-maturity securities, a change in market price of a forward contract or purchased option should be recognized if there has been a *permanent decline* in value. The permanent loss is presented in the current year's income statement.

STRUCTURED NOTES

Structured notes are debt instruments whose cash flows are tied to the change in some index (e.g., Consumer Price Index, or CPI), foreign exchange rate, interest rate (e.g., prime interest rate), price of some item (e.g., commodity), etc. The notes usually include a nondetachable forward or option component (e.g., calls, caps). The cash flow associated with the payment of interest and/or principal will change in timing and amount over time depending on the linked index, interest rate, or other market factor.

Income on structured notes classified as held to maturity or available for sale should be accounted for under the *retrospective interest method* as long as at least one or more of the following criteria exist:

- The maturity date of the note depends on a particular index or happening of a given event not within the control of the participants to the transaction. An example is the maturity date tied to the prime interest rate or price of wheat.
- The interest on the note varies over its life such as an inverse floating-rate note.
- The maturity value of the note may change, such as when the principal at the maturity date is tied to the S&P 100 index.

When the retrospective interest method is used, the interest income for the year equals the difference between the amortized cost of the security at year-end versus at the beginning of the year, plus the cash received for the year on the note. Amortized cost is based on the discounted value of projected future cash flows using the effective yield. If a permanent decline in value occurs, a write-down of the amortized cost is required. The loss is reported in the income statement.

BOND QUOTES

A *basis point* is one one-hundredth of one percentage point, usually used in quoting of spreads between interest rates or describing changes in yields of securities. Quotes for notes and bonds are expressed in thirty-seconds. However, quotes may be in sixty-fourths by using pluses. For example, a trade at 100 : 08 bid means a bid of 100 and 8 thirty-seconds. A quote of 103 : 12 + bid means a bid of 103 and 12½ thirty-seconds, or 103 25/64. Refer to the "bid" column in a financial newspaper for the current average price for a note or bond.

STATEMENT OF CASH FLOWS

In the statement of cash flows, cash flows from buying or selling trading securities are presented in the operating activities section. However, cash flows from buying, selling, or maturing available-for-sale or held-to-maturity securities are shown in the investing activities section. Realized gains or losses, dividend income, or interest income are included in the operating section because they affect earnings.

GENERAL ACCOUNTING FOR INVESTMENTS

Dividend and interest income (revenue) are included in "Other (Financial) Income" as earned and as an element of net income.

EXAMPLE

You own 1,000 shares of a stock. The company declares a $.30 dividend per share. The entry is

Dividend receivable	300	
Dividend revenue		300

EXAMPLE

You own a $20,000 face value bond having a coupon interest rate of 10% paid annually. The entry is

Cash	2,000	
Interest income		2,000

Interest income is shown net of the amortization of discount or premium for held-to-maturity securities.

Realized gains and losses on the sale of securities for all three types (trading, available-for-sale, and held-to-maturity securities) are included as a separate item in the income statement in the year of sale. The gain or loss equals the difference between the net proceeds and the adjusted cost basis. The net proceeds equal the selling price less brokerage commissions less service fees less any transfer taxes. The adjusted cost basis equals the purchase price plus brokerage commissions plus service fees plus taxes.

EXAMPLE

You buy 100 shares of ABC stock having a market price of $20. The brokerage fee is $50. You later sell the shares at a market price of $25. The brokerage commission upon sale is $75. The net gain or loss equals

Net sales proceeds (100 shares × $25) − $75	$2,425
Less: Adjusted cost basis (100 shares × $20) + $50	2,050
Capital gain	$ 375

Gains and losses on financial instruments used to hedge trading securities should be included in the income statement. However, gains and losses on instruments that hedge available-for-sale securities should initially be presented as a separate item in the stockholders' equity section and then amortized as an adjustment to yield.

Permanent losses (e.g., due to bankruptcy, liquidity crisis) on either available-for-sale or held-to-maturity securities are considered a realized loss and included in earnings. The carrying amount of the investment is similarly reduced. When the security is written down, fair value at that date becomes the new cost basis. Declines are measured by individual security.

Losses in value of one security cannot be offset by gains in another. Factors in considering whether a permanent impairment in value has occurred include an adverse event or condition, how long and how much market value has been less than cost, financial status of issuing company, poor economic conditions, industry problems, reduction or cessation in dividends, missing interest payments, and investor's ability to wait for a possible recovery in value. A subsequent recovery (gain) in the fair value of available-for-sale securities which had been written down because of a permanent loss should be added to the investment account and included as a separate component in the stockholders' equity section of the balance sheet. The journal entry for a recovery in fair value is

> Available-for-sale securities
>> Unrealized gain

Note: Even though a permanent loss on available-for-sale securities is presented in the income statement, recovery in fair value is reported in the stockholders' equity section and in the comprehensive income statement (other comprehensive income).

If held-to-maturity securities are similarly permanently written down as a loss, the fair value increase will not be reported in the balance sheet, although disclosure will usually be made in the footnotes.

EXAMPLE

A company held available-for-sale debt securities having an amortized cost of $250,000. The fair market value of the securities is $200,000. The unrealized loss on these securities presented in the comprehensive income statement (other comprehensive items) and as a reduction of stockholders' equity is $50,000. It is now determined that a permanent loss exists because the investor will not be able to collect all amounts due. Therefore, the unrealized loss of $50,000 is now considered a permanent loss to be included in earnings. The entry is

Permanent loss	50,000	
Valuation allowance	50,000	
Unrealized loss		50,000
Available-for-sale securities		50,000

The new cost basis of the debt securities is $200,000. Any later change in fair market value of the impaired securities is included in the stockholders' equity section and in the comprehensive income statement (other comprehensive income).

EXAMPLE

Available-for-sale securities were written down because of a permanent loss by $18,000. A subsequent recovery of such loss was $7,000. The appropriate journal entry for the recovery is

Available-for-sale securities	7,000	
Unrealized gain		7,000

Unrealized (holding) gains and losses on trading securities and available-for-sale securities are not recognized for tax purposes until realized by sale. Therefore, differences between the tax basis and financial reporting basis of trading securities (shown in the income statement) and available-for-sale securities (presented in the stockholders' equity section) are temporary differences. A deferred tax liability (asset) is recognized for unrealized gains (losses).

Note: Permanent declines in value of available-for-sale and held-to-maturity securities also result in temporary differences because the loss is not deductible on the tax return until the securities are sold.

Deferred tax liabilities and deferred tax assets are reported in the balance sheet. The corresponding tax provisions will be presented in the income statement for trading securities or in the stockholders' equity section for available-for-sale securities. **Note:** No deferred taxes exist for temporary declines in price of held-to-maturity securities because no recognition is given for such a decline.

EXAMPLE

A trading security was bought at a cost of $200,000. At year-end, the fair market value of the security was $150,000, resulting in a temporary decline. The tax rate is 40%. The journal entries to record the fair value adjustment and the tax effect follow:

Unrealized loss	50,000	
Valuation allowance		50,000
Deferred tax asset	20,000	
Tax provision		20,000

If the security was available for sale instead of trading, the credit for $20,000 would go to unrealized loss (presented in the stockholders' equity section). If the security was held to maturity, no entry is made for temporary declines in price. However, if we assumed a permanent loss, then deferred taxes would be recognized. In such a case, the entries would be:

Realized loss	50,000	
Held-to-maturity securities		50,000
Deferred tax asset	20,000	
Tax provision		20,000

The tax provision would be presented in the income statement for held-to-maturity securities.

In an unclassified balance sheet, the portfolio is considered noncurrent.

Equity securities acquired by exchanging noncash consideration (property or services) are recorded at either the fair market value of the consideration given or received, whichever is more clearly evident. Fair market value may be based on appraisal.

Table 10–2 presents the accounting and reporting for trading, available-for-sale, and held-to-maturity securities.

Table 10–2

Accounting and Reporting for Investments

	Trading	Available for Sale	Held to Maturity
Valuation	Fair value	Fair value	Amortized cost
Unrealized (holding) gain or loss	Income statement	Comprehensive income statement (other comprehensive income) stockholders' equity	Not reported
Realized gain or loss	Income statement	Income statement	Income statement
Classification in balance sheet	Current assets	Current or noncurrent assets	Noncurrent assets
Type of security	Equity or debt	Equity or debt	Debt only
Periodic income	Dividend or interest revenue	Dividend or interest revenue	Interest revenue

Blocks of Stock

A company's stock may be bought on different dates and then later sold. The sale can be based on specific identification (preferred), FIFO, or average cost. FIFO is the method typically used in practice. The realized gain or loss on sale is presented in the income statement.

EXAMPLE

On January 1, 19X5, you bought 100 shares of L Company Stock at $9 per share. On February 3, 19X5, you bought another 200 shares at $10 per share. On March 6, 19X5, you sold 50 shares at $11 per share. The FIFO method is used. The journal entry is

Cash (50 × $11)	550	
Investment in L Company (50 × $9)		450
Gain on sale		100

The T-account looks as follows:

L Company

1/1/19X5	100 @ $9	900	3/6/19X5	50 @$9	450
2/3/19X5	200 @ $10	2,000			
	300	2,900			
Balance	250	2,450			

Lump-Sum Purchase

If two or more stocks are bought for one price, the cost is allocated to the securities proportionately based on their market values.

EXAMPLE

You pay for 100 shares of stock A having a market price per share of $40 and 200 shares of stock B having a market price of $10 per share. The cost allocation follows:

Stock	*Market Value*	*Allocated Cost*
A 100 shares × $40	$4,000	$3,867[a]
B 200 shares × $10	2,000	1,933[b]
Total	$6,000	$5,800

[a] $4,000/$6,000 × $5,800 = $3,867
[b] $2,000/$6,000 × $5,800 = $1,933

The journal entry is

Investment—Stock A	3,867	
Investment—Stock B	1,933	
Cash		5,800

If market value is available for one security but not the other, the incremental method must be used. Under this method, cost is first assigned to the market value of the security for which it is known, with the balance assigned to the other security.

EXAMPLE

You pay $50,000 for 1,000 shares of stock X with a market price of $30 and 300 shares of stock Y, which does not have a market price because it is a closely held company. The cost allocation follows:

Stock		Allocated Cost
Stock X	1,000 shares @ $30	$30,000
Stock Y	Balancing figure	$20,000 ($50,000 − $30,000)
Total		$50,000

Exchange (Conversion) of Securities

A conversion of securities may include exchanging preferred stock or bonds for common stock. The security received is recorded at its market value. The difference between the market value of the security received and the cost basis of the security given up represents a gain or loss on conversion. The gain or loss is reported in the income statement.

EXAMPLE

You own preferred stock costing $10,000, which you convert into 1,000 shares of common stock having a market price of $15 per share. The journal entry is

Investment in common stock	15,000	
Investment in preferred stock		10,000
Gain—Conversion of stock investment		5,000

Stock Dividends

A stock dividend increases the number of shares held without increasing the cost. Since total cost remains the same, the cost per share after the stock dividend is received decreases. A stock dividend only involves a memo entry.

EXAMPLE

You own 100 shares of DEF Company at a total cost of $1,000. Therefore, the cost per share is $10. A 20% stock dividend is received, so the shares owned now are 120. It costs you nothing to get those shares. Because total cost remains at $1,000, the cost per share decreases to $8.33 ($1,000/120). The T-account looks as follows:

		Investment in DEF	
100	$10	$1,000	
20		0	
120	$8.33	$1,000	

EXAMPLE

On April 3, 2003, Robert Company bought 1,000 shares of DEF common stock at $82 per share. On October 15, 2003, Robert received 1,000 stock rights to buy an additional 1,000 shares at $95 per share. On October 30, 2003, DEF common stock had a market value, ex-rights, of $100 per share, and the stock rights had a market value of $6 each. At October 30, 2003, the investment in stock rights has a carrying value equal to $4,920, computed as follows:

Original cost of stock	$82,000
Ratio of value of stock rights to value of stock	× $6/$100
Investment in stock rights	$ 4,920

Stock Splits

A stock split increases the number of shares held without increasing the cost. After a stock split, the cost per share is proportionately reduced. A stock split only involves a memo entry.

EXAMPLE

You own 500 shares of PQ Company at a total cost of $10,000. Therefore, the cost per share is $20. A 2 for 1 stock split is issued. As a result, you will now have 1,000 shares. Because total cost remains the same ($10,000), the cost per share is proportionately reduced to $10. The T-account looks as follows:

		Investment in PQ Company	
500	$20	$10,000	
1,000	$10	$10,000	

RECLASSIFICATION ADJUSTMENTS RELATING TO INVESTMENTS

As indicated in previous discussions, any unrealized holding gains or losses relating to the available-for-sale portfolio are reported in an enterprise's comprehensive income statement as part of other comprehensive income. These gains or losses are then closed to the accumulated other comprehensive income section of stockholders' equity. However, when securities from this portfolio are actually sold, then double counting may occur. This is due to the recognition of realized gains and losses from the sale of available-for-sale securities in the income statement (and comprehensive income statement) as well as their disclosure in comprehensive income from the current or prior periods. The latter may have occurred as part of the recognition of unrealized holding gains or losses derived from the mark-to-market entry made on the available-for-sale portfolio at the end of the current or prior periods. To ensure that such double counting does not occur when the sale of available-for-sale securities occurs, it is necessary to ascertain the extent of the duplication and record a reclassification adjustment in the comprehensive income statement. This adjustment(s) may either be shown on the face of the financial statement in which comprehensive income is shown or may be disclosed in the notes to the financial statements.

EXAMPLE

X Company has the following securities in its available-for-sale portfolio at December 31, 2001. This was the company's first year of operations

	Cost	Fair Value	*Unrealized Gain (Loss)*
Y Company stock	$ 60,000	$40,000	$(20,000)
Z Company stock	50,000	20,000	(30,000)
	$110,000	$60,000	$(50,000)

In its comprehensive income statement for the year, 2001, the unrealized holding losses of $50,000 will be included in other comprehensive income, as follows:

X Company
Statement of Comprehensive Income
For the Year Ended December 31, 2001

Net income	$XX,XXX
Other comprehensive income	
Unrealized holding losses on available for-sale securities	$(50,000)
Comprehensive income	$XX,XXX

At the beginning of the next year, 2002, X Company sells its Y Company stock and incurs a realized loss of $20,000 on the sale. At December 31, 2002, the fair value of Z Company stock (the remaining security in its available-for-sale portfolio) dropped to $30,000 (from $20,000). This represented an additional $10,000 unrealized holding loss in the year 2002 and is disclosed in X Company's statement of comprehensive income (as part of other comprehensive income). Also assume that X Company had net income of $150,000 for the year 2002, which included the realized loss of $20,000 from the sale of Y Company stock. The X Company comprehensive income statement for the year 2002 appears as follows:

X Company
Statement of Comprehensive Income
For the Year Ended December 31, 2002

Net income		$150,000
Other comprehensive income		
Less: Unrealized holding losses on available for-sale securities	$10,000	
Add: Reclassification adjustment for losses included in net income	20,000	10,000
Comprehensive income		$160,000

In the year 2001, the unrealized loss of $20,000 was included in the X Company's comprehensive income statement. The next year, 2002, the company sold its Y Company stock and incurred a realized loss of $20,000, which decreased its net income and comprehensive income for the period. A reclassification adjustment (shown in the preceding statement of comprehensive income) is required, causing an unrealized gain of $10,000 to avoid double counting.

TRANSFERS OF SECURITIES BETWEEN CATEGORIES

The reasonableness of a security's classification should be reevaluated at each reporting date. For example, there may have been a change in circumstances, such as a change in financial condition (e.g., cash flow, liquidity, profitability).

All types of transfers between categories should be accounted for at fair market value on the transfer date. This requirement assures that a company cannot avoid fair value recognition by transferring a security from one category to another. If, for example, a security is transferred from the trading to the available-for-sale portfolio, it is recorded in the available-for-sale portfolio at fair value (at the date of transfer), and any unrealized holding gain or loss (due to the difference between fair value and cost) is recorded as part of net income and closed to retained earnings in stockholders' equity. Fair value at the date of transfer becomes the new cost basis of the security. At the next reporting date, an adjusting entry is made to record any new changes in the fair value of the available-for-sale portfolio. FASB Statement Number 115 notes, however, that transfers of this nature should, in fact, be rare. The same parameters apply to the transfer of a security from the available-for-sale to the trading portfolio. For a debt security transferred from the held-to-maturity to the available-for-sale portfolio, any unrealized holding gain or loss (due to the difference between cost and fair value increases and decreases) is disclosed in the comprehensive income statement as other comprehensive income and is ultimately transferred to the accumulated other comprehensive income section of stockholders' equity (as a separate component of stockholders' equity). A securities valuation account is also used in this transfer because its balance must always equal the balance in the unrealized holding gain or loss account (unlike the prior types of transfers, where net income was changed). Net income in this situation is not affected. The same guidelines apply to the transfer of a debt security from the available-for-sale to the held-to-maturity portfolio except that any unrealized gain or loss at the date of transfer represents a component of stockholders' equity and is amortized over the remaining life of the debt security. A securities valuation account (held to maturity) is also used in this transfer. Both the unrealized holding gain or loss account and its equivalent securities valuation account (held to maturity) are amortized over the remaining life of the debt securities. The results of these calculations are netted against each other so there is no effect on net income. In addition, if the debt security was sold at a discount or premium, the discount or premium should be amortized over the life of the debt security as well. All of the aforementioned guidelines presume that end-of-period adjusting entries to report portfolio changes in fair value were not yet recorded.

Table 10–3 presents the accounting for the transfers between categories.

Table 10–3
Transfer Between Classifications

Nature of Transfer	How Measured	Effect on Income	Effect on Stockholders' Equity
1. Trading to available for sale	Transfer at market value, which becomes new cost basis at the date of transfer	Unrealized gain or loss is recognized as part of income	Unrealized gain or loss is recognized as part of stockholders' equity
2. Available for sale to trading	Same as above	Same as above	Same as above
3. Held to maturity to available for sale	Transfer security at market value on transfer date	None	The separate component of stockholders' equity is increased or decreased by the unrealized gain or loss at the date of transfer
4. Available for sale to held to maturity	Same as above	None	Amortize balance of unrealized gain or loss as part of stockholders' equity over the remaining life of the security

EXAMPLE

On December 31, 19X4, a company elects to transfer from trading to available for sale one stock of many stocks. On the transfer date, the stock's cost is $100,000 and its market value is $120,000. The transfer will be made at fair market value, which becomes the new cost basis. Assuming that the adjusting entry to record any change of fair value for the current period has not been made, the entry is

Available-for-sale securities	120,000	
Trading securities		100,000
Unrealized holding gain—net income		20,000

The unrealized holding gain increases net income for the period.

EXAMPLE

A company elects to transfer from available for sale to trading one stock in its portfolio. On the transfer date, cost equals $100,000 and market value equals $90,000 of that stock. Assuming that the adjusting entry to record any change of fair value for the current period has not been made, the entry is:

Trading securities	90,000	
Unrealized holding loss—net income	10,000	
Available-for-sale securities		100,000

The unrealized loss will decrease net income for the period.

EXAMPLE

A company decides to transfer one of its corporate bonds in its portfolio from held to maturity to available for sale. The amortized cost is $40,000 and the fair market value is $55,000. The transfer is made at fair market value. Assuming that the adjusting entry to record any change of fair value for the current period has not been made, the entry is

Valuation adjustment (available for sale)	15,000	
Available-for-sale securities	40,000	
Unrealized holding gain—stockholders' equity		15,000
Held-to-maturity securities		40,000

Note that the unrealized gain of $15,000 will be reflected in the other comprehensive income section of comprehensive income as well as stockholders' equity.

DISCLOSURES

The following information should be disclosed about investments in equity and debt securities:

- Valuation basis used
- Total portfolio market value

- Method used to determine cost (e.g., FIFO, average cost, specific identification) in computing the realized gain or loss on sale of securities

- Unrealized (holding) gains and losses for trading and available-for-sale securities

- Reasons for selling or transferring securities

- Gains and losses from transferring available-for-sale securities to trading included in the income statement

- Market value and cost by major equity security

- Fair value and amortized cost basis by major debt security type

- Proceeds from selling available-for-sale securities, with associated realized gains and losses

- Subsequent event disclosure in the form of significant changes in market value taking place after year-end but before the issuance of the financial statements

- Name of companies owned when ownership is significant

Disclosure for debt securities classified as available for sale or held to maturity should include contractual maturity dates.

Financial institutions should disclose their holdings in equity securities, corporate debt securities, mortgage-backed securities, U.S. government securities, foreign government securities, and other debt securities. Financial institutions should disclose fair value and amortized cost of debt securities in maturity groupings, including within one year, in 1 to 5 years, after 5 to 10 years, and after 10 years.

FINANCIAL STATEMENT ANALYSIS

Held-to-maturity securities for analytical purposes should be valued at market value rather than amortized cost to reflect current prices. However, this is not GAAP.

THE GI CORP. MAKES THE FOLLOWING DEBT AND EQUITY INVESTMENTS:

Bonds	Par Value:	$200,000
	Nominal interest rate:	8%
	Market interest rate:	10%
	Years to maturity:	5
	Interest paid:	Annually
Stocks	Number of shares:	4,000
	Par value stock:	$20.00
	Purchase price:	$25.00

Purchase price of investments is calculated as follows:

Bonds	Present value of amount due at maturity	$124,184	
	Present value of interest payments	$ 60,653	
	Purchase priced of bonds		$184,837
Stocks	Purchase price of stocks		$100,000
	[4,000 shares at $25 each]		
	Total purchase price of investments (Bonds & stocks):		$284,837

Figure 10–1 *Comprehensive Example of FASB Statement Number 115*

The bond discount will be amortized using the effective interest method over a period of five years as follows:

Year	(I) Interest Income	(II) Cash Received	(III) Discount Amortization	(IV) Discount Remaining	(V) Carrying Amount
1/1/01				15,163	184,837
12/31/01	18,484	16.000	2,484	12,679	187,321
12/31/02	18,732	16,000	2,732	9,947	190,053
12/31/03	19,005	16,000	3,005	6,942	193,058
12/31/04	19,306	16,000	3,306	3,636	196,364
12/31/05	19,636	16,000	3,636	—	200,000

[I] Interest income is calculated by multiplying previous year's carrying amount (V) by the market interest rate of 10%.

[II] Cash received is calculated by multiplying the par value of bonds by the nominal interest rate: 200,000 × 8%.

[III] Discount amortization is (I) – (II).

[IV] Discount remaining is prior year's carrying amount (V) minus current year's discount (III).

[V] Carrying amount is par value of bonds, $200,000, minus the discount remaining (IV).

Assume that the market values for the investments are as follows:

	12/31/01	12/31/02
Bonds	180,000	170,000
Stocks	150,000	125,000
Total Investments	330,000	295,000

Dividend is paid on Common Stock as follows:

8/31/01	10.00 dollars per share
8/31/02	5.00 dollars per share

Figure 10–1   *Comprehensive Example of FASB Statement Number 115 (Cont.)*

TRADING SECURITIES

Assume that these investments are classified as trading securities.

1/1/01	Investments—Trading	$184,837	
	Cash		$184,837
	Purchase of bonds classified as trading		
1/1/01	Investments—Trading	$100,000	
	Cash		$100,000
	Purchase of common stocks classified as trading		
8/31/01	Cash	$ 40,000	
	Dividend income		$ 40,000
	Dividends received on common stocks		
12/31/01	Investments—Trading	$ 2,484	
	Cash	$ 16,000	
	Interest income		$ 18,484
	Interest received and amortization of bond discount		
12/31/01	Investments—Trading*	$ 42,679	
	Unrealized gain on investments*		$ 42,679

*The unrealized GAIN is calculated as follows:

Market value of bonds and stocks at 12/31/01	330,000
[180,000 + 150,000]	
Carrying value of bonds and stocks at 12/31/01	287,321
[187,321 + 100,000]	
Unrealized Gain	$ 42,679

Figure 10–1 *Comprehensive Example of FASB Statement Number 115 (Cont.)*

In the second year, the journal entries will be as follows:

8/31/02	Cash	$ 20,000	
	Dividend income		$ 20,000
	Dividends received on common stocks		
12/31/02	Investments—Trading	$ 2,732	
	Cash	$ 16,000	
	Interest income		$ 18,732
12/31/02	Unrealized Loss on investments**	$ 37,732	
	Investments—Trading**		$ 37,732
	Adjustment to market value for trading investments		

**The unrealized loss is calculated as follows:

Market value of bonds and stocks at 12/31/02	295,000
[170,000 + 125,000]	
Carrying value of bonds# and stocks at 12/31/02	332,732
[182,732 + 150,000]	
Unrealized Loss	(37,732)

#The carrying value of bonds on 12/31/02 is calculated as follows:

Market value of bonds at 12/31/01:	180,000
Plus: Bond discount amortization for year 2:	2,732
	182,732

The trading investments will be presented in the financial statements as follows:

	Year 1	Year 2
INCOME STATEMENT:		
Interest income	18,484	18,732
Dividend income	40,000	20,000
Unrealized gain (loss) on investments	42,679	(37,732)
BALANCE SHEET:		
Current Assets:		
Investments—Trading	330,000	295,000
STATEMENT OF CASH FLOWS:		
Operating Activities:		
Interest	16,000	16,000
Dividends	40,000	20,000
Investment purchases	284,837	—

Figure 10–1 *Comprehensive Example of FASB Statement Number 115 (Cont.)*

SECURITIES AVAILABLE FOR SALE

Assume that these investments are now classified as available for sale.

When securities are available for sale, the unrealized gain or loss is presented as part of "other comprehensive income" in the income statement.

The journal entries to record the unrealized gain or loss are

12/31/01	Investments—Available for Sale	$ 42,679	
	Unrealized gain on investments		$ 42,679
	Adjustment to market value for available-for-sale investments		
12/31/02	Unrealized loss on investments	$ 37,732	
	Investments—Available for sale		$ 37,732
	Adjustments to market value for available-for-sale investments		

The available-for-sale investments will be presented in the financial statements as follows:

	Year 1	Year 2
INCOME STATEMENT:		
Interest income	18,484	18,732
Dividend income	40,000	20,000
OTHER COMPREHENSIVE INCOME:		
Unrealized gain or (loss) on investments available for sale	42,679	(37,732)
BALANCE SHEET:		
Asset (current or long-term based upon intent):		
Investments—Available for sale	330,000	295,000
STATEMENT OF CASH FLOWS:		
Operating Activities:		
Interest	16,000	16,000
Dividends	40,000	20,000
INVESTMENT ACTIVITIES:		
Investment Purchases	284,837	—

Figure 10–1   *Comprehensive Example of FASB Statement Number 115 (Cont.)*

SECURITIES HELD-TO-MATURITY

Assume that the bonds are now classified as investments held to maturity. Recall that common stocks do not have a maturity date and are therefore not included in this example.

Journal entries for discount amortization and cash received are the same as entries for trading securities. However, no journal entries are required at the end of the year to record unrealized gain or loss.

The financial statement presentation for securities held to maturity is as follows:

For Bonds Only

	Year 1	Year 2
INCOME STATEMENT:		
Interest income	18,484	18,732
BALANCE SHEET:		
Asset:		
Investments—held to maturity	187,321	190,053
STATEMENT OF CASH FLOWS:		
Operating Activities:		
Interest	16,000	16,000
INVESTMENT ACTIVITIES:		
Investment purchases	184,837	—

Figure 10–1   *Comprehensive Example of FASB Statement Number 115 (Cont.)*

EQUITY METHOD

APB Opinion Number 18 covers the accounting, reporting, and disclosures under the equity method to account for investments in other companies. The investor is the owner and the investee is the company owned. The equity method is used if

- An investor owns between *20 and 50%* of the investee's voting common stock.

- The investor owns less than 20% of the investee's voting common stock but has effective control (significant influence). Significant influence may be indicated by a number of factors, including substantial intercompany transactions, exchanges of executives between investor and investee, investor's significant input in the investee's decision-making process, investor's representation on the investee's board of directors, investee's dependence on investor (e.g., operational, technological, or financial support), and substantial ownership of the investee by investor relative to other widely disbursed shareholder interests. The factors indicating that significant influence may not exist, thereby precluding the equity method, are that significant influence exists by a small group of stockholders excluding the investor representing majority ownership of investee, the investee sues the investor, the investee makes a formal complaint to governmental bodies regarding the investor, and the investor is unable to obtain needed financial data from the investee to use the equity method. Under FASB Interpretation Number 35, if there is a standstill agreement stipulating that either the investor has relinquished major rights as a stockholder or that significant influence does not exist, it may indicate that the equity method is not appropriate. Interpretation Number 35 also may preclude the equity method if the investor attempts unsuccessfully to obtaining representation on the investee's board of directors.

- The investor owns in excess of 50% of the investee's voting common stock, but a negating factor exists, preventing consolidation. According to FASB Statement Number 94 (*Consolidation of All Majority Owned Subsidiaries*), negating factors prohibiting consolidation might be temporary control, noncontrol, and foreign exchange restrictions. However, under FASB Statement Number 94, the equity method is used to account for nonconsolidated majority-owned subsidiaries.

- There is a joint venture. A joint venture is an entity that is owned, operated, and jointly managed by a common group of investors.

The accounting under the equity method is illustrated in selected T-account form:

Investment in Investee	
Cost	Ordinary loss
Ordinary profit	Extraordinary loss
Extraordinary gain	Dividends
	Permanent decline in market price
	Amortization of goodwill
	Depreciation on excess of fair market value less book value of specific assets

Equity in Earnings of Investee	
Amortization expense	Ordinary profit
Depreciation expense on excess value	
Ordinary loss	

Extraordinary Gain	
	Extraordinary Gain

The accounting process as explained by these T-accounts involves the following:

- The cost of the investment includes brokerage charges. The investor recognizes its percentage ownership interest in the investee's ordinary earnings by debiting investment in investee and crediting equity in earnings of investee. The latter is like a revenue account.

- The investor's share in the investee's profits is determined after subtracting cumulative preferred dividends, whether or not declared. **Note:** The investor's share of investee earnings in excess of dividends paid is referred to as undistributed investee earnings. The investor's share is based on the investee's most recent income statement provided the time lag in reporting each year is consistent. In other words, if the investor and investee have different year-ends, the investor may compute its share of investee's profits or losses based on the investee's financial statements for its fiscal year-end.

- Extraordinary gains or losses and prior period adjustments are recognized by the investor exactly as presented on the investee's financial statements. Such items are separately reported if material.

- The investor's share of the investee's dividends reduces the carrying value of the investment in investee account. **Note:** The final financial effect on the investor's financial statements is identical whether the equity method or full consolidation is used. The only difference lies in the detail within the financial statements.

- The excess paid by the investor for the investee's net assets is first assigned to the specific assets and liabilities and is depreciated. The unidentifiable part of the excess is goodwill which is amortized over the period benefited not exceeding 40 years. The investment in investee account is credited, and the equity in earnings account is debited for both the amortization of goodwill and the depreciation on excess of fair market value less book value of specific assets acquired.

- While the equity method makes no adjustment for temporary declines in market price of the investment, permanent declines in value are recognized by debiting loss and crediting investment in investee.

EXAMPLE

Mavis Company acquires 30% of Blake Company's stock under the equity method for $500,000. Blake's net income and dividends for the year are $100,000 and $20,000, respectively. The carrying value of the investment at year-end equals

Initial cost	$500,000
Add: Share of net income $100,000 × 30%	30,000
Less: Share of dividends $20,000 × 30%	(6,000)
Carrying value—year-end	$524,000

If, at the beginning of the next year, Mavis sells 50% of its interest in Blake for $275,000, the journal entry for the sale would be

Cash	275,000	
Investment in Blake (50% × $524,000)		262,000
Gain on sale of investment		13,000

Other accounting aspects exist. If the investor's share of the investee's losses exceeds the carrying value of the investment account, the equity method should be discontinued at the zero amount. Thereafter, the investor should not record additional losses unless it has guaranteed the investee's debts, is otherwise committed to provide additional financial support to the investee, or immediate profitability is forthcoming. If the investee later shows net income, the investor can reinstate using the equity method only after its share of profit equals the share of unrecorded losses when the equity method was suspended. If the investor sells the investee's stock, a realized gain or loss is recognized for the difference between the selling price and carrying value of the investment in investee account at the time of sale. The realized gain or loss appears in the investor's income statement.

The equity method basically uses the consolidation approach by eliminating intercompany profits and losses. Such profits and losses are eliminated by reducing the investment balance and the equity earnings in investee for the investor's share of the unrealized intercompany profits and losses. Investee capital transactions affecting the investor are treated as in consolidation. The investee is treated as if it were a consolidated subsidiary. For example, the purchase or sale by the investee of its treasury stock, which changes the investor's ownership interest, is accounted for by the investor as if the investee were a consolidated subsidiary. Use of the equity method generally results in the investor's stockholders' equity and net earnings being the same as if the investor and investee were consolidated. For example, if the investee issues its common stock to third parties at a price above book value, the investment value increases, with a related increase in the investor's paid-in-capital. Similar results occur when holders of options or convertible securities exchange them for investee's common stock.

EXAMPLE

An investor sells merchandise "downstream" to an investee. At year-end, $100,000 of profit resides in inventory from intercompany sales. The investor owns 30% of the investee. The tax rate is 25%. The elimination entry for intercompany profits is

Equity in earnings of investee ($100,000 × 30%)	30,000	
Deferred tax asset ($30,000 × 25%)	7,500	
Investment in investee		30,000
Income tax expense		7,500

Assuming that the intercompany sales were "upstream" (investee to investor), the elimination entry would be

Equity in earnings of investee ($30,000 × 1 – .25)	22,500	
Deferred tax asset	7,500	
Inventory		30,000

EXAMPLE

On January 3, 19X8, Klemer Corporation buys a 25% interest (4,000 shares) in Jones Company's outstanding stock for $160,000. The cost equals both the book and fair values of Klemer's interest in Jones's underlying net assets. On January 14, 19X8, Jones purchases 2,000 shares of its stock from other shareholders for $100,000. Because the price paid ($50 per share) is more than Klemer's per share carrying value of its interest of $40 per share, Klemer has experienced a loss by the transaction. Further, Klemer's percentage interest in Jones has increased because the shares held by third parties have been reduced.

Klemer's new interest in Jones's net assets follows:

$$\frac{4,000 \text{ shares owned by Klemer}}{14,000 \text{ shares outstanding in total}} \times \text{Jones's net assets}$$
$$.2857 \times (\$640,000 - \$100,000) = \$154,278$$

Klemer's interest has been increased by $160,000 – $154,278, or $5,722. In consequence, the following entry is required:

Paid-in-capital (or retained earnings)	5,722	
Investment in Jones		5,722

Paid-in-capital is charged for the loss if such an account arose from previous similar transactions. If not, retained earnings is charged. If a gain arose, paid-in-capital would be credited.

A temporary tax difference arises under the equity method because the investor recognizes the investee's earnings for financial reporting purposes but recognizes dividend income on the tax return. This will cause a deferred tax liability.

If ownership falls below 20%, or if the investor loses effective control over the investee, the investor should stop recording the investee's earnings. The equity method is discontinued, but the balance in the investment account is retained. The market value method (under FASB 115) will then be applied in the future.

If the investor increases its ownership in the investee to 20% or more (e.g., 30%), the equity method should be used for current and future years. The effect of using the equity method instead of the market value method on previous years at the old percentage (e.g., 10%) should be recognized as a retroactive adjustment to retained earnings and other affected accounts (e.g., investment in investee). The retroactive adjustment on the investment, earnings, and retained earnings should be applied in a similar way as a step-by-step acquisition of a subsidiary.

The investor must disclose the following information in the footnotes, in separate schedules, or parenthetically:

- Statement that the equity method is being used
- Identification of investee along with percent owned
- Quoted market price of investee's stock
- Investor's accounting policies
- Significant subsequent events between the date and issuance of the financial statements
- Reason for not using the equity method even though the investor owned 20% or more of the investee's common stock
- Reason why the equity method was used even though the investor owned less than 20% of the investee's common stock
- Summarized financial information as to assets, liabilities, and earnings of significant investments in unconsolidated subsidiaries
- Significant realized and unrealized gains and losses applying to the subsidiary's portfolio taking place between the dates of the financial statements of the parent and subsidiary
- Restatement of prior periods because of a change to the equity method
- Significant effects of possible conversion and exercises of investee common stock
- A statement when income taxes have not been provided for on a foreign subsidiary's undistributed profits and the reasons therefore (The cumulative amount of undistributed earnings must be specified.)

EXAMPLE

On January 1, 19X7, ABC Company purchased 40,000 shares for a 30% interest in the common stock of XYZ Company at $35 per share. Brokerage fees were $7,000. During the year, XYZ's net income was $200,000 and dividends were $50,000. On January 1, 19X8, ABC received 20,000 shares of common stock because of a stock split by XYZ. On January 6, 19X8, ABC sold 4,000 shares at $25 per share of XYZ stock. The journal entries are

1/1/19X7		
Investment in investee	1,400,000	
Cash		1,400,000
12/31/19X7		
Investment in investee	60,000	
Equity in earnings of investee		60,000
30% × $200,000 = $60,000		
Cash	15,000	
Investment in investee		15,000
30% × $50,000 = $15,000		
1/1/19X8 Memo for stock split of 20,000 additional shares		
1/6/19X8		
Cash (4,000 × $25)	100,000	
Investment in investee*		96,320
Gain on sale of investment		3,680

*(4,000 shares × $24.08) = $96,320.

Investment in Investee			
1/1/19X7	1,400,000	12/31/19X7	15,000
12/31/19X7	60,000		
	1,460,000		
Balance	1,445,000		

EXAMPLE

On January 1, 2005, Harvest Company bought a 25% interest in Levine Company for $500,000. On this date, Levine's net assets were $900,000. All assets had the same book and fair values except for land, which had a fair value exceeding its book value by $300,000. Levine's net income for the year was $200,000. Goodwill is amortized over 20 years. Using the equity method, the December 31, 2005 balance sheet will present the investment in subsidiary account at $540,000, computed as follows:

Cost of investment			$500,000
Share of Levine's net income: $200,000 × 25%		$50,000	
Amortization of goodwill:			
Cost of investment	$500,000		
Less: Equity acquired: $900,000 × 25%	225,000		
Difference	$275,000		
Less: Share of undervalued land			
$300,000 × 25%	75,000		
Goodwill	$200,000		
Amortization of goodwill ($200,000/20)		(10,000)	
Net addition			40,000
Investment in subsidiary—12/31/2005			$540,000

EXAMPLE

On January 1, 19X2, Gonzalez Corporation bought 200,000 shares of Richardson Corporation's 800,000 shares outstanding for $5,000,000. The book value of net assets acquired was $4,000,000. Of the $1,000,000 excess paid over book value, $700,000 is applicable to undervalued tangible assets, with the balance attributable to goodwill. The depreciation period is 10 years, and the amortization period for goodwill is 30 years. In 19X2, the investee's net income was $150,000, including an extraordinary loss of $10,000. Dividends of the investee paid on August 1, 19X2 were $80,000. The required journal entries for these events follow:

1/1/19X2		
Investment in investee	5,000,000	
Cash		5,000,000
8/1/19X2		
Cash	20,000	
Investment in investee		20,000
25% × $80,000 = $20,000		
12/31/19X6		
Investment in investee	40,000	
Equity in earnings of investee		40,000
$160,000 × 25% = $40,000		
Extraordinary loss	2,500	
Investment in investee		2,500
$10,000 × 25% = $2,500		
Equity in earnings of investee	80,000	
Investment in investee		80,000
Computations follow:		
Depreciation on undervalued depreciable assets		
$700,000/10 years	$	70,000
Amortization on unrecorded goodwill		
$300,000/30 years		10,000
	$	80,000

EXAMPLE

An investor purchases 500,000 shares of an investee at an average cost per share of $5, or $2,500,000. The investee's total shares outstanding are 2,000,000. Therefore, the investor's percentage ownership interest is 25% (500,000/2,000,000). In effect, the relative cost paid by the investor for the investee was $625,000 ($2,500,000 × 25%). The *overall value* of the investee equals $10,000,000, computed as follows:

Actual cost/Percentage ownership

$2,500,000/25% = $10,000,000

If the book value of the net assets of the investee is $7,000,000, the excess of fair market value over book value is $3,000,000 ($10,000,000 − $7,000,000). This $3,000,000 excess is assigned to the investee's net assets as follows:

Excess		$3,000,000
Excess of fair market value over book value attributable to		
Land	$500,000	
Fixed assets	1,000,000	
Less: Deferred income taxes		
30% × $1,500,000	(450,000)	1,050,000
Total goodwill of investee company		$1,950,000

The investor's share of the total goodwill of the investee company would be *$487,500* ($1,950,000 × 25%). **Note:** Deferred income taxes are based on the investee's effective tax rate of 30% applicable to the excess of fair value over book value of investee's net assets.

EQ Inc. uses the equity method for its investment in CHL Inc.

Assume the following:

Percentage of shares of CHL owned by EQ:	40%
Date of acquisition:	1/1/2001
Purchase price:	400,000
CHL's stockholders' equity on acquisition date:	900,000
Income for CHL during year 2001:	120,000
Dividends paid by CHL during year 2001:	80,000
Purchase price over book value is amortized over (years):	10

The purchase price paid by EQ is in excess of the book value of the stockholders' equity of CHL. This excess must be amortized.

Purchase price:	400,000
EQ's share in CHL's stockholders' equity:	360,000
[40% multiplied by 900,000]	
Amount to be amortized:	40,000

The entries for this investment are as follows:

1. Investment in CHL   400,000
     Cash   400,000
   To record initial investment using equity method

2. Investment in CHL*   44,000
     Income from CHL*   44,000
   To record EQ's share of CHL's net income

*EQ's share in CHL's income is calculated as follows:	
[40% multiplied by 120,000]	48,000
Less: Amortization per year:	
[40,000 divided by 10 years]	4,000
EQ's share in CHL's income (net of amortization):	44,000

3. Cash**   32,000
     Investment in CHL**   32,000
   To record EQ's share of CHL's net income

**EQ's share in dividends paid by CHL is calculated as follows:	
[40% multiplied by 80,000]	32,000

Figure 10–2 *Equity Method of Accounting for Investments*

Appendix:
Investments by Banks
In Debt Securities

Banks can only invest in debt securities that satisfy their suitability criteria. Banks may buy

- *Revenue Anticipation Notes (RANs)* These are short-term debt securities pledged with specific source revenues, such as sales taxes.
- *Tax Anticipation Notes (TANs)* These are short-term debt securities used to finance expenditures pending the pledged receipt of anticipated real estate taxes.
- *Bond Anticipation Notes (BANs)* These are a community's short-term debt securities repaid from amounts received from permanent financing.

Banks may invest in all federal government securities without limitation except for those of the Tennessee Valley Authority, which is limited to 10% of capital and surplus. Banks may invest in state and municipal bonds as follows:

- General obligation municipals may be bought by banks in unlimited amounts.
- Revenue bonds issued by municipals may be bought by banks only up to 10% of capital and surplus.

Banks may invest in corporate debt securities with the following restrictions:

- Banks are not legally allowed to invest in junk bonds because of the high risk.

- National banks cannot invest in privately placed corporate debt because of limited marketability due to the number and type of potential investors. However, a national bank may buy privately placed corporate securities and consider them loans.

The yield on government agency investments exceed the yield on U.S. Treasury investments. The reasons for the higher yield are that there is less liquidity and more risk with agency issues, the interest income is often taxable, and many agencies' debts are not guaranteed by the U.S. government.

Banks can deduct for tax purposes 80% of the interest expense on deposits used to buy obligations of "small issuer" municipalities (those in which debt obligations do not exceed $10 million per year).

Amortization of discount or premium is based on the effective interest method. Amortization is from the date of purchase to the maturity date. However, if it is probable that the security will be redeemed before maturity, amortization will be from the purchase date to the call date.

Gains and losses on sale of securities are reported at the trade date. However, if immaterial, the settlement date may be used.

Annual Report References

GENERAL MOTORS
1998 ANNUAL REPORT

3. Marketable and Other Securities

Marketable securities held by GM are classified as available-for-sale, except for certain mortgage related securities of GMAC, which are classified as trading securities. The aggregate excess of fair value over cost, net of related income taxes, for available-for-sale securities is included as a separate component of stockholders' equity. The excess of fair value over cost for trading securities is included in income on a current basis. GM determines cost on the specific identification basis.

Automotive, Electronics and Other Operations
Investments in marketable securities were as follows (in millions):

December 31, 1998	Cost	Fair Value	Unrealized Gains	Unrealized Losses
Type of Security				
Bonds, notes, and other securities				
United States government and governmental agencies and authorities	$291	$291	$—	$—
States, municipalities, and political subdivisions	11	11	—	—
Corporate debt securities and other	98	105	7	—
Total marketable securities	$400	$407	$7	$—

December 31, 1997	Cost	Fair Value	Unrealized Gains	Unrealized Losses
Type of Security				
Bonds, notes, and other securities				
United States government and governmental agencies and authorities	$ 621	$ 623	$ 2	$—
Corporate debt securities and other	3,188	3,203	15	—
Total marketable securities	$3,809	$3,826	$17	$—

Debt securities totaling $136 million mature within one year and $271 million mature after one through five years. Proceeds from sales of marketable securities totaled $4.4 billion in 1998, $10.9 billion in 1997, and $3.4 billion in 1996. The gross gains related to sales of marketable securities were $17 million, $121 million, and $106 million in 1998, 1997, and 1996, respectively. The gross losses related to sales of marketable securities were $11 million, $51 million, and $4 million in 1998, 1997, and 1996, respectively.

Other securities classified as cash equivalents which consisted primarily of commercial paper, repurchase agreements and certificates of deposit, were $9.2 billion and $10.0 billion at December 31, 1998 and 1997, respectively

Financing and Insurance Operations

Investments in securities were as follows (in millions):

December 31, 1998	Cost	Fair Value	Unrealized Gains	Unrealized Losses
Type of Security				
Bonds, notes, and other securities				
United States government and governmental agencies and authorities	$ 445	$ 456	$ 12	$ 1
States, municipalities, and political subdivisions	1,495	1,600	117	12
Mortgage-backed securities	415	383	6	38
Corporate debt securities and other	1,895	1,926	66	35
Total debt securities available-for-sale	4,250	4,365	201	86
Mortgage-backed securities held for trading purposes	3,173 3,173	—	—	

December 31, 1998	Cost	Fair Value	Unrealized Gains	Unrealized Losses
Total debt securities	7,423	7,538	201	86
Equity securities	779	1,210	534	103
Total investment in securities	$8,202	$8,748	$735	$189
Type of Security				
Bonds, notes, and other securities				
United States government and governmental agencies and authorities	$ 687	$ 694	$ 7	$—
States, municipalities, and political subdivisions	1,576	1,686	121	11
Mortgage-backed securities	110	113	3	—
Corporate debt securities and other	2,401	2,441	50	10
Total debt securities available-for-sale	4,774	4,934	181	21
Mortgage-backed securities held for trading purposes	2,063	2,063	—	—
Total debt securities	6,837	6,997	181	21
Equity securities	523	899	416	40
Total investment in securities	$7,360	$7,896	$597	$61

Debt securities totaling $317 million mature within one year, $1.3 billion mature after one through five years, $1.5 billion mature after five years through 10 years, and $4.5 billion mature after 10 years. Proceeds from sales of marketable securities totaled $3.6 billion in 1998, $2.7 billion in 1997, and $2.3 billion in 1996. The gross gains related to sales of marketable securities were $218 million, $176 million, and $130 million in 1998, 1997, and 1996, respectively. The gross losses related to sales of marketable securities were $49 million, $45 million and $29 million in 1998, 1997, and 1996, respectively. Other securities classified as cash equivalents, which consisted primarily of commercial paper, repurchase agreements, and certificates of deposit, were $155 million and $293 million at December 31, 1998 and 1997, respectively.

GENERAL ELECTRIC
1998 ANNUAL REPORT

(In millions)	Amortized Cost	Gross Unrealized Gains	Gross Unrealized Losses	Estimated Fair Value
December 31, 1998				
GE				
Equity securities	$ 233	$ 26	$ —	$ 259
GECS				
Debt securities				
U.S. corporate	27,888	1,293	(325)	28,856
State and municipal	12,483	727	(8)	13,202
Mortgage-backed	11,641	413	(109)	11,945
Corporate — non-U.S.	8,692	409	(90)	9,011
Government — non-U.S.	5,415	258	(9)	5,664
U.S. government and federal agency	2,706	207	(7)	2,906
Equity securities	5,651	1,415	(192)	6,874
	74,476	4,722	(740)	78,458
Consolidated totals	$74,709	$ 4,748	$(740)	$78,717
December 31, 1997				
GE				
Equity securities	$ 257	$ 13	$ (5)	$ 265
GECS				
Debt securities				
U.S. corporate	24,580	1,028	(53)	25,555
State and municipal	10,780	636	(2)	11,414
Mortgage-backed	12,074	341	(30)	12,385
Corporate — non-U.S.	7,683	310	(12)	7,981
Government — non-U.S.	3,714	150	(3)	3,861
U.S. government and federal agency	2,413	103	(4)	2,512
Equity securities	5,414	1,336	(102)	6,648
	66,658	3,904	(206)	70,356
Consolidated totals	$66,915	$3,917	$(211)	$70,621

The majority of mortgage-backed securities shown in the table above are collateralized by U.S. residential mortgages.

At December 31, 1998, contractual maturities of debt securities, other than mortgage-backed securities, were as follows:

Contractual maturities of debt securities
(excluding mortgage-backed securities)

(In millions)	Amortized cost	Estimated fair value
Due in		
1999	$ 5,370	$ 5,574
2000–2003	14,145	14,497
2004–2008	13,068	13,538
2009 and later	24,601	26,030

It is expected that actual maturities will differ from contractual maturities because borrowers have the right to call or prepay certain obligations. Proceeds from sales of investment securities by GE and GECS in 1998 were $16,707 million ($14,728 million in 1997 and $11,868 million in 1996). Gross realized gains were $1,126 million in 1998 ($1,018 million in 1997 and $638 million in 1996). Gross realized losses were $308 million in 1998 ($173 million in 1997 and $190 million in 1996).

HALLIBURTON COMPANY
1998 ANNUAL REPORT

5. Related Companies

The Company conducts some of its operations through various joint ventures which are in partnership, corporate and other business forms, which are principally accounted for using the equity method.

The larger unconsolidated entities include European Marine Contractors, Limited (EMC), Bredero-Shaw and Ingersoll-Dresser Pump (IDP). EMC which is 50% owned by a subsidiary of the Company and part of the Energy Services Group, specializes in engineering, procurement and construction of marine pipelines. Bredero-Shaw, which is 50% owned by a subsidiary of the Company and part of the Energy Services Group, specializes in pipe coating. Effective February 29, 1996, a subsidiary of the Company entered into an agreement to form a joint venture with Shaw Industries Ltd. (Shaw) by contributing its Bredero Price assets and Shaw contributing its Shaw Pipe Protection assets on a worldwide basis. During the fourth quarter of 1997, the Company and Shaw agreed to a long-term extension of their strategic pipe coating alliance, Bredero-Shaw. In connection with the new agreement, Shaw agreed to pay a subsidiary of the Company $50 million over a four-year period. This transaction resulted in a fourth quarter pretax gain of $41.7 million which is reported in the consolidated statements of income in the caption "special charges and credits."

For balance sheet purposes, at year-end 1997 the subsidiary of the Company deconsolidated Bredero-Shaw and accounted for its 50% interest in the joint venture as an equity investment. The subsidiary of the Company includes its share of equity earnings in the results of operations beginning January 1, 1998 under the equity method. IDP which is 49% owned by a subsidiary of the Company and part of the Dresser Equipment Group, manufactures a broad range of pump products and services.

In the second quarter of 1996, M-I, formerly a 36% owned joint venture, purchased Anchor Drilling Fluids. The Company's share of the purchase price was $41.3 million and is included in cash flows from other investing activities. The Company sold its 36% ownership interest in M-I to

Smith International, Inc. (Smith) on August 31, 1998. This transaction completed Halliburton's commitment to the U.S. Department of Justice to sell its M-I interest in connection with its merger with Dresser. The purchase price of $265 million was paid by Smith in the form of a non-interest bearing promissory note due April 1999. This receivable is included in "notes and accounts receivable" on the consolidated balance sheets. All of M-I's debt remains an obligation of M-I.

Summarized financial statements for all combined jointly-owned operations which are not consolidated are as follows:

Combined Operating Results

MILLIONS OF DOLLARS	1998	1997	1996
Revenues	**$5,244.0**	$3,958.9	$3,505.5
Operating income	**$ 478.3**	$407.3	$325.7
Net income	**$341.0**	$316.2	$236.3

Combined Financial Position

MILLIONS OF DOLLARS	1998	1997
Current assets	**$1,854.2**	$1,779.5
Noncurrent assets	**322.3**	576.0
Total	$2,176.5	**$2,355.5**
Current liabilities	**$1,074.6**	$ 859.6
Noncurrent liabilities	**118.2**	245.3
Minority interests	**3.9**	8.1
Shareholders' equity	**979.8**	1,242.5
Total	$2,176.5	**$2,355.5**

BOEING
1999 ANNUAL REPORT

5. Equity in Income (Loss) from Joint Ventures

Equity in income (loss) from joint ventures in the Consolidated Statements of Operations included recognized losses of $65, $127 and $102 for the years ended December 31, 1999, 1998 and 1997, respectively, representing the Company's share of losses from joint venture arrangements in the developmental stages accounted for under the equity method. The Company's principal joint venture arrangement in the developmental stages is a 40% partnership in Sea Launch, a commercial satellite launch venture with Norwegian, Russian and Ukrainian partners. The Sea Launch program entered the production phase with its first revenue-producing launch in the fourth quarter of 1999.

Additionally, the Company recognized income of $69, $60, and $59 for the years ended December 31, 1999, 1998 and 1997, respectively, attributable to non-developmental joint venture arrangements. The Company's 50% partnership with Lockheed Martin in United Space Alliance is the principal non-developmental joint venture arrangement. United Space Alliance is responsible for all ground processing of the Space Shuttle fleet and for space-related operations with the U.S. Air Force.

As of December 31, 1999 and 1998, other assets included $164 and $117 attributable investments in joint ventures.

Chapter 11

Business Combinations

Business combinations are accounted for in accordance with APB Opinion Number 16 (*Business Combinations*), Accounting Interpretations of APB Opinion Number 16, FASB Interpretation Number 4 (Applicability of FASB Statement Number 2 to Business Combinations Accounted for by the Purchase Method), FASB Statement Number 38 (*Accounting for Preacquisition Contingencies of Purchased Enterprises*), and FASB Technical Bulletin 85–5 (*Issues Relating to Accounting for Business Combinations*).

A business combination takes place when two or more entities combine to form a single company. A business combination occurs before the consolidation process. Consolidation is discussed in the next chapter (Chapter 12). Business combinations are accounted for under either the pooling-of-interests method or the purchase method. In using a method, consideration should be given to the criteria, accounting and reporting requirements, and footnote disclosure.

The pooling-of-interests method is used when the acquirer issues its voting common stock for 90% or more of the voting common stock of the acquired company and all of the 12 criteria for a pooling are met. If one or more criteria are not satisfied, the purchase method must be used. Because of the restrictive criteria for a pooling, most business combinations are accounted for as purchases. These criteria are fully discussed in this chapter.

A pooling of interests presumes that for accounting purposes both companies were always combined. No purchase or sale is assumed to have occurred. A pooling is a union of ownership interests of the two previously separate stockholder groups. Shareholders of the combining entities do not invest or take out assets, but exchange stock based on their proportionate ownership interests. In other words, stockholders of the combining companies become stockholders in the combined company. On the other hand, the purchase method considers the combination as an acquisition of one company by the other.

The purchase method is used when cash or other assets are given or liabilities are incurred for the other company. In a purchase, more than 50% of the voting common stock of the acquired company still has to be acquired. An acquisition of a minority interest is always a purchase at a subsequent date even if the pooling method was used for the initial acquisition.

POOLING-OF-INTERESTS METHOD

There are twelve criteria, all of which must be satisfied for the pooling-of-interests method to be used. The criteria follow:

1. There is autonomy between the combining companies, meaning that a combining company was not a subsidiary or division of any other company within two years before the initiation date. The initiation date is the earlier of the date the major provisions of the agreement (e.g., exchange ratio) are made public or issued in writing to the shareholders of one of the combining entities. A new company incorporated within two years qualifies unless it is a successor to a company not deemed autonomous. A company would still qualify under this criterion if it was a previously owned one that was divested because of a governmental regulation or dictate.

2. The combining companies are independent. A combining company is not independent if it owns 10% or more of another combining company's voting common stock at the initiation or consummation dates or at any time in between. If there is a change in the exchange ratio, a new initiation date is established. The consummation date is the date on which the net assets are transferred to the acquiring company. However, temporary assets (e.g., cash, trading securities) may be held to pay liabilities and contingent items.

A pooling of interests does not apply when net assets are transferred or shares exchanged between companies under common control. An example is a partly owned subsidiary exchanging its common stock for that of its parent (referred to as a downstream merger). In this case, the purchase method would be used.

The existence of a joint venture between the combining entities should not be taken into account in determining if the combining companies hold as intercorporate investments no more than 10% of another combining company's common stock. Hence, a joint venture relationship does not negate the independence criterion for a pooling. **Exception:** A pooling is negated if the fair market value of an investment in a common joint venture constitutes in excess of 50% of the estimated fair value of one of the combining companies.

3. The combining companies are brought forth in a single transaction or within one year after the initiation date. A delay is permitted for a lawsuit or government intervention. For example, if the combination took 16 months, of which 5 months arose from litigation, this criterion is met.

4. The acquiring company issues voting common stock in exchange for substantially all (90% or more) of the voting common stock of the acquired business. The 90% rule is determined at the consummation date. The consummation date is usually the date the issuing company receives the transferred assets. The following shares of the combiners are excluded from the 90% minimum:

- Shares of the acquired company outstanding after the consummation date

- Shares owned by the issuer or its subsidiaries before the initiation date

- Shares acquired by the initiating company other than by issuing its own common stock between the initiation and consummation dates

In ascertaining whether 90% of the combiner's stock has been transferred to the issuing corporation, the number of shares transferred is reduced by the equivalent number of shares (based on the exchange ratio) of the issuing company owned by the combiner before combination. This number of shares is then compared to 90% of the total outstanding shares of the combiner, to ascertain if the requirement is met.

Intercompany investments among combining companies are excluded in determining if 90% or more of voting common stock is exchanged. However, the intercompany investments are considered in determining the total voting common shares outstanding.

A lottery feature in connection with stock issuance by the acquirer does *not* violate the 90% criterion.

An acquiring company may pay cash or issue common stock for debt or preferred stock of an acquired business and qualify as a pooling only if the debt securities and preferred stock were not issued in an exchange for voting common stock of the acquired business within two years prior to the initiation date.

According to Emerging Issues Task Force Issue Number 88–26, the acquirer's issuance of voting preferred stock in exchange for the voting preferred stock of the acquired company does not satisfy the 90% rule. Common stock must be issued to obtain a controlling interest. However, if the merging entities both convert their preferred shares to common shares before the transaction is affected, then pooling accounting could be used.

A combination plan may not provide for a proportionate cash distribution, but may within certain limitations have a cash payment for either fractional shares or shares of dissenting stockholders. Cash may also be used in a combination plan to retire or redeem callable debt and equity securities.

If there are outstanding stock warrants, they also apply to the 90% rule, meaning that they must be exchanged for the acquirer's stock. Stock warrants are considered similar to common shares in applying the 90% criterion. However, cash may be exchanged for convertible debt.

Emerging Issues Task Force Issue Number 87–16 applies to whether the 90% test for a pooling of interests is applied separately to each company or on a combined basis. If more than two companies are combined, the criteria must be satisfied for each one. Further, pooling accounting is required where a new entity is formed to effect the merger, provided pooling would have been indicated if one or more of the combining companies served as the issuer/acquirer.

5. None of the combining companies change the equity interest of voting common stock in expectation of the combination in the two years before the initiation date or between the initiation and consummation dates. The voting common stock is considered altered if there are abnormal dividends after considering earnings and previous years' dividends.

6. Treasury stock is acquired by a combining company and is not to be used for business combination purposes between the initiation and consummation dates. Any treasury stock purchases must be a normal amount after taking into account previous experience. Otherwise, such purchase may be suspicious. A reacquisition of treasury stock within six months after consummation of the combination is presumed to be a part of the plan of combination. A systematic plan of buying treasury stock for a stock option or compensation plan is allowed. **Note:** A planned transaction to reacquire treasury stock that is deferred until after the combination does not of itself negate this criterion.

7. The proportionate ownership percentage of each stockholder remains the same after combination as before combination. For example, if X and Y each owned 3% of ABC Company, they should still own the same percentages in the newly formed entity (e.g., 2%).

A pooling is negated if the issuer has a right of first refusal to repurchase shares issued in certain cases irrespective of the fact that the shares issued are identical to other outstanding shares.

As a general rule, restrictions placed on the issuance of shares to the public to comply with governmental law do not preclude a pooling as long as after the combination the issuer has begun the registration process for the stock.

8. Voting rights of stockholders in the combined entity are not restricted in any way. For example, shares may not be placed in a voting trust.

9. The combination is complete at the consummation date, with no pending provisions. For example, there cannot be any provision for contingently issuable shares or asset distributions to former stockholders of the combined entity. **Exception:** It is allowed to have contingently issuable shares to adjust for differences in amounts at the consummation date. Any differences adjust the combined stockholders' equity. This criterion is negated if there exist contingencies based on profits or market prices. This criterion is still satisfied if there is a settlement of a contingency such as arising from a tax credit or litigation.

10–12. There must be an absence of planned transactions for the following:

10. Repurchase of shares issued to effect the combination. However, the issuer may have the right of first refusal on a later resale of shares to effect the combination.

Emerging Issues Task Force Issue Number 93–2 (*Effect of Acquisition of Employer Shares for/by an Employee Benefit Trust on Accounting for Business Combinations*) states that unallocated shares of a sponsoring entity held by an employee stock option plan are allowable treasury shares and are therefore consistent with pooling treatment.

11. Financial arrangement of benefit to former stockholders of the combining entities. An example is cosigning a loan for a stockholder who needs cash.

12. Disposal of a major part of the combined company's assets within two years after the combination. An example is the sale of a division. **Exception:** A disposal to comply with court or government dictate is allowable. According to Emerging Issues Task Force Issue Number 84–35 (*Business Combinations: Sale of Duplicate Facilities and Accrual of Liabilities*), the disposal of a duplicate warehouse would be permissible. **Note:** The disposal of a significant part of the assets or segment of a combining company within two years after consummation results in extraordinary gain or loss.

Accounting and Reporting

In accounting for a pooling of interests, do the following:

1. Net assets of the acquired business are carried forward at book value. No assets or liabilities are added or withdrawn by the acquirer or acquired.

2. Retained earnings and paid-in-capital of the acquired business are brought forth at book value. While total stockholders' equity does not change, the equity components do change. Any necessary adjustments are made to paid-in-capital. If paid-in-capital is inadequate to absorb the difference, retained earnings would be reduced for the balance.

3. A deficit in retained earnings for a combining company is retained in the combined entity.

4. Net income of the acquired company is carried forth for the entire year regardless of the acquisition date.

5. Expenses of the pooling are charged against earnings immediately. Examples are consulting charges, finders' fees, costs to provide information to stockholders, registration fees, and costs incurred to combine operations of the prior separate companies.

6. A gain or loss from disposing of a major part of the assets of the acquired business (e.g., duplicate warehouse) within two years after combination is treated as an extraordinary item (net of tax).

Comparative prior years' financial statements must be restated retroactively on a combined basis to account for the pooling. It should be clearly stated that the combined information is for the previously separate companies.

The journal entry to record the typical pooling of interests is:

Investment in subsidiary	xx	
Common stock		xx
Paid-in-capital		xx
Retained earnings		xx

EXAMPLE

The accounting procedure of a pooling of interests follows:

	Company A	Company B	Combined
Assets	$700	$800	$1,500
Liabilities	100	300	400
Stockholders' equity	600	500	*

*Addition of
—Capital stock of company A before
—Capital stock issued in the pooling
—Retained earnings of both
—Paid-in-capital absorbs the difference

Note: New assets do not arise from a pooling of interests. In the year of pooling, recurring intercompany transactions should be eliminated from the beginning of the year. Nonrecurring intercompany transactions applying to long-term assets and liabilities need not be eliminated, but their nature and impact on earnings per share should be disclosed.

In a pooling, the stockholders' equities of the separate companies are combined. The combined entity's outstanding common stock at par value may not equal those of the separate companies' combined amounts of common stock. If this occurs, do the following: If the combined entity's outstanding common stock at par value is less than those of the separate companies' combined amounts of common stock, increase paid-in-capital.

EXAMPLE

Company X had 4,000 shares of $30 par value common stock outstanding and Company Y had 2,000 shares of $40 par value common stock outstanding. Assuming that Company X issues 2,000 shares of its common stock in exchange for all the shares of Company Y, the combined entity's common stock and paid-in-capital figures would be calculated as follows:

Company X's common stock prior to combination	
(4,000 × $30)	$120,000
Company Y's common stock prior to combination	
(2,000 × $40)	80,000
	$200,000

Combined company's common stock	
(6,000 × $30)	$180,000
Increase in paid-in-capital	$ 20,000

If the combined company's outstanding common stock at par value is more than the separate companies' combined amounts of common stock, the difference reduces the combined paid-in-capital. If the paid-in-capital balance is insufficient to absorb the entire deduction, then combined retained earnings would be reduced for the balance.

EXAMPLE

Assume the same information as the previous example except that Company X issues 4,000 shares of its common stock in exchange for all of Company Y's common stock. The combined company's common stock, paid-in-capital, and retained earnings accounts would be as follows:

Company X's common stock prior to the combination	
(4,000 × $30)	$120,000
Company Y's common stock prior to the combination	
(2,000 × $40)	80,000
	$200,000
Combined company's common stock	
(8,000 × $30)	$240,000
Decrease in paid-in-capital (and retained earnings, if needed)	$ 40,000

Note: The $40,000 is used to reduce paid-in-capital to zero. If a balance still remains, retained earnings is reduced for the residual.

POOLING-OF-INTERESTS COMBINATION

EX Corp. issues common stock shares to acquire 100% of the shares of WHY Corp. and Zee Corp. to be accounted for as a pooling of interests. The separate balance sheets of the three entities is as follows:

	EX Corp.	WHY Corp.	ZEE Corp.
Assets	$45,000,000	$8,500,000	$12,000,000
Liabilities	23,000,000	2,500,000	5,000,000
Common stock			
par $100	10,000,000		
par $ 10		5,000,000	
par $ 1			2,000,000
Additional paid-in-capital	4,000,000		1,000,000
Retained earnings	8,000,000	1,000,000	4,000,000
Liabilities & equity	$45,000,000	$8,500,000	$12,000,000

Shares issued by EX to acquire WHY	30,000	Par Value:	$3,000,000
Shares issued by EX to acquire ZEE	50,000	Par Value:	$5,000,000

In a pooling of interests, assets and liabilities retain their historical values. Thus, after EX, WHY, and ZEE combine, their assets will still total $65,500,000, liabilities will still be $30,500,000, and total equity will be 35,000,000. While total equity remains the same, before and after the combination, the allocation between paid-in-capital and retained earnings can vary. Postcombination retained earnings may be equal to or less than the sum of original retained earnings but cannot be more than the original amount.

Balance Sheet after merger of only EX Corp. and WHY Corp.

	EX Corp.	WHY Corp.	Combined EX and WHY
Assets	$45,000,000	$8,500,000	$53,500,000
Liabilities	23,000,000	2,500,000	25,500,000
Common stock			
par $100	10,000,000		13,000,000
par $ 10		5,000,000	
Additional paid-in-capital	4,000,000		6,000,000
Retained earnings	8,000,000	1,000,000	9,000,000
Liabilities & equity	$45,000,000	$8,500,000	$53,500,000

The postacquisition par value of the EX Corp.'s common stock is $13,000,000 plus $2,000,000 of additional paid-in-capital. Neither retained earnings can be increased nor contributed capital decreased as a result of pooling.

Balance Sheet after merger of only EX Corp. and ZEE Corp.

	EX Corp.	ZEE Corp.	Combined EX and ZEE
Assets	$45,000,000	$12,000,000	$57,000,000
Liabilities	23,000,000	5,000,000	28,000,000
Common stock			
par $100	10,000,000		15,000,000
par $ 1		2,000,000	
Additional paid-in-capital	4,000,000	1,000,000	4,000,000
Retained earnings	8,000,000	4,000,000	10,000,000
Liabilities & equity	$45,000,000	$12,000,000	$57,000,000

The postacquisition par value of the EX Corp.'s common stock is $15,000,000. As a result of the combination, we "capitalized" retained earnings in the amount of $2,000,000. This can be avoided if pooling of interests takes place simultaneously, as illustrated in the following combination.

Balance Sheet after merger of EX Corp., WHY Corp., and ZEE Corp.

	EX Corp.	WHY Corp.	ZEE Corp.	Combined
Assets	$45,000,000	$8,500,000	$12,000,000	$65,500,000
Liabilities	$23,000,000	$2,500,000	$ 5,000,000	$30,500,000
Common stock				
par $100	$10,000,000			18,000,000
par $ 10		$5,000,000		
par $ 1			$ 2,000,000	
Additional				
paid-in-capital	$ 4,000,000		$ 1,000,000	4,000,000
Retained earnings	$ 8,000,000	$1,000,000	$ 4,000,000	$13,000,000
Liabilities & equity	$45,000,000	$8,500,000	$12,000,000	$65,500,000

The postacquisition par value of the EX Corp.'s common stock is $18,000,000. Net assets of $13,000,000 were acquired and additional common stock of $8,000,000 was issued. All retained earnings of WHY and ZEE were transferred to EX Corp.

When one combining firm uses a different GAAP than another (e.g., different inventory methods), the firm is allowed to change to the GAAP used by the other combining company and to record the cumulative effect of a change in accounting principle. Previous years' financial statements, when issued on a pooled basis, should be restated for a change in accounting principle.

An issuing company may impact a pooling by distributing treasury stock (bought before two years before combination). The transfer of this stock is accounted for as if the shares were retired and then reissued to effect the combination. The stock reissuance is accounted for similarly as to the issuance of new shares.

Combining companies may invest in the stock of each other. The accounting follows:

- Investments in the common stock of the other combining companies. This is an investment in the kind of stock exchanged for the new shares issued. It should be treated as retired stock.

- Investment of a combiner in the common stock of the issuing entity. In essence, the stock is retired to the resulting combined company and should be treated as treasury stock.

Disclosures

Disclosures for a pooling of interests should be placed within financial statement captions or in the footnotes. The disclosures include the name and description of combined entities, a statement that this is a pooling, a description and the number of shares issued, the accounting method for intercompany transactions, a reconciliation of earnings previously reported by the issuing company to combined amounts currently presented, the net income of the prior separate entities, adjustments to net assets to conform accounting methods, the effect of retained earnings because of a change in the fiscal year of a combining company, and the nature of and effects on earnings per share of nonrecurring intercompany transactions involving noncurrent assets and liabilities that were not eliminated in the current year.

A combining company should disclose financial data concerning a business combination that took place before its issuance of separate financial statements but is either incomplete or not initiated at year-end. The disclosure includes the impact of the merger on revenue, profit, and earnings per share along with the effects of expected changes in accounting principle, assuming that the combination had been consummated at year-end. If a pooling of interests occurs after year-end but before the audit report date, disclosure is required of the financial effects of the pooling on prior and current years if the pooling occurred at the balance sheet date.

Advantages and Disadvantages

The major advantage of a pooling is the retention of historical cost. The major disadvantage from the point of view of a financial statement reader is the possible overstatement of profits because of the following: (1) sale of low-cost basis assets at a gain, (2) lower depreciation expense relative to using the purchase method, and (3) bringing forth the net income of the acquired company for the entire year irrespective of the acquisition date.

PURCHASE METHOD

If any one of the 12 criteria is not met for a pooling, the purchase method would be used. In a purchase, there is usually either the payment of assets or liability incurrence for the other business. In a purchase, one party acquires a controlling interest in another party in a bargained transaction between independent parties.

A purchase combination may occur in one of two ways. The acquirer may buy the assets of the target company, which is then usually liquidated and only one entity remains. Alternatively, the acquirer purchases more than 50% of the acquired (target) company's outstanding voting common stock. In this case, the two entities are consolidated.

The purchase method is an application of the cost principle in that assets acquired are recorded at the price paid (which is their fair market value), fair values of other assets distributed, or fair values of the liabilities incurred. This gives rise to a new basis for the net assets acquired.

Under the purchase method, none of the equity accounts of the acquired business appears on the acquirer's records or on the consolidated financial statements. In effect, ownership interests of the acquired company's stockholders are not continued after the combination.

Accounting and Reporting

In accounting for a purchase, we do the following:

1. Net assets of the acquired business are brought forth at fair market value. Trading securities are at market value. Receivables are recorded at the present value of amounts to be received using current interest rates, less allowance for bad debts and collection costs. Raw materials are recorded at current replacement cost. Work-in-process is recorded at estimated net realizable value of finished goods less the costs to complete and the profit allowance. Finished goods are recorded at estimated net realizable value less a reasonable profit allowance (lower limit). Fixed assets to be used in the business are recorded at replacement cost. If the fixed assets are to be sold, they are recorded at fair value less cost to sell. Intangibles and other assets are recognized at appraised values. Any duplicate assets which are to be disposed of are recorded at estimated net salvage value. If there is no net salvage value, then a zero valuation is assigned. Liabilities are typically recorded at present value of amounts to be paid based on current interest rates.

2. The excess of cost over the fair market value of net tangible assets is assigned to goodwill, which is to be amortized over the period benefited using the straight-line method not exceeding 40 years. **Note:** If contingent consideration is given based on the acquired company's future profits, the value of the additional consideration increases the original cost of the acquisition. This usually increases the value of the goodwill recorded.

3. Goodwill of the acquired business is not brought forth.

4. The excess of the fair market value of net tangible assets over the cost is considered negative goodwill. Negative goodwill reduces on a proportionate basis the noncurrent assets acquired (except for long-term investments). Any remaining balance is a deferred credit to be amortized over a period not exceeding 40 years.

5. None of the stockholders' equity accounts of the acquired company (e.g., retained earnings) is shown on the acquirer's books.

6. Net income of the acquired business is recognized from the acquisition date to year-end.

7. Direct costs of the acquisition (e.g., legal, accounting, consulting, engineering evaluation, appraisal, and finders' fees) are an element of the acquisition cost and are charged to the investment in subsidiary account. Indirect and general costs (internal costs) are expensed as incurred. If the acquirer pays fees to an investment banker for advice and assistance, such costs should usually be considered a direct cost of the acquisition and therefore an element of the purchase price. The costs of registering and issuing any securities to effect the combination are accounted for as any other issue cost; that is, the issuance cost for debt is deferred and amortized over the term of the debt using the interest method, and the cost of issuing stock (e.g., underwriting fees) is a reduction of paid-in-capital. Liabilities and commitments for the costs of closing an acquired company's plant are considered direct costs of the acquisition. They are recorded at the present value amounts to be paid. However, the costs of closing a duplicate plant of the acquirer are not part of the acquisition cost.

According to Emerging Issues Task Force Issue Number 95–3 (*Recognition in Connection with a Purchase Business Combination*), costs associated with leaving an operation of the acquiree and employee termination or relocation costs should be considered in allocating the purchase price. However, if these costs do not generate revenue for the combined entity subsequent to acquisition, they should be immediately expensed. On the other hand, if these costs are associated with the acquirer itself, then they are immediately expensed in all cases. Disclosures include the terms of an exit or relocation plan.

According to Emerging Issues Task Force Issue Number 96–5, termination or employee relocation costs arising because of a business combination should be accrued when the combination is consummated.

A purchase of stock appreciation rights (awards) or stock options by an acquired company related to a business combination should be accounted for as compensation expense rather than as an element of acquisition cost by the acquirer.

If debt securities are issued in the acquisition, they should be recorded at their fair value based on the present value of the debt payments discounted at the market interest rate. Any difference between face value and present value is recorded as discount or premium on the debt.

In determining the fair value of securities issued in a business combination, consideration should be given to the quantity issued, price variability, and issue costs.

There is a step-by-step acquisition process to be followed:

- ■ If control is not achieved on the initial purchase, the subsidiary is not included in consolidation until control has been achieved.

- ■ After the parent owns more than 50% of the subsidiary, a retroactive adjustment is required, including the subsidiary's profits in consolidated retained earnings, in a step-by-step manner starting with the original investment.

- ■ The subsidiary's profits are included in ownership years at the applicable percentage owned.

- ■ Once control is achieved, fair market value and goodwill adjustments will be made retroactively step by step. Each purchase is separately determined.

EXAMPLE

On October 31, 20X2, Kravis Company bought for cash at $10 per share all 300,000 of Hartman's outstanding common stock. At October 31, 20X2, Hartman's balance sheet showed a book value of net assets of $2,500,000. At that date, the fair market value of Hartman's fixed assets exceeded its book value by $300,000. In the October 31, 20X2 consolidated balance sheet, Kravis will present goodwill as $200,000, computed as follows:

Price paid ($10 × 300,000 shares)	$3,000,000
Book value of net assets acquired	2,500,000
Excess of cost over book value	$ 500,000
Excess of fair value over book value of fixed assets	300,000
Goodwill	$ 200,000

EXAMPLE

ABC Co. bought a 90% interest in common stock and a 50% interest in the preferred stock of DEF Co. for $1,800,000. At the purchase date, the stockholders' equity section of DEF was

Common stock, 100,000 shares at $6 par value	$ 600,000
Preferred stock, 4%, 9,000 shares	900,000
Paid-in-capital	250,000
Retained earnings	350,000
Total stockholders' equity	$2,100,000

Goodwill is computed as follows:

Cost of 90% of common stock and 50% of preferred stock		$1,800,000
Less: DEF Equity		
Common stock ($600,000 × 90%)	$540,000	
Preferred stock ($900,000 × 50%)	450,000	
Paid-in-capital ($250,000 × 90%)	225,000	
Retained earnings ($350,000 × 90%)	315,000	
Total		1,530,000
Goodwill		$ 270,000

The journal entry to reflect the investment owned is

Investment in DEF Company	1,800,000	
Cash		1,800,000

EXAMPLE

Moses Company bought 100% of Rolo Company in a business combination on September 30, 20X3. During 20X3, Moses declared dividends of $20,000 per quarter while Rolo declared quarterly dividends of $5,000. The dividends declared to be reported in December 31, 20X3 consolidated retained earnings under the purchase method are $80,000 (those paid by Moses only) and under the pooling-of-interests method they are $95,000 (Moses's $80,000 plus those paid by Rolo before the business combination of $15,000 [$5,000 × 3]).

EXAMPLE

On June 30, 20X3, Harris Company exchanged 300,000 shares of its $10 par value common stock for all of Blake Company's common stock. The fair market value of Harris Company's common stock issued equals the carrying value of Blake's net assets. Both entities will continue their separate businesses and operations. The following data are presented:

	Harris	Blake
Retained earnings—12/31/20X2	$3,000,000	$900,000
Dividends paid—4/1/20X3	700,000	
Net income—1/1/20X3 to 6/30/20X3	850,000	250,000

Assuming that the pooling method is used, the retained earnings to be presented by Harris in its June 30, 20X3 consolidated balance sheet are

Balance, 12/31/20X2 ($3,000,000 + $900,000)	$3,900,000
Net income—1/1/20X3–6/30/20X3 ($850,000 + $250,000)	1,100,000
Dividends paid—4/1/20X3	(700,000)
Retained earnings—6/30/20X3	$4,300,000

On the other hand, if the purchase method was used, the balance in retained earnings to be presented by the Harris Company in its June 30, 20X3 consolidated balance sheet would be based on the parent's retained earnings as follows:

Balance, 12/31/20X2	$3,000,000
Net income—1/1/20X3–6/30/20X3	850,000
Dividends paid—4/1/20X3	(700,000)
Retained earnings—6/30/20X3	$3,150,000

If there is an exchange by a partly owned subsidiary of its common stock for the voting common stock of the parent company, this *downstream merger* transaction is treated as a purchase.

EXAMPLE:
BUSINESS COMBINATION
ACCOUNTED FOR AS A PURCHASE

ABC Company issues shares on December 1, 2007 to acquire all of XYZ Company's outstanding shares. This transaction will be accounted for as a purchase, where the XYZ Company will remain as a separate corporation.

ABC Company

Shares issued to acquire XYZ Company:		50,000
Par value:	$ 3	
Fair value:	$10	

XYZ Company

Total shares outstanding:		10,000
Par value:	$10	

OUT-OF-POCKET COSTS OF BUSINESS COMBINATION

Legal fees related to business combination:	$35,000
SEC registration related costs:	$15,000
Total:	$50,000

ABC Company and XYZ Company
Separate Balance Sheets (prior to combination)
As of Dec. 31, 2007

	ABC Company	*XYZ Company*
ASSETS		
Current assets	900,000	135,000
Property, plant, and equipment (net)	2,500,000	400,000
Goodwill (net)	—	35,000
Total Assets	3,400,000	570,000

LIABILITIES & EQUITY

Current liabilities	500,000	120,000
Long-term liabilities	1,200,000	200,000
Common stock, ABC Company	900,000	
Common stock, XYZ Company		100,000
Paid-in-capital	300,000	50,000
Retained earnings	500,000	100,000
Total liabilities and equity	3,400,000	570,000

We will assume that there were no intercompany transaction prior to the business combination. Moreover, there were no contingent considerations related to this combination. We will disregard the effect of income taxes.
ABC will record its investment in XYZ as follows:

12/31/2007	Investment in XYZ Company	500,000	
	Common stock		150,000
	Paid-in-capital in excess of par		350,000

To record issuance of ABC shares in exchange for all of XYZ shares in a purchase type business combination.

12/31/2007	Investment in XYZ Company	35,000	
	Paid-in-capital in excess of par	15,000	
	Cash		50,000

To record out-of-pocket costs.

The fair value for XYZ Company's assets and liabilities differs from the carrying amount as follows:

	Carrying Amount	*Fair Value*
Inventory	100,000	125,000
Plant assets	400,000	550,000
Long-term liabilities	250,000	220,000

Thus, XYZ's assets and liabilities in terms of fair values are as follows:

ASSETS

Current assets	160,000	
Property, plant, and equipment (net)	550,000	
Goodwill (net)	35,000	
Total assets		745,000

LIABILITIES

Current liabilities	120,000	
Long-term liabilities	170,000	
Total liabilities		290,000
Fair value of XYZ		455,000

The Goodwill generated by the purchase may be calculated as follows:

ABC's total investment in XYZ	535,000
Less: fair value of XYZ	455,000
Goodwill	80,000

ABC Company and Subsidiary
Consolidated Balance Sheet
As of Dec. 31, 2007

	ABC Company	XYZ Company	Eliminations Increases (Decreases)	Consolidated
ASSETS				
Current assets	850,000	135,000	25,000	1,010,000
Investment in XYZ	535,000		(535,000)	—
Property, plant, and equipment (net)	2,500,000	400,000	150,000	3,050,000
Goodwill (net)		35,000	80,000	115,000
Total assets	3,885,000	570,000	(280,000)	4,175,000
LIABILITIES & EQUITY				
Current liabilities	500,000	120,000		620,000
Long-term liabilities	1,200,000	200,000		1,400,000
Discount on long-term debt			(30,000)	(30,000)
Common stock, ABC Company	1,050,000			1,050,000
Common stock, XYZ Company		100,000	(100,000)	—
Paid-in-capital	635,000	50,000	(50,000)	635,000
Retained earnings	500,000	100,000	(100,000)	500,000
Total liabilities and equity	3,885,000	570,000	(280,000)	4,175,000

Contingent Considerations

Any business combination providing for contingent consideration must be accounted for as a purchase.

A preacquisition contingency (asset or liability) is a contingency of a company that is bought under the purchase method. An example of a contingent (uncertain) liability is a pending lawsuit. FASB Statement Number 38 requires the recording of "preacquisition contingencies" during the allocation period as a cost element of the investment. The allocation period ends when the acquirer no longer needs information. The existence of a preacquisition contingency for which an asset or liability cannot be estimated does not, of itself, extend the allocation period. In general, the allocation period does not exceed one year from the consummation date. If the contingency is resolved after one year, it is reported in current year earnings.

Preacquisition contingencies are includable in allocating purchase cost. The allocation basis is based on the fair market value of the preacquisition contingency. If fair market value is not reliably ascertainable, the following criteria are followed:

- Information available prior to the end of the allocation period indicates that is probable that an asset existed, a liability had been incurred, or an asset had been impaired at the consummation date. It must be probable that one or more future occurrences will confirm the existence of the asset, liability, or impairment.

- The amount of the asset or liability can be reasonably estimated.

Adjustments required by a preacquisition contingency taking place after the end of the allocation period must be included in net income.

According to Emerging Issues Task Force Issue Number 87–11 (*Allocation of Purchase Price to Assets to Be Sold*), any profit or loss aspects associated with the sale of a division should not be included in net income if the sale occurred within one year after combination but rather accounted for as a reallocation of the purchase price since these aspects deal with a resolution of a preacquisition contingency.

A contingent additional consideration should be disclosed but not recorded as a liability. Examples of contingent considerations are those based on accomplishing a given profit level or market price per share in the future. If the contingent consideration is tied to profit, it is recorded at its fair value when the profit level is achieved. If the contingent consideration applies to achieving a specified market price per share, the acquirer will need to issue additional shares or transfer other assets to satisfy the contingency terms. The additional securities issued will be based on their current fair value. An example of a contingent consideration is a company agreeing to issue 2,000 shares of its common stock to a seller for an acquisition. Assume that at the time of sale the market price of the stock is $20 per share. The company guarantees that if, at the end of three years, the market price falls below $20 per share, it will issue additional shares to make up the difference.

If contingent debt securities are issued in accordance with an agreement, a discount account may have to be recorded to reflect any decline in value. The discount is amortized over the life of the securities beginning with the date the additional securities were issued.

Note: We do not recognize contingently issuable debt or equity securities until resolution of the contingency.

Interest or dividends accrued or paid on contingent securities are recorded as interest expense or dividend distributions only when the contingency is resolved.

If the contingent consideration is for services or property use, it is recorded as an expense when the contingency is resolved.

Minority Interest

If some or all of the shares owned by minority stockholders in one subsidiary are exchanged for the stock in another subsidiary of the same parent, the transaction is accounted for under the purchase method. The parent treats the transaction as a purchase of shares from the minority interest.

Pension Aspects

If a defined benefit pension plan is acquired in connection with a business combination using the purchase method, the amount by which the projected benefit obligation exceeds the plan assets is reported as a liability. In the opposite case, an asset is recorded. The recognition of such new liability or new asset results in eliminating any prior unrecognized net gain or loss, or any unrecognized prior service cost for that pension plan. In later years, the difference between the amount funded and the pension expense adjusts the new liability or new asset recognized at the combination date.

Tax Considerations

An acquiring company is not allowed to record any deferred income taxes on the acquired company's books before the business combination. However, a deferred tax asset or liability should be recorded based on the temporary differences between the assigned values on the books versus the tax bases of the net assets acquired. Further, any deferred tax benefits the acquired company had may be recognized by the acquirer after acquisition if allowed under the tax law.

The tax benefit of an unrecognized net operating loss carryforward arising from a purchase business combination may be used prospectively to reduce goodwill to zero. If a balance still remains, other identifiable intangibles are then reduced to zero. If there remains a residual balance after that, it serves to reduce the current year's tax expense. **Note:** Prior years' earnings are never restated for the net operating loss benefit.

Disclosures

Disclosures for the purchase method include the name and brief description of the combined companies, the fact that the purchase method was used, the period for which operating results of the acquired companies are included, the cost of the acquired company and the number of shares issued or issuable and the amount assigned, the plan for amortization of acquired goodwill (including the amortization method and amortization period), contingencies and options remaining under the acquisition agreement and their proposed accounting treatments, unresolved issues, commitments made, consideration issuable at the end of a contingency period or that is held in escrow, and operating results for the current and immediately preceding periods as though the companies had combined at the beginning of the year. (The latter is pro forma disclosure to make the purchase method comparable to the pooling method.) The exit plan should be described, including exit costs (e.g., relocation, employee termination). The minimum disclosure includes revenue, operating income, net income, and earnings per share amounts. Minor acquisitions may be combined.

An illustrative disclosure under the purchase method appears in Note 2: Acquisition.

> **Note 2: Acquisition**   On February 9, 1996, the Company completed its acquisition of ABC. Pursuant to the acquisition, aggregate consideration paid to ABC shareholders consisted of $10.1 billion in cash and 155 million shares of Company common stock valued at $8.8 billion based on the stock price as of the date the transaction was announced.
>
> The acquisition has been accounted for as a purchase and the acquisition cost of $18.9 billion has been allocated to the assets acquired and liabilities assumed based on estimates of their respective fair values. Assets acquired totaled $4.8 billion (of which $1.5 billion was cash) and liabilities assumed were $4.4 billion. A total of $18.3 billion, representing the excess of acquisition cost over the fair value of ABC's net tangible assets, has been allocated to intangible assets and is being amortized over forty years.
>
> In connection with the acquisition, all common shares of the Company outstanding immediately prior to the effective date of the acquisition were canceled and replaced with new common shares and all treasury shares were canceled and retired.
>
> The Company's consolidated results of operations have incorporated ABC's activity from the effective date of the acquisition. The unaudited pro forma information below presents combined results of operations as if the acquisition had occurred at the beginning of the respective periods presented. The unaudited pro forma information is not necessarily indicative of the results of operations of the combined company had the acquisition occurred at the beginning of the periods presented, nor is it necessarily indicative of future results.

In addition, during the second quarter, the Company recognized a $225 million charge for costs related to the acquisition,
which are not included in the above pro forma amounts. Acquisi-
tion-related costs consist principally of interest costs related to
imputed interest for the period from the effective date of the
acquisition until March 14, 1996, the date that cash and stock consideration was issued to ABC shareholders.

The Company entered into an agreement to sell its independent Los Angeles television station as a result of the ABC
acquisition. The sale of KCAL-TV for $387 million was completed
on November 22, 1996, resulting in a gain of approximately $135
million which will be recognized in 1997's income statement.

Advantage and Disadvantages

An advantage of the purchase method is that fair value is used to recognize the acquired company's assets just as in the case of acquiring a separate
asset. The disadvantages of the purchase method are the difficulty in determining both fair value and a suitable amortization period for goodwill, and
the mixing of fair value of the acquired company's assets and historical cost
of the acquiring company's assets.

Annual Report References

BROADCOM
1999 ANNUAL REPORT

2. Business Combinations
Pooling-of-Interests Transactions

On May 31, 1999 the Company completed the acquisitions of Maverick Networks ("Maverick"), Epigram, Inc. ("Epigram"), and Armedia, Inc. ("Armedia"). Maverick develops highly integrated silicon for multi-layer switching equipment in enterprise networks, Epigram makes advanced semiconductor products for high-speed home networking, and Armedia is a developer of high performance digital video decoders. In connection with the acquisitions, the Company issued 12,727,644 shares of its Class B common stock and reserved an additional 1,332,924 shares of its Class B common stock for issuance upon exercise of outstanding employee stock options, warrants and other rights assumed by the Company.

On August 31, 1999 the Company completed the acquisition of HotHaus Technologies Inc. ("HotHaus") and AltoCom, Inc. ("AltoCom"). HotHaus is a provider of OpenVoIP™ (Voice over Internet Protocol) embedded communications software that enables transmission of digital voice, fax and data packets over data networks, including the Internet. AltoCom offers complete software data/fax modem implementations for general purpose embedded processors, PC CPUs and digital signal processors. In connection with the acquisitions, the Company issued 6,723,142 shares of its Class B common stock and reserved an additional 516,526 shares of its

Class B common stock for issuance upon exercise of outstanding employee stock options and other rights assumed by the Company. Each of the acquisitions was accounted for as a pooling of interests. Accordingly, the Company's consolidated financial statements have been restated to include the pooled operations of Maverick, Epigram, Armedia, HotHaus, and AltoCom (collectively, the "Acquired Companies"). A reconciliation of revenue, net income (loss) and diluted earnings (loss) per share originally reported for the years ended December 31, 1998 and 1997 top the restated amounts presented in the accompanying Consolidated Statements of Operations is as follows:

Years Ended December 31, (*In thousands, except per share data*)	1998	1997
Revenue		
Broadcom (as originally reported)	$203,095	$36,955
Maverick, Epigram and Armedia	200	913
HotHaus and AltoCom	13,161	4,473
Total	$216,456	$42,341
Net income (loss)		
Broadcom (as originally reported)	$ 36,398	$(1,173)
Maverick, Epigram and Armedia	(14,774)	(5,379)
HotHaus and AltoCom	2,968	623
Total	$ 24,592	$(5,929)
Diluted earnings (loss) per share		
Broadcom (as originally reported)	$.19	$ (.01)
Maverick, Epigram and Armedia	(.08)	(.05)
HotHaus and AltoCom	.01	.01
Total	$ .12	$ (.05)

The restated consolidated financial statements give effect to the business combinations as if they had occurred prior to the beginning of each period presented and reflect adjustments made to (i) comform the accounting policies of the combined companies and (ii) eliminate intercompany accounts and transactions.

The historical numbers of shares of the Acquired Companies' respective common stock and common stock equivalents have been converted to equivalent shares of the Company's common stock based on the applicable exchange ratios used to convert the respective outstanding shares of each Acquired Company on the respective acquisition dates.

Included in revenue for the year ended December 31, 1999 were aggregate revenues of $8.3 million from the Acquired Companies incurred prior to the respective closings of the acquisitions. Included in net income for the year ended December 31, 1999 were aggregate net losses of $8.8 million from the Acquired Companies incurred prior to the respective closings of the acquisitions.

AltoCom recorded approximately $6.4 million and $2.2 million in the years ended December 31, 1999 and 1998, respectively, representing accretion to redemption value of its preferred stock. Such amounts have been presented as reductions to retained earnings in the accompanying Consolidated Statements of Shareholders' Equity.

Merger-Related Costs

In connection with the acquisitions of the Acquired Companies, the Company recorded approximately $15.2 million in charges during the year ended December 31, 1999 for direct and other merger-related costs and certain restructuring programs. Merger transaction costs of approximately $11.9 million consisted primarily of fees for investment bankers, attorneys, accountants and other related charges. Restructuring costs of approximately $3.3 million included provisions for the disposal of duplicative facilities and assets, write-down of unutilized assets, and adjustments to conform accounting policies to those of the Company.

INTERNATIONAL PAPER
1997 ANNUAL REPORT

Note 5

In September 1997, the Company acquired Merbok Formtec, a company that has pioneered the development of door facing products through post-forming medium-density fiberboard. In November 1997, the stock of Taussig Graphics Supply, Inc. was acquired.

On March 12, 1996, the Company completed the merger with Federal Paper Board (Federal), a diversified paper and forest products company. Under the terms of the merger agreement, Federal shareholders received, at their election and subject to certain limitations, either $55 in cash per share or a combination of cash and International Paper common stock worth $55 for each share of Federal common stock. Federal shares were acquired for approximately $1.3 billion in cash and $1.4 billion in International Paper common stock, and approximately $800 million of debt was assumed.

In August 1996, the Company acquired Forchem, a tall oil and turpentine processor in Finland. In September 1996, Carter Holt Harvey acquired Forwood Products, the timber-processing business of the South Australian Government.

In late April 1995, the Company acquired approximately 26% of Carter Holt Harvey, a New Zealand-based forest and paper products company, for $1.1 billion. The acquisition increased International Paper's ownership to just over 50%. As a result, Carter Holt Harvey was consolidated into International Paper's financial statements beginning on May 1, 1995. Prior to this date, the equity accounting method was utilized. As a result of this consolidation, the Company's consolidated cash and temporary investments balance increased by $241 million, representing approximately 74% of Carter Holt Harvey's cash and temporary investments balance as of the acquisition date. This is reflected in the consolidated statement of cash flows as the consolidation of an equity investment. The acquisition of Carter

Holt Harvey is presented net of 26% of its cash and temporary investments as of the acquisition date.

In January 1995, the assets of both Seaman-Patrick Company and Carpenter Paper Company, two paper distribution companies, were acquired for approximately 988,000 shares of common stock. In September, Micarta, the high-pressure laminates business of Westinghouse, was acquired. In October, the inks and adhesives resin business of DSM, located in Niort, France, was acquired.

All of the 1997, 1996 and 1995 acquisitions were accounted for using the purchase method. The operating results of these mergers and acquisitions have been included in the consolidated statement of earnings from the dates of acquisition.

CBS CORPORATION
1997 ANNUAL REPORT

3. Acquisitions

On September 30, 1997, the Corporation acquired Gaylord's two major cable networks: TNN and CMT. The acquisition included the domestic and international operations of TNN, the U.S. and Canadian operations of CMT, and approximately $50 million in working capital. The total purchase price of $1.55 billion was paid through the issuance of 59 million shares of the Corporation's common stock. The acquisition was accounted for under the purchase method. Based on preliminary estimates, which may be revised at a later date, the excess of the consideration paid over the estimated fair value of net assets acquired of approximately $1.2 billion was recorded as goodwill and is being amortized on a straight-line basis over 40 years.

Prior to the acquisition, the Corporation provided certain services to TNN and CMT for which it received a commission. Additionally, the Corporation owned a 33% interest in CMT.

On December 31, 1996, the Corporation acquired Infinity for $3.8 billion of equity and $.9 billion of debt. The acquisition, which was accounted for under the purchase method, resulted in an increase in the Corporation's shareholders' equity at year-end 1996 of $3.8 billion from the issuance of 183 million shares of common stock and the conversion of Infinity options into options to acquire approximately 22 million additional shares of the Corporation's common stock.

The estimated fair values of assets acquired and liabilities assumed are summarized in the following table:

Fair Values of Assets Acquired and Liabilities Assumed
(in millions)

	TNN and CMT At September 30, 1997	INFINITY At December 31, 1996
Cash	$ 8	$ —
Receivables	63	180
Program rights	22	—
Investments	—	107
Assets held for sale	—	70
Property and equipment	49	39
Identifiable intangible assets:		
FCC licenses	—	996
Cable license agreements	506	—
Other	—	277
Goodwill	1,177	3,630
Other assets	4	31
Liabilities for talent, program rights, and similar contracts	(8)	—
Debt	—	(149)
Deferred income taxes	(200)	(328)
Other liabilities	(71)	(146)
Total purchase price	$1,550	$4,707

The following unaudited pro forma information combines the consolidated results of operations of the Corporation with those of TNN and CMT and Infinity as if these acquisitions had occurred at the beginning of 1996. The pro forma results give effect to certain purchase accounting adjustments, including additional depreciation expense resulting from a step-up in the basis of fixed assets, additional amortization expense from goodwill and other identifiable intangible assets, increased interest expense from acquisition debt, related income tax effects, and the issuance of additional shares in connection with the acquisitions.

Pro Forma Results
(unaudited, in millions except per-share amounts)

Year Ended December 31,	1997	1996
Revenues	**$5,566**	$5,137
Interest expense	**(386)**	(482)
Loss from continuing operations	**(129)**	(242)
Loss per common share—		
continuing operations	**(.23)**	(.45)

This pro forma financial information is presented for comparative purposes only and is not necessarily indicative of the operating results that actually would have occurred had the TNN and CMT and Infinity acquisitions been consummated on January 1, 1996. In addition, these results are not intended to be a projection of future results and do not reflect any synergies that might be achieved from combined operations.

JOHNSON & JOHNSON 1998 ANNUAL REPORT

17. Mergers, Acquisitions and Divestitures

Certain businesses were acquired for $3.8 billion during 1998 and the purchase method of accounting was employed. The most significant 1998 acquisition was DePuy, Inc., a leading orthopedics company. DePuy's product lines include reconstructive products (implants for hips, knees and extremities), spinal implants, trauma repair and sports-related injury products.

The excess of purchase price over the estimated fair value amounted to $3.3 billion. This amount has been allocated to identifiable intangibles and goodwill. Approximately $164 million has been identified as the value of IPR&D associated with the acquisitions. The majority of the value is associated with DePuy projects that focus on spinal and hip implants, which were near regulatory approval as of the acquisition date. The remaining effort and cost to complete these projects is not expected to be material. The Company is in the process of finalizing a plan to reconfigure and integrate DePuy's operations, which will be completed within one year of acquisition. This effort is expected to result in employee terminations, facility closures and other related costs, which will be recorded as adjustments to the opening balance sheet and are not expected to be material. Pro forma information is not provided since the impact of the acquisitions does not have a material effect on the Company's results of operations, cash flows or financial position.

During 1997, certain businesses were merged with Johnson & Johnson at a value, net of cash, of $737 million. The mergers have been accounted for as poolings of interests; prior period financial statements have not been restated since the effect of these mergers would not materially effect previously issued financial statements. The 1997 mergers included Biopsys Medical, Inc., Biosense, Inc. and Gynecare, Inc. Biopsys Medical, Inc. is an innovator and marketer of the MAMMOTOME Breast Biopsy System. Biosense, Inc. is a leader in developing medical sensor technology and is developing several applications that will facilitate a variety of diagnostic and therapeutic interventional and cardiovascular procedures. Gynecare, Inc. is the developer and marketer of innovative, minimally invasive medical devices utilized in the treatment of uterine disorders.

Certain businesses were acquired for $180 million during 1997 and the purchase method of accounting was employed. The most significant 1997 acquisition was Innotech, Inc., a developer and marketer of eyeglass lens products.

The excess of purchase price over the estimated fair value of 1997 acquisitions amounted to $157 million. This amount has been allocated to identifiable intangibles and goodwill. Pro forma information is not provided for in 1997 as the impact of the acquisition does not have a material effect on the Company's results of operations, cash flows or financial position.

Divestitures in 1998 and 1997 did not have a material effect on the Company's results of operations, cash flows or financial position.

ALCOA
1998 ANNUAL REPORT

C. Acquisitions

In July 1998, Alcoa acquired Alumax Inc. (Alumax) for approximately $3,800, consisting of cash of approximately $1,500, stock of approximately $1,300 and assumed debt of approximately $1,000. Alumax operates over 70 plants and other manufacturing facilities in 22 states, Canada, Western Europe and Mexico.

The following unaudited pro forma information for the years ended December 31, 1998 and 1997 assumes that the acquisition of Alumax had occurred at the beginning of each respective year. Adjustments that have been made to arrive at the pro forma totals include those related to acquisition financing, the amortization of goodwill, the elimination of transactions between Alcoa and Alumax and additional depreciation related to the increase in basis that resulted from the transaction. Tax effects from the pro forma adjustments noted above have been included at the 35% U.S. statutory rate.

December 31 (unaudited)	1998	1997
Net sales	$16,766.3	$16,160.2
Net income	875.5	770.2
Earnings per share:		
Basic	2.36	2.02
Diluted	2.35	2.00

The pro forma results are not necessarily indicative of what actually would have occurred if the transaction had been in effect for the periods presented, are not intended to be a projection of future results and do not reflect any cost savings that might be achieved from the combined operations.

In February 1998, Alcoa completed its acquisition of Inespal, S.A. of Madrid, Spain. Alcoa paid approximately $150 in cash and assumed $260 of debt and liabilities in exchange for substantially all of Inespal's businesses. The acquisition included an alumina refinery, three aluminum smelters, three aluminum rolling facilities, two extrusion plants and an administrative center.

In 1996, Alcoa made various acquisitions totaling $302. They include the purchase of Alumix, Italy's state-owned integrated aluminum producer, and Alcan's extrusion operations in Brazil.

Alcoa's acquisitions have been accounted for using the purchase method. The purchase price has been allocated to the assets acquired and liabilities assumed based on their estimated fair market values. Any excess purchase price over the fair market value of the net assets acquired has been recorded as goodwill. In the case of the Alumax acquisition, the allocation of the purchase price resulted in goodwill of approximately $945, which will be amortized over a forty-year period. Operating results have been included in the statement of consolidated income since the dates of the acquisitions. Had the Inespal acquisition, and those made in 1996, occurred at the beginning of each respective year, net income for the year would not have been materially different.

Chapter 12

Consolidation

Consolidated financial statements present the financial position, operating results, and statement of cash flows of a single entity, even though multiple, separate legal entities exist. The major authoritative pronouncements governing consolidated financial statements are Accounting Research Bulletin Number 43, covering comparative financial statements; Accounting Research Bulletin Number 51, dealing with consolidated financial statements; and FASB Statement Number 94, covering consolidation of all majority-owned subsidiaries.

Consolidation takes place when the parent owns more than 50% of the voting common stock of the subsidiary. The purpose behind consolidation is to report as one economic unit the financial position and operating performance of a parent and its majority-owned subsidiaries. It presents the group as a single company with one or more branches or divisions, instead of as separate companies. Consolidated financial statements are a reporting mechanism for accounting purposes, ignoring legal distinctions.

A consolidation is negated, even if more than 50% of voting common stock is owned by the parent, in the following cases:

This chapter was co-authored by Chansog Kim, Ph.D., assistant professor of accounting at Queens College.

- Parent is not in actual control of subsidiary, such as when the subsidiary is in receivership (arising from bankruptcy or receivership) or in a politically unstable foreign region. When control is temporary, consolidation is negated. **Note:** Significant foreign exchange restrictions may be a negating factor.

- Parent has sold or agreed to sell the subsidiary shortly after year-end. In this case, the subsidiary is a temporary investment.

Majority-owned subsidiaries not consolidated because of the existence of one of the preceding exceptions should usually be accounted for under the equity method.

A proposal of the FASB is being reviewed that provides guidance in determining whether control exists. According to the proposal, control would be indicated if the parent can nominate candidates for the subsidiary's board of directors so as to achieve a voting majority, hold convertible securities that would accomplish majority voting rights, have an ability to dissolve an entity and assume control of its assets, and have a sole general partnership interest in a limited partnership.

Note: Unincorporated joint ventures and/or partnerships that are directly controlled (majority control) must be consolidated.

Emerging Issues Task Force Consensus Summary Number 85–28 (*Consolidation Issues Relating to Collateralized Mortgage Obligations*) states that a special-purpose subsidiary created to originate collateralized mortgage debt must be consolidated if the parent formed it so the subsidiary would originate the mortgages, which the parent previously did itself.

The companies comprising the consolidated group retain their individual legal identities. Adjustments and eliminations are only for financial statement presentation. They are never posted on the books of either the parent or the subsidiary.

A subsidiary whose primary business activity is leasing to a parent should be consolidated.

Note: Consolidation is still appropriate even if the subsidiary has a substantial debt position.

ACCOUNTING IN CONSOLIDATION

The equity method is typically used to account for a majority-owned unconsolidated subsidiary when the parent has effective control over the subsidiary. In rare circumstances, a majority-owned subsidiary may not be controlled by the parent. In such instances, the parent would use the cost method to account for the investment when the stock does not have a readily determinable fair value. (If the stock has a fair value we would use the marketed value method.) Regardless of which method is used, the consolidated financial statement will be identical. The parent will include its share of the subsidiary earnings after acquisition as part of consolidated retained earnings. When the parent carries its investment at cost, the investment will be adjusted to equity for purposes of the consolidated financial statements.

Note: Control is typically affected when the parent owns, directly or indirectly, more than 50% of the outstanding voting common stock of the subsidiary. **Important:** FASB Statement Number 94 eliminated the requirement that unconsolidated subsidiaries must be accounted for by the equity method. When majority-owned subsidiaries are not consolidated, a particular method of accounting is not specified in FASB Number 94, although the equity method is often viewed as the appropriate choice depending on the circumstances.

If a parent purchases a subsidiary in more than one block of stock, each acquisition is on a step-by-step basis, and consolidation does not take place until control exists. Any goodwill or negative goodwill is determined at each step-by-step transaction. When control is accomplished, we must adjust to the equity method any prior step acquisition accounted for by the cost method. In consequence, the parent's portion of the subsidiary's undistributed earnings for the period before achieving control increases the parent's investment account.

The retained earnings of a subsidiary at the acquisition date are not included in the consolidated financial statements.

In consolidation by purchase when the equity method is used, the parent includes its share of changes in subsidiary retained earnings on the books. In consolidation by purchase under the cost method, there are three elements of subsidiary retained earnings: retained earnings at acquisition, changes in retained earning after acquisition but before the current period, and net income of the current period. Retained earnings at acquisition will be offset in the elimination of the investment account since the consolidated entity has no interest in preacquisition earnings. Changes in retained earnings after acquisition but prior to the current period will not be provided for in the elimination of the investment account under the cost method. The consolidated entity is entitled to its portion of this element of retained earnings. On a practical basis, this amount can be arrived at by considering the difference between retained earnings at acquisition and retained earnings at the beginning of the current year. Net income of the current period in retained earnings depends on whether a consolidated income statement is to be prepared (and, therefore, the books are open) or whether no income statement is to be prepared (and, therefore, the books are closed). Where the books are open, after the minority interest in net income of the current period is provided for, the consolidated portion of net income of the current period results from extension of worksheet balances. In effect, where the books are closed, the consolidated portion of net income of the current period becomes a part of retained earnings after acquisition but prior to the current period.

Consolidated financial statements do not reflect capitalized earnings in the form of stock dividends by subsidiaries after acquisition.

There may occur the acquisition of stock directly from an investee. The target company is selling some of its own capital stock to another company. In this case, the amount paid for the capital stock increases the stockholders' equity prior to determining the acquirer's stock interest.

If a subsidiary is disposed of during the year, the parent should report its equity in the subsidiary's earnings before the disposal date as a separate line item in the consolidated income statement in conformity with the equity method.

A parent may transfer a wholly owned subsidiary's net assets to itself and liquidate the affiliate, or it may transfer its interest in a number of partly owned subsidiaries to a new wholly owned subsidiary. A transfer or exchange between entities under common control should be reflected at historical cost in a similar way as in a pooling. In other words, the acquirer records the net assets acquired at their book values.

Since the parent and subsidiary are separate legal entities, any transactions between them must be given accounting recognition in their respective accounting records. For consolidated financial statement purposes, they are viewed as one entity; therefore, any intercompany transactions must be eliminated.

Unrealized intercompany profit is the excess of the transaction price over an item's (e.g., inventory, fixed asset) carrying value transferred from or to a parent or subsidiary. It is internal and not sold to an outside entity. In terms of consolidated financial statements, recognition should not occur until realized through a transaction with an unrelated party.

EXAMPLE

Information from the individual and consolidated income statements and balance sheets of Hand Inc. and its subsidiary, Foot Co., for the year ended December 31, 2002 and as of the year then ended are as follows:

	Hand	Foot	Consolidated
INCOME STATEMENT ACCOUNTS			
Revenues	$200,000	$140,000	$308,000
Cost of goods sold	150,000	110,000	231,000
Gross profit	$ 50,000	$30,000	$77,000
BALANCE SHEET ACCOUNTS			
Accounts receivable	$26,000	$19,000	$39,000
Inventory	30,000	25,000	52,000

ADDITIONAL DATA

During 2004, Hand sold goods to Foot at the same markup on cost that Hand uses for all of its sales.

The following questions relate to the aforementioned data:

- What was the amount of intercompany sales from Hand to Foot during 2004?

- What was the amount of Foot's payable to Hand for intercompany sales?

- In Hand's consolidated worksheet, what amount of unrealized intercompany profit was eliminated?

GAAP requires that in the preparation of consolidated financial statements, all intercompany transactions must be eliminated so that only those transactions between the consolidated entity and its outside parties are included in the financial statements.

The amount of intercompany sales from Hand to Foot must be ascertained from Hand's revenue, Foot's revenue, and consolidated revenues. Hand's revenue, it should be noted, includes intercompany sales to Foot. That is, part of the Hand's $200,000 includes sales that were made to Foot. The $308,000 of consolidated revenues represents the amount that has already been reduced for intercompany sales. Therefore, the amount of intercompany sales may be computed as follows:

Total combined revenues of Hand and Foot ($200,000 + 140,000)	$340,000
Less: Consolidated revenues	308,000
Intercompany sales for 2002	$ 32,000

In computing the amount of Foot's payable to Hand, the consolidated balance sheet should include only those amounts due to or from those outside the consolidated entity. The computation, therefore, of Foot's payable to Hand may be computed as follows:

Total combined accounts receivable of Hand and Foot ($26,000 + 19,000)	$45,000
Less: Consolidated receivables	39,000
Foot's payable to Hand for intercompany sales	$ 6,000

Finally, with respect to the inventory purchased by one member of the consolidated group from another, from the perspective of consolidated entity, the inventory must be stated at historical cost. That is, the difference between the selling price of the inventory and its historical cost at the date of consolidated financial statements should be considered unrealized intercompany profit and eliminated in consolidation. Thus, the following computation must be made to determine the unrealized intercompany (gross) profit in inventory that was eliminated:

Total combined inventory of Hand and Foot ($30,000 + $25,000)	$55,000
Less: Consolidated inventory	52,000
Unrealized intercompany (gross) profit in ending inventory that was eliminated	$ 3,000

Emerging Issues Task Force Summary Number 88–2 discusses the transfer of noncash assets to acquire a company and simultaneous common control mergers. A company may transfer investments accounted for by the equity method or subsidiary shares to an unrelated company in exchange for new equity interests of the transferee so the acquirer achieves control of the transferee. The cost of the transferee should be based on the fair market value of the transferred assets or equity interest received, whichever is more evident.

Emerging Issues Task Force Consensus Summary Number 86–32 covers the early extinguishment of a subsidiary's mandatorily redeemable preferred stock. The extinguishment is a capital stock transaction involving no gain or loss recognition. Dividends are included in minority interest as a reduction of income.

Emerging Issues Task Force Consensus Summary Number 84–33 covers the acquisition of a tax loss carryforward when there is a temporary parent-subsidiary relationship. It deals with a situation where one company has a significant net operating loss carryforward while the other company is very profitable. In a highly leveraged purchase combination, the companies' financial statements should not be consolidated. Income should be recognized on the equity method only until the carrying amount of the investment equals the probable repurchase price.

Consolidated financial statements are prepared in a similar way for a pooling-of-interests as for a purchase.

EXAMPLE OF ACQUIRING A COMPANY IN STAGES

Page Company acquired an 85% interest in Sage Company in two stages. In the first year, Page acquired a 25% interest in Sage Company's common stock for $450,000. In the second year, Sage acquired an additional 60% for $1,500,000. The equity book value for Sage Company was $2,000,000 in the first year and $2,200,000 in the second year.

First Year

Cost of 25% interest in Sage	$ 450,000
25% of equity book value of $2,000,000	$ (500,000)
Excess of book value over cost (negative goodwill)	$ (50,000)

Second Year

Cost of 60% interest in Sage	$ 1,500,000
60% of equity book value of $2,200,000	$(1,320,000)
Excess of cost over book value (goodwill)	$ 180,000

Note that at the date of second acquisition, the investment account needs to be adjusted to reflect the amount that should have existed if the equity method had been used for the initial holding.

EXAMPLE OF ACQUIRING STOCK DIRECTLY FROM SUBSIDIARY COMPANY

Sage Company's stockholders' equity is as follows:

Common stock (20,000 shares @ $10 par)	$200,000
Additional paid-in-capital	0
Retained earnings	150,000
Total	$350,000

Sage Company issues an additional 80,000 shares at $15 per share and sells them directly to Page Company. Sage Company's stockholders' equity section is now as follows:

Common stock (100,000 shares @ $10 par)	$1,000,000
Additional paid-in-capital	400,000
Retained earnings	150,000
Total	$1,550,000

Page Company's investment in Sage can be determined as follows:

	Minority Interest (20%)	Page Company (80%)
Common stock	$200,000	$ 800,000
Additional paid-in-capital	$ 80,000	$ 320,000
Retained earnings	$ 30,000	$ 120,000
Total	$310,000	$1,240,000
Page Company's investment		$1,200,000
Negative goodwill		$ 40,000

EXAMPLE

On January 1, 2003, Josh Corp. purchased all of Barb Corp. common stock for $600,000. On that date, the fair values of Barb's assets and liabilities equaled its carrying amounts of $660,000 and $160,000, respectively. Josh's policy is to amortize intangibles over 20 years. During 2003, Barb paid cash dividends of $10,000. Selected information from the separate balance sheets and income statements of Josh and Barb as of December 31, 2003 and for the year then ended follows:

Balance Sheet Information	*Josh*	*Barb*
Investment in subsidiary	$650,000	
Retained earnings	620,000	$280,000
Total stockholders' equity	1,310,000	560,000

Income Statement Information		
Operating income	210,000	100,000
Equity in earnings of Barb	60,000	—
Net income	200,000	140,000

The following questions relate to the aforementioned data:

■ What amount should be reported for amortization of goodwill in Josh's 2003 consolidated income statement?

■ What amount should be reported as total retained earnings in Josh's December 31, 2003 consolidated balance sheet?

In a business combination accounted for as a purchase, the assets that are acquired should be presented in the consolidated balance sheet based on their fair values at the date of the combination. Any excess of the purchase price over the fair values of the identifiable net assets that were acquired should be allocated to goodwill. Goodwill should always be amortized to expense over a period not to exceed 40 years. In the problem at hand, the amortization period is 20 years. The computation of goodwill amortization for 2003 is as follows:

Cost of investment	$600,000
Fair value of identifiable net assets acquired: $660,000 – $160,000	500,000
Goodwill	$100,000
Amortization of goodwill for 2003: $100,000/20 years	$ 5,000

When the purchase method of accounting for a consolidation is used, the parent company (Josh Corp.) is not entitled to any preacquisition retained earnings of the subsidiary. Any such earnings should be eliminated against the investment account in the preparation of the consolidated balance sheet.

When the consolidated balance sheet is prepared, it should include the parent's retained earnings plus the parent's share of the subsidiary's retained earnings subsequent to the date of acquisition. The parent company, it is assumed, utilizes the equity method, since the equity method is typically used to account for a majority-owned subsidiary when the parent has effective control of the subsidiary. (Nothing is mentioned in this problem that contradicts this assumption.) Since the equity method is used on the parent's balance sheet and the acquisition took place on January 1, 2003, the parent's retained earnings account already includes the parent's share of changes in the subsidiary's retained earnings since the date of acquisition. Thus, examining the balance sheets given, the consolidated retained earnings of the Josh Corp. is Josh Corp.'s (the parent company) retained earnings balance at December 31, 2003. That amount is $620,000.

ELIMINATION ENTRIES

Consolidated financial statements consist of combining parent and subsidiary accounts and eliminating intercompany balances and transactions. Thus, all gains and losses on transactions between the parent and subsidiaries, or between subsidiaries, should be eliminated.

Intercompany eliminations include those for intercompany payables and receivables, advances, investments, and profits. The existence of a minority interest in a subsidiary does not affect the amount of intercompany profit to be eliminated. That is, the entire intercompany profit should be eliminated, not just the portion related to the controlling interest. In the case of certain regulated companies, intercompany profits do not need elimination to the degree that the profit constitutes a reasonable return on investment. Subsidiary investment in the parent's shares is not consolidated outstanding stock in the consolidated balance sheet.

Intercompany sales and purchases require elimination because revenue and expenses are not realized for consolidated purposes until the inventory is sold to outsiders. The elimination of intercompany profits will result in inventory being valued at cost on the consolidated balance sheet and is accomplished as indicated in the following discussion.

Intercompany profits in ending inventory are eliminated by crediting inventory and debiting cost of sales or retained earnings (if books are closed). Further, cost of sales and beginning retained earnings must be adjusted for intercompany profit in beginning inventory stemming from intercompany transactions in the prior year. Unless intercompany profits in inventories are eliminated, consolidated net income and ending inventory will be misstated.

If merchandise, including an intercompany profit, is reduced from the acquisition price to market value and the reduction equals or exceeds the intercompany inventory profit, there is no need for a deferral of profit entry in consolidation. For example, if merchandise costing one affiliate $15,000 is sold to another affiliate for $18,000, who reduces it to market value of $16,500, the consolidated work paper adjustment for unrealized intercompany profits should be only $1,500.

Profits or losses on sales and/or purchases before an affiliation are not adjusted in consolidation.

In summary, assuming that the books are open and assuming the use of a perpetual inventory system, the elimination of intercompany transactions in inventory is accomplished as follows:

Cost of sales	xx	
Inventory		xx
To eliminate unrealized profit in ending inventory.		
Beginning retained earnings	xx	
Cost of sales		xx
To eliminate unrealized profit in beginning inventory.		
Sales	xx	
Cost of sales		xx
To eliminate intercompany sales and purchases.		

If the books are closed, the elimination of the unrealized gross profit in ending inventory follows:

Retained earnings	xx	
Inventory		xx

EXAMPLE OF INTERCOMPANY SALE OF INVENTORY

Page Company purchased inventory from its wholly owned subsidiary, Sage Company, during year ended December 31, 2001 as follows:

	Selling Price	Cost	Gross Profit
Beginning inventory	400,000	320,000	80,000
Sales	700,000	560,000	140,000
Ending inventory	300,000	240,000	60,000
Cost of goods sold	800,000	640,000	160,000

The journal entry to eliminate intercompany profits is as follows:

Retained earnings—Page	80,000	
Intercompany sales—Page	700,000	
Intercompany cost of goods sold—Page		560,000
Cost of goods sold—Sage		160,000
Inventories—Sage		60,000

All intercompany receivables, payables, notes, advances, etc. are eliminated for the purposes of consolidation. An illustrative entry is

Accounts (notes) payable xx
   Accounts (notes) receivable xx

If the balance sheet includes discounted receivables from another affiliate, it must be eliminated by debiting discounted receivables and crediting receivables. As to notes receivable, where the holder of an intercompany note has discounted the instrument with an outsider, the contingent liability for notes receivable discounted is considered a primary liability.

When an intercompany sale/purchase of a fixed asset occurs, such assets remain within the consolidated group. Intercompany profits on the sale and/or acquisition of fixed assets between affiliates are eliminated in consolidation so as to reflect the carrying value of the fixed assets at cost to the consolidated group. A similar adjustment for intercompany profit is made for depreciable and nondepreciable long-lived assets. An adjustment must also be made for any depreciation recorded on the intercompany profit so that depreciation is adjusted based upon cost of the asset to the consolidated entity. Illustrative entries follow:

In the year a fixed asset is sold, the elimination entry is

Accumulated depreciation
Gain
   Fixed asset
   Depreciation

In the years after sale, the elimination entry would be

Retained earnings (beginning)
Accumulated depreciation
   Fixed asset
   Depreciation

This elimination is cumulative until the asset is fully depreciated.

EXAMPLE

A parent had equipment with a five-year remaining life and a carrying value of $30,000. The parent sold the equipment to its subsidiary for $40,000. The parent's journal entry for the sale was

Cash	40,000	
Accumulated depreciation	30,000	
Equipment		60,000
Gain on sale of equipment		10,000

The subsidiary recorded its purchase as

Equipment	40,000	
Cash		40,000

The subsidiary will record depreciation expense each year at $8,000 ($40,000/5 years).

The gain of $10,000 must be eliminated along with the difference in depreciation of $2,000 ($8,000 − $6,000). The $6,000 in depreciation is based on a $30,000 carrying value.

The elimination entry is:

Gain on sale of equipment	10,000	
Accumulated depreciation	2,000	
Depreciation expense		2,000
Equipment		10,000

The depreciation adjustment will be required at each year-end over the life of the asset.

EXAMPLE OF INTERCOMPANY SALE OF EQUIPMENT

On January 1, 2001, Page Company paid $250,000 to purchase equipment that cost Sage Company, its 90% owned subsidiary, $200,000. The equipment is to be depreciated on a straight-line basis over a 20-year period.

At December 31, 2001, year-end, the intercompany gain is eliminated as follows:

Gain on sale of equipment	$50,000	
Equipment		$50,000

The following entry is made to eliminate depreciation expense:

Accumulated depreciation	$ 2,500	
Depreciation expense		$ 2,500

The elimination entries are not posted to books and therefore entries are required in subsequent years. If the equity method was not used by Page Company, then the following entries would be necessary:

Retained earnings—Page Company	$45,000	
Retained earnings—Sage Company	$ 5,000	
Equipment		$50,000
Accumulated depreciation	$ 5,000	
Retained earnings—Page Company		$ 2,250
Retained earnings—Sage Company		$ 250
Depreciation expense		$ 2,500

Once the asset is fully depreciated, the following entry would be necessary:

Accumulated depreciation	$50,000	
Equipment		$50,000

Note that if the sale had been made by Page to Sage, then retained earnings adjustments are necessary only for Page Company's accounts.

An affiliate experiencing an intercompany profit on the sale of a long-lived asset to another affiliate may have to pay income taxes on that gain. In this instance, the intercompany profit on the sale should be reduced by the tax effect in making the consolidated adjusting entry.

Intercompany bonds bought by an affiliate are considered as being retired in the year of purchase. In other words, intercompany bonds (along with any premium or discount) are eliminated and treated as if the bonds were retired in exchange for the investment. A resulting gain or loss is recognized in the consolidated income statement. The gain or loss is allocated between the consolidated (parent) interest and the minority interest in transactions where a parent holds bonds of a partially owned subsidiary or where one subsidiary holds bonds of another subsidiary. However, an intercompany gain or loss on bonds does not arise when an affiliate makes the purchase directly from an affiliated issuer since the selling price will equal the cost.

An illustrative entry to eliminate an intercompany transaction in bonds follows:

Bonds payable	xx	
Discount on bonds	xx	
Extraordinary gain	xx	
Investment in bonds		xx

EXAMPLE

An affiliate buys $40,000 face value 10% bonds from an affiliated issuer for $39,000. The following entry is recorded on the affiliated investor's books:

Investment in bonds	39,000	
Cash		39,000

The affiliated issuer makes the following entry:

Cash	39,000	
Discount on bonds payable	1,000	
Bonds payable		40,000

The elimination in consolidation is

Bonds payable	40,000	
Discount on bonds payable		1,000
Investment in bonds		39,000

An intercompany gain or loss on bonds does not occur if the acquisition price is the same as the book value of the bonds on the affiliated issuer's records.

In order for an affiliated investor to recognize a gain or loss on intercompany bondholdings, the following must exist:

■ The bonds are bought outside of the affiliated group.

■ The price paid differs from the carrying value of the affiliated issuer.

■ The bonds are outstanding.

Intercompany dividends are eliminated in consolidation. Consolidated retained earnings should include the accumulated earnings of the consolidated group arising after acquisition that have not been distributed to stockholders of the parent company.

EXAMPLE

On September 30, 19X1, a parent acquired a 100% interest in another company using the pooling-of-interests method. During 19X1, the parent declared quarterly dividends of $25,000 and the subsidiary declared quarterly dividends of $20,000. The amounts reported as dividends declared on the consolidated December 31, 19X1 statement are

■ Those paid by the parent: $100,000 ($25,000 × 4)

■ Those paid by the subsidiary prior to combination: $60,000 ($20,000 × 3)

When eliminating the investment account if consolidation by purchase is involved, the following should be noted:

■ Eliminate the subsidiary's equity accounts.

- Make fair value adjustments.
- Provide for a minority interest.
- Eliminate preacquisition retained earnings.

The typical elimination entries under purchase are

Common stock	xx	
Paid-in-capital	xx	
Retained earnings	xx	
Property, plant, and equipment	xx	
Goodwill	xx	
Investment in subsidiary		xx
Minority interest		xx

The typical elimination entries under pooling-of-interests are

Common stock	xx	
Paid-in-capital	xx	
Retained earnings	xx	
Investment in subsidiary		xx
Minority interest		xx

Offsetting revenue and expense items such as interest or rent are eliminated in the preparation of a consolidated income statement in order to avoid double-counting. This is a consideration separate from the treatment of intercompany profits, as discussed next. The elimination entry is

Interest revenue
Interest expense

Once a parent-subsidiary relationship exists, all of the intercompany profits are eliminated in the preparation of a consolidated financial statement. The intercompany profit elimination is allocated between the consolidated (parent) interest and the minority interest in transactions involving sales by a partially owned subsidiary to the parent or by one subsidiary to another. In all other transactions, the elimination is allocated only to the consolidated interest.

MINORITY INTEREST

Minority interest refers to the investment by third parties in the voting stock of a subsidiary and thus is not held by the parent. Thus, minority interest in a subsidiary is the stockholders' equity in the partly owned subsidiaries outside the parent's controlling interest. It is a separate element of stockholders' equity. Minority interests are theoretically limited to the degree of their equity capital. If losses associated with the minority interest in a subsidiary are more than the minority interest's equity capital, the excess and any later losses applicable to the minority interest are charged to the parent. If profit later occurs, the parent's interest is credited to the extent of previous losses absorbed.

EXAMPLE

On January 2, 2004, Suz Co. purchased 75% of the Levita Co.'s outstanding common stock. Selected balance sheet data at December 31, 2004 follow:

	Suz	Levita
Total assets	$210,000	$90,000
Liabilities	$ 60,000	$30,000
Common stock	50,000	25,000
Retained earnings	100,000	35,000
	$210,000	$90,000

During 2004, Suz and Levita paid cash dividends of $12,500 and $2,500, respectively, to their shareholders. There were no other intercompany transactions.

The following questions relate to the data just presented:

■ In Suz's December 31, 2004 consolidated balance sheet, what amount should be reported as minority interests in net assets?

■ What amount should Suz report as dividends paid on its December 31, 2004 consolidated statements of retained earnings?

■ In its December 31, 2004 consolidated balance sheet, what amount should Suz report as common stock?

The minority interest represents the portion of total stockholders' equity owned by investors in a subsidiary who are not part of the controlling interest. That is, they are not part of the parent entity. The minority interest is computed by referring to the stockholders' equity accounts of the subsidiary standing alone. Any adjustments made for consolidated financial statements are ignored in this calculation. Examination of the data given in the illustration enumerated previously indicates that the minority interest in Levita's net assets at December 31, 2004 is $15,000. This amount is computed by multiplying Levita's net assets ($60,000) by the portion of Levita's stock (25%) that is not owned by the parent company (Suz Co.). The computation is as follows:

$$\$60,000 \ (\$25,000 + \$35,000) \times 25\% = \$15,000$$

When a business combination is accounted for under the purchase method, any preacquisition dividends are not accounted for. Only those transactions of the subsidiary subsequent to the date of the purchase are presented in the consolidated financial statements. Thus, any dividends paid by the subsidiary to the parent should be eliminated in preparing the consolidated financial statements. In general, all dividends paid to minority shareholders of the subsidiary should be accounted for as a reduction of the minority interest in the subsidiary's net assets. In this illustration, Suz should report dividends as $12,500 in its December 31, 2004 consolidated statement of retained earnings. This is the amount Suz paid to its shareholders that year.

In the preparation of Suz's consolidated balance sheet, the entire stockholders' equity of the subsidiary must be eliminated. Thus, Suz's December 31, 2004 balance sheet should report common stock as $50,000. This amount represents the par value of the company's common stock that was issued at that date.

When consolidated financial statements are presented, the net assets in the balance sheet and the revenue and expenses in the income statement of the subsidiary are typically shown. Therefore, a contra must be presented for the part of these financial statement items not belonging to the parent. In the balance sheet, the contra for the minority interest in consolidated net assets based on the minority's percentage ownership in the net assets of the subsidiary must be presented. If a debt balance for minority interest arises, it may be shown as a deduction to stockholders' equity or a reduction to the parent's retained earnings.

There are acceptable alternative presentations to presenting minority interests in the balance sheet. Minority interest may be shown as a part of stockholders' equity but segregated from the equity of the controlling interest. This presentation is also suggested in the FASB's proposed FASB Statement on Consolidated Financial Statements: Policy and Procedures. This presentation is as follows:

STOCKHOLDERS' EQUITY	
Controlling interests:	
Common stock	$100,000
Retained earnings	800,000
Total	$900,000
Minority interests	70,000
Total	$970,000

Minority interests may be presented between the liabilities and stockholders' equity sections in the consolidated statement of financial position (balance sheet). This presentation is mandated in SEC filings. An acceptable but rare alternative treatment is to present minority interests as other liabilities. The minority interest is computed by multiplying the subsidiary's total realized stockholders' equity by the percentage of the subsidiary's stock held by the minority interest. The subsidiary's realized stockholders' equity is its reported equity adjusted for any unrealized intercompany profit or loss still present in the subsidiary's retained earnings.

In the consolidated income statement, minority interests are presented as a deduction (expense) if there is a consolidated profit. If there is a consolidated net loss, the minority interest will be an income item since the minority interest would decrease the consolidated loss. The minority interest is calculated by multiplying the subsidiary's profit (after elimination for intercompany profits) by the percentage of the subsidiary's stock held by the minority interest. The minority interest may be presented in the income statement as a separate item if material after income taxes but before extraordinary items.

Losses may be incurred by the subsidiary, with their concurrent negative financial effect on minority interests. If minority interest in the subsidiary's net assets has been reduced to zero because of the losses, and if a net debit minority interest will not be recorded for the losses, the minority's interest in additional losses should not be recorded. A footnote explanation, however, is required. If past minority losses have not been recorded, the minority's interest in the current profits will not be presented until the cumulative profits equals the cumulative unrecognized losses.

In the statement of cash flows, the income applicable to minority interests should be added back to consolidated net income to derive cash earnings, because minority interest income is a noncash item.

When two subsidiaries, of which one or both are partly owned by the parent, exchange stock, the parent accounts for its minority interest at historical cost if the minority stockholders are not involved in the exchange transaction. In this case, the minority interest continues outstanding and is not impacted by the exchange transaction.

The purchase of all or part of a minority interest between entities under common control is not construed as a transfer or exchange by the companies under the common control.

The purchase of some or all of the stock held by minority shareholders of a subsidiary is accounted for by the purchase method at fair value. The minority interest is impacted by this transaction, and in consequence a new minority interest is created in a different subsidiary. This arises whether the minority interest shareholders' stock is bought by the parent, the subsidiary itself, or another affiliate.

Minority interests in net income are deducted to determine consolidated net income.

Minority interests do not affect the adjustment for unrealized intercompany profits in inventories. However, consolidated profit and minority interests in the net income of a subsidiary are affected by the adjustment because the change in beginning or ending inventory of a partly owned subsidiary does impact net income determination.

SPINOFFS

A parent may transfer a wholly or partly owned subsidiary or an investee to the entity's stockholders. The accounting for a spinoff varies with the percentage of the company that is owned. If ownership is minor (e.g., 20%), the transfer is considered a dividend in kind (property dividend) and is accounted for at the fair value of the shares in the investee transferred. If the spinoff is for a majority or wholly owned subsidiary, the impact is to remove its operations from the former parent and to vest them with the parent's stockholders. This transaction is clearly a spinoff of substance. Such a spinoff is accounted for at the recorded book values of the net assets transferred. The profit of the subsidiary to be disposed should be included in the parent's earnings up to the actual date of spinoff.

Emerging Issues Task Force Consensus Summary Number 87–17 deals with spinoffs or other distributions of loans receivable to shareholders. A transfer of loans receivable to a newly formed subsidiary in consideration for stock of the subsidiary should be accounted for at fair market value. Because the subsidiary is not an operating company, the transaction is treated as a dividend in kind instead of as a spinoff.

CONSOLIDATION REPORTING

If a subsidiary holds shares in the parent, the shares should not be reported as outstanding stock in the consolidated balance sheet but rather treasury shares to be deducted from consolidated stockholders' equity.

If an investment in subsidiary is sold during the year, the parent should include in its income statement its percentage interest in the subsidiary's profits up to the disposal date and any gain or loss on sale.

Purchased preacquisition earnings under the purchase method are presented as a deduction, along with minority interest, to arrive at consolidated net income.

Consolidation is still allowed without adjustments if the parent and subsidiary have fiscal year-ends of three months or less apart. There should be footnote disclosure of significant occurrences during the intervening time period.

There are situations where parent company statements are required in addition to consolidated statements so as to provide information to lenders, suppliers, and preferred stockholders. In this case, dual columns are warranted: one column for the parent and the other for the subsidiary.

TAXES

There is a deferral of income taxes on any intercompany profits if the asset remains within the consolidated group. If consolidated tax returns are prepared, no adjustment is required for deferred income taxes since the intercompany profits are eliminated in deriving the consolidated tax liability.

Consolidated income tax expense may be recorded on the parent's books or allocated among the affiliates so each affiliate will recognize its share of consolidated income tax expense on its own books. However, if affiliates issue their own separate financial statements in addition to consolidated statements being prepared, the income tax expense must be allocated to the affiliates.

If the parent and subsidiary prepare separate tax returns instead of a consolidated tax return, the parent or a subsidiary may include in its accounts income taxes paid on intercompany profits. In this case, the taxes should be deferred or the intercompany profits that have been eliminated in consolidation reduced.

EXAMPLE

A subsidiary sells inventory costing $200,000 to its parent and records a $50,000 profit on the transaction. The subsidiary files a separate tax return from its parent and pays $15,000 in income taxes from the transaction. If consolidated financial statements were prepared, the following consolidating entries are required:

Sales	250,000	
Cost of sales		200,000
Inventory		50,000
To eliminate intercompany profits in sales.		
Deferred income tax asset	15,000	
Income tax expense		15,000
To defer tax expense on intercompany profits eliminated in consolidation.		

When a parent owns 80% or more of the voting common stock of a subsidiary and consolidated financial statements and tax returns are prepared, there are no temporary differences. However, if consolidated financial statements are prepared but not a consolidated tax return, a dividends received deduction of 100% is permissible. Hence, the temporary difference between books and the tax return is zero if the parent assumes that the undistributed earnings will be realized in dividends.

DISCLOSURES

Disclosure is required on the financial statements or footnotes of the company's consolidation policy (e.g., composition of companies consolidated, intercompany transactions eliminated), intervening events affecting financial position when the reporting periods of subsidiaries differ from that of the parent, tax implications on the accounts, and allocation methods (e.g., taxes among members of the consolidated group).

COMBINED FINANCIAL STATEMENTS

Combined financial statements present the financial status and operating results of legally separate entities, related by common ownership, as if they were a single entity.

Consolidated financial statements are typically prepared because the parent has control over its affiliates. However, when control does not exist, combined financial statements may be more suitable than consolidated statements. Examples of when combined statements should be prepared are when one stockholder owns a controlling interest in several related operating companies (brother-sister corporation), companies are under common management, subsidiaries cannot be consolidated for some reason, and combined statements are more meaningful than separate statements. For example, combined financial statements may be suitable for a combination of a partnership and a corporation that are commonly owned.

Combined financial statements are prepared in a similar manner as consolidated statements. In other words, intercompany transactions and profits are eliminated. There is similar accounting treatment for minority interests, foreign operations, income taxes, and differences in fiscal year-ends among the consolidated group.

The major difference between combined and consolidated financial statements is that in the former none of the combining companies has an ownership interest in any of the other combining companies. The equity accounts of the combining companies are added. The equity section of the combined balance sheet incorporates the paid-in-capital accounts of the combining entities. However, there is only a single combined retained earnings account. Combined statements are unlike consolidation, in which the equity accounts are offset against the investment in subsidiaries held by the parent company.

Comprehensive Examples
and Applications

PROBLEM 1

APB Opinion Number 16, *Business Combinations*, specified 12 conditions for business combinations that were to be accounted for as poolings. Assume that all 11 out of the 12 conditions were satisfied for pooling to be appropriate, except for *the substantially all voting common stock test*, which requires that at least 90% of the combinee's outstanding common stock be exchanged for the combinor's common stock. On June 5, 19X2, Peace Corporation and Southern Company initiated a plan of business combination. Peace Corporation offered to exchange three shares of its common stock for each share of Southern Company common stock. Peace owned 9,000 shares of Southern's common stock and Southern owned 6,000 shares of Peace's common stock on June 5, 19X2. Peace acquired in the open market 8,500 shares of Southern's outstanding common stock on June 9, and Southern acquired 3,000 shares of Peace's outstanding common stock on July 1. At all times the number of shares of common stock outstanding for Southern was 200,000 shares. The business combination was consummated on July 25. On that date, Peace owned 200,000 shares of Southern common stock.

Required: Determine the number of shares of Southern Company common stock considered exchanged for *the substantially all voting common stock test.*

Solution (Problem 1)

Three shares of Peace's common stock are going to be exchanged with one share of Southern's common stock.

Southern's number of shares outstanding		200,000
Southern's shares owned by Peace on June 5	9,000	
Southern's shares acquired by Peace on June 9	8,500	
Equivalent number of Southern shares represented by Peace's common stock owned by Southern on June 5 (6,000/3)	2,000	
Equivalent number of Southern shares represented by Peace's common stock acquired by Southern on July 1 (3,000/3)	1,000	20,500
Effective number of Southern's shares acquired on July 25		179,500

Because the effective number of Southern's shares (179,500 shares) is less than 90% of Southern's 200,000 shares outstanding (180,000 shares), the business combination does not qualify for pooling-of-interests accounting.

PROBLEM 2

Popular Corporation owns 80% of Sun Corporation, acquired on January 2, 19X1. Peace Corporation sells merchandise to Steve Corporation at a markup of 30% on selling price. Steve Corporation sells merchandise to Peace at a markup of 25% on cost. Intercompany sales of merchandise between the two companies for the year ended December 31, 19X2 were as follows:

	Downstream Intercompany Sale (Popular sales to Sun)	Upstream Intercompany Sale (Sun sales to Popular)
January 2, 19X2 inventories	$ 200,000	$ 90,000
Intercompany sales during 19X2	3,200,000	1,500,000
December 31, 19X2 inventories	340,000	95,000

Required: Prepare working paper elimination journal entries on December 31, 19X2 for Peace Corporation and its subsidiary. (Assume that both Peace and Steve Corporation use the FIFO inventory system.)

Solution (Problem 2)

Downstream Intercompany Sale (Popular sales to Sun)		
Retained earnings—Popular (200,000 × 30%)	60,000	
Intercompany sales—Popular	3,200,000	
Intercompany cost of goods sold—Popular ($3,200,000 × 70%)		2,240,000
Cost of goods sold—Sun ($3,060,000 × 30%)		918,000
Inventories—Sun ($340,000 × 30%)		102,000

To eliminate intercompany sales and cost of goods sold and unrealized gross profits in ending inventories.

	Selling Price	Cost	Markup	
January 2, 19X2 inventories	$ 200,000	$ 140,000	$ 60,000	← Realized
Intercompany sales during 19X2	3,200,000	2,240,000	960,000	
December 31, 19X2 inventories	(340,000)	(238,000)	(102,000)	← Unrealized
Cost of goods sold	$3,060,000	$2,142,000	$918,000	← Realized

Upstream Intercompany Sale (*Sun sales to Popular*)

Retained earnings—Sun ($18,000 × 60%)	10,800	
Minority interest in net assets of subsidiary ($18,000 × 40%)	7,200	
Intercompany sales—Sun	1,500,000	
Intercompany cost of goods sold—Sun ($1,500,000 × 80%)		1,200,00
Cost of goods sold—Popular ($1,495,000 × 20%)		299,000
Inventories—Popular ($95,000 × 20%)		19,000

To eliminate intercompany sales and cost of goods sold and unrealized gross profits in ending inventories.

Minority interest in net assets of subsidiary*	400	
Minority interest in net income of subsidiary		400

To establish minority interest in subsidiary's adjusted net income:

* ($1,500,000 – $1,050,000 – $299,000) × 40% = $400

	Selling Price	Cost	Markup	
January 2, 19X2 inventories	$ 90,000	$ 72,000	$ 18,000	← Realized
Intercompany sales during 19X2	1,500,000	1,200,000	300,000	
December 31, 19X2 inventories	(95,000)	(76,000)	(19,000)	← Unrealized
Cost of goods sold	$1,495,000	$1,196,000	$299,000	← Realized

PROBLEM 3

On December 31, 19X2, Star Company, a 90% owned subsidiary of Paul Corporation, sold its parent company for $120,000 a machine with a carrying amount of $96,000, a five-year economic life, and no residual value. Both Paul and Star use the straight-line method of depreciation for all machinery.

Required: Prepare working paper eliminations (in journal entry format) on December 31, 19X2 and December 31, 19X3 for Paul and Star.

Solution (Problem 3)

12/31/19X2

Intercompany gain on sale of machinery—Star	24,000	
Machinery—Paul		24,000

Minority interest in net assets of subsidiary	2,400	
Minority interest in net income of subsidiary		2,400

To eliminate unrealized intercompany gain on sale of machinery and establish minority interest in subsidiary's adjusted net income.

12/31/19X3

Retained earnings—Star	21,600	
Minority interest in net assets of subsidiary	2,400	
Accumulated depreciation—Paul	4,800	
Machinery—Paul		24,000
Depreciation Expense—Paul		4,800

Minority interest in net income of subsidiary	480	
Minority interest in net assets of subsidiary		480

To eliminate unrealized intercompany gain on sale of machinery and establish minority interest in subsidiary's adjusted net income.

PROBLEM 4 (Use Exhibit 12–1)

On December 31, 19X1, Popular Corporation issued 21,040 shares of its $1 par (current fair value $10) common stock for *all* the outstanding common stock of Sky Company in a statutory merger. Assume that the business combination must be recorded as a *purchase*.

Required: Prepare Popular Corporation's journal entries on December 31, 19X1, (a) to record the stock exchange, (b) to record payment of the out-of-pocket costs incurred in merger with Sky Company, and (c) to record the merger with Sky Company.

PROBLEM 5 (Use Exhibits 12–1 and 12–2)

On December 31, 19X1, Popular Corporation issued 22,800 shares of its $1 par (current fair value $10) common stock to stockholders of Sky Company in exchange for 15,200 of the 16,000 outstanding shares of Sky's $5 par common stock in a *purchase-type* business combination.

Required:

1. Prepare the elimination entries for the consolidated working paper on December 31, 19X1.

2. Prepare the journal entries Popular Corporation should make on its books (a) to record dividend declared by Sky Company on November 24, 19X2, (b) to record net income of Sky Company for the year ended December 31, 19X2, (c) to amortize differences between current fair values and carrying amounts of Sky Company's identifiable net assets, and (d) to amortize goodwill for 19X2.

3. Prepare the elimination entries for the consolidated working paper on December 31, 19X2.

4. Complete the working paper for Consolidated Financial Statements (use Exhibit 12–2).

PROBLEM 6 (Use Exhibits 12–1 and 12–3)

On December 31, 19X1, Popular Corporation issued 22,800 shares of its $1 par (current fair value $10) common stock to stockholders of Sky Company in exchange for 15,200 of the 16,000 outstanding shares of Sky's $5 par common stock in a *pooling-type* business combination.

Required:

1. Prepare the elimination entries for the consolidated working paper on December 31, 19X1.

2. Prepare the elimination entries for the consolidated working paper on December 31, 19X2.

3. Complete the working paper for Consolidated Financial Statements (use Exhibit 12–3).

Exhibit 12–1

Out-of-pocket costs of the business combination paid in cash by Popular on December 31, 19X1 were as follows:

Finder's and legal fees to business combination	$10,450
Costs associated with SEC registration statement	14,550
Total out-of-pocket costs of business combination	$25,000

Popular and Sky's modified balance sheets and current fair values (*prior* to the business combination) on December 31, 19X1 follow:

	Popular Carrying Amounts	Sky Carrying Amounts	Sky Current Fair Values	Excess of Current Fair Value Over Book Value
ASSETS				
Cash	$ 40,000	$ 20,000	$ 20,000	$ 0
Inventory	160,000	100,000	105,200	5,200
Other current assets	110,000	43,000	43,000	0
Plant assets (net)	*700,000*	*220,000*	*258,000*	*38,000*
Land	200,000	50,000	62,000	12,000
Building (economic life = 20 years)	260,000	120,000	136,000	16,000
Machinery (economic life = 5 years)	240,000	50,000	60,000	10,000
Patent (economic life = 6 years)	0	0	42,000	42,000
Goodwill (net) (economic life = 40 years)	20,000	0	?	?
Total assets	$1,030,000	$383,000		
LIABILITIES & STOCKHOLDERS' EQUITY				
Current liabilities	$20,000	$ 3,200	$ 3,200	$ 0
Long-term liabilities	490,000	186,000	222,000	36,000
Common stock, $1 par	200,000			
Common stock, $5 par		80,000		
Additional paid-in-capital	110,000	47,000		
Retained earnings	210,000	66,800		
Total liabilities & stockholders' equity	$1,030,000	$383,000		

Additional Information

1. Assume that Sky Co. on November 24, 19X1, declared and paid in cash $0.50 a share dividend and that Sky had a net income of $16,800 for the year ended December 31, 19X1, and on November 24, 19X2, declared and paid in cash $0.50 a share dividend and that Sky had a net income of $18,000 for the year ended December 31, 19X2.

2. On December 31, 19X1, the current fair value of Sky's identifiable total assets and total liabilities was $468,200 and $225,200, respectively.

3. Assume that on January 2, 19X2, Sky company purchased inventories of $150,000 from Bernstein Company; and Sales by Sky amounted to $217,800; Sky's cost of merchandise sold was $140,000 during 19X2. Assume that Sky uses the last-in, first-out (LIFO) inventory cost system.

4. Assume that Sky Co. allocates machinery depreciation, patent amortization, and building depreciation to operating expenses.

Exhibit 12–2

POPULAR CORPORATION AND SUBSIDIARY
Working Paper for Consolidated Financial Statements
For Year Ended December 31, 19X2

	Popular	Sky	Eliminations Dr.	Eliminations Cr.	Consolidated
INCOME STATEMENT					
Revenue:					
Net sales	1,122,200	217,800			
Intercompany investment income	7,790				
Total revenue	1,129,990	217,800			
Costs and expenses:					
Cost of goods sold	785,000	140,000			
Operating expenses	111,390	25,800			
Interest and income taxes expense	142,000	34,000			
MI* in net income of subsidiary					
Total costs and expenses	1,038,390	199,800			
Net income	91,600	18,000			
STATEMENT OF RETAINED EARNINGS					
Retained earnings, beginning of year	210,000	66,800			
Net income	91,600	18,000			
Subtotal	301,600	84,800			
Dividends declared	26,010	8,000			
Retained earnings, end of year	275,590	76,800			

*MI = minority interest.

(continued)

	Popular	Sky	Eliminations Dr.	Cr.	Consolidated
BALANCE SHEET					
ASSETS					
Inventories	172,200	110,000			
Other current assets	133,000	52,000			
Investment in Sky common stock	238,450				
Plant assets (net)	720,000	230,000			
Patent (net)	0	0			
Goodwill (net)	19,500	0			
Total assets	1,283,150	392,000			
LIABILITIES AND STOCKHOLDERS' EQUITY					
Liabilities	484,110	188,200			
Minority interest in net assets of subsidiary					
Common stock, $2 par	211,400				
Common stock, $10 par	0	80,000			
Additional paid-in-capital	312,050	47,000			
Retained earnings	275,590	76,800			
Total liabilities & stockholders' equity	1,283,150	392,000			

Exhibit 12–3

POPULAR CORPORATION AND SUBSIDIARY
Working Paper for Consolidated Financial Statements
For Year Ended December 31, 19X2

	Popular	*Sky*	*Dr.*	*Cr.*	*Consolidated*
			Elimi	nations	
INCOME STATEMENT					
Revenue:					
Net sales	1,122,200	217,800			
Intercompany investment income	17,100				
Total revenue	1,139,300	217,800			
Costs and expenses:					
Cost of goods sold	785,000	140,000			
Operating expenses	111,200	25,800			
Interest and income taxes expense	142,000	34,000			
Minority interest in net income of subsidiary					
Total costs and expenses	1,038,200	199,800			
Net Income	101,100	18,000			
STATEMENT OF RETAINED EARNINGS					
Retained earnings, beginning of year	185,000	66,800			
Net income	101,100	18,000			
Subtotal	286,100	84,800			
Dividends declared	26,010	8,000			
Retained earnings, end of year	260,090	76,800			

(continued)

	Popular	Sky	Eliminations Dr.	Cr.	Consolidated
BALANCE SHEET					
ASSETS					
Inventories	172,200	110,000			
Other current assets	133,000	52,000			
Investment in Sky common stock	193,610				
Plant assets (net)	749,340	230,000			
Patent (net)	0	0			
Goodwill (net)	19,500	0			
Total Assets	1,267,650	392,000			
LIABILITIES AND STOCKHOLDERS' EQUITY					
Liabilities	484,110	188,200			
Minority interest in net assets of subsidiary					
Common stock, $2 par	211,400				
Common stock, $10 par		80,000			
Additional paid-in-capital	312,050	47,000			
Retained earnings	196,630	76,800			
Retained earnings of subsidiary	63,460				
Total liabilities & stockholders' equity	1,267,650	392,000			

Solution (Problem 4)

(a) 12/31/19X1

Investment in Sky's common stock	210,400	
Common stock		21,040
Additional paid-in capital		189,360

(b) 12/31/19X1

Investment in Sky's common stock	10,450	
Additional paid-in-capital	14,550	
Cash		25,000

(c) 12/31/19X1

Cash	20,000	
Inventories	105,200	
Other current assets	43,000	
Plant assets	238,951	
Patent	38,899	
Current liabilities		3,200
Long-term debts		186,000
Premium on long-term debts		36,000
Investment in Sky's common stock		220,850

Solution (Problem 5)

(1) 12/31/19X1

Investment in Sky's common stock	228,000	
Common stock		22,800
Additional paid-in-capital		205,200
Investment in Sky's common stock	10,450	
Additional paid-in-capital	14,550	
Cash		25,000
Common stock—Sky	80,000	
Additional paid-in capital—Sky	47,000	
Retained earnings—Sky	66,800	
Inventories—Sky	5,200	

(continued)

Plant assets—Sky	38,000	
Patent—Sky	42,000	
Goodwill—Popular	7,600	
Investment in Sky's common stock—Popular		238,450
Minority interest in net assets of subsidiary		12,150
Premium on long-term debts—Sky		36,000

(2-a) 12/31/19X1

Cash	7,600	
Investment in Sky's common stock		7,600

(2-b)

Investment in Sky's common stock	17,100	
Intercompany investment income		17,100

(2-c)

Intercompany investment income	9,310	
Investment in Sky's common stock		9,310

(2-d)

Amortization Expenses	190	
Investment in Sky's common stock		190

(3) 12/31/19X2

Common stock—Sky	80,000	
Additional paid-in capital—Sky	47,000	
Retained earnings—Sky	66,800	
Inventories—Sky	5,200	
Plant assets—Sky	35,200	
Patent—Sky	35,000	
Goodwill—Popular	7,410	
Intercompany investment income—Popular	7,790	
Operating expenses—Sky	9,800	
Minority interest in net income of subsidiary	410	
Investment in Sky's common stock—Popular		238,450
Minority interest in net assets of subsidiary		12,160
Dividends declared—Sky		8,000
Premium on long-term debts—Sky		36,000

Exhibit 12–2

POPULAR CORPORATION AND SUBSIDIARY
Working Paper for Consolidated Financial Statements
For Year Ended December 31, 19X2

	Popular	Sky	Eliminations Dr.	Cr.	Consolidated
INCOME STATEMENT					
Revenue:					
Net sales	1,122,200	217,800			1,340,000
Intercompany investment income	7,790		7,790		
Total revenue	1,129,990	217,800	7,790		1,340,000
Costs and expenses:					
Cost of goods sold	785,000	140,000			925,000
Operating expenses	111,390	25,800	9,800		146,990
Interest and income taxes expense	142,000	34,000			176,000
Minority interest in net income of subsidiary			410		410
Total costs and expenses	1,038,390	199,800	10,210		1,248,400
Net income	91,600	18,000	18,000		91,600
STATEMENT OF RETAINED EARNINGS					
Retained earnings, beginning of year	210,000	66,800	66,800		210,000
Net income	91,600	18,000	18,000		91,600
Subtotal	301,600	84,800	84,800		301,600
Dividends declared	26,010	8,000		8,000	26,010
Retained earnings, end of year	275,590	76,800	84,800	8,000	275,590

(continued)

	Popular	Sky	Eliminations Dr.	Eliminations Cr.	Consolidated
BALANCE SHEET					
ASSETS					
Inventories	172,200	110,000	5,200		287,400
Other current assets	133,000	52,000			185,000
Investment in Sky common stock	238,450			238,450	0
Plant assets (net)	720,000	230,000	35,200		985,200
Patent (net)	0	0	35,000		35,000
Goodwill (net)	19,500	0	7,410		26,910
Total Assets	1,283,150	392,000	82,810	238,450	1,519,510
LIABILITIES AND STOCKHOLDERS' EQUITY					
Liabilities	484,110	188,200		36,000	708,310
Minority interest in net assets of subsidiary				12,160	12,160
Common stock, $2 par	211,400				211,400
Common stock, $10 par	0	80,000	80,000		0
Additional paid-in-capital	312,050	47,000	47,000		312,050
Retained earnings	275,590	76,800	76,800		275,590
Total liabilities & stockholders' equity	1,283,150	392,000	203,800	48,160	1,519,520

Solution (Problem 6)

(1) 12/31/19X1

Investment in Sky's common stock	184,110	
Common stock		22,800
Additional paid-in-capital		97,850
Retained earnings of subsidiary		63,460
Expenses of business combination	25,000	
Cash		25,000
Common stock—Sky	80,000	
Additional paid-in-capital—Sky	47,000	
Retained earnings of subsidiary—Popular	63,460	
Retained earnings—Sky	2,900	
Minority interest in net income of subsidiary	840	
Investment in Sky's common stock—Popular		184,110
Minority interest in net assets of subsidiary		9,690
Dividend declared—Sky		400

(2) 12/31/19X2

Common stock—Sky	80,000	
Additional paid-in-capital—Sky	47,000	
Retained earnings of subsidiary—Popular	63,460	
Retained earnings—Sky	3,340	
Minority interest in net income of subsidiary	900	
Intercompany investment income—Popular	17,100	
Investment in Sky's common stock—Popular		193,610
Minority interest in net assets of subsidiary		8,000
Dividend declared—Sky		10,190

Exhibit 12–3

POPULAR CORPORATION AND SUBSIDIARY
Working Paper for Consolidated Financial Statements
For Year Ended December 31, 19X2

	Popular	Sky	Eliminations Dr.	Cr.	Consolidated
INCOME STATEMENT					
Revenue:					
Net sales	1,122,200	217,800			1,340,000
Intercompany investment income	17,100		17,100		
Total revenue	1,139,300	217,800	17,100		1,340,000
Costs and expenses:					
Cost of goods sold	785,000	140,000			925,000
Operating expenses	111,200	25,800			137,000
Interest and income taxes expense	142,000	34,000			176,000
Minority interest in net income of subsidiary			900		900
Total costs and expenses	1,038,200	199,800	900		1,238,900
Net income	101,100	18,000	18,000		101,100
STATEMENT OF RETAINED EARNINGS					
Retained earnings, beginning of year	185,000	66,800	3,340		248,460
Net income	101,100	18,000	18,000		101,100
Subtotal	286,100	84,800	21,340		349,560
Dividends declared	26,010	8,000		8,000	26,010
Retained earnings, end of year	260,090	76,800	21,340	8,000	323,550

	Popular	Sky	Eliminations Dr.	Cr.	Consolidated
BALANCE SHEET					
ASSETS					
Inventories	172,200	110,000			282,200
Other current assets	133,000	52,000			185,000
Investment in Sky common stock	193,610			193,610	0
Plant assets (net)	749,340	230,000			979,340
Patent (net)	0	0			0
Goodwill (net)	19,500	0			19,500
Total Assets	1,267,650	392,000	0	193,610	1,466,040
LIABILITIES AND STOCKHOLDERS' EQUITY					
Liabilities	484,110	188,200			672,310
Minority interest in net assets of subsidiary				10,190	10,190
Common stock, $2 par	211,400				211,400
Common stock, $10 par		80,000	80,000		0
Additional paid-in-capital	312,050	47,000	47,000		312,050
Retained earnings	196,630	76,800	13,340		260,090
Retained earnings of subsidiary	63,460		63,460		0
Total liabilities & stockholders' equity	1,267,650	392,000	203,800	10,190	1,519,520

Annual Report References

TELEPHONE AND DATA SYSTEMS 1997 ANNUAL REPORT

8. Minority Interest in Subsidiaries

The following table summarizes the minority shareholders' and partners' interests in the equity of consolidated subsidiaries.

(Dollars in thousands)	December 31, 1997	1996
U.S. Cellular		
U.S. Cellular shareholders	$305,478	$285,835
U.S. Cellular subsidiaries' partners	53,908	48,715
	359,386	334,550
Aerial shareholders	33,692	75,897
TDS Telecom telephone subsidiaries	23,293	21,810
Other	195	86
	$416,566	$432,343

Sale of Stock by Subsidiaries

Aerial issued 12.3 million Common Shares in 1996 in an initial public offering (at a price of $17 per share). The initial public offering reduced TDS's ownership percentage from 100% to 82.8%. The Aerial Common Share offering was recorded at a fair market value which was more than TDS's book value investment in Aerial. TDS adjusted its book value investment as a result of this issue and increased capital in excess of par value $114.1 million in 1996.

BAUSCH & LOMB
1997 ANNUAL REPORT

12. Minority Interest

Four wholly-owned subsidiaries of the company have contributed operating and financial assets to a limited partnership for an aggregate 72% in general and limited partnership interests. The partnership is a separate legal entity from the company whose purpose is to own and manage a portfolio of assets. Those assets include portions of the company's biomedical operations, those used for the manufacture and sale of rigid gas permeable contact lenses and lens care products, cash and cash equivalents, a long-term note guaranteed by the company and certain floating-rate demand notes due from certain of the company's subsidiaries. For financial reporting purposes, the assets, liabilities and earnings of the partnership entities have continued to be included in the company's consolidated financial statements. The outside investor's limited partnership interest in the partnership has been recorded as minority interest totaling $403.0 at both December 27, 1997 and December 28, 1996.

UNION CARBIDE
1998 ANNUAL REPORT

The following are financial summaries of 33 percent- to 50 percent-owned joint ventures included in *Companies carried at equity*. The corporation's most significant joint ventures, classified as partnerships, include UOP LLC; Petromont and Company, Limited Partnership; Aspell Polymeres SNC; World Ethanol Company and Univation Technologies, LLC (formed in 1997).

| | | Partnerships | |
Millions of dollars	*1998*	*1997*	*1996*
Net sales[a]	**$1,905**	$2,076	$2,109
Cost of sales	**1,210**	1,242	1,338
Depreciation	**116**	83	83
Partnership income	**154**	249	242
UCC share of partnership income	**$ 33**[b]	$ 133	$ 144
Current assets	**$799**	$ 746	$ 704
Noncurrent assets	**937**	886	806
Total assets	**1,736**	1,632	1,510
Current liabilities	**430**	451	608
Noncurrent liabilities	**828**	711	385
Total liabilities	**1,258**	1,162	993
Net assets	**478**	470	517
UCC equity	**$ 286**	$ 278	$ 251

(a) Includes $140 million net sales to the corporation in 1998 ($208 million in 1997 and $159 million in 1996).

(b) Includes $53 million of losses associated with Aspell Polymeres SNC.

The corporation's joint ventures, classified as corporate investments, include Polimeri Europa S.r.l.; EQUATE Petrochemical Company K.S.C.; Nippon Unicar Company Limited; Alberta & Orient Glycol Company Limited; Asian Acetyls Co., Ltd. and several smaller entities.

| | Corporate Investments | | |
Millions of dollars	*1998*	*1997*	*1996*
Net sales[a]	$2,151	$2,248	$2,059
Cost of sales	1,732	1,814	1,693
Depreciation	256	109	129
Net income (loss)	(195)	75	(6)
UCC share of net income (loss)	$ (66)	$ 3	$ (16)
Current assets	$1,037	$ 933	$ 877
Noncurrent assets	2,932	3,252	2,918
Total assets	3,969	4,185	3,795
Current liabilities	963	872	888
Noncurrent liabilities	2,371	2,347	1,891
Total liabilities	3,334	3,219	2,779
Net assets	635	966	1,016
UCC equity	$ 338	$ 412	$ (444

(a) Includes $157 million net sales to the corporation in 1998 ($156 million in 1997 and $153 million in 1996).

Dividends and distributions received from joint ventures and partnerships aggregated $123 million in 1998 ($126 million in 1997 and $141 million in 1996).

Chapter 13

Leases

The accounting, presentation, and disclosures for lease arrangements are provided in various authoritative pronouncements, including FASB Statement Number 13 (*Accounting for Leases*), FASB Statement Number 23 (*Inception of the Lease*), FASB Statement Number 91 (*Accounting for Nonrefundable Fees and Costs Associated with Originating or Acquiring Loans and Initial Direct Costs of Leases*), FASB Statement Number 98 (*Accounting for Leases*), FASB Interpretation Number 24 (*Leases Involving Only Part of a Building*), FASB Technical Bulletin Number 88–1 (*Issues Relating to Accounting for Leases*), FASB Technical Bulletin Number 79–14 (*Upward Adjustment of Guaranteed Residual Values*), Emerging Issues Task Force Consensus Summary Number 90–15 (*Impact of Nonsubstantive Lessors, Residual Value Guarantees, and Other Provisions in Leasing Transactions*), Emerging Issues Task Force Consensus Summary Number 88–12 (*Accounting for the Sale of Property Subject to the Seller's Preexisting Lease*), and Emerging Issues Task Force Consensus Summary Number 84–25 (*Offsetting Nonrecourse Debt with Sales-Type or Direct Financing Lease Receivables*).

Leases are usually of a long-term noncancellable nature. *Noncancellable* means either the lease cannot be terminated or it is cancellable only upon the happening of either a remote contingency, the lessor's approval, or

---

This chapter was co-authored by Robert Fonfeder, Ph.D., CPA, professor of accounting at Hofstra University.

643

entering into a new lease with the same lessor; or the lease imposes a substantial penalty on the lessee for cancellation. The lessee obtains the right to use property (tangible or intangible) for a specified time period from the lessor, who owns it by paying a rental fee. Although title is not transferred, the lease may in some cases transfer substantial risks and benefits of ownership. Theoretical substance comes before legality in accounting so that the lessee in a capital lease arrangement will have to record an asset and related liability. Other leases are simply a rental of property. A lessor's classification of a lease does not affect the accounting treatment for the lease by the lessee. Leases may be structured to derive certain tax benefits.

In certain situations, a lease may be transacted among related parties. This arises when one company has substantial influence over the operating and financial activities of the other business.

The inception date of a lease is the earlier date of the rental contract or commitment. A commitment must be in written form, it must be signed, and it must contain the major terms. If principal provisions are to be negotiated at a later date, no binding commitment is deemed to exist.

Leases may include contracts that are not referred to as leases as such but have the attributes of one, including the right to use property. An example is a contract requiring the rendering of services in order to operate equipment.

This chapter discusses the accounting, reporting, and disclosures of leases by lessees and lessors. It includes a discussion of sale-leasebacks, subleases, renewals and extensions, terminations, leveraged leases, and other issues.

LESSEE

Leasing has many advantages for the lessee, including the following:

- Immediate cash outlay is not required.
- Typically, a purchase option exists, allowing the lessee to obtain the property at a bargain price at the expiration of the lease.
- The lessor's expert service is made available.

- There are usually fewer financing restrictions (e.g., limitations on dividends) placed on the lessee by the lessor than are imposed when obtaining a loan to buy the asset.

- The obligation for future rental payment does not have to be reported on the balance sheet in the case of an operating lease.

- Leasing allows the lessee under a capital lease, in effect, to depreciate land, which is not allowed if land is purchased.

- In bankruptcy or reorganization, the maximum claim of lessors against the company is three years of lease payments. In the case of debt, creditors have a claim for the total amount of the unpaid financing.

- The lessee may avoid having the obsolescence risk of the property if the lessor, in determining the lease payments, fails to estimate accurately the obsolescence of the asset.

There are several drawbacks to leasing, including the following:

- There is a higher cost in the long run than if the asset is purchased.

- The interest cost associated with leasing is typically higher than the interest cost on debt.

- If the property reverts to the lessor at termination of the lease, the lessee must either sign a new lease or buy the property at higher current prices. Also, the salvage value of the property is realized by the lessor.

- The lessee may have to retain property no longer needed (i.e., obsolete equipment).

- The lessee cannot make improvements to the leased property without the lessor's permission.

The lessee may account for a lease under either the operating method or capital lease method.

Operating Method

In an operating lease, there is a regular rental of property. In such a case, rent expense is charged as incurred under the accrual basis. The credit is either to payables or cash. Rent expense is usually reflected on a straight-line basis over the lease term even if the payments are not on a straight-line basis.

Note: According to FASB Technical Bulletin Number 85–3 (*Accounting for Operating Leases with Scheduled Rent Increases*), if a more suitable and rational method exists reflective of the time pattern that the leased property is used, it may be used, although this is a rare occurrence. Since the lessee is just engaged in a regular rental, there is no property shown on the lessee's balance sheet.

EXAMPLE

This example shows rent expense on a straight-line basis even though the payments are not on such a basis. A lessee leases property for a 10-year period but as an incentive will not pay a rental in the first year. After the first year, the monthly rental is $400. Therefore, total rent under the rental agreement equals $43,200 ($400 × 108 months). The 108 months represents 9 years multiplied by 12 months in a year. As a result, the amount charged to rent expense each month will be $360 ($43,200/120 months). One hundred and twenty months represents 10 years multiplied by 12 months a year. In the first year, the journal entry each month would be to debit rent expense and credit an accrued liability since no cash payment is being made. After the first year, as payments are made the accrued liability will be reduced by the excess of the monthly payment over the monthly rent expense, amounting to $40 ($400 – $360).

EXAMPLE

The lease may provide that the lessee will pay lower rentals in the early years and higher rentals in the later years of a lease. Assume a six-year rental in which the rentals per month for years 1 and 2 are $250, $375 for years 3 to 4, and $500 for years 5 and 6. The total rental over the six-year period equals $27,000 ($6,000 + $9,000 + 12,000), which must be amortized over the rental term on a straight-line basis. Hence, the monthly amortization for years 1 and 2 is $375 ($27,000/72 months) even though $250 is being paid.

As per FASB Statement Number 29 (*Determining Contingent Rentals*), a rental based on some factor or event not determinable at the inception of the lease (e.g., units sold, units produced, inflation rate, prime interest rate) is referred to as a contingent rental. However, a contingent rental does not apply to a variable dependent only upon the passage of time. Further, a contingent rental does not include passthrough increases (escalation) in construction cost or the purchase cost of leased property. According to Emerging Issues Task Force Consensus Summary Number 86–33 (*Tax Indemnification in Lease Agreements*), tax indemnification payments do not qualify as contingent rentals. A contingent rental payment is charged to rent expense as incurred.

FASB Technical Bulletin Number 88–1 includes coverage of lease incentives in an operating lease. Lease incentives include giving a bonus payment to the lessee for signing the rental contract, reimbursing the lessee for certain costs (e.g., moving costs), and paying a third party an amount on behalf of the lessee (e.g., loan payment to the lessee's bank, payment for a leasehold improvement, assumption of a lessee's obligation under a preexisting lease). Lease incentive payments should be amortized by the lessee against rental expense over the rental time period. When a lease incentive is received, the lessee debits cash and credits a deferred rental incentive account. This latter account is amortized and reduces rent expense over the rental period using the straight-line method. (The lessor recognizes in a similar manner lease incentives given to the lessee by reducing rental income on a straight-line basis over the term of the new rental agreement.)

With regard to the costs or losses incurred by the lessee related to a lease incentive, the lessee will account for such costs or losses as usual. For example, moving costs will be expensed, and losses will be recognized on abandoned leasehold improvements. If the lessor incurs a loss because it provides the lessee with an incentive, the lessor will account for such loss as part of the new rental transaction.

EXAMPLE

A lessee receives a lease incentive of $25,000 to sign a 10-year lease requiring annual rentals of $75,000. The lessee's entry to record the incentive is to debit cash and credit deferred rental incentive for $25,000. The deferred rental incentive account will be amortized over the lease term using the straight-line method. The amortization each year will be $2,500 ($25,000/10 years). The journal entries each year to record the rental payment and the amortization of the incentive follow:

Rent expense	75,000	
Cash		75,000
Deferred rental incentive	2,500	
Rent expense		2,500

The net rental cost each year is $72,500 ($75,000 – $2,500).

A lease may stipulate escalated amounts that must be provided for in rent expense to the lessee. The escalated amounts are to be accounted for under the straight-line method over the rental period. If the contract gives the lessee control over additional property, the escalated rent applicable to the original leased property is charged to rent expense on a pro rata basis to the additional leased property in the years the lessee has control over the additional property. The lessor records the escalated amounts on the initial leased property as additional rental income. The rental expense of the lessee or rental income of the lessor should be on a pro rata basis dependent upon the relative fair market value of the additional leased property as stipulated in the rental contract for the period the lessee controls such additional property.

An operating lease may contain a penalty clause. The lessee's payment of a penalty should be expensed as incurred. A penalty may be in the form of a cash payment, performance of services, liability incurrence, or significant extension of the lease term. A penalty should be so significant that the lessee will want to abide by contractual terms or reasonably assure the lessee's renewal of the lease.

Any moving costs incurred by the lessee to move from one location to another are usually expensed as incurred.

The lessee can determine the periodic rental payments to be made under a lease by dividing the value of the leased property by the present value factor associated with the future rental payments.

EXAMPLE

Gonzalez Corporation enters into a lease for a $100,000 machine. It is to make equal annual payments at year-end. The interest rate is 14%.

The periodic payment equals $100,000/5.2161 = $19,171

Note: The present value of an ordinary annuity factor for $n = 10$, $i = 14\%$, is 5.2161.

Assuming the same information except that the annual payments are to be made at the beginning of each year, the periodic payment would equal $100,000/5.9464 = $16,817.

The interest rate associated with a lease agreement may also be computed. Divide the value of the leased property by the annual payment to obtain the factor, which is then used to find the interest rate using a present value of ordinary annuity table.

EXAMPLE

Coleman Company leased $300,000 of property and is to make equal annual payments at year-end of $40,000 for 11 years. The interest rate in the lease agreement is 7%. The factor equals $300,000/$40,000 = 7.5.

Going to the present value of an ordinary annuity table and looking across 11 years to a factor closest to 7.5 gives 7.4987 at a 7% interest rate. Therefore, the interest rate in the lease is 7%.

Capital Lease Method

A capital lease exists if any one of the following four criteria exists:

1. The lessee is to get property ownership at the end of the lease term. This criterion is still satisfied if ownership is transferred shortly after the end of the lease term.

2. A bargain purchase option exists in which the lessee can either buy the property at a minimal amount or renew the lease at very low rental payments relative to the "going rates."

3. The lease term is 75% or more of the life of the property.

4. The present value of minimum lease payments at the start of the lease equals or exceeds 90% of the fair market value of the property. Minimum lease payments do not include executory costs to be paid by the lessor, which are being reimbursed by the lessee. Examples of such costs are property taxes, insurance, and maintenance. Executory costs also include lessee payments to an unrelated third party to guarantee the residual value. When the lessor pays executory costs, any lessor's profit on such costs is construed the same as the executory costs.

If the lease term starts within the last 25% of the total life of the property (including earlier years of use), criteria 3 and 4 do not apply because the property has already been used for most of its life.

If criterion 1 or 2 is satisfied, the property is depreciated over its life. On the other hand, if criterion 3 or 4 is met, the lease term is the depreciation period.

The lease period cannot go past the date of exercisability of a bargain purchase option because it is presumed that the option will be exercised and the lease will terminate on that date.

The inception date of a lease is the date of agreement or commitment (if before) of the major provisions that are fixed in nature, with no major provisions yet to be settled.

The term of a lease may represent either a stated noncancellable period, a period covered by a bargain renewal option, the time period including a renewal term because of significant penalties that, in effect, assure renewal, the time period including extensions or renewals at the lessor's option, and the time period including renewal options because of the lessee's guarantee of the lessor's debt that is related to the leased property.

If a lease has a noncancellable period followed by cancelable renewal periods (e.g., yearly, semiannually), then only the noncancellable period should be taken into account when making a determination as to the classification of the lease.

In a capital lease, there is a transfer of substantial benefits and there are risks of property ownership to the lessee. A capital lease is treated for accounting purposes as if the lessee borrowed funds to buy the property.

In a capital lease, the asset and liability are presented at the inception date at the present (discounted) value of minimum lease payments plus the present (discounted) value of any bargain purchase option. It is anticipated that the lessee will take advantage of the nominal acquisition price. However, the asset cannot be recorded at more than its fair market value because that would violate conservatism. In other words, the asset would be recorded at the lower of the present value computation or the fair market value of the property. The liability is presented in the balance sheet at its current and noncurrent amounts.

In determining present value, the lessee uses as its discount rate the lower of the lessee's incremental borrowing rate if it was to buy the property outright at the inception of the lease or the lessor's desired (implicit) rate of return on the lease. According to FASB Technical Bulletin Number 79–12 (*Interest Rate Used in Calculating the Present Value of Minimum Lease Payments*), the lessee may use its secured borrowing interest rate as its incremental borrowing rate as long as such rate is logical in the circumstances.

The lessee's minimum lease payments typically include

- The lessee's penalty payment arising from not renewing or extending the lease upon expiration.

- Minimum lease payments over the rental period plus the lessee's guaranteed salvage value. The guarantee is the stated amount that the lessee agrees to pay the lessor for any deficiency below the stipulated amount in the lessor's realization of the residual value. FASB Technical Bulletin Number 79–14 (*Upward Adjustment of Guaranteed Residual Values*) does not allow any upward adjustments of guaranteed residual values in lease agreements. Reference should also be made to FASB Interpretation Number 19 (*Lessee Guarantee of the Residual Value of Leased Property*). Besides executory costs, minimum lease payments exclude the lessee's guarantee of the lessor's debt and any contingent rentals.

The executory costs paid by the lessee are expensed as incurred. Therefore, unless paid directly with cash, executory costs will be accrued.

If during the lease term the recorded value of a leased asset exceeds its market value, it should be written down recognizing a loss.

Each minimum lease payment is debited to the liability account for the principal portion and is debited to interest expense for the interest portion. Interest expense is computed under the interest method (sometimes termed the effective interest method), which results in a constant periodic interest rate. Interest expense equals the interest rate multiplied by the carrying (book) value of the liability at the beginning of the period.

The lessee will record depreciation expense on capitalized leased property. Depreciation expense equals the cost of the asset less the estimated residual value divided by the depreciable period.

Financial Accounting Standards Board Interpretation Number 26 provides that if a lessee purchases a leased asset during the lease term that was originally capitalized, the transaction is deemed an extension rather than a termination of a capital lease. The difference between the purchase price and the book value of the lease obligation is treated as an adjustment of the carrying value of the asset. No loss recognition is required on an extension of a capital lease.

In general, under the capital lease method, the lessee's journal entries are as follows:

AT INCEPTION OF LEASE:

    Asset (present value of future payments)

        Liability

AT THE END OF EACH YEAR, ASSUMING EACH PAYMENT IS MADE ON DECEMBER 31:

    Interest expense (interest)

    Liability (principal)

        Cash (interest and principal)

    Depreciation

        Accumulated depreciation

Under the capital lease method, the lessee reports in its balance sheet the leased asset and the associated liability. In the income statement, the lessee presents interest expense and depreciation expense.

EXAMPLE

On January 1, 19X3, the lessee engages in a capital lease for property. The minimum lease payment is $30,000 per year for six years payable at year-end. The interest rate is 5%. The present value of an ordinary annuity factor for $n = 6$, $i = 5\%$ is 5.0757. The journal entries for the first two years follow:

1/1/19X3		
Asset	152,271	
Liability		152,271
$30,000 \times 5.0757 = \$152,271$		
12/31/19X3		
Interest expense	7,614	
Liability	22,386	
Cash		30,000
$5\% \times \$152,271 = \$7,614$		
Depreciation expense	25,379	
Accumulated depreciation		25,379
$\$152,271/6$ years $= \$25,379$		

The liability as of December 31, 19X3 is

Liability

12/31/19X3	22,386	1/1/19X3	152,271
		12/31/19X3 Balance	129,885

12/31/19X4		
Interest expense	6,494	
Liability	23,506	
Cash		30,000
$5\% \times \$129,885 = \$6,494$		
Depreciation expense	25,379	
Accumulated depreciation		25,379

EXAMPLE

Levsee Corp. entered into a 10-year capital lease on a building on December 31, 2002. Lease payments of $62,000, which include real estate taxes of $2,000, are due annually, beginning December 31, 2003 and every December 31 thereafter for the lease term. Levsee does not know the interest implicit in the lease, but its (Levsee's) incremental borrowing rate is 10%. The rounded present value of an ordinary annuity for 10 years at 10% is 6.1. What amount should Levsee report as capitalized lease liability at December 31, 2002?

The problem indicates that this lease is a capital lease. In addition, since payments are due at the end of the period (year), we are dealing with an ordinary annuity. The question is to determine the initial lease liability of the lessee. In order to compute this number, we must calculate the present value of the minimum lease payments discounted at the incremental borrowing rate since the implicit rate in the lease is not known. In general, we choose the lessee's incremental borrowing rate. However, the implicit rate in the lease is substituted if it is known and it is lower than the incremental rate.

$$
\begin{aligned}
\text{Capitalized lease liability} &= \text{minimum lease payments} \\
&\quad \times \text{present value of an ordinary} \\
&\quad \text{annuity of 1 for ten years at 10\%} \\
&= (\$62{,}000 - \$2{,}000) \times 6.1 \\
&= \$60{,}000 \times 6.1 \\
&= \$366{,}000
\end{aligned}
$$

Levsee Corp., the lessee, should report the capitalized lease liability as $366,000.

EXAMPLE

Joel Co. leased a machine for 10 years, its useful life, and agreed to pay $25,000 at the start of the lease term on December 31, 2001. As part of the agreement, it was also required to continue such payments each December 31 for the next nine years. The present value on December 31, 2001 of the 10 lease payments over the lease term, using the implicit rate of interest known to Joel Co. of 8%, is \$181,250. The present value of the lease payments using Joel's incremental borrowing rate of 10% is \$169,000. Joel Co. made a timely second lease payment. What amount should Joel report as its capital lease liability in its December 31, 2002 balance sheet?

In this problem, it is stated that the lease is a capital lease. In addition, because all lease payments are being made at the beginning of the period by the lesee, the lease represents an annuity due. Also, since the implicit rate in the lease is known and it is lower than Joel's incremental rate (10%), the discount rate that should be used is the 8% rate. Therefore, Joel should originally record the capitalized lease (long-term asset and liability) at \$181,250. This amount was derived in the following way:

Present value of minimum lease payments = \$25,000 × present value
of 1 for 10 years at 8%
= \$25,000 × 7.25
= \$181,250

Present value of minimum lease payments at 12/31/2001		\$181,250
Less: Payment at 12/31/2001		25,000
Liability balance, 1/1/01–12/31/02		\$156,250
Less: Payment at 12/31/02	\$25,000	
Less: Portion of payment applicable to interest during 2002, \$156,200 × 8%	12,496	12,504
Capital lease at December 31, 2002		\$143,746

There are a number of considerations regarding residual value. A contractual clause mandating the lessee to pay for a deficiency in residual value applicable to unusual wear and tear, damage, or very significant usage is not deemed a lease guarantee in computing the discounted value of the minimum lease payments. This kind of guarantee is indeterminable at the lease inception date. As a result, it should be treated as a contingent rental. If a lessee receives a residual value guarantee from an unrelated third party to benefit the lessor, the guarantee should not be used to reduce the minimum lease payments unless the lessor releases the lessee from the obligation to make up all or part of the residual value deficiency. Any payments by a lessee to a third party to secure a guarantee are treated as executory costs. As such, they are not included in computing the minimum lease payments. According to FASB Technical Bulletin Number 86–2 (*Accounting for an Interest in the Residual Value of a Leased Asset*), the purchase by a third party from a lessor of the unconditional right to own property at the end of the lease term should be accounted for as a purchase of an asset at the time the right is acquired.

The capital lease is presented in the lessee's balance sheet under noncurrent assets as follows:

Asset under lease
Less: Accumulated depreciation
Book value

In the lessee's income statement, the capital lease shows interest expense and depreciation expense.

In the beginning years, expenses reported under a capital lease (interest expense and depreciation expense) exceed those under an operating lease (rent expense).

The lessee should make the following footnote disclosures:

- Assets under lease by category
- Sublease rentals
- Contingent rentals (rentals depending on something other than time such as sales) (Contingent rentals may increase or reduce rental payments.)
- Future minimum lease payments in the aggregate and for each of the next five years
- Description of the rental arrangement, such as expiration date of lease, purchase options, escalation clauses, renewal term, and leasing restrictions (e.g., additional leasing activity, additional debt, dividend ceilings)
- Nature and degree of leasing activity with related parties

FASB Technical Bulletin Number 82–1 (*Disclosure of the Sale or Purchase of Tax Benefits Through Tax Leases*) requires disclosure of information concerning tax leases.

LESSOR

There are three possible methods a lessor may use to account for leases as follows:

- Operating method
- Direct financing method
- Sales-type method

Operating Method

The operating method is a regular rental by the lessor, such as Hertz's leasing of automobiles to companies. With the operating method, the lessor recognizes rental income less applicable expenses (e.g., repairs, depreciation, insurance, taxes). Rental income is recognized as earned under the straight-line method over the lease period except if another method is more appropriate. Contingent rentals are accrued as earned. Therefore, the lessor's income statement under the operating method will show rental revenue less expenses. The balance sheet presents the asset under lease less accumulated depreciation to derive book value.

Initial direct costs are deferred and amortized proportionately over the lease term based on the rental revenue recognized. However, if initial direct costs are insignificant in amount, they may be immediately charged against earnings. Initial direct costs are those related to negotiating and closing a lease. Reference should be made to the FASB Implementation Guide (*Questions and Answers*) to FASB Statement Number 91 (*Accounting for Refundable Fees and Costs Associated with Originating or Acquiring Loans and Initial Direct Costs to Leases*).

If the lessor makes incentive payments to the lessee to motivate the lessee to sign the contract, such payments should be amortized against rental revenue over the lease term. The payment is charged to a deferred lease incentive account (an asset) and credited to cash. The amortization of the deferred lease incentive account should be based on the straight-line method.

If the lessor assumes a lessee's preexisting lease with a third party, the lessor should treat any resulting loss as a rent incentive. The loss should be determined after taking into account the costs incurred less any anticipated benefits arising from a sublease or use of the property.

EXAMPLE

Dan Company leased office space from Ron Co. for a five-year term beginning January 2, 2002. Under the requirements of the operating lease, rent for the first year would be $9,000 and rent for the following year through year 5 (that is, year 2 through year 5) would be $12,000 per year. Ron Co. offered Dan Company an inducement to enter the lease. The inducement consisted of waiving the rental payments for the first six months of the lease, making this period rent free for Dan. In its December 31, 2002 income statement, what amount should Ron report as rental income?

The problem specifies that this is an operating lease. Under an operating lease, rental revenue should be recognized on a straight-line basis unless it is shown that some other systematic methodology is deemed to be more representative. Therefore, total rental revenue should be evenly recognized over all the years of the operating lease.

The following computation should be made. The total revenue over the life of the lease is

1. $\frac{1}{2} \times 9,000 = \$4,500$ for the first year (since the first six months are rent free) plus

2. $\$12,000 \times 4$ years $= \$48,000$ (years 2 through 5)

   Therefore, total rental revenue over the life of the lease $= \$4,500 + \$48,000 = \$52,500$.

In its December 31, 2002 income statement, Ron should record $52,500/5 years $= \$10,500$.

EXAMPLE

On April 1, 19X2, XYZ Company manufactured equipment costing $600,000, which it leased out under the operating method. The lease is for 10 years, with equal monthly payments of $6,000 payable at the beginning of each month. The first payment was made on April 1, 19X2. The depreciation period is 12 years, with a salvage value of $40,000.

The lessor reports the following for 19X2 for the period 4/1 to 12/31:

Rental revenue ($6,000 × 9 months)	$54,000
Less: Depreciation expense ($600,000/12 years × 9/12)	37,500
Income before tax	$16,500

The lessor determines the amount of rental based on its desired rate of return. The return the lessor will seek depends on such factors as the financial standing of the lessee, period of rental, and technological risk. The rental payment is often based on a present value computation.

EXAMPLE

The fair market value of leased equipment is $300,000 and the discounted (present) value of the residual (salvage) value is $20,000. There will be five beginning-of-year lease payments to yield a 10% return. The annual rental payments are computed as follows:

Fair market value of leased equipment	$300,000
Less: Present value of residual value	20,000
Recoverable amount	$280,000
Annual rental equals	
Recoverable amount/present value factor for $n = 5$, $i = 10\%$	

$$\$280,000/4.16986 = \$67,149$$

Direct Financing Method

The direct financing method meets one of the four criteria for a capital lease by the lessee plus both of the following two criteria for the lessor:

1. No significant uncertainties are present with respect to future costs to be incurred. However, a performance guarantee might present a significant uncertainty, negating this condition. Unusual and uncustomary warranties and commitments represent important uncertainties that violate this condition. **Note:** FASB Statement Number 23 (*Inception of the Lease*) states that if leased property has not been built or bought by the lessor at the lease date, this criterion is applied at the construction completion date or the date the property is bought.

2. There is assurance of lease payments being collected. This condition is met even if some uncollectibility is expected as long as payment can be reasonably estimated. However, if credit risks are substantial, this criterion is negated.

The lessor is not a manufacturer or dealer in the item. The lessor buys the property only to lease it out for a profit. The lease is treated as a financing arrangement. An example is an insurance company renting electronic equipment.

In a direct financing lease, the book value and fair value of the leased property are the same at the inception of the lease. In consequence, no gain or loss arises.

Note: Although in a direct financing arrangement, the fair value of the property is usually the same as its cost, market conditions need to be taken into account, particularly when there is a long time period between the time of lease and the purchase or construction of the property.

The lessor uses as the discount rate in determining the present value of future minimum lease payments its desired rate of return (implicit rate). The implicit rate is the rate that discounts the lease payments and the unguaranteed residual value to the property's fair value at the time of lease.

Note: The lessor's minimum lease payments are identical to the lessee's except that the lessor includes a guarantee of the lease payments or residual value after the lease term by a third party as long as that party is financially healthy to meet its commitments.

Interest revenue is computed under the interest method. Interest revenue equals the interest rate multiplied by the carrying (book) value of the receivable at the beginning of the period. In effect, unearned interest revenue is amortized over the lease term, resulting in a constant interest rate. Contingent rentals are recognized as earned.

The lessor's minimum lease payments include

- The minimum lease payments to be paid by the lessee
- Any guarantee of residual value of the leased item or of rental payments after the lease term, made by an unrelated, financially sound third party

If a change in lease term occurs that would have meant an initially different lease classification, then the lease is deemed to be a new arrangement and should be classified and treated for accounting purposes under the new terms. However, exercising a renewal option is not considered an alteration of the lease. Further, a change in estimate does not mean a new lease.

An escalation clause related to the minimum lease payments during a construction or preacquisition period may be involved. The ensuing increase in minimum lease payments is used to determine the leased item's fair value at the time of lease. Further, a change in residual value may also arise due to the escalation provision.

Initial direct costs are paid or accrued by the lessor to negotiate and finalize a lease. Examples are finders' commissions, attorney fees, credit appraisal, negotiating and processing fees, and an allocated portion of salesperson and employee compensation. In a direct financing lease, such costs are included in the gross receivable (investment). Initial direct costs do not include costs for failed lease opportunities, advertising and solicitation, and indirect costs (e.g., administrative, supervisory). The initial direct costs under a direct financing lease are amortized over the lease period using the interest method.

A portion of unearned income equal to the initial direct costs is recorded as income in the same accounting period.

If the leasing contract includes a penalty clause for not renewing and the penalty does not apply because of renewal or time extension, an adjustment must be made to the unearned interest income account for the difference between the present values of the original and revised agreements. The discounted value of future minimum lease payments under the new contract should be determined using the rate in the original lease.

Lease termination is accounted for by the lessor through eliminating the net investment and recording the leased property at the lower of cost or fair value. The net investment is then charged against earnings.

Contingent rentals are immediately recognized in earnings. They are not included in computing minimum lease payments.

Note: Contingent rentals do not include lessee reimbursement to the lessor of any tax savings because of a change in tax legislation.

FASB Statement Number 91 (*Accounting for Nonrefundable Fees and Costs Associated with Originating or Acquiring Loans*) provides for the accounting treatment of nonrefundable fees and expenses related to lending activities, including buying loans. The lessor's loan origination charges and associated costs are deferred and amortized over the loan period. Yield is adjusted accordingly.

In general, the journal entries under the direct financing method follow:

AT DATE OF LEASE

    Gross receivable (total payments equal to principal + interest)

      Asset (principal)

      Unearned interest revenue (total interest)

Note: The difference between the gross receivable (investment) and the carrying value of the leased property (asset) equals unearned interest revenue.

AT EACH DATE OF RECEIPT OF RENTAL PAYMENT

> Cash (amount of receipt including principal and interest portion)
> > Gross receivable
> Unearned interest revenue
> > Interest revenue (interest earned for period)

On the balance sheet, the lessor reports as gross receivables (investment) the total minimum lease payments (net of any included executory costs and associated profits to be paid by the lessor) plus the unguaranteed residual value of the property belonging to the lessor at the end of the lease period. The unearned interest revenue account is deducted from gross receivables (investment) to obtain net receivables (investment). In summary, net receivables (investment) equals the gross receivables plus unamortized initial direct costs less the unearned interest income. The net receivables is classified as current or noncurrent depending upon whether collection will be made within one year from the balance sheet date. The presentation in the balance sheet follows:

> Gross lease payments receivable (principal + interest)
> Less: Unearned interest revenue (interest)
> Net Lease payments receivable (principal)

In the income statement, the following is presented:

> Interest revenue
> Less: Executory costs
> Net Income

Note: The income statement may also include a loss associated with a permanent decline in the unguaranteed residual value requiring a write-down of the net receivable (investment) in the lease. However, the unguaranteed residual value should not be written up because to do so violates conservatism.

Sales-Type Method

A sales-type lease is sometimes entered into by the lessor in order to improve the marketability of a costly asset. A sales-type lease must meet the same criteria as that of a direct financing lease. The only difference is that the former involves a lessor who is either the producer or dealer in the leased item. Therefore, a manufacturer or dealer profit arises. In a sales-type arrangement the book value of the leased property differs from its fair value (price the property may be exchanged for between unrelated parties in an arms-length agreement), resulting in a gain or loss to the lessor. Even though no legal sale has occurred, theoretical substance comes before legal form, and a sale is presumed to have occurred. An example of a sales-type lease is a manufacturer of a computer or photocopy system leasing it to a lessee with the option of the lessee purchasing it.

The differentiation between a sales-type lease and a direct financing lease is only of concern to the lessor. The lessee still uses the capital lease method irrespective of which of the two methods the lessor uses.

In a sales-type lease, profit on the assumed sale of the property is recorded in the year of the lease as well as interest income over the lease term. The interest income calculation is based on the interest method. At inception of the lease, the cost and fair value (usually the normal selling price) of the leased item are different. Therefore, under the sales-type method, there is both a profit and financial income component.

Each year the salvage value of the property should be evaluated. Such appraisal may require loss recognition with a reduction of the net receivable (investment).

Against the sales price is matched the cost of the leased item so as to obtain the assumed profit in the year of lease. Cost of sales equals the cost (or carrying value) of the leased property reduced by the discounted value of any unguaranteed residual value. In a sales-type lease, initial direct costs are immediately expensed.

Note: A lessor must recognize immediately in the current year's income statement a loss on selling peripheral equipment as a marketing strategy.

In general, under the sales-type method, the journal entries are

AT DATE OF LEASE

> Gross receivable (total payments equal to principal + interest)
>> Sales (assumed selling price of leased item)
>> Unearned Interest revenue (total interest)
> Cost of sales (cost of assumed item sold)
>> Inventory

Note: The gross receivable (investment) in lease equals the total minimum lease payments to be received (net of executory costs and any associated profits to be paid by the lessor) plus the unguaranteed salvage (residual) value accruing to the lessor at the termination date of the lease. However, the estimated unguaranteed residual value may not be more than the amount of residual value estimated at lease inception. If the salvage value was guaranteed, it would be included in the minimum lease payments.

AT EACH DATE OF RENTAL RECEIPT

> Cash (amount received equal to principal and interest)
>> Gross receivable
> Unearned interest revenue
>> Interest Revenue (interest earned)

Under the sales type method, the balance sheet is identical to that of the direct financing method, namely

> Gross lease payments receivable (principal + interest)
> Less: unearned interest revenue (interest)
> Net lease payments receivable (principal)

Note: The lease payments receivable to be collected within one year should be classified as a current asset.

Under the sales-type method, the income statement in the first year only will show

> Interest revenue
> Gross profit on leased item (sales less cost of sales)
> Less: executory costs
>> Initial direct costs (e.g., attorney fees, commissions)

In the second year and thereafter the income statement will show

> Interest revenue
>
> Less: executory costs

The journal entries under the sales-type method are generally the same as those under the direct financing method, with the exception of the initial entry. This is illustrated in the following example.

EXAMPLE

On January 1, 19X3, the lessor leases property to the lessee. The lessee accounts for the lease under the capital lease method. The minimum lease payments are $30,000 per year for six years payable at year-end. The interest rate is 5%. The present value of an ordinary annuity factor for $n = 6$, $i = 5\%$ is 5.0757. The cost of the leased property is $120,000. (Note that this problem is identical to the one illustrated previously under the capital lease method used by the lessee. The calculations were provided in that example.) The lessor's accounting, assuming a direct financing lease and a sales-type lease, follows:

Direct Financing Lease		
1/1/19X3		
Gross receivable (6 × $30,000)	180,000	
Asset (5.0757 × $30,000)		152,271
Unearned interest revenue		27,729
12/31/19X3		
Cash	30,000	
Gross Receivable		30,000
Unearned interest revenue	7,614	
Interest Revenue (5% × $152,271)		7,614

The balance sheet as of December 31, 19X3 presents the following:

Gross Receivable	$150,000
Less: Unearned interest revenue ($27,729 − $7614)	20,115
Net Receivables	$129,885

The income statement for 19X3 presents interest revenue of $7,614.

12/31/19X4		
Cash	30,000	
Gross receivable		30,000
Unearned interest revenue	6,494	
Interest revenue (5% × $129,885*)		6,494

*$30,000 – $7,614 = $22,386. $152,271 – $22,386 = $ 129,885.

The balance sheet as of December 31, 19X4 shows

Gross receivable	$120,000
Less: Unearned interest revenue ($20,115 – $6,494)	13,621
Net Receivable	$106,379

The income statement for 19X4 presents interest revenue of $6,494.

Sales-Type Lease

1/1/19X3		
Gross receivable	180,000	
Sales		152,271
Unearned interest revenue		27,729
Cost of sales	120,000	
Inventory		120,000

All other entries at year-end 19X3 and 19X4 are the same as that under the direct financing method in this set of facts.

The balance sheets at year-end 19X3 and 19X4 are also the same as that under the direct financing method. However, the income statement in the year of lease (19X3) will not only show the interest revenue of $7,614 but also the assumed gross profit on the sale of the item in the year of lease. In this example, the gross profit equals $32,271 (sales of $152,271 less cost of sales of $120,000). The income statement after 19X3 will be the same as that under the direct financing method based on the facts in this particular example.

EXAMPLE

On January 1, 19X2, Coleman Company leased equipment to a lessee under a sales-type lease. There will be 11 annual rentals of $10,000 beginning on January 1, 19X2. Further, the lessee will make an initial payment of $5,000 on the date of lease. The lessee will buy the property at the termination date of the lease for $5. The implicit interest rate is 10%. The book value of the leased property on Coleman Company's records is $45,000.

On January 1, 19X2, the gross receivable in the lease equals $115,000, calculated as follows:

Total lease payments($10,000 × 11 payments)	$110,000
Down payment	5,000
Gross receivable (investment)	$115,000

The present (discounted) value of the gross receivable (investment) equals $76,450, computed as follows:

Present value of future payments ($10,000 × 6.145*)	$61,450
Payment made on 1/1/19X2 ($10,000 + $5,000)	15,000
Total	$76,450

*The present value factor for $n = 10$, $i = 10\%$ is 6.145

The journal entry on January 1, 19X2 follows:

Gross lease receivable	115,000	
Equipment		45,000
Unearned interest income ($115,000 – $76,450)		38,550
Gain on sale of asset		31,450

EXAMPLE

On October 1, 19X4, Mavis Company leased machinery to Buyko Company. The lease is treated as a sales type by the lessor and as a capital lease by the lessee. The lease period is 10 years, with equal annual payments of $400,000 due on October 1 each period. The first payment was made on October 1, 19X4. The machinery cost Mavis $1,800,000. It has a life of 12 years with a salvage value of $200,000. The relevant interest rate is 10%.

Buyko, the lessee, will make the following calculations:

> Present value of lease payments equals
>   ($400,000 × 5.868*) = $2,347,200
>   ─────────────────────────────────
>   *Present value of ordinary annuity factor.

Therefore, the asset will be recorded at $2,347,200.

Buyko presents the following in its income statement for 19X4:

Depreciation expense:	
[($2,347,200 – $200,000)/12 years × 3/12]	$44,733
Interest expense ($1,947,200* × 10% × 3/12)	$48,680

*Present value of lease payments	$2,347,200
Less: Initial payment	400,000
Balance at beginning of lease	$1,947,200

Mavis, the lessor, presents the following in its income statement for 19X4:

Interest revenue		$48,680
Gross profit:		
Sales	$2,347,200	
Less: Cost	1,800,000	547,200

EXAMPLE

Carol Company leased a truck to Queens Corp. on January 2, 2002 for a seven-year period. Equal lease payments of $500,000 are due at the beginning of each year beginning January 2, 2002. The carrying cost of the machine is $1,800,000. The lease expires January 2, 2009. The lease is accounted for as a sales-type lease. The lessor's interest rate is 10%. What amount of profit on the sale should Carol report for the year ended December 31, 2002?

The problem denotes that the lease is appropriately accounted for by the lessor (Carol) as a sales-type lease. The machine's sales price may be derived by calculating present value of the lease payments discounted at the lessor's interest rate (10%).

Sales price of the machine = $500,000 × present value of an annuity due
of 1 for 7 years discounted at 10%

= $500,000 × 5.35526

= $2,677,630

The profit on the sale is the difference between the sales price of the
machine and the lessor's carrying value of the asset sold. That is,

$$\$2,677,630 - \$1,800,000 = \$877,630$$

EXAMPLE

Dauber Company, a dealer in equipment and machinery, leased equipment
to Greene, Inc. on July 1, 19X1. The lease is appropriately accounted for as
a sale by Dauber and as a purchase by Greene. The lease is for a 10-year
period (the useful life of the asset). The first of 10 equal annual payments
of $500,000 was made on July 1, 19X1. Dauber had purchased the equip-
ment for $2,675,000 on January 1, 19X1 and set a list selling price of
$3,375,000 on the equipment. Assume that the present value at July 1, 19X1
of the minimum rental payments over the lease term discounted at 12%
(the appropriate interest rate) was $3,165,000.

The entries for the lessor using the sales-type method follow:

TO RECORD THE SALE ON JULY 1, 19X1:

Lease payments receivable	5,000,000	
Sales		3,165,000
Unearned interest revenue		1,835,000
Cost of sales	2,675,000	
Equipment		2,675,000

TO RECORD THE PAYMENT ON JULY 1, 19X1:

Cash	500,000	
Lease payments receivable		500,000

TO RECORD INTEREST REVENUE ON DECEMBER 31, 19X1:

Unearned interest revenue	159,900	
Interest revenue		159,900*

*Sales price	$3,165,000
Payment, 7/1/19X1	500,000
Outstanding balance, 7/1/19X1	$2,665,000

Interest $2,665,000 x 12% x 6/12 = $159,900

The entries for the lessee follow:

TO RECORD THE PURCHASE ON JULY 1, 19X1:

Leased equipment	3,165,000	
Liability		3,165,000

TO RECORD THE PAYMENT ON JULY 1, 19X1:

Liability	500,000	
Cash		500,000

TO RECORD INTEREST EXPENSE AND DEPRECIATION ON DECEMBER 31, 19X1:

Interest expense ($2,665,000 × .12 × 6/12)	159,900	
Depreciation expense ($3,165,000/10 × 6/12)	158,250	
Accrued interest payable		159,900
Accumulated depreciation		158,250

Lessors should footnote the following:

- Major types of assets leased
- Components of the net investment
- Lease provisions, including interest rate, term, restrictions, renewal options, escalation clauses, and disposition of property when the lease expires
- Executory costs
- Initial direct costs
- Unearned interest revenue
- Contingent rentals
- Future minimum lease payments in the aggregate and for each of the next five years

■ Lessee defaults and allowance for uncollectibles

■ Unguaranteed residual values accruing to the lessor's benefit

■ Nature and amount of third-party financing

■ Leasing activities with related parties

■ Tax treatment of the lease

RESIDUAL VALUE CONSIDERATIONS

A leased asset's residual (salvage) value is how much it is worth at the end of the lease. In most cases residual value goes to the lessor's benefit. However, it occasionally may accrue to a nonlessor (e.g., lessee, lease broker).

Unguaranteed residual value is defined as the expected residual value of the leased property excluding any part guaranteed by the lessee, by a related party to the lessee, or by a third party. However, if the guarantor is associated with the lessor, the residual value is deemed unguaranteed.

A periodic review (at least yearly) should be made to ascertain whether there has been a permanent decline in the estimated unguaranteed residual values associated with direct financing or sales-type leases. If a permanent decline has occurred, the new estimated life should be used and any ensuing loss recognized in the year the change in estimate was made. However, no adjustment is made for a temporary decline. As noted before, an upward adjustment is prohibited either to unguaranteed or guaranteed residual values.

FASB Statement Number 23 (*Inception of the Lease*) allows an increase in the estimated residual value taking place because of an escalation clause in the lease contract for leased property bought or built by the lessor. Assume that the residual value was estimated at $50,000 when the lease was originally signed and during the construction period the leased property increased in fair value by $5,000. The escalation provision allows for an increase in residual value to $55,000.

FASB Statement Number 125 (*Transfers of Financial Assets and Extinguishment of Liabilities*) and FASB Technical Bulletin Number 86–2 (*Accounting for an Interest in the Residual Value of a Leased Asset*) discuss the transfers of residual value. When there has been a purchase of interests in residual values of leased property by companies whose major business activity is not leasing nor financing, such rights should be accounted for by the buyer at the fair value of the assets received. The purchaser may be either buying the right to own the leased property or the right to receive the sales proceeds of the leased property at the end of the lease period. If there has been an increase in value of the financial interest in the residual value after purchase but before the end of the lease period, it may be recorded for guaranteed residual values since they are financial assets. However, no accreditation in residual value is allowed for unguaranteed residual values. A permanent loss in residual value should be recognized immediately.

TRANSFER OF LEASE RECEIVABLE

The lessor may transfer a lease receivable. The gain on sale equals the cash received less both the portion of the gross investment sold applicable to the minimum lease payments and the unearned income related to the minimum lease payments.

EXAMPLE

A lessor has on its books a lease receivable with an unguaranteed residual value. Unlike guaranteed residual value, unguaranteed residual value does not qualify as a financial asset. The lessor sells an 80% interest in the minimum lease payments for $100,000. The lessor retains a 20% interest in the minimum lease payments and a 100% interest in the unguaranteed residual value. Other data follow:

Minimum lease payments		$110,000
Unearned income in minimum lease payments		75,000
Gross investment in minimum lease payments		$185,000
Unguaranteed residual value	$7,000	
Unguaranteed income in residual value	13,000	
Gross investment in residual value		20,000
Gross investment in lease receivable		$205,000

The journal entry for the sale of the lease receivable is

Cash	100,000	
Unearned income ($75,000 × 80%)	60,000	
Lease receivable ($185,000 × 80%)		148,000
Gain on sale		12,000

SALES-LEASEBACK

As per FASB Statement Number 28 (*Accounting for Sales with Leasebacks*), a sales-leaseback takes place when the lessor sells the asset (e.g., equipment) and then leases all or some of it back. However, there is no physical transfer of the property. The seller is referred to as the seller-lessee, while the buyer is termed the buyer-lessor. Possible reasons for a sale-leaseback are to raise needed funds or to achieve a tax benefit.

The profit or loss on the sale is deferred and amortized proportionately as an adjustment to depreciation expense if a capital lease, or proportionately to rent expense if an operating lease. (The deferred gain is classified as a deferred credit if an operating lease or an asset valuation offset if a capital lease.) However, if the fair value of the equipment at the date of sales-leaseback is less than its book value, a loss is immediately recognized for that difference. Emerging Issues Task Force Consensus Summary Number 89–16 (*Considerations of Executory Costs in Sale-Leaseback Transactions*) specifies that executory costs are excluded in computing the profit to be deferred on a sale-leaseback. Emerging Issues Task Force Consensus Summary Number 86–17 applies to the deferred profit on a sale-leaseback transaction with lessee guarantee of residual value.

If the seller leases back just a minor part (discounted value of lease-back rentals is 10% or less of the fair market value of the property sold) of the remaining use of the property sold, the gain or loss is immediately recognized. However, part of the gain or loss must be deferred and amortized so as to adjust the rental to a reasonable figure if the rental amount differs from prevailing market conditions.

If the seller leases back more than a minor but less than significantly all of the use of the sold property, there is immediate recognition of part of the gain if it is more than the discounted value of the minimum lease payments if the leaseback is an operating lease or it is more than the amount capitalized when the leaseback is considered a capital lease. The excess amount in both cases is recognized immediately, with the balance being deferred and amortized.

The journal entries associated with a sales-leaseback arrangement are

> *AT THE TIME OF SALE:*
> Cash (amount received)
>> Asset (cost)
>> Deferred gross profit (deferred profit)
>
> *AT YEAR-END, WHEN A RENTAL PAYMENT IS MADE ASSUMING AN OPERATING LEASE:*
> Rent expense (rental payment)
>> Cash
> Deferred gross profit (amortized profit for the period)
>> Rent expense

EXAMPLE

On January 1, 19X1, an asset costing $200,000 was sold for $280,000. The property was then leased back under an operating lease. The deferred profit on the sales-leaseback is $80,000 ($280,000 – $200,000). Assume that rental expense in 19X1 was $15,000 and total rentals are estimated at $120,000. The journal entries are

1/1/19X1

Cash	280,000	
Asset		200,000
Deferred gross profit		80,000

12/31/19X4

Rent expense	15,000	
Cash		15,000
Deferred gross profit	10,000	
Rent expense		10,000

$$\$80,000 \times \$15,000/\$120,000 = \$10,000$$

Rental expense is adjusted as follows:

Rental expense	$15,000
Less: Amortization of deferred gross profit	10,000
Net Rental Expense	$ 5,000

EXAMPLE

X Company sold property and then leased it back as a capital lease for 20 years. The selling price was $1,000,000, the fair value of the property was $1,150,000, and the book value was $1,250,000. The transaction results in a loss of $250,000 (selling price of $1,000,000 less book value of $1,250,000). The loss recognized immediately is $100,000 (book value of $1,250,000 less fair market value of $1,150,000). The remaining loss of $150,000 ($250,000 less $100,000) is deferred and amortized over the useful life of the property. The journal entry for the sales-leaseback transaction follows:

Cash	1,000,000	
Deferred loss	150,000	
Recognized loss (sales-leaseback)	100,000	
Property		1,250,000

EXAMPLE

Travis Company sells a building and then leases part of it for 10 years. The selling price was $500,000 and the book value was $400,000 (cost of

$450,000 less accumulated depreciation of $50,000). The discounted value of the minimum leaseback rental is $20,000.

The leaseback represents a minor part of the building because $20,000 is less than $50,000 ($500,000 × 10%). As such, the sale is a separate transaction. The journal entry is

Cash	500,000	
Accumulated depreciation	50,000	
Building		450,000
Gain		100,000

The buyer-lessor must classify the lease as either an operating or direct financing one. It cannot treat it as a sales-type lease.

As per FASB Statement Number 98 (*Accounting for Leases*), a partial sale transaction may preclude the use of sale-leaseback accounting if there is a continuing involvement of the seller-lessee in ownership of the property. Sales-leaseback accounting is also not appropriate when the seller-lessee requires a buyer-lessor to refinance the debt associated with the property and pass through any interest savings to the seller-lessee.

If a sale-leaseback arrangement does not qualify for sale-leaseback accounting and reporting, it should be handled under either the deposit method or the financing method, enumerated as follows:

- The deposit method involves crediting the down payment and collections on the note (principal and interest) to a deposit liability account. As rental payments are made, the liability is reduced.

- The financing method credits a liability for the down payment and collections on the note (principal and interest). Lease payments are allocated to interest expense and reducing the financing obligation. Interest expense is computed under the interest method, in which the effective interest rate is multiplied by the carrying value of the liability at the beginning of the period.

Even though the deposit method or financing method has been used, the seller-lessee should convert to sale-leaseback accounting when the conditions for sale-leaseback treatment are satisfied.

According to Emerging Issues Task Force Consensus Summary Number 88–21 (*Accounting for the Sale of Property Subject to the Seller's Preexisting Lease*), a sale-leaseback transaction is still recognized if a preexisting lease is modified in accordance with the terms of sale. An exercise of a renewal option or sublease clause in the preexisting lease does not affect the accounting for the transaction.

Emerging Issues Task Force Consensus Summary Number 93–8 discusses the accounting for the sale and leaseback of an asset that is leased to another party.

Emerging Issues Task Force Consensus Summary Number 84–37 applies to sale-leaseback transactions with repurchase options.

Emerging Issues Task Force Consensus Summary Number 90–14 deals with an unsecured guarantee by a parent of its subsidiary's lease payments in a sale-leaseback transaction. Sales-leaseback accounting may still be used even if there is an unsecured guarantee of one member of the consolidated group for the lease payments of another member of that group.

Emerging Issues Task Force Consensus Summary Number 90–20 considers the impact of an uncollateralized irrevocable letter of credit on a real estate sale-leaseback transaction.

Refer to Emerging Issues Task Force Consensus Summary Number 95–4 for the treatment of revenue recognition on equipment sold and subsequently repurchased subject to an operating lease.

Footnote disclosure for a sale-leaseback includes the provisions of the agreement, such as the terms regarding future commitments, duties, and responsibilities of the parties.

SUBLEASES AND SIMILAR ARRANGEMENTS

A sublease occurs when the original lessee re-leases the leased property to a third party, called the *sublessee*. The original lessee is termed the *sublessor*. In most cases, the sublease contract does not impact the original lease agreement. The original lessee, who is now the sublessor, still has primary liability.

There are three kinds of subleases:

- The new lease replaces and cancels the old one.
- The new lease is substituted under the initial agreement. The original lessee may still be secondarily liable.
- The original lessee rents the property to a third party. The lease contract of the original parties continues.

The original lessor continues its current accounting method if the initial lessee subleases or sells to a third party. If the original lease is substituted by a new arrangement with a new lessee, the lessor terminates the initial lease and accounts for the new lease in a separate transaction.

In accounting by the original lessee, if the original lessee is relieved of primary obligation by a transaction other than a sublease, the original lease should be terminated. The accounting procedure is as follows:

- If the original lease was a capital lease, remove the asset and liability and recognize a gain or loss for the difference, including any consideration paid or received. In addition, if a secondary liability exists, a loss contingency should be accrued.
- If the original lease was an operating lease and the initial lessee is secondarily responsible, a loss contingency should be accrued.

If the original lessee is not relieved of the primary obligation under a sublease, the initial lessee (now sublessor) accounts in the following way:

- If the original lease satisfied criterion 1 or 2 of a capital lease, the new lease should be classified as per the lessor's normal classification criteria. If the sublease is a sales type or direct financing one, the unamortized asset balance becomes the cost of the leased property. Otherwise, it is an operating lease. The original lease obligation should continue to be accounted for as previously.

- If the original lease satisfied criterion 3 or 4 of a capital lease, classify the new lease using lessor criteria 1 and 2. Classify as a direct financing lease. The unamortized balance of the asset becomes the cost of the leased equipment. Otherwise, it is an operating lease. Continue to account for the original lease obligation as previously.

If the original lease was an operating lease, account for the old and new leases as operating leases.

As per FASB Technical Bulletin Number 79–15 (*Accounting for Loss on a Sublease Not Involving the Disposal of a Segment*), losses on subleases should be immediately recognized. The amount of loss is the excess of costs to be incurred over the expected revenue to be received over the term of the sublease.

If a lessee is secondarily liable for a lease, disclosure should be made of that contingency and any associated risks.

MODIFICATIONS AND TERMINATIONS

If the terms of a lease are changed and the revisions thereto would have caused a different classification if they existed when the lease was originally signed, the revised lease should be considered as a new agreement over its remaining life and classified accordingly. Accounts may need adjustment to what they would have been assuming the revised terms had been in effect at the inception date of the lease.

With regard to the lessee, assume that the revised terms apply to what was accounted for as a capital lease. If the revised lease would have been an operating one rather than a capital lease, the asset and liability should be eliminated, with a gain or loss recorded for the difference. The modified lease would be accounted for as an operating one in future years. On the other hand, if the modification changes the remaining minimum lease payments but remains intact, the capital lease classification, the asset, and the lease liability should be revised to the discounted value of the remaining minimum lease payments. No gain or loss is recognized. If the modified provisions in an operating lease would have resulted in it being a capital lease at inception, the revised lease is considered a new contract. An asset and liability is recorded for the discounted value of the future minimum lease payments.

With regard to the lessor, if there is a revision to the terms of a direct financing lease or sales-type lease that would have resulted in it being considered an operating lease at inception, the following accounting adjustments are necessary: (1) Write off the net investment in the lease; (2) show the leased asset at the lower of initial cost, current fair value, or current carrying value; (3) recognize a loss for the difference between the net investment in the lease and the amount the asset is recorded at on the lessor's books (a gain will not occur since the asset cannot be presented at more than the net investment); and (4) account for the lease in later years as an operating one. If the modified terms to a direct financing lease or sales-type lease only change the remaining minimum lease payments and not the classification, the following adjustments are needed: (1) Adjust the gross investment in the lease to conform to the new minimum lease payments receivable and the revised salvage value (however, the residual value estimate cannot be more than the amount originally estimated), and (2) decrease or increase unearned income for the net adjustment. If modifications to an operating lease would have resulted in it being considered as a sales-type or direct financing one at inception, the revised lease should be considered as a new agreement.

Emerging Issues Task Force Consensus Summary Number 95–17 (*Accounting for Modifications to an Operating Lease That Do Not Change the Lease Classification*) states that if a modification is made to future rental payments, the increase should be amortized over the remaining period of the revised lease. However, if the modification is considered a termination penalty, it should be recognized in the year of revision. The termination penalty, is the amount by which the revised rentals exceed the original rentals that would have been made over the shortened lease period.

According to FASB Interpretation Number 26 (*Accounting for Purchase of a Leased Asset by the Lessee during the Term of the Lease*), when a capital lease is terminated because the lessee buys the property from the lessor, the lessee eliminates the lease liability. The lessee records the difference between the acquisition cost and the obligation as an adjustment to the carrying value of the asset. The asset is then presented in the balance sheet and accounted for in a way similar to that of other owned assets. If a capital lease is terminated due to a reason other than the lessee buying the property, the lessee must eliminate from its books the leased asset and related liability recognizing the difference as a gain or loss. The lessee should accrue a loss contingency if it is secondarily liable on the lease.

There is no accounting adjustment required by the lessee when an operating lease is terminated. However, the lessee should accrue a loss contingency if it is secondarily liable on the lease.

The lessor recognizes the effect on income of a termination of a lease in the period it occurs. The lessor eliminates the carrying value of the net investment in lease. The leased property is recorded as an asset based on the lower of its initial cost, current fair value, or current carrying amount. The difference between the net investment and the amount the asset is recorded on the lessor's records represents a loss in the year of termination.

Emerging Issues Task Force Consensus Summary Number 88–10 (*Costs Associated with Lease Modification or Termination*) covers the situation when a lessee contracts for a new lease for replacement property before the end of a preexisting lease. If the preexisting lease is ended, costs related to that preexisting lease must be expensed if the leased property no longer benefits the lessee. Examples of such costs are moving costs, write-off of abandoned leasehold improvements, and termination charges. If the lease is not terminated and is not used by the lessee, the amount expensed, including any remaining costs and future rental payments, is reduced by any sublease income. If the preexisting lease is assumed by the new lessor,

lessor incentives to the lessee are treated as incentives for accounting purposes. The incentives are amortized on a straight-line basis to rent expense or rent revenue over the life of the new lease. Moving costs are typically expensed.

RENEWALS AND EXTENSIONS

A renewal or extension to an existing lease contract impacts the accounting by both the lessor and lessee.

FASB Statement Number 27 (*Classification of Renewals or Extensions of Existing Sales-Type or Direct Financing Leases*) states that a renewal or extension of a sales-type or direct financing lease shall be treated as a sales-type lease only if it satisfies the criteria for a sales-type lease and takes place at or near the end of the lease term (within the last few months). If a renewal or extension does not take place at or near the end of the lease period, such lease must be treated as a direct financing lease. When a renewal or extension is classified as a direct financing lease, the balances in the lease receivable and the estimated residual value accounts must be modified in accordance with the revised agreement. However, the estimated residual value may not be increased. The net adjustment increases or reduces an unearned income account. If the renewal or extension is treated as an operating lease, the balance in the new investment under the current direct financing or sales-type lease must be eliminated. The leased asset will be recorded at the lower of its original cost, current fair value, or current carrying amount. Any difference between the net investment and the amount of the leased asset is charged against income. The renewal or extension is then treated as an operating lease.

An occurrence that extends the lease term except to cancel a residual guarantee or a penalty for failing to renew the lease results in a new lease agreement that may need to be classified by different criteria.

If a penalty or guarantee no longer applies due to a renewal or extension of the lease period, or if a new lease arises involving the rental of the same property by the lessee, the asset and liability from a capital lease must be adjusted for the difference in amount between the discounted values of future minimum lease payments between the original and revised lease contracts. The present value determinations for the original and revised lease agreements must be based on the original interest rate.

If a renewal or extension is classified as an operating lease, the current capital lease continues to be treated by the lessee as a capital lease until the expiration of its lease period. At the end of the lease term, the balances in the asset and liability accounts are eliminated, with any resulting gain or loss recognized for the difference. The renewal or extension is considered an operating lease.

If leased property accounted for as a capital lease is bought by the lessee, it is treated as a renewal or extension of a capital lease. The difference between the book value of the property and the acquisition price adjusts the property's carrying value.

A renewal or extension of an operating lease is accounted for as a new agreement.

LEVERAGED LEASES

A leveraged lease occurs when the lessor (equity participant) finances a minimal amount of the purchase but has total equity ownership. A third party (debt participant) finances the remainder. The property is leased to a lessee. Rental receivable is reduced by the difference between the amounts received from the lessee and payments made to the third-party creditor. The lessor maximizes its leveraged return by recognizing lease revenue and an income tax shelter (e.g., interest deduction, accelerated depreciation). A leveraged lease is structured so as to generate tax savings to the lessor without it being entirely at risk for lack of performance on the part of the lessee.

A leveraged lease must satisfy *all* of the following conditions:

■ There are three participants: lessee, lessor, and long-term creditor. The creditor provides nonrecourse financing, with the lessor having substantial leverage (usually 60% or more of the lessor's cost of the property).

- The lessor's net receivable (investment) decreases in the early years of lease and then increases in later years.

- The lease meets the test for being a direct financing lease. A sales-type lease is not a leveraged lease. **Note:** Used assets of the lessor rarely qualify as direct financing leases and thus cannot be treated as leveraged leases.

FASB Technical Bulletin Number 88–1 (*Issues Relating to Accounting for Leases*) stipulates that the book value of an asset must be the same as its fair market value for the lease to qualify as a leveraged lease.

A lessee classifies and accounts for a leveraged lease in the same way as a nonleveraged lease. The lessee follows its normal leasing policy.

The lessor presents the investment in the leveraged lease net of the nonrecourse obligation. The net of the following balances constitutes the initial and continuing investment:

- Rentals receivable net of principal and interest associated with non-recourse debt

- Estimated salvage value

- Unearned income

The initial entry to record the leveraged lease follows:

> Lease receivable
> Salvage value of the asset
>   Cash invested in asset
>   Unearned income

The lessor's net investment in the leveraged lease for deriving net income is the investment in the leveraged lease less deferred income taxes.

Net income is computed as follows using the net investment in the leveraged lease:

- Compute annual cash flow equal to the following:

Gross lease rental (add salvage value)
Less: Interest payments on debt
Less: Income tax charges
Add: Income tax credits
Less: Principal reduction
Annual cash flow

The return rate on the net investment in the leveraged lease should be determined. It is the rate that when applied to the net investment will distribute cash flow.

The net investment will be

- Positive in the early years but decline because of accelerated depreciation and interest expense
- Negative in the middle years
- Again positive in the later years due to a declining tax shelter

In the event that at any time expected net cash receipts over the remaining lease period are less than the lessor's investment in the lease, a loss must be recorded immediately.

FASB Emerging Issues Task Force Consensus Summary Number 85–16 (*Leveraged Leases*) provides that recourse debt arising from a delayed equity investment may be treated as a leveraged lease if all other criteria except for the nonrecourse condition are met. The lessor's liability should be based on the discounted value of future payments.

FASB Technical Bulletin 79–16 (*Effect of a Change in Income Tax Rate on the Accounting for Leveraged Leases*) requires the effect on a leveraged lease of a change in tax rate to be recognized as a gain or loss in the year in which the tax rate changes.

Emerging Issues Task Force Consensus Summary Number 86–43 also discusses the effect of a change in income tax law or rate on the accounting for leveraged leases.

If there is an investment tax credit retained by the lessor, it should be deferred and amortized to income over the lease term.

Disclosure for leveraged leases should be made of

- Assumptions related to estimating the net income associated with the lease
- Components of the net investment
- Deferred taxes

RELATED PARTIES

A related party is one whom has substantial influence in financial or operating terms over another in a leasing arrangement, such as an owner, parent company, investor, creditor, or officer or director of the company. Substantial influence may be exercised through extending credit, owning debt or equity securities, or the guaranteeing indebtedness. In a related party lease where significant influence is involved, the lease should be accounted for according to its economic substance, not its legal form. If substantial influence does not exist, the related party lease should be classified and accounted for as if the participants were unrelated.

FASB Statement Number 13 (*Accounting for Leases*) requires a parent to consolidate a subsidiary whose major business activity is leasing property from a parent or other affiliates.

According to Emerging Issues Task Force Consensus Summary Number 90–15 (*Impact of Nonsubstantive Lessors, Residual Value Guarantees, and Other Provisions in Leasing Transactions*), a related party lease arrangement involving substantial influence may require consolidation accounting for the lessor and lessee if all of the following criteria exist:

- Most of the lessor's activities relate to leasing assets to one particular lessee.
- The lessee incurs the risks and rewards associated with the rented property along with any related debt. This may arise if the lease contract gives the lessee control and management over the leased property, the lessee guarantees the lessor's debt or residual value of the leased item, and the lessee has the right to buy the property at a lower than fair value price.

■ The lessor's owners do not have a significant residual equity capital investment that is at risk.

If the consolidation criteria are not satisfied, combined financial statements rather than consolidated financial statements may be appropriate.

FASB Statement Number 57 (*Related Party Disclosures*) requires disclosure of the nature and extent of leasing transactions between related parties.

MONEY-OVER-MONEY LEASE

FASB Technical Bulletin Number 88–1 covers money-over-money lease transactions. This transaction occurs when an entity manufactures or buys an asset, leases it to the lessee, and receives nonrecourse financing exceeding the cost of the asset. The collateral for the borrowing is the leased asset and any future rentals derived therefrom. A money-over-money lease transaction is accounted for as the production or acquisition of an asset, the leasing is under one of the lessor's acceptable methods (operating, direct financing, or sales type), and the receipt of borrowed funds. The lessor is prohibited from offsetting the asset (in an operating lease) or the lease receivable (in other than an operating lease) and the nonrecourse obligation unless there is a legal right of setoff. In other words, the leasing and borrowing are considered separate transactions. If a sales-type lease is involved, the lessor may record a profit at the inception of the lease.

THIRD PARTIES

If a direct financing or sales-type lease is sold or assigned by a lessor to a third party, the original accounting policies are still retained; they should not be reversed. When the sale or assignment occurs, the profit or loss is recorded by the lessor except if the seller retains substantial risks. If the transfer qualifies as a sale, the transferor (seller) must record the proceeds received at fair value, credit the asset sold, and book the ensuing gain or loss. In the case when the seller is assuming significant risk of ownership (e.g., seller guarantees the buyer's investment, seller promises to repurchase the leased property if the lessee defaults), the transaction is accounted for as a secured borrowing rather than a sale.

If the lessor has an operating lease, the lessor (seller) records rental receipts as income even if the lessee pays the rentals to a third party. The rental payment includes imputed interest (charged to interest expense) and a reduction of the obligation. A sale or assignment of rentals received from lessees under an operating lease is treated for accounting purposes as a borrowing if the seller retains substantial risks of ownership in the leased property. The seller records the sales proceeds as an obligation on its books. The lessor (seller) records rent receipts as revenue and continues to keep the leased asset on its balance sheet. However, the asset is depreciated over a period not exceeding the period of the obligation.

If the lessee defaults or the rental terminates, the seller may buy the property or lease, substitute an existing lease, get a substitute lessee, or enter into a remarketing arrangement.

The accounting treatment just specified also applies even if the leased property is sold to a third party that intends to lease the property to another party.

WRAP LEASES

FASB Technical Bulletin Number 88–1 (*Issues Related to Accounting for Leases*) states that the following scenario related to a wrap lease arrangement should be accounted for as a sale-leaseback transaction: (1) The company buys an asset, (2) it leases the property to a lessee, (3) the company (now the lessor) receives nonrecourse financing in which the asset and rentals derived therefrom are used as collateral, (4) lessor sells the asset and related nonrecourse debt to a third party (e.g., financial institution), and (5) the company leases the asset back while still being the principal (substantive) lessor under the initial lease (continuing to service the leased property). (Nonrecourse financing is a borrowing transaction in which the lender does not have general recourse against the borrower directly but instead has recourse against the collateralized property.) The company cannot offset the subleased asset and the related nonrecourse debt unless a legal right of offset exists.

In a wrap lease transaction the lessor may or may not be responsible for leaseback payments in the case of lessee default or receive a fee to service the lease. The leaseback payments do not necessarily have to coincide with the collections under the note. Further, the leaseback provisions do not necessarily have to agree with the provisions of the initial lease.

In a sales-leaseback transaction, the sale portion is recognized by the seller-lessee as a sale. The seller-lessee eliminates from its balance sheet the asset sold and its associated liabilities. The lease portion of the sale-leaseback transaction is either treated as an operating or capital lease depending on the criteria met.

Emerging Issues Task Force Consensus Summary Number 87–7 (*Sale of an Asset Subject to a Lease and Nonrecourse Financing: Wrap Lease Transactions*) states that an original lessor should defer recognizing the revenue associated with future remarketing rights until such services are conducted. Further, the original lessor should present any retained interest in the salvage value of a leased asset in its balance sheet as an asset.

EXAMPLE

A lessor leases property with a book value of $100,000 to a lessee for five years (60 months) at $2,000 per month. The residual value of the leased property at the end of the lease period is $15,000. The interest rate is 8%. The lessor treats the lease as a direct financing lease. The journal entries follow:

Lease receivable (60 × $2,000)	120,000	
Residual value of leased asset	15,000	
Asset		100,000
Unearned revenue		35,000

The lease receivable and the asset are used as collateral when the lessor signs a nonrecourse financing contract with the bank for $24,753 (discounted value of $2,000 per month rental for 60 months at an 8% interest rate, or $2,000 × 12.3766 = $24,753). The journal entry to record the nonrecourse debt is

Cash	24,753	
Nonrecourse debt		24,753

BUSINESS COMBINATIONS

FASB Interpretation Number 21 (*Accounting for Leases in a Business Combination*) states that a business combination by itself has no bearing on the classification of a lease.

The terms of a business combination may affect the classification, accounting, and reporting of a lease. A lease should be treated and accounted for as a new one if its provisions are modified and such revisions would have resulted in another classification at the inception date. In a purchase transaction, the acquirer may assign a new value to a capitalized lease because of the allocation of acquisition price to the net assets of the acquired company. However, as long as the lease terms are not revised, the lease should be accounted for using the initial terms and classification. A similar treatment is afforded under the pooling-of-interests method in that the new lease would retain its classification provided the terms are still intact.

In the case of a leveraged lease when the purchase method is used in a business combination, the following guidelines are followed:

- The classification continues as a leveraged lease.
- The net investment in the leveraged lease should be recorded at fair market value, including tax effects. Fair market value is usually based on the discounted value of future cash flows.
- The three elements of the net investment are net rentals receivable (investment), expected salvage value, and unearned interest income.
- The usual accounting for a leveraged lease should be practiced.

DISPOSAL OF A BUSINESS SEGMENT

FASB Interpretation Number 27 (*Accounting for a Loss on a Sublease*) states that expected costs and expenses directly tied to a disposal of a business segment decision should include future rental payments less amounts to be received from subleases on those properties. The difference between the unamortized cost of the leased property and the discounted value of the minimum lease payments to be received from the sublease is recognized as a gain or loss. This gain or loss is includable in the overall gain or loss on disposing of the business segment.

CURRENT VALUE FINANCIAL STATEMENTS

FASB Technical Bulletin Number 79–13 covers the applicability of FASB Statement Number 13 to current value financial statements.

REAL ESTATE LEASES

A lessee will classify the lease as a capital lease if any of the following factors are present at the inception of the lease:

- *Ownership*   At the end of the lease term, the ownership of the property is transferred to the lessee.

- *Bargain*   The lease contains a bargain purchase option.

- *Life*   The lease term is for 75% or more of the estimated economic life of the property. This does not apply, however, to leases that begin in the last 25% of the original estimated economic life of the property.

- *Value*   The present value of minimum lease payments is equal to 90% or more of the fair value of the property. To determine the present value of minimum lease payments, one needs to consider the minimum lease payment, executory costs, and discount rate. Executory costs, such as insurance, maintenance, and taxes, should be excluded if they are to be paid by the lessor. This does not apply, however, to leases that begin in the last 25% of the original estimated economic life of the property.

Real estate leases are of four types:

- Land only
- Land and building
- Land, building, and equipment
- Portion of a building

Land Only

Lessee

Leases involving land only are classified by the lessee as a capital lease only if either the ownership or bargain criterion is met. The lease should be accounted for as an operating lease if either of these conditions is not met.

Lessor

The lessor classifies a lease involving land only as a sales-type lease if the transaction yields manufacturer's or dealer's profit or loss and the ownership criterion is met. Such a transaction is accounted for according to the provisions of FASB Statement Number 66.

If the transaction does not yield manufacturer's or dealer's profit and the ownership criterion is met, the lease is classified as a direct financing lease or leveraged lease, as appropriate, as long as both the collectibility and no material uncertainties criteria are met.

If a lease satisfies both the collectibility and no material uncertainties criteria, and the lease contains a bargain purchase option, then the lease should be accounted for as a direct financing, leveraged, or operating lease, as applicable. All other leases should be accounted for as operating leases.

Land and Building

There are three main categories of leases involving land and building:

- Leases that satisfy the ownership or bargain criterion
- Leases where the land is valued at less than 25%
- Leases where the land is valued at 25% or more

Lessee

If the lease agreement transfers the title (ownership) or the agreement contains a bargain purchase option, the lessee should separate the land and building components and capitalize each. The present value of the minimum lease payments (less executory costs to be paid by the lessor and any profits) should be allocated to the land and building components according to their fair values. The building component should be depreciated.

When a lease does not satisfy the ownership or bargain criterion, the fair value of the land must be determined.

- If the fair value of the land component is less than 25% of the total land and building lease, then the land is considered immaterial. Thus, the lease should be accounted for as a single unit. The lease should be capitalized and depreciated over the economic life if either the life or value criterion is met.

- The land is considered material if the fair value of the land component is 25% or more of the total fair value of the lease, and each component should be accounted for separately. The minimum lease payment attributable to the land should be determined using the lessee's incremental borrowing rate and the fair value of the land. The remaining balance of the lease payment is attributable to the building component. The land component should *always* be accounted for as an operating lease. The building component of the lease should be capitalized and depreciated over the economic life if either the life or value criterion is met.

Lessor

If the lease satisfies the ownership criterion and results in dealer's profit or loss, the lessor is required to classify the lease as a sales-type lease. Such a lease should be accounted for as a single unit in a manner similar to a seller of the property, in accordance with FASB Number 66.

If the lease satisfies the bargain criterion and results in dealer's/manufacturer's profit or loss, then the lease should be classified as an operating lease. If the lease satisfies the bargain criterion and meets both the collectibility and no material uncertainties criteria, but does *not* result in dealer's/manufacturer's profit or loss, then the lease should be classified as direct financing or a leveraged lease, as appropriate.

If the lease does not satisfy either the ownership or the bargain criterion, the lessor should follow the same rules as the lessee in accounting for leases.

- If the fair value of the land is less than 25% of the total fair value of the leased property at the inception of the lease, and either the life or value criterion is met, and the lease gives rise to a dealer's or manufacturer's profit/loss, then the lease should be classified as an operating lease.

- If the fair value of the land is less than 25% of the total fair value of the leased property at the inception of the lease, and either the life or value criterion is met, but the lease does *not* give rise to a dealer's or manufacturer's profit/loss, then the lease should be classified as a direct financing or a leveraged lease, as appropriate, provided that the collection and no material uncertainties criteria are satisfied. Otherwise, the lease should be classified as an operating lease.

- If the fair value of the land is 25% or more of the total fair value of the leased property at the inception of the lease, and either the life or value criterion is met, and the lease gives rise to a dealer's or manufacturer's profit/loss, then the lease should be classified as an operating lease.

- If the fair value of the land is 25% or more of the total fair value of the leased property at the inception of the lease, and either the life or value criterion is met, but the lease does *not* give rise to a dealer's or manufacturer's profit/loss, then the building portion of the lease should be classified as a direct financing or a leveraged lease, as appropriate, provided that the collection and no material uncertainties criteria are satisfied. Otherwise, the building portion of the lease should be classified as an operating lease. The land portion of the lease should *always* be accounted for as an operating lease.

Land, Building, and Equipment

When a lease involves land, building, and equipment, the equipment component, if material, should be estimated and accounted for separately. The capitalization requirements for equipment should be considered separately from the land and building components for both the lessee and lessor.

Portion of a Building

Frequently, a lease involves only a portion of a building. The classification of such leases depends upon the ability of lessee and lessor to determine objectively the cost or fair value of the leased property.

Lessee

If the lessee can objectively determine the fair value of the property, the lease should be classified according to the criteria discussed for land and building leases in the previous sections. If the lessee cannot objectively determine the fair value of the property, then only the life criterion should be used to determine the lease classification. If the lease is for a period greater than 75% of economic life of building, the lease is classified as a capital lease. In all other instances, it should be treated as an operating lease.

Lessor

If the lessor can objectively determine *both* the cost and fair value of the property, the lease should be classified according to the criteria discussed for land and building leases in the previous sections. If the lessor cannot objectively determine both the cost and fair value of the property, the lessor should classify the lease as an operating lease.

Sale-Leaseback Involving Real Estate

In a sale-leaseback, the seller-lessee sells property and then leases back from the purchaser-lessor all or part of the same property. Real estate is classified as a sales-type lease only if the title to the leased property is transferred to the lessee at or shortly after the end of the lease term.

Three conditions must exist for the seller-lessee to use sale-lease-back accounting. First, the leaseback should be a "normal leaseback." A leaseback is considered normal when the seller-lessee actively uses the leased-back property in a trade or business (up to 10% of the property may be subleased). Second, the buyer-lessor's initial and continuing investment in the property should be adequate. FASB Statement Number 66 (*Accounting for Sales of Real Estate*) is used to determine the adequacy of the initial investment. Third, risk and reward are transferred to the buyer, the sale is complete, and the seller-lessee has no continuing involvement. The following factors indicate continuing involvement by the seller-lessee and preclude the use of sale-leaseback accounting:

- A specific residual value is guaranteed by the seller-lessee, where the seller-lessee will pay the buyer-lessor for a decline in fair value below estimated residual value, as long as the decline is not associated with excess wear and tear.

- Nonrecourse financing is provided by the seller-lessee to the buyer-lessor for any portion of the sales proceeds.

- Recourse financing is provided by the seller-lessee to the buyer-lessor where the only recourse is the leased property.

- Collateral, other than the property involved in the sale-leaseback transaction, is provided by the seller-lessee on behalf of the buyer-lessor.

- The seller-lessee is not relieved of the obligation under any existing debt related to the property, including secondary liability.

- The buyer-lessor's debt is guaranteed by the seller-lessee or a party related to the seller-lessee.

- Any appreciation on the property will be shared by the seller-lessee.

Subleases

Subleasing involves the original lessee leasing the property to a third party during the time period in which original lease is in force. Sometimes a new lessee is substituted for the original lessee and the new lessee becomes primarily obligated. The original lease may be canceled and substituted with a new lessee. The accounting for such transactions depends upon whether the original lessee is or is not relieved of primary liability.

Annual Report References

HOME DEPOT
1999 ANNUAL REPORT

5. Leases

The Company leases certain retail locations, office space, warehouse and distribution space, equipment and vehicles. While the majority of the leases are operating leases, certain retail locations are leased under capital leases. As leases expire, it can be expected that in the normal course of business, leases will be renewed or replaced.

In June 1996, the Company entered into a $300 million operating lease agreement for the primary purpose of financing construction costs for selected new stores. The Company increased its available funding under the operating lease agreement to $600 million in May 1997. In October 1998, through a second operating lease agreement, the Company further increased the available funding by $282 million to $882 million. Under the agreements, the lessor purchases the properties, pays for the construction costs and subsequently leases the facilities to the Company. The initial lease term for the $600 million agreement is five years with five 2-year renewal options. The lease term for the $282 million agreement is 10 years with no renewal options. Both lease agreements provide for substantial residual value guarantees and include purchase options at original cost on each property. The Company financed a portion of its new stores in fiscal 1997, 1998 and 1999, as well as an office building in fiscal 1999, under the operating lease agreements. The Company anticipates utilizing these facilities to finance selected new stores and an additional office building in fiscal 2000.

699

During 1995, the Company entered into two operating lease arrangements under which the Company leases an import distribution facility, including its related equipment, and an office building for store support functions. The operating lease agreement for the office building terminated in 1999 when the Company refinanced the property under the $600 million operating lease agreement. The initial lease term for the import distribution facility is five 5-year renewal options. The lease agreement provides for substantial residual value guarantees and includes purchase options at the higher of the cost or fair market value of the assets.

The maximum amount of the residual value guarantees relative to the assets under the lease agreements described above is projected to be $799 million. As the leased assets are placed into service, the Company estimates its liability under the residual value guarantees and records additional rent expense on a straight-line basis over the remaining lease terms.

Total rent expense, net of minor sublease income for the fiscal years ended January 30, 2000, January 31, 1999 and February 1, 1998 was $389 million, $321 million and $262 million, respectively. Real estate taxes, insurance, maintenance and operating expenses applicable to the leased property are obligations of the Company under the building leases. Certain of the store leases provide for contingent rentals based on percentages of sales in excess of specified minimums. Contingent rentals for the fiscal years ended January 30, 2000, January 31, 1999 and February 1, 1998 were approximately $11 million, $11 million and $10 million, respectively.

The approximate future minimum lease payments under capital and operating leases at January 30, 2000 were as follows (in millions):

Fiscal Year	Capital Leases	Operating Leases
2000	$ 35	$ 466
2001	35	462
2002	35	415
2003	36	384
2004	36	359
Thereafter	505	3,969
	682	$6,055
Less imputed interest	(466)	

(Cont.)

Fiscal Year	Capital Leases	Operating Leases
Net present value of capital lease obligations	216	
Less current installments	(3)	
Long-term capital lease obligations, excluding current installments	$213	

Short-term and long-term obligations for capital leases are included in the Company's Consolidated Balance Sheets in Current Installments of Long-Term Debt and Long-Term Debt, respectively. The assets under capital leases recorded in Net Property and Equipment, net of amortization, totaled $208 million and $180 million, at January 30, 2000 and January 31, 1999, respectively.

CHEVRON
1999 ANNUAL REPORT

11. Lease Commitments

Certain noncancelable leases are classified as capital leases, and leased assets are included as part of "Properties, plant and equipment." Other leases are classified as operating leases and are not capitalized. Details of the capitalized leased assets are as follows:

	At December 31	
	1999	1998
Exploration and Production	**$ 86**	$ 5
Refining, Marketing and Transportation	**779**	757
Total	**865**	762
Less: accumulated amortization	**425**	398
Net capitalized leased assets	**$440**	$364

Rental expenses incurred for operating leases during 1999, 1998 and 1997 were as follows:

	Year ended December 31		
	1999	1998	1997
Minimum rentals	**$465**	$503	$443
Contingent rentals	**3**	5	5
Total	**468**	508	448
Less: sublease rental income	**3**	3	5
Net rental expense	**$465**	$505	$443

At December 31, 1999, the future minimum lease payments under operating and capital leases are as follows:

	At December 31	
	Operating Leases	Capital Leases
Year		
2000	$ 157	$ 81
2001	180	77
2002	180	72
2003	178	103
2004	177	46
Thereafter	312	889
Total	$1,184	$1,268
Less: amounts representing interest and executory costs		625
Net present values		643
Less: capital lease obligations included in short-term debt		332
Long-term capital lease obligations		$ 311
Future sublease rental income	$ 1	$ —

Contingent rentals are based on factors other than the passage of time, principally sales volumes at leased service stations. Certain leases include escalation clauses for adjusting rentals to reflect changes in price indices, renewal options ranging from one to 25 years, and/or options to purchase the leased property during or at the end of the initial lease period for the fair market value at that time.

U.S. STEEL GROUP
1998 ANNUAL REPORT

12. Leases

Future minimum commitments for capital leases (including sale-leasebacks accounted for as financings) and for operating leases having remaining noncancelable lease terms in excess of one year are as follows:

(In millions)	Capital Leases	Operating Leases
1999	$10	$ 229
2000	11	293
2001	11	200
2002	11	116
2003	11	82
Later years	117	208
Sublease rentals	—	(16)
Total minimum lease payments	171	$1,112
Less imputed interest costs	(76)	
Present value of net minimum lease payments included in long-term debt	$95	

Operating lease rental expense from continuing operations:

(In millions)	1998	1997	1996
Minimum rental	**$293**	$237	$227
Contingent rental	**29**	25	15
Sublease rentals	**(8)**	(8)	(8)
Net rental expense	**$314**	$254	$234

USX leases a wide variety of facilities and equipment under operating leases, including land and building space, office equipment, production facilities and transportation equipment. Most long-term leases include renewal options and, in certain leases, purchase options. In the event of a change in control of USX, as defined in the agreements, or certain other circumstances, operating lease obligations totaling $115 million may be declared immediately due and payable.

DOW CHEMICAL
1999 ANNUAL REPORT

H. Leased Property

The Company routinely leases premises for use as sales and administrative offices, warehouses and tanks for product storage, motor vehicles, railcars, computers, office machines and equipment under operating leases. In addition, gas turbines at two U.S. locations are leased and a Canadian subsidiary leases an ethylene plant. The Company has the option to purchase the ethylene plant and certain other leased equipment and buildings at the termination of the leases.

Rental expenses under operating leases were $394 for 1999, $408 for 1998, and $406 for 1997.

Minimum Operating Lease Commitments at December 31, 1999	
2000	$ 321
2001	184
2002	144
2003	122
2004	101
2005 and thereafter	1,076
Total	$1,948

Chapter 14

Pension Plans and Other Postretirement Benefit Plans

This chapter discusses pension plans and other postretirement benefits other than pensions. The major types of pension plans are defined contribution and defined benefit. The reporting by a trustee for the plan is also presented, including the requirements surrounding pension plan financial statements. The accounting for settlements, curtailments, and terminations is presented. Postretirement benefit plans other than pensions are also discussed. Finally, the accounting and reporting for postemployment benefits are presented.

PENSION PLANS

Pension plans provide benefits to employees at retirement, death, disability, or some other covered event. Many pension plans allow for early retirement or termination of service.

Although a company is not required to have a pension plan, if it does it must follow Financial Accounting Standards Board and government accounting and presentation dictates. Under FASB Statement Number 87 (*Employers' Accounting for Pensions*) and the FASB Implementation Guide (*Questions and Answers*) to FASB Statement Number 87, pension costs must be accounted for under the accrual basis. Pension expense is accrued as services are rendered. Reasonable estimates and averages may be used for future events in computing pension expense. Pension expense is presented in the income statement as a single amount. The American Institute of CPAs has issued an Industry Audit and Accounting Guide for Employee Benefit Plans.

Note: FASB Statement Number 87 does not apply if a plan provides only for life or health insurance benefits.

Pension expenses for administrative personnel are expensed, but those for factory workers are inventoriable.

A depiction of the relationship among the parties in a pension plan follows:

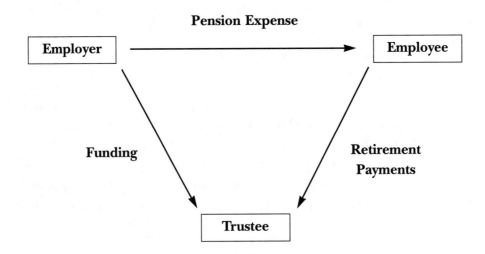

There are two kinds of pension plans:

- *Defined Contribution*   The amount to be contributed each year by the employer is specified. The benefits to be paid at retirement are not specified or known. Defined contribution plan benefits equal the value of each participant's account balance. Examples of such plans include employee stock ownership, profit sharing, and money purchase.

■ *Defined Benefit*   The amount to be received by retirees is specified. The employer contributes amounts to fund the accumulation benefit. In most cases, annuity payments are made.

Note: The requirements of FASB Statement Number 87 also apply to pension plans outside the United States as long as they are similar to U.S. plans. In some countries, it may be the custom to pay employee benefits upon voluntary or involuntary termination of employees.

Employers usually design a pension plan so it qualifies under the federal tax law. This allows for the tax deductibility of pension expense as well as tax-free status of income generated from pension fund assets.

Terminology

Terminology peculiar to pension plans follows:

■ *Benefit Information Date*   The date that actuaries use to determine the present value of accumulated benefits.

■ *Vested Benefits*   The employee is entitled to pension benefits at retirement even if he or she leaves the employ of the company. In a single-employer plan, the employee must vest after five years, while in a multiemployer plan the employee must vest after 10 years. While disclosure is required of the vested benefit obligation, it is not a component of the net periodic pension expense. If a pension plan is terminated, the employer is liable for the vested benefit obligation. According to Emerging Issues Task Force Consensus Summary Number 88–1 (*Determination of Vested Benefit Obligation for a Defined Benefit Pension Plan*), the vested benefit obligation can be the discounted value of vested benefits the worker is eligible to receive if he or she leaves immediately or the discounted value of vested benefits the employee is presently entitled to based on his or her anticipated date of departure or retirement. This is mostly of concern to foreign plans.

■ *Net Assets Available for Pension Benefits*   The excess of pension assets over pension liabilities. The pension liability does not include employees' accumulated benefits.

■ *Actuarial Assumptions*   Assumptions used by actuaries to compute pension expense and cash payment to the trustee. Examples of assumptions needed for mathematical computations are turnover rate, return rate, salary levels, retirement age, withdrawal, disablement, administrative costs, and life expectancy.

■ *Actuarial Cost Method*   The funding method actuaries use to calculate the employer's contribution so adequate funds will be available when workers retire. The method will determine the pension expense and associated liability. The American Institute of CPAs recommends the unit credit method.

■ *Unrecognized Net Gain or Loss*   The cumulative net gain or loss that has not been recognized as a component of pension expense.

■ *Actuarial Present Value of Accumulated Plan Benefits*   The discounted (time value) amount of money necessary to meet retirement obligations for current and retired employees. The calculation considers such factors as withdrawal, death, and disability.

■ *Accumulated Benefit Obligation (ABO)*   The year-end pension obligation based on past and current salaries, not future compensation levels. It is the actuarial present value of vested and nonvested benefits attributable to the pension plan based on services rendered to date. It assumes that compensation to plan participants does not change. While attrition of current participants is considered, there is no consideration given to employees who will enter the plan in later years. If the pension plan is terminated, the amount of any unfunded accumulated benefit obligation continues as a liability of the employer. The accumulated benefit obligation is used in calculating the minimum pension liability.

■ *Projected Benefit Obligation (PBO)*   The year-end pension obligation based on future projected salaries. It relates to the discounted value of benefits (whether vested or nonvested) earned to date. The employer does not record the projected benefit obligation on its books. It is only maintained on a worksheet record.

Examples of plans based on future salary levels are career average pay, pay related, and final pay. These plans take into account compensation increases and employee turnover rates. The projected benefit obligation equals the anticipated increase (progression) in salaries plus the accumulated benefit obligation. For example, if the accumulated benefit obligation is $150,000 and the expected progression in wages is $20,000, the projected benefit obligation will equal $170,000.

In the case of pension plans with flat-benefit or non-pay-related pension benefit formulas, the accumulated benefit obligation and the projected benefit obligation amounts will be the same.

The projected benefit obligation is used to calculate interest cost, prior service cost, and corridor amounts in the actuarial gains or losses computation.

■ *Market-Related Asset Value*   The fair market value of pension plan assets or a calculated value (e.g., moving average) that recognizes the changes in the actual fair value of pension assets over a period not exceeding five years. Market-related asset value is an average of fair values and is used because fair value may change significantly over the years, which would cause significant differences in pension expense each period. The valuation method must be used consistently. Market-related values may be assigned to different asset classes.

EXAMPLE

A calculated moving average value is to be used in measuring pension plan assets. The actual fair value of plan assets at the end of each of the last six years was $16,000, $20,000, $25,000, $28,000, $32,000, and $26,000. The net gain for the five years is $10,000 ($4,000 + $5,000 + $3,000 + $4,000 − $6,000). The five-year net gain is over a five-year period, or 20% (1/5). Therefore, only 20% of the $10,000 net gain, or $2,000, is included in deriving the calculated market-related value of the pension plan assets for the current period.

Note: The amount by which the actual fair value differs from the calculated market-related value is the net gain or loss from prior years that still has not been recognized in the calculated market-related value.

■ *Contributory Plan*   A plan in which employees must contribute their share to the pension and to its cost. The contribution rate is usually specified as a percentage. For example, a pension plan may require employees to contribute 5% of their annual salary while the employer contributes 10% of the salary. In some plans, employees have the option to contribute in order to receive increased benefits. In a noncontributory plan, employees do not contribute to the pension plan. The employer is the only one who funds the plan.

■ *Measurement Date*   The date in which pension plan assets and liabilities are measured. They should usually be measured at the employer's fiscal year-end. However, the measurement date may be three months or less before the fiscal year-end if used consistently.

■ *Attribution*   The procedure used to assign pension benefits or cost to the years of employee service. The attribution period usually starts when the employee is hired and ends when the employee becomes fully eligible under the plan. Each year of service is usually considered equal in application. However, a benefit formula may be used, attributing more or less benefits to later service years.

■ *Full Eligibility*   The date the employee achieves complete eligibility for pension benefits. The benefits may be received by either the employee or his or her beneficiaries in the case of death. Full eligibility may be based on reaching a predetermined number of service years, or age, or a combination of service and age.

■ *Mortality Rate*   The ratio of the number of deaths relative to the number of living persons in a particular group. This is one consideration used by actuaries in determining pension expense and related funding. Actuaries refer to mortality tables, which indicate the death rates by age.

■ *Annuity Contract*   An irrevocable agreement in which the insurer has the unconditional obligation to pay employees of the employer either specific periodic benefits or a lump-sum payment to another party. The employer pays the insurance company premiums over the life of the contract. In so doing, the employer transfers its risk to the insurer.

Defined Contribution Pension Plan

In a defined contribution plan, the employer and employees make contributions to a plan so as to provide pension benefits to employees when they retire.

Under a defined contribution pension plan, pension expense is accrued each year based on services rendered. The amount funded (contributed) equals the pension expense for the period. The entry is to debit pension expense and credit cash. As a result, a deferred charge or deferred credit is not recorded.

In the event that the plan provides for contributions after retirement or termination, the associated expense should be accrued during the service years.

At retirement, the employee will receive pension benefits based on the amounts contributed to his or her account, income earned on investments, and forfeitures of amounts of other participants who leave employment before being vested.

The following should be footnoted:

- Cost recognized for the year
- Method and basis in computing contributions
- Description of the terms
- Categorization of covered employees
- Discussion of items affecting comparability over the years

The American Institute of CPAs' Statement of Position Number 94–4 discusses the reporting of investment contracts held by defined contribution pension plans.

Emerging Issues Task Force Consensus Summary Number 86–27 covers the measurement of excess contributions to a defined contribution plan or employee stock ownership plan.

Practice Bulletin 12 covers the reporting of separate investment fund option information of defined contribution pension plans.

Defined Benefit Pension Plan

Under a defined benefit plan, pension expense is charged to operations over the time period employees perform services. A benefit formula considers the pension benefits employees will receive for their employment. The employer's contribution (cash funded) into the plan is based on the anticipated pension benefits employees will receive when they retire. When benefits are paid, plan assets are reduced.

In a defined benefit plan, pension expense consists of the following components:

- Service cost (+)
- Amortization expense on prior (past) service cost (+)
- Return on pension plan assets (−)
- Interest on projected benefit obligation (+)
- Actuarial loss (+) or gain (−)

Total Pension Expense

Each of these pension elements are now discussed.

Service Cost   Pension cost assigned for services rendered in the current year. It is based on the actuarial determined present value of future payments to be made using a benefit formula. It is charged in the current period. Service cost should take into account benefit changes per the pension agreement, such as cost increases arising from some inflation measure (e.g., Consumer Price Index). In other words, if the benefit formula includes benefits tied to expected future employee salaries, this must be considered in computing service cost for the current year. Future compensation levels should incorporate changes arising from productivity, promotion, seniority, additional responsibilities, etc.

Amortization Expense on Prior Service Cost   Pension expense assigned for services performed prior to adopting or modifying a pension plan. The cost associated with granting retroactive benefits increases the projected benefit obligation at the amendment date. Prior service cost arising for an amendment to the plan is accounted for as a change in estimate. Prior service cost is allocated over current and future years using the straight-line method in equal amounts based on the average remaining service life of eligible active employees. (An alternative accelerated amortization method to straight-line may be used but must be followed consistently and disclosed in the footnotes.) However, if most of the pension plan participants are inactive, the prior service cost attributable to the benefits of the inactive participants is amortized over their remaining life expectancy. The unamortized (unrecognized) prior service balance is presented in a footnote.

A company may grant employees this privilege for one or more reasons, such as enhancing worker morale, reducing turnover rates, improving productivity, and controlling raises.

In most cases, a modification to a pension plan will increase pension benefits as well as the projected benefit obligation. However, the opposite effect from an amendment is also possible. If the amendment actually reduces pension benefits, the employer shall reduce the balance of the unamortized prior service cost.

Emerging Issues Task Force Consensus Summary Number 87–13 covers the amortization of prior service cost for a defined benefit plan when there is a history of plan amendments.

EXAMPLE

On January 1, 19X3, XYZ adopted a pension plan giving a retroactive pension benefit for services rendered in the two years before adoption. The prior service cost amounted to $500,000. It is to be amortized over 10 years. Therefore, the amortization expense on prior service cost for 19X3 will be $50,000. The unamortized prior service cost to be disclosed in a footnote will be $450,000.

EXAMPLE

A company reported the following on January 1, 19X5:

Projected benefit obligation—1/1/19X5	$800,000
Fair market value of plan assets—1/1/19X5	600,000

The unamortized prior service cost on January 1, 19X5 equals

Projected benefit obligation—1/1	$800,000
Fair market value of plan assets—1/1	600,000
Unamortized prior service cost—1/1	$200,000

If the amortization period is 20 years, the amortization expense on prior service cost for 19X5 would be $10,000 ($200,000/20 years), resulting in unamortized prior service cost on December 31, 19X5 of $190,000 ($200,000 − $10,000).

EXAMPLE

ABC Company modifies its pension formula from 3% to 4% of the last four years of pay multiplied by the service years on January 1, 19X1. This causes the projected benefit obligation to increase by $400,000. It is expected that employees will receive benefits over the next 10 years.

Total future service years equal:

$$\frac{n\,(n+1) \times P}{2}$$

n = service years to be made

P = annual population decrease

$$\frac{10\,(10+1) \times 9}{2} = 495$$

Amortization expense on prior service cost for 19X1 equals

$$\frac{\$400,000 \times 10 \times 9}{495} = \$72,727$$

Return on Pension Plan Assets   Pension plan assets may include bank accounts, stocks, bonds, real estate, etc. The return on plan assets may be expressed in the form of expected or actual. The total expected return equals the long-term return rate multiplied by the market-related value of pension plan assets at the beginning of the year. The total expected return reduces pension expense. **Note:** It is possible for the return to be negative, such as in a stock market crash. In such a case, the negative return would increase pension expense.

The actual return on pension plan assets equals the difference between the fair value of pension assets at the start and end of the year adjusted for employer contributions and benefit payments to retirees. In other words, the actual return results from realized and holding gains or losses on plan assets plus the periodic income earned (e.g., dividends, interest) on the plan assets.

EXAMPLE

The fair values of plan assets at the beginning and end of the year were $2,800 and $3,086, respectively. The employer's contribution to the plan during the year was $290. Benefit payments to retirees were $320. The actual return is computed as follows:

Fair value of plan assets—1/1	$2,800
Plus: Employer contributions	290
Plus: Actual return	?
Less: Benefit payments	(320)
Fair value of plan assets—12/31	$3,086

Solving for the unknown, the actual return equals $316.

Alternatively, the following formula may be used to derive the actual return:

Actual return = Fair value of assets (end of year) − fair value of assets (beginning of year) − employer contributions + benefit payments
Actual return = $3,086 − $2,800 − $290 + $320 = $316

EXAMPLE

The following data apply to a company's defined benefit pension plan for the year:

Fair market value of plan assets—1/1	$400,000
Fair market value of plan assets—12/31	570,000
Employer contributions	140,000
Benefits paid	100,000

The actual return on plan assets equals $130,000, computed as follows:

Fair market value of plan assets—12/31		$570,000
Fair market value of plan assets—1/1		400,000
Change in plan assets		$170,000
Adjusted for		
Employer contributions	$140,000	
Less: Benefits paid	100,000	40,000
Actual return on plan assets		$130,000

EXAMPLE

Based on the following information, the actual return on pension plan assets will be computed as follows:

Benefit payments	$100,000	
Contribution	130,000	
Fair market value of plan assets:		
End of year		600,000
Beginning of year		400,000

The actual return equals $170,000, computed as follows:

Change in fair market value of plan assets		$200,000
Adjustments:		
Employer contribution	$130,000	
Benefit payments	100,000	30,000
Actual return on plan assets		$170,000

Interest on Projected Benefit Obligation This is computed by multiplying the interest (settlement discount) rate by the projected benefit obligation (discounted present value of employee benefits earned based on future salaries) at the beginning of the year. The interest (settlement) rate is usually based on the company's average borrowing cost. The settlement rate should be reviewed each year. It represents the time value of money. The interest cost increases pension expense and the projected benefit obligation. The interest cost equals the increase in the projected benefit obligation over time.

Actuarial Losses or Gains   Actuarial losses or gains are the difference between actual experience and estimates. For example, an actuarial loss would arise if the actual interest rate earned was 6% when the anticipated interest rate was 8%. Actuarial losses or gains arise from the difference between the expected versus actual projected benefit obligation and/or fair value of plan assets at year-end. **Caution:** While FASB Statement Number 87 refers to the gains or losses associated with the change in the projected benefit obligation as actuarial gains and losses, it refers to the change in the fair value of pension plan assets as net asset gain or loss. However, for purposes of accounting they are not distinguished separately. Actuarial gains or losses include unrealized and realized amounts. A change in actuarial assumptions will also result in actuarial gains or losses.

Actuarial losses or gains are deferred and amortized as an adjustment to pension expense over future years. Recognition of actuarial gains or losses is based on the corridor method. This method lowers the amount of gain or loss to be reflected as an adjustment of pension cost. Under the corridor (materiality threshold) approach, recognition is given to certain gains or losses exceeding 10% of the greater of the beginning of year balances of the projected benefit obligation or the market-related value of plan assets. The excess over the corridor (test) is amortized over the average remaining service period for active employees expected to receive benefits in the plan. The amortization of actuarial losses increases pension expense, while the amortization of actuarial gains reduces pension expense. If the balance of the unrecognized net gain or loss is below the corridor, no amortization occurs. The unrecognized net gain or loss balance is carried forward as is.

EXAMPLE

At the beginning of the year, the projected benefit obligation was $250,000 and the market-related value of plan assets was $325,000. The corridor equals $32,500 (10% × $325,000). Actuarial gain or loss is not recognized unless it exceeds $32,500. The excess over $32,500 (corridor) is amortized. Thus, if the actuarial gain was $40,000, $7,500 ($40,000 – $32,500) would be amortized as a reduction to pension expense over the average remaining service period for active employees in the plan. If the actuarial gain was $30,000, there would be no amortization because the corridor ($32,500) had not been exceeded.

However, actuarial losses or gains applicable to a single event unrelated to the pension plan and not in the ordinary course of business are immediately recognized in the current year's income statement. This may arise in the case of disposing of a business segment or closing a plant.

If the employer wishes to use an approach other than the minimum amortization of unrecognized gains and losses discussed previously, it can use an alternative amortization method as long as it is logical, consistently applied to both gains and losses, disclosed, and reduces the unamortized balance by an amount more than that which would arise from the minimum amortization method.

Although actuarial gains and losses are reflected on the books of the pension plan, the employer does not record such gains or losses on its books. The employer only shows its amounts in its worksheet records.

Emerging Issues Task Force Consensus Summary Number 91–7 provides the accounting for pension benefits paid by employers after insurance companies fail to provide annuity benefits.

Pension Plan Benefit Formula

In the case where a pension plan benefit formula assigns all or a disproportionate share of total pension benefits to future years, the employee's total projected benefit is computed and used as the basis to assign total pension plan benefits. In this case, it is presumed that the employee's total projected benefit will accumulate proportionately based on the ratio of completed service years to date to the total completed service years ending when the benefit is fully vested.

Some benefit formulas are as follows:

- *Career-average-pay formula* This formula bases pension benefits on the worker's salary for his or her working career with the employer.

- *Final-pay formula* A benefit formula in which pension benefits are based on the employee's salary over a stipulated time period close to the retirement date or based on the period of time in which the worker earns the most.

- *Flat-benefit formula* A benefit formula in which benefits are a constant dollar amount per year of service. An example is a retirement benefit of $30 of biweekly retirement income for each service year.

Types of Methods

The unit credit method is used for flat-benefit plans. Under such a plan, benefits are expensed as a constant amount per service year. Pension expense and the related liability is based on estimating future salaries for total benefits paid. Under final pay plans, the projected unit credit method is used.

Plan Assets

Pension plan assets are typically maintained in a trust account. In is unusual for an employer to withdraw plan assets from the trust fund. However, a withdrawal may occur if the value of plan assets exceeds the pension obligation when the plan is ended. The plan contract may allow for employer withdrawal in this case as long as all pension obligations have been met by the employer. Pension plan assets do not include those that are unrestricted for purposes other than paying pension benefits or those which are not segregated in a pension trust fund. Plan assets are increased from income thereon, such as capital gains, interest, and dividends. Plan assets are reduced by capital losses, administrative costs, and benefit payments to retirees.

Plan assets used to operate the pension plan are recorded at book value. These assets include office building, office equipment, and furniture and fixtures.

Pension plan assets held as investments so as to have sufficient funds to pay pension benefits to retirees are recorded at their fair market value.

Pension plan assets are recorded on the books of the pension plan. The employer only keeps worksheet records to track the cost and fair market value of those assets. Fair value of plan assets is measured in the following preferential order: market price, selling price of comparable investments, and present value of cash flows. Fair value is the price negotiated between a willing buyer and seller. It is not based on liquidation value.

Fair market value of plan assets at the end of the year equals the fair market value of plan assets at the beginning of the year plus employer contributions plus actual return on plan assets less benefit payments.

EXAMPLE

A company reports the following information regarding pension plan assets:

Fair market value of plan assets—1/1	$700,000
Employer contributions	100,000
Actual return on plan assets	50,000
Benefit payments to retirees	40,000

The fair market value of plan assets on December 31 equals $810,000, computed as follows:

Fair market value of plan assets—1/1	$700,000
Employer contributions	100,000
Actual return	50,000
Benefit payments	(40,000)
Fair market value of plan assets—12/31	$810,000

Underfunding or Overfunding

Pension expense will in most cases not equal the amount of cash funded into the plan by the employer. If pension expense is more than the cash funded (underfunded), a deferred (accrued) pension liability (credit) arises. On the other hand, if pension expense is less than the cash funded (overfunded), a deferred (prepaid) pension asset (charge) arises.

EXAMPLE

Pension expense	800,000	
Cash		700,000
Deferred pension liability		100,000
Pension expense	800,000	
Deferred (prepaid) pension asset	100,000	
Cash		900,000

EXAMPLE

The following data relate to a company's defined benefit pension plan:

Deferred (prepaid) pension asset—1/1	$4,000
Service cost	22,000
Interest cost	30,000
Actual return on plan assets	25,000
Amortization of past service cost	43,000
Employer contribution	37,000

Assume that the fair market value of plan assets exceeds the accumulated benefit obligation at year-end. On December 31 the deferred pension liability (unfunded accrued pension cost) equals $29,000, computed as follows:

Pension expense:

Service cost	$22,000	
Interest cost	30,000	
Actual return on plan assets	(25,000)	
Amortization of prior service cost	43,000	$70,000
Less: Deferred (prepaid) pension asset—1/1	$ 4,000	
Employer contributions	37,000	(41,000)
Deferred pension liability—12/31		$29,000

EXAMPLE

The following data apply to Lake's defined benefit pension plan:

Prepaid pension cost—beginning of year	$ 5,000
Employer contribution	60,000
Service cost	40,000
Interest on projected benefit obligation	25,000
Actual return on plan assets	30,000
Amortization of unamortized prior service costs	50,000

The company's fair market value of pension plan assets exceeded the accumulated benefit obligation. At December 31, the amount to be reported as unfunded accrued pension cost is computed as follows:

Pension expense ($40,000 + $25,000 − $30,000 + $50,000)		$85,000
Less: Prepaid pension cost—1/1	$5,000	
Employer contribution	60,000	65,000
Unfunded accrued pension cost—12/31		$20,000

Minimum Pension Liability

A minimum pension liability (MPL) arises and must be recognized at year-end when the accumulated benefit obligation (ABO) exceeds the fair value (not market-related asset value) of pension plan assets at year-end. (A minimum pension liability is synonymous with unfunded accumulated benefit obligation.) Liability recognition is based on the conservatism principle. However, a minimum pension asset would not be recognized because it violates conservatism. (A minimum pension asset is synonymous with overfunded accumulated benefit obligation.)

EXAMPLE

Accumulated benefit obligation—12/31	$400,000
Less: Fair value of pension plan assets—12/31	500,000
Minimum pension asset	$100,000

This minimum pension asset cannot be recorded.

The minimum pension liability is the total liability to be shown in the balance sheet broken down into two accounts (either a deferred pension liability or deferred pension asset) and the additional pension liability. If there exists a deferred pension liability, it is subtracted from the minimum pension liability to arrive at the additional pension liability. If there exists a deferred pension asset, it is added to the minimum pension liability to arrive at the additional pension liability. While there is no account called minimum pension liability, it consists of the additional pension liability plus the deferred pension liability (or less the deferred pension asset).

EXAMPLE

Accumulated benefit obligation—12/31	$600,000
Less: Fair value of pension plan assets—12/31	400,000
Minimum pension liability	$200,000
Less: Deferred (accrued) pension liability	60,000
Additional pension liability	$140,000

PROOF

Minimum pension liability = Additional pension liability
+ Deferred pension liability
$200,000 = $140,000 + $60,000

EXAMPLE

Accumulated benefit obligation—12/31	$600,000

Less: Fair value of pension plan assets—12/31	400,000
Minimum pension liability	$200,000
Add: Deferred pension asset	60,000
Additional pension liability	$260,000

PROOF

Minimum pension liability = Additional pension liability
– Deferred pension asset
$200,000 = $260,000 – $60,000

When an additional pension liability is recorded, the debit is to intangible asset (pension plan) and the credit is to additional pension liability. The intangible asset (pension plan) is not amortized.

EXAMPLE

Using the same information as the preceding example, the journal entry would be

Intangible asset(pension plan)	260,000	
Additional pension liability		260,000

Exception: The intangible asset(pension plan) cannot exceed the unamortized prior service cost shown in the footnote. If it does, the excess is presented in a separate account called minimum pension liability adjustment (net of tax) in the other comprehensive income section of the income statement. While these items may be adjusted periodically, they are not amortized.

EXAMPLE

Assume in the prior example that the unamortized prior service cost shown in the footnote was $340,000. No additional entry is needed because the intangible asset (pension plan) of $260,000 does not exceed the unamortized prior service cost.

Assume instead that the unamortized prior service cost disclosed in the footnote was $210,000. The exception would now apply and the journal entry would be

Intangible asset (pension plan)	210,000
Minimum pension liability adjustment*	50,000
Additional pension liability	260,000

*The account may also be described as excess of additional pension liability over unamortized prior service cost.

In this case, the intangible asset (pension plan) cannot exceed $210,000.

Note: If not needed at the end of the next year, the foregoing entry would be reversed.

EXAMPLE

On January 1, 20X3, a company started a defined benefit pension plan. The service cost for the year was $130,000, which was completely funded at the year-end 20X3. The amount contributed to fund prior service cost was $50,000. Amortization expense on prior service cost was $23,000. The amount to be presented as prepaid pension cost at December 31, 20X3 is $27,000 ($50,000 − $23,000). Note that because the service cost was fully funded, no prepaid or accrued pension cost arises. The prepaid pension cost only applies to the excess of the amount funded over the amortized prior service cost.

EXAMPLE

The following data apply to Marco Company's defined benefit pension plan at December 31, 20X6:

Pension expense	$32,000
Unamortized prior service cost	48,000
Unfunded accumulated benefit obligation	90,000

There were no contributions to the pension plan during the year. The additional pension liability to be reported is $58,000 determined as follows:

Unfunded accumulated benefit obligation (minimum pension liability)	$90,000
Less: accrued pension cost	32,000*
Additional pension liability—12/31/20X6	$58,000

*Since no funding was made during the year, pension expense was fully accrued.

The excess of additional pension liability over unamortized prior service cost equals $10,000, computed as follows:

Additional pension liability	$58,000
Less: Unamortized prior service cost	48,000
Excess amount	$10,000

EXAMPLE

A company started a defined benefit pension plan on January 1, 19X4. The following information exists on December 31, 19X4:

Accumulated benefit obligation	$140,000
Fair market value of plan assets	80,000
Pension expense	53,000
Employer's contribution	50,000

The additional pension liability at December 31, 19X4 equals $57,000, computed as follows:

Accumulated benefit obligation	$140,000
Fair value of plan assets	80,000
Minimum pension liability	$ 60,000
Less: Deferred pension liability	3,000
Additional pension liability	$ 57,000

EXAMPLE

Yaho Company started a defined benefit pension plan on January 1, 20X0. The following information was provided for the year 20X0, as of December 31, 20X0:

Accumulated benefit obligation	$200,000
Employer contribution	130,000
Pension expense	150,000
Fair market value of plan assets	145,000
Deferred pension cost liability	20,000

The additional pension liability at December 31, 20X0 is computed as follows:

Accumulated benefit obligation	$200,000
Fair market value of plan assets	145,000
Minimum pension liability	$ 55,000
Less: Deferred pension cost	20,000
Additional pension liability	$ 35,000

EXAMPLE

A company presents the following information at December 31, 19X6:

Minimum pension liability	$37,000
Unamortized prior service cost	18,000
Pension expense	15,000

The company made no contributions during the year. Therefore, the deferred pension liability equals $15,000 since the journal entry would be

| Pension expense | 15,000 | |
| Deferred pension liability | | 15,000 |

On December 31, 19X6, the additional pension liability equals $22,000, computed as follows:

Minimum pension liability	$37,000
Less: Deferred pension liability	15,000
Additional pension liability	$22,000

The minimum pension liability adjustment equals $4,000, computed as follows:

Additional pension liability	$22,000
Less: Unamortized prior service cost	18,000
Minimum pension liability adjustment	$ 4,000

EXAMPLE

The following information applies to Smith Company's defined benefit pension plan as of December 31, 20X3:

Deferred pension cost	$90,000
Unamortized prior service cost	50,000
Unfunded accumulated benefit obligation	160,000

The excess of the additional pension liability over the unamortized prior service cost to be presented in the statement of stockholders' equity is as follows:

Unfunded accumulated benefit obligation	$160,000
Less: Deferred pension cost	90,000
Additional pension liability	$ 70,000
Less: Unamortized prior service cost	50,000
Excess amount	$ 20,000

EXAMPLE

The following information applies to a company's defined benefit pension plan at year-end:

Minimum pension liability (unfunded accumulated benefit obligation)	$170,000
Unrecognized (unamortized) prior service cost	60,000
Deferred pension liability (accrued pension cost)	90,000

The minimum pension liability adjustment to be charged equals $20,000, computed as follows:

Minimum pension liability	$170,000
Less: Deferred pension liability	90,000
Additional pension liability	$ 80,000
Less: Unamortized prior service cost	60,000
Minimum pension liability adjustment	$ 20,000

The journal entry is

Intangible asset—pension plan	60,000	
Minimum pension liability adjustment	20,000	
Additional pension liability		80,000

EXAMPLE

A company reports the following information for its defined benefit pension plan:

Pension expense	$ 700,000
Employer contribution for year	620,000
Accumulated benefit obligation—12/31	1,600,000
Fair market value of plan assets—12/31	1,300,000
Unamortized prior service cost—12/31	250,000

The journal entry to record pension expense and the funding of the plan is

Pension expense	700,000	
Cash		620,000
Deferred pension liability		80,000

The computation of minimum pension liability and additional pension liability follow:

Accumulated benefit obligation—12/31	$1,600,000
Fair market value of plan assets—12/31	1,300,000
Minimum pension liability	$ 300,000*
Less: Deferred pension liability	80,000
Additional pension liability	$ 220,000

*If the fair market value of plan assets—12/31 exceeded the accumulated benefit obligation—12/31, a minimum pension asset would not be recorded because it violates conservatism.

The journal entry is

Intangible asset—pension plan	220,000*	
Additional pension liability		220,000

*The exception to the rule does not apply because the unamortized prior service cost—12/31 ($250,000) exceeds the additional pension liability ($220,000).

EXAMPLE

The following information is provided about a company's pension plan for the year 19X2:

Service cost	$340,000
Projected benefit obligation—1/1/19X2	900,000
Accumulated benefit obligation—12/31/19X2	800,000
Fair market value of plan assets—12/31/19X2	700,000
Actual return on pension plan assets	30,000
Unamortized prior service cost—1/1/19X2	130,000
Interest (settlement) rate	10%
Amortization period for prior service cost	10 years
Employer contribution to plan	450,000

Pension expense equals $413,000, computed as follows:

Service cost	$340,000
Interest on projected benefit obligation (10% × $900,000)	90,000
Actual return on plan assets	(30,000)
Amortization of prior service cost ($130,000/10 years)	13,000
Pension expense	$413,000

The unamortized prior service cost on December 31, 19X2 equals $117,000, computed as follows:

Unamortized prior service cost—1/1/19X2	$130,000
Amortization of prior service cost for 19X2	13,000
Unamortized prior service cost—12/31/19X2	$117,000

If the cash funded for the year was $450,000, the journal entry to fund the plan would be

Pension Expense	413,000	
Deferred Pension Asset	37,000	
Cash		450,000

The minimum pension liability and the additional pension liability are computed as follows:

Accumulated benefit obligation—12/31/19X2	$800,000
Less: Fair market value of plan assets—12/31/19X2	700,000
Minimum pension liability	$100,000
Add: Deferred pension asset	37,000
Additional pension liability	$137,000

The journal entry to record the additional pension liability is

Intangible asset—pension plan	117,000*	
Minimum pension liability adjustment	20,000	
Additional pension liability		137,000

*The intangible asset—pension plan cannot be recorded at more than the unamortized prior service cost at December 31, 19X2, which is $117,000. The excess of $20,000 is charged to the account entitled "minimum pension liability adjustment."

If instead we assumed that the unamortized prior service cost on 12/31/19X2 was more than $137,000, the journal entry would have been

Intangible asset—pension plan	137,000	
Additional pension liability		137,000

In general, pension assets and liabilities may be netted in the employer's balance sheet if there is a right of offset, even if a liability has not yet been settled.

Retirement Benefit

A retirement benefit may be determined by considering such factors as salary and service years.

EXAMPLE

Mr. Paul has eight years before retirement. The expected salary at retirement is $60,000. The pension benefit is 4% of final salary for each service year payable at retirement. The retirement benefit is calculated as

Final annual salary	$60,000
× Formula rate	× 4%
	$ 2,400
× Service years	× 8
Retirement benefit	$19,200

Comprehensive Examples

EXAMPLE

On January 1, 19X4, Travis Company adopts a defined benefit pension plan.

The return rate on assets is 12% and the interest rate on debt is 15%. Service costs for 19X4 and 19X5 are $200,000 and $215,000, respectively. The amounts funded for 19X4 and 19X5 are $170,000 and $195,000, respectively.

The journal entry for 19X4 is

Pension expense	200,000	
Cash		170,000
Deferred pension liability		30,000

The journal entry for 19X5 is

Pension Expense	215,600	
Cash		195,000
Deferred pension liability		20,600

Computation:

Service cost	$215,000
Interest on projected benefit obligation (15% × $200,000)	30,000
Return on plan assets (12% × $170,000)	(20,400)
Pension expense	$215,600

At December 31, 19X5 we have

Projected benefit obligation = $200,000 + $215,000 + $30,000 = $445,000
Pension plan assets = $170,000 + $195,000 + $20,400 = $385,400

EXAMPLE

Coleman Company has a defined benefit plan for its 1,000 employees. On January 1, 19X8, the fair market value of pension plan assets is $500,000, the accumulated benefit obligation is $540,000, and the projected benefit obligation is $650,000. It is anticipated that 10 workers eligible for pension benefits will leave each year over the next 10 years. Service cost for 19X1 is $90,000. On December 31, 19X8, the projected benefit obligation is $680,000, the fair market value of pension plan assets is $510,000, and the accumulated benefit obligation is $570,000. The return on plan assets is 9% and the interest rate on debt is 10%. There are no actuarial gains or losses for the year. Cash funded to the trustee for the year is $120,000.

Pension expense equals

Service cost	$ 90,000
Interest on projected benefit obligation (10% × $650,000)	65,000
Return on plan assets (9% × $500,000)	(45,000)
Amortization of actuarial gains or losses	—
Amortization of prior service cost	27,273
Pension expense	$137,273

Calculation of the amortization of prior service cost follows:

Projected benefit obligation—1/1	$650,000
Less: Fair value of pension plan assets—1/1	500,000
Initial net obligation—1/1	150,000

Amortization = $150,000/5.5 months = $27,273

$$\frac{n(n+1) \times P}{2} = \frac{10\,(10+1) \times 10}{2} = 55 \times 10 = 550$$

550/100 = 5.5 years

P = population decrement each year

The journal entries at December 31, 19X8 are

Pension expense	137,273	
Cash		120,000
Deferred pension liability		17,273
Intangible asset (pension plan)	42,727	
Additional pension liability		42,727

Computations follow:

Accumulated benefit obligation—12/31/19X8	$570,000
Less: Fair value of pension plan assets—12/31/19X8	510,000
Minimum pension liability—12/31/19X8	60,000
Less: Deferred pension liability	17,273
Additional pension liability	$ 42,727

Business Combinations

If a single-employer defined benefit pension plan is acquired as part of a purchase method acquisition of another company, a liability must be recognized for the excess of the projected benefit obligation over the fair value of the pension plan assets. On the other hand, an asset would be recorded if the plan assets exceed the projected benefit obligation. The projected benefit obligation includes the impact of an anticipated curtailment or termination of the acquired pension plan. Because a new pension asset or liability is recorded at the purchase date, an elimination will be made of both the unrecognized prior service cost and the unrecognized net gain or loss. In later years, the asset or liability recognized at the purchase date will be adjusted for the differences between the acquiring company's net pension cost and the amounts contributed.

Emerging Issues Task Force Consensus Summary Number 96–5 covers the recognition of liabilities for contractual termination benefits or changing benefit plan assumptions in anticipation of a business combination.

Discontinued Operations

If a disposal of a business segment occurs, any termination benefits must be recognized and reported as a component of discontinued operations in the income statement.

Employers Having More than One Defined Benefit Plan

As per FASB Statement Number 87, if an employer has more than one pension plan, it must make separate computations of pension expense, fair value of plan assets, and liabilities for each plan.

The employer may not offset assets or liabilities of different pension plans unless there is a legal right to use the assets on one plan to satisfy the debt or benefits of another plan.

Disclosures may be aggregated for all pension plans maintained by the employer except for the following:

- U.S. pension plans may not be combined with foreign pension plans unless there are similar assumptions used for both.

- A minimum pension asset of one plan may not be used to offset a minimum pension liability of another, and vice versa. (As you recall, a minimum pension liability is the only one that a company can show under GAAP. A minimum pension asset is prohibited because it violates conservatism. As previously stated, a minimum pension liability occurs when the accumulated benefit obligation at year-end exceeds the fair value of pension assets at year-end.)

Multiemployer Plans

A multiemployer plan usually includes participation of two or more unrelated employers. It often ensues from a collective bargaining arrangement with the union. The plan is usually administered by a board of trustees. In this case, plan assets contributed by one employer may be used to pay employee benefits of another participating employer. Thus, the assets are aggregated for all employers and are available and unrestricted to pay benefits to all employees regardless of whom they are employed by. In other words, there is no segregation of assets in a particular employer's account or any restrictions placed on that employer's assets. An example is a plan contributed to by all employers employing the members of a particular union regardless of whom the employees are employed by. Retirees of different employers receive payment from the same pooled fund. The Teamster's Union is a case in point.

In a multiemployer plan, the employer's pension expense equals its contribution to the plan for the year. If a contribution is due but yet unpaid, the employer must recognize it as a liability.

If an employer withdraws from the multiemployer plan, it may incur a liability for its part of the unfunded benefit obligation of the plan. If an employer would probably incur a liability if it withdraws from the plan and the amount is reasonably determinable, a loss must be accrued with a concurrent liability. However, if the loss is reasonably possible, only footnote disclosure is required.

Emerging Issues Task Force Consensus Summary Number 90–3 (*Accounting for Employer's Obligations for Future Contributions to a Multiemployer Pension Plan*) stipulates that an employer need not record a liability for an amount beyond that currently due.

The following must be disclosed by employers participating in a multiemployer plan:

- A description of the plan including workers covered
- The benefits to be provided
- Nature of matters impacting on the comparability of information for the years presented
- Pension expense for the period.

Multiple-Employer Plans

These plans are similar to multi-employer plans. They also consist of two or more unrelated employers. However, multiple-employer plans are, in effect, aggregated single-employer plans that are combined so that assets of all may be totaled to lower administrative costs. The assets are also merged to improve the overall rate of return from investing them. In many cases, participating employers may use different benefit formulas for their respective pension contributions. Each employer in the plan accounts for its particular interest separately. An example of such an arrangement is when companies in an industry have their trade association handle the plans of all the companies. Each company retains its responsibilities only for its own workers. Multiple-employer plans are usually not associated with collective bargaining contracts.

Annuity (Allocated) Contracts

An employer may sign a valid and irrevocable insurance contract to pay benefit obligations arising from a defined benefit plan. Annuity contracts are used to transfer the risk of providing employee benefits from the employer to the insurance company.

If the annuity contracts are the basis for funding the pension plan and paying plan obligations thereto, the insurance premium paid by the employer is the pension expense for the period covering all currently earned benefits. In this case, the company and plan do not report plan assets, accumulated benefit obligation, or a projected benefit obligation. On the other hand, if the annuity contracts cover just part of the benefit obligation, the employer is liable for the uncovered obligation. Such uncovered obligation is accounted for as per the usual requirements under FASB Statement Number 87 specified in this chapter for pension plans.

In a participating annuity contract, the insurer pays the employer part of the income earned from investing the insurance premiums. In most cases, income earned (e.g., dividends, interest) reduces pension cost. A drawback to the employer of a participating contract is that it costs more than one which is nonparticipating because of the participation right. This additional cost associated with the participation privilege should be recognized as a pension plan asset. Therefore, except for the cost of participation rights, pension plan assets exclude the cost of annuity contracts. In later years, fair value should be used in valuing the participation right included in plan assets. In the event that fair value may not be reasonably determined, the asset should be recorded at cost, with amortization based on the dividend period specified in the agreement. However, unamortized cost cannot exceed the net realizable value of the participation right.

Caution: If the terms of the participating annuity contract are such that the employer retains all or most of the risk related to the benefit obligation, the purchase of this contract does not represent a settlement of the employer's obligations under the pension plan.

Insurance contracts other than annuity contracts are considered investments. They are reported as pension plan assets and reported at fair value. Fair value may be in terms of conversion value, contract value, cash surrender value, etc., depending on the circumstances.

In terms of accounting for pension plans, the definition of an annuity contract is not satisfied if one or more of the following exists:

- There is a captive insurance company, meaning that the insurance entity has as its major client the employer or any of its associated parties.

- There is uncertainty as to whether the insurance company will be able to pay its obligations because of financial problems.

Emerging Issues Task Force Consensus Summary Number 91–7 (*Accounting for Pension Benefits Paid by Employers after Insurance Companies Fail to Provide Annuity Benefits*) stipulates that the employer must record a loss when it assumes the obligation to pay retirees because the insurance company is financially unable to do so (e.g., bankruptcy). The loss is recorded at the lower of any gain associated with the original insurance contract or the amount of benefit obligation assumed. Any unrecognized additional loss should be treated as an amendment to the pension plan.

Disclosures

A single-employer pension plan requires the following footnote disclosures:

- Description of the plan, including categorization of workers covered, retirement age, funding policy, benefit formula, and benefits provided
- Pension plan commitments, such as to increase benefits
- Elements (components) of pension expense

- Assumptions and changes therein used in determining pension expense and related funding, such as turnover rate, mortality rate, and interest rate

- Unamortized prior service cost and a description of the amortization policy

- Unrecognized net gain or loss

- Annuity benefits due employees

- Weighted-average assumed discount rate and the rate of compensation increases used in measuring the projected benefit obligation

- Weighted-average long-term return rate on pension plan assets

- Discounted value of vested and nonvested benefits

- Fair value and type of pension plan assets

- Amounts and type of securities included in pension plan assets (Further, other pension plan assets should be identified.)

- Accumulated benefit obligation

- Projected benefit obligation (Included is the rate of compensation increase to measure the projected benefit obligation.)

- Additional pension liability

- Nonbenefit liabilities

- Vested benefits

- Liabilities of the pension plan other than those applicable for plan benefits (Examples of these types of liabilities are unsecured borrowings and unsettled stock purchases.)

- Reconciling the plan's funded status with employer amounts recognized in the balance sheet (e.g., unamortized prior service cost, fair value of plan assets, projected benefit obligation)

- Specific investments representing 5% or more of pension plan assets

- Insurance coverage for the pension plan, if any (Reference to annuity contracts agreed to by the employer and insurer should be specified.)

- Related party transactions
- Nature and impact of matters bearing upon the ability to compare pension data over the years (The amount of annual benefits to retirees covered by the annuity contracts should be indicated.)
- Modification in cost-sharing arrangements

Optional disclosures for single-employer plans may also be provided, including the following:

- Categorization of pension plan assets by major type
- Cash flow information with regard to employer funding and benefits paid during the period
- Percentage of pension expense to total salaries
- Change in the projected benefit obligation that would arise from a one-percentage change in the assumed discount rate and the assumed rate of compensation increase

The preceding disclosures may be aggregated for all of the employer's pension plans or presented in groups. Disclosures associated with U.S. plans should be separate from those outside the United States unless the plans are similar and use the same assumptions.

Financial Statement Analysis

For financial statement analysis purposes, an unrecorded liability exists for the amount by which the projected benefit obligation exceeds the accumulated benefit obligation. Although a minimum pension asset is not recorded for accounting purposes when the fair value of pension assets exceed the accumulated benefit obligation, it should be considered for analytical purposes as an unrecorded asset.

An analysis should be made of the components making up pension plan assets. Are there risky or speculative investments in the portfolio? Is there an excessive percentage of assets invested in a particular stock? If the company needs to be liquidated, how much of pension plan assets are protected to meet pension plan deficiencies?

Employee Retirement Income Security Act (ERISA)

This Act was passed in 1974. It enumerates law for pension plans so as to improve their financial viability and to safeguard employee interests. A Pension Benefit Guaranty Corporation (PBGC) was created to protect against employees losing their pension benefits. The PBGC guarantees that employees will receive a minimum amount of benefits based on their service years in the event of employer bankruptcy. To provide funds to pay employees, employers are required to pay insurance premiums to the PBGC. The Act requires certain employee participation in the pension plan. The PBGC has the authority to administer a terminated plan. The Act mandates that annual reports on the pension plan be provided, including plan assets and liabilities as well as a description of the plan. The Act generally provides for full vesting of pension benefits when an employee has been in the service of the employer for 15 years. Minimum funding levels for employers are specified. Past service costs must be funded over a period not exceeding 40 years. An employer's violation of the statute's provisions may result in penalties, liens on or seizure of assets, and the loss of tax deductions.

SETTLEMENT, CURTAILMENT, AND TERMINATION

FASB Statement Number 88 (*Employers' Accounting for Settlements and Curtailments of Defined Benefit Pension Plans and for Termination Benefits*) covers situations in which modifications are made to a pension plan.

Settlement

A settlement of a pension plan is an action that discharges an employer from his or her primary responsibility for an entity's pension obligation and the associated elimination of the risks associated with having sufficient assets available to satisfy this obligation. Examples of settlements include

1. Acquiring annuity contracts to cover participants' vested benefits
2. Making lump sum payments to pension plan participants in satisfaction of their right to receive pension benefits

A settlement has to meet each of the following criteria:

- Significantly reduces risk of the pension obligation
- Relieves pension benefit responsibility
- Is irrevocable

After the settlement of a pension plan, the employer may choose to provide pension benefits in a new plan or may decide to continue the old plan.

In accounting for a settlement, the amount of the gain or loss is a function of the percentage of the projected benefit obligation (PBO) that has been reduced. That is, if only a portion of the PBO is settled, then only a proportionate part of the maximum gain or loss is recognized. The maximum gain or loss that could be recognized is the unrecorded net gain or loss existing at the date of settlement and the unrecognized net asset or obligation that existed when FASB Statement Number 87 was initially applied. If, for example, the PBO is reduced by 60%, then 60% of the gain or loss is recognized in the current year's income statement. Correspondingly, if the employer's PBO is completely discharged, then the total gain or loss at the date of settlement is recognized. Settlement gains or losses do not, in most situations, meet the requirements of extraordinary items and therefore are considered ordinary. Full disclosure should always be made of the nature of the settlement.

EXAMPLE

1. On December 31, 19A, X Company made a lump sum payment to retirees to satisfy the benefits of all retired individuals.

2. On December 31, 19A, the plan's projected benefit obligation consisted of the following two components:

Cost of settling retirees benefits	$100,000
Benefits owed to active employees—not settled	70,000
Total Projected Benefit Obligation	$170,000

3. On December 31, 19A, the Company disclosed the following on its balance sheet related to pension disclosure:

Projected Benefit Obligation	$(170,000)
Plan assets	200,000
Funded status	$ 30,000
Unrecognized prior service costs	24,000
Net loss	20,000
Net obligation at the time FASB Number 87 was adopted	(50,000)
Prepaid pension cost	$ 24,000

MAXIMUM GAIN (LOSS) ON SETTLEMENT

Unrecognized net loss prior to settlement	$(20,000)
Net Obligation at time FASB Number 87 was adopted	50,000
Maximum gain recognizable	$ 30,000

Settlement Reduction of the Projected Benefit Obligation:

$$\frac{\text{Projected benefit obligation settled}}{\text{Total project benefit obligation}} = \frac{\$100,000}{\$170,000} = 59\%$$

SETTLEMENT GAIN

Maximum gain recognizable	$30,000
Reduction in projected benefit obligation	× 59%
Settlement gain	$17,700

The same application would apply, for example, if an employer gives employees a lump sum payment in exchange for their pension rights. The gain or loss on settlement is recognized in the current year's income statement. If there is a settlement of only part of the plan, only a proportionate share of the gain or loss, as before, is recognized.

Curtailment

A curtailment takes place when an occurrence materially reduces the future years of service of current employees or eliminates for most workers the accumulation of defined benefits for future services. An example is the closing of a plant, terminating employment.

The gain or loss arising from curtailment is recognized in the current year's income statement. The gain or loss is composed of the following components:

- Unamortized (unrecognized) prior service cost for employee service no longer required
- Change in the pension benefit obligation

In a curtailment some of the future pension benefits for employees currently employed are reduced, resulting in a gain (PBO decrease) or loss (PBO increase). For example, the PBO may be decreased by the amount of the pension benefits that the entity does not have to pay as a result of some employees being terminated. If, on the other hand, these employees (those who are terminated) are eligible for subsidized early retirement and benefits earlier than expected, an increase in the PBO occurs.

It is important to note that a pension plan curtailment may occur by itself or in conjunction with a settlement. If, for example, years of future service are cut back as a result of the discontinuance of a segment of a business, but the pension plan continues overall for the employees of the entity, a curtailment has occurred but a settlement has not. If, on the other hand, the employer totally terminates the entity's pension plan and then fully settles the pension obligation with employees, both a settlement and curtailment have occurred.

In accounting for curtailments, a curtailment gain is computed as the difference between the amount of the PBO decrease as a result of the curtailment less any related unrecognized net loss. A curtailment loss, on the other hand, is the difference between the amount of the PBO increase less any related unrecognized gain. In computing curtailment gains and losses, any unrecognized net asset or liability at transition is also considered part of the unrecognized gain or loss.

EXAMPLE

As a result of a termination of employees' services earlier than expected due to the closing of a facility, the following occurred:

Increase in projected benefit obligation from curtailment	$600,000
Unrecognized net gain	(360,000)
Curtailment loss	$240,000

Assume the same circumstances as in the prior situation; however, in this case assume the following:

Decrease in projected benefit obligation from curtailment	$(600,000)
Unrecognized net loss	360,000
Curtailment Gain	$(240,000)

Termination

If early retirement benefits are offered by an employer, are accepted by employees, and the amount of the benefits can be reasonably estimated, an expense provision should be recorded by debiting expense, crediting cash (for the down payment), and crediting a liability (for future payments). The amount accrued equals the down payment plus the discounted value of future employer payments. In addition, there should be a footnote describing the particulars of the agreement.

Note: A gain or loss arising from a settlement or curtailment of a pension plan or termination benefits that are directly associated with disposing of a business segment is included in the gain or loss on the disposal of the segment.

EXAMPLE

Assume that ABC Company offers special termination benefits to employees that are accepted by the employees and can reasonably estimated. The employees accept the offer on July 15, 19A. The cost of the termination benefits includes a lump sum payment of $2,500,000, and the present value of expected future payments amounts to $2,600,000. The entry that should be made for the accrual of termination benefits follows:

Retirement termination benefits expense	5,100,000	
Estimated liability for termination benefits		5,100,000

TRUSTEE REPORTING IN A DEFINED BENEFIT PENSION PLAN

FASB Statement Number 35 (*Accounting and Reporting by Defined Benefit Pension Plans*) specifies the accounting, reporting, and footnote disclosures required of the trustee of a defined benefit plan. The trustee reports for the plan as a separate accounting and legal entity for which books of record are kept. Accrual accounting must be followed. The trustee is not required to prepare financial statements for the plan. However, if issued, the financial statements must be prepared in accordance with certain rules. The major purpose of reporting is to allow one to evaluate the adequacy of the plan to pay employees' benefits after retirement.

In the balance sheet, pension assets are netted against pension liabilities. Operating assets are expressed at book value. Investments are reported at market value. One asset presented is "Contributions Receivable Due from Employer."

The pension plan liability presented by the employer excludes the employees' accumulated benefits because in reality plan participants are equity holders and not creditors of the plan.

The trustee must make the following footnote disclosure:

■ Description of the plan, including changes therein

- Accounting and funding policies

- Net assets available for benefits and changes therein during the year, such as from capital appreciation of equity and debt securities (Capital appreciation or depreciation by source must be given.)

- Actuarial present value of accumulated plan benefits separately presented for that attributable to current employees, retirees, and beneficiaries (Changes in the discounted value of accumulated benefits should also be disclosed.)

There may be an annuity contract whereby an insurance company agrees to provide specified pension benefits based on premiums received.

POSTRETIREMENT BENEFIT PLANS OTHER THAN PENSIONS

The authoritative GAAP of accounting, reporting, and disclosures for postretirement benefit plans other than pensions is FASB Statement Number 106 (*Employers' Accounting for Postretirement Benefits Other Than Pensions*). Reference should also be made to the FASB Implementation Guide (*Questions and Answers*) titled *A Guide to Implementation for Statement 106.* Emerging Issues Task Force Consensus Summary Number 93–3 covers the reporting of plan assets under FASB Statement Number 106.

FASB Statement Number 106 provides the accounting provisions for health care and welfare benefits (such as dental care, medical care, eye care, legal services, tuition assistance, day care assistance, and other services) that are provided to retirees, their spouses, dependents, and beneficiaries other than pension benefits. Health care benefits are generally considered the most important and largest postretirement benefit. Most employers, prior to FASB Statement Number 106, accounted for postretirement benefits on a cash basis (pay-as-you-go basis). However, the accrual basis of accounting requires that the employer's obligation regarding the payment of future postretirement benefits be measured and the resulting cost be accrued during the employees' service period. This, of course, is also required by FASB Statement Number 87 in accounting for pensions. In fact, FASB Statement Number 106 on health care and nonpension benefits was actually modeled after FASB Statement Number 87 and is very similar to it. However, measuring future payments for health care benefits is more difficult than for pension plans. The level of health care costs is difficult to measure because of constant changes in medical technology, increased longevity of retirees and their dependents and beneficiaries, as well as new and unexpected illnesses that surface and are expensive to cure. In addition, many postretirement plans do not limit the amount of health care benefits that can be utilized by retirees.

Accounting

As was noted, the accounting requirements for postretirement benefits other than pensions are similar to those of pension plans. However, there are several differences as well.

Accrual of postretirement benefits expense must be made of the benefits employees are entitled to receive based on services performed. In the case of a defined contribution plan, the cash funded for the year represents the postretirement benefits expense. However, in a defined benefit plan the amount funded and the expense will be different.

Postretirement benefits expense is based on actuarial calculations. The benefits are allocated over the employees' service years. The benefits must be completely accrued by the time that the employee is fully vested (eligible) to receive them. Even if the employee resigns after the full eligibility date, he or she is entitled to those benefits.

The expected postretirement benefit obligation is the actuarial present value as of a particular date of the benefits expected to be paid to employees, beneficiaries, or covered dependents. It is used to calculate service cost.

In accounting for postretirement benefits, the health care and other postretirement benefits for current and future retirees are accrued over a period of time known as the attribution period. This period represents the period of service during which the employee earns the postretirement benefit. This period begins when the employee is hired and terminates when the employee terminates performing services and therefore is not eligible to receive benefits. The employee becomes vested for postretirement benefits on this date and is eligible to receive benefits.

Some new terms that were established by the FASB in FASB Statement Number 106 for postretirement benefits accounting that are different from FASB Statement Number 87 include the following:

- *Expected Postretirement Benefit Obligation (EPBO)*   This is the total benefits expected to be paid after retirement to employees and their dependents. It is disclosed at its actuarial present value off balance sheet. However, it is used in computing periodic postretirement expense.

- *Accumulated Postretirement Benefit Obligation (APBO)*   This is the actuarial present value of future benefits related to employers' services rendered as of a particular date. The difference between the EPBO and APBO is that the APBO does not include active employees not yet eligible for benefits. That is, before an employee achieves full eligibility, the APBO is only a portion of the EPBO.

Another unique issue of FASB 106 is the accounting for the transition amount. The transition amount is an obligation or asset at the beginning of the year of adopting FASB Statement Number 106. It is computed as the difference between the APBO and the fair value of the plan assets plus any accrued obligation or less any prepaid cost (asset). Generally, large transition obligations occur because most companies are only now starting to begin to accrue postretirement benefit costs for the first time.

The accounting treatment for the transition amount includes a choice of the following:

1. *Immediate recognition*   The transition amount is immediately written off and is disclosed in the income statement as a change in accounting principle, net of taxes, and in the balance sheet as a long-term liability termed Postretirement Benefit Obligation. Previously issued financial statements are not permitted to be restated.

2. *Deferred recognition* Employers choosing this option must amortize the transition amount on a straight-line basis over the average remaining service period to expected retirement of the employees working at the time of transition and expected to receive benefits. If the remaining service period is less than 20 years, the employer may elect a 20-year amortization period. The transition amount, however, may not be amortized more slowly than it is paid.

It is important to note that once a method of accounting for the transition amount is chosen, it cannot be changed.

Disclosures

Required footnote disclosures for postretirement benefits include

- Description of the plan, including nature of benefits to be paid
- Health care cost trend factors
- Effect of a one-percentage-point increase in trend rates
- Trend in compensation cost
- Discount rate
- Funding policy
- Components of postretirement expense
- Unamortized prior service cost
- Accumulated postretirement benefit obligation
- Fair market value of plan assets
- Return on plan assets on an after-tax basis

FASB STATEMENT NUMBER 132
Employers' Disclosures about Pension and Other Postretirement Benefits

Newly issued FASB Statement Number 132, *Employers' Disclosures about Pension and Other Postretirement Benefits*, standardizes disclosures for retiree benefits. In general, it revises and improves the effectiveness of current note disclosure requirements for employers' pensions and other retiree benefits. Recognition or accounting measurement issues are not addressed. In addition, the statement eliminates certain disclosures that have been deemed to be no longer useful by the FASB and requires additional information to enhance financial analysis.

PENSION PLAN FINANCIAL STATEMENTS

FASB Statement Number 35 (*Accounting and Reporting by Defined Benefit Pension Plans*) provides authoritative guidance in accounting and reporting for defined benefit pension plans. Additional guidance is provided by FASB Statement Number 110 (*Reporting by Defined Benefit Pension Plans of Investment Contracts*) and the AICPA Accounting Standards Executive Committee (AcSEC) Practice Bulletin, *Reporting Separate Investment Fund Option Information of Defined-Benefit Pension Plans*. Other related information is given by

- Emerging Issues Task Force (EITF) Issue Number 89–1, *Accounting by a Pension Plan for Bank Investment Contracts and Guaranteed Investment Contracts*

- AICPA Industry Audit and Accounting Guide, *Audits of Employee Benefit Plans*

- Practice Bulletin Number 12, *Reporting Separate Investment Fund Option Information of Defined Contribution Pension Plans*

- Statement of Position (SOP) 94–4, *Reporting of Investment Contracts Held by Health and Welfare Benefit Plans and Defined Contribution Pension Plans*

A defined benefit plan pays specified or determinable retirement benefits to participants either on retirement or on the occurrence of certain events, such as death, disability, or termination of employment. Benefits are paid based on factors such as the participant's age, salary, length of service, and other factors. The employers' contributions in defined benefit plans are calculated actuarially based upon specified benefits and may be periodically adjusted.

A defined contribution plan, unlike a defined benefit plan, maintains separate accounts for each participant, and the employer deposits a specified amount in each participant's account on a periodic basis. Defined contribution plans include 401(k) and 403(b) plans, employee stock ownership plans, profit sharing plans, and money purchase plans. Participants' benefits in a defined contribution plan are simply equal to the amount accumulated in their respective accounts. (**Note:** The information in this section applies only to defined benefit plans and not to defined contribution plans.)

Defined benefit plans are not required by FASB Statement Number 35 to present financial statements. However, if the plan chooses to present financial statements, FASB Statement Number 35 requires the following information:

- Net assets available to pay benefits
- Changes in net assets available to pay benefits
- Actuarial present value of accumulated plan benefits
- Factors affecting the change in actuarial present value of accumulated plan benefits

This information may be disclosed either in the statement or otherwise. Certain disclosures about the plan and its accounting policies are also required.

The primary purpose of these financial statements is to provide information to assess the present and future ability of pension plans to pay promised benefits. The following information should be disclosed in the financial statements:

- Resources of the pension plan
- Accumulated benefits

- Transactions affecting the plan's resources and benefits
- Additional information to clarify financial statement presentation and make it understandable

Financial statements should be prepared as of the most recent year-end period. However, if the actuarial present value of accumulated plan benefits is unavailable or cannot be determined, then beginning of period information may be presented. Use of an interim date is not allowed by GAAP. Approximations may be used to determine benefit information at the beginning or end of the fiscal year, if such information becomes available during the fiscal year, as long as the method used to estimate benefits produces results comparable to those required by FASB Statement Number 35. Information about the actuarial present value of accumulated plan benefits and changes to the benefits may be presented as a separate statement or on the face of the statement of net assets or in notes to financial statements.

Comparative financial statements *must* be presented if the plan presents the actuarial present value of accumulated plan benefits as of the beginning of the plan period. Comparative financial statements are preferable even when they are not required. Information from several years may be more useful in assessing a plan's ability to pay benefits.

A statement of cash flows is not required of defined benefit plans. However, GAAP encourages its presentation when such information would be relevant in assessing a plan's ability to meet future obligations, such as when the assets lack liquidity or when financing is obtained for investments.

Exhibit 14–1

Statement of Net Assets Available for Benefits
For Year Ended December 31, 2001

ASSETS

Investments (fair value):

Government securities	$ 1,000,000	
Corporate debt securities	$ 1,500,000	
Investment contracts	$ 2,300,000	
Common stock	$ 4,500,000	
Preferred stock	$ 1,700,000	
Mortgages	$ 850,000	
Real estate	$ 1,200,000	
	$13,050,000	
Receivables		
Employees' contributions	$ 235,000	
Employer's contributions	$ 354,000	
Accrued interest	$ 400,000	
Accrued dividends	$ 325,000	
	$ 1,314,000	
Cash	$ 1,600,000	
Total assets		$15,964,000
LIABILITIES		
Accounts payable	$ 365,000	
Accrued expenses	$ 475,000	
Total liabilities		$ 840,000
NET ASSETS AVAILABLE FOR BENEFITS		$15,124,000

Net Assets Available for Benefits

The resources available to pay benefits to participants are identified in the statement of net assets. The statement of net assets (see Exhibit 14–1 above) is prepared using accrual accounting and includes information about a plan's assets and liabilities.

Investments

Benefit plans own many types of investments, such as marketable securities, restricted or unregistered securities, real estate, mortgages, leases, interests in limited partnerships, repurchase agreements, futures and options, and contracts with insurance companies that do not subject the insurance company to risks arising from policyholders' mortality or morbidity. Such investments must be identified in reasonable detail and presented at fair value in the financial statements. Fair value is defined as the amount that the plan could reasonably expect to receive in an arm's-length sale between willing buyers and sellers when neither is compelled to buy or sell. In an active market, quoted market values may be used. If an active market does not exist, the fair value may be determined using another method, such as discounted cash flow or estimates from independent expert appraisers. The method used should be disclosed in the financial statements or its footnotes. Brokerage commissions and other selling costs, if significant, should be considered in determining the fair value.

Contributions Receivable

Contributions receivable from participants, employers, and other sources should be recorded as of the reporting date and identified in the financial statements. All amounts that are formally committed to be paid to the plan as well as amounts that are legally or contractually due should be included in contributions receivable. Note, however, that an employer's accruing a liability to the pension plan does not, by itself, constitute sufficient basis for the plan to record a receivable. The following factors may provide evidence that the employer has formally committed to make a contribution to the plan:

- A formal approval, such as a resolution, by the employer's governing body to make a contribution
- A consistent pattern of making payments after the pension plan's year-end in accordance with an established funding policy that attributes the payments to the preceding plan year

- A federal income tax deduction, taken by the employer for periods ending on or before the reporting date for the pension plan

Insurance Contracts

Insurance contracts generally have two characteristics. The purchaser of the insurance contract makes payments to the insurance company before the insured event. The insurance company generally does not know if, when, or how much will have to be paid on the insurance contract at that time the contract is made.

Insurance contracts are required by FASB Statement Number 110 to be presented in the same format as specified in annual reports filed with certain governmental agencies pursuant to ERISA. The contracts are presented either at fair value or at amounts determined by the insurance company. If an insurance plan is not subject to ERISA, it still presents its insurance contracts as if the plan was subject to the reporting requirements of ERISA. Insurance contracts that do not relate to policyholders' mortality or morbidity are investments, not insurance contracts. Mortality or morbidity risk exists if the insurance company is required to make payments or forgo required premiums contingent upon the death or disability (life insurance contracts) or continued survival of specific individuals or groups of individuals (annuity contracts). An investment contract, such as a guaranteed interest contract, generally provides for a set return on principal over a given time period.

Operating Assets

Operating assets such as property, plant, equipment, and leasehold improvements are reported at historical costs less accumulated depreciation/amortization. If such assets are held for investment, rather than in operations, they should be a reported at fair value with other investments.

Liabilities

Liabilities for expenses related to investment purchases, trustee fees, and administrative fees should be accrued. Benefit obligations, however, should not be recorded by a defined benefit plan as a liability.

Statement of Changes in Net Assets Available for Benefits

Significant changes in net assets available for benefits should be identified in the statement of changes in net assets available for benefits (see Exhibit 14–2). Investment income, excluding realized or unrealized gains or losses, should be disclosed separately in reasonable detail. It is not necessary to report separately interest, dividends, etc. Realized and unrealized gains or losses on investment with quoted market values are reported separately from investments presented at otherwise determined fair value. The net change in fair value for each significant class of investments should be reported. Cash and noncash contributions from the employer, participants, and others should be reported separately at fair value. The nature of non-cash contributions should be described in footnotes. Benefits paid to participants, as well as administrative or operating expenses, should be identified and reported separately. Payment for insurance contracts that are excluded from the plan's assets, such as allocated contracts, is reported separately. Dividend income from such contracts may be netted against the purchase price. Footnote disclosure should be made about the dividend income policy.

Exhibit 14–2

Statement of Changes in Net Assets Available for Benefits
For Year Ended December 31, 2001

Investment Income	
Interest	$ 325,000
Dividend	415,000
Rental income	225,000
Increases (decreases) in fair value of investments	575,000
Less: Investment expenses	(125,000)
	1,415,000
Contributions	
Employees' contributions	685,000
Employer's contributions	1,200,000
	1,885,000
Benefits paid directly to participants	(877,000)
Annuity contracts purchased	(1,125,000)
Administrative expenses	(195,000)
	(2,197,000)
Net increase (Decrease) in Assets	1,103,000
Net assets available for benefits	
Beginning of year	18,357,000
End of year	$19,460,000

Exhibit 14–3

Statement of Accumulated Plan Benefits
For Year Ended December 31, 2001

Actuarial present value of vested benefits	
Participants currently receiving payments	$2,900,000
Other participants	1,700,000
	4,600,000
Actuarial present value of nonvested benefits	1,200,000
Total actuarial present value of accumulated plan benefits	$5,800,000

Actuarial Present Value
of Plan Benefits

Certain information about the actuarial present value of accumulated plan benefits of participants must be disclosed. FASB Statement Number 35 requires disclosure of vested and nonvested benefits. Vested benefits are not contingent upon future services by employees. The total actuarial present value of accumulated plan benefits may be divided into three categories:

1. Vested benefits of participants presently receiving payments, including benefits due and payable as of the benefit information date
2. Vested benefits of other participants
3. Nonvested benefits

Benefit obligation information may be presented as a separate statement (see Exhibit 14–3 on page 760), on another statement, or in footnotes to financial statements. Benefit obligation information, however, is not a liability on the statement of net assets. It also should not be disclosed as supplementary information. It is preferable to present benefit obligation information as of year-end. If this is not feasible due to difficulties in making actuarial determinations, information may be presented as of the beginning of the plan's year. An interim date, however, may not be used.

FASB Statement Number 35 assumes that the pension plan is a going concern and will continue to exist. Each actuarial assumption should be based on the plan's most likely expectations. The assumed rate of return should reflect the expected rate of return. It should be consistent with returns typically achieved on the types of assets held by the plan. The inflation rate assumed in determining the automatic cost-of-living adjustments should also be consistent with the assumed rates of return. Administrative expenses to be paid by the plan may be recognized using two methods. The assumed rate of return may be adjusted to reflect administrative expenses. Disclosure should be made about the adjustment. Alternatively, the administrative expenses may be assigned to the future and discounted to the benefit information date. The actuarial present value of accumulated plan benefits may alternatively be determined using the assumptions an insurance company would use if it were to issue a contract providing the same benefits to the same participants.

Pension plan benefits are usually based on years of service. Benefits can generally be determined through the provisions of the plan. However, if the benefits cannot be determined from the provisions, FASB Statement Number 35 requires the use of the following formula to determine the benefits includable in vested benefits:

$$
\begin{array}{l}
\text{Percentage of} \\
\text{plan benefits} \quad = \\
\text{accumulated}
\end{array}
\dfrac{\text{Number of years of service completed to the benefit information date}}{\text{Number of years service that will have been completed when the benefits will first be fully vested}}
$$

For benefits not includable in vested benefits, the following formula may be used:

$$
\begin{array}{l}
\text{Percentage of} \\
\text{plan benefits} \quad = \\
\text{accumulated}
\end{array}
\dfrac{\text{Number of years of service completed to the benefit information date}}{\text{Number of years service upon anticipated separation from covered employment}}
$$

Employees' history of earnings and service should be used to determine accumulated plan benefits. When benefits increase periodically, the employees' projected years of service should be used to determine death benefits, early retirement benefits, and disability benefits. Automatic benefit increases specified in the plan, even though subsequent to the benefit information date, should be recognized in determining accumulated plan benefits. Amendments adopted after the benefit information date do not affect the calculation of accumulated plan benefits. Benefits that will be provided by a contract should not be considered if the contract is excluded from the plan's financial statements. Social Security benefits may need to be determined in an integrated plan. It is assumed that the participant's pay will remain the same during his or her assumed service years. We ignore scheduled or future changes in the wage base or benefit level under Social Security.

Changes in Actuarial Present Value of Plan Benefits

All factors affecting the actuarial present value of accumulated plan benefits should be identified, if significant either individually or in the aggregate, in the financial statements or the footnotes (see Exhibit 14–4). Such changes include amendments to the plan, changes in the nature of the plan (such as a merger with another plan or a spinoff of a plan), and changes in actuarial assumptions. Other factors, such as the amount of accumulated benefits, change in the discount period, and the amount of benefits paid, should be disclosed.

Exhibit 14–4

Statement of Changes in Accumulated Plan Benefits
For Year Ended December 31, 2001

Actuarial present value of accumulated plan benefits, beginning of year	$16,755,000
Amendments to plan	(425,000)
Changes in actuarial assumptions	385,000
Other factors	175,000
Actuarial present value of accumulated plan benefits, end of year	$16,890,000

Required Disclosures

GAAP requires defined benefit plans to make several disclosures. A plan should disclose its accounting policies, including assumptions and methods used to derive the fair value of investments and the reported value of insurance contracts. Disclosure should be made of significant assumptions and methods used to determine the actuarial present value of accumulated plan benefits, including the rates of return, the inflation rate, and the retirement age of participants. A description of the provisions of pension plan vesting and benefit provisions should be presented. If that information is available elsewhere, making a reference to that published source is also acceptable. Amendments adopted on or before the latest benefit information date, if significant, should be described. A disclosure, including the effect on present value of accumulated plan benefits, is required if significant amendments are adopted after the benefit information date but before the plan's year-end. Disclosure is required of the order of priority of participants' claims to plan assets upon termination. If benefits are guaranteed by the Pension Benefit Guaranty Corporation, the disclosure should include this information and a description of the applicability of any PBGC guaranty to recent plan amendments.

If the employer is absorbing significant plan administration costs, this should be disclosed. Any changes in the plan's funding policy, including the method for determining participants' contributions, should be described. For plans subject to ERISA, whether the minimum funding requirements have been met or if a waiver has been granted or is pending must be discussed. Insurance contracts that are excluded from the plan's assets, as well as the plan's policy concerning these assets, should be disclosed. Disclosure should be made of whether or not a favorable determination letter has been obtained for federal income tax purposes, and the plan's federal income tax status. Disclosure is also required of all investments that represent 5% or more of a plan's net assets available for benefits. A disclosure should be made of any significant real estate or other transactions between the plan and the sponsor, employer, or the employee organization. Finally, disclosure is required of all unusual or infrequent events that occur after the latest benefit information date, but before the financial statements are issued, if these events are significant and have an affect on the plan's present and future ability to pay benefits.

EMPLOYER'S ACCOUNTING FOR POSTEMPLOYMENT BENEFITS

FASB Statement Number 112 (*Employers' Accounting for Postemployment Benefits*) provides authoritative guidance in accounting and reporting for postemployment benefits. It concerns benefits provided to former or inactive employees, their beneficiaries, and dependents after employment but before retirement. Former or inactive employees include individuals on disability and those that have been laid off. However, individuals on vacation or holiday or who are ill are not considered inactive.

Postemployment benefits differ from postretirement benefits. Postemployment benefits may be in cash or in kind and include salary continuation benefits, supplemental unemployment benefits, severance benefits, disability-related benefits, job training and counseling benefits, life insurance benefits, and health care benefits.

Postemployment benefits that meet certain conditions of FASB Number 43 require accrual in accordance with FASB Statement Number 112. These conditions include the following:

- Benefits are related to services already performed.
- Benefit obligations vest or accumulate.
- Payment of benefits is probable.
- The amount of benefits can be reasonably estimated.

Postemployment benefits that do not meet the conditions of FASB Statement Number 43 should be accounted for in accordance with FASB Statement Number 5.

- It is probable that an asset has been impaired or liability incurred at the date of the financial statements based on information available prior to the issuance of financial statements.
- The amount of loss can be reasonably estimated.

If the amount cannot be estimated in accordance with FASB Statement Number 43 or FASB Statement Number 5, the financial statements should disclose this information.

PROFIT SHARING PLANS

A profit sharing plan may be discretionary (contributions are at the discretion of the Board of Directors) or nondiscretionary (contributions are based on a predetermined formula and depend on attaining a specified level of profit). In a discretionary plan, an accrual of expense should be made when set by the Board of Directors. The entry is to debit profit sharing expense and credit accrued profit sharing liability. In a nondiscretionary plan, an accrual is made when required under the terms of the plan.

Annual Report References

GENERAL ELECTRIC
1999 ANNUAL REPORT

5. Pension Benefits

GE and its affiliates sponsor a number of pension plans. Principal pension plans are discussed below; other pension plans are not significant individually or in the aggregate.

Principal pension plans are the GE Pension Plan and the GE Supplementary Pension Plan.

The GE Pension Plan provides benefits to certain U.S. employees based on the greater of a formula recognizing career earnings or a formula recognizing length of service and final average earnings. Benefit provisions are subject to collective bargaining. At the end of 1999, the GE Pension Plan covered approximately 470,000 participants, including 124,000 employees, 153,000 former employees with vested rights to future benefits, and 193,000 retirees and beneficiaries receiving benefits.

The GE Supplementary Pension Plan is a pay-as-you-go plan providing supplementary retirement benefits primarily to higher-level, longer-service U.S. employees.

The effect on operations of principal pension plans is as follows:

Effect on operations (In millions)	**1999**	1998	1997
Expected return on plan assets	**$3,407**	$3,024	$2,721
Service cost for benefits earned (a)	**(693)**	(625)	(596)
Interest cost on benefit obligation	**(1,804)**	(1,749)	(1,686)
Prior service cost	**(151)**	(153)	(145)
SFAS No. 87 transition gain	**154**	154	154
Net actuarial gain recognized	**467**	365	295
Special early retirement cost	**—**	—	(412)
Total pension plan income	**$1,380**	$1,016	$331

(a) Net of participant contributions.

Funding policy for the GE Pension Plan is to contribute amounts sufficient to meet minimum funding requirements as set forth in employee benefit and tax laws plus such additional amounts as GE may determine to be appropriate. GE has not made contributions since 1987 because the fully funded status of the GE Pension Plan precludes current tax deduction and because any GE contribution would require payment of excise taxes.

Changes in the projected benefit obligation for principal pension plans follow.

Projected benefit obligation December 31 (In millions)	**1999**	1998
Balance at January 1	**$27,572**	$25,874
Service cost for benefits earned (a)	**693**	625
Interest cost on benefit obligation	**1,804**	1,749
Participant contributions	**122**	112
Actuarial (gain)/loss (b)	**(2,790)**	1,050
Benefits paid	**(1,879)**	(1,838)
Balance at December 31	**$25,522**	$27,572

(a) Net of participant contributions.

(b) Principally associated with discount rate changes.

Changes in the fair value of assets for principal pension plans follow.

Fair value of assets December 31 (In millions)	**1999**	1998
Balance at January 1	**$43,447**	$38,742
Actual return on plan assets	**8,472**	6,363

(Cont.)

Fair value of assets December 31 (In millions)	**1999**	1998
Employer contributions	**81**	68
Participant contributions	**122**	112
Benefits paid	**(1,879)**	(1,838)
Balance at December 31	**$50,243**	$43,447

Plan assets are held in trust and consist mainly of common stock and fixed-income investments. GE common stock represented 9.8% and 7.5% of trust assets at year-end 1999 and 1998, respectively.

GE recorded assets and liabilities for principal pension plans as follows:

Prepaid pension asset December 31 (In millions)	**1999**	1998
Fair value of plan assets	**$50,243**	$43,447
Add (deduct) unrecognized balances		
Prior service cost	**699**	850
SFAS No.87 transition gain	**(154)**	(308)
Net actuarial gain	**(16,850)**	(9,462)
Projected benefit obligation	**(25,522)**	(27,572)
Pension liability	**981**	797
Prepaid pension asset	**$ 9,397**	$ 7,752

Actuarial assumptions used to determine costs and benefit obligations for principal pension plans follow.

Actuarial assumptions December 31	**1999**	1998	1997
Discount rate	**7.75%**	6.75%	7.0%
Compensation increases	**5.0**	5.0	4.5
Return on assets for the year	**9.5**	9.5	9.5

Experienced gains and losses, as well as the effects of changes in actuarial assumptions and plan provisions, are amortized over the average future service period of employees.

ALLIED SIGNAL
1998 ANNUAL REPORT

21. Pension and Other Postretirement Benefits

The Company's pension plans, most of which are defined benefit plans and almost all of which are noncontributory, cover substantially all employees. The Company's U.S. retiree medical plans cover employees who retire with pension eligibility for hospital, professional and other medical services. The following table summarizes the balance sheet impact, including the benefit obligations, assets, funded status and rate assumptions associated with the Company's significant pension and retiree medical benefit plans.

	Pension Benefits		Other Postretirement Benefits	
	1998	**1997**	**1998**	**1997**
Change in benefit obligation				
Benefit obligation at January 1	$ **5,941**	$ **5,419**	$ **1,634**	$ **1,533**
Service cost	**139**	**124**	**21**	**21**
Interest cost	**422**	**412**	**103**	**111**
Plan amendments	**20**	—	**5**	**(121)**
Actuarial (gains) losses	**352**	**470**	**(27)**	**188**
Acquisitions	**91**	—	—	**16**
Benefits paid	**(447)**	**(454)**	**(127)**	**(114)**
Settlements and curtailments	**(65)**	**(8)**	**(32)**	—
Translation effect	**2**	**(22)**	—	—
Benefit obligation at December 31	**6,455**	**5,941**	**1,577**	**1,634**
Change in plan assets				
Fair value of plan assets at January 1	**6,428**	**5,843**	—	—
Actual return on plan assets	**853**	**1,018**	—	—
Company contributions	**46**	**40**	—	—
Participants' contributions	—	**1**	—	—
Acquisitions	**63**	—	—	—
Settlements	**(48)**	**(9)**	—	—
Benefits paid	**(447)**	**(454)**	—	—
Translation effect	**(10)**	**(11)**	—	—
Fair value of plan assets at December 31	**6,885**	**6,428**	—	—
Funded status of plans	**430**	**487**	**(1,577)**	**(1,634)**
Unrecognized transition (asset)	**(22)**	**(26)**	—	—
Unrecognized net (gain) loss	**(569)**	**(659)**	**(99)**	**(77)**
Unrecognized prior service cost	**102**	**93**	**(188)**	**(221)**
(Accrued) benefit cost	$ **(59)**	$ **(105)**	$**(1,864)**	$**(1,932)**
Assumptions as of December 31				
Discount rate	**6.75%**	**7.25%**	**6.75%**	**7.25%**
Assumed rate of return on plan assets	**10.00%**	**10.00%**	—	—
Assumed annual rate of compensation increase	**5.00%**	**5.00%**	—	—

The projected benefit obligation, accumulated benefit obligation and fair value of plan assets for the pension plans with accumulated benefit obligations in excess of the fair value of plan assets were $328, $281 and $43 million, respectively, as of December 31, 1998 and $285, $246 and $31 million, respectively, as of December 31, 1997.

Net periodic pension and other postretirement benefit costs include the following components.

	Pension Benefits			Other Postretirement Benefits		
	1998	1997	1996	1998	1997	1996
Service cost	$139	$124	$133	$ 21	$ 21	$ 24
Interest cost	422	412	398	103	111	111
Assumed return on plan assets	(580)	(519)	(458)	—	—	—
Amortization of transition asset	(4)	(7)	(7)	—	—	—
Amortization of prior service cost	12	11	11	(19)	(15)	(10)
Recognition of actual (gains) losses	1	1	1	(2)	(9)	(4)
Benefit cost (credit)	$(10)	$ 22	$ 78	$103	$108	$121

Most of the U.S. retiree medical plans require deductibles and copayments and virtually all are integrated with Medicare. Retiree contributions are generally required based on coverage type, plan and Medicare eligibility. The retiree medical plans are not funded. Claims and expenses are paid from the general assets of the Company.

For most non-union employees retiring after July 1, 1992, the Company implemented an approach which bases the Company's contribution to retiree medical premiums on years of service and also establishes a maximum Company contribution in the future at approximately twice the current level at the date of implementation. Effective July 1, 1997, the Company adopted a plan amendment that will encourage Medicare eligible non-union retirees to join Company sponsored Medicare managed care programs.

For measurement purposes, the assumed annual rates of increase in the per capita cost of covered health care benefits for 1998 were 6.5% for indemnity programs and 6% to 8% for managed care programs, which reduce to 6% for all programs in the year 2000 and remain at that level thereafter (except for Medicare managed care programs which continue at 8%).

Assumed health care cost trend rates have a significant effect on the amounts reported for the retiree medical plans. A one-percentage-point change in assumed health care cost trend rates would have the following effects.

	One-Percentage-Point Increase	One-Percentage-Point Decrease
Effect on total of service and interest cost components	$ 11	$ (10)
Effect on postretirement benefit obligation	$122	$(109)

JOHNSON & JOHNSON
1998 ANNUAL REPORT

13. Retirement and Pension Plans

The Company sponsors various retirement and pension plans, including defined benefit, defined contribution and termination indemnity plans, which cover most employees worldwide. The Company also provides postretirement benefits, primarily health care to all domestic retired employees and their dependents. Most international employees are covered by government-sponsored programs and the cost to the Company is not significant.

Retirement plan benefits are primarily based on the employee's compensation during the last three to five years before retirement and the number of years of service. The Company's objective in funding its domestic plans is to accumulate funds sufficient to provide for all accrued benefits. International subsidiaries have plans under which funds are deposited with trustees, annuities are purchased under group contracts, or reserves are provided.

In certain countries other than the United States, the funding of pension plans is not a common practice as funding provides no economic benefit. Consequently, the Company has several pension plans which are not funded.

The Company does not fund retiree health care benefits in advance and has the right to modify these plans in the future.

Effective December 29, 1997, the Company adopted Statement of Financial Accounting Standards (SFAS) No. 132, "Employers' Disclosures about Pensions and Postretirement Benefits," which standardizes the disclosure requirements for pensions and other postretirement benefits. The Statement addresses disclosure only. It does not address liability measurement or expense recognition. There was no effect on financial position or net income as a result of adopting SFAS No. 132.

Net periodic benefit costs for the Company's defined benefit retirement plans and other benefit plans for 1998, 1997 and 1996 include the following components:

	Retirement Plans			Other Benefit Plans		
(Dollars in Millions)	**1998**	1997	1996	**1998**	1997	1996
Service cost	**$185**	166	159	**20**	17	16
Interest cost	**254**	239	230	**50**	46	46
Expected return on plan assets	**(291)**	(256)	(231)	**(14)**	(3)	(3)
Amortization of prior service cost	**17**	16	14	**2**	1	1
Amortization of net transition assets	**(14)**	(13)	(13)	—	—	—
Recognized actuarial (gain)/loss	**(24)**	(19)	2	**8**	(6)	(1)
Curtailments and settlements	**2**	1	—	—	—	—
Net periodic benefit cost	**$129**	134	161	**66**	55	59

The net periodic cost attributable to domestic retirement plans included above was $40 million in 1998, $50 million in 1997 and $84 million in 1996.

The following tables provide the weighted-average assumptions used to develop net periodic benefit cost and the actuarial present value of projected benefit obligations:

	Retirement Plans			Other Benefit Plans		
Domestic Benefit Plans	**1998**	1997	1996	**1998**	1997	1996
Weighted average discount rate	**6.75%**	7.25%	7.75%	**6.75%**	7.25%	7.75%
Expected long-term rate of return on plan assets	**9.0**	9.0	9.0	**9.0**	9.0	9.0
Rate of increase in compensation levels	**5.0**	5.0	5.5	**5.0**	5.0	5.5
International Benefit Plans						
Weighted average discount rate	**5.50%**	6.25%	6.50%	**6.00%**	7.00%	7.25%
Expected long-term rate of return on plan assets	**7.75**	7.75	7.75	—	—	—
Rate of increase in compensation levels	**3.50**	4.25	4.75	**4.25**	5.00	5.00

Health care cost trends are projected at annual rates grading from 10% for employees under age 65 and 7% for employees over age 65 down to 5% for both groups by the year 2008 and beyond. The effect of a 1% change in these assumed cost trends on the accumulated postretirement benefit obligation at the end of 1998 would be a $99 million increase or an $88 million decrease and the effect on the service and interest cost components of the net periodic postretirement benefit cost for 1998 would be a $12 million increase or a $10 million decrease.

The following tables set forth the change in benefit obligations and change in plan assets at year-end 1998 and 1997 for the Company's defined benefit retirement plans and other postretirement plans:

(Dollars in Millions)	Retirement Plans		Other Benefit Plans	
Change in Benefit Obligation	1998	1997	1998	1997
Benefit obligation—beginning of year	**$3,704**	3,412	**691**	591
Service cost	**185**	166	**20**	17
Interest cost	**254**	239	**50**	46
Plan participant contributions	**11**	10	—	—
Amendments	**13**	27	—	—
Actuarial loss	**325**	123	—	66
Curtailments & settlements	**(7)**	1	—	—
Total benefits paid	**(203)**	(175)	**(33)**	(28)
Effect of exchange rates	**33**	(99)	**(2)**	(1)
Benefit obligation—end of year	**$4,315**	3,704	**726**	691

Change in Plan Assets				
Plan assets at fair value—beginning of year	**$3,694**	3,330	**46**	41
Actual return on plan assets	**606**	547	**14**	8
Company contributions	**45**	35	**29**	24
Plan participant contributions	**11**	10	—	—
Settlements	**(4)**	—	—	—
Benefits paid from plan assets	**(193)**	(158)	**(32)**	(27)
Effect of exchange rates	**14**	(70)	—	—
Plan assets at fair value—end of year	**$4,173**	3,694	**57**	46

Amounts recognized in the Company's balance sheet consist of the following:

	Retirement Plans		Other Benefit Plans	
(Dollars in Millions)	**1998**	1997	**1998**	1997
Plan assets less than projected benefit obligation	**$(142)**	(10)	**(668)**	(645)
Unrecognized actuarial gains	**(511)**	(543)	**(117)**	(107)
Unrecognized prior service cost	**98**	102	**(11)**	(8)
Unrecognized net transition asset	**(37)**	(51)	—	—
Total recognized in the consolidated balance sheet	**$(592)**	(502)	**(796)**	(760)
Book reserves	**$(726)**	(592)	**(796)**	(760)
Prepaid benefits	**109**	75	—	—
Intangible assets	**25**	15	—	—
Total recognized in the consolidated balance sheet	**$(592)**	(502)	**(796)**	(760)

Plans with accumulated benefit obligations in excess of plan assets consist of the following:

	Retirement Plans		Other Benefit Plans	
(Dollars in Millions)	**1998**	1997	**1998**	1997
Accumulated benefit obligation	**$(558)**	(435)	**(696)**	(691)
Projected benefit obligation	**$(723)**	(566)	—	—
Plan assets at fair value	**$162**	126	**57**	46

EASTMAN AND KODAK 1998 ANNUAL REPORT

13. Nonpension Postretirement Benefits

The Company provides health care, dental and life insurance benefits to U.S. eligible retirees and eligible survivors of retirees. In general, these benefits are provided to U.S. retirees that are covered by the Company's principal pension plan (KRIP). These benefits are funded from the general assets of the Company as they are incurred. Certain non-U.S. subsidiaries offer health care benefits; however, the cost of such benefits is insignificant to the Company.

Changes in the Company's benefit obligation and funded status are as follows:

(In millions)	1998	1997
Net benefit obligation at beginning of year	$2,366	$2,281
Service cost	19	21
Interest cost	161	159
Plan participants' contributions	3	1
Plan amendments	(158)	—
Actuarial loss	78	55
Curtailments	(29)	—
Benefit payments	(160)	(151)
Net benefit obligation at end of year	$2,280	$2,366
Funded status at end of year	$(2,280)	$(2,366)
Unrecognized net actuarial loss	443	410
Unrecognized plan amendments	(773)	(788)
Net amount recognized and recorded at end of year	$(2,610)	$(2,744)

Weighted-average assumptions were as follows:

	1998	1997
Discount rate	6.8%	7.0%
Salary increase rate	4.3%	4.5%
Health care cost trend(a)	7.0%	8.0%

(a) decreasing to 5.0% by 2002

(In millions)	**1998**	1997	1996
Components of net postretirement benefit cost			
Service cost	**$ 19**	$ 21	$ 25
Interest cost	**161**	159	166
Amortization of:			
Prior service cost	**(70)**	(69)	(71)
Recognized actuarial loss	**16**	2	8
	126	113	128
Curtailment credit	**(103)**	—	(97)
Total net postretirement benefit cost	**$ 23**	$113	$ 31

The Company recorded a $103 million curtailment gain in 1998 as a result of the reduction in employees in 1998 from the 1997 restructuring program. The Company recorded a $97 million curtailment gain in 1996 as a result of the sale of the Office Imaging business, which was included in the loss on the sale.

In 1998, the Company moved to a new managed-care base health plan in order to effectively manage health care costs while maintaining the quality of care. This change resulted in a reduction of $25 million for 1998 postretirement benefit costs.

Assumed health care cost trend rates have a significant effect on the amounts reported for the health care plans. A one percentage point change in assumed health care cost trend rates would have the following effects:

	1% increase	1% increase
Effect on total service and interest cost components	$ 8	$ (6)
Effect on postretirement benefit obligation	68	(56)

GENERAL ELECTRIC
1998 ANNUAL REPORT

6. Retiree Health and Life Benefits

GE and its affiliates sponsor a number of retiree health and life insurance benefit plans. Principal retiree benefit plans are discussed below; other such plans are not significant individually or in the aggregate.

Principal retiree benefit plans generally provide health and life insurance benefits to employees who retire under the GE Pension Plan (see note 5) with 10 or more years of service. Retirees share in the cost of health care benefits. Benefit provisions are subject to collective bargaining. At the end of 1998, these plans covered approximately 250,000 retirees and dependents.

The effect on operations of principal retiree benefit plans is shown in the following table.

Effect on operations			
(In millions)	**1998**	1997	1996
Retiree health plans			
Service cost for benefits earned	**$ 79**	$ 90	$ 77
Interest cost on benefit obligation	**205**	183	166
Prior service cost	**14**	(3)	(20)
Net actuarial loss recognized	**28**	16	20
Special early retirement cost	**—**	152	—
Retiree health plan cost	**326**	438	243
Retiree life plans			
Expected return on plan assets	**(149)**	(137)	(132)
Service cost for benefits earned	**17**	17	16
Interest cost on benefit obligation	**114**	116	106
Prior service cost	**(6)**	(8)	(11)
Net actuarial loss recognized	**11**	16	23
Special early retirement cost	**—**	13	—
Retiree life plan cost (income)	**(13)**	17	2
Total cost	**$313**	$455	$245

Funding policy for retiree health benefits is generally to pay covered expenses as they are incurred. GE funds retiree life insurance benefits at its discretion.

Changes in the accumulated postretirement benefit obligation for retiree benefit plans follow.

Accumulated postretirement benefit obligation	Health plans		Life plans	
December, 31 (In millions)	**1998**	1997	**1998**	1997
Balance at January 1	**$3,098**	$2,415	**$1,677**	$1,539
Service cost for benefits earned	**79**	90	**17**	17
Interest cost on benefit obligation	**205**	183	**114**	116
Participant contributions	**24**	21	—	—
Plan amendments	—	325	—	44
Actuarial loss	**177**	245	**91**	56
Benefits paid	**(363)**	(333)	**(112)**	(108)
Special early retirement cost	—	152	—	13
Balance at December 31	**$3,220**	$3,098	**$1,787**	$1,677

Changes in the fair value of assets for retiree benefit plans follow.

Fair value of assets	Health plans		Life plans	
December, 31 (In millions)	**1998**	1997	**1998**	1997
Balance at January 1	**$ —**	$ —	**$1,917**	$1,682
Actual return on plan assets	—	—	**316**	343
Employer contributions	**339**	312	—	—
Participant contributions	**24**	21	—	—
Benefits paid	**(363)**	(333)	**(112)**	(108)
Balance at December 31	**$ —**	$ —	**$2,121**	$1,917

Plan assets are held in trust and consist mainly of common stock and fixed-income investments. GE common stock represented about 5% and 4% of trust assets at year-end 1998 and 1997, respectively.

GE recorded assets and liabilities for retiree benefit plans as follows:

Retiree benefit liability/asset

	Health plans		Life plans	
December, 31 (In millions)	**1998**	1997	**1998**	1997
Accumulated postretirement benefit obligation	**$3,220**	$3,098	**$1,787**	$1,677
Add (deduct) unrecognized balances				
Net actuarial gain/(loss)	**(572)**	(423)	**214**	127
Prior service cost	**(157)**	(171)	**49**	55
Fair value of plan assets	**—**	—	**(2,121)**	(1,917)
Retiree benefit liability/ (asset)	**$2,491**	$2,504	**$ (71)**	$ (58)

Actuarial assumptions used to determine costs and benefit obligations for principal retiree benefit plans are shown below.

Actuarial assumptions

December, 31	**1998**	1997	1996
Discount rate	**6.75%**	7.0%	7.5%
Compensation increases	**5.0**	4.5	4.5
Health care cost trend (a)	**7.8**	7.8	8.0
Return on assets for the year	**9.5**	9.5	9.5

(a) For 1998, gradually declining to 5.0% after 2003.

Increasing or decreasing the health care cost trend rates by one percentage point would not have had a material effect on the December 31,1998, accumulated postretirement benefit obligation or the annual cost of retiree health plans.

Experience gains and losses, as well as the effects of changes in actuarial assumptions and plan provisions, are amortized over the average future service period of employees.

Chapter 15

Income Tax Accounting

Under FASB Statement Number 109 (*Accounting for Income Taxes*), income tax allocation is required. Temporary differences take place between book income and taxable income. The deferred tax liability or asset is measured at the tax rate that will arise when the temporary difference reverses. In determining the tax rate, consider that different rates exist for ordinary income and capital gains. The deferred tax liability or asset must be adjusted for changes in tax law or in tax rate. As a result, the asset and liability method (hereafter referred to simply as the liability method) must be used to account for deferred income taxes. The liability method is balance sheet oriented because the major goal is to present the estimated actual taxes to be paid in future years. Comprehensive deferred tax accounting is followed, meaning that all income tax effects of all revenues, expenses, gains, losses, and other items creating differences between tax and financial reporting are considered. Tax expense equals taxes payable plus the tax impact of all temporary differences. In other words, the total provision for income taxes is the sum of the amount of tax currently payable (current tax expense) and the net change in the deferred tax assets and deferred tax liabilities (deferred tax expense or benefit). Interperiod tax allocation is followed to account for temporary differences affecting the current year's results. Tax effects of future events should be reflected in the year they occur. Besides temporary differences, FASB Statement

Number 109 deals with the recognition of taxes currently payable or refundable.

Deferred tax assets and liabilities also take into account operating loss carryforwards for tax reporting purposes.

Deferred tax assets are reduced by a valuation allowance account representing the amount of tax benefits not expected to be realized.

In effect, the tax provision is basically the residual amount computed as the current tax provision plus the difference between the beginning and ending deferred tax balances.

If tax rates are graduated based on taxable income, aggregate calculations may be made using an estimated average rate.

FASB Statement Number 109 applies to federal, state, local, and foreign income taxes; consolidated and combined financial statements; investments under the equity method; and foreign companies issuing their financial statements in conformity with GAAP.

Of note to the reader is the FASB Implementation Guide (*Accounting for Income Taxes*) providing questions and answers regarding the implementation of FASB Statement Number 109.

TEMPORARY DIFFERENCES

Most transactions entered into by a company are accounted for in the same way for financial and tax reporting purposes. However, some transactions are accounted for differently. Temporary differences apply to the period in which revenue or expenses will be recognized. Temporary differences can be caused by four types of transactions as follows:

1. Revenue is included on the tax return after being presented on the books (financial records). An example is an installment sale which is recognized for the books in the year of sale but is recognized for tax purposes when cash collections are received. Another example is using the percentage-of-completion construction contract method on the books but the completed contract method on the tax return. This also occurs if the equity method is used by the investor because the investees' earnings are recognized for book purposes by the investor but the investor recognizes only the investees' dividends for tax reporting.

2. Revenue is included on the tax return before being presented on the books. An example is deferred (unearned) revenue, such as an advance payment (retainer) which is recognized for tax purposes when the advance payment is received but is not recognized for book purposes until the services are performed.

3. Expenses are deducted on the tax return after being deducted on the books. For example, bad debts are deducted on the books in the year of sale (allowance method) but are not deductible on the tax return until the customer's balance is uncollectible (direct writeoff method). Warranty expense is deducted on the books in the year of sale but is deducted on the tax return when paid. Another example is a contingent loss accrual for book purposes before being deductible for tax purposes. Sales returns and allowances are accrued for book purposes but not deducted on the tax return until the product is returned.

4. Expenses are deducted on the tax return before being deducted on the books. An example is accelerated depreciation on the tax return but straight-line depreciation on the books. Another example is a shorter depreciable life of fixed assets for tax purposes relative to book purposes. A deferred tax liability also arises when certain preoperating costs and certain capital interest costs are deductible for tax purposes in the current year.

Other examples of temporary differences follow:

1. Unrealized losses or gains on trading securities or available-for sale securities which are recorded for financial reporting purposes (On the tax return, losses or gains are only recognized when the securities are sold.)

2. The amortization of goodwill for tax purposes over 15 years but over a different period of years for book purposes

3. Use of the equity method for book purposes but the cost method for tax reporting

4. Gross profit recognized on the cost recovery method for book purposes but on the cash basis for tax purposes

5. The use of the capital lease method for book purposes but the operating method for tax reporting

6. Amortizing capitalized leases over different time periods for book and tax purposes

7. Gains or losses on fixed assets recognized for book purposes but deferred for tax purposes because of a trade-in on similar fixed assets

8. Gains on appreciation in assets distributed associated with a liquidation recognized for financial reporting and on distribution for tax purposes

9. The use of different amortization periods for intangible assets for book and tax purposes

10. The use of cost depletion for financial reporting while using statutory depletion for tax purposes

11. A net capital loss recognized in the current year for book purposes but carried forward to offset future capital gains on the tax return

12. An excess charitable contribution carried over to future years for tax reporting

13. Deferred compensation accrued for books while employee services are performed but not deductible on the tax return until actually paid

14. The amortization of bond issue costs under the interest method for book purposes but the straight-line method on the tax return

15. The accrual of sick or vacation pay as employee services are rendered for book purposes but when paid on the tax return

16. The deferral of intangible drilling costs for book purposes while expensing them on the tax return

17. Interest revenue used to offset capitalized interest on the books but recognized as income on the tax return

18. Inventories valued at the lower of cost or market value for books but at cost for tax reporting

19. Loss provision for obsolete inventory for books but not deductible on the tax return until the inventory is available for sale at discounted values or discarded

20. Inventory-related costs deducted on the books but capitalized for tax reporting

21. Use of the accrual basis for book purposes but the cash basis on the tax return

22. The effect of a change from the cash basis to the accrual basis recognized equally over four years for tax purposes

23. Imputed interest for book purposes that differs from the amount recognized for tax purposes

24. A reduction in the tax basis of depreciable assets due to tax credits

25. An increase in the tax basis of assets due to indexing whenever the local currency is the functional currency

26. Tax consequences of differences between the assigned values and the tax bases of assets and liabilities in a purchase business combination

27. Tax basis adjustments required by the tax law

28. Items relating to foreign currency denominated assets and liabilities

Some items may be considered temporary differences in one case but not in another. For example, the amount by which the cash surrender value of life insurance exceeds insurance premiums paid is a temporary difference if there is an anticipation that the cash surrender value will be recovered. It is not a temporary difference if it is anticipated that the cash surrender value will not be recovered when the insured dies.

DEFERRED TAX LIABILITY

If book income (BI) exceeds taxable income (TI), then tax expense (TE) exceeds tax payable (TP), resulting in a deferred tax liability (credit). The deferred tax liability may also be calculated by multiplying the temporary difference by the applicable tax rate.

EXAMPLE

Assume that book income and taxable income are both $200,000. Depreciation expense for book purposes is $20,000 using the straight-line method, but depreciation for tax purposes is $30,000 using an accelerated depreciation method. Assuming a 30% tax rate, the entry is

Income tax expense ($180,000 × 30%)	54,000	
Income tax payable ($170,000 × 30%)		51,000
Deferred tax liability ($10,000 × 30%)		3,000

At the end of the life of the asset, the deferred tax liability of $3,000 will be completely reversed.

EXAMPLE 1: INTERPERIOD TAX ALLOCATION WITH TEMPORARY DIFFERENCE

XYZ Corp.'s pretax financial income is $500,000 for year 2001. It has a $200,000 temporary difference at the end of 2001 that will reverse and result in taxable amounts as follows:

Year	Taxable Amount
2002	$40,000
2003	$70,000
2004	$90,000

The tax rate is 30% for all years. There were no deferred taxes at the beginning of year 2001.

The taxes payable for year 2001 are calculated as follows:

Pretax financial income for 2001	$500,000
Temporary difference at end of 2001	(200,000)
Taxable income for 2001	$300,000
Tax rate	30%
Taxes payable for 2001	$ 90,000

The deferred tax liability is calculated as follows:

	2002	2003	2004	Total
Future taxable amount	$40,000	$70,000	$90,000	$200,000
Tax rate	30%	30%	30%	30%
Deferred tax liability	$12,000	$21,000	$27,000	$ 60,000

Total tax expense for year 2001 is as follows:

Current tax expense for 2001	$ 90,000
Deferred tax expense for 2001	$ 60,000
Total tax expense for 2001	$150,000

The journal entry to record tax expense is:

Income tax expense	150,000	
Income tax payable		90,000
Deferred tax liability		60,000

EXAMPLE 2: INTERPERIOD TAX ALLOCATION WITH TEMPORARY DIFFERENCE AND BEGINNING DEFERRED TAXES

XYZ Corp.'s pretax financial income is $600,000 and taxable income is $450,000 for year 2001. Its beginning deferred tax liability account has a balance of $75,000. Its cumulative temporary difference for year end 2001 is equal to $300,000 and will reverse and result in taxable amounts as follows:

Year	Taxable Amount
2002	$100,000
2003	$ 75,000
2004	$125,000

The tax rate is 30% for all years.

The taxes payable for year 2001 are calculated as follows:

Pretax financial income for 2001	$600,000
Temporary difference at end of 2001	(150,000)
Taxable income for 2001	$450,000
Tax rate	30%
Taxes payable for 2001	$135,000

The deferred tax liability is calculated as follows:

	2002	2003	2004	Total
Future taxable amount	$100,000	$75,000	$125,000	$300,000
Tax rate	30%	30%	30%	30%
Deferred tax liability	$ 30,000	$22,500	$ 37,500	$ 90,000

Total tax expense for year 2001 is as follows:

Current tax expense for 2001		$135,000
Deferred tax liability at end of 2001	$90,000	
Deferred tax liability at beginning of 2001	75,000	
Deferred tax expense for 2001 (additional)		15,000
Total tax expense for 2001		$150,000

The journal entry to record tax expense is

Income tax expense	150,000	
Income tax payable		135,000
Deferred tax liability		15,000

EXAMPLE

On January 1, 1996, Levita Company purchased an $800,000 machine with an estimated useful life of 10 years with no salvage value. The machine was depreciated using a accelerated method for both book and tax purposes. On December 31, 1998, the carrying value of the machine was $380,000. At the beginning of the next year (January 1, 1999), Levita changed to the straight-line method for financial statement purposes. Levita's tax rate was 40%. On January 1, 1999, what amount should Levita report as a deferred income tax liability as a result of the change?

After the change in accounting method was made (to the straight-line method), there would be a temporary difference since the machine was being depreciated using the straight-line method for financial statement purposes and an accelerated method for tax purposes. The temporary difference may be computed in the following manner*:

Carrying amount of the machine for financial statement purposes after the change on 1/1/99:	
$800,000 − (3/10 × $800,000)	$560,000
Less: Carrying amount of machine for tax purposes on 1/1/99	380,000
Temporary Difference —(Future Taxable Amount)	$180,000

Because the machine was being depreciated using the straight-line method for financial statement purposes and an accelerated method for tax purposes, the temporary difference represents a future taxable amount and therefore results in a deferred tax liability. FASB Statement Number 109 (*Accounting for Income Taxes*) requires that the deferred tax liability be measured by multiplying the amount of the temporary difference by the tax rate scheduled to be in effect when the temporary difference reverses. Therefore, the deferred income tax liability is computed in the following way:

Deferred income tax liability, Jan. 1, 1999: $180,000 × .4 = $72,000

DEFERRED TAX ASSET

If book income (BI) is less than taxable income (TI), then tax expense (TE) is less than tax payable (TP), causing a deferred tax asset (charge). The deferred tax asset equals the temporary difference multiplied by the tax rate scheduled to be in effect when the difference reverses.

---

*The carrying value of the machine was the same for both financial statement purposes and tax purposes prior to the change because during that period the machine was depreciated using an accelerated method for both book and tax purposes.

A net deferred tax asset may be recorded if it is more likely than not that the tax benefit will be realized in the future (probability of more than 50% of occurring). The gross deferred tax asset is reduced by a valuation allowance (contra account) if it is more likely than not that some or all of the gross deferred tax asset will not be realized. The net deferred tax asset represents the amount likely to be realized. The deferred tax asset is presented in the following balance sheet, assuming a temporary difference of $500,000, a tax rate of 40%, and $350,000 of the tax benefit having more than a 50% probability of being realized.

Gross deferred tax asset ($500,000 × .40)	$200,000
Less: Valuation allowance ($150,000 × .40)	60,000
Net deferred tax asset ($350,000 × .40)	$140,000

EXAMPLE

Assume a temporary difference of $300,000, a 30% tax rate, and that the entire temporary difference has more than a 50% probability of being realized. The balance sheet presentation follows:

Gross deferred tax asset ($300,000 × .30)	$90,000
Less: Valuation allowance	0
Net deferred tax asset ($300,000 × .30)	$90,000

EXAMPLE

Assume in the previous example that the entire deferred tax asset of $300,000 had less than a 50% probability of being realized. The balance sheet presentation follows:

Gross deferred tax asset ($300,000 × .30)	$90,000
Less: Valuation allowance ($300,000 × .30)	90,000
Net deferred tax asset	$ 0

The following factors are reflective of there being more than a 50% probability of future realization of a temporary difference presented as a deferred tax asset:

- There has been a relatively consistent strong earnings history.

- Future earnings are assured.

- There is expected adequate future taxable income arising from the reversal of a temporary difference (deferred tax liability) to realize the benefit of the tax asset.

- Sound and prudent tax planning strategies are in place which would allow for the realization of the deferred tax asset.

- The amount per books of asset values exceeds their tax bases sufficient to realize the deferred tax asset.

- Lucrative contracts exist.

- There is a significant sales backlog.

The following factors indicate that there is a 50% or less probability of future realization of a deferred tax asset:

- A history of losses in prior years

- An expectation of future operating losses even though prior years showed profitability

- Tax benefits which have expired

- Significant contingencies and uncertainties, such as lawsuits that could have a disastrous effect on the business

The valuation allowance reduces the deferred tax asset to its realizable value. The determination of whether a valuation allowance is necessary involves considering the positive and negative factors related to whether the deferred tax asset is more likely than not to be realized. The valuation allowance account should be evaluated periodically at each year-end to determine if any adjustments are required. For example, the valuation allowance account would be eliminated in full if positive evidence now exists indicating that the deferred tax asset is no longer impaired. Any entry required to the valuation allowance account is coupled with a related adjustment to income tax expense. For example, if the valuation allowance account is increased, so is income tax expense. The entry is to debit income tax expense and credit valuation allowance.

EXAMPLE

XYZ Company has income before taxes of $1,100,000. The only temporary difference is warranty expense, which is recorded at $100,000 on the books based on sales but is recognized for tax purposes at $30,000 (which is based on the amount paid). The tax rate is 34%. Therefore, the amount of the temporary difference is $70,000 ($100,000 – $30,000). It is concluded that $60,000 of this temporary difference has a greater than 50% probability of being realized, while $10,000 of the temporary difference has a 50% or less probability of being realized. Relevant computations follow:

	Book Income	Tax Income
Income before taxes	$1,100,000	$1,100,000
Warranty expense	100,000	30,000
Income	$1,000,000	$1,070,000

The journal entry to record the temporary difference is:

Income tax expense (.34 × $1,000,000)	340,000	
Deferred tax asset (.34 × $70,000)	23,800	
Income tax payable (.34 × $1,070,000)		363,800

The entry to record the valuation allowance is:

Income tax expense (.34 × $10,000)	3,400	
Valuation allowance (.34 × $10,000)		3,400

The balance sheet presentation follows:

Gross deferred tax asset (.34 × $70,000)	$23,800
Less: Valuation allowance (.34 × $10,000)	3,400
Net deferred tax asset (.34 × $60,000)	$20,400

The valuation allowance for a particular tax jurisdiction should be allocated proportionately (pro rata) between the current and noncurrent deferred tax assets for that jurisdiction.

EXAMPLE

Temporary differences at year-end related to accounts receivable and fixed assets were $40,000 and $10,000, respectively. The company determines that the valuation allowance should be $8,000 at year-end. The tax rate is 30%. Therefore, the valuation allowance must be proportionately allocated between current and noncurrent deferred tax assets as follows:

		Percent	*Allocation*
Amount			
Current:			
Deferred tax asset (for accounts receivable):			
$40,000 × .30	$12,000	80%	$6,400
Noncurrent:			
Deferred tax asset (for fixed assets)			
$10,000 × .30	3,000	20%	1,600
	$15,000	100%	$8,000

At year-end, the amounts presented in the balance sheet follow:

Current:	
Deferred tax asset	$12,000
Less: Valuation allowance	6,400
Net deferred tax asset	$ 5,600
Noncurrent:	
Deferred tax asset	$ 3,000
Less: Valuation allowance	1,600
Net deferred tax asset	$ 1,400

A deferred tax asset may be recognized up to an existing deferred tax liability balance.

EXAMPLE

In 19X3, a company sold a fixed asset at a gain of $40,000 for book purposes, which was deferred for tax purposes (installment method) until 19X4. Also in 19X3, $25,000 of deferred revenue was received. The income was reflected on the current year's tax return but was deferred for book purposes until the next year. The deferred tax asset may be recognized because the deductible amount in the future ($25,000) offsets the taxable amount ($40,000). Using a 25% tax rate and income taxes payable of $42,000, the entry in 19X3 is

Income tax expense (balancing figure)	45,750	
Deferred tax asset ($25,000 × .25)	6,250	
Deferred tax liability ($40,000 × .25)		10,000
Income tax payable		42,000

A deferred tax asset can also be recognized for the tax benefit of deductible amounts realizable by carrying back a loss from future years to lower taxes paid in the current year or in prior years.

A deferred tax asset is recognized for the excess of the tax basis over the amount for book purposes of an investment in a subsidiary or joint venture that is permanent in nature if it is expected that the temporary difference will reverse in the future years.

PERMANENT DIFFERENCES

Permanent differences do not reverse in subsequent years and therefore do not require tax allocation. They either affect book income or taxable income, but not both. Examples of expenses that are not tax deductible are penalties and fines. Premiums paid on an officer's life insurance policy for which the company is the beneficiary are not tax deductible. Some organization and startup costs are not deductible for tax purposes (e.g., costs associated with raising capital). The amount of wages used to derive the jobs credit is not tax deductible. An example of an expense that is only partly deductible on the tax return is 50% for meals and entertainment. An example of tax-exempt income is interest on municipal bonds. The proceeds of life insurance arising from an officer's death for which the company is the beneficiary are not subject to tax. An example of income that is fully or partly nontaxable is dividends received by a corporation.

EXAMPLE

Roberta Co. began its operation in 1998. In that year, it reported income before operations of $425,000. In 1998, Roberta Co.'s tax depreciation exceeded its book depreciation by $55,000. Roberta's tax rate for 1998 was 35%. Recent legislation that was enacted boosted this rate to 40% for years after 1998. *Roberta Co. also had nondeductible book expenses of $20,000 related to permanent differences.* According to FASB Statement Number 109 (*Accounting for Income Taxes*), what amount of deferred income tax liability should be reported by Roberta in its December 31, 1998 balance sheet?

FASB Statement Number 109 requires that a deferred tax liability be measured by multiplying the amount of temporary tax difference by the tax rate that is scheduled to be in effect when the temporary difference reverses. In the problem at hand, tax depreciation exceeded book depreciation by $55,000. That is, there are future taxable amounts of $55,000, which will result in a deferred tax liability currently that will reverse in the future (after 1998). To compute the amount of the deferred tax liability, we must do the following:

$$\$55,000 \times 40\% \text{ (the enacted tax rate after 1998)} = \$22,000$$

Thus, the deferred tax liability is $22,000. As was noted previously, permanent differences do not reverse in subsequent years and therefore do not require tax allocation. They either affect book income or taxable income, but not both. In this case, the $20,000 represents a permanent difference and as such should be ignored in computing the deferred income tax liability.

Some permanent differences arise because of different bases used for financial and tax purposes. Examples are investments in a leveraged lease, the excess of the tax bases of assets in a buyer's tax jurisdiction over the financial bases of assets as presented in consolidated financial statements, and different bases for tax versus book arising from foreign currency remeasurements.

A permanent difference is the permanent excess of the amount for financial reporting over that for tax reporting of an investment in a foreign subsidiary or a foreign corporate joint venture.

INTRAPERIOD TAX ALLOCATION

Intraperiod tax allocation occurs when tax expense is presented in different parts of the financial statements for the current year. The income statement shows the tax impact of income from continuing operations, of income from discontinued operations, of extraordinary items, and of the cumulative effect of a change in accounting principle. In the retained earnings statement, prior period adjustments are shown net of tax.

EXAMPLE 3: INTRAPERIOD TAX ALLOCATION

XYZ Corp.'s financial information for year ended Dec. 31, 2002 is as follows:

Income from continuing operations	$600,000
Loss from discontinued operations	(150,000)
Extraordinary gain	80,000
Correction of accounting error	(30,000)
Taxable income	$500,000

There are $150,000 in deductible temporary differences at year-end Dec. 31, 2001. No change occurs in year 2002. $10,000 of tax credit is available for year 2002. The tax rate structure is as follows:

Taxable Income	Rate
1 to 100,000	20%
100,001 to 200,000	25%
200,001 to 300,000	40%
300,001 and above	50%

Future tax rates are expected to increase from 25% on Dec. 31, 2001 to 35% on Dec. 31, 2002.

Tax on income from continuing operations is $225,000 (including a credit of $10,000). Based on taxable income of $500,000 and a credit of $10,000, the tax due is $175,000. The $50,000 difference should be allocated between discontinued operations, extraordinary gain, and correction of error. Deferred taxes are adjusted by $15,000 [$150,000 · (35% − 25%)] for increase in estimate of expected tax rate.

The combined statement of income and retained earnings is as follows:

Income from continuing operations, before taxes		$600,000
Tax on income from continuing operations		
Current	$235,000	
Deferred	(15,000)	
Tax credits	(10,000)	
		210,000
Income from continuing operations, net of taxes		$390,000
Loss from discontinued operations, net of tax benefit of $75,000		(75,000)
Extraordinary gain, net of tax of $40,000		40,000
Net income		$355,000
Retained earnings, Jan. 1, 2002		435,000
Correction of accounting error, net of tax of $15,000		(15,000)
Retained earnings, Dec. 31, 2002		$775,000

BALANCE SHEET PRESENTATION

FASB Statement Number 37 deals with balance sheet classification of deferred income taxes. In the balance sheet, deferred tax assets are offset against deferred tax liabilities and shown as (1) net current or (2) net noncurrent. However, you cannot offset a current account against a noncurrent account. Further, you cannot offset (net) current or noncurrent accounts for different tax-paying components or for different tax jurisdictions (e.g., federal versus local) because offsetting is prohibited unless there is a legal right of setoff.

Deferred tax assets or deferred tax liabilities are classified based on the related asset or liability they apply to. For example, a deferred tax liability due to depreciation on a fixed asset would be presented as noncurrent. A deferred tax asset related to accounts receivable would be classified as current.

Deferred taxes not related to specific assets or liabilities are classified as current or noncurrent depending on the anticipated reversal dates of the temporary differences. Temporary differences reversing within one year are current, but those reversing after one year are noncurrent. In some cases, a given temporary difference may be a mix of current and noncurrent, such as a three-year warranty in which the first year is shown as a current account while years 2 and 3 are presented as a noncurrent account. Other examples are deferred tax assets related to a loss carryforward, and deferred tax liabilities arising when a long-term contract is accounted for by the percentage-of-completion method for financial reporting and by the completed contract method for tax purposes. Under the latter circumstances, the temporary difference becomes taxable when the contract is completed.

If a valuation allowance account exists as a reduction of a gross deferred tax asset, there must be a proration of the valuation allowance between current and noncurrent relative to the classification of the gross deferred tax asset.

INCOME STATEMENT PRESENTATION

Income tax expense should be presented in the income statement as two components—namely, the tax currently payable (the liability) and the deferred portion (portion of the expense based on temporary differences). The total income tax expense provision is based on financial reporting income excluding permanent differences. Presentation of these two expense portions would be as follows:

Income tax expense:		
Amount currently payable	$40,000	
Deferred portion	(32,000)	8,000

The amount currently payable is the current year's taxable income multiplied by the current year's tax rate. The deferred portion equals the temporary difference times the tax rate, or the change in the deferred tax balance during the year (ending balance less beginning balance).

As indicated previously, the deferred tax provision is added to the current tax provision to derive the total tax provision for the year. The current tax provision is the income taxes for the year as reported on the tax return.

LOSS CARRYBACKS

Tax effects of net operating loss carrybacks are allocated to the loss period (the current year). A company may carry back a net operating loss three years and receive a tax refund for taxes paid in profitable years. The tax benefit is recognized as a receivable for the refundable amount. Further, the tax benefit reduces the current year's tax expense, but the amount is based on the tax rate(s) in effect in the carryback period. The loss is first applied to the earliest year, with any remaining loss carried forward. (A company may elect to forgo the carryback.) The latter is discussed in the next section.

The presentation of a loss carryback with recognition of the refund during the loss year follows:

Loss before refundable income taxes	$120,000
Refund of prior years' income taxes arising from carryback of operating loss	40,000
Net loss	$ 80,000

Note: The refund should be computed at the amount actually refundable regardless of current tax rates.

EXAMPLE

In 19X5, a net loss of $100,000 occurred. In the prior years the net incomes were $250,000 in 19X2, $60,000 in 19X3, and $80,000 in 19X4. The tax rates over the years were 19X2 30%, 19X3 31%, 19X4 33%, and 19X5 32%.

The 19X5 net loss may be carried back starting in 19X2. The loss carryback of $100,000 can be used in 19X2 because the net profit that year was higher. The tax benefit of the carryback is calculated based on the 19X2 tax rate of 30% since 19X2 was when the tax was paid. The amount of the tax benefit is $30,000 ($100,000 × 30%). The journal entry in 19X5 to recognize the loss carryback benefit is

Receivable from the IRS	30,000	
Income tax expense		30,000

EXAMPLE

Assume the same facts as in the previous example except that the net income in 19X2 was $75,000. In that case, the tax benefit of the carryback loss is first applied to 19X2, with the balance ($25,000) in 19X3. The relevant computations follow:

19X2 $75,000 × 30%	$22,500
19X3 $25,000 × 31%	7,750
Total	$30,250

The journal entry in 19X5 to reflect the loss carryback benefit is

Receivable from the IRS	30,250	
Income tax expense		30,250

NOTE: For net operating losses occurring on or after August 6, 1997, the carryback period is two years.

LOSS CARRYFORWARDS

A net operating loss may be carried forward up to 15 years. A loss carryforward may be recognized to the extent that there are net taxable amounts in the carryforward period (deferred tax liabilities) to absorb them. A loss carryforward benefit may also be recognized if there exists more than a 50% probability of future realization. In this case, a net deferred tax asset may be recorded for the tax benefit (the gross deferred tax asset amount becomes the net deferred tax asset balance because the valuation allowance is zero). In other words, the tax benefit of a loss carryforward is recognized as a deferred tax asset if the loss is to be carried forward to offset future amounts of taxable income. The tax benefit is measured at the tax rate(s) scheduled to be in effect for the carryforward period. When the net deferred tax asset is recorded, income tax expense is reduced. In later years, as income is realized, the deferred tax asset is reduced. If there is a 50% or less probability of future realization, a net deferred tax asset is not recorded (the valuation allowance equals the gross deferred tax asset, resulting in a zero balance in the net deferred tax asset). In this case, the tax effect of the operating loss carryforward cannot be recognized until the year realized (the year in which the tax liability is reduced). In other words, the amount of the gross deferred tax asset is reduced by a valuation allowance if it is more likely than not that some or all of the benefit of the loss carryforward will not be realized (that is, sufficient taxable income will not be earned in the carryforward period). When the tax benefit of a loss carryforward is recognized when realized in a later year, it is classified in the same way as the income enabling recognition (typically reducing tax expense).

Presentation of the loss carryforward with recognition of benefit in the year realized follows:

Income tax expense:		
Without carryforward	$50,000	
Reduction of income taxes arising from carryforward of prior years' operating losses	(30,000)	$20,000

NOTE: For net operating losses occurring on or after August 6, 1997, the carryforward period is twenty years.

EXAMPLE 4: INTERPERIOD TAX ALLOCATION AND CARRYBACK AND CARRYFORWARD OF NET OPERATING LOSS

XYZ Corp.'s pretax financial income (or loss) is as follows:

Year	Income (Loss)	Tax Rate	Tax Expense
2001	$200,000	40%	$ 80,000
2002	$300,000	40%	$120,000
2003	$100,000	30%	$ 30,000
2004	($200,000)	30%	
2005	($500,000)	30%	
2006	$150,000	30%	$ 45,000
2007	$120,000	30%	$ 36,000

The taxable income (or loss) is the same as the financial income (or loss).

The journal entries to record income tax expense and the net operating loss carrybacks and carryforwards at Dec. 31 year-end are as follows:

12/31/01	Income tax expense	80,000	
	Income tax payable		80,000
12/31/02	Income tax expense	120,000	
	Income tax payable		120,000
12/31/03	Income tax expense	30,000	
	Income tax payable		30,000
12/31/04	Income tax refund receivable	80,000	
	Benefit due to loss carryback		80,000
	[$200,000 · 40%]		
12/31/05	Income tax refund receivable	150,000	
	Benefit due to loss carryback		150,000
	[$300,000 · 40% + $100,000 ' 30%]		
	Deferred tax asset	30,000	
	Benefit due to loss carryforward		30,000
	[($500,000 − $300,000 − $100,000) · 30%]		

12/31/06	Income tax expense	45,000	
	Income tax payable		15,000
	Deferred tax asset		30,000
12/31/07	Income tax expense	36,000	
	Income tax payable		36,000

Special rules and exceptions exist. The tax benefit of operating losses arising in a business combination accounted for under the purchase method subsequent to the acquisition date should be applied first to reduce goodwill and other noncurrent intangible assets related to the purchase to zero. The tax benefits of carryforwards related to contributed capital and expenses for employee stock options should be allocated to the related equity components. The tax benefit of operating losses as of the date of a quasi-reorganization that are later recognized usually should be added to contributed capital.

There should be footnote disclosure of the amount and expiration dates of operating loss carryforwards.

TAX RATES

Deferred taxes are recorded at the amounts of settlement when the temporary differences reverse.

EXAMPLE

Assume that in 19X2 a total temporary difference of $300,000 will reverse in later years, resulting in the following taxable amounts and tax rate:

	19X3	*19X4*	*19X5*	*Total*
Reversals	$110,000	$140,000	$50,000	$300,000
× Tax rate	× .30	× .28	× .25	
Deferred tax liability	$ 33,000	$ 39,200	$12,500	$ 84,700

On 12/31/19X2, the deferred tax liability has an $84,700 balance.

According to federal tax law, there is a graduated tax rate structure (tax rates increase when taxable income reaches the next tax level). However, GAAP requires deferred federal taxes to be based on a flat tax rate (currently 35%) unless the effect of the graduated rate is significant or special rates apply to the temporary difference.

If the use of a flat tax rate results in a significant difference than if graduated tax rates were used, then an average tax rate should apply in computing deferred taxes. The average tax rate equals the tax divided by taxable income.

EXAMPLE

Assume that the first $100,000 of income is taxed at 15%, the next $100,000 is taxed at 25%, and income above $200,000 is taxed at 35%. If taxable income in the next year is estimated at $240,000, the expected average graduated tax rate is computed as follows:

<table>
<tr><td colspan="2" align="center">Tax Computation</td></tr>
<tr><td>$100,000 × .15</td><td>$15,000</td></tr>
<tr><td>$100,000 × .25</td><td>25,000</td></tr>
<tr><td>$ 40,000 × .35</td><td>14,000</td></tr>
<tr><td>Total tax</td><td>$54,000</td></tr>
<tr><td colspan="2">Average tax rate = $54,000/$240,000 = 22.5%</td></tr>
</table>

The use of a single average graduated tax rate based on average estimated annual taxable income during the reversal period will usually suffice.

EXAMPLE

Assume that a company has a taxable temporary difference of $400,000. The difference is anticipated to reverse $300,000 in year 1 and $100,000 in year 2. The company also anticipates $120,000 of taxable income from other sources per year. The relevant computations follow:

Year 1: expected taxable income ($300,000 + $120,000)	$420,000
Year 2: expected taxable income ($100,000 + $120,000)	$220,000
Average taxable income = ($420,000 + $220,000) =	$320,000

The company should use an average graduated tax rate based on the estimated annual taxable income of $320,000. This is computed as follows:

$100,000 × .15	$15,000
$100,000 × .25	25,000
$120,000 × .35	42,000
Total Tax	$82,000

Average tax rate = $82,000/$320,000 = 25.63%

A change in tax rate or other provisions of the tax law (e.g., tax deductibility of expenses) must immediately be reflected by adjusting tax expense and deferred taxes. If less taxes are owed, tax expense and deferred taxes will be decreased. If more taxes are owed, tax expense and deferred taxes will be increased.

EXAMPLE

On December 31, 19X2, a new tax law increases the tax rate from 28% to 33%. The effective date of the increase is January 1, 19X4. If the temporary difference is expected to reverse in 19X4, the company should calculate the deferred tax liability at December 31, 19X2 at the newly enacted tax rate of 33%.

EXAMPLE

At the end of 19X4, a new tax law reduces the tax rate from 36% to 30% starting in 19X6. In 19X4, the business had a deferred profit of $400,000 and showed a deferred tax liability of $144,000. The gross profit is to be reflected equally in 19X5, 19X6, 19X7, and 19X8. Thus, the deferred tax liability at year-end 19X4 of $18,000 is derived as follows:

	19X5	*19X6*	*19X7*	*19X8*	*Total*
Reversals	$100,000	$100,000	$100,000	$100,000	$400,000
× Tax rate	× .36	× .30	× .30	× .30	
Deferred tax liability	$ 36,000	$ 30,000	$ 30,000	$ 30,000	$126,000

The required journal entry in 19X4 is

Deferred tax liability	18,000	
Income tax expense		18,000
($144,000 – $126,000)		

A short-cut to obtain $18,000 follows:

Income subject to change in tax rate	$300,000
× Change in tax rate	.06
Adjustment	$ 18,000

If a new tax law occurs after year-end but before the audit report date, the company should use the tax rate in effect at the year-end financial statement date but disclose in a footnote as a subsequent event the new rate.

EXAMPLE

After December 31, 19X2 but before the financial statements are issued, a new tax law reduces the tax rate from 32% to 31%. The decrease in rate is effective January 1, 19X5. The 32% tax rate should be used in computing the deferred tax liability at December 31, 19X2 because that is the rate expected to be in effect in 19X5 based on the tax law in effect on the balance sheet date. However, the effect of the rate change should be a subsequent event footnote disclosure in the December 31, 19X2 financial statements. Of course, on the December 31, 19X3 financial statements, the company should compute the deferred tax liability at the newly enacted tax rate of 31%.

MULTIPLE TAX JURISDICTIONS

The determination of tax liability for federal reporting purposes may differ from that of state and/or city reporting requirements. As a consequence, temporary differences, permanent differences, and loss carrybacks or carryforwards may be different between federal and local reporting. If the temporary differences are significant, separate deferred tax calculations and recording will be required.

If temporary differences are treated the same for federal and local reporting purposes, a combined tax rate may be used in determining deferred taxes. The combined tax rate equals

$$\text{Federal tax rate} \times (1 - \text{state tax rate}) + \text{state tax rate}$$

TAX CREDITS

According to Emerging Issues Task Force Consensus Summary Number 95–10 (*Accounting for Tax Credits Related to Dividend Payments in Accordance with FASB Statement No. 109*), if a company pays a dividend, any tax credit associated with it acts to reduce income tax expense.

TAX STATUS CHANGES

The effect of any change in tax status affecting a company requires an immediate adjustment to deferred tax liabilities (or assets) and to income tax expense. For example, if a company changes to S corporation status, a tax advantage generally arises, resulting in a reduction in both the deferred tax liability and income tax expense. Another example of a tax status change requiring an adjustment on the accounts is a company electing C corporation status. There should be a footnote explaining the nature of the status change and its affect on the accounts.

If an entity's tax status changes from nontaxable to taxable, a deferred tax asset or liability should be recorded for any temporary differences at the time the status changes. On the other hand, if the status change is from taxable to nontaxable, any deferred tax asset or liability should be eliminated.

BUSINESS INVESTMENTS

If the cost method is used to account for an investment in the common stock of other companies, no temporary difference arises. However, if the equity method is used to account for an investment in another company, a temporary difference arises because, as discussed in Chapter 10, the investor recognizes in its earnings the profit of the investee but recognizes for tax purposes the dividends received from the investee. As a result, the investor's book income exceeds its tax income because profit is usually in excess of dividends. In consequence, a deferred tax liability will likely arise.

BUSINESS COMBINATIONS

In a business combination accounted for under the purchase method, the costs assigned to the acquired company's net assets may differ from the valuation of those net assets on the tax return. This may result in a temporary difference arising in either a deferred tax liability or deferred tax asset reported on the acquirer's consolidated financial statements.

      Goodwill may arise in a purchase combination if the cost to the acquirer exceeds the fair market value of the acquired company's net assets. The amortization of goodwill for tax purposes is over a mandatory 15-year amortization period, while for the books goodwill may be amortized over a period not exceeding 40 years. This will give rise to a temporary difference. If negative goodwill arises because the acquirer's cost is less than the fair market value of the acquired company's net assets, noncurrent assets (except for long-term investments) are proportionately reduced. This will result in a temporary difference arising from the difference of depreciation expense for book and tax purposes.

      In some cases, companies may have unrecognized tax benefits associated with operating losses or tax credits arising from a business combination accounted for under the purchase method. This may give rise to other similar tax advantages subsequent to the date of combination. In the absence of a provision in the tax law to the contrary, the tax benefits realized should be apportioned for book reporting between pre- and post-acquisition tax benefits.

Under the pooling-of-interests method to account for a business combination, if the combined company will be able under the tax law to use an operating loss or tax credit carryforward, the deferred tax benefits should be recognized when prior years' financial statements are restated. If the benefits cannot be used under the tax law in the consolidated tax return, the tax benefits cannot be recognized in the restated financial statements.

In some instances, a pooling of interests is taxable, requiring a step up of the net assets of a combining company for tax reporting. The difference between the stepped-up basis and the book value of net assets on the books constitutes a temporary difference.

EXAMPLE 5: TAX EFFECTS OF PURCHASE BUSINESS COMBINATION

XYZ Corp.'s information about a nontaxable purchase business combination is as follows:

1. The acquisition cost is $800,000.

2. The fair value of assets acquired is $950,000 and XYZ's carryforward tax bases is $700,000.

3. The $250,000 difference between the fair and tax carryforward bases of assets acquired consists of taxable temporary differences of $350,000 and deductible temporary differences of $100,000.

4. The fair and carryforward tax bases of liabilities assumed is $150,000.

5. Assume deductible temporary differences will be realized.

6. The tax rate is a flat 30%.

The allocation of the purchase price is as follows:

Purchase price		$800,000
Allocation to Identifiable assets and (liabilities)		
Fair value of assets	$950,000	
Fair value of liabilities	(150,000)	
Deferred tax benefits	30,000	
Deferred tax obligations	(105,000)	
		725,000
Allocation to goodwill		$ 75,000

EXAMPLE 6

On 1/1/19X2, XYZ Company bought ABC Company for $4,000,000 in a purchase business combination. Goodwill was not involved. The tax basis of the net assets is $12,000,000. Therefore, deductible temporary differences equal $8,000,000. The tax rate is 40%. It has been determined that a valuation allowance for the entire amount of the deferred tax asset is required. However, at year-end 19X3, it is determined that the valuation allowance account is no longer needed. Income results for 19X2 and 19X3 are as follows:

	19X2	*19X3*
Before-tax for book income	$3,000,000	$1,800,000
Reversal of acquired deductible temporary differences	(3,000,000)	(1,800,000)
Taxable income	0	0

On the purchase date the deferred tax asset is recorded at $3,200,000 ($8,000,000 × 40%), with a valuation allowance for $3,200,000. On 12/31/19X2, the deferred tax asset is $2,000,000 equal to 40% of $5,000,000 ($8,000,000 − $3,000,000), with a valuation allowance for the same amount ($2,000,000). On 12/31/19X3 the valuation allowance account, which is no longer required, is eliminated, resulting in a deferred tax benefit or in a reduction of deferred tax expense. **Caution:** If goodwill arose in the purchase business combination, the tax benefit would first reduce goodwill to zero, with any residual balance left reducing to zero any acquired intangible assets.

The journal entries applicable to deferred taxes follow:

1/1/19X2 (date of purchase combination)		
Net assets	4,000,000	
Deferred tax asset	3,200,000	
Cash		4,000,000
Valuation allowance		3,200,000
12/31/19X2		
Valuation allowance	1,200,000	
Deferred tax asset		1,200,000
$3,200,000 – $2,000,000		
12/31/19X3		
Valuation allowance	2,000,000	
Deferred tax asset		800,000
Income tax benefit deferred		1,200,000

SEPARATE FINANCIAL STATEMENTS OF A SUBSIDIARY

If separate financial statements are prepared, the consolidated income tax expense should be allocated to each of the subsidiaries. The allocation basis should be logical and in conformity with the liability method of tax allocation.

LEASES

Emerging Issues Task Force Consensus Summary Number 86–43 (*Effect of a Change in Tax Law or Rates on Leveraged Leases*) states that the components of a leveraged lease have to be recomputed from the beginning of the rental when modifications occur in tax laws or other relevant financial variables (e.g., cash flows). The effects of a change must be accounted for and reflected in the income statement for the year of change. Lease calculations must incorporate the impact of the alternative minimum tax.

FASB Technical Bulletin Number 82–1 applies to disclosures of the sale or purchase of tax benefits through tax leases.

EMPLOYEE STOCK OWNERSHIP PLANS (ESOPs)

Retained earnings are increased for the tax benefit arising from deductible dividends paid on unallocated shares held by an ESOP. However, dividends paid on allocated shares are includable in income tax expense.

QUASI-REORGANIZATION

The tax benefits associated with deductible temporary differences and carryforwards on the date of a quasi-reorganization should typically be recorded as an increase in paid-in-capital if the tax benefits will occur in later years.

DISCLOSURES

Disclosure is required of

- Current tax expense or benefit
- Deferred tax expense or benefit
- Types of temporary differences and cumulative amounts
- Reconciliation between tax expense per books and tax payable per the tax return
- Reconciliation between the actual and expected tax rates
- Components of the net deferred tax liability or asset
- Valuation allowance provision and changes therein during the year (The reasons for the changes should be specified.)

- Factors considered in determining the realizability of deferred tax assets

- Adjustments to tax expense due to a change in tax law, tax rates, or tax status

- Operating loss carryforwards and their tax benefits, including expiration dates

- Amount of any unrecognized deferred tax liability because of undistributed foreign earnings

- Amount of any unrecognized deferred tax liability for temporary differences applicable to undistributed domestic earnings

- Tax expense arising from allocating tax benefits to contributed capital or to reduce the goodwill of an acquired company

- Major aspects of the method used by which consolidated tax expense is allocated to subsidiaries

- Method to account for the sale or purchase of tax benefits arising through tax leases

- Investment tax credit

- Government grants that reduce tax expense

- Intercorporate tax sharing arrangements

- Tax-related balances due to or from affiliates

INDEFINITE REVERSAL

Deferred taxes should not be recognized for the following types of temporary differences unless it is evident that they will reverse in the future years:

- Temporary differences applicable to an investment in a foreign subsidiary or foreign corporate joint venture that is permanent in nature

■ Undistributed earnings of a domestic subsidiary or domestic joint venture that is permanent in nature that arose in fiscal years beginning on or before December 15, 1992

COMPREHENSIVE EXAMPLE

ABC Company uses the accelerated depreciation method for tax reporting and the straight-line depreciation method for financial reporting. At December 31, 19X2, there was a taxable temporary difference of $250,000, which will reverse equally over 19X3 and 19X4. The current and expected future tax rate is 30%. Therefore, on December 31, 19X2 the company presented a noncurrent deferred tax liability of $75,000 ($250,000 × 30%) for this temporary difference.

During 19X3, ABC earned book income of $600,000. The following differences arose between financial and tax reporting:

1. Nondeductible officers' life insurance premiums recorded in 19X3 were $30,000.

2. Gross profit on installment sales in 19X3 of $150,000 will be taxed evenly in 19X4, 19X5, and 19X6.

3. Depreciation for books exceed that for tax by $125,000 in 19X3. This represents the reversal of 50% of the $250,000 temporary difference referred to previously as of December 31, 19X2.

4. An estimated loss provision was made in 19X3 for $40,000. The loss is deductible in 19X5 for tax purposes because that is when it will be paid. Of course, as on December 31, 19X3, the accrued liability is a noncurrent liability.

5. A valuation allowance is not required at December 31, 19X3.

A schedule follows, presenting the taxable income and the current portion of income tax expense for 19X3:

Pretax financial statement income	$600,000
Reversal of 19X2 depreciation temporary difference	125,000
Deferral of gross profit on installment sales	(150,000)
Contingent loss	40,000
Officers' life insurance premium	30,000
Taxable income	$645,000

Current income tax expense and liability equals

$$\$645,000 \times 30\% = \$193,500$$

The deferred tax liability at December 31, 19X3 is $70,500 calculated as follows:

Depreciation temporary difference	
($250,000 − $125,000)	$125,000
Deferred gross profit on installment sales	150,000
Contingent loss	(40,000)
Net temporary difference	$235,000
Deferred tax liability $235,000 × 30%	$ 70,500

The deferred portion of tax expense as of December 31, 19X3 is $4,500 calculated as follows:

Deferred tax liability—12/31/19X2	$75,000
Deferred tax liability—12/31/19X3	70,500
Net change in deferred tax liability (expense credit)	$4,500

Total income tax expense for the year ended December 31, 19X3 is $189,000 computed as follows:

Current portion	$193,500
Deferred portion (credit)	(4,500)
Total income tax expense	$189,000

The composition of the deferred tax liability as of December 31, 19X3 follows:

Current portion (based on the installment sales temporary difference) $150,000 × 30%		$45,000
Noncurrent portion:		
Depreciation temporary difference		
$125,000 × 30%	$37,500	
Less contingent loss temporary difference		
$ 40,000 × 30%	12,000	25,500
Total deferred tax liability—12/31/19X3		$70,500

On December 31, 19X3, the following journal entry is made:

Income tax expense	189,000	
Deferred tax liability (noncurrent)	49,500	
Income taxes payable		193,500
Deferred tax liability (current)*		45,000

*$150,000 × 30% = $45,000.

With respect to the journal entry, note the following:

1. The $49,500 charge to deferred tax liability (noncurrent) adjusts the December 31, 19X2 balance of $75,000 to the required $25,500 net noncurrent balance at December 31, 19X3. The two elements of this account are noncurrent because they apply to items classified as non-current in the balance sheet (the depreciation difference applying to fixed assets, and the loss contingency applying to a reversal in more than one year).

2. The deferred tax liability (current) of $45,000 applies to the install-ment sales temporary difference. A current classification is appro-priate because installment receivables are typically considered current based on the operating cycle of the business.

PROPERTY TAXES

Accounting Requirements

Real and personal property taxes are based, by law, on the assessed valuation of property as of a particular date. Although the states differ as to when this date should be, generally, taxes are recognized on the date on which they are assessed by the taxing authority. Although the exact amount owed may not be known on the assessment date, a reasonable estimate should be made by the taxpayer (on that date) so that the expected amount of taxes and related liability may be accrued and recognized. The entry should be accounted for as a debit to the deferred property taxes account and a credit to a property taxes payable account, a current liability. After this entry is made (on the assessment date), a portion of the property taxes should be recognized in income by amortizing the deferred property taxes account over the fiscal period of the taxing authority.

When the exact amount of property taxes is determined, an adjustment to the estimated tax liability of the prior year is made. Frequently, this adjustment is made to the current year's property tax provision (either increasing it or reducing it) in the current income statement (the year in which the exact amount of the tax liability is determined) or as a separate item there.

Property taxes assessed on property that will be sold to customers or under construction for an entity's own use are generally capitalized as part of the cost of these items.

Reporting Requirements

Since real and personal taxes are considered bona fide expenses of doing business, they should be disclosed and reported as either

1. Expenses allocated to other related expense accounts, such as manufacturing, overhead, and, general and administrative expenses

2. Operating expenses

3. Deductions from income

Real and property taxes should not be combined with income taxes.

EXAMPLE

On October 1, 19A, Levita Company is assessed property taxes of $24,000 for the city's fiscal period from October 1, 19A through September 30, 19B. Levita Company's accounting and financial reporting year ends December 31, 19A.

Levita Company should record its property taxes on October 1, 19A, the assessment day, and make the following entry:

```
October 1 19A:  Deferred property taxes        24,000
                    Property taxes payable              24,000
```

Each month a portion of the deferred property taxes should be amortized, providing recognition for the appropriate amount of property tax expense. The entry that should be made follows:

```
Property tax expense          2,000 (1/12 × $24,000)
    Deferred property taxes           2,000
```

SAFEWAY
1999 ANNUAL REPORT

G. Taxes on Income

The components of income tax expense are as follows (in millions)

	1999	1998	1997
Current:			
Federal	$333.7	$398.8	$303.6
State	62.3	80.0	57.5
Foreign	62.4	52.0	37.8
	458.4	530.8	398.9
Deferred:			
Federal	188.9	44.4	40.4
State	38.1	12.2	8.4
Foreign	17.7	2.8	7.1
	244.7	59.4	55.9
	$703.1	$590.2	$454.8

Extraordinary losses are presented net of related tax benefits. Therefore, 1997 income tax expense excludes the $41.1 million tax benefit on an extraordinary loss related to the early retirement of debt. Tax benefits from the exercise of employee stock options of $77.0 million in 1999, $85.2 million in 1998 and $42.2 million in 1997 were credited directly to paid-in capital and, therefore, are excluded from income tax expense.

The reconciliation of the provision for income taxes at the U.S. federal statutory income tax rate to the Company's income taxes is as follows (dollars in millions):

	1999	*1998*	*1997*
Statutory rate	**35%**	35%	35%
Income tax expense using federal statutory rate	**$585.9**	$488.9	$376.7
State tax on income net of federal benefit	**65.2**	59.9	42.8
Taxes provided on equity in earnings of unconsolidated affiliates at rates below the statutory rate	**(12.1)**	(10.0)	(9.4)
Taxes on foreign earnings not permanently reinvested	**8.3**	7.9	8.9
Nondeductible expenses and amortization	**32.9**	17.6	13.6
Difference between statutory rate and foreign effective rate	**16.6**	11.1	10.6
Other accruals	**6.3**	14.8	11.6
	$703.1	$590.2	$454.8

Significant components of the Company's net deferred tax liability at year-end were as follows (in millions):

	1999	*1998*	*1997*
Deferred tax assets:			
Workers' compensation and other claims	**$144.7**	$158.5	$138.8
Accruals not currently deductible	**111.3**	106.6	80.3
Accrued claims and other liabilities	**28.9**	48.0	48.8
Employee benefits	**46.1**	34.7	18.4
U.S. operating loss carryforward	**—**	12.1	—
Other assets	**42.7**	51.5	14.6
	$373.7	$411.4	$300.9

	1999	*1998*	*1997*
Deferred tax liabilities:			
Property	**$(387.8)**	$(315.7)	$(280.8)
Prepaid pension costs	**(165.4)**	(166.4)	(161.3)
LIFO inventory reserves	**(171.3)**	(125.7)	(106.0)
Investments in unconsolidated affiliates	**(5.8)**	(16.7)	(15.3)
Cumulative translation adjustments	**(4.9)**	(3.8)	(16.2)
Other liabilities	**(17.6)**	—	(18.3)
	(752.8)	(628.3)	(597.9)
Net deferred tax liability	**$(379.1)**	$(216.9)	$(297.0)

ALLIED SIGNAL
1998 ANNUAL REPORT

7. Taxes on Income

Income before taxes on income

Years ended December 31,	1998	1997	1996
United States	$1,600	$1,526	$1,099
Foreign	343	190	454
	$1,943	$1,716	$1,553

Taxes on income

Years ended December 31,	1998	1997	1996
United States	$478	$466	$359
Foreign	134	80	174
	$612	$546	$533

Years ended December 31,	1998	1997	1996
Taxes on income consist of:			
Current:			
United States	$298	$292	$190
State	16	54	41
Foreign	65	62	89
	379	408	320
Deferred:			
United States	100	98	133
State	64	22	(5)
Foreign	69	18	85
	233	138	213
	$612	$546	$533

Years ended December 31,	1998	1997	1996
The U.S. statutory federal income tax rate is reconciled to the Company's overall effective income tax rate as follows:			
U.S. statutory federal income tax rate	35.0%	35.0%	35.0%
Taxes on foreign earnings over U.S. tax rate	.8	.2	.4
Asset basis differences	(1.9)	(2.4)	(.1)
Nondeductible amortization	1.3	1.4	2.1
State income taxes	2.5	2.6	1.3
Tax benefits of Foreign Sales Corporation	(2.6)	(3.0)	(1.9)
Dividends received deduction	—	(.3)	(.2)
ESOP dividend tax benefit	(.6)	(.7)	(.7)
Tax credits	(1.5)	(.2)	—
All other items—net	(1.5)	(.8)	(1.6)
	31.5%	31.8%	34.3%

Deferred income taxes

Years ended December 31,	1998	1997
Included in the following balance sheet accounts:		
Other current assets	$ 408	$ 394
Other assets	84	117
Accrued liabilities	(8)	—
Deferred income taxes	(795)	(694)
	$(311)	$(183)

Deferred tax assets (liabilities)

Years ended December 31,	1998	1997
The principal components of deferred tax assets and (liabilities) are as follows:		
Property, plant and equipment basis differences	$(660)	$(690)
Postretirement benefits other than pensions and postemployment benefits	786	795
Investment and other asset basis differences	(508)	(567)
Other accrued items	406	561
Net operating losses	209	218
Deferred foreign gain	(39)	(48)
Undistributed earnings of subsidiaries	(55)	(45)
All other items–net	(420)	(381)
	(281)	(157)
Valuation allowance	(30)	(26)
	$(311)	$(183)

The amount of federal tax net operating loss carryforwards available for 1998 is $197 million. These loss carryforwards were generated by certain subsidiaries prior to their acquisition in 1997 and have expiration dates through the year 2011. The use of pre-acquisition operating losses is subject to limitations imposed by the Internal Revenue Code. The Company does not anticipate that these limitations will affect utilization of the carryforwards prior to their expiration. The Company also has foreign net operating losses of $429 million which are available to reduce future income tax payments in several countries, subject to varying expiration rules.

Deferred income taxes have not been provided on approximately $552 million of undistributed earnings of foreign affiliated companies, which are considered to be permanently reinvested. Any U.S. taxes payable on foreign earnings which may be remitted, however, will be substantially offset by foreign tax credits.

BORDERS
1999 ANNUAL REPORT

5. Income Taxes

The income tax provision consists of:

	1999	1998	1997
Current:			
Federal	$44.5	$40.9	$42.7
State and local	7.0	7.9	4.3
Foreign	0.2	—	0.4
Deferred:			
Federal	9.1	11.7	3.2
State and local	0.7	—	—
Foreign	(3.5)	(1.5)	—
Total income tax provision	$58.0	$59.0	$50.6

A reconciliation of the federal statutory rate to the Company's effective tax rate follows:

	1999	1998	1997
Federal statutory rate	$51.9	$52.9	$45.8
State and local taxes, net of federal tax benefit	5.0	5.2	3.5
Other	1.1	0.9	1.3
Total income tax provision	$58.0	$59.0	$50.6

Deferred tax assets and liabilities resulted from the following:

	1999	1998
Deferred tax assets:		
Federal benefit for state deferred taxes	$ 0.9	$ 1.6
Accruals and other current liabilities	8.6	11.2
Deferred revenue	7.0	7.0
Other long-term liabilities	2.6	1.5
Deferred compensation	8.1	7.4
Deferred rent	19.4	16.8
Net operating losses	5.0	1.5
FAS 121 impairment	6.3	7.9
Total deferred tax assets	57.9	54.9

(continued)

	1999	1998
Deferred tax liabilities:		
Inventory	9.1	8.6
Property and equipment	35.3	26.5
Other	3.4	3.4
Total deferred tax liabilities	47.8	38.5
Net deferred tax assets	$10.1	$16.4

The Company has tax net operating loss carryforwards in foreign jurisdictions totaling $16.3 as of January 23, 2000, $5.7 as of January 24, 1999 and $1.2 as of January 25, 1998. These losses have an indefinite carry-forward period.

COLGATE-PALMOLIVE
1997 ANNUAL REPORT

8. Income Taxes

The provision for income taxes consists of the following for the years ended December 31:

	1997	*1996*	*1995*
United States	**$ 91.0**	$ 67.2	$ 18.0
Overseas	**270.9**	252.4	173.5
	$361.9	$319.6	$191.5

Differences between accounting for financial statement purposes and accounting for tax purposes result in taxes currently payable being (lower) higher than the total provision for income taxes as follows:

	1997	*1996*	*1995*
Excess of tax over book depreciation	**$(12.7)**	$(15.9)	$(18.9)
Net restructuring (spending) accrual	**(47.5)**	(26.3)	70.5
Other, net	**5.2**	21.5	(5.3)
	$(55.0)	$(20.7)	$ 46.3

The components of income before income taxes are as follows for the three years ended December 31:

	1997	*1996*	*1995*
United States	**271.8**	$171.3	$(121.1)
Overseas	**830.5**	783.3	484.6
	$1,102.3	$954.6	$ 363.5

The difference between the statutory United States federal income tax rate and the Company's global effective tax rate as reflected in the Consolidated Statements of Income is as follows:

Percentage of Income Before Tax	1997	1996	1995
Tax at U.S. statutory rate	**35.0%**	35.0%	35.0%
State income taxes, net of federal benefit	**.6**	.3	.6
Earnings taxed at other than U.S. statutory rate	**(1.8)**	(1.4)	(.4)
Restructured operations	—	—	18.4
Other, net	**(1.0)**	(.4)	(.9)
Effective tax rate	**32.8%**	33.5%	52.7%

In addition, net tax benefits of $49.2 in 1997 and $32.6 in 1996 were recorded directly through equity.

The components of deferred tax assets (liabilities) are as follows at December 31:

	1997	1996
Deferred Taxes—Current:		
Accrued liabilities	**$ 78.8**	$ 63.7
Restructuring	**27.7**	24.5
Other, net	**17.9**	28.2
Total deferred taxes current	**124.4**	116.4
Deferred Taxes—Long-term:		
Intangible assets	**(251.6)**	(212.9)
Property, plant and equipment	**(188.4)**	(175.7)
Postretirement benefits	**65.6**	73.1
Restructuring	—	50.7
Tax loss and tax credit carryforwards	**159.5**	116.3
Other, net	**54.7**	29.1
Valuation allowance	**(124.3)**	(114.9)
Total deferred taxes long-term	**(284.5)**	(234.3)
Net deferred taxes	**$(160.1)**	$(117.9)

The major component of the 1997 and 1996 valuation allowance relates to tax benefits in certain jurisdictions not expected to be realized.

Part III

FOREIGN OPERATIONS AND DERIVATIVE INSTRUMENTS

Chapter 16

Foreign Currency Translation and Transactions

This chapter discusses the process of translating financial statements from foreign currency into U.S. dollars. It also covers the accounting and reporting of foreign currency transactions. Forward contracts may be entered into for hedging or speculative purposes. A sale or liquidation of an investment in a foreign entity may occur. The tax impact related to foreign currency dealings is also presented. Footnote disclosures are necessary so readers can properly appraise a company's exposure in overseas operations to variability in foreign exchange rates.

FASB Statement Number 52 (*Foreign Currency Translation*) requires that the assets, liabilities, and operations of an entity be measured in the functional currency of that business. The pronouncement applies to

- Foreign currency financial statements of divisions, branches, and other investees included in the financial statements of a U.S. company by consolidation, combination, or the equity method
- Foreign currency transactions, including imports and exports denominated in a currency other than the company's functional currency

An essential purpose in translating foreign currency is to preserve the financial performance and relationships expressed in the foreign currency. This is achieved by using the foreign entity's functional currency.

833

The functional currency is then converted into the reporting entity's reporting currency. It is presumed under FASB Statement Number 52 that the reporting currency for a company is U.S. dollars. However, it is possible that the reporting currency may be other than U.S. dollars.

A U.S. company should usually include the profits from foreign activities in its financial statements only to the degree that it receives funds in the United States or has unrestricted funds available to be transferred to the United States. If losses are expected, they should be provided for. In accounting and reporting of assets located in foreign countries, consideration should be given to possible problems of expropriation or restriction, if any exist.

The American Institute of CPAs' Statement of Position 93–4 deals with foreign currency accounting and financial statement presentation for investment companies.

TERMINOLOGY

Key terms in foreign dealings are defined as follows:

- *Foreign Entity* An operation (e.g., division, subsidiary, branch, joint venture) whose financial statements are prepared in a currency other than the reporting currency of the reporting entity.

- *Spot Rate* The exchange rate for immediate delivery of currencies exchanged.

- *Conversion* The exchange of one currency for that of another.

- *Exchange Ratio* The ratio of one unit of a currency to that of another at a given date. If a temporary lack of exchangeability exists between the two currencies at the transaction date or balance sheet date, the first rate available thereafter should be used.

- *Foreign Currency Translation* Stating in a company's reporting currency those amounts denominated or measured in a different currency.

- *Measure*   Translating into a currency other than the original reporting currency. Foreign financial statements are expressed in U.S. dollars by using the relevant exchange rate.

- *Denominate*   Pay or receive in the same foreign currency. The account can only be denominated in one currency (e.g., lira). It is a real account (asset or liability) fixed in terms of a foreign currency regardless of the exchange rate.

- *Local Currency*   The currency of a particular foreign country.

- *Reporting Currency*   The currency the business prepares its financial statements in, typically U.S. dollars.

- *Foreign Currency*   A currency other than the functional currency of a business. For example, the dollar could be a foreign currency for a foreign entity. Composites of currencies (e.g., special drawing rights) may be used to establish prices or denominate amounts of loans.

- *Foreign Currency Transactions*   Transactions in which the terms are denominated in a currency other than the entity's functional currency. Foreign currency transactions occur when a company (1) purchases (imports) or sells (exports) on credit merchandise or services the prices being denominated in a foreign currency; (2) buys or sells assets or incurs or settles liabilities denominated in foreign currency; (3) takes out or gives international loans in which the amounts payable or receivable are denominated in a foreign currency; (4) is a participant in an unperformed forward exchange contract; and (5) borrows or lends money, and the amounts payable or receivable are expressed in a foreign currency.

- *Currency Swap*   The exchange between two business entities of the currencies of two different countries in accordance with a contract to re-exchange the two currencies at the same exchange rate at an agreed upon future date.

- *Functional Currency*   A company's functional currency is the currency of the primary economic environment in which the company operates. It is usually the currency of the environment in which the business mostly receives and pays cash. Once determined, the functional currency should be used consistently unless significant changes clearly indicate a change. **Note:** The currency of a highly inflationary environment (three-year rate of 100% or more) is not stable enough to be used for this purpose. In such circumstances, the U.S. dollar is the functional currency. The functional currency of a foreign operation may be the same as that of a related affiliate where a foreign activity is a "key" component or extension of a related affiliate.

If remeasurement (restatement) of a subsidiary's foreign currency financial statements is required before translation can be accomplished (i.e., when the functional currency is the U.S. dollar), a transaction gain or loss results.

- *Foreign Currency Statements*   Financial statements using as the measuring unit a functional currency other than the reporting currency of the business.

- *Translation Adjustments*   Adjustments derived from translating financial statements from the entity's functional currency into the reporting one.

- *Monetary Assets and Liabilities*   Cash, receivables, and obligations to pay a fixed amount of debt.

- *Nonmonetary Items*   All balance sheet items except for cash, claims to cash, and cash obligations.

- *Transaction Gain or Loss*   Transaction gain or loss is produced from redeeming receivables/payables that are fixed in terms of amounts of foreign currency received/paid. An example is a French subsidiary having a receivable denominated in francs from a Swiss customer. A transaction gain or loss takes place when there is a change in exchange rates between the functional currency and the currency in which a foreign currency transaction is denominated. It constitutes an increase or decrease in (1) the actual functional currency cash flows realized upon settlement of foreign currency transactions and (2) the expected functional currency cash flows on unsettled foreign currency transactions.

THE FUNCTIONAL CURRENCY

In most instances, the functional currency is the currency of the country in which the company is located. In other instances, it may be the currency of another country. For example, if a foreign subsidiary's activities are situated within one country, are basically self-contained, and do not rely on the parent's economic environment, the subsidiary's functional currency is the currency of the country in which it is located. Conversely, if a foreign subsidiary's daily activities are a direct and important element of the parent's operations and environment, then the parent's currency will be the functional currency. If the company carries out major operations in more than one currency, management must make a determination of which currency to use as the functional currency. However, a company may have more than one distinct operation (e.g., branch, division). If conducted in different economic settings, each operation may have a different functional currency.

Before translating, the foreign country figures are remeasured in the functional currency.

EXAMPLE

If a French company is an independent entity and received cash and incurred expenses in France, the franc is the functional currency. However, if the Italian company is an extension of an Italian parent, the functional currency is the lira.

There should be consistent use of the functional currency except if significant economic changes required a change. A change in the functional currency is accounted for as a change in estimate. Previously issued financial statements are not restated for a change in the functional currency. Further, when there is a change in functional currency, the translation adjustments for previous years are still kept as a separate component of stockholders' equity.

If a company's books are not maintained in the functional currency, remeasurement into the functional currency is required. The remeasurement process takes place prior to translation into the reporting currency. When a foreign entity's functional currency is the reporting currency, remeasurement into the reporting currency obviates translation. The objective of the remeasurement process is to generate the same result as if the company's books had been kept in the functional currency.

EXAMPLE

A foreign entity's records are maintained in Mexican pesos, but the functional currency is Canadian dollars. The foreign entity's accounts must be remeasured into Canadian dollars before the financial statements are translated into the reporting entity's currency. An ensuing translation gain or loss from Mexican pesos to Canadian dollars is included in the remeasured net profit. However, if the foreign entity's functional currency is the Mexican peso, there is only a need to translate to the reporting currency. If the foreign entity's functional currency is the same as that of the reporting entity, remeasurement is only from the Mexican peso to the reporting currency.

The following guidelines are used to determine the functional currency of a foreign activity:

- *Market*   The functional currency is the foreign currency when the foreign activity has a strong local sales market for products or services, even though a substantial amount of exports may arise. The functional currency is the parent's currency when the foreign operation's sales market is primarily in the parent's country.

- *Financing*   The functional currency is the foreign currency if financing the foreign activity is in foreign currency and funds obtained by the foreign activity are adequate to meet debt obligations. The functional currency is the parent's currency when financing of foreign activity is provided by the parent or occurs in U.S. dollars. Funds received by the foreign activity are adequate to meet debt requirements.

- *Selling Price*   The functional currency is the foreign currency when the foreign operations' selling prices of products or services arise from local factors such as competition and government law. It is not because of changes in exchange rate. The functional currency is the parent's currency when the foreign operation's selling prices mostly apply in the short-term to variability in the exchange rate due to international reasons such as global competition.

- *Expenses*   The functional currency is the foreign currency when the foreign operation's manufacturing costs or services are typically incurred locally. However, some foreign imports may exist. The functional currency is the parent's currency when the foreign operations' manufacturing and service costs are mostly component costs obtained from the parent's country.

- *Intercompany Transactions*   If there is a limited number of intercompany transactions, the functional currency is the foreign currency— that is, when minor interrelationship occurs between the activities of the parent and foreign entity except for competitive advantages (e.g., patents, trademarks). If there are many intercompany transactions, the functional currency is the parent's currency—that is, when substantial interrelationship exists between the parent and foreign entity.

- *Cash Flow*   The functional currency is the foreign currency when the foreign operation's cash flows are mostly in foreign currency not directly impacting the parent's cash flow. The functional currency is the parent's currency when the foreign operation's cash flows directly affect the parent's cash flows. Cash flows are typically available for remittance via intercompany accounting settlement.

FOREIGN CURRENCY TRANSACTIONS

Foreign currency transactions may result in receivables or payables fixed in the amount of foreign currency to be received or paid. A foreign currency transaction requires payment in a currency other than the reporting entity's functional currency.

When a transaction is entered into, each asset, liability, revenue, expense, gain, or loss arising from that transaction should be measured and recorded based on the reporting company's functional currency at the exchange rate on that date. At each balance sheet date, balances that will be settled should be brought up to date at the current exchange rate.

A change in exchange rates between the functional currency and the currency in which a transaction is denominated increases or decreases the expected amount of functional currency cash flows upon settlement of the transaction.

The change in expected functional currency cash flows is a foreign currency transaction gain or loss that is presented separately as an element of income from continuing operations in the income statement for the period in which the exchange rate changed. In other words, if the exchange rate changes between the date of a purchase or sale and the time of actual payment or receipt, a foreign exchange transaction gain or loss arises.

EXAMPLE

A transaction may result in a gain or loss when an Italian subsidiary has a receivable denominated in lira from a Canadian customer. In other words, a transaction gain or loss (measured from the transaction date or the most recent intervening balance sheet date, whichever is later) realized upon settlement of a foreign currency transaction should typically be included in arriving at net income for the period in which the transaction is settled.

EXAMPLE

An exchange gain or loss takes place when the exchange rate changes between the purchase and payment dates. Assume that merchandise is purchased for 300,000 francs. The exchange rate is 3 francs to 1 dollar. The journal entry is

Purchases	$100,000	
Accounts Payable		$100,000

$$300,000 \text{ francs}/3 = \$100,000$$

When the goods are paid for, the exchange rate is 3.5 francs to 1 dollar. The journal entry is

Accounts Payable	$100,000	
Cash		$85,714
Foreign Exchange Gain		14,286

$$300,000 \text{ francs}/3.5 = \$85,714$$

The $85,714, using an exchange rate of 3.5 to 1, can buy 300,000 francs. The transaction gain is the difference between the cash required of $85,714 and the initial liability of $100,000.

EXAMPLE

On January 15, 2001, ABC Company, which uses a perpetual inventory system, shipped merchandise costing $45,000 to XYZ Company, a German company, for 100,000 Deutsche marks (DM). On February 15, 2001, ABC Company received a draft for DM 100,000 from XYZ Company. The draft was immediately converted. The spot rates were as follows:

	DM 1 =	
	Buying Rate	Selling Rate
January 15, 2001	0.60	0.65
January 31, 2001	0.65	0.70
February 15, 2001	0.55	0.60

Assuming that monthly statements are prepared, ABC Company will make the following journal entries:

1/15/01 Accounts receivable [DM 100,000 · $.60]	$60,000	
Sales		$60,000
1/15/01 Cost of goods sold	$45,000	
Inventory		$45,000
1/31/01 Accounts receivable [DM 100,000 · ($0.65–$0.60)	$ 5,000	
Transaction gain or loss		$ 5,000
2/15/01 Cash [DM 100,000·0.55]	$55,000	
Transaction gain or loss	$10,000	
Accounts receivable [$60,000 – $5,000]		$65,000

EXAMPLE

Klemer Corporation bought merchandise for 240,000 pesos when the exchange rate was 12 pesos to a dollar. The journal entry expressed in dollars follows:

Purchases	$20,000	
Accounts payable		$20,000

When the merchandise is paid for, the exchange rate changed to 15 : 1. The journal entry in dollars is

Accounts payable	$20,000	
Cash		$18,667
Foreign exchange gain		$ 1,333

At a 15 : 1 exchange rate the $18,667 can buy 240,000 pesos. The difference between the $18,667 and the initial liability of $20,000 represents a foreign exchange gain. If payment is made when the exchange rate is below 12 pesos to a dollar, a foreign exchange loss would arise.

EXAMPLE

On September 1, 19X4, a U.S. company bought foreign goods requiring payment in francs in 30 days after their receipt. Title to the merchandise passed on November 15, 19X4. The goods were still in transit on November 30, 19X4, the fiscal year-end. The exchange rates were one dollar to 22 francs, 20 francs, and 21 francs on September 1, November 15, and November 30, 19X4, respectively.

The transaction was recorded on November 15, 19X4, when title to the merchandise passed, and was recorded at an exchange rate of one dollar to 20 francs (i.e., it would cost $.05 to buy one franc). At November 30, 19X4, the exchange rate increased to 21 francs (it would cost less than $.05 to buy one franc). Because the dollar equivalent of the liability declined from November 15 to November 30, it gave rise to a gain included in income before extraordinary items.

Note: A foreign transaction gain or loss needs to be determined at each balance sheet date on all recorded foreign transactions that have not been settled. The difference between the exchange rate that would have settled the transaction at the date it occurred and the exchange rate that could be used to settle the transaction at a later balance sheet date is the gain or loss to be recorded.

EXAMPLE

A U.S. company sells merchandise to a customer in Italy on 10/1/19X8 for 20,000 lira. The exchange rate is 1 lira to $.40. Hence, the transaction is valued at $8,000 (20,000 lira × $.40). The terms of sale require payment in four months. The journal entry for the sale is

        10/1/19X8
        Accounts receivable—Italy $8,000
            Sales $8,000

Accounts receivable and sales are measured in U.S. dollars at the transaction date using the spot rate. Even though the accounts receivable are measured and reported in U.S. dollars, the receivable is fixed in lira. Hence, a transaction gain or loss can occur if the exchange rate changes between the date of sale (10/1/19X8) and the settlement date (2/1/19X9).

Because the financial statements are prepared between the transaction date (date of sale) and settlement date, receivables denominated in a currency other than the functional currency (U.S. dollar) must be restated to reflect the spot rate on the balance sheet date. On 12/31/19X8, the exchange rate is 1 lira equals $.45. Thus, 20,000 lira are now valued at 9,000 (20,000 × $.45). In consequence, the accounts receivable denominated in lira should be increased by $1,000.

The journal entry to do this on 12/31/19X8 is:

Accounts receivable—Italy	$1,000	
Foreign exchange gain		$1,000

The income statement for the year ended 12/31/19X8 shows an exchange gain of $1,000. It should be pointed out that sales is not affected by the exchange gain because sales relates to operational activity.

On 2/1/19X9, the spot rate is 1 lira equals $.43. The journal entry is

Cash	$8,600*	
Foreign exchange loss	$ 400	
Accounts receivable—Italy		$9,000

*20,000 lira × $.43 = $8,600

The 19X9 income statement presents an exchange loss $400.

EXAMPLE

On September 14, 1997, ABC company bought goods from an unaffiliated foreign company for 30,000 units of the foreign company's local currency. On that date, the spot rate was $.57. ABC paid the bill in full on March 27, 1998, when the spot rate was $.64. The spot rate was $.68 on December 31, 1997. ABC should report as a foreign currency transaction loss $3,300 in its income statement for the year ended December 31, 1997, calculated as follows:

Liability—12/31/1997: 30,000 × $.68	$20,400
Liability—9/22/1997: 30,000 × $.57	17,100
Foreign currency transaction loss	
at 12/31/1997: 30,000 × $.11	$ 3,300

Exception: Gains or losses on some types of foreign currency trans-actions are not included in profit but rather are treated as translation adjustments. Such gains and losses include

- Intercompany foreign currency transactions of a long-term investment nature (settlement is not planned or anticipated in the foreseeable future), when the entities to the transactions are consolidated, combined, or accounted for under the equity method in the reporting company's financial statements.

- Foreign currency transactions engaged in as economic hedges of a net investment in a foreign entity, beginning as of the designation date.

A foreign currency transaction is deemed a hedge of an identifiable foreign currency commitment provided both of the following two conditions exist:

- The foreign currency commitment is firm.
- The foreign currency transaction is intended as a hedge.

Note: A dealer in foreign exchange may account for transaction gains or losses as dealer gains or losses.

In conclusion, when the balance sheet falls between the transaction and final settlement dates, receivables/payables must be adjusted to the dollar equivalent as of the balance sheet date; the difference is an exchange gain or loss. Upon settlement of the transaction, there will be a further gain or loss based on the recorded balance at that time.

TRANSLATION PROCESS

Translation of foreign currency statements is usually needed when a foreign subsidiary's statements or equity-method investee has a functional currency other than the U.S. dollar included in a domestic company's financial statements, such as through consolidation or using the equity method.

If a foreign entity's functional currency is the U.S. dollar and the parent's currency is also the U.S. dollar, no translation adjustment is required. A translation adjustment only occurs if the foreign entity's functional currency is different from that of the parent.

The objectives of translation include

■ *Preserving the operating results and relationships measured in the foreign currency.* This is achieved by measuring assets, liabilities, and operating results in the foreign entity's functional currency and, when required, converting them to the parent's reporting currency.

■ *Providing information in consolidated financial statements about the financial performance of each foreign consolidated entity.*

■ *Providing information on the anticipated effects of changes in exchange rates on cash flow and equity.*

The following steps are required in translating the foreign country's financial statements into U.S. reporting requirements:

1. Conform the foreign currency financial statements into U.S. generally accepted accounting principles. The foreign currency financial statements must be in conformity with U.S. GAAP before they are translated to the functional or reporting currency.

2. Ascertain the functional currency of the foreign entity.

3. Remeasure the financial statements in the functional currency, if required. Gain or loss from remeasurement is included in the remeasured net income.

   Note: If the foreign company keeps its records in a currency other than the functional or reporting currency, its balance sheet and income statement accounts have to be remeasured into the functional currency before translation into the reporting currency. For example, a parent maintains its financial statements in U.S. dollars and owns a foreign subsidiary whose functional currency is British pounds. If some or all of the foreign subsidiary's records are kept in Italian lira, its financial statements must be remeasured into British pounds before translation into U.S. dollars.

4. Convert from the foreign (functional) currency into U.S. dollars (reporting currency). If a foreign company's functional currency is other than the reporting currency, translation into the reporting currency is necessary before the entity may be consolidated, combined, or accounted for on the equity method.

> **Note:** A permanent impairment of a foreign investment must be provided for before translation and consolidation.

In the usual case, when the foreign currency is the functional currency, balance sheet items (assets and liabilities) are translated at the current exchange rate at the balance sheet date of the foreign entity. Capital accounts are translated using the historical exchange rate in effect when the foreign entity's stock was issued, or reacquired retained earnings are translated at the translated amount at year-end of the previous year, plus the translated amount of net income for the current year, less the translated amount of dividends during the current year. If the current exchange rate is unavailable at the balance sheet date, the first available exchange rate after that date should be used. The current method is required under FASB Statement Number 52 (except when there is a highly inflationary environment, to be discussed shortly). The current method assures that financial relationships remain the same in both local currency and U.S. dollars.

In the statement of cash flows, cash flows are translated based on the exchange rates in existence at the time of the cash flows. If reasonable and practical, a weighted-average rate for the year may be used as long as the result is similar. Disclosure should be made in the statement of cash flows for the impact of any exchange rate changes on cash flow.

In the usual case (when high inflation does not exist), income statement items (revenue, expenses, gains, and losses) are translated at the exchange rate at the dates those items are recognized. Because translation at the exchange rates at the dates of many revenues, expenses, gains, and losses is usually impractical, a weighted-average exchange rate for the year is typically used in translating income statement items. However, average quarterly or monthly rates may be used if significant revenues and expenses occur at particular times during the year.

If a company's functional currency is a foreign currency, translation adjustments occur from translating the company's financial statements into the reporting currency. Translation adjustments are unrealized. They are reported separately as a component of "other comprehensive income" in the income statement for the current year amount with the cumulative translation adjustment reported as "accumulated other comprehensive income" in the stockholders' equity section of the balance sheet. Translation adjustments shall not be included in net income unless and until there is a sale or liquidation of the investment in the foreign entity.

Exception: If remeasurement from the recording currency to the functional currency is needed before translation, the gain or loss is included in the income statement.

EXAMPLE

Blake Company's wholly owned subsidiary, David Company, keeps its records in German marks. Since David Company's branch offices are located in Switzerland, its functional currency is the Swiss franc. Remeasurement of David Company's 19X8 financial statements resulted in an $8,700 gain, and translation of its financial statements resulted in a $9,200 gain. Blake should report as a foreign exchange gain $8,700 in its income statement for the year ended December 31, 19X8. The translation gain of $9,200 should be included in the cumulative translation adjustment, which is a separate component of stockholders' equity.

HIGHLY INFLATIONARY ENVIRONMENT IN FOREIGN COUNTRY

According to FASB Statement Number 52, a highly inflationary environment is one with a cumulative inflation rate of 100% or more over a three-year period. In other words, the inflation rate must be increasing at a rate of about 33% per year for three consecutive years. **Note:** The International Monetary Fund of Washington, D.C. publishes information about the international inflation rates. **Tip:** In some cases, the inflation trend may be as important as the absolute rate of inflation.

The foreign entity's financial statements in a very inflationary environment are unstable and should be remeasured as if the functional currency were the reporting currency. In this case, the investor's reporting currency is used directly. Consequently, if a foreign entity's financial statements in a highly inflationary economy are expressed in a currency different from the reporting currency, they have to be remeasured into the reporting currency.

If the U.S. dollar is used directly as the functional currency because of high inflation, balance sheet conversion would be as follows:

- Cash, receivables, and payables are converted at the foreign exchange rate in effect at the balance sheet date.

- Other assets and liabilities are converted at foreign exchange rates (historical rates) in effect at the date of transaction, except that the exchange rate in effect at the balance sheet date is used to translate assets and liabilities that are accounted for on the basis of current prices, such as marketable securities carried at market and estimated warranty obligations.

If the U.S. dollar is used as the functional currency because of high inflation, translation of income statement items is based on the weighted-average rate for the period. However, revenues and expenses that relate to assets and liabilities translated at historical rates should be translated at such historical rates. Examples are depreciation on fixed assets, amortization expense on intangible assets, and amortized revenue arising from deferred revenue.

In a highly inflationary environment in a foreign country requiring the use of the reporting currency directly, gains and losses from converting foreign currency financial statements into reporting currency financial statements are recognized in net income rather than reported in stockholders' equity.

According to Emerging Issues Task Force Consensus Summary Number 92–4 (*Accounting for a Change in Functional Currency When an Economy Ceases to be Considered Highly Inflationary*), when a foreign subsidiary's environment is no longer highly inflationary, the entity must convert the amounts expressed in the reporting currency into the local currency based on the exchange rates on the date of change.

EXAMPLE 1: REMEASURING ACCOUNTS
OF A FOREIGN SUBSIDIARY

FNC is a wholly owned German subsidiary of MNC. The functional currency is U.S. dollars. The following accounts, for year ended December 31, 2004, are stated in Deutsche marks (DM).

Rent expense	150,000
Allowance for doubtful accounts	60,000
Patent amortization expense*	85,000

*Acquired on March 23, 2002

The exchange rates for the DM for various dates and time periods are as follows:

March 23, 2002	0.65
December 31, 2004	0.55
Average for year ended December 31, 2004	0.6

The remeasured accounts in U.S. dollars are as follows:

	DM	Exchange Rate	U.S. dollars
Rent expense	150,000	0.60	$90,000
Allowance for doubtful accounts	60,000	0.55	33,000
Patent amortization expense	85,000	0.65	55,250
	295,000		$178,250

EXAMPLE 2: REMEASURING ACCOUNTS
OF A FOREIGN SUBSIDIARY

The trial balance of the German branch of XYZ Corp. for its first month of operations in Deutsche Marks (DM) is as follows:

XYZ Corporation
German Branch Trial Balance (in DM)
January 31, 2002

Cash	50,000	
Accounts receivable	250,000	
Inventory	500,000	
Investment in German branch		700,000
Sales		1,200,000
Cost of goods sold	650,000	
Selling expenses	125,000	
Administrative expenses	325,000	
	1,900,000	1,900,000

Inventory was shipped from the main office on January 1, 2002, when the exchange rate was 1 DM = $0.65. The exchange rate on January 31, 2002 was 1 DM = $0.55.

The investment in German branch appears on XYZ Corp.'s at $105,000 on January 31, 2002.

The remeasured trial balance of the German branch in the functional currency (U.S. dollars) is as follows:

	Balance in DM debit/(credit)	Exchange Rate	Balance in U.S. Dollars debit/(credit)
Cash	50,000	0.55	$ 27,500
Accounts receivable	250,000	0.55	137,500
Inventory	500,000	0.65	325,000
Investment in German branch	(700,000)		–105,000
Sales	(1,200,000)	0.60	–720,000
Cost of goods sold	650,000	0.65	422,500
Selling expenses	125,000	0.60	75,000
Administrative expenses	325,000	0.60	195,000
	$0		$357,500
Transaction gain	$0		($357,500)
Total	$0		$0

HEDGING

Foreign currency transaction gains and losses on assets and liabilities, denominated in a currency other than the entity's functional currency, can be hedged if the U.S. company enters into a forward exchange contract (discussed in the next section).

A hedge can arise if a forward exchange contract does not exist.

EXAMPLE

A foreign currency transaction can serve as an economic hedge offsetting a parent's net investment in a foreign entity when the transaction is entered into for hedging purposes and is effective.

EXAMPLE

A U. S. parent owns a British subsidiary with net assets of $6 million in pounds. The U.S. parent can borrow $6 million pounds to hedge its net investment in the British subsidiary. Assume that the British pound is the functional currency, and the $6 million obligation is denominated in pounds. Fluctuation in the exchange rate for pounds does not have a net effect on the parent's consolidated balance sheet, because increases in the translation adjustment balance arising from translation of the net investment will be netted against reductions in this balance caused from adjusting the liability denominated in pounds.

EXAMPLE 3: PURCHASE OF INVENTORY—USE OF HEDGING

On January 3, 2001, ABC Inc. purchased merchandise from a German company goods costing 100,000 Deutsche marks (DM) on 30-day open account. On the same day, ABC Inc. acquired a 30-day forward exchange contract for DM 100,000, to hedge its commitment. The exchange rates were as follows:

Spot rates:			
Buying:	DM 1 = $0.60		
Selling:	DM 1 = $0.65		
Selling spot rate for February 2, 2001: DM 1 = $0.65			
30-day forward rate: DM 1 = $0.70			
1/3/01	Inventory [DM 100,000 · $0.65]	$65,000	
	Accounts payable		$65,000
	To record purchase of inventory.		
1/3/01	Investment in forward exchange contract [DM 100,000 · $0.65]	$65,000	
	Inventory [DM 100,000 · ($0.70 – $0.65)]	$ 5,000	
	Forward exchange contract payable [DM 100,000 · $0.70]		$70,000
	To record acquisition of 30-day forward exchange contract.		
2/2/01	Forward exchange contract payable	$70,000	
	Investment in DM	$65,000	
	Investment in forward exchange contract		$65,000
	Cash		$70,000
	To record payment of contract and receipt of DM.		
2/2/01	Accounts payable	$65,000	
	Investment in DM		$65,000
	To record payment of liability.		

Emerging Issues Task Force Consensus Summary Number 90–17 covers hedging foreign currency risks with purchased options.

FORWARD EXCHANGE CONTRACTS

A forward exchange contract is an agreement to exchange different currencies at a particular future date at a specified rate (forward rate). A forward contract is a foreign currency transaction. A forward exchange contract is usually constructed to hedge a position or for speculative purposes. Gains or losses on foreign exchange contracts typically are recognized in net income in the year the exchange rate changes. Gains and losses that are exceptions to this general rule are deferred.

A gain or loss on a forward contract not satisfying the conditions enumerated next are included in net income.

Note: Currency swaps are accounted for in a similar way.

Condition 1

A gain or loss on a forward contract designed as a hedge (excluding a speculative forward contract) should be computed by multiplying the foreign currency principal amount of the forward contract by the difference between the spot rate at the balance sheet date and the spot rate at the inception date of the forward contract. A gain or loss on a forward exchange contract (or other foreign currency transaction) that is for hedging purposes of a particular foreign currency commitment should be deferred until the associated foreign currency commitment is settled. The foreign currency commitment must be a firm one.

EXAMPLE

A U.S. company commits itself to buy merchandise from a Mexican company at a future date and when delivery occurs to pay 800,000 pesos. The U.S. company seeks to insulate itself from a declining exchange rate by buying a forward exchange contract to purchase 800,000 pesos at the exchange rate existing when the purchase commitment was made. The following must be taken into account when deferring the gain or loss on such transactions:

1. A loss should not be deferred if it will probably be recognized in future years.

2. If the hedging transaction is terminated prior to the transaction date of the commitment, the gain or loss will continue to be deferred until the associated commitment is settled.

3. The gain or loss associated with the forward exchange contract should usually be deferred only to the degree that the contract does not exceed the firm, identifiable commitment.

However, the gain or loss applicable to an amount exceeding the commitment should be deferred to the extent the contract serves as a hedge in after-tax terms. Such deferred gains or losses should offset the related tax effects in the years the taxes are recorded. In the event that the gain or loss associated with the hedge of an identifiable foreign currency commitment is deferred, the discount or premium on the forward contract may be either accounted for separately and amortized over the contract's life as an adjustment to net income, or deferred and included in the basis of the associated foreign currency transaction when it is recorded. Gains or losses exceeding the amount of commitment on an after-tax basis cannot be deferred. Further, any gains or losses on a forward exchange contract applicable to a period subsequent to the transaction date of the related commitment cannot be deferred.

Deferred gain or loss on hedging a foreign currency commitment that is sold or terminated is not recorded until the associated identifiable transaction occurs, except if the transaction is likely to result in a loss.

A forward exchange contract may be entered into to hedge an identifiable foreign currency commitment. A gain or loss on a forward exchange contract that is intended to hedge a foreign currency commitment (such as an agreement to purchase or sell equipment) shall be deferred and included in the measurement of the related foreign currency transaction (i.e., the purchase or sale).

A forward exchange contract may be entered into to hedge exposure from a recognized receivable or payable denominated in a foreign currency. A gain or loss is recognized for changes in the spot rate of the applicable currency; however, this gain or loss is offset by the transaction loss or gain recognized from the associated receivable or payable.

EXAMPLE

A U.S. company buys equipment from a Mexican company for 50,000 pesos at the time the exchange rate is 5 : 1 (5 pesos to one dollar). The equipment is to be delivered next year, when it will be paid for in Mexican pesos. The U.S. company hedges against a change in the exchange rate of the peso by purchasing a $1,500 forward contract to buy 50,000 Mexican pesos in one year at the exchange rate of 5 : 1. In this way, the U.S. company can hedge against an increase or decrease in the peso. After six months, the exchange rate of Mexican pesos is 6 : 1. Hence, the equipment will now cost in U.S. dollars $8,333, or 50,000 Mexican pesos, while at the purchase date the cost in U.S. dollars was $10,000, or 50,000 Mexican pesos. After one year, the company will receive 50,000 Mexican pesos from the forward exchange contract after paying $10,000. At the interim six-month date, however, there is a deferred loss on the forward contract of $3,167 ($1,667 plus the cost of the contract of $1,500). The loss is not deferred if the cost of the equipment, including the deferred loss on the forward exchange contract, is anticipated to be more than the estimated net realizable value of the equipment.

Emerging Issues Task Force Consensus Summary Number 91–1 (*Hedging Intercompany Foreign Currency Risks*) states that transactions engaged in by members of a consolidated group with different functional currencies can cause foreign currency risks in need of hedging.

Condition 2

The discount or premium on a forward contract (the foreign currency amount of the contract multiplied by the difference between the contracted forward rate and the spot rate at the inception date of the contract) should be accounted for separately from the gain or loss on the contract. It is included in determining net income over the forward contract period. In other words, the discount or premium on a hedge contract should be amortized to income over the contract's life, usually on a straight-line basis. The amortization of discount or premium is recorded in a separate revenue or expense account. It is not an adjustment to the foreign currency transaction gain or loss account. Under this accounting approach, there will not be a net foreign currency transaction gain or loss if the assets and liabilities denominated in foreign currency are fully hedged at the transaction date.

Condition 3

A gain or loss on a speculative forward contract (a contract that does not hedge an exposure) should be determined by multiplying the foreign currency principal amount of the forward contract by the difference between the forward rate available for the remaining maturity of the contract and the specified contracted forward rate (or the forward rate last used to measure a gain or loss on that contract for an earlier period). In other words, a speculative forward exchange contract is essentially accounted for like an investment in a trading security. The gain or loss is based on the change in the fair value of the contract. **Note:** No separate accounting recognition is given to the discount or premium on a speculative forward contract.

EXAMPLE

On November 1, 19X5, Ace Company bought a foreign exchange contract as a speculative investment. It bought 100,000 Deutsche marks for delivery in 60 days. The rates to exchange $1 for 1 Deutsche mark are as follows:

	11/1/19X5	*11/30/19X5*
Spot rate	.95	.90
30-day forward rate	.93	.91
60-day forward rate	.94	.93

In its November 30, 19X5 income statement, Ace Company will report a foreign exchange loss of $3,000 calculated as follows:

100,000 Deutsche marks × ($.94 less $.91) = $3,000

Emerging Issues Task Force Consensus Summary Number 87–2 deals with the net present value method of valuing speculative foreign exchange contracts.

Key Point: The spot or forward rate last used in an earlier period may be the basis to determine the gain or loss on a hedging or speculative forward exchange contract, if required.

Note: Hedges and other futures contracts not related to foreign currency transactions are recorded in conformity with FASB Statement Number 80 (*Accounting for Futures Contracts*). This is discussed in Chapter 17.

SALE OR LIQUIDATION OF AN INVESTMENT IN A FOREIGN ENTITY

If there is a sale or liquidation of an investment in a foreign entity, the amount attributable to that entity and accumulated in the translation adjustment component of equity is removed from the stockholders' equity section. It is considered a part of the gain or loss on sale or liquidation of the investment in the income statement for the period during which the sale or liquidation occurs.

As per FASB Interpretation Number 37 (*Accounting for Translation Adjustment Upon Sale of Part of an Investment in a Foreign Entity*), sale of an investment in a foreign entity may include a partial sale of an ownership interest. In that event, a proportionate amount of the cumulative translation adjustment reflected as a stockholders' equity component is included in determining the gain or loss on sale.

EXAMPLE

If a business sells 30% ownership in a foreign investment, 30% of the translation adjustment applicable to it is included in computing gain or loss on sale of that ownership interest.

INTERCOMPANY PROFITS

In the elimination of intercompany profits, the company should use the exchange rate in existence at the date of the intercompany transaction. A transaction is either at the date of sale or transfer. However, a reasonable average or estimated rate may be used when there are frequent intercompany transactions during the year.

Emerging Issues Task Force Consensus Summary Number 91–1 covers the hedging of intercompany foreign currency risks.

EXCLUDING A FOREIGN ENTITY FROM FINANCIAL STATEMENTS

In some cases a foreign entity may be excluded from consolidated or combined financial statements. This may arise if serious political problems exist in the foreign country (e.g., civil war) or if exchange restrictions are extremely restrictive, inhibiting any reliability to exchange rates. In this situation, profits of a foreign activity should be included in the financial statements only to the degree of receipt of unrestricted cash. When the foreign entity is excluded from the financial statements, proper disclosure should be made of the reasons therefor, other pertinent information, and dollar effect. Such disclosure may be in a supplemental schedule or in footnote form.

FOREIGN OPERATIONS IN THE UNITED STATES

An entity in the United States may be a subsidiary of a parent company domiciled in a foreign country. In this case, the local company's financial statements may be presented separately in the United States or combined with the financial statements in the foreign country.

TAXES

Deferred taxes will typically be recorded for the future tax impact of temporary differences, resulting in taxable translation and/or transaction gains or losses. Tax effects may be presented in either the income statement or stockholders' equity section, depending on the nature of the taxable item. However, deferred taxes may not need to be recorded for a foreign subsidiary's unremitted earnings. In such a case, proper disclosure should be made.

According to Emerging Issues Task Force Consensus Summary Number 92–8 (*Accounting for the Income Tax Effects under FASB Statement Number 109 of a Change in Functional Currency When an Economy Ceases to Be Considered Highly Inflationary*), deferred taxes on temporary differences arising because of a change in the functional currency are accounted for as an adjustment to the cumulative translation adjustments presented in stockholders' equity.

DISCLOSURES

Footnote disclosure is required of:

- Profits earned from overseas. This also includes the amount of foreign earnings in excess of amounts received in the United States.
- Foreign currency transaction gains or losses, including that associated with forward exchange contracts.

- The impact on unsettled balances regarding foreign currency transactions.

- Cumulative translation adjustments reported in stockholders' equity. This includes the reasons for the change in the balance from the beginning to the end of the year.

- Gains or losses arising from hedging a foreign currency position.

- Effect of exchange rate changes on operating results and financial position. This disclosure includes the impact of a change in exchanges rates from the prior year to the current year associated with translation of revenues and expenses. It also includes the effect of a change in exchange rate on revenue and cost components, such as sales volume, sales price, and cost of sales. The nature of restated figures should be noted.

- A significant change in exchange rate taking place after year-end and before the audit report date. This is a subsequent event disclosure.

SUMMARY

If the foreign statements have any accounts expressed in a currency other than their own, they have to be converted into the foreign statement's currency prior to translation into U.S. dollars or any other reporting currency.

In most cases, assets and liabilities are translated at the current exchange rate at the balance sheet date. Revenue and expenses are usually translated at the weighted-average exchange rate for the period. Translation adjustments are reported as a part of comprehensive income and ultimately as a separate component of stockholders' equity as accumulated other comprehensive income. Foreign currency transaction gains and losses are reported in the income statement.

Annual Report References

TEXACO
1998 ANNUAL REPORT

8. Foreign Currency

Currency translations resulted in a pre-tax loss of $80 million in 1998, $59 million in 1997 and 60 million in 1996. After applicable taxes, 1998 included a loss of $94 million compared to a gain of $154 million in 1997 and a loss of $66 million in 1996.

After-tax currency impacts for the years 1998 and 1997 were largely due to currency volatility in Asia. In 1998, our Caltex affiliate incurred significant currency-related losses due to the strengthening of the Korean won and Japanese yen against the U.S. dollar. In contrast, those currencies weakened against the U.S. dollar in 1997 which resulted in significant currency-related gains.

Results for 1996 through 1998 were also impacted by the effect of currency rate changes on deferred income taxes denominated in British pounds. In 1998 and 1996, the U.S. dollar weakened against that currency causing us to record losses of 5 million and $58 million. In 1997, when the U.S. dollar strengthened, we recorded a gain of $28 million.

Effective October 1, 1997, Caltex changed the functional currency for its operations in its Korean and Japanese affiliates to the U.S. dollar.

Currency translation adjustments shown in the separate stockholders' equity account result from translation items pertaining to certain affiliates of Caltex. For the years 1998, 1997 and 1996 these adjustments were losses of $2 million, $40 million and $126 million. The year 1996 includes the reversal of $60 million of previously deferred gains which were recognized in earnings due to the sale by Caltex of its investment in its Japanese affiliate, NPRC.

PHARMACIA AND UPJOHN 1998 ANNUAL REPORT

14. Currency Risk Management

The company is exposed to currency exchange rate fluctuations related to certain intercompany and third-party transactions, primarily intercompany sales from Sweden and Italy to other European countries, the U.S. and Japan. The exposures and related hedging program are managed centrally using forward currency contracts, cross-currency swaps and currency options to hedge a portion of both net recorded currency transaction exposures on the balance sheet as well as net anticipated currency transactions. The company also has hedged part of its net investment in Japan. Financial instruments for trading purposes are neither held nor issued by the company.

The company's program to hedge net anticipated currency transaction exposures is designed to protect cash flows from potentially adverse effects of exchange rate fluctuations. At December 31, 1998, the contract amount of the company's outstanding contracts used to hedge net transaction exposure was $690. Of these contracts, 20 percent were denominated in Japanese yen, 11 percent were denominated in U.S. dollars, 8 percent were denominated in German marks, and 17 percent were denominated in mainly other European currencies all against Swedish krona; 10 percent were denominated in various currencies, mainly Japanese yen and U.S. dollars, against Italian lira; and 34 percent in various currencies, mainly European currencies and Japanese yen, against U.S. dollars.

Gains and losses on hedges of intercompany loans and deposits offset the currency exchange gains and losses of the underlying loans and deposits. At December 31, 1998, the contract amount of forward exchange contracts held for balance sheet financial exposure hedging program was $756. Of these contracts, 59 percent were denominated in U.S. dollars against European currencies; 17 percent were denominated in U.S. dollars against Japanese yen; 4 percent were denominated in Swedish krona against various European currencies; and 20 percent were denominated in various other currencies mainly against the Swedish krona and the U.S. dollar.

Because the contract amounts are stated as notional amounts, the amount of contracts disclosed above is not a direct measure of the exposure of the company through its use of derivatives. These contracts generally have maturities that do not exceed twelve months and require the company to exchange currencies at agreed-upon rates at maturity. The counterparties to the contracts consist of a limited number of major international financial institutions. The company does not expect any losses from credit exposure.

AMR CORPORATION
1997 ANNUAL REPORT

15. Foreign Operations

American conducts operations in various foreign countries. American's operating revenues from foreign operations were (in millions):

	Year Ended December 31,		
	1997	*1996*	*1995*
Latin America	**$2,716**	$2,438	$2,316
Europe	**2,035**	1,967	2,059
Pacific	**356**	336	373
Foreign operating revenues	**$5,107**	$4,741	$4,748

The SABRE Group also conducts operations in various foreign countries. THE SABRE Group's operating revenues from foreign operations were $339 million, $284 million and $251 million for 1997, 1996 and 1995, respectively.

MOBIL
1997 ANNUAL REPORT

13. Foreign Currency

Foreign exchange transaction gains of $7 million in 1995, and losses of $21 million in 1996 and $52 million in 1997, have been included in income.

The effect of foreign currency translation on Mobil's balance sheet accounts is shown below.

| *Cumulative foreign exchange translation adjustment* | *(In millions)* | | |
at December 31	*1995*	*1996*	*1997*
Properties, plants and equipment, net	$(124)	$ (27)	**$(940)**
Deferred income taxes	(252)	(256)	**(103)**
Working capital, debt and other items, net	349	210	**222**
Total	$ (27)	$ (73)	**$(821)**[1]

[1] The change in 1997 from 1996 reflects the strengthening U.S. dollar relative to local currencies in certain countries, including several in the Asia-Pacific region, in which the company has significant operations.

17

Derivatives, Repurchase Agreements, and Disclosures of Credit Risk and Fair Values: Accounting, Reporting, and Disclosures

TERMINOLOGY

Accounting Loss   Loss recorded on the financial books due to changes in the market, credit, or other risk arising from a financial instrument.

Arbitrage   The simultaneous purchase and sale of similar financial instruments with the purpose of taking advantage of perceived disparities in the relative value of these instruments.

Cap, Collar, or Floor   An option contract that provides the purchaser with protection against price movements outside a predefined range, e.g., an interest rate cap protects the purchaser from interest rate increases above a certain level.

Carrying Amount (Carrying Value)   Amount recorded on the financial books.

Compound Instrument   A financial instrument that contains two or more embedded financial instruments. For example, a callable bond consists of a bond and a call option.

Comprehensive Income   Change in equity (net asset) arising from either transactions or other occurrences with non-owners. For more information, see Chapter 1.

Contractual Rights and Obligations   Specific legal obligations of the parties to an agreement. Based on the contract terms, rights may result in an asset being recorded, obligations may result in a liability or an off-balance-sheet contingency may exist.

Credit Risk　Risk of a loss due to the failure of a counterparty to perform as per contractual terms.

Derivative Financial Instrument (derivative)　Contract in which the value is tied to the return on stocks, debt, currencies, or commodities. Thus, there may be an underlying interest rate, commodity price, stock price index, foreign exchange rate, and/or other variable.

Duration　The expected actual life, in years. For example, prepayments significantly shorten the expected duration.

Equity Instrument　A security evidencing ownership interest in a business.

Fair Value　A price set in the ordinary course of business by willing buyers and sellers. The best measure of fair value is a quoted market price when the market is liquid. If a quoted price does not exist, then use an estimate of fair value. When possible, such estimate should take into account quoted market prices for comparable instruments. If comparable instruments with quoted prices are not available, other valuation approaches include the discounted value of expected future cash flows (using a suitable discount rate), or model-derived prices (option-pricing models, matrix pricing, fundamental analysis, option-adjusted spread models). In arriving at a valuation, consideration should be given to expectations regarding: future revenues, future expenses, interest rates, and volatility. In valuing foreign currency forward contracts by discounting techniques, expected cash flows generally are based on the forward rate (not the spot rate). In valuing liabilities by discounting, the discount rate generally is based on a rate the company would need to pay a financially sound third party to assume a similar obligation.

Financial Asset　Cash, an ownership interest in another company, or a contract to receive cash or another asset from a third party.

Financial Instrument　Financial assets and liabilities. Includes derivatives and non-derivatives.

Financial Liability　Obligation to deliver cash or another financial asset to a third party.

Firm Commitment　Legal agreement or other obligation to perform. The failure to perform results in possible damages. The terms of the commitment should be stated, such as price, date and amount.

Forecasted Transaction　Expected transaction, but without firm commitment. A forecasted transaction does not give the company current rights to later benefits or duties for future sacrifices.

Forward Contract　An over-the-counter contract similar to futures. Unlike a futures contract, a forward contract is not uniform or standardized, and is not traded on an exchange. In such a contract, the contract is settled when the underlying is actually delivered at a future date—or settlement may be in cash, based on the net change in value of the underlying. A forward contract may be based on a commodity or a financial instrument. The contract fixes the quantity, price, and date of purchase or sale. In most cases, money is not paid until the delivery date.

Forward Exchange Rate   Agreed-upon rate at which two currencies will be exchanged at some future date, usually 30, 90, or 180 days from the day the transaction is negotiated.

Futures Contract   Agreement to buy or sell a specified amount of a commodity or financial instrument at a particular future date at a given price. With futures, physical delivery of the underlying asset almost never occurs; the position instead is closed out by the purchase of an offsetting contract. The contracts are standardized and traded on an exchange, usually subject to daily margin requirements. Examples of the underlying include commodities, debt instruments, composite stock indexes, or foreign currencies.

Hedge   An action taken to reduce risk, e.g., exposure to market price volatility. For example the purchase of an equity put option can protect the holder against a declining stock price.

Interest Rate Swap   Agreement to exchange future cash flows based on a reference rate. In a single currency interest rate swap, one party pays a fixed interest rate and one party pays a floating interest rate (e.g., LIBOR) based on a notional principle amount.

LIBOR   London Inter-Bank Offered Rate. Floating-rate index that can be contrasted with the prime rate in the US.

Market Risk   Risk associated with changes in market value of financial instruments.

Market Risk Valuation Adjustments   A valuation adjustment may be used to account for uncertainty in a market price or model-derived value. Such uncertainties include high concentrations in a particular security, or liquidity concerns when trading for a particular security is thin.

Notional Amount   Number of shares, currency, or goods stated in a contract, e.g. the number of bushels in a corn futures contract.

Option Contract   Giving buyers the right, but not the obligation, to purchase or sell a specified amount of an asset at a set price for a given time period. The value of an option is typically a minor percentage of the underlying value of the asset.

Other-Than-Temporary Decline   Permanent decrease in the market price of an equity security. The permanent impairment reduces the carrying value of the asset, and establishes a new "cost" basis.

Realized Gain (Loss)   Excess or (deficiency) in selling price relative to carrying value of a financial instrument. For instruments that are not marked to market, realized gains or losses are included in net income in the year of the sale.

Repurchase Agreement (Repo)   Contract in which the company sells a security to a third party for cash and at the same time commits to repurchase that security at a later date of a stated price plus interest. Interest is due for the period of transfer. Examples of securities involved might be mortgage-backed securities and US Treasuries. "Dollar roll" repurchase agreements are contracts to sell and repurchase similar but not identical securities; the securities are collateralized by different, but similar, mortgage pools and will typically have different principal amounts. These transactions are also referred to as collateralized borrowings.

Reverse Repo   A repurchase agreement contract from the perspective of the company that purchases the security.

Risk of Accounting Loss   Likelihood of loss arising from changes in credit, market or operational risks.

Spot (or Cash) Rate   Exchange rate for a foreign currency for immediate delivery in accordance with normal market conventions.

Securities Lending   Similar to a repurchase agreement except that the company that lends (sells) the security may accept other securities or other financial instruments as collateral, instead of cash.

Swap   Contractual agreement to exchange something, usually obligations to pay streams of money. Typically, there is no exchange of the underlying instrument itself. A swap may be tied to various underlying financial instruments, indices, or commodities. Examples are currency swaps and interest rate swaps. A swap is not publicly traded on an exchange.

Swaption   Option on a swap giving the holder the right but not the obligation to contract a swap at a particular future date at specified terms or to lengthen or terminate an existing swap.

Underlying Commodity   Price, interest rate, share price, foreign exchange rate, index of prices, or other variable applied to a notional amount to compute cash settlement or other exchange per the derivative contract provisions. While an underlying may be the price of an asset or liability, it is not itself an asset or liability of the derivative holder.

Unrealized Gain (Loss)   Difference between market price and carrying (book) value of an unsold financial instrument.

Valuation Adjustments (holdbacks)   Adjustments to model-derived values to arrive at fair value. This can be necessary due to systems limitations, structural complexity of the instrument, hedging costs, etc. For derivatives that are marked to market, models that are used to derive fair value often do not take into account changes in the counterparties' creditworthiness, or certain operational costs. For example, a portion of the initial model-generated mark-to-market may be deferred to take into account potential credit losses. This deferred income is recognized over in revenue over time to create a matching of revenue and expense at the portfolio level. A similar treatment may be used to account for normal, recurring operations costs that are not factored into the valuation model.

Value at Risk   A measure of expressing a potential gain or loss on a financial instrument due to market risk over a period of time with a degree of probability.

Warrants   Refers to a call option in the company's stock. Typically, warrants have longer terms than other call options. For transactions in the company's own stock, see the chapter on Stockholders' Equity.

This chapter addresses the accounting and disclosure requirements related to derivative financial instruments (derivatives), including those specific to mortgage servicing and repurchase agreements. The accounting for these types of products has been redeliberated by the FASB in recent years, and several changes have been recently issued/proposed. This chapter should be read in conjunction with the previous chapter on foreign currency translation and transactions.

This chapter addresses selected disclosure requirements for other financial instruments, primarily those related to fair value and concentrations of credit risk. Such disclosures have not been significantly changed by recent developments.

BACKGROUND

FASB Statement Number 107 (Disclosures about Fair Value of Financial Instruments) defines a financial instrument as cash (including currencies of other countries), evidence of an ownership interest in another company (e.g., common or preferred stock), or a contract that both:

1. imposes on one company the obligation to (a) deliver cash or another financial instrument to another company or (b) exchange financial instruments with another company on potentially unfavorable terms, and

2. conveys to the other company the right (a) to receive cash or another financial instrument from the first company, or (b) exchange other financial instruments on potentially favorable terms with the first company.

From the preceding definition, conventional assets and liabilities (e.g. accounts and notes receivable, accounts and notes payable, investment in equity and debt securities, and bonds payable) are deemed to be financial instruments. The definition also encompasses many derivative contracts, e.g. options, swaps, caps, and futures. Figure 17-1 provides examples of conventional and derivative financial instruments.

Figure 17-1
Conventional and Derivative Financial Instruments

Conventional Financial Instruments	Derivative Financial Instruments
Corporate bonds and notes	Interest rate swaps and options
Corporate equities	Stock-index futures and options
Municipal bonds	Fixed rate loan commitments
Mortgages	Mortgage servicing rights
Foreign Currencies	Currency futures and options
Accounts receivable and payable	Swaptions
Bank certificates of deposit	Commodity futures and options
Treasury bonds, bills and notes	Interest rate caps, floors, and collars

DERIVATIVE FINANCIAL INSTRUMENTS

A primary purpose of using derivative financial instruments is to reduce risk, such as risk of changes in market price of interest rates, currency exchange rates, and fluctuations in commodity prices. Derivatives are contracts that may hedge the company from adverse movement in the underlying base. However, derivatives are not without their own risks. If used for speculation, then derivatives can be extremely risky. If leveraged, minor adverse price or interest rate changes can result in huge losses. Leverage significantly multiplies return or losses.

Other risks besides leverage exist, such as the following:

- *Credit risk.* The risk that the other party to a contract may default. Investors in "hedge funds" rely on the ability of the fund to meet its obligations.
- *Market risk.* The risk of loss in the market value of the underlying instrument.
- *Operational (business) risk.* The risk of internal operational errors (such as failure to accurately reflect counterparty obligations) or poor internal controls.
- *Legal risk.* A judge may rule the contract illegal.

- *Valuation risk.* The risk that profit from a transaction is misstated.

- *Liquidity risk.* Inability to sell a financial instrument quickly because of an illiquid market.

- *Correlation risk.* Risk that the value of another position (e.g., in derivatives, conventional securities) in response to changing market conditions.

- *Systemic risk.* A problem with a particular instrument that may disrupt the entire market.

- *Settlement risk.* Risk of not receiving timely payment on a contract.

Figure 17-2 lists major financial institutions and the notional value of their derivative contracts.

Figure 17-2
Notional Value of Derivative Contracts for Major U.S. Financial Institutions
Per 1998 Annual Reports
(Billions of Dollars)

	Interest Rate	Notional Principal Foreign Exchange	Other	Total	Credit Exposure Total
Chase Manhattan	$ 8,172	$ 2,041	$ 141	**$10,353**	**$ 33**
JP Morgan	8,090	565	86	**8,741**	**48**
Citigroup	5,553	2,222	212	**7,987**	**37**
Bank of America	3,458	771	55	**4,285**	**15**
Merrill Lynch	2,698	590	182	**3,470**	**24**
Morgan Stanley	1,759	903	198	**2,860**	**21**
Bankers Trust	1,666	800	87	**2,553**	**17**

Figure 17-3 presents some companies that recognized large losses on derivatives. However, derivatives do not introduce risks that are fundamentally different from the risks already existing in the financial markets.

Figure 17-3

Sampling of Companies with Losses from Derivatives

Company	Pre-Tax Losses ($millions)	Year	Type of Derivative/Loss
Sumitomo Corporation	$2,600	1996	Estimate of copper trading losses by unauthorized trading positions over 10 years
Barings	$1,390	1995	Unauthorized derivatives transactions
Yakult Hoshna	$ 498	1998	Derivatives trading • Lost more than $800 million over four years ended 3/98
Union Bank of Switzerland	$ 241	1997	Equity derivatives • $138 million in pricing model errors and unexpected tax legislation • $103 million losses in "ordinary equity derivatives business"
Fuji Bank	$ 114	1998	Projected maximum loss on derivatives, primarily futures
Kanematsu	$ 90	1994	Crude oil futures at Hong Kong subsidiary
Bankers Trust	$ 14	1994	Unconfirmed reports on settlement on leveraged derivatives that Procter & Gamble had with BT Securities Corp

Derivatives can be either on the balance sheet or off the balance sheet (unrecorded). They include:

1. Futures

2. Option contracts

3. Fixed-rate loan commitments

4. Interest rate caps and floors

5. Interest rate collars

6. Forward contracts

7. Forward interest rate agreements

8. Swaps

9. Instruments with similar characteristics

The FASB's current definition of derivatives excludes on-balance-sheet receivables and payables, such as:

1. principal-only obligations,

2. interest-only obligations,

3. indexed debt,

4. mortgage-backed securities, and

5. other optional attributes incorporated within those receivables and payables (e.g., convertible debt conversion or call provisions)

The FASB definition of a derivative currently excludes contracts that either mandate exchange for a nonfinancial good or allow settlement by delivering a nonfinancial commodity. Hence, most product futures contracts are excluded, while swaps (payable in cash) are included.

A company enters into derivative contracts for either trading or hedging purposes. However, only certain hedges qualify to be treated as hedges for accounting purposes. Therefore, a company may enter into a derivative contract as an economic a hedge of an item that is not carried at fair value, but the contract may be required to be marked to market. For such contracts, the timing of the recognition of the mark-to-market value of the derivative may not match the timing of the recognition of the changes in value of the hedged item. If hedge accounting is allowed, the gain(loss) on the hedge is deferred to the accounting period in which the offsetting (loss)gain is recognized on the hedged item. Either way, if the hedge is serving its intended purpose, eventually these timing differences will offset, although it will be in different reporting periods.

If the derivative is entered into for trading purposes or hedge accounting is not allowed, then the instrument is marked to market, and any unrealized gain or loss is recorded in income. Generally, an end user of derivatives will obtain the fair value of a derivative by getting a quote from a market maker. Market makers use complex models based on discounted cash flows to calculate the fair value. If the cash instrument underlying the derivative is illiquid, market risk adjustments may be used to reduce the model-derived value to realizable value. In addition, valuation adjustments, or holdbacks, may be used to take into account operational costs or changes in counterparty credit risk that are not contemplated in the models. Fair values are also used to evaluate hedge effectiveness, if mark-to-market accounting is not used.

Accounting loss may arise from writing off a contractual right or from settling a contractual obligation applicable to a financial instrument. An accounting loss that may arise from credit or market risk is required to be footnoted.

1. Credit risk is the possibility that a loss may occur because of the failure of another party to carry out the terms of a contract. An example is a borrower's failure to repay a loan.

2. Market risk is the possibility that future changes in market prices may cause a financial instrument to decline in value. An example is a decline in the price of a security.

It is possible that accounting risk associated with a financial instrument may already be reflected in the balance sheet. In other instances, the risk exceeds the amount recorded, which is called unrecorded risk, or off-balance-sheet risk (OBSR). An example is a guarantee of another company's debt. The estimated amount of potential credit losses is set up as an allowance for bad debt on the balance sheet. For recorded risks, the bad debt allowance is shown as a contra-asset. For unrecorded risks, the allowance is classified in liabilities. Credit risk is generally limited to the amount recorded on the balance sheet, while market risk is unlimited.

Figure 17-4 lists certain derivative financial instruments with OBSR.

Cash positions (e.g., securities, loans) have little or no off-balance sheet risk, although they expose the company to credit and market risks. Accounting loss is limited to the amount recorded on the balance sheet. Thus, there can be no credit loss if no asset is recorded. However, market risk often exists, i.e., the market value the next day may be lower, thereby causing the company to record a loss. Many disclosures relate to communicating risk of loss to financial statement users.

Figure 17-4

Examples of Derivative Financial Instruments with Off-Balance-Sheet Risk

| | Risk of Accounting Loss to Reporting Company | |
Financial Instrument	Credit Risk	Market Risk
Over-the-Counter Contracts—marked to market		
In a gain position (i.e., receivable)	Yes	Yes
In a loss position (i.e., payable)	No	Yes
Over-the-Counter Contracts—hedges (marked to market, but with the gain or loss deferred)		
In a gain position	Yes	Yes
In a loss position	No	Yes
Over-the-Counter Contracts, settled net under a qualifying netting arrangement		
In a net gain position	Yes	Yes
In a net loss position	No	Yes
Exchange-Traded Contracts—marked to market		
In a gain position	Yes, but minimal credit risk if margin settles daily	Yes
In a loss position	No	Yes

RECENT DEVELOPMENTS RELATED TO DERIVATIVES

We are currently at a crossroads in accounting for derivatives used for hedging purposes. As described later in this Chapter, FASB Statement Number 133 (Accounting for Derivative Instruments and Hedging Activity, as amended) essentially is abandoning the historical accounting approach in that it no longer permits companies to defer gains and losses on derivatives, even on hedge contracts. This is the longest FASB statement to date, and the FASB has established a "Derivatives Implementation Group" that has begun to formulate detailed guidance. We cannot now fully contemplate the rules that will be in effect for 2001 annual reports. Thus, the primary focus is on the accounting and disclosure requirements in effect for 2000 reporting.

FASB Statement Number 133 is effective for fiscal periods beginning after June 15, 2000. This means that for the next year, we are living in two worlds:

- For a company's 2000 accounting and 2000 annual report disclosures, derivatives financial transactions will be accounted for under existing authoritative guidance ("pre-Statement Number 133").

- For financial years beginning after June 15, 2000, all open derivative transactions must be accounted for under the new rules ("post-Statement Number 133").

Much of the material related to derivatives in this chapter is divided into two sections.

- Accounting for derivatives "pre-FASB Statement Number 133," i.e., under the current rules.

- Accounting for derivatives "post-FASB Statement Number 133", i.e., under the rules that will be effective for fiscal periods beginning after June 15, 2000.

Pages 893–901 are disclosures and accounting rules specific to derivative financial instruments "pre-FASB Statement Number 133." Then, beginning on page 901 is a section describing FASB Statement Number 133 requirements. Other changes to disclosures of fair values and concentrations of credit risk are indicated in the applicable sections.

CONCENTRATIONS OF CREDIT RISK FOR ALL FINANCIAL INSTRUMENTS

FASB Statement Number 105 (Disclosure of Information about Financial Instruments with Off-Balance-Sheet Risk and Financial Instruments with Concentrations of Credit Risk) will be superseded by FASB Statement Number 133. Under FASB Statement Number 105, the company must footnote credit risk applicable to all financial instruments. Some requirements of FASB Statement Number 105 will be retained by FASB Statement Number 133, but moved to FASB Statement Number 107 and are discussed later in this section. Under the superseded portions of FASB Statement Number 105, i.e., for 2000 annual reports only, if a financial instrument has off-balance-sheet risk (credit or market), then the following disclosures should be footnoted by major type of financial instrument:

1. Face, contract, or notional principal amount.

2. The nature and terms, including a discussion of credit and market risk, cash requirements, and accounting policy.

   FASB Statement Number 119 (Disclosure about Derivative Financial Instruments and Fair Value of Financial Instruments), which will also be superseded by FASB Statement Number 133, requires similar disclosures for options held and other derivative financial instruments that are not included above because off-balance-sheet risk of accounting loss does not exist.

   Under the superseded portions of FASB Statement Number 105, the company must also footnote the following for each category of financial instrument with off-balance-sheet credit risk:

1. The company's collateral policy and access to the collateral. (Disclosure includes a summary description of the collateral plus any other information that may prove useful in helping to understand the extent of market risk.) And,

2. The amount of accounting loss due to a party's failure to perform, after consideration of the value of available collateral. Additional disclosures are encouraged.

   A distinction is to be made between financial instruments held or issued for trading purposes from those held or issued for other purposes for all of the above credit risk disclosures.

   Under FASB Statement Number 105 (and under FASB Statement Number 107, as amended by FASB Statement Number 133), the company must disclose concentrations of credit risk for financial instruments that could cause the company to be adversely impacted by economic conditions.

Examples of credit risk are sales to companies concentrated in one industry or locality. In this case, disclosures includes

1. the amount of possible accounting loss,
2. the policy regarding security or collateral, and
3. particulars regarding the area of concentration (e.g., economic sector, class of customer, geographic region, and activity).

Under FASB Statement Number 107, as amended by FASB Statement Number 133, requirement 1, above, will be required to be presented on a gross basis, before consideration of netting agreements. The company then will be required to disclose the nature of netting agreements and how they impact the credit exposure. See the discussion later in this chapter regarding netting agreements.

Under current and future rules, certain instruments are excluded from the disclosure requirements, e.g., postretirement benefits, insurance contracts.

FAIR VALUE DISCLOSURES FOR ALL FINANCIAL INSTRUMENTS

Some financial instruments are carried on the books at fair value, while others are not. Accordingly, FASB Statement Number 107 requires that disclosures regarding fair value be made in the body of the financial statements or in the footnotes. Disclosure includes the methods and assumptions used to estimate fair value. The fair value amounts disclosed should be cross-referenced to carrying value amounts presented in the balance sheet. The disclosures should distinguish between financial instruments held or issued for trading purposes and financial instruments held or issued for purposes other than trading. However, fair values of non-derivative financial instruments should not be aggregated or netted with fair values of derivative financial instruments unless netting is permitted as per FASB Interpretation Number 39 (Offsetting of Amounts Related to Certain Contracts). Disclosure may point out that fair value is a subjective approximation.

If it is not practical to estimate the fair value of a financial instrument, then information relevant to estimating fair value should be disclosed, including the financial instrument's carrying value, maturity, and interest rate. The reasons why fair value is not determinable should also be provided.

HOW TO ARRIVE AT FAIR VALUE

The fair value of a financial instrument is the amount at which the instrument could be exchanged in a current transaction between willing parties, other than in a liquidation sale. Quoted market prices are best to use, if available. FASB Statement Number 107 specifies the following types of markets in which financial instruments can be transacted:

- *Exchange markets*, for listed stocks, bonds, options, and certain futures contracts.

- *Dealer markets*, e.g., the NASDAQ or other over-the-counter markets, are the major exchanges for more thinly traded securities. Dealer markets also exist for commercial loans, asset-backed securities, mortgage-backed securities, and municipal securities. In most cases, quotations on this market properly reflect fair value. However, if evidence exists to the contrary, then the company may opt for another indicator of fair value, such as an internally developed model. Market quotations for dealer markets are usually in the form of bid and ask prices. Fair value determination should take into account the size of an issue and its possible dilutive effect on price of the financial instrument. **Note:** The basis used for a price quote should be disclosed.

- *Principal-to-principal markets* in principal-to-principal transactions, transactions occur independently, with no intermediary and basically no public information available to approximate market price, e.g., an interest rate swap.

- *Brokered markets*, in which intermediaries match buyers and sellers but do not trade for their own accounts, usually provide less reliable information as to price. The broker is aware of the prices bid and asked by the parties, but each participant is usually unaware of the other party's price requests. Prices of completed transactions may be available in some cases. If more than one quoted price for a financial instrument is available, then use the one in the most active market. When possible, get more than one quotation when quoted prices vary widely in the market.

The company may want to disclose additional information about the fair value of a financial instrument, e.g., if the fair value of long-term debt is below its carrying value. In this case, the company may want to provide the reasons and whether the debt could be settled at the lower amount.

For financial institutions, loans receivable may be a major financial instrument. If market prices are available (e.g., securities backed by residential mortgages may be a proxy for valuing residential mortgages), then they should be used to arrive at fair value. If no quoted market price exists for a category of loans, particularly fixed rate loans, then an approximation may be based on:

1. market prices of similar traded loans (similarity may be in the forms of terms, interest rates, maturity dates, and credit scoring),
2. current prices for similar loans that the company has originated and sold, or
3. valuations derived from loan pricing services.

Fair value of a loan may be determined by using the present value of future cash flows, using a risk-adjusted discount rate. Different discount rates may be used for different categories of loans, such as

1. a risk-free interest rate, adjusted for counterparty and prepayment risk,
2. a single discount rate for homogeneous types of loans, or
3. a rate considering the impact of changing interest rates, adjusted for modified cash flow estimates and credit risk.

Fair value of financial liabilities having no quoted market prices should be approximated using the same approaches used for estimating fair value of financial assets. For example, a loan payable may be valued based on the discounted amount of future cash flows. The discount rate chosen should be the company's incremental borrowing rate. For banks and thrifts, the fair value of deposit liabilities may also be based on the discounted value of future cash flows to be expended. The rate used could be the current rate for comparable deposits with similar maturities. If no maturity dates exist, then disclose the fair value based on the amount payable on demand at the end of the accounting period, i.e., no explicit recognition is given to the value of "core deposits" (demand deposits that have no stated maturity).

Certain instruments are excluded from fair value disclosures (e.g., leases, warranties, equity investments in consolidated subsidiaries and affiliates, instruments that are transacted in the company's own stock, certain insurance contracts). Fair value disclosures do not apply to trade receivables and payables unless their carrying values do not reflect fair value.

EXAMPLE

A sample fair value disclosure is reported in Figure 17-5 for ABC, Inc.

Companies transacting in derivative financial instruments for trading purposes disclose the following:

1. End-of-period and average fair value of derivative financial instruments reported separately for assets and liabilities

2. Net trading revenues segregated by category, business activity, risk, or other distinguishing features. (Net trading gains or losses are presented separately in the income statement.)

It is preferred to compute average fair value based on daily balances. However, another practical time period may be used.

OTHER RELATED DISCLOSURES FOR FINANCIAL INSTRUMENTS

Under FASB Statement Number 119, companies are encouraged, but not required, to disclose quantitative data about foreign exchange, interest rate,

Figure 17-5

Disclosure of Fair Value of Financial Instruments Company ABC, Inc.

(dollars in thousands)

	December 31, 20X1	
	Carrying Amount	*Estimated Fair Value*
Assets		
Cash and cash equivalents	$ 250	$ 250
Accounts receivable	103,000	101,000
Investment in joint ventures	34,000	
Liabilities		
Accounts payable	240,000	240,000
Short-term debt	500,000	502,000
Long-term debt	700,000	750,000
Off-balance-sheet financial instruments - unrealized gains(losses)		
Interest rate swap agreements-net		5,000
Foreign currency contracts		(4,500)

- *Cash and cash equivalents, accounts receivable, and accounts payable.* The carrying amounts of these items are a reasonable estimate of their fair value.

- *Investments in joint ventures.* Management was not able to estimate practicably the fair value of the Company's equity investments in nonconsolidated real estate ventures. At December 31, 20X1, the total assets reported by these ventures were $340 million, the total shareholders' equity was $96 million, and net income for the year then ended was $11.3 million.

- *Short-term debt and long-term debt.* Interest rates that are currently available to the Company for issuance of debt with similar terms and remaining maturities are used to estimate fair value for debt issues that are not quoted on an exchange.

- *Interest rate swap agreements and foreign currency contracts.* The fair value of interest rate swaps and foreign currency contracts is the amount at which they could be settled, based on estimates obtained from dealers. The estimated unrealized net gain on the interest rate swaps of $5 million consists of unrealized gains and losses of $14 million and $9 million, respectively.

The fair value estimates presented herein are based on pertinent information available to management as of December 31, 20X1. Although management is not aware of any factors that would significantly affect the estimated fair value amounts, such amounts have not been comprehensively revalued for purposes of these financial statements since that date, and current estimates of fair value may differ significantly from the amounts presented herein.

commodity price, or other market risks of derivatives consistent with the company's strategies and manner in which it manages risk. The FASB suggests five approaches the company may use when presenting quantitative data in its financial statements:

- In-depth information for current positions, such as time maturity profile, contract rates, indexes, and provisions of contract—as well as activity during the period.

- Hypothetical changes in market prices and their impact on net income and equity.

- Gap analysis to measure interest rate risk associated with repricing of assets and liabilities at their maturity. The interest rate gap is the difference between assets and the liabilities within a maturity band, e.g., within one-year and two-year maturities. Gap analysis is used within traditional Treasury asset/liability management. It does not, however, incorporate the effect of options, and it may be erroneous if all of the financial instruments are not expressed in one currency.

- Duration of the financial instruments. FASB Statement Number 119 describes duration "as the result of a calculation based on the timing of future cash flows." It can be thought of "as the life, in years, of a zero-coupon bond in which fair value would change by the same amount as the real bond or portfolio in response to a change in market interest rates."

- Value at risk. The expected loss over a specified period of time from an adverse price movement, with a stated probability.

Other approaches are permitted.

FASB Statement Number 107, as amended by FASB Statement Number 133, carries forward the above requirement, and extends it to all financial instruments.

Public companies should provide the following data related to accounting policies for derivative financial instruments as per Rule 4-08(n) of Regulation S-X:

- The method used to account for derivatives (i.e., the fair value "mark to market" method, the deferral method, or the accrual method)

- Types of derivatives used and how accounted for
- The conditions required to use a particular method, such as risk reduction correlation, and effectiveness
- The accounting method used if certain criteria are absent
- The accounting policy for the termination of hedging derivatives
- The accounting policy for derivatives if the hedged item matures or is sold, extinguished, terminated, or, if the related expected transaction is no longer likely to occur
- How derivatives are reported in the primary financial statements [Rule 4-08(n) of Regulation S-X requires registrants to distinguish between accounting policies used for derivatives engaged for trading purposes and those that are contracted for purposes other than trading.]

The following example illustrates the disclosure requirements of FASB Statement Number 119 for a bank that serves as a dealer or intermediary in some derivative financial instrument markets and holds and issues derivative financial instruments for trading and asset-liability management purposes.

EXAMPLE

The Bank has active trading positions in a number of derivative financial instruments. Many of the Bank's trading activities are customer-oriented. Trading positions are set as needed to satisfy customers' demands. The Bank has an inventory of capital market instruments. It keeps its access to market liquidity by quoting competitive bid and offer prices. It trades with other market makers. The Bank's positions are carried at fair value. Changes in fair values are reported as trading income in the income statement.

The amounts presented in Figure 17-6 are the end-of-period and average fair values for derivative financial instruments held or issued for trading purposes. Allowable offsetting of transactions is included.

Net Trading Gains and Losses

Net trading gains recognized in earnings on interest rate contracts outstanding totaled $86 million in 20X2, $84 million in 20X1, and $16 million

Figure 17-6

Fair Value and Average Fair Value of Derivative Financial Instruments

Dollars in millions	Fair Value (Carrying Amount) at 12/31		Average Face Value	
	20X2	20X1	20X2	20X1
Interest rate contracts				
Forwards and futures:				
Assets	$XXX	$XXX	$XXX	$XXX
Liabilities	(XXX)	(XXX)	(XXX)	(XXX)
Swaps				
Assets	XXX	XXX	XXX	XXX
Liabilities	XXX	XXX	XXX	XXX
Options, caps, and floors held	XXX	XXX	XXX	XXX
Options, caps, and floors written	XXX	XXX	XXX	XXX
Foreign exchange contracts				
Forwards, swaps, and futures:				
Assets	XXX	XXX	XXX	XXX
Liabilities held	XXX	XXX	XXX	XXX
Options held	XXX	XXX	XXX	XXX
Options written	XXX	XXX	XXX	XXX

in 20X0. Net trading gains from foreign exchange forward, futures, swap, and option contracts outstanding totaled $105 million in 20X2, $109 million in 20X1, and $89 million in 20X0.

Credit Risk from Trading

The Bank's credit exposure resulting from interest rate and foreign exchange contracts held for trading purposes is the sum of current exposure limited to the (current fair value of contracts with a positive fair value) plus potential future exposure if the contracts move more "in the money". The Bank's total credit exposure from interest rate and foreign exchange contracts held for trading purposes as of December 31, 20X2 is $1.7 billion. The Bank manages the potential credit exposure through careful appraisal of counterparty credit standing, collateral dictates, and other contractual terms. The potential credit exposure from future market movements is forecasted by using a statistical model considering possible changes in interest rates, exchange rates, and other applicable concerns. Options written do not expose the Bank to credit risk, except to the degree of the underlying risk in the debt instrument that the Bank may be obligated to acquire because of particular written put options. Caps and floors written do not make the Bank susceptible to credit risk.

Companies holding or issuing derivative financial instruments for purposes other than trading must disclose the following:

1. Company's objectives and strategies in dealing with derivative financial instruments (e.g., using a put option on assets at risk).

2. Types of derivatives used.

3. Recognition and reporting of derivatives in the financial statements, including balance sheet presentation, and policies for recognition of gains and losses in the income statement. And,

4. For anticipated transactions both firm commitment and forecasted transactions, include the amount of hedging gains and losses deferred, and recognized gains and losses (see the following example).

EXAMPLE

A company's revenue consists of approximately 38% from export sales to Japan. The company is expecting to increase its export sales to Japan by 10% in the following eleven months. To manage its foreign exchange risk, the company has entered into foreign currency option contracts to hedge its anticipated foreign transactions. The Yen option contracts will expire in one year. Gains and losses on these specific options are deferred and recognized as export revenue at the same date as the transaction that the company is hedging. As of December 31, 1994, a net realized loss of $112,000 was deferred on these Yen options. This loss will be recognized in sales from exports.

Disclosure should also be made of the following:

1. risks associated with derivative financial instruments, amounts reported in the financial statements (see the following examples), and

2. accounting policies followed.

EXAMPLE

Note 1—Significant Accounting Policies: In addition to its trading activities, the corporation, as an end user, utilizes various types of derivative products (principally interest rate and currency swaps) to manage the interest, currency and other market risks arising from certain of its assets and liabilities. Revenue or expense pertaining to management of interest rate exposure is predominantly recognized over the life of the contract as an adjustment to interest revenue or expense. Realized gains and losses on hedges of equities classified as other assets are included in the carrying amounts of those assets and are ultimately recognized in income when those assets are sold. Derivatives are also used to manage the risks associated with securities available for sale. These derivatives are carried at fair value, with the resulting net unrealized gains and losses recorded in stockholders' equity as securities valuation allowance. The discount or premium on foreign exchange forward contracts and the periodic cash settlement on swaps used as hedges of net investments in foreign entities, as well as the net unrealized gains and losses from revaluing these contracts to spot exchange rates, are recorded in stockholders' equity as cumulative translation adjustments.

The following example illustrates the information that may be disclosed by a nonfinancial company that has signed interest rate cap agreements and also hedges specified foreign exchange and commodity price exposures. The corporation does not trade in derivative financial instruments.

EXAMPLE

The JKS Corporation enters into interest rate cap agreements to reduce the impact of increases in interest rates on its floating-rate long-term debt. At December 31, 20X2, the Company had one interest rate cap agreement outstanding. The agreement effectively entitles the company to receive from a bank the amount, if any, by which the company's interest payments on its $50 million floating-rate notes due in 20X5 exceed 9%. The $2 million premium paid for this interest rate cap agreement is included in other assets and is being amortized to interest expense over the remaining three-year term of the cap. Payments received when actual interest rates exceed the cap are amortized accrued as a reduction of interest expense on the floating-rate notes.

The company enters into forward exchange contracts to hedge certain firm sales commitments denominated in foreign currencies and purchases currency options to hedge certain anticipated but not yet committed sales expected to be denominated in foreign currencies. The purpose of the company's foreign currency hedging activities is to protect the company from the risk that the eventual dollar cash flows resulting from the sale of products to international customers will be adversely affected by changes in exchange rates. At December 31, 20X2 and 20X1, the company had forward exchange contracts and purchased currency options, all having maturities of less than two years to exchange various foreign currencies for U.S. dollars in the amount of $27.6 million and $24.9 million, respectively. Figure 17-7 summarizes by currency the contractual amounts of the company's forward exchange and options contracts at December 31, 20X2.

Figure 17-7

Sample Disclosure of Contractual Amounts of Forward Exchange and Options

Dollars in millions	Forward Contracts	Purchased Option Contracts	Total Contracts	Unrealized Gain/(Loss)
Currency:				
Deutsche mark	$ 3.7	$ 6.0	$ 9.7	$ .8
Yen	4.2	3.2	7.4	(.5)
Pound sterling	2.2	4.0	6.2	1.1
Other	3.1	4.0	4.3	(.2)
Total	$13.2	$14.4	$27.6	$1.2

Gross deferred realized gains and losses from hedging firm sales commitments and anticipated but not yet committed sales transactions were a $2.4 million gain and a $1.0 million loss, respectively, at December 31, 20X2, and a $.8 million gain and a $1.6 million loss, respectively, at December 31, 20X1. Deferred gains and losses are included in other assets and liabilities and recognized in earnings when the future sales occur or at the point in time when a sale is no longer expected to occur. Of the amounts deferred at December 31, 20X2, $2.0 million of gains and $.7 of losses are expected to be recognized in earnings within one year; the remainder in the following year.

The company also uses oil swap agreements to hedge exposures under certain firm commitments to deliver petroleum-based products at fixed prices. Under the oil swap agreements, the company receives or makes payments to an investment bank based on the differential between a fixed and a variable price for crude oil. At December 31, 20X2, the company had swap agreements to exchange payments each quarter based on 2.2 million barrels of oil over the next two years. Under the swap agreements, the company pays fixed prices averaging $17 per barrel and receives a variable price (based on a published index of crude oil prices) that was $14 per barrel at December 31, 20X2 and averaged $12 during 20X2.

Those swap agreements are intended to hedge the crude oil cost component of virtually all of the company's firm commitments to deliver petroleum-based products. Expected profits on the firm commitments exceed the $6.6 million unrealized losses on the swap agreements, which will be recognized in income as the petroleum-based products are sold.

The company is exposed to credit loss in the event of nonperformance by counterparties to interest rate caps, foreign exchange contracts, and oil swaps. The amount of such exposure is the current unrealized gains on such contracts, plus any future unrealized gains.

PRE-FASB STATEMENT NUMBER 133 *ACCOUNTING FOR DERIVATIVES*

Forward Foreign Exchange Contracts

A forward foreign exchange contract is an agreement to exchange different currencies at some future date at a given rate (the forward rate).

1. Premium = Forward (future) rate in excess of spot (cash) rate (spot rate is the rate today)

2. Discount = Forward rate less than spot rate

The purpose of engaging in a forward exchange contract is to do either of the following:

1. *Hedge*—Hedging may reduce exchange rate variation risk to protect an exposed net asset or liability.

2. *Proprietary trading*—Speculation by attempting to profit from correctly "guessing" the future price movement on the item being traded, e.g., foreign exchange rates.

Gain or loss from hedging equals spot rate at the balance sheet date versus the spot rate at the date the forward contract was signed (or the spot rate last used to measure a gain or loss on that contract for an earlier period) multiplied by the foreign currency amount.

Note: The discount or premium on a forward contract should be computed separately from the contract gain or loss.

The gain or loss on a hedge against a firm foreign currency commitment should be deferred and included in the measurement of the associated foreign currency transaction (e.g., the acquisition or sale of machinery). A loss should not be deferred if to do so would result in recognizing later losses. A discount or premium on a hedge against a firm foreign commitment may also be deferred and amortized over the term of the forward contract.

A gain or loss from a hedge against an exposed net asset or liability position is not included in the income statement but rather is presented as a translation adjustment in the stockholders' equity section under "accumulated other comprehensive income." Any associated discount or premium may be either similarly treated or amortized over the time period of the forward contract.

A gain or loss from speculation (i.e., the forward contract does not hedge a commitment or exposure) is determined by the difference between the forward rate available for the remainder of the contract and the contracted forward rate (or the forward rate last used to measure a gain or loss on that contract for an earlier period) multiplied by the foreign currency amount.

Figure 17-8 presents the current accounting treatment for major types of forward foreign exchange contracts.

The following examples illustrate the appropriate accounting for a hedge against a net asset or liability position that is denominated in a foreign currency.

Figure 17-8
Current Accounting Treatment for Forward Foreign Exchange Contract

Type of Contract	Gain or Loss	Discount or Premium
Hedge of an identifiable firm foreign currency commitment	Measured based on the change in the spot rate; deferred and included in the basis of the associated foreign currency transaction; any excess gain or loss is offset against tax effects	Measured by the difference between the forward rate and the spot rate at the beginning of the contract; may be amortized over the period of the contract or deferred and included on the basis of the related foreign currency transaction
Hedge against a net asset or liability exposure	Measured the same as above; deferred and reported in the same way as translation adjustments	Measure the same as above; may be deferred and reported in the same way as translation adjustments or amortized over the period of the contract
Speculation	Measured by the difference between the forward rate available for the remaining period of the contract and the contracted forward rate	Not accounted for separately

EXAMPLE

ABC Company finds itself in an exposed net liability position with regard to its German subsidiary, DEF Company, on June 1, 1999. On that date, ABC Company signs a forward exchange contract with a currency broker for the purchase of 200,000 deutschemarks (DM 200,000) in 90 days. Exchange rates are as follows:

- June 1, 1999 spot rate: DM = $0.50

- June 1, 1999 3-month Forward rate: DM = $0.53

- July 31, 1999 spot rate: DM = $0.54

- September 1, 1999 spot rate: DM = $0.55

The journal entry required at June 1, 1999 is:

Dr.	Due from currency broker (DM 200,000 × $.50	$100,000	
Dr.	Premium (DM 200,000 x $0.03)	6,000	
Cr.	Due to currency broker (DM 200,000 x $0.53)		$106,000

To record the exchange gain.

At July 31, 1999, the gain is calculated as follows:

Forward contract amount		DM 200,000
Spot rate at 7/31/99	$.54	
Spot rate at 6/1/99	$.50	
		× $.04
Exchange gain		$8,000

The journal entries at July 31, 1999 are:

Dr.	Due from currency broker	$ 8,000	
Cr.	Forward exchange gain		$ 8,000

To record the exchange gain.

Dr.	Amortization of premium [($6,000/ 3 months ×) 2]	$ 4,000	
Cr.	Premium Income		$ 4,000

To record the premium amortization.

In the 1999 consolidated financial statements, the $8,000 gain is presented as a credit translation adjustment (i.e., addition to stockholders equity). The premium amortization is presented on the income statement. Alternatively, the $6,000 premium could be deferred as an offset to the exchange gain and included as part of the translation adjustment.

On September 1, 1999, the currency broker delivers the DM 200,000 to ABC Company for the price of $106,000 ($.53 on $200,000) (as agreed on 6/1/99).The spot rate on September 1, 1999 is $0.55; the gain on that date equals the difference between the spot rate at September settlement and the spot rate at July 31, 1999 as follows:

Forward contract amount		*DM 200,000*
Spot rate at 9/01/99	$.55	
Spot rate at 7/31/99	$.54	
		× $.01
Exchange gain		$2,000

The journal entry to be made at September 1, 1999 is:

Dr.		Due from currency broker	$106,000	
Dr.		Amortization of premium	2,000	
Dr.		Cash (DM 200,000 × $0.55)	110,000	
	Cr.	Cash in U.S. dollars		$106,000
	Cr.	Forward exchange gain		2,000
	Cr.	Due from currency broker ($100,000 +		108,000
		previously recorded $8,000 gain)		

To record the close-out of the contract.

The following example illustrates the current accounting for a hedge against a foreign currency commitment.

EXAMPLE

ABC Company agrees on June 1, 1999 to buy machinery from a West German manufacturer for DM 250,000. Payment and delivery are to be made on September 1, 1999. On June 1, 1999, ABC Company signs a forward exchange contract for delivery of DM 250,000 on September 1, 1999. Exchange rates are as follows:

- June 1, 1999 spot rate: DM = $0.50
- June 1, 1999 3-month forward rate: DM = $0.51
- July 31, 1999 spot rate: DM = $0.52
- September 1, 1999 spot rate: DM = $0.55

The journal entry on June 1, 1999 is:

Dr.		Due from currency broker (DM 250,000 × $0.50)	$125,000
Dr.		Premium (DM 250,000 × $0.01)	2,500
	Cr.	Due to currency broker (DM 250,000 × $0.51)	$127,500

To record purchase of foreign exchange contract.

On July 31, 1999, the gain is calculated as follows:

Forward contract amount		DM 250,000
Spot rate at 7/31/99	$.52	
Spot rate at 6/1/99	$.50	
		× $.02
Exchange gain		$5,000

The $5,000 gain is deferred on 7/31/99, and the journal entry is:

Dr.	Due from currency broker	$5,000	
Cr.	Deferred forward exchange gain		$5,000

To record deferred exchange gain.

The $2,500 premium may either be amortized into income for 1999 or deferred with the exchange gain. Here, the assumption is that the premium is deferred. When the machinery is delivered on September 1, 1999, the gain is determined as follows:

Forward contract amount		*DM 250,000*
Spot rate at 9/01/99	$.55	
Spot rate at 7/31/99	$.52	
		× $.03
Exchange gain		$7,500

The journal entries to be made at September 1, 1999 are:

Dr.		Due from currency broker	$ 7,500	
Dr.		Due to currency broker	127,500	
	Cr.	Deferred forward exchange gain		$ 7,500
	Cr.	Cash		127,500
To record payment to broker.				
Dr.	Cash		$137,500	
	Cr.	Due from currency broker		$137,500
		($125,000 + $5,000 gain at 7/31/99 +		
		$7,500 gain at 9/1/99)		

To record payment from broker (DM 250,000 × $0.55 spot rate).

Dr.		Deferred forward exchange gain	$ 12,500	
		($5,000 + $7,500)		
Dr.		Equipment	127,500	
	Cr.	Premium		$ 2,500
	Cr.	Cash (DM 250,000 × $0.55)		137,500

To record purchase of equipment based on hedged price.

Because of the hedge, the cost of the machinery is fixed at the forward rate of $127,500 (DM 250,000 x $0.51). It can also be computed as the amount paid at 9/1/99 of $137,500 less the deferred gain of $12,500 plus the premium of $2,500.

The following example illustrates the accounting for a foreign currency transaction that does not meet the current accounting requirements of a hedge transaction.

EXAMPLE

ABC Company signs a forward foreign exchange contract on June 1, 1999 that does not meet FASB hedge criteria. The contract requires delivery from the currency broker to ABC Company of DM 800,000 in exchange for dollars on September 1, 1999 (90 days). Exchange rates are as follows:

- June 1, 1999 90-day forward rate: DM = $0.54
- July 31, 1999 30-day forward rate: DM = $0.52
- September 1, 1999 spot rate: DM = $0.53

Since this contract does not meet FASB hedging criteria it must be "marked to market" (carried on the books at fair value). In a speculative transaction, discount or premium is not separately computed.

The journal entry on June 1, 1999 is:

Dr.		Due from currency broker	$432,000	
		(DM 800,000 × $0.54)		
	Cr.	Due to currency broker		$432,000

To record the purchase of the forward foreign exchange contract.

At July 31, 1999, an exchange loss is calculated as follows:

Forward exchange contract		DM 800,000
90-day forward rate at 6/1/99	$.54	
30-day forward rate at 7/31/99	.52	
Due to currency broker		× $.02
Exchange loss		$16,000

The journal entry required is:

Dr.	Forward exchange loss	$16,000	
Cr.	Due from currency broker		$16,000

The $16,000 loss is recognized in 1999.

On September 1, 1999, ABC Company computes the gain as follows:

Forward exchange contract		DM 800,000
Spot rate at 9/1/99	$.53	
30-day forward rate at 7/31/99	.52	
Due to currency broker		× $.01
Exchange gain		$8,000

The entries required on September 1, 1999 are:

Dr.	Due from currency broker	$ 8,000	
Cr.	Forward exchange gain		$ 8,000
Dr.	Due to currency broker	$432,000	
Cr.	Cash		$432,000

To record payment of amount due to broker..

Dr.	Cash (DM 800,000 × $0.53)	$424,000	
Cr.	Due from currency broker		$424,000
	($432,000 − $16,000 loss + $8,000 gain)		

To record payment from broker.

The transaction resulted in a $8,000 net loss—a $16,000 loss at 7/31/99 and an $8,000 gain on 9/1/99.

Futures Contracts

The accounting for futures contracts except for futures contracts on foreign currencies (governed by FASB Statement Number 52) is covered by FASB Statement Number 80. The following disclosure is required:

For a futures contract qualifying as a hedge, disclose

1. accounting treatment utilized,

2. nature of assets, liabilities, from commitments or anticipated transactions that are hedged with financial futures, and

3. particulars of the hedging transaction.

POST-FASB STATEMENT NUMBER 133 *ACCOUNTING FOR DERIVATIVES*

FASB Statement Number 133 is among the most complex that FASB has issued. Despite its issuance in June 1998, the FASB a year later agreed to postpone its effective date until 2001 for companies on a calendar fiscal year. This means that it will not be until early 2002 that readers of financial statements of calendar fiscal year companies will be able to assess the impact of the new standard. There are two principal reasons for the postponement:

- Significant changes, that will be required by the new standard and the concern how this might impact "Y2K" preparation.

- The complexity of the standard and need to study it in great detail.

A FASB "Derivatives Implementation Group" has been working since late 1998 in dealing with how to account for situations encountered in practice. Not surprisingly, this text cannot capture every nuance associated with the Statement, nor can it anticipate the final guidance to be provided by the Derivatives Implementation Group. The purpose is to give the reader a solid foundation relating to the basic principles and to illustrate several practical applications.

View From "50,000 Feet"

1. All derivatives have to put on the balance sheet at their fair value, i.e., marked to market.

2. Changes in the fair value of derivatives must be recognized in the financial statements as they occur,

■ Changes in value of *qualified* hedges of foreign currency exposure are reported as part of comprehensive income (not as part of the income statement).

■ Changes in value of other *qualified* hedges will be recognized in income along with an offsetting adjustment to item being hedged.

■ Changes in value of all other derivatives are recognized income.

Discussion

There are three types of qualified hedges discussed in FASB Statement Number 133: fair value hedges, cash flow hedges, and foreign currency hedges.

Simply stated, a *fair value hedge* is protection against adverse changes in the value of an existing asset, liability or unrecognized firm commitment.

A *cash flow hedge* protects against changes in the value of future cash flows—for instance interest payments on fixed rate debt, if the company is concerned about falling interest rates and the fact that would not be able to renegotiate the terms of the debt to capitalize on lower rates.

A *foreign currency hedge* protects against adverse movement of exchange rates impacting any foreign currency exposure—which, for instance, can involve either fair value or cash flow hedges in foreign currency or a net investment in a foreign business activity, e.g., concern over the impact that a devaluation of a foreign currency would have on the company's investment in an overseas subsidiary.

In all of these three hedges, a hedge effectiveness test must be met in order to achieve hedge accounting. This test is described in further detail in the next section, where illustrations of the accounting are provided.

Definition of Derivative Financial Instrument Under FASB Statement Number 133

A derivative must contain all of the following attributes:

- one or more underlying instrument and one or more notional amounts/payment provisions,

- no initial net investment (no cash outlay) or a smaller net investment than would otherwise be expected for such contract, and

- its terms require or permit net settlement of amounts due.

Figure 17-9 lists some common derivative-like contracts, along with whether they are covered by FASB Statement Number 133.

Figure 17-9

Impact on FASB Statement Number 133 on Selected Financial Instruments

What financial instruments are covered by FASB Statement Number 133?	*Yes*	*No*
Interest rate caps, floor, collars	✔	
Interest rate and currency swaps	✔	
Financial guarantees		✔
Financial futures contracts	✔	
Forward contracts with no net settlement		✔
Mortgage backed security		✔
Option to purchase securities	✔	
Adjustable rate loan		✔
Variable annuity contract		✔
Swaptions	✔	
Commodities	✔	

Currently, the accounting for compound instruments is based primarily on practice. FASB Statement Number 133 requires that many derivatives that are components of a compound instrument be bifurcated and accounted for under the new rules. An exception is provided if:

- the instrument is subject to mark-to-market accounting,

- the embedded derivative does not meet the FASB Statement Number 133 definition of a derivative, or

- the embedded derivative is "clearly and closely" related to the embedded cash instrument. For example, if a deposit pays an interest rate based on a stock index, then the deposit must be bifurcated such that the deposit is separated from the embedded stock index because the embedded derivative is not "clearly and closely" related.

Fair Value Hedges

If a hedge qualifies as reducing the risk of changes in value of an on balance sheet asset or liability or an unrecognized firm commitment—then, both the hedge and the underlying risk exposure are "marked to market" through the income statement. In the case of a perfect hedge, the gain or loss on the hedging derivative instrument will offset the impact of the valuation of the exposure that is being hedged. For an imperfect hedge, any "breakage" between the valuation of the hedge and the underlying risk exposure will flow through earnings.

The following example illustrates the FASB Statement Number 133 accounting for interest rate swaps used to hedge the fair value of fixed-rate debt.

EXAMPLE

On June 1, 20X2, ABC Corporation enters into an agreement with its bank to borrow $10 million over 3 years at a fixed interest rate of 7%, with no prepayment permitted. The Company wishes to convert this debt to floating rate so as to not run the risk of paying an above market interest rate, if the general level of interest rate declines.

An interest rate swap is structured that will require the Company's counterparty to pay it a fixed rate of interest (assumed to be 7%) equal to what the Company owes its bank. In return, the company will pay its counterparty a floating market rate of interest based on six month LIBOR. This effectively converts the Company's fixed rate debt to floating rate debt. Assume that expiration of the swap matches the maturity of the borrowing and that the periodic payments under the swap are with the same frequency, as payments required under the borrowing agreement.

The changes in value of the fixed rate debt and the interest rate swap are assumed to move in equal and opposite directions. When interest rates rise, the fair value of the fixed rate debt increases (the company is receiving cheaper funding than the market level of interest rates), while the fair value of the interest rate swap decreases (the company is paying a market interest rate—LIBOR—that is higher than when the swap was originally contracted).

Assume the following value of the swap and the debt:

	Value of Swap	Value of Debt
June 1, 20X2	+$200,000	$10,200,000
December 31, 20X2	-$100,000	$ 9,900,000

The following is the calculation of the periodic six-month settlements, assuming LIBOR rates in effect as indicated.

Month LIBOR	Pay Six Fixed	Received Debt	Principal Amount Settlement	Interest
June 20X2	6%	7%	$10 million	$ 50,000
July 20X2—December 20X2	7¼%	7%	$10 million	$(12,500)

Accounting Entries

June 20X2:

Dr.	Interest Expense	$350,000	
Cr.	Accrued Interest Payable		$350,000

To accrue six months contractual interest due on outstanding debt.

Dr.	Funds Borrowed	$200,000	
Cr.	Gain on Valuation of Debt		$200,000

To record gain in the value of fixed rate debt in a rising interest rate environment.

Dr.	Loss on Swap Hedge	$200,000	
Cr.	Swap Hedge (Balance Sheet Liability)		$200,000

To record loss in value of the swap hedge contract that is "marked to market."

Dr.	Cash	$50,000	
Cr.	Interest Expense		$50,000

To record six-month settlement of the swap as a reduction of interest expense.

December 20X2:

Dr.	Interest Expense	$350,000	
	Cr.	Accrued Interest Payable	$350,000

To record contractual interest due.

Dr.	Loss on Valuation of Debt	$300,000	
	Cr.	Funds Borrowed	$300,000

To record the cumulative loss in the value of the fixed rate debt in a falling interest rate environment.

Dr.	Swap Hedge (Balance Sheet Asset)	$300,000	
	Cr.	Gain on Swap Hedge	$300,000

To record gain in value of swap hedge contract that is marked to market.

Dr.	Interest Expense	$12,500	
	Cr.	Cash	$12,500

To record cash payment on semi-annual settlement of the swap as an adjustment to, i.e., increase in, interest expense.

Cash Flow Hedges

Companies are often interested in protecting (hedging) the value of future cash flows that they will either receive or pay. The nature of cash flows that require protection is one where there is variability/uncertainty of what those future flows will be. In some instances transactions that are hedged relate to contractual future cash flows, while in other instances they may relate to forecasted transactions.

Examples of transactions that may be eligible for cash flow hedge treatment include:

- A hedge of future cash interest outflows associated with floating rate debt.
- A hedge of a forecasted future purchase of a commodity to protect against rising prices.
- A hedge to protect against rising rates for prime based mortgages.
- A hedge to lock in the future cost of borrowing for the company.
- A hedge to anticipate future repricings of certificates of deposit.

Accounting for cash flow hedges involves reporting the effective portion of the hedge in Other Comprehensive Income. It is later reclassified into earnings in the same period as the forecasted cash flow affects earnings. Any ineffective portion of the hedge is reported as earnings. This will be clear in the example below.

EXAMPLE

XYZ Corporation has issued $100 million of six-month fixed interest rate commercial paper that is rolled over at each expiration date. Rising interest rates will increase its cost of funds when the commercial paper comes up for repricing and this is an exposure XYZ wishes to minimize.

Since XYZ is attempting to take action to protect its future cash interest outflows, in this example there is a cash flow hedge. To hedge its interest rate risk, XYZ sells 100 Treasury bill futures contracts (these are sold in contract units of $1 million). Management has determined that this strategy meets the hedge effectiveness test—discussed later in this chapter—and thereby qualifies for hedge accounting treatment under FASB Statement Number 133.

Assume the following changes in interest rates and their impact on future cash flows. For simplicity purposes, this example does not deal with any initial or variation margin that would be required on the futures contract.

Assumptions:

- Six-month commercial paper issued January 1, 20X2 at 6% interest, due June 30.

- At June 30, 20X2, interest rates increase to 6.5%, resulting in an additional cost of funds of .5% or $250,000 for the second half of the year.

- Assume the future contract is removed at June 30 and has a gain of $240,000.

The following are the financial accounting entries to reflect this transaction.

January 1, 20X2

Dr.	Cash	$100,000,000	
	Cr.	Commercial Paper Outstanding		$100,000,000

To record issuance of commercial paper.

June 30, 20X2

Dr.	Interest Expense	$ 3,000,000	
	Cr.	Accrued Interest Payable		$ 3,000,000

To record contractual interest due for six months.

Dr.	Cash	$ 240,000	
	Cr.	Other Comprehensive Income		$ 240,000

To record gain on the settlement of the futures contract. The entire futures contract is assumed to be an effective hedge.

July 31, 20X2

Dr.	Interest Expense	$ 541,667	
	Cr.	Accrued Interest Payable		$ 541,667

To record one month of interest after the rollover of the commercial paper to 6.5%.

Dr.	Other Comprehensive Income	$ 40,000	
	Cr.	Interest Income		$ 40,000

To reclassify one month of hedge gain as a reduction of interest expense on the rolled over commercial paper debt.

The result of the cash flow hedge is that interest expense beginning at the rollover date of the commercial paper has been reduced from what it otherwise would have been if the hedge had not been put in place. In the example, the effective interest rate after the rollover comes to 6.02% (6.5% − .48% hedge gain).

Foreign Currency Hedges

With respect to *foreign currency hedges*, there are two areas of difference in the accounting previously prescribed by FASB Statement Number 52:

1. FASB Statement Number 133 permits the company to hedge *forecasted transactions* with foreign currency forward contracts, and

2. it permits the company to hedge an exposure with a *tandem currency*, assuming hedge effectiveness can be proven.

See also Chapter 16, Foreign Currency Translation and Transactions.

Hedge Effectiveness Criteria

In order to receive the benefit of hedge accounting, there must be a highly effective relationship between the item to be hedged and the hedging instrument. This effective relationship must exist both at the initiation of the hedge, and throughout the life of the hedge. The relationship must be evaluated quarterly and whenever financial statements for the company are issued.

The company must indicate how hedge effectiveness is defined and measured, and then stay with the criteria. It also needs to be able to measure the ineffective part of the hedge. Statistical methods, including regression analysis are means of assessing initial and ongoing effectiveness. In order for a hedging relationship to qualify as "highly effective," the change in fair value or cash flows of the hedge must fall between 80% and 125% of the opposite change in fair value or cash flows of the exposure that is hedged.

If a transaction no longer meets the "highly effective" test, then hedge accounting is to be terminated.

Disclosure Requirements under FASB Statement Number 133

There are both qualitative and quantitative disclosures required under FASB Statement Number 133. The company should provide qualitative disclosures of:

- The business reason for holding or issuing derivatives, for both trading and hedging. Discussion of hedging should differentiate by hedge type (fair value hedge, cash flow hedge, and hedges of a foreign currency exposure of a net investment in a foreign operation).

- The company's risk management strategy and which risks are hedged with derivatives. The discussion should differentiate by hedge type and detail the items or transactions for which the company hedges risks. A discussion of the company's overall risk management strategy is encouraged.

■ When FASB Statement Number 133 will be adopted by the company. And,

■ A discussion of the impact of FASB Statement Number 133 on the financial statements or other aspects of the company's business (e.g., violation of debt covenants).

Similar separate qualitative disclosures should be made for non-derivative instruments used for hedging purposes.

The company's quantitative disclosures for derivatives and non-derivatives by hedge type (for cash flow hedges and fair value hedges) should include the amount of gains or losses recognized in earnings because: (a) of hedge ineffectiveness, or (b) they are related to the derivative, but are excluded in assessing hedge effectiveness. The company should disclose the income statement classification. In addition:

■ For fair value hedges, the company should disclose the amount recognized that resulted from previously hedged firm commitments that no longer were firm.

■ For cash flow hedges, the company should disclose the amount of gains or losses currently included in other comprehensive income that is expected to be recognized in the income statement within the next 12 months. The disclosure should include a discussion of the: (a) events that would cause the earnings to be recognized, and (b) expected maximum duration of hedges of forecasted transactions other than those related to outstanding floating rate financial instruments. The company should disclose the amount recognized that resulted from previously hedged firm commitments that no longer were firm. The company's comprehensive earnings include the net gain or loss on derivative instruments designated and qualifying as cash flow hedging instruments. Consistent with FASB Statement Number 130 (Reporting Comprehensive Income), the company must present a reconciliation of changes in the accumulated derivative gain or loss, including, the net change related to hedging transactions, and the net amount recognized in earnings.

For hedges of the net investment in a foreign operation, the company should disclose the amount of gains or losses included in the cumulative translation adjustment.

The company is encouraged to provide quantitative disclosures that provide the context for derivatives by activity.

Transition to the New Standard

Once the new standard is adopted, the company must recognize all outstanding derivatives on the balance sheet at fair value. Any prior deferred gains and losses from outstanding derivative hedging transactions must be removed from the balance sheet. All hedging documentation must be reviewed to ensure that outstanding designated hedges meet the criteria under FASB Statement Number 133.

There are transition adjustments that include the determination of the impact on the income statement and comprehensive income if the hedge is designated as a fair value hedge or cash flow hedge, respectively. In addition, since held to maturity securities cannot be hedged under the provisions of Statement 133, the FASB is permitting a one time opportunity to change the designation of such securities as to either be available for sale or trading.

OFFSETTING OF ASSETS AND OBLIGATIONS

Offsetting of assets and liabilities is not permitted unless all of the following criteria are satisfied:

1. Each of two parties owes the other determinable amounts.

2. The company has the right to set off the amount it owes with the amount owed by the other party.

3. The company intends to set off.

4. The right of setoff is enforceable under law.

FASB Interpretation Number 39 states that the requirements for offsetting also relate to conditional contracts and to exchange contracts, such as options, currency swaps, forward contracts, and interest rate swaps, caps, or collars. In a conditional contract, obligations or rights depend on a future occurrence. In an exchange contract, these will be a future exchange of assets or liabilities. Unless the criteria for the right of setoff are satisfied, the fair value of conditional contracts in a gain position should not be offset against other contracts with a loss position. In a similar vein, if accrued receivables and accrued payables are recognized in conditional or exchange contracts, then they should not be offset against each other except if the above four conditions are met.

Recorded amounts, whether accrued or at fair value associated with conditional or exchange contracts, are assets and liabilities in their own right. The fair value of conditional or exchange contracts recognized and executed with the same counterparty may be offset under a master netting agreement. A master netting arrangement is when a reporting company has multiple contracts, with one counterparty stipulating net settlement of all contracts in a single sum in one currency if default or cancellation of any one contract takes place. The contracts need not be of the same type. The offsetting in a master netting situation results in recording the fair value of one asset or liability constituting the net fair value of all positions for all contracts with one counterparty.

The post-FASB Statement Number 133 requirement to disclose netting agreements and their impact on credit risk is described earlier in this chapter.

FASB Interpretation Number 41 permits (but does not require) offsetting of payables under repurchase arrangements against receivables under reverse repurchase agreements if all of the following criteria are satisfied:

1. The securities underlying the repurchase and reverse repurchase contracts are in "book entry" form.

2. The repurchase and reverse repurchase agreements are with the same counterparty.

3. The repurchase and reverse repurchase agreements are executed under a master netting arrangement.

4. The company expects to use the same account at the clearing bank on the settlement date in transacting the cash flows from both the

reverse repurchase agreement and the offsetting repurchase agreement.

5. The repurchase and the reverse repurchase agreements have the same settlement date when initiated. And,

6. The repurchase and reverse repurchase agreements will be settled on a qualifying securities transfer system that allows for daylight overdrafts or a comparable settlement facility.

The company's offsetting policy must be consistently followed.

TRANSFERS AND SERVICING OF FINANCIAL ASSETS AND EXTINGUISHMENTS OF LIABILITIES

Most transfers of financial assets involve the transfer of control over an asset to the buyer/transferee and are accounted for as sales and purchases by the respective parties. Each company recognizes the financial and servicing assets it controls and derecognizes liabilities it extinguishes. The transferor may continue to be involved with assets transferred either through servicing arrangements or agreements to repurchase assets prior to maturity. FASB Statement Number 125 (Accounting for Transfers and Servicing of Financial Assets and Extinguishments of Liabilities) provides accounting guidance with respect to certain mortgage servicing rights and collateral pledged in repurchase agreements and securities lending arrangements.

Sale Accounting Under FASB Statement Number 125

The accounting and reporting standards of FASB Statement Number 125 are based on a financial-components approach, in which receivables and liabilities are separated into various rights and activities.

Control over transferred assets is surrendered if all of the following conditions are satisfied:

1. The transferee obtains the right to pledge or exchange the transferred assets or the transferee is a qualifying off balance sheet special purpose entity,

2. control over the transferred assets is not retained by the transferor, and

3. transferred assets have been segregated from the transferor.

Subsequent to financial assets being transferred, the transferor should retain its interest in the transferred assets on its balance sheet.

For transfers satisfying the criteria to be accounted for as a sale, the transferor (seller) should:

1. record the assets received and liabilities incurred as proceeds from the sale,

2. report assets received and liabilities incurred at fair value,

3. remove from the balance sheet any assets sold, and

4. record the gain or loss on the sale.

In determining asset recognition or derecognition, consider whether the transferor has surrendered control of the assets and whether the assets are isolated from the seller. This will depend on the facts surrounding the transaction, such as:

1. The transferor's ability to revoke the transfer.

2. Bankruptcy statutes related to the transfer. To receive sale treatment the assets must be beyond the reach of the transferor, even in bankruptcy.

3. Whether the transfer would be considered a "true sale" at law.

4. The transferor and transferee affiliation, if any.

5. Whether the transferee has the right to sell or exchange the collateral.

6. Whether an agreement exists requiring the transferor to reacquire the transferred assets.

Note: Put options held by the buyer typically do not preclude sale treatment if the seller satisfies the conditions for surrender of control over the financial assets. Since the put owner had control over whether to exercise the option, put options are not an indication that the transferor has maintained control over the transferred assets.

The transferee must recognize the assets obtained and liabilities incurred at fair value. If the transfer does not satisfy the conditions for sale, then the transferor and transferee should treat the transfer as a collateralized borrowing. If the transferor enters into a contract with the transferee that, in effect, results in the transferor keeping effective control over the assets, then the transaction should be accounted for as a secured borrowing. A contract maintains the transferor's effective control over transferred assets if the transferor must repurchase transferred assets from the transferee and if all of the following criteria exist:

1. The repurchase or redemption price before maturity is fixed or determinable.

2. The contract occurs at the same time as the transfer.

3. The assets to be repurchased are similar to the transferred assets. Similarity may be in the form of risk characteristics, identical form and type, maturity, interest rate, and collateral requirements. And,

4. Transferor can redeem the transferred assets on basically the same terms even in the event of default.

If fair value is not determinable, then record transferred assets obtained at zero. If the transferor cannot estimate the fair values of liabilities incurred, then no gain should be recorded.

Mortgage Servicing Rights

Typical transfer and servicing transactions include collateralized mortgage obligations, securitizations, options for repurchase, transfers of loans with recourse, loan participations, and factoring arrangements. For example, a bank that has mortgages may wish to sell those receivables to another financial institution.

A pool of mortgages that are bundled together to form a negotiable instrument is referred to as a mortgage-backed security. Car loans, credit cards, and other assets pooled together are called asset-backed securities. However, in selling these receivables the bank may retain the rights to service the loans (collect the principal, interest, and escrow payments and pay taxes and insurance payments from the escrow). Servicing activities that generate revenue in excess of the costs of the servicing activity are called servicing assets, and they are termed servicing liabilities if the costs are more than the revenues. Therefore, the financial components of a loan receivable might include as assets the following: cash, calls or puts, servicing assets, and swaps. The liability components may include servicing liabilities and recourse obligations.

If the company is required to service financial assets, then it should record a servicing asset or a servicing obligation for the servicing contract. Servicing may include activities such as collecting principal, interest and escrow payments from the borrower, following upon delinquencies, remitting taxes and insurance out of escrow accounts, etc. Accounting for the servicing of financial assets is as follows:

1. Servicing assets or servicing liabilities are recorded at fair value.

2. The balance sheet should present separately servicing assets and servicing liabilities.

3. Servicing assets retained in the sale or securitization of the assets being serviced are presented at their allocated previous carrying amount based on proportionate fair values.

4. Servicing assets are amortized proportionately to and over the period of estimated net servicing income.

5. Impairment of servicing assets are recorded in a valuation allowance account and adjusted subsequently as measurement of the impairment changes. This can occur when the future servicing costs exceeds future servicing income.

6. Servicing liabilities are amortized proportionately to estimated net servicing loss. However, if later events cause an increase in the fair value of the servicing liability, then an expense provision should be made. An example is a sudden and drastic increase in servicing expenses.

7. Rights to future interest income derived from serviced assets exceeding agreed upon servicing fees should be shown separately from servicing assets.

FASB Statement Number 125 does not require a servicing asset or liability to be recognized when the company securitizes the financial assets, keeps all the resulting securities, and treats them as debt securities held to maturity.

In the case of previously recognized servicing receivables exceeding fees specified in the contract, they should be reclassified as interest-only strips receivable.

The company must disclose the following information for its servicing assets and servicing liabilities: (1) amounts recognized and amortized, (2) fair values, (3) risk factors of the underlying financial assets, (4) movement of the balances in the valuation allowance for impaired activities.

Collateral Pledged in Repurchase Agreements and Securities Lending Arrangements

Under FASB Statement Number 125, assets received as collateral in repurchase agreements and securities lending arrangements are considered assets of the company (secured party) if:

1. the company is able to sell or repledge the collateral, *and*

2. the party pledging the collateral does *not* have the ability to redeem the collateral on short notice by substituting other collateral or terminating the contract.

In that case, the company recognizes the collateral and an obligation to return the collateral, and the pledging party reclassifies the securities pledged to "securities receivable":

Figure 17-10

Current Accounting for Collateral in Certain Repurchase Transactions

Secured Party (Reverse Repo)		*Pledging Party (Repo)*
Dr. Securities Purchased Under Resale Agreements Cr. Cash	Cash →	Dr. Cash Cr. Securities Sold Under Repurchase Agreements
Dr. Trading Securities—Collateral Received Cr. Trading Liabilities—Liability to Return Collateral	←Collateral	(Securities are reclassified to a segregated Securities Receivable account)

Under an amendment proposed by the FASB, when the company has the right to sell or repledge the collateral, it would recognize only the right to use such collateral and would no longer record the full value of the collateral and an obligation to return the asset. Effectively, the right to use the collateral would be accounted for as an option and marked to market through income. The pledging party would recognize the granting of that right by reducing the carrying amount of the pledged asset (or, if the debtor has pledged another entity's asset, by recognizing a liability to that entity).

Figure 17-11

Proposed Future Accounting for Collateral in All Repurchase Transactions

Secured Party (Reverse Repo)		*Pledging Party (Repo)*
Dr. Securities Purchased Under Resale Agreements	Cash →	Dr. Cash
Dr. Securities—Rights Received to Use Securities 　　Cr. Cash	← Collateral	Cr. Securities Sold Under Repurchase Agreements 　Cr. Contra Securities—Rights Granted to Use Securities

The fair value of the collateral and the portion of such collateral that has been sold or repledged would be a required disclosure.

OPTIONS ON ISSUER'S SECURITIES

A company may sign contracts that are tied to, and/or settled in, it's own stock. Examples are written put or call options, purchased put or call options, and forward sale or purchase contracts. These contracts may be settled using various settlement approaches as follows:

1. *Physical settlement*—the buyer pays cash while seller delivers the shares.

2. *Net cash settlement*—the party incurring a loss delivers to the party having a gain the cash payment equal to the gain.

3. *Net share settlement*—the party incurring a loss delivers to the party having a gain the shares with a current fair value equal to the gain.

4. A combination of the above.

Such derivatives are excluded from the scope of FASB Statement Number 133 if they are indexed to the company's stock and classified in Stockholders' Equity.

AUTHORITATIVE LITERATURE

FASB Statement Number 80
Accounting for Futures Contracts

This Statement is superseded by FASB Statement Number 133.

FASB Statement Number 105
Disclosure of Information about Financial Instruments with Off-Balance-Sheet Risk and Financial Instruments with Concentrations of Credit Risk

This statement requires companies to disclose information concerning financial instruments with off-balance-sheet risk of accounting loss. Companies are required to disclose the following information about financial instruments with off-balance-sheet risk of accounting loss:

1. The nature and terms of the instruments including information about credit and market risk, cash needs, and accounting policies

2. The face, contract, or notional principal amount

3. The accounting loss arising if any party to the financial instrument failed to conduct contractual responsibilities

4. Collateral requirements and description

Disclosure is required of significant concentrations of credit risk from one or more counterparties for all financial instruments.

The Statement is superseded by FASB Statement Number 133, which creates comparable requirements under FASB Statement Number 107.

FASB Statement Number 107
Disclosures about Fair Value of Financial Instruments

The fair value of financial instruments, whether assets or liabilities, must be presented. If estimating fair value is not possible, then disclosure should be made descriptive information relevant to estimating the value of a financial instrument. FASB Statement Number 133 will amend this Statement to require disclosures of concentrations of credit risk that previously were required by FASB Statement Number 105.

FASB Statement Number 119
Disclosure about Derivative Financial Instruments and Fair Value of Financial Instruments

This statement mandates disclosures about derivative financial instruments—futures, forward, swap, and option contracts, and other financial instruments with comparable characteristics. It amends the requirements of FASB Statement Number 105 and FASB Statement Number 107.

This statement requires disclosures about amounts, characteristics, and provisions of derivative financial instruments that do not follow FASB Statement Number 105 because they do not result in off-balance-sheet risk of accounting loss. A distinction must be made between financial instruments held or issued for trading purposes versus non-trading purposes. For derivative financial instruments held for trading purposes, disclosure must be made of the reasons held and how they are presented in financial statements. Disclosure must also be made of average fair value and of net trading gains or losses. For derivative financial instruments designed to hedge the company's position, disclosure must be made of the current or expected transactions that are hedged, types of instruments used, deferred hedging gains and losses, and recognized gains or losses. Disclosure of risks associated with the derivative products is also recommended. Hedging activities must be described and explained.

This statement amended FASB Statement Number 105 to require disaggregation of information concerning financial instruments with off-balance-sheet risk of accounting loss by category, business function, and risk. This statement amends FASB Statement Number 107 to require that fair value information be shown without combining or netting the fair value of derivatives with the fair value of non-derivatives. Disclosure may be in the footnotes, in a separate schedule, or in the body of the financial statements.

FASB Statement Number 119 will be superseded by FASB Statement Number 133.

FASB Statement Number 125
Accounting for Transfers and Servicing of Financial Assets and Extinguishments of Liabilities

This statement addresses distinguishes between sales and secured borrowings, and requires that all financial instruments that are transferred are to be valued at fair value. It provides guidance specific to mortgage servicing rights and repurchase agreements.

FASB Statement Number 133
Accounting for Derivative Instruments and Hedging Activities

This statement provides a comprehensive rewrite of the accounting for derivative financial instruments.

FASB Statement Number 137
Accounting for Derivative Instruments and Hedging Activities—Deferral of the Effective Date of FASB Statement Number 133

Delays the effective date of FASB Statement Number 133 to the first quarter of fiscal years commencing after June 15, 2000.

FASB Interpretation Number 39
Offsetting of Amounts Related to Certain Contracts

Defines the right of set-off and the criteria for reporting assets and liabilities on a net basis in the balance sheet.

FASB Interpretation Number 41
Offsetting of Amounts Related to Certain Repurchase and Reverse Repurchase Agreements

Defines the right of set-off and the criteria for reporting repurchase and reverse repurchase agreements on a net basis in the balance sheet.

Annual Report References

BAUSCH & LOMB

Notes to Financial Statements
1. Accounting Policies

Derivative Financial Instruments

The company enters into foreign currency and interest rate derivative contracts for the purpose of minimizing risk and protecting earnings.

The company uses principally foreign currency forward contracts to hedge foreign exchange exposures. The portfolio of contracts is adjusted at least monthly to reflect changes in exposure positions as they become known. When possible and practical, the company matches the maturity of the hedging instrument to that of the underlying exposure. Net settlements are generally made at contract maturity based on rates agreed to at contract inception. Gains and losses on hedges of transaction exposures are included in income in the period in which exchange rates change. Gains and losses related to hedges of foreign currency firm commitments are deferred and recognized on the basis of the transaction when completed, while those on forward contracts hedging non-U.S. equity investments are offset against the currency component in accumulated other comprehensive income. The receivable or payable with the counterparty to the derivative contract is reported as either other current assets or accrued liabilities. Deferred gains and losses totaled less than $0.5 at December 26, 1998 and December 27, 1997 and are expected to be recognized within one year.

(info obtained from 10k from http://edgarscan.pwcglobal.com)

923

The company enters into interest rate swap and cap agreements to effectively limit exposures to interest rate movements within the parameters of its interest rate hedging policy. This policy requires that interest rate exposures from floating-rate assets be offset by a substantially similar amount of floating-rate liabilities. Interest rate derivatives are used to read-just this natural hedge position whenever it becomes unbalanced beyond policy limits. Net payments or receipts on these agreements are accrued as other current assets and accrued liabilities and recorded as adjustments to interest expense or interest income. Interest rate instruments are entered into for periods no longer than the life of the underlying transactions being hedged or, in the case of floating-rate to fixed-rate swaps, for periods no longer than the underlying floating-rate exposure is expected to remain outstanding. Interest rate derivatives are normally held to maturity, but may be terminated early, particularly if the underlying exposure is similarly extinguished. Gains and losses on prematurely terminated interest rate derivatives are recognized over the remaining life, if any, of the underlying exposure as an adjustment to interest income or interest expense.

The company amortizes premium income or expense incurred from entering into derivative instruments over the life of each agreement as non-operating income and expense.

New Accounting Guidance

In June 1998, the Financial Accounting Standards Board (FASB) issued SFAS No. 133, Accounting for Derivative Instruments and Hedging Activities, which the company is required to adopt effective no later than the first quarter of 2000. SFAS No. 133 will require the company to record all derivatives on the balance sheet at fair value. Changes in derivative fair values will either be recognized in earnings as offsets to the changes in fair value of related hedged assets, liabilities and firm commitments or for fore-casted transactions, deferred and recorded as a component of accumulated other comprehensive income until the hedged transactions occur and are recognized in earnings. The ineffective portion of a hedging derivative's change in fair value will be immediately recognized in earnings. The impact of SFAS No. 133 on the company's financial statements will depend on a variety of factors, including the future level of forecasted and actual for-eign currency transactions, the extent of the company's hedging activities, the types of hedging instruments used and the effectiveness of such instruments. The company is currently evaluating the impact of adopting SFAS No. 133 to its financial statements.

Notes to Financial Statements
14. Financial Instruments

The carrying amount of cash, cash equivalents, current portion of long-term investments and notes payable approximated fair value because maturities are less than one year in duration. The company's remaining financial instruments consisted of the following:

	December 26, 1998		December 27, 1997	
	Carrying Value	Fair Value	Carrying Value	Fair Value
Nonderivatives				
Other investments	$249.2	$249.2	$546.4	$546.4
Long-term debt, including current portion	(1,312.4)	(1,302.7)	(515.2)	(516.4)
Derivatives held for purposes other than trading				
Foreign exchange instruments				
Other current assets	$ 7.6		$ 45.3	
Accrued liabilities	(15.7)		(40.5)	
Net foreign exchange instruments	$ (8.1)	$ (8.3)	$ 4.8	$ 2.4
Interest rate instruments				
Other current assets	$ 22.1		$ 17.5	
Accrued liabilities	(15.2)		(12.6)	
Net interest rate instruments	$ 6.9	$ 14.9	$ 4.9	$ 20.7

Fair value of other investments was determined based on contract terms and an evaluation of expected cash flows and investment risk. Fair value for long-term debt was estimated using either quoted market prices for the same or similar issues or the current rates offered to the company for debt with similar maturities. The fair value for foreign exchange and interest rate instruments was determined using a model that estimates fair value at market rates, or was based upon quoted market prices for similar instruments with similar maturities.

The company, as a result of its global operating and financing activities, is exposed to changes in interest rates and foreign currency exchange rates that may adversely affect its results of operations and financial position. In seeking to minimize the risks and/or costs associated with such activities, the company manages exposures to changes in interest rates and foreign currency exchange rates by entering into derivative contracts. The company does not generally use financial instruments for trading or other speculative purposes, nor does it use leveraged financial instruments.

The company enters into foreign exchange forward contracts primarily to hedge foreign currency transactions and equity investments in non-U.S. subsidiaries. At December 26, 1998 and December 27, 1997, the company hedged aggregate exposures of $1,063.0 and $1,559.0, respectively, by entering into forward exchange contracts requiring the purchase and sale of U.S. and foreign currencies. The company selectively hedges firm commitments that represent both a right and an obligation, mainly for committed purchase orders for foreign-sourced inventory. In general, the forward exchange contracts have varying maturities up to, but not exceeding, two years with cash settlements made at maturity based upon rates agreed to at contract inception. At December 26, 1998 and December 27, 1997, the company deferred gains of less than $0.1 relating to hedged firm commitments.

The company's exposure to changes in interest rates results from investing and borrowing activities. The company enters into interest rate swap and cap agreements to effectively limit exposure to interest rate movements within the parameters of its interest rate hedging policy. At December 26, 1998 and December 27, 1997, the company was party to swap contracts that had aggregate notional amounts of $869.5 and $866.3, respectively. At year-end 1998 and 1997, the company had an outstanding interest rate cap with a notional amount of NLG15.5 million that protects the company from exposures to rising NLG interest rates.

Counterparties to the financial instruments discussed above expose the company to credit risks to the extent of non-performance. The credit ratings of the counterparties, which consist of a diversified group of major financial institutions, are regularly monitored and thus credit loss arising from counterparty non-performance is not anticipated.

THE CHASE MANHATTAN CORPORATION

Notes to Financial Statements
19. Derivative and Foreign Exchange Contracts

Chase utilizes derivative and foreign exchange financial instruments for both trading and non-trading activities, such as ALM. A discussion of the credit and market risks involved with these instruments is included in the first six paragraphs of the Derivative and Foreign Exchange Contracts section of the Management's Discussion and Analysis ("MD&A"), and paragraphs one through four of the Market Risk Management section of the MD&A.

Derivative and Foreign Exchange Instruments Used for Trading Purposes

The credit risk associated with Chase's trading activities is recorded on the balance sheet. The effects of any market risk (gains or losses) on Chase's trading activities have been reflected in trading revenue, as the trading instruments are marked-to-market daily. See Summary of Significant Accounting Policies.

Derivative and Foreign Exchange Instruments Used for ALM Activities

A discussion of Chase's objectives and strategies for using these instruments for ALM activities is included in the first four paragraphs of the Asset/Liability Management discussion of the MD&A in Market Risk Management.

Chase believes the best measure of credit risk is the mark-to-market exposure amount of the derivative or foreign exchange contract. This is also referred to as repayment risk or the replacement cost.

While notional principal is the most commonly used volume measure in the derivative and foreign exchange markets, it is not a useful measure of credit or market risk. The notional principal typically does not change hands, but is simply a quantity upon which interest and other payments are calculated. The notional principal amounts of Chase's derivative and foreign exchange products greatly exceed the possible credit and market loss that could arise from such transactions.

The following table summarizes the aggregate notional amounts of derivative and foreign exchange contracts as well as the credit exposure related to these instruments (after taking into account the effects of legally enforceable master netting agreements).

December 31 (in billions)	Notional Amounts[a]		Credit Exposure	
	1998	1997	1998	1997
Interest Rate Contracts				
Interest Rate Swaps				
Trading	$4,882.4	$3,206.0	$10.8	$14.0
ALM	97.8	98.2	0.3	0.6
Futures, Forwards and Forward Rate Agreements				
Trading	2,090.0	1,643.7	0.4	0.3
ALM	74.6	42.6	—	—
Purchased Options				
Trading	443.8	316.1	1.5	1.7
ALM	52.6	13.1	—	—
Written Options				
Trading	503.2	395.7	—	—
ALM	27.5	0.2	—	—
Total Interest Rate Contracts	$8,171.9	$5,715.6	$13.0	$16.6
Foreign Exchange Contracts				
Spot, Forward and Futures Contracts				
Trading	$1,532.6	$1,521.7	$11.0	$14.4
ALM	54.0	72.6	—	—
Other Foreign Exchange Contracts[b]				
Trading	449.8	358.7	5.0	5.8
ALM	4.2	5.2	—	—
Total Foreign Exchange Contracts	$2,040.6	$1,958.2	$16.0	$20.2
Debt, Equity, Commodity and Other Contracts				
Trading	$140.5	$64.4	$4.3	$1.6
Total Debt, Equity, Commodity and Other Contracts	$140.5	$64.4	$4.3	$1.6
Total Credit Exposure Recorded on the Balance Sheet			$33.3	$38.4

[a]The notional amounts of exchange-traded interest rate contracts, foreign exchange contracts, and equity, commodity and other contracts were $699.3 billion, $3.3 billion and $3.9 billion, respectively, at December 31, 1998, compared with $691.2 billion, $22.8 billion and $6.1 billion, respectively, at December 31, 1997. The credit risk for these contracts was minimal as exchange-traded contracts principally settle daily in cash.

[b]Includes notional amounts of purchased options, written options and cross-currency interest rate swaps of $137.0 billion, $137.9 billion and $179.1 billion, respectively, at December 31, 1998, compared with $123.9 billion, $126.6 billion and $113.4 billion, respectively, at December 31, 1997.

Classes of Derivative and Foreign Exchange Instruments

The following instruments are used by Chase for purposes of both trading and ALM activities.

Derivative and foreign exchange instruments may be broadly categorized as exchange-traded or over-the-counter ("OTC"). Exchange-traded instruments are executed through a recognized exchange as standardized contracts, and are primarily futures and options. OTC contracts are executed between two counterparties who negotiate specific agreement terms, including the underlying instrument, notional amount, exercise price and maturity. In this context the underlying instrument may include interest rates, foreign exchange rates, commodities, debt or equity instruments.

Interest rate swaps are contracts in which a series of interest rate flows in a single currency are exchanged over a prescribed period. Interest rate swaps are the most common type of derivative contract that Chase utilizes for both assets and liabilities. An example of a situation in which Chase would utilize an interest rate swap would be to convert its fixed -rate debt to a variable rate. By entering into the swap, the principal amount of the debt would remain unchanged but the interest streams would change. Cross-currency interest rate swaps are contracts that generally involve the exchange of both interest and principal amounts in two different currencies.

Interest rate futures and forwards are contracts for the delayed delivery of securities or money market instruments. The selling party agrees to deliver on a specified future date, a specified instrument, at a specified price or yield.

Forward rate agreements are contracts to exchange payments on a specified future date, based on a market change in interest rates from trade date to contract settlement date.

Interest rate options, including caps and floors, are contracts to modify interest rate risk in exchange for the payment of a premium when the contract is initiated. As a writer of interest rate options, Chase receives a premium in exchange for bearing the risk of unfavorable changes in interest rates. Conversely, as a purchaser of an option, Chase pays a premium for the right, but not the obligation, to buy or sell a financial instrument or currency at predetermined terms in the future. Foreign currency options are similar to interest rate options, except that they are based on foreign exchange rates.

Chase's use of written options as part of its ALM activities is permitted only in those circumstances where they are specifically linked to purchased options. All unmatched written options are included in the trading portfolio at fair value.

Foreign exchange contracts are used for the future receipt or delivery of foreign currency at previously agreed-upon terms.

Debt, equity, commodity and other contracts include swaps and options and are similar to interest rate contracts, except that the underlying instrument is debt, equity or commodity-related. Credit derivatives are considered debt-related and are included in this category of derivatives.

These instruments are all subject to market risk, representing potential loss due to adverse movements in the underlying instrument. Credit risk arises primarily from OTC contracts, since exchange-traded contracts are generally settled daily.

Market risk is reduced by entering into offsetting positions using other financial instruments.

Credit risk is reduced significantly by entering into legally enforceable master netting agreements. To further reduce exposure, management may deem it necessary to obtain collateral. The amount and nature of the collateral obtained is based on management's credit evaluation of the customer. Collateral held varies, but may include cash, securities, accounts receivable, inventory, property, plant and equipment and real estate.

MERCK & CO.

Notes to Financial Statements
6. Financial Instruments

The Company has established revenue and balance sheet hedging programs to protect against reductions in value and volatility of future foreign currency cash flows caused by changes in foreign exchange rates. The objectives and strategies of these programs are described in the Analysis of Liquidity and Capital Resources section of the Financial Review.

The Company partially hedges forecasted revenues denominated in foreign currencies with purchased currency options. When the dollar strengthens against foreign currencies, the decline in the value of foreign currency cash flows is partially offset by the recognition of gains in the value of purchased currency options designated as hedges of the period. Conversely, when the dollar weakens, the increase in the value of foreign currency cash flows is reduced only by the recognition of the premium paid to acquire the options designated as hedges of the period. Market value gains and premiums on these contracts are recognized in Sales when the hedged transaction is recognized. The carrying value of purchased currency options is reported in Prepaid expenses and taxes or Other assets.

The Company continually reviews its portfolio of purchased options and will adjust its portfolio to accommodate changes in exposure to forecasted revenues. The most cost-effective means of decreasing coverage provided by purchased options is to write options with terms identical to purchased options that are no longer necessary. Deferred gains or losses that accumulate on purchased options prior to writing an offsetting position will remain deferred and are recognized when the hedged transaction occurs. Subsequent changes in the market value of the written options and related purchased options are recorded in earnings. Because the changes in market value of the purchased options equally offset the written options, there is no net impact on earnings. The carrying value of written currency options is reported in Accounts payable and accrued liabilities or Deferred income taxes and noncurrent liabilities. The Company also hedges certain exposures to fluctuations in foreign currency exchange rates that occur prior to conversion of foreign currency denominated monetary assets and liabilities into U.S. dollars. Prior to conversion to U.S. dollars, these assets and liabilities are translated at spot rates in effect on the balance sheet date. The effects of changes in spot rates are reported in earnings and included in Other (income) expense, net. The Company hedges its exposure to changes in foreign exchange principally with forward contracts. Because monetary assets and liabilities are marked to spot and recorded in earnings, forward contracts designated as hedges of the monetary assets and liabilities are also marked to spot with the resulting gains and losses similarly recognized in earnings. Gains and losses on forward contracts are included in Other (income) expense, net, and offset losses and gains on the net monetary assets and liabilities hedged. The carrying values of forward exchange contracts are reported in Accounts receivable, Other assets, Accounts payable and accrued liabilities or Deferred income taxes and noncurrent liabilities.

Deferred gains and losses on currency options used to hedge forecasted revenues amounted to $12.6 million and $45.3 million at December 31, 1998 and $95.4 million and $5.9 million at December 31, 1997, respectively.

The Company also hedges certain exposures to fluctuations in foreign currency exchange rates that occur prior to conversion of foreign currency denominated monetary assets and liabilities into U.S. dollars. Prior to conversion to U.S. dollars, these assets and liabilities are translated at spot rates in effect on the balance sheet date. The effects of changes in spot rates are reported in earnings and included in Other (income) expense, net. The Company hedges its exposure to changes in foreign exchange principally with forward contracts. Because monetary assets and liabilities are marked to spot and recorded in earnings, forward contracts designated as hedges of the monetary assets and liabilities are also marked to spot with the resulting gains and losses similarly recognized in earnings. Gains and losses on forward contracts are included in Other (income) expense, net, and offset losses and gains on the net monetary assets and liabilities hedged. The carrying values of forward exchange contracts are reported in Accounts receivable, Other assets, Accounts payable and accrued liabilities or Deferred income taxes and noncurrent liabilities.

At December 31, 1998 and 1997, the Company had contracts to exchange foreign currencies, principally the Japanese yen, French franc and Deutschemark, for U.S. dollars in the following notional amounts: yen, French franc and Deutsche mark, for U.S. dollars in the following notional amounts:

Dollars in Millions	1998	1997
Purchased currency options	$4,583.5	$1,462.7
Forward sales contracts	1,972.3	1,500.9
Forward purchase contracts	542.8	412.1

Interest Rate Risk Management

The Company uses interest rate swap contracts on certain borrowing and investing transactions. Interest rate swap contracts are intended to be an integral part of borrowing and investing transactions and, therefore, are not recognized at fair value. Interest differentials paid or received under these contracts are recognized as adjustments to the effective yield of the underlying financial instruments hedged. Interest rate swap contracts would only be recognized at fair value if the hedged relationship is terminated. Gains or losses accumulated prior to termination of the relationship would be amortized as a yield adjustment over the shorter of the remaining life of the contract or the remaining period to maturity of the underlying instrument hedged. If the contract remained outstanding after termination of the hedged relationship, subsequent changes in market value of the contract would be recognized in earnings. The Company does not use leveraged swaps and, in general, does not use leverage in any of its investment activities that would put principal capital at risk.

In 1995, the Company entered into a five-year combined interest rate and currency swap contract with a notional amount of $231.3 million at December 31, 1998 and $313.6 million at December 31, 1997 and, in 1997, a seven-year interest rate and currency swap contract with a notional amount of $344.1 million at December 31, 1998 and $334.2 million at December 31, 1997. In 1998, a portion of the 1995 swap contract was terminated in conjunction with the sale of a portion of the related asset with an immaterial impact on net income. These swaps convert two different variable rate Dutch guilder investments to variable rate U.S. dollar investments. The market values of these contracts are reported in Other assets or Deferred income taxes and noncurrent liabilities with unrealized gains and losses recorded, net of tax, in Accumulated other comprehensive income.

At December 31, 1997, the Company had one variable maturity interest rate swap contract outstanding with a notional amount of $85.0 million to convert 7.25% U.S. dollar callable debt issued in 1997 to variable rate U.S. dollar debt. This swap contract was terminated in February 1998 in conjunction with the retirement of the callable debt.

Fair Value of Financial Instruments

Summarized below are the carrying values and fair values of the Company's financial instruments at December 31, 1998 and 1997. Fair values were estimated based on market prices, where available, or dealer quotes.

| | 1998 | | 1997 | |
| | Carrying Value | Fair Value | Carrying Value | Fair Value |
Dollars in Millions				
Assets				
Cash and cash equivalents	**$2,606.2**	**$2,606.2**	$1,125.1	$1,125.1
Short-term investments	**749.5**	**749.5**	1,184.2	1,184.2
Long-term investments	**3,607.7**	**3,604.3**	2,533.4	2,531.8
Purchased currency options	**170.2**	**137.5**	54.6	144.1
Forward exchange contracts and currency swaps	**72.8**	**72.8**	197.0	197.0
Interest rate swaps	**—**	**—**	.1	.3
Liabilities				
Loans payable and current portion of long-term debt	**$ 624.2**	**$ 654.7**	$ 902.5	$ 900.5
Long-term debt	**3,220.8**	**3,336.5**	1,346.5	1,387.0
Forward exchange contracts and currency swap	**86.1**	**86.1**	22.0	22.0

A summary of carrying values and fair values of the Company's investments at December 31 is as follows:

| | 1998 | | 1997 | |
| | Carrying Value | Fair Value | Carrying Value | Fair Value |
Dollars in Millions				
Available-for-sale				
Debt securities	**$2,639.0**	**$2,639.0**	$1,947.2	$1,947.2
Equity securities	**1000.6**	**1000.6**	887.6	887.6
Held-to-maturity securities	**717.6**	**714.2**	882.8	881.2

A summary of gross unrealized gains and losses on the Company's investments at December 31 is as follows:

| | 1998 | | 1997 | |
Dollars in Millions	Carrying Value	Fair Value	Carrying Value	Fair Value
Available-for-sale				
Debt securities	$ 22.1	$ (12.5)	$ 11.1	$ (2.8)
Equity securities	124.1	(64.2)	111.3	(91.9)
Held-to-maturity securities	.6	(4.0)	2.9	(4.5)

Gross unrealized gains and losses with respect to available-for-sale investments are recorded, net of tax and minority interests, in Accumulated other comprehensive (loss) income. Available-for-sale debt securities and held-to-maturity securities maturing within one year totaled $535.5 million and $214.0 million, respectively, at December 31, 1998. Of the remaining debt securities, $1.8 billion mature within six years. At December 31, 1998, $507.3 million of held-to-maturity securities maturing within five years set off $507.3 million of 5.0% nontransferable note obligations due by 2003 issued by the Company.

Concentrations of Credit Risk

As part of its ongoing control procedures, the Company monitors concentrations of credit risk associated with financial institutions with which it conducts business. Credit risk is minimal as credit exposure limits are established to avoid a concentration with any single financial institution. The Company also monitors the creditworthiness of its customers to which it grants credit terms in the normal course of business. Concentrations of credit risk associated with these trade receivables are considered minimal due to the Company's diverse customer base. Bad debts have been minimal. The Company does not normally require collateral or other security to support credit sales.

WALT DISNEY

Notes to Financial Statements
12. Financial Instruments

Investments

As of September 30, 1998 and 1997, the company held $126 million and $137 million, respectively, of securities classified as available for sale. In 1998, 1997 and 1996, realized gains and losses on available for-sale securities, determined principally on an average cost basis, and unrealized gains and losses on available-for-sale securities were not material.

Interest Rate Risk Management

The company is exposed to the impact of interest rate changes. The company's objective is to manage the impact of interest rate changes on earnings and cash flows and on the market value of its investments and borrowings. The company maintains fixed rate debt as a percentage of its net debt between a minimum and maximum percentage, which is set by policy.

The company uses interest rate swaps and other instruments to manage net exposure to interest rate changes related to its borrowings and to lower its overall borrowing costs. Significant interest rate risk management instruments held by the company at September 30, 1998 and 1997 included pay-floating and pay-fixed swaps, interest rate caps and swaption contracts. Pay-floating swaps effectively converted medium-term obligations to LIBOR-based or commercial paper variable rate instruments. These swap agreements expire in one to fourteen years. Pay-fixed swaps and interest rate caps effectively converted floating rate obligations to fixed rate instruments. These instruments expire within one year. Swaption contracts were designated as hedges of floating rate debt and expired in 1998.

The following table reflects incremental changes in the notional or contractual amounts of the company's interest rate contracts during 1998 and 1997. Activity representing renewal of existing positions is excluded.

	September 30, 1997	Additions	Maturities/ Expirations	Terminations	September 30, 1998
Pay-floating swaps	$2,086	$950	$(50)	$(100)	**$2,886**
Pay-fixed swaps	950	6,000	(4,050)	—	**2,900**
Interest rate caps	—	3,100	(2,000)	—	**1,100**
Swaption contracts	300	—	(300)	—	—
	$3,336	$10,050	$(6,400)	$(100)	**$6,886**

	September 30, 1996	Additions	Maturities/ Expirations	Terminations	September 30, 1997
Pay-floating swaps	$1,520	$2,479	$ —	$(1,913)	**$2,086**
Pay-fixed swaps	900	850	(200)	(600)	**950**
Swaption contracts	—	1,100	—	(800)	**300**
Option contracts	—	593	—	(593)	—
Spreadlock contracts	—	470	(470)	—	—
	$2,420	$5,492	$(670)	$(3,906)	**$3,336**

The impact of interest rate risk management activities on income in 1998, 1997 and 1996, and the amount of deferred gains and losses from interest rate risk management transactions at September 30, 1998 and 1997 were not material.

Foreign Exchange Risk Management

The company transacts business in virtually every part of the world and is subject to risks associated with changing foreign exchange rates. The company's objective is to reduce earnings and cash flow volatility associated with foreign exchange rate changes to allow management to focus its attention on its core business issues and challenges. Accordingly, the company enters into various contracts which change in value as foreign exchange rates change to protect the value of its existing foreign currency assets and liabilities, commitments and anticipated foreign currency revenues. By policy, the company maintains hedge coverage between minimum and maximum percentages of its anticipated foreign exchange exposures for periods not to exceed five years. The gains and losses on these contracts offset changes in the value of the related exposures.

It is the company's policy to enter into foreign currency transactions only to the extent considered necessary to meet its objectives as stated above. The company does not enter into foreign currency transactions for speculative purposes.

The company uses option strategies which provide for the sale of foreign currencies to hedge probable, but not firmly committed, revenues. While these hedging instruments are subject to fluctuations in value, such fluctuations are offset by changes in the value of the underlying exposures being hedged. The principal currencies hedged are the Japanese yen, French franc, German mark, British pound, Canadian dollar and Italian lira. The company also uses forward contracts to hedge foreign currency assets, liabilities and foreign currency payments the company is committed to make in connection with the construction of a cruise ship (*see* Note 13). Cross-currency swaps are used to hedge foreign currency-denominated borrowings.

At September 30, 1998 and 1997, the notional amounts of the company's foreign exchange risk management contracts, net of notional amounts of contracts with counterparties against which the company has a legal right of offset, the related exposures hedged and the contract maturities are as follows:

Dollars in Millions	*Notional Amount*	*Exposures Hedged*	*Fiscal Year Maturity*
1998			
Option contracts	**$2,966**	**$1,061**	**1999-2000**
Forward contracts	2,053	1,773	**1999-2000**
Cross-currency swaps	1,678	1,678	**1999-2003**
	$6,697	**$4,512**	
1997			
Option contracts	$3,460	$1,633	1998-1999
Forward contracts	2,284	1,725	1998-1999
Cross-currency swaps	1,812	1,812	1998-2001
	$7,556	$5,170	

Gains and losses on contracts hedging anticipated foreign currency revenues and foreign currency commitments are deferred until such revenues are recognized or such commitments are met, and offset changes in the value of the foreign currency revenues and commitments. At September 30, 1998 and 1997, the company had deferred gains of $245 million and $486 million respectively, and deferred losses of $118 million and $220 million, respectively, related to foreign currency hedge transactions. Deferred amounts to be recognized can change with market conditions and will be substantially offset by changes in the value of the related hedged transactions. The impact of foreign exchange risk management activities on operating income in 1998 and in 1997 was a net gain of $227 million and $166 million, respectively.

Fair Value of Financial Instruments

At September 30, 1998 and 1997, the company's financial instruments included cash, cash equivalents, investments, receivables, accounts payable, borrowings and interest rate and foreign exchange risk management contracts.

At September 30, 1998 and 1997, the fair values of cash and cash equivalents, receivables, accounts payable and commercial paper approximated carrying values because of the short-term nature of these instruments. The estimated fair values of other financial instruments subject to fair value disclosures, determined based on broker quotes or quoted market prices or rates for the same or similar instruments, and the related carrying amounts are as follows:

| | 1998 | | 1997 | |
| | Carrying Value | Fair Value | Carrying Value | Fair Value |
Dollars in Millions				
Investments	$ 686	$ 765	$ 769	$ 1,174
Borrowings	(10,914)	(11,271)	(10,313)	(10,290)
Risk Management contracts				
Foreign exchange forwards	49	18	43	93
Foreign exchange options	58	178	177	367
Interest rate swaps	30	181	20	54
Cross-currency swaps	25	(89)	17	(77)

MEAD
1999 ANNUAL REPORT

Financial Instruments

The company uses various derivative financial instruments as part of an overall strategy to manage the company's exposure to market risks associated with interest rate and foreign currency exchange rate fluctuations. The company uses foreign currency forward contracts to manage the foreign currency exchange rate risks associated with its international operations. The company utilizes rate swap and cap agreements to manage its interest rate risks on its debt instruments, including the reset of interest rates on variable-rate debt. The company does not hold nor issue derivative financial instruments for trading purposes.

The risk of loss to the company in the event of nonperformance by any counterparty under derivative financial instrument agreements is not considered significant by management. All counterparties are rated A or higher by Moody's and Standard & Poor's. Although the derivative financial instruments expose the company to market risk, fluctuations in the value of the derivatives are mitigated by expected offsetting fluctuations in the matched instruments.

As part of an overall strategy to maintain an acceptable level of exposure to the risk of interest rate fluctuation, the company has developed a targeted mix of fixed-rate and cap-protected debt versus variable-rate debt. To efficiently manage this mix, the company may utilize interest rate swap, cap and option agreements to effectively convert the debt portfolio into an acceptable fixed-rate, capped-rate and variable-rate mix.

Under interest rate swap agreements, the company agrees with other parties to exchange, at specified intervals, the difference between fixed-rate and variable-rate interest amounts calculated by reference to an agreed-upon notional principal amount. The company utilizes interest rate cap agreements to limit the impact of increases in interest rates on its floating rate debt. The interest rate cap agreements require premium payments to counterparties based upon a notional principal amount. Interest rate cap agreements entitle the company to receive from the counterparties the amounts, if any, by which the selected market interest rates exceed the strike rates stated in the agreements.

The fair values of the interest rate swap and cap agreements are estimated using quotes from brokers and represent the cash requirement if the agreements had been settled at year-end. Selected information related to the company's interest rate swap and cap agreements is as follows:

	Swap Agreements		Cap Agreements	
December 31 (all dollar amounts in millions)	*1999*	*1998*	*1999*	*1998*
Notional amount	**$114.2**	$114.2	**$50.0**	$50.0
Fair value	**(3.1)**	$ (4.6)	**$**	$
Carrying amount	**(1.5)**	(3.2)	**.1**	.2
Net unrecognized (loss)	**$ (1.6)**	$ (1.4)	**$ (.1)**	$ (.2)

The company utilizes foreign currency forward contracts to reduce exposure to exchange rate risks primarily associated with transactions in the regular course of the company's international operations. The forward contracts establish the exchange rates at which the company will purchase or sell the contracted amount of specified foreign currencies at a future date. The company utilizes forward contracts which are short-term in duration (generally one month) and receives or pays the difference between the contracted forward rate and the exchange rate at the settlement date. The major currency exposures hedged by the company are the Canadian dollar, British pound, Japanese yen and euro. Selected information related to the company's foreign currency forward contracts is as follows:

	Foreign Currency Forward Contracts	
December 31 (all dollar amounts in millions)	*1999*	*1998*
Notional amount	**$239.7**	$127.2
Fair Value	**$ 6.9**	$ (.2)
Carrying amount	**6.9**	(.2)
Net unrecognized gain (loss)	**$**	$

The fair value of the company's long-term debt is estimated based on quoted market prices for the same or similar issues or on current rates offered to the company for debt of the same remaining maturities. The fair value of long-term debt was $1,295.0 million and $1,439.8 million at December 31, 1999 and 1998, respectively, and the related carrying amounts were $1,333.7 million and $1,367.4 million, respectively. The carrying amount of the notes payable and the current maturities of long-term debt are reasonable estimates of their fair value.

At December 31, 1999 and 1998, the company held short-term investments which are included in cash and cash equivalents. The carrying amount of these short-term investments is a reasonable estimate of fair value. See Note D for disclosure regarding the investment in convertible debentures.

Part IV

GAAP IN SPECIALIZED INDUSTRIES

Chapter 18

Accounting in Specialized Industries

BROADCASTING INDUSTRY

Primary Source of Authoritative GAAP

The primary source of authoritative GAAP relating to guidance in the broadcasting industry is

- SFAS Statement Number 63 (*Financial Reporting by Broadcasters*)

GAAP Abstract and Introduction

A program agreement for program material for features, specials, series, or cartoons generally covers several programs (a package) and grants a television station, group of stations, network, pay television, or cable television system (the licensee) the right to broadcast either a specified number or an unlimited number of showings over some defined specified period. The agreement usually consists of separate licenses for each program in the package. The licensee must pay the required fee for the program materials even though the rights may not be used. If the rights of use are not exercised, then they revert back to the licensor with no refund to the licensee. The license period specified in the license agreement defines a reasonable period of time within which the licensee can exercise its purchased rights for programming use. It does not delineate the period of time in which a licensee may use programming material on a continuing basis.

A broadcaster's acquisition of a license agreement to broadcast program material should be accounted for as a group of rights or privileges. The rights that have been acquired and the related obligation incurred should be reported by the licensee as an asset and liability. They may be shown at either the gross amount or the present value of the liability when the license period begins and certain other conditions are satisfied. Broadcasters may also participate in barter transactions. That is, they exchange unsold advertising time for programs, fixed assets, merchandise, travel and hotel arrangements, entertainment and other products, or services. These events should be accounted for as nonmonetary transactions and therefore their recognition and disclosure should adhere to the guidance of APB Opinion Number 29 (*Accounting for Nonmonetary Transactions*). A network affiliation agreement should be accounted for as an intangible asset and should be amortized to expense over the lesser of its useful life or 40 years.

Primary GAAP

Program License Agreements

SFAS Statement Number 63 requires that a broadcaster's acquisition of a license agreement for program material should be reported as an asset purchased and liability incurred when the license period commences and all of the following conditions have been satisfied:

1. The program material has been accepted by the licensee in accordance with the conditions of the license agreement.

2. The cost of each program constituting the program package is known or is reasonably determinable.

3. The program is available for its first showing or telecast. This condition is not met when a conflicting license prevents program broadcasting. However, any restriction under this license or another license with the same licensor regarding programming should not be construed as causing this condition to fail.

Any program license agreement which has been executed but did not meet the aforementioned three criteria and were not reported as an asset and liability should be fully disclosed in the notes to the financial statements.

GAAP requires that the license program agreement be classified as a current and noncurrent asset based on its estimated future usage. The related liability should also be dichotomously classified as current or non-current based on the future payment terms.

The amount of the recorded asset and liability that is to be reported by the licensee for a broadcast license agreement should be shown at either (1) the gross amount of the liability or (2) the present value of the liability (computed in accordance with APB Opinion Number 21 (*Interest on Receivables and Payables*). If the latter option is chosen, the difference between the gross and net liability shall be accounted for as interest (in accordance with APB 21). The use of the present value approach enumerated in (2) is used more limitedly than the gross method in (1) because APB 21 may only be used to impute interest when the liability exceeds one year and bears an unreasonable amount of interest or none at all. If the debt instrument that is generated in the broadcast license acquisition reflects a reasonable amount of interest, the present value of the debt would be equal to its gross amount and the gross presentation would be appropriate.

Cost Allocation and Amortization of Capitalized Program License Agreement

The total capitalized cost of the program license agreement should be proportionally allocated to the individual programs that compose it based on the relative value of each program to the broadcaster. These amounts are commonly specified in the program license agreement contract. Amortization of the allocated cost should then be based on the estimated number of future showings of each program. If a particular program license provides for an unlimited number of showings, as is usually the case for cartoons and related type of programming, then the amortization of the costs should take place over the period of the license agreement since the number of showings cannot be determined.

License agreements for feature programs should be amortized on a program-by-program basis. Program series and other syndicated products should be amortized as a series. Since television series license agreements commonly provide for rerun rights, the licensee must also ascertain whether the first showing of the series is more valuable to the station than its reruns. If so, then the amortization should be based on an accelerated method. If it is deemed that all showings are equally valuable, then the straight-line method may be used.

Balance Sheet Valuation of Capitalized Program License Agreement

The capitalized program license agreement should be reported on the balance sheet of the licensee at the lower of amortized cost or estimated net realizable value. Each component of the license agreement (programs, series, packages, dayparts [collection of programs broadcast during a particular time of the day, e.g., daytime, evening, late night]) should be valued separately. If the licensee's management decides that the usefulness of a program, series, package, or daypart is to be revised downward, then it may be necessary to write its amortized cost down to a lower estimated realizable value. This lower amount then becomes the new cost basis of the capitalized program license agreement. (SFAS Statement Number 121, *Accounting for the Impairment of Long-Lived Assets to be Disposed*, is not applicable to specialized industries such as the broadcast industry.) Once written down to a new cost basis, the asset cannot later be written up for a recovery in value.

Network Affiliation Agreements

A broadcaster may be affiliated with a network under a network affiliation agreement. If a station has signed such an agreement, it receives compensation for the network programming that it carries based on a pre-agreed formula. This formula is designed to compensate the station for advertising sold on a network basis that is included in network programming. Program costs for stations that have network affiliation agreements are generally lower for the station that is affiliated with a network compared to an independent station because the affiliate does not have to incur costs for network programs. These programs generally represent a major expense for television stations.

Network affiliation agreements should be classified as intangible assets. If a network affiliation agreement is terminated and is not immediately replaced or under agreement to be replaced, then any remaining unamortized capitalized cost should be charged to expense. However, if there is immediate replacement or there is an agreement for such a replacement, then a loss should be recognized equal to the excess of the unamortized cost of the terminated affiliation agreement over the fair value of the new affiliation agreement that replaced it. If, on the other hand, the fair value of the replacement agreement exceeds the unamortized cost of the terminated affiliation agreement, no gain should be recognized in the accounting record nor disclosed in the financial statements.

Barter Transactions

Broadcasters commonly exchange unsold advertising time for products or services. That is, they frequently engage in barter transactions in which no material amounts of cash exchange hands between the parties involved. All barter transactions (with the exception of trading advertising time for network programming) should be accounted for at the estimated fair value of the products or services received or advertising time given up, whichever is more clearly determinable. The accounting parameters that must be followed in these transactions may be found in APB Opinion Number 29 (*Accounting for Nonmonetary Transactions*). Barter revenue should be recognized when commercials are broadcast, and merchandise or services received should be reported when received or used. Thus, if advertising time is broadcast before the products or services are compensatorily received, then a receivable should be recorded at the same time that the advertising revenue is reported. Correspondingly, if merchandise or services are received prior to the broadcast of an advertising commercial, a liability should be recorded.

BANKING AND THRIFT INDUSTRY

Primary Sources of Authoritative GAAP

The primary sources of authoritative GAAP relating to guidance in the banking and thrift industry are

- SFAS Statement Number 72 (*Accounting for Certain Acquisitions of Banking or Thrift Institutions*)

- SFAS Statement Number 91 (*Accounting for Nonrefundable Fees and Cost Associated with Originating or Acquiring Loans and Initial Direct Costs of Leases*)

- FASB Interpretation Number 9 (*Applying APB Opinions 16 and 17 When a Savings and Loan Association or a Similar Institution is Acquired in a Business Combination Accounted for by the Purchase Method*)

GAAP Abstract and Introduction

GAAP in the banking and thrift industry emphasizes the determination of goodwill and the valuation of other assets acquired as a result of a business combination. In the acquisition of a troubled bank or thrift institution, if the fair value of the liabilities assumed exceeds the fair value of the identifiable tangible and intangible assets acquired, the excess should be recognized as a an unidentifiable intangible asset (i.e., goodwill). Goodwill recognized in this manner should be amortized to expense using the interest method over a period not to exceed a period no greater than the estimated remaining life of the long-term interest-bearing assets acquired. An accelerated amortization method of amortizing goodwill is generally used when a savings and loan association is acquired if it can be shown that (1) the goodwill was acquired as payment for the ability of existing savings and loan accounts to generate future income as well as other factors (which cannot be otherwise allocable) and (2) the economic benefits derived from these factors are expected to decline over their useful lives.

If a regulatory agency grants financial assistance to an entity that has acquired a banking or thrift institution, the financial assistance should be accounted for as part of the business combination in the period in which its receipt is probable and the amount to be received can be reasonably estimated. The financial assistance should be reported as a reduction of the goodwill that was recorded in the acquisition. Subsequent amortization of the goodwill should also be accordingly adjusted. Any financial assistance recognized in excess of the unidentifiable intangible asset should be reported as income.

Primary GAAP

Acquiring Banking and Thrift Institutions

When a banking or thrift institution (including commercial banks, savings and loan associations, mutual savings banks, credit banks, etc.) is acquired using the purchase method, each asset acquired and liability assumed is allocated a portion of the purchase price based on their fair value at the date of acquisition. That is, each item is separately valued at the date of acquisition. This technique, known as the separate valuation technique, is used to value all of the tangible and identifiable intangible assets that are acquired. In general, the difference between the fair value of the tangible and identified intangible assets acquired and liabilities assumed using this method is viewed as goodwill. However, special considerations relating to the identification and recording of intangible assets and goodwill in the banking and thrift institutions are discussed further in this section. FASB Interpretation Number 9 concluded that the net-spread method, an alternative technique for valuing and recording the acquisition of a savings and loan institution, is not appropriate and should not be used. Under the latter method, the acquisition of a banking or thrift institution is not viewed as a purchase of separate assets and liabilities. Rather, it is viewed as an acquisition of an entire business. Based on the acquired institution's spread between the rates paid on its mortgage loans and the rates paid on its savings accounts for a given market or area, determination is made on whether the acquiree's carrying amounts or fair value should be used in accounting for the acquisition. The net-spread method, however, is not allowed under GAAP.

Identified and Unidentified Intangible Assets Acquired in the Acquisition of Banking and Thrift Industries

The purchase price paid for a banking or thrift institution in a business combination may include one or more of the following identified intangible assets:

1. Capacity of existing savings accounts and loan accounts to generate future income.

2. Capacity of existing savings accounts and loan accounts to generate additional business or new business.

3. Nature of territory served.

The fair values relating to depositor and borrower relationships [i.e., described in (1) and (2) in the preceding list] should be based on estimated benefits that are expected to be derived from these associations at the time of acquisition and not to any new depositors or borrowers that might replace them at a later date. Amortization of the allocated cost should occur over the estimated lives of the existing relationships. Other intangible assets that might be identified in such a combination may include contracts and customer lists. If the amount paid for these can be determined, that amount should not be included in goodwill. The amount paid for such separately identified assets should be recorded as the cost of such intangibles and then amortized over their useful lives as well.

Unidentifiable assets such as goodwill should only be assigned to that portion of the purchase price of the acquired entity that cannot be assigned to such specifically identifiable tangible and intangible assets acquired less liabilities assumed.

In general, APB Opinion Number 17 requires that recognized goodwill be amortized using the straight-line method unless a company can demonstrate that another systematic method is more appropriate. However, the accelerated method should not be used unless the company can demonstrate that (1) although it is known that the goodwill represents amounts paid for factors such as the capacity of existing savings accounts and loan accounts to generate future income previously noted, it cannot come up with a satisfactory basis for assigning dollar values to those individual factors; and (2) the benefits that are expected to derived from the aforementioned factors are expected to decline over their useful lives. Only if both (1) and (2) exist can an accelerated method be utilized. When a portion of the financial institution that has been acquired is sold or liquidated, the portion of unamortized goodwill relating to the goodwill is considered part of the cost of the assets that are sold. If the entire entity is sold, then all of remaining goodwill is considered part of the asset's cost.

If, in a given acquisition of a troubled banking or thrift institution, the excess of the fair value of liabilities assumed exceeds the fair value of tangible and identified intangible assets acquired, the excess constitutes an unidentifiable intangible asset (i.e., another source of goodwill). The goodwill acquired in this manner should be amortized to expense over a period no greater than the estimated remaining life of the long-term interest-bearing assets acquired. Amortization should be computed on the carrying amount of the interest-bearing assets expected to be outstanding at the beginning of each subsequent period.If the assets acquired in the acquisition do not include a significant amount of long-term interest-bearing assets, the goodwill should be amortized over a period not to exceed the estimated average remaining life of the existing customer deposit base acquired. Regardless of the guideline applicable, the amortization term should not exceed 40 years, as required by APB Opinion Number 17.

Considerations Related to Regulatory Financial Assistance Provided in the Acquisition of a Bank or Thrift Institution

A regulatory agency may grant financial assistance in the course of an entity acquiring a particular bank or thrift institution. For example, a regulatory agency may agree to pay the extent (the amount) by which future interest received or receivable on the interest-bearing assets acquired is less than the interest cost of carrying those assets for a period by a stated margin.

The projected assistance (computed at the date of acquisition) should be considered additional interest on the interest-bearing assets acquired in determining their fair values for the purpose of applying the purchase method in accounting for the combination. Actual assistance should be reported as income in the period in which it accrues.

Other forms of assistance may also be granted to either party by a regulatory authority in a combination accounted for by the purchase method. If (1) the assistance is probable and (2) the amount that is expected to be received is reasonably estimatable, then the assistance should be accounted for as part of the combination. If either of these two criteria were not met, then any assistance subsequently recognized in the financial statements should be reported as a reduction of the unidentifiable intangible asset (i.e., goodwill previously described). Subsequent amortization of the goodwill should also be adjusted. Any assistance recognized in excess of that intangible assets should be reported as income of the period. In general, any assets and liabilities that have been or will be transferred to or assumed by a regulatory authority should not be recognized in the acquisition.

When financial assistance is granted in connection with the acquisition of a banking or thrift institution,the combined entity may agree to repay all or a part of the assistance that was provided if certain levels of operations are met. Such a repayment obligation should be met by recognizing a liability and charge to income when the repayment contingency is probable and the amount of repayment can be reasonably estimated.

The nature and amount of any financial assistance which was granted to an entity during a given period by a regulatory agency in connection with the acquisition of a bank or thrift institution should be fully disclosed.

Savings and Loan Association's Bad Debts Reserves

Governmental regulatory bodies require that savings and loan associations allocate part of their earnings to general reserves as a means of protecting depositors against the possibility of loss. In addition, the IRS allows these entities to deduct an amount as a reserve for bad debts in determining taxable income. This amount is generally different from the amount that is deducted on the income statement in determining pretax financial income (i.e., under GAAP for financial accounting purposes). Therefore, as would be assumed, taxable income and pretax financial income will differ. Under GAAP, a savings and loan association is precluded from providing deferred taxes on the difference between taxable income and pretax accounting income attributable to its bad debts reserve that arose in tax years beginning December 31, 1997. However, if circumstances indicate that an association is likely to pay income taxes, either currently or in later years (because of known or expected reductions in the bad debts reserve), income taxes attributable to that reduction should be accrued as tax expense for the current period. The income tax expense that is accrued in this manner should not be accounted for as an extraordinary item.

Specialized Disclosure Requirements

Banks, savings institutions, and credit unions are not required to report the gross amounts of cash receipts and cash payments for the following:

1. Deposits placed with other financial institutions and withdrawals of deposits.
2. Loans made to customers and principal collections of loans.
3. Time deposits accepted and repayments of deposits.

When a banking or thrift association is part of a consolidated entity, net amounts of cash receipts and cash payments for deposit and lending activities of these entities should be reported separately from the gross amounts of cash receipts and payments for the other investing and financing activities of the consolidated entity. That is, the net amounts of cash receipts and payments of the bank, savings institutions, and credit unions should be reported separately from the gross cash receipts and payments of the consolidated enterprise.

Supplemental GAAP Guidance: Emerging Issues Task Force Issues Relating to the Banking and Thrift Industries

The following are the titles of supplemental guidance issued by the Emerging Issue Task Force relating to topics of the banking and thrift industries:

- Issue Number 84–9 (*Deposit Loan of Banks*)
- Issue Number 84–19 (*Mortgage Loan Payment Modifications*)
- Issue Number 84–21 (*Sale of a Loan with a Partial Participation Retained*)
- Issue Number 84–22 (*Prior Years' Earnings Per Share Following a Savings and Loan Association Conversion and Pooling*)
- Issue Number 84–31 (*Equity Certificates of Deposits*)
- Issue Number 85–3 (*Tax Benefits Relating to Asset Dispositions Following an Acquisition of a Financial Institution*)
- Issue Number 85–8 (*Amortization of Thrift Intangibles*)
- Issue Number 85–33 (*Disallowance of Income Tax Deduction for Core Deposit Intangibles*)
- Issue Number 85–41 (*Accounting for Savings and Loan Association Under FSLIC Management Consignment Program*)
- Issue Number 85–42 (*Amortization of Goodwill Resulting from Recording Time Savings Deposits at Fair Values*)
- Issue Number 85–44 (*Differences between Loan Loss Allowances for GAAP and RAP*)
- Issue Number 86–31 (*Reporting the Tax Implications of a Pooling of a Bank and a Savings and Loan Association*)
- Issue Number 87–22 (*Prepayment to the Secondary Reserve of the FSLIC*)
- Issue Number 88–17 (*Accounting for Fees and Costs Associated with Loan Syndications and Loan Participation*)
- Issue Number 88–19 (*FSLIC—Assisted Acquisitions of Thrift*)

- Issue Number 88–20 (*Difference Between Initial Investment and Principal Amount of Loans in a Purchased Credit Card Portfolio*)

- Issue Number 88–22 (*Securitization of Credit Card Portfolio*)

- Issue Number 88–25 (*Ongoing Accounting and Reporting for a Newly Created Liquidating Bank*)

- Issue Number 89–3 (*Balance Sheet Presentation of Savings Accounts in Financial Statement of Credit Unions*)

- Issue Number 90–11 (*Accounting for Exit and Entrance Fees Incurred in a Conversion from the Savings and Association Insurance Fund to the Bank Insurance Fund*)

- Issue Number 90–18 (*Effect of a "Removal of Accounts" Provision on the Accounting for a Credit Card Securitization*)

- Issue Number 92–5 (*Amortization Period for Net Deferred Credit Card Origination Costs*)

- Issue Number 92–10 (*Loan Acquisitions Involving Table Funding Arrangements*)

- Issue Number 94–9 (*Determining a Normal Servicing Fee Rate for the Sale of an SBA Loan*)

CABLE TELEVISION

Primary Sources of Authoritative GAAP

The primary sources of authoritative GAAP relating to guidance in the cable television industry are

- SFAS Statement Number 51 (*Financial Reporting by Cable Television Companies*)

- SFAS Statement Number 121 (*Accounting for the Impairment of Long-Lived Assets and for Long-Lived Assets to be Disposed Of*)

GAAP Abstract and Introduction

SFAS Statement Number 51 presents the standards of financial reporting and disclosure for certain revenues and expenses related to cable television systems. The emphasis of the SFAS is on special accounting rules applicable to the prematurity period. During this period a cablevision television system is partly in use and partly under construction. The prematurity period generally begins with the first earned subscriber revenue and ends when the first major construction period has been completed or the achievement of a specified predetermined subscriber level has been reached. Prematurity status is very common in this industry. For example, over time it is usual for cable companies to expand throughout the geographical area that they have franchised. For large- and medium-size entities this effort results in many parts of their system being "energized" while construction progresses in others. Thus, except for the smallest systems, programming is delivered to parts of the area being serviced (with revenues being earned)before construction of the entire system is complete. Thus, virtually every medium- and large-size franchise cable television system experiences a prematurity period during which it receives some revenue while continuing to incur substantial costs related to its completion. During the prematurity period, costs incurred that relate to both current and future operations shall be partially capitalized and partially expensed.

Primary GAAP

Establishment of the Prematurity Period

Before revenue is earned from the first subscriber, the management of a cable television entity should establish the beginning and end of the prematurity period. By definition, the prematurity period begins with the first earned subscriber revenue. Its end will vary with the circumstances of the system but will be determined based on plans for completion of the system's first major construction period. The end of the prematurity period can also be based on the achievement of a specified predetermined subscriber level at which no additional investment will be required for other than cable television plants. Under GAAP, there is a presumption that the prematurity period will not exceed two years. A longer period is justified only in major urban markets. After its establishment, a premature period should not be changed except under highly unusual circumstances. The part of the cable television system that is in the prematurity period should be accounted for separately from the rest of the system and should be clearly distinguished from it. The portion that is in the prematurity period should have most of the following characteristics:

1. It should be in a geographically different area or different franchise area.

2. It should have mechanical differences, such as different equipment and facilities. For example, it might have separate equipment used to receive the signals of distant television or radio stations whether directly from a transmitter or from a microwave relay system. Equipment used to receive television and radio signals, called head-end, may also include separate studio facilities required for operator-originated programming, if such activities take place in this portion of the cable television system.

3. There should be timing differences. For example, its construction or marketing should start at dates significantly different from the other portions of the system.

4. There should be investment decision differences. The portion of the cable television system that is in the prematurity period should have different breakeven and return-on-investment analyses or different construction start approvals.

5. It should have separate accounting records, separate budgets and forecasts, or other accountability differences.

Accounting for Costs during the Prematurity Period

In general, costs incurred by the system should be charged to the portion of the cable television system in the prematurity period only if they are specifically identified with the operations of that portion. Separate projections for the portion shall be developed, and the portion's capitalized costs should be evaluated separately during the prematurity period for recoverability. Other guidance related to accounting in the prematurity period includes the following:

1. Subscriber-related costs and general and administrative expenses shall be expensed as period costs. Subscriber-related costs are those costs incurred to obtaining and retaining subscribers to the cable television system. They include

   (a) cost of billing and collection

   (b) bad debts

   (c) mailings

   (d) repairs and maintenance of subscriber connections

   (e) franchise fees related to revenue or the number of subscribers

   (f) salary of the system manager and office rent

   (g) programming cost for additional channels used in the marketing effort or costs related to revenues from, or the number of subscribers to, channels or program services

   (h) direct selling costs

2. Costs of the cable television plant should be capitalized in full. These include materials, direct labor, and construction overhead.

3. Programming and other systems costs that are incurred in anticipation of servicing a fully operating system should be allocated between current and future operations. These costs do not change based on the number of subscribers. They include such items as property taxes based on valuation of the cable entity as a fully operating system; pole, underground duct, antenna site, and microwave rental based on rental costs for a fully operating system; and local origination programming to satisfy franchise requirements.

The proportion attributable to current operations shall be expensed currently, and the remainder of the expenditures should be capitalized. The amount that should be expensed in the current period is derived by multiplying the total expenditures for the month by the following fraction:

	The greatest of
	(**a**) the average number of subscribers expected that month as estimated at the beginning of the prematurity period
	(**b**) the average number of subscribers that would be attained using at least equal (straight-line) monthly progress in adding new subscribers towards the estimate of subscribers that would be attained at the end of the prematurity period
Amount to be expensed = currently	(**c**) the average number of actual subscribers ———divided by the——— Total number of subscribers that are expected at the end of the prematurity period

The preceding fraction should be determined each month of the prematurity period.

In addition, depreciation and amortization expense should be determined by multiplying the monthly depreciation and amortization based on total capitalized costs expected on completion of the prematurity period by the aforementioned fraction using the depreciation that will be applied by the entity after the prematurity period.

Capitalization of Interest Costs during the Prematurity Period

The interest costs that should be capitalized during the prematurity period should be done in accordance with SFAS Statement Number 34 (*Capitalization of Interest Costs*). SFAS 34 requires that the interest costs that should be capitalized should be determined by multiplying an interest capitalization rate to the average amount of qualifying assets for the system during the period. During the prematurity period, a portion of the system is in use in the earnings activity of the enterprise and therefore is not eligible for interest capitalization. In addition, interest should not be capitalized on phases of the project that are complete and ready for service. In total, the amount of interest cost that is capitalized should not exceed the total amount of interest cost incurred by the total cablevision system for the period.

Recognition of Hookup Revenue and Amortization of Capitalized Costs

Hookup revenue should be recognized as revenue to the extent of the direct selling costs incurred. Direct selling costs include

1. Commissions.
2. The portion of a salesperson's compensation other than commissions for obtaining new subscribers.
3. Local advertising targeted for acquisition of new subscribers.
4. Costs of processing documents related to new subscribers acquired.

Direct selling costs do not include supervisory and administrative expenses or indirect expenses such as rent and costs of facilities.

Subscriber installation costs, including material, labor, and overhead costs, should be capitalized and depreciated over a period no longer than the depreciation period used for the cable television plant. Costs of subsequently disconnecting and reconnecting should be charged to expense of the current period.

The cost of a successful franchise application should be capitalized and subsequently amortized over its useful life or the life of the franchise, whichever is shorter. However, APB Opinion Number 17 requires that this period not exceed 40 years. Costs of unsuccessful franchise applications and abandoned franchises should be expensed.

Recoverability of Capitalized Assets

The carrying amounts of the capitalized assets and identifiable intangible assets are subject to the requirement of SFAS Statement Number 121 (*Accounting for the Impairment of Long-Lived Assets and for Long-Lived Assets to be Disposed Of*). Even if it is determinable that the entity's capitalized costs are not recoverable, capitalization of costs should not cease. Instead, the provision required to reduce capitalized costs to their recoverable value should also be increased.

COMPUTER SOFTWARE DEVELOPMENT

Computer Software to be Sold, Leased, or Otherwise Marketed

Primary Sources of Authoritative GAAP

The primary sources of authoritative GAAP relating to guidance in computer software to be sold; leased, or otherwise marketed are:

- SFAS Statement Number 2 (*Accounting for Research and Development Costs*)

- SFAS Statement Number 86 (*Accounting for the Costs of Computer Software to Be Sold, Leased, or Otherwise Marketed*)

GAAP Abstract and Introduction

GAAP in the area of computer software to be sold, leased, or otherwise marketed relates to computer software that is developed internally and to software that is purchased. In creating a computer software product, costs incurred internally should be expensed when incurred to research and development costs until technological feasibility for the product has been established. Technological feasibility is deemed established when a detailed program design or working model for the product is completed. Thereafter, all software production costs should be capitalized and amortized to current and future periods. In computing amortization expense, companies are required to use the greater of the ratio of current revenues to current and anticipated revenues or the amount derived through straight-line amortization computed over the remaining estimated economic life of the computer product. With respect to financial statement disclosure, computer software costs should be reported in the financial statements at the lower of amortized cost or net realizable value.

Primary GAAP

SFAS Statement Number 86 discusses the accounting for the costs of computer software to be sold, leased, or otherwise marketed as a separate product or as part of a product or process. It applies to computer software developed internally and to purchased software. It does not address the accounting and reporting of cost incurred for computer software created for the internal use of an entity or for the development of software for others under a contractual arrangement.

Research and Development Costs

All costs incurred in establishing the technological feasibility of a computer software product to be sold, leased, or otherwise marketed should be charged to research and development expense when incurred. A computer software product's technological feasibility is established when the developing entity has performed all planning, designing, coding, and test activities that are required to meet its design specifications. Such specifications generally include the product's technical performance, functions, and features. Coding refers to generating the software product's detailed instructions in computer language. These make the computer perform all that has been called for in the detailed program design. Testing refers to performing the steps necessary to ensure that the coded computer software is doing what it was designed to do.

At a minimum, the entity developing the software product must perform the following activities before evidence is provided that technological feasibility has been achieved. These activities are dicotomized into two categories based on whether or not a detailed program design has been created. A detail program design is a blueprint of a computer product's function, features, and technological requirements derived to the their most detailed, logical form.

1. If the software product development process includes a detail program design, then

   (a) The product design and detail program design must be completed and the entity developing the software has established that the necessary skills, hardware, and software technology are available to it to produce the product. The product design is a logical enumeration of all the product functions and serves as the product specifications.

   (b) The consistency between the product design and detail program design and the completeness of the latter has been confirmed by documenting and tracing the detail program design to the product specifications found in the product design.

   (c) The detail program design has been reviewed for what are termed high-risk development issues. These include such items as novel, unique, or unproven functions and features, technological innovations, etc. Assurance has been derived that any uncertainties related to these issues have been resolved through coding and testing.

2. If the software product development process does not have a detail program design, then

   (a) A product design and working model must be completed. A working model is an operative version of the computer software product that will be marketed. It is written in the same software language as the computer software product and performs all the functions planned for the product.

   (b) The completeness of the working model and its consistency with the product design have been confirmed by testing.

Capitalization of Computer Software Subsequent to the Establishment of Technological Feasibility

Product master production cost incurred subsequent to the establishment of technological feasibility should be capitalized. These costs generally include the performance of coding and testing. SFAS Statement Number 86 indicates that no software production costs shall be capitalized until technological feasibility has been established for the software and all R&D activities for the other components of the product or process have been completed. The capitalization process should be discontinued when the product is ready and available for general release to customers.

Maintenance and customer support costs should be charged to expense when these costs are incurred or the related revenue is recognized from the product's sale. When the sales price of a computer software product includes customer support for several periods and the price of that support is not separately stated, the estimated cost of the customer support should accrued in the same period that the sales revenue is recognized.

Purchased Computer Software with No Alternative Future Uses

The cost of purchased computer software that is to be sold, leased, or otherwise marketed and that has no alternative future uses should be charged to expense in the period incurred like R&D expenditures. If, on the other hand, the purchased software has alternative future uses, then it should be capitalized and amortized based on its future expected application.

Amortization of Capitalized Software Costs

Capitalized software computer costs should be amortized on a product-by-product basis. SFAS Statement Number 86 requires that the annual amortization that is recognized should be based on the greater of the following two computations after the product is available for general release to customers:

1. Result derived by computing the ratio of current gross revenues of the product to its current and anticipated gross revenues.

2. The straight-line method taken over the remaining estimated economic life of the product, including the period being reported on.

Duplication Costs Charged to Inventory

All costs incurred in duplicating the computer software and related materials (documentation, training materials, etc.) from the product masters as well as the physical packaging needed for its distribution should be recorded as inventory on a unit-specific basis. When the sale of the unit is recognized, then the cost of the inventory should also be recognized and charged to the cost of sales. If the unit is unsold, its costs remains as unsold inventory.

End of Period Evaluation and Disclosure on the Financial Statements

At each balance date, the unamortized capitalized costs of the computer software product should be compared to its net realizable value. Any excess of the unamortized capitalized computer product over its net realizable value should be written off. The amount of the writeoff should not be subsequently restored. In addition, the remaining unamortized capitalized computer software costs at the close of the entity's annual fiscal period then become its new cost for subsequent accounting periods.

SFAS Statement Number 86 requires that the following disclosure requirements be satisfied relating to computer software costs each period:

1. Unamortized computer software costs should be included in each balance sheet presented.

2. The total amount that was charged to expense should be disclosed in each income statement presented (e.g., amortization of capitalized computer software costs as well as the amounts that were written off in bringing the amortized costs down to their net realizable values).

ACCOUNTING FOR THE COSTS OF COMPUTER DEVELOPED OR OBTAINED FOR INTERNAL USE

Authoritative Guidance

- SOP 98-1—*Accounting for the Costs of Computer Software Developed or Obtained for Internal Use*[1]

- SFAS 2—*Accounting for Research and Development Costs*

Abstract and Introduction

Accounting guidance in the area of computer software developed or obtained for internal use is primarily provided by SOP 98-1, *Accounting for the Costs of Computer Software Developed or Obtained for Internal Use.* This statement outlines the steps that must be followed in accounting for software that has been acquired, internally developed or modified for the specific purpose of meeting an entity's internal needs. Throughout the software development process, it is assumed that the entity has no plan or no plan is being developed to market the software externally.

      The statement discusses three stages of computer software development that are applicable. These are: the preliminary project stage; the application development stage; and the post-implementation/operation stage. During the preliminary project stage and post-implementation/operation stage, costs incurred are to be expensed in the period they are incurred. During the application development stage, costs incurred should be capitalized.

---

[1]Statements of Position are publications of the AICPA's Accounting Standards Executive Committee (AcSEC). Under Statement on Auditing Standards No. 69, *The Meaning of "Present Fairly in Conformity with Generally Accepted Accounting Principles" in the Independent Auditors Report,* Statements of Position are not construed as Generally Accepted Accounting Principles covered by Rule 203 of the AICPA's Code of Professional Ethics.

Authoritative Guidance

Statement of Position 98-1 discusses the parameters of accounting for the costs of computer software developed or obtained for internal use. Internal use software is software that was acquired or internally developed to meet an entity's internal needs rather than for external marketing purposes. In general, any internally used computer software that was utilized in the research and development activities of an entity should be accounted for in conjunction with SFAS No. 2, *Accounting for Research and Development Costs.*

SOP 98-1 establishes three stages of computer software development for internal use. These include: (1) The preliminary project stage; (2) The application/development stage; and (3) The post-implementation/operation stage. The following is a brief discussion of each of the aforementioned categories.

Preliminary Project Stage—During this stage, the entity is in the midst of evaluating alternatives regarding the software project and hasn't yet determined which strategy to use nor which vendor will be chosen. Activities that occur during this stage include assembling the evaluation team, evaluating proposals from vendors, and determining the viability of other related reengineering needs. All costs incurred during this period should be expensed as incurred.

Application Development Stage—This stage commences when management decides how the internal software development work will be performed. From this chronological point, all costs incurred to develop or obtain computer software for internal use is required to be capitalized and treated as a long-lived asset. Capitalization should begin when the following occur:

- The Preliminary Project Stage has been completed, and

- Management commits to funding a computer software project. It is believed that the completion of this project is probable and that it will be used to perform its intended function.

The capitalization of costs should terminate when the software is complete and ready for use. Typical costs that should be capitalized include: Any direct material and/or services contributing to the project, payroll costs, any interest costs that were incurred during the development process, and testing and installation software costs. (Note: General and administrative costs, training, and overhead should not be capitalized as costs of the computer software.)

Post-Implementation/Operation Stage—This stage commences once the internal use software is put into use. In addition, the costs that have been capitalized should be amortized over the period that is expected to be benefitted. In general, capitalized cost should be amortized on a straight-line basis over the estimated useful life of the internally-used software. The estimated useful life of this software is commonly short and should be frequently reassessed considering the obsolescence, competition, and other factors.

It is possible for a company to decide to subsequently market the computer software that it developed for internal use. If this occurs, then the entity should not recognize any profit until the aggregate proceeds from the sales of the software exceeds its carrying amount. All subsequent proceeds received should be recognized as being earned.

FRANCHISING: ACCOUNTING BY FRANCHISORS

Primary Sources of Authoritative GAAP

The primary source of authoritative GAAP relating to guidance in accounting by franchisors is

- SFAS Statement Number 45 (*Accounting for Franchise Fee Revenue*)

GAAP Abstract and Introduction

A franchise is a written business agreement in which a franchisor, for a specified period and delineated geographical area, allows a franchisee to use certain tradenames and trademarks, sell certain products, perform certain services, etc., for which the franchisor has exclusive legal rights. The franchisor is the entity that grants the rights under the franchise contract to the franchisee, who then operates the franchised business and, in turn, compensates the franchisor for the privilege. SFAS Statement Number 45 discusses the accounting and reporting requirements from the perspective of the franchisor. Individual and area franchise sales should be recognized as franchise fee revenue when all material services or conditions related to the sale have been substantially performed and satisfied by the franchisor. Other areas of the standard for which guidance is rendered are contractual arrangements between franchisor and franchisee, allocation of initial franchise fee, continuing franchise fees, product sales made to franchisee on a continuing basis, agency sales, franchising costs, repossessed franchises, business combinations, and required disclosures.

Initial Individual Franchise Sales

Franchise fee revenue from individual franchise sales should be recognized when the franchisor has substantially performed and satisfied all material services or conditions relating to the sale. SFAS Statement Number 45 indicates that *substantial performance on the part of the franchisor* means

1. There is no obligation or intent to refund any cash received or forgive any unpaid notes or receivables.

2. All initial services that the franchisor was contractually required to do by the signed franchise agreement have been completed.

3. No significant responsibilities related to substantial performance by the franchisor remain.

In addition, a provision for estimated uncollectible initial franchise fees should be recorded to ensure a proper matching of revenues and costs. In exceptional cases, when franchise fee revenue is collected over an extended period and no reasonable basis exists for estimating collectibility, it may be necessary to use the installment or cost recovery methods to account for revenue recognition.

Unless there are unusual circumstances, substantial performance cannot take place before the franchisee starts his or her operation. Often, a franchise agreement calls for a large initial franchise fee and relatively small continuing franchise fees providing for future services that the franchisor agrees to perform throughout the term of the franchise agreement. If it is determined that the continuing fee will not cover the cost of the continuing services performed by the franchisor as well as earning a reasonable profit, then a portion of the initial franchise fee should be deferred and subsequently amortized over the life of the franchise. That is, the portion of the initial franchise fee that is deferred should be sufficient to cover the estimated cost in excess of continuing franchise fees and the earning of a reasonable profit on the continuing services themselves.

Area Franchise Sales

An area franchise is an agreement that transfers franchise rights within a geographical area, permitting the opening of a number of franchised outlets. A franchisor may sell an area franchise to a franchisee, who may decide to operate the franchised outlets, or the franchisor may sell an area franchise to an intermediary franchisee, who then may decide to sell the individual franchises to other franchisees who will operate the outlets.

Sometimes the cost and efforts relating to the initial services performed by the franchisor are not affected by the number of outlets opened in an area, and therefore the area franchise sale is very similar to an individual franchise sale. In that situation, any initial franchise fees relating to area franchise sales should be accounted for in the same manner as individual franchise sales, and substantial performance on the part of the franchisor should be evaluated using the same parameters.

However, when the efforts and total cost related to the initial services are materially affected by the number of outlets opened in an area, it may be necessary to view the area franchise agreement differently. In this circumstance, an area franchise agreement should be viewed as a divisible contract, and area franchise fees should be recognized in proportion to the number of outlets opened. For example, the more the outlets that are opened, the proportionally greater part of the area franchise fee should be recognized (assuming substantial performance has taken place). This may require an estimate on the part of the franchisor regarding the expected number of outlets guided by, perhaps, the minimum or maximum outlets indicated in the franchise contract. Any change in estimate resulting from a change in circumstance should result in recognizing the remaining fees as revenues in proportion to the remaining services that have yet to be performed.

Contractual Arrangements between Franchisor and Franchisee

A franchisor and franchisee may have several contractual business relationships outstanding at any given point in time. For example, a franchisor may have guaranteed the borrowings of a franchisee, have a creditor interest in the franchisee, or control a franchisee's operations by sales or other agreements. The extent of these associations may effectively make the franchisee an affiliate of the franchisor. This relationship (between franchisor and franchisee) does not change the GAAP requirement that revenue should not be recognized if all material services, conditions, or obligations relating to the sale have not been substantially performed or satisfied.

A franchisor may have an option (delineated in the franchise agreement) to purchase a franchisee's business. A franchisor may choose to repurchase a franchise business because it is profitable or because it is having financial difficulties or other problems that may tarnish the reputation and goodwill of the entire franchise system. If such an option exists, the likelihood of the franchisor's acquiring the franchised business should be considered in accounting for the initial franchise fee. If it is probable that the franchisor will eventually repurchase the franchise, the initial fee must be deferred and considered as a reduction of the repurchase price when the option is exercised.

Allocation of Initial Franchise Fee

A franchise agreement commonly establishes an initial franchise fee that is to be paid to a franchisor for the franchise rights and services that are to be performed by the franchisor. However, that fee may also include the sale of such tangible property as franchise signs, equipment, inventory, land, and buildings. In this situation, a portion of the fee related to the sale of the tangible assets based on their fair market value may be recognized before or after recognizing the portion applicable to the initial services. For example, a franchisor may recognize a portion of the fee related to the sale of specific tangible assets when their title passes although the balance of the fee relating to services would be recognized as revenue when those services have been substantially performed or satisfied.

A franchise agreement may specify that certain portions of the franchise fee relate to specific services that the franchisor will provide the franchisee. If, however, the services that the franchisor will provide are interrelated to such an extent that the amount that applies to each service cannot be objectively segregated, then the revenue for a specific purpose should not be recognized until all services noted by the franchise agreement are substantially performed. If, on the other hand, transaction prices for the services are available, then a part of the revenue may be recognized when that service is performed.

Continuing Franchise Fees

A franchisee may be contractually required to pay continuing franchise fees to a franchisor for the continued use of the franchised rights as well as for services performed by the franchisor. These fees should be reported by the franchisor as revenue as the fees are earned and become a receivable to the franchisor. In addition, any costs incurred by the franchisor related to the franchise fees should be expensed as incurred. The earnings process must be honored even though a portion of the continuing fee is designated for a particular purpose, such as an advertising program. It should not be recognized as revenue until the fee is earned and becomes receivable from the franchisee. An exception exists when a franchise arrangement is an agency arrangement under which a portion of the continuing fee is required to be segregated and used for a special purpose. In this situation, the segregated amount should be recorded as a liability by the franchisor against which costs incurred by the franchisee would be charged.

Product Sales Made to Franchisee on a Continuing Basis

In the course of franchisee operations, the franchisee may purchase some or all of its supplies and equipment from the franchisor. As part of this arrangement, the franchisee may be given the right to purchase these items at a bargain price. If this price is lower than the selling price of the product to other customers or the price that is paid does not generate a reasonable profit on the equipment or supplies, then a portion of the initial franchise fee should be deferred and accounted for as an adjustment of the selling price when the equipment or supplies are purchased. The portion that should be deferred should be one of the following:

1. The difference between the selling price of the equipment or products and the bargain purchase price that the franchisee is receiving.

2. An amount that would cover any cost in excess of the bargain purchase price and provide a reasonable profit to the franchisor.

Agency Sales

Some franchisors may act as an agent for franchisees by placing orders for inventory and equipment and selling them to franchisees at no profit. Franchisors involved in such transactions should account for these transactions as receivables and payables and not as revenues and expenses.

Franchising Costs

Direct costs relating to franchise sales should be recognized in the same accounting period as the revenue that they helped generate. If revenue is not yet recognized, costs incurred should be deferred until the revenue is recognized. However, deferred costs shall not exceed anticipated revenue less estimated additional estimated costs. Indirect costs of a regular and recurring nature that are incurred independent of the level of sales, such as general, administrative, and selling costs, should be expensed as incurred.

Repossessed Franchises

If a franchisee decides not to open a franchise business, then a franchisor may recover the franchise rights through repossession. If repossession occurs, then two possible outcomes may occur. The franchisor may decide to (1) refund the money received from the franchisee or (2) not refund the money. A description of these contingencies follow:

1. *A refund is made.* If the franchisor refunds the franchisee's money, then the original sale is canceled and the revenue previously recognized is accounted for as a reduction in revenue in the period in which the franchise is repossessed.

2. *No refund is made.* If the franchisor does not refund the franchisee's money, then:

   (a) The transaction should be regarded as a canceled sale.

   (b) No adjustment should be made to any previously recognized revenue.

   (c) Any uncollectible amounts resulting from receivables that have not been paid should be accounted for and a provision for bad debts should be provided for.

   (d) Any money that was previously received and accounted for as deferred revenue should now be recognized as earned revenue.

Business Combinations

If a franchisor acquires an operating business from a franchisee, it should be accounted for as a business combination in accordances with APB Opinion Number 16 (*Business Combinations*). Accounting for the transaction is predicated on whether the combination was accounted for as a pooling or purchase.

1. *Accounted for as a pooling* If the business combination is accounted for as a pooling of interests, then the financial statements of the two

entities are considered to be retroactively combined and the original franchise sales transaction as well as any product sales should be removed from present and prior years' combined financial statements.

2. *Accounted for as a purchase* If the business combination was accounted for as a purchase, the financial statements of the two entities are not considered to be retroactively combined and the revenue that was recorded relating to the franchise prior to the date of purchase should not be adjusted. The two entities are only considered to be combined as of the date of purchase of the franchisee's operation. If, on the other hand, the acquisition of the franchisee's operation is, in substance, a cancellation of the original franchise sale, then the transaction should be considered a franchise repossession and should be accounted for as such (see prior section on repossessed franchises).

Required Disclosures

SFAS Statement Number 45 requires that the following information be disclosed in the body of the franchisor's financial statements or notes:

■ The nature of all significant commitments and obligations resulting from the franchise agreement, including a description of the services that the franchisor has agreed to provide that has not yet been substantially performed.

■ If no basis exists for estimating the collectibility of specific franchise fees, then the notes to the financial statements should disclose the following:

1. Whether the installment or cost recovery method is being used to account for the related franchise fee revenue

2. The sales price of the franchise

3. Revenue and related costs deferred both currently and on a cumulative basis

4. The periods in which the franchise fees become payable by the franchisee

5. Amounts that were originally deferred but later recognized because the uncertainty relating to the franchise fee's collectibility was resolved

- If material, initial franchise fees should be separated from other franchise revenue.

- Predictable decline in future initial franchise fee revenues because sales have reached a saturation point. (This disclosure is desirable but not required.)

- Separate disclosure of the amount of initial franchise fees relative to the amount of net income when such amounts are not apparent. (This disclosure is desirable but not required.)

- Revenue and costs related to franchisor related businesses should be shown separately from those related to franchisee related businesses when practicable.

- If there are significant changes in the ownership of franchisor-owned outlets or franchised outlets during the period, the following should be disclosed:

  1. Number of franchises sold
  2. Number of franchises purchased during the period
  3. Number of franchised outlets in operation during the fiscal year
  4. Number of franchisor-owned outlets in operation during the fiscal year

INSURANCE INDUSTRY

Primary Sources of Authoritative GAAP

The primary sources of authoritative GAAP relating to guidance in the Insurance Industry are

- SFAS Statement Number 5 (*Accounting for Contingencies*)

- SFAS Statement Number 60 (*Accounting and Reporting by Insurance Companies*)

- SFAS Statement Number 91 (*Accounting for Nonrefundable Fees and Costs Associated with Originating or Acquiring Loans and Initial Direct Costs of Leases*)

- SFAS Statement Number 97 (*Accounting and Reporting by Insurance Enterprises for Certain Long-Duration Contracts and for Realized Gains and Losses from the Sale of Investments*)

- SFAS Statement Number 109 (*Accounting for Income Taxes*)

- SFAS Statement Number 113 (*Accounting and Reporting for Reinsurance of Short-Duration and Long-Duration Contracts*)

- SFAS Statement Number 114 (*Accounting by Creditors for Impairment of a Loan*)

- SFAS Statement Number 115 (*Accounting for Certain Investments in Debt and Equity Securities*)

- SFAS Statement Number 120 (*Accounting and Reporting by Mutual Life Insurance Enterprises and by Insurance Enterprises for Certain Long-Duration Participating Contacts*)

- SFAS Statement Number 121 (*Accounting for the Impairment of Long-Lived Assets and for Long-Lived Assets to be Disposed Of*)

- SFAS Statement Number 124 (*Accounting for Certain Investments Held by Not-for-Profit Organizations*)

- SFAS Statement Number 125 (*Accounting for Transfers and Servicing of Financial Assets and Extinguishments of Liabilities*)

- FASB Interpretation Number 40 (*Applicability of Generally Accepted Accounting Principles to Mutual Life Insurance and other Enterprises*)

GAAP Abstract and Introduction

Insurance is purchased to provide economic protection from identified risks occurring within a specified period. Types of risks usually covered by insurance include death, damage, injury to others, and business interruption. Insurance contracts may be classified either as short-duration or long-duration contracts. Long-duration insurance contracts include those that are expected to remain in force for an extended period, such as whole life, universal life, guaranteed renewable term life, endowment, annuity, title insurance, and participating life insurance contracts. Long-duration contracts with terms that are not fixed and guaranteed are called universal-life-type contracts. All other insurance are considered short-duration contracts. Short-duration contracts consist mainly of most property and liability contracts.

Insurance contracts that do not involve the assumption of significant insurance risks by the insurance company are referred to as investment contracts and are not accounted for as insurance. Instead, they are accounted for as an interest-bearing financial instrument.

Short-term duration contract premiums are recognized as revenue evenly as insurance protection is provided. Claim costs (including estimates of costs for claims relating to events that have occurred but have not been reported to the insurer) are recognized when the insured event occurs. Premiums from long-duration contracts other than universal-life-type contracts are recognized as revenue when they are due from policy holders over the premium paying periods. Universal insurance contracts differ from other long-duration contracts in the flexibility that they provide to one or both of the parties to the contract. Amounts that the insurance company assesses against policy holders for contract services, other than premiums, should be reported as revenue.

Costs that are incurred related to the acquisition of insurance contracts other than universal-life-type contracts are capitalized and charged to expense in proportion to premium revenue recognized. Acquisition costs related to universal-life-type contracts are capitalized and amortized in proportion to the gross profit amounts that are derived from the operations of these contracts.

Insurance companies that reinsure insurance contracts should account for their reinsurance receivables and prepaid reinsurance premiums as assets. Guidelines for the accounting and reporting standards used in recording and disclosing these types of transactions are fully described.

In general, insurance transactions are characterized by the following two situations:

1. The purchaser of an insurance contract makes an initial payment or deposit to the insurance company in advance of the possible occurrence.

2. When the insurance contract is consummated, the insurance company does not know if, how much, or when amounts will be payable to the insured.

These two classifications reflect the nature of the insurance company's obligation and the policy holder's rights under the insurance contract.

Primary GAAP

Classification of Insurance Contracts

In general, insurance contracts are classified as short-duration or long-duration. SFAS Statement Number 60 discusses each category in the following way:

- *Short-duration contracts*   Most property and liability insurance contracts are considered short duration. These contracts cover expected claim costs resulting from insured events that occur during a fixed period of short duration. The insurance company, in this situation, has the right to cancel the contract or revise the premium at the beginning of each contract period covering insured events. This enables the insurer to adjust the amount of the premiums charged or coverage provided at the end of each period. As was noted, short-duration contracts include most property and liability insurance contracts. They also include certain term life insurance contacts, such as credit life insurance. (Credit life insurance is decreasing term insurance issued on the lives of borrowers to cover the payment of debt of the insured.) Accident and health insurance contracts, for example, may be short duration or long duration based on whether the contract is expected to remain in force for an extended period. *Premiums from short-duration contracts are earned and recognized as revenue evenly as the insurance protection is consumed.*

■ *Long-duration contracts* Long-duration contracts include those insurance contracts that are expected to remain in force for an extended period, such as whole life, universal life, guaranteed renewable term life, endowment, annuity, title insurance, and participating life insurance contracts. These types of contracts are generally not subject to unilateral changes in their provisions. For example, policies that are of long duration may be noncancelable or may be a guaranteed renewable contract. Premiums from long-duration insurance contracts are generally level even though the policy benefits and services provided do not occur evenly over the contract periods. They are recognized as revenue throughout the pay periods of the contract. Since this premium revenue generally exceeds the policy benefits that will be derived in the early years of the contract, the insurer is required to accrue a liability for the costs that are expected to be paid in the later years of the contract. Thus, for most types of long-duration contracts, a liability is accrued for current and expected renewal contract periods. The amount of the liability is equal to the present value of estimated future policy benefits to be paid policy holders less the present value of estimated future net premiums to be collected from policy holders. These estimates are based on several assumptions, such as investment yields, mortality, morbidity (the incidence of disability due to disease or physical impairment), terminations, and other expenses.

Universal-life-type contracts are long-duration insurance contracts that lack the fixed or guaranteed terms that are characteristic of most of the life insurance policies. They provide either death or annuity benefits and have any one of the following features:

1. One or more of the amounts assessed by the insurer against the policy holder, such as amounts for mortality coverage, contract

administration, initiation, or surrender, are not fixed or guaranteed by the terms of the contract.

2. Amounts accruing to the policy holder, such as accrued interest on policy balances, are not fixed or guaranteed by the contract terms.

3. The policy holder may vary the premiums within the contract limits and without the permission of the insurer.

Premium Revenue Recognition for Short-Duration Contracts

Premiums derived from short-duration contracts should be recognized as revenue over the insurance contract period in proportion to the amount of insurance protection provided. SFAS Statement Number 60 notes, however, that if the period of risk differs significantly from the contract period, revenue should be recognized over the period of risk in proportion to the amount of insurance provided. As a result, premiums are generally recognized as revenue evenly over the contract period (or period of risk if that differs from the contract period). The only exception to the generalization is if the insurance protection declines according to some predetermined schedule.

Under certain circumstances, premiums may be subject to adjustment. For example, certain insurance contracts may be experience rated. That is, the premium may be determined after the period of the contract based on the insured's claim experience. In such a situation, the premium revenue should be recognized in accordance with the following guidelines:

1. If the ultimate premium can be reasonably estimated, then it should be recognized as revenue over the contract period with appropriate revision to reflect the experience of the insurance company.

2. If the ultimate premium cannot be reasonably estimated, the cost recovery method or deposit method should be used until the ultimate premium is reasonably estimable. Under the cost recovery method, premiums are recognized as revenue in an amount equal to estimated claim costs as insured events occur. Under the deposit method, the recognition of income is deferred until the ultimate

premium can be reasonably estimated. That is, premiums are not recognized as revenue and claim costs are not correspondingly recorded as expenses until a reasonable estimate is derived of the ultimate premium that will be earned by the insurer.

Premium Revenue Recognition for Long-Duration Contracts

Premiums derived from long-duration contracts (other than universal-type insurance contracts) such as whole life contracts, guaranteed renewable term life contracts, and title insurance contracts should be recognized as revenue when due from policy holders. (Revenue from universal-type policies will be discussed momentarily.) In the case of title insurance, for example, the premium is considered due from policy holders on the effective date of the insurance policy. It is on this date that premium revenue should be recognized. If the binder date (the date a commitment to issue the policy is given by the insurer) is earlier, then it may be used as the date of premium revenue recognition.

Premiums collected on universal-life-type contracts should be recognized as revenue in the period in which the amounts were assessed against policy holders unless the amounts collected represent compensation to the insurer for more than one period. If this is the case, then the amounts received for future services should be accounted for as unearned revenue and should be accounted for as income in the period earned.

Recognition of Claim Costs

Unpaid claim costs, including estimates of cost relating to claims that have been incurred but not reported, should be accrued when the insured events occur. The exception to this relates to title insurance contracts, where estimated claim costs (including estimates of costs) are incurred but not reported. In this case, claims should be accrued when title insurance premiums are recognized as revenue.

The recorded liability for unpaid claims should be based on the cost of settling the claim, which, in turn, should be based on past experience adjusted for current trends as well as any other factors that would help make past experiences more current and realistic. If there are changes in the estimates of claim costs due to differences between estimates and payments for claims, these changes should be recognized in the period in which the estimates are changed or payments are made. Estimated recoveries from unsettled claims, such as from salvage, subrogation, or potential interests from real estate, should be evaluated for their estimated realizable value and should be deducted from the recorded liability for unpaid claims. Any estimated recoveries on settled claims (other than mortgage guaranty and title insurance claims) should also be deducted from the liability on unpaid claims.

In the settlement of mortgage guaranty and title insurance claims, real estate is often acquired by the insurer. The real estate should be reported at its fair value. This is the amount that could be expected to be received in a current sale between a buyer and seller. If market value is not available, expected cash flows (anticipated sales price less maintenance and selling costs of the real estate) may be used in estimating the fair value of the asset. The real estate acquired in settling claims should be reported in the balance sheet separately and should not be categorized as an investment. If there are any subsequent reductions in the reported amount of real estate or if gains or losses are realized as a result of its sale in settling claims, then these amounts should be used as an adjustment of the claim costs incurred.

Catastrophe Losses of Property and Liability Insurance Enterprises

Property and liability insurance enterprises are entities that issue insurance contracts that protect against (1) damage to or loss of property caused by perils such as fire and theft or (2) legal liability resulting from injuries to other persons or to their property. Typically, property and liability insurance enterprises are fire and casualty insurance entities.

When a property and liability insurance entity issues an insurance policy against loss from catastrophes, the insurance entity assumes a contingency relating to the risk of loss from such events. That is, it assumes the risk of loss from the occurrence of covered catastrophes that may occur during the period of the insurance contract. It incurs no potential asset impairment or liability incurrence with respect to any catastrophes that may occur beyond the insurance term.

In general, SFAS Statement Number 5 requires that an estimated loss from a contingency should be accrued by a charge against income if both of the following conditions occur:

1. Information becomes known prior to the issuance of the financial statements that indicates that it is probable that an asset had been impaired or a liability had been incurred at the date of the financial statements.

2. The amount of the loss can be reasonably estimated.

Thus, in order for a loss contingency to be accrued, it is necessary that the possibility of catastrophic occurrence be reasonably predictable within the insurance contract period and the amount of the loss be reasonably estimatible. Actuarial techniques are utilized by insurance companies to predict the rate of occurrence and amounts that would have to paid as a result of losses from catastrophes over long periods of time for insurance rate-setting purposes. Predictions over relatively short periods of time, such as an an individual accounting period or the periods of coverage of a large number of outstanding insurance contracts, are subject to significant deviations. Thus, the assumption of risk of loss by accrual (by property and liability insurance companies) relating to catastrophes fails the criteria of SFAS Statement Number 5. In addition, deferral of unearned premiums within the coverage periods of "in force" insurance policies represents the unknown liability for unpaid claims, including catastrophe claim liabilities. An accrual, therefore, of an additional liability for potential losses is inappropriate under SFAS 5. Disclosure, however, of the loss contingency is required. An insurance entity should accrue a net loss on insurance contracts that will probably be incurred in excess of deferred premiums when the liability can be reasonably estimated.

Liability for Future Policy Benefits

When premium revenue is recognized, a liability for long-duration contracts (other than title insurance contracts or universal insurance) should be accrued. The liability equals the present value of future benefits to be paid to policy holders and related expenses less the present value of future net premiums (portion of gross premiums required to provide all benefits and expenses). The liability is estimated based on expected investment yields, mortality, morbidity (the relative incidence of disability due to disease and impairment), terminations, and other applicable expenses that are incurred at the time that the insurance contracts are consummated. Changes in the liability for future policy benefits that result from periodic estimation for financial reporting purposes should be recognized in the period in which the changes occur. It is assumed that all original assumptions continue into subsequent accounting periods for purposes of determining the liability for future policy benefits.

Liability for Universal-Life-Type Contracts

The liability for policy benefits for universal-life-type contracts should be equal to the sum of the following components:

1. The balance that accrues to the benefit of policy holders at the date of the financial statements.

2. Any amounts that have been assessed against policy holders to compensate the insurer for services to be performed over future periods.

3. Any amounts that have previously been assessed against policy holders that are refundable in the termination of the contract.

4. Any probable loss (premium deficiency).

Acquisition Costs

Acquisition costs are those costs that vary with and are primarily related to the acquisition of new and renewal insurance contracts. Acquisition costs should be capitalized and charged to expense in proportion to the revenue that is recognized. To ensure that a proper matching is achieved, acquisition costs should be allocated by the insurer by categories of insurance contracts. Unamortized acquisition cost should be classified on the balance sheet as an asset.

For universal-life-type contracts, capitalized acquisition costs should be amortized over the life of a book of universal-life-type contracts at a constant rate based on the present value of the estimated gross profit amounts expected to be realized over the life of such book of contracts.

The present value of estimated gross profits should be computed using the specified contract rate, (i.e., the rate of interest that accrues to policy holder balances).

Premium Deficiency

Short-Duration Contracts   A short-duration contract premium deficiency occurs if unearned premiums do not exceed the sum of related expected claim costs and claim adjustment expenses, expected dividends to policy holders, unamortized acquisition costs, and maintenance costs. The premium deficiency should first be recognized by expensing any unamortized acquisition costs to the extent required to eliminate the deficiency. If the premium deficiency is greater than the unamortized acquisition costs, a liability should be accrued for the excess deficiency.

Long-Duration Contracts   A long-duration contract premium deficiency exists if the insurer's actual experience with respect to investment yields, mortality, morbidity, terminations, or expenses indicates that existing contract liabilities, together with the present value of future gross premiums, will not be sufficient to

1. Cover the present value (PV) of future benefits to be paid to or on behalf of policy holders as well as settlement and maintenance relating to long-duration contracts.

2. Recover any unamortized acquisition costs.

Based on the aforementioned, a premium deficiency should be computed as follows:

PV of future payments for benefits and related settlements and maintenance costs, determined by using revised assumptions based on actual and anticipated experience	$XXXX
Less: PV of future gross premiums, determined by using revised assumptions based on actual and anticipated experience	XXXX
Liability for future policy benefits using revised assumptions	$XXXX
Less: Liability for future policy benefits at the valuation date, reduced by unamortized acquisition costs	XXXX
Premium deficiency	$XXXX

The premium deficiency should be recognized by a charge to income and (1) a reduction of unamortized costs or (2) an increase in the liability for future policy benefits. If a premium deficiency does occur, future changes in the liability should be based on the insurer's revised assumptions. No loss should be reported currently if it ultimately results in creating future income.

Internal Replacement Transactions

Policy holders frequently acquire universal-life-type contracts as replacements for other insurance contracts issued by the same insurer. A policy holder commonly uses the cash surrender value of the previous contract to pay an initial lump sum premium for the new replacement contract. When a replacement occurs with a universal-life-type contract, any unamortized acquisition costs associated with the replaced contract and any difference between the cash surrender value and its previously recorded liability should not be deferred in connection with the replacement. Rather, any gain or loss should be recognized in the period of replacement.

Policy Holder Dividends

Policy holder dividends are paid on participating insurance contracts of life insurance enterprises. Participating contacts are those that allow the policy holder to participate in the earnings or surplus of the insurance entity.

SFAS Statement Number 60 requires that policy holder dividends should be accrued using an estimate of the amount that will be paid. Two situations prevail here

1. For life insurance companies that use life insurance dividend scales unrelated to actual net income earned, policy holder dividends should be accrued over the premium paying periods of the contract.

2. If limitations exist on the amount of net income from participating insurance contracts that may be distributed to stockholders, then the amount of the policy holder's share of net income that cannot be distributed to stockholders should be excluded from stockholders' equity by a charge to current operations and a credit to a liability relating to participating policy holders' funds. Dividends declared or paid to participating policy holders should then reduce this liability. Any dividends declared or paid in excess of the liability should be charged to current operations.

Contingent Commission Arrangements

Experience-rated insurance contacts sometimes provide that an insurance agent should be paid additional commissions under an experience refund arrangement. For example, if a particular policy that an insurance agent sold has had a positive experience in a given period, then that agent is due additional commission. Income in any period should not include amounts that are expected to be paid to agents in the form of experience refunds or additional commissions. Instead, contingent commissions payables or receivables should be accrued over the period in which related income is recognized.

Investments of an Insurance Entity

An insurance enterprise should account for its investments in debt and equity securities that have readily determinable fair values in accordance with SFAS Statement Number 115 (*Accounting for Certain Investments in Debt and Equity Securities*).

Investments that are not addressed by SFAS 115 because they do not have a readily determinable fair value should also be reported at fair value with changes in such values accounted for as unrealized gains and losses and reported net of taxes in a separate component of equity.

Mortgage loans should be reported at their outstanding principal balance if acquired at par value. If they were purchased at a discount or premium, they should be reported at amortized cost with an allowance for estimated uncollectible amounts. Amortization of the discount or premium and related charges or credits should be charged or credited to investment income.

Investments in assets in which the holder would not recover substantially its recorded investment (such as interest-only strips, loans, other receivables, retained interests in securitizations) should be classified as investments in debt securities and reported in the available-for-sale or trading portfolio.

Real estate investments should be reported at their cost less any accumulated depreciation. Depreciation and related charges or credits should be charged or credited to investment income.

Real Estate Used in the Business

Real estate acquired by an insurance enterprise is classified in one of two ways: as an investment or as real estate that is being used in the entity's operations. Thus, depreciation and other real estate operating expenses should either be classified as investment expenses or as operating expenses based on how the real estate is categorized.

Separate Accounts

Insurance entities frequently maintain separate assets and liabilities accounts for a contract holder for purposes of funding fixed-benefit plans, pension plans, variable annuity contracts, etc. The insurance enterprise, in this circumstance, receives a fee for investment management, administrative expenses, and other related functions. It is the contract holder, however, who assumes the investment risk, as it is he or she who directs the portfolio management.

Investments in the separate accounts described previously should be reported at market value except for those with guaranteed investment returns. For those separate accounts, the related assets should be reported as investments of the insurance enterprise described in the investments section previously noted. In addition, the assets and liabilities of separate accounts should be reported as summary totals in the insurance entity's financial statements.

Income Taxes

Insurance enterprises are required to recognize a deferred tax liability or asset for the deferred tax consequences of temporary differences necessitated by SFAS Statement Number 109. However, an insurance entity should not recognize deferred taxes on taxable temporary differences related to policy holder's surplus that arose in fiscal years beginning December 15, 1992. If, on the other hand, there is an expected reduction in policy holders' surplus, and it is likely that the insurance entity is likely to pay income taxes either currently or in subsequent years, then the income tax expense attributable to this reduction should be accrued and recognized in the current period.

Reinsurance

Insurance entities frequently seek to obtain indemnification against loss or liability from claims associated with contracts they wrote. They do this by entering into a reinsurance contract with another insurance entity called the reinsurer or assuming entity. When such a contract is consummated, the original insurer, known as the ceding enterprise, pays an amount to the reinsurer and the latter agrees to reimburse the insurer for a specified portion of the claims paid under the reinsurance contract. The legal rights of the insured remain unaffected by the reinsurance transaction. Although the insurer is indemnified for contracted losses under this arrangement, it is not relieved of obligation to the original policy holder, who, incidentally, is usually unaware of the reinsurance arrangement. In addition, the reinsurer may enter into reinsurance contracts with other reinsurers to be indemnified for loss and liability in a process known as retrocession.

Indemnification against Loss or Liability Relating to Insurance Risk

Ascertaining whether an reinsurer's insurance contract with a ceding enterprise provides indemnification against loss or liability relating to insurance risk requires an understanding of the arrangement between the parties involved.

Short-Duration Contracts In a short-duration contract, the reinsurer is required to assume significant insurance risk under the reinsured portions of the underlying insurance contracts. In this situation, it is assumed that both the timing and amount of the reinsurer's payments will depend on and vary directly with the amounts and timing of claims settled under the reinsured contract. Provisions in the reinsurance contract that delay timely reimbursement to the ceding entity would prevent the assumption of significant risk by the reinsurer. Contractual features may also prevent the reinsurer's payments from directly varying with the claims settled under the reinsured contract.

There must be a reasonable possibility (more than remote and less than probable) that the reinsurer may realize a significant loss from the transaction. The determination of whether a loss is reasonably possible is predicated on comparing the present value of all cash flows between the ceding and assuming entities under reasonable possible outcomes compared with the present value of amounts paid or deemed to have been paid to the reinsurer. If this comparison indicates that the reinsurer is not exposed to the reasonable possibility of significant loss, the ceding entity may only be considered indemnified against loss if substantially all of the insurance risk relating to the reinsured portions of the underlying insurance contracts has been assumed by the reinsurer.

Long-Duration Contracts There must be a reasonable possibility that the reinsurer will realize a significant loss from indemnifying a ceding insurance entity against loss or liability in assuming the insurance risk in a reinsurance contract. Long-duration contracts that do not subject the insurance enterprise to mortality or morbidity risks should be classified as investment contracts rather than insurance contracts.

Reinsurance Transactions

Reinsurance contracts that are legal replacements of one insurer by another eradicate the ceding entity's liability to the policy holder and result in the removal of related assets and liabilities from that entity's financial statements. Some reinsurance contracts do not extinguish the ceding entity's legal liability to the policy holder. In this situation, the ceding entity should not remove the related assets and liabilities from its financial statements.

Estimated reinsurance receivables arising from those contracts with enterprises that reinsure insurers should be reported separately as assets. In addition, amounts prepaid to the reinsurer relating to reinsurance contracts should also be reported as assets.

Receivables and payables between a reinsurer and the ceded entity should be offset only when a right of setoff exists. Earned premiums ceded (paid to the reinsurer) and recoveries recognized under reinsurance contracts should be reported in either the statement of earnings or in the footnotes to the financial statements.

Recognition of Revenues and Costs

The parameters for revenue and cost recognition relating to reinsurance by the insurer depend on whether the contract is in fact a bona fide reinsurance contract (see section on indemnification against loss or liability relating to insurance risk). Recognition also depends on whether the contract is of a short duration or long duration.

Contracts That Do Not Meet the Conditions for Reinsurance Accounting

1. If, despite its form, the reinsurance contract does not provide for indemnification of the ceding entity against loss and liabilities, then the premiums paid less the premium that is to be retained by the reinsurer should be accounted for as a deposit by the ceding entity. A net credit that results from the contract is reported as a liability by the ceding entity. A net charge resulting from the contract, on the other hand, should be reported as an asset by the reinsurer.

2. In addition, proceeds from reinsurance transactions that represent recovery of acquisition costs should reduce unamortized acquisition costs so that net acquisition costs are capitalized and charged to expense in proportion to net revenue recognized. If the ceded entity has agreed to service all related insurance contracts without reasonable compensation, a liability should be accrued for estimated excess servicing costs under the reinsurance contract. Any net cost should be accounted for as an acquisition cost.

Contracts That Meet the Conditions for Reinsurance Accounting

Short-duration contracts. Amounts paid for prospective reinsurance by the ceded enterprise should be accounted for and reported as prepaid insurance premiums and amortized over the remaining contract period in proportion to the amount of insurance protection provided. If the amounts paid in are subject to adjustment, then the basis for amortization should be the amount that is estimated to be paid.

Amounts that are paid for retroactive reinsurance should be reported as reinsurance receivables to the extent those amounts do not exceed the recorded liabilities relating to the underlying reinsured contracts. If the recorded liabilities, in fact, exceed the amounts paid, then the reinsurance receivables should be increased to reflect the difference and the resulting gain that is deferred. This gain should then be amortized over the estimated remaining settlement period. The settlement period is the estimated period over which the ceding entity expects to recover amounts from the reinsurer under the terms of the reinsurance contract. If the amounts and timing of the reinsurance recoveries can be reasonably estimated, the gain should be amortized using the interest method. If, on the other hand, the amounts and timing of recoveries cannot be estimated, then the recovery method should be used. The recovery method bases the amount of amortization on the proportion of actual recoveries to the total estimated recoveries. If the amount that was paid for retroactive reinsurance exceeds the recorded liabilities relating to the reinsured contracts, then the ceding entity should increase the related liabilities or reduce the reinsurance receivable or both at the time that the reinsurance contract has been effected so that the excess is charged to earnings.

The amortization of deferred amounts (under both the interest method and recovery method) should be based on estimates of the ceding entity's estimates of the expected timing and amounts of cash flows. The timing of changes in these estimates should not change the recognition of revenues and reinsurance costs.

SFAS Statement Number 113 requires that any changes in estimates relating to the amount that will be recovered from the insurer be accounted for consistently at both the beginning of and after the reinsurance transactions. Changes in the estimated amount of liabilities relating to the underlying insurance contracts should be recognized in income in the period of the change. Reinsurance receivables should reflect any adjustment in the amount recoverable from the reinsurer, and a gain should be adjusted or established.

Reinsurance contracts include both prospective and retroactive provisions. For example, a given reinsurance contract may insure liabilities relating to contracts relating to one or more prior years and may at the same time insure losses under contracts covering one or more future periods. When possible, prospective and retroactive provisions should be accounted for separately. If separate accounting within a single contract is not practicable, the contract should be accounted for as a retroactive contract.

Long-duration contracts The insurance enterprise should amortize the estimated cost of reinsurance of long-duration contracts over the remaining life of the underlying reinsured contracts. This compares to the cost of reinsurance of short-duration contracts where the cost is amortized over the reinsurance contract period. Determining whether an insurance contract that reinsures a long-duration contract is long or short duration is a matter of professional judgment. However, the assumptions relating to accounting for reinsurance costs should be consistent with those used for the the reinsured contract. Any difference between the amount paid for a reinsurance contract and the amount of liabilities for policy benefits relating to the underlying reinsured contract is part of the estimated cost to be amortized.

Disclosure Requirements

Insurance entities should disclose the following information in their financial statements:

1. The basis for estimating liabilities for unpaid claims and claim adjustment expenses.

2. The methods and assumptions used in estimating the liability for future policy benefits. This should include the disclosure of the average rate of assumed investment yields in effect for the current year.

3. The nature of acquisition costs that were capitalized. In addition, the method of amortizing those costs and the amount that was amortized for the period should be shown.

4. The carrying amount of liabilities for unpaid claims and claim adjustment expenses on short-duration contracts. These should be presented at their present value in the financial statements with the range of interest rates that were used to discount those liabilities.

5. Determination of whether the insurance entity considered anticipated investment income in determining whether a short-duration contract premium deficiency exists.

6. The relative percentage of participating insurance, the method of accounting for policy holder dividends, the amount of dividends, and the amount of any additional income that was allocated to participating policy holders.

7. The amount of statutory capital and surplus.

8. The amount of statutory capital and surplus needed to satisfy regulatory requirements based on current operations if material in relation to the entity's statutory capital and surplus.

9. The nature of statutory restrictions on the payment of dividends and the amount of retained earnings that is not available for the payment to stockholders.

10. The nature, purpose, and effect of ceded reinsurance transactions on the insurance entity's operations. In addition, the ceded enterprise must disclose the fact that it is not relieved of its primary obligation to the policy holder in a given reinsurance transaction.

11. For short-duration contracts, premiums from direct business; reinsurance assumed; and reinsurance ceded on both a written and earned basis.

12. For long-duration contracts, premiums and amounts assessed against policy holders from direct business; reinsurance assumed and ceded; and premiums and amounts earned.

13. Methods used for income recognition on reinsurance contracts.

Ceding insurance entities are required to disclose concentrations of credit risk associated with reinsurance receivables and prepaid reinsurance premiums.

MOTION PICTURE INDUSTRY

Primary Sources of Authoritative GAAP

The primary source of authoritative GAAP relating to guidance in the motion picture industry is

■ SFAS Statement Number 53 (*Financial Reporting by Producers and Distributors of Motion Picture Films*)

GAAP Abstract and Introduction

Producers and distributors of motion picture films license film exhibition rights to movie theaters and to television. When film exhibition rights are licensed to movie theaters, the revenue generated by producers and distributors is generally recognized when the films are shown. The sale of exhibition rights to television broadcasters should be accounted for as revenue by the licensor. The revenue is recognized when the license period begins and certain conditions are met. Accounting for related film costs and participation agreements is fully discussed in the following paragraphs.

Primary GAAP: Accounting and Reporting by Producers and Distributors of Motion Picture Films

Recognizing Revenue by Licensing Films to Movie Theaters

Exhibition rights to motion pictures are sold through the process of licensure based on either (1) a flat fee or (2) a percentage of the box office receipts. The entities licensing the motion picture may be motion picture production companies, independent producers, or distributors. Distributors own the rights to distribute films to movies theaters, individual television station, groups of stations, networks, etc. The licensing entities may require a nonrefundable guarantee against a percentage of the box office receipts. The guarantee in some markets (e.g., foreign markets) constitutes the amount that the motion picture exhibition rights are sold for because the licensors have no means of controlling the distribution of the movie and ascertaining the actual percentage of box office receipts due with any degree of accuracy.

Motion picture revenues should be recognized on a percentage of box office receipts or flat fee basis when the film is actually shown. Thus, the date of exhibition is the date on which revenue is realized and accordingly recognized. If a nonrefundable guarantee is prepaid, it should be deferred and recognized as revenue on the date that the motion picture is run. SFAS Statement Number 53 notes that guarantees received by licensors that are in substance outright sales due to the circumstances previously noted (e.g., foreign markets) should be considered revenue if all of the following conditions are met when the license period begins:

1. The license fee for each film is known.

2. The cost of each film is known or reasonably determinable.

3. Collectibility of the full license fee is reasonably assured.

4. The film has been accepted by the licensee in accordance with the conditions of the license agreement.

5. The film is available for its first showing or telecast. Restrictions under the same license agreement or another license agreement with the same licensee preventing usage should not affect this condition. However, a conflicting license that prevents usage by the licensee does represent a bona fide obstacle to satisfying this condition.

Films Licensed to Television

A license agreement for television program material is granted by either motion picture producers, independent producers, or distributors (licensors) granting a broadcaster (licensee) the right to telecast either a specified or unlimited number of showings over a specified maximum period of time for a specified fee. A license agreement typically covers several films and contains a separate license for each film in the package covered by the overall license agreement. The licensee must pay the contracted fee whether or not exhibition rights are exercised, and the rights revert to the licensor with no refund if they are not exercised.

SFAS Statement Number 53 notes that revenue is to be recognized for television programming licensure when the license period begins and all of the following conditions have been met:

1. The license fee for each film is known.

2. The cost of each film is known or reasonably determinable.

3. Collectibility of the full license fee is reasonably assured.

4. The film has been accepted by the licensee in accordance with the conditions of the license agreement.

5. The film is available for its first showing or telecast. Restrictions under the same license agreement or another license agreement with the same licensee preventing usage should not affect this condition. How-

ever, a conflicting license that prevents usage by the licensee shall represent a bona fide obstacle to satisfying this condition.

When the aforementioned conditions have been satisfied, the licensor and licensee are contractually bound and are required to comply with all the terms of the license agreement. If considerations arise which indicate doubt regarding one or both of the parties ability to perform contractually, then revenue recognition should be deferred until these considerations no longer exist.

Revenues derived from licensing a film should be recognized in the same order as the market-by-market utilization of the film and at the time the licensee is able to exercise rights under the contractual agreement. That time would be the later of (1) the beginning of the license period or (2) the expiration of a conflicting license, making the licensor able to deliver the right to the licensee. The amount of sales revenue that should be recognized should be accounted for at the present value of the license fee specified in the contract.

Production Costs

Costs incurred to produce a film are known as production costs. They include the cost of the story and scenario to be used for the film and other costs typically consisting of

1. Salaries of cast, directors, producers, extras, and miscellaneous staff.
2. Cost of set construction and operations, wardrobe, and accessories.
3. Cost of sound synchronization.
4. Production overhead, including depreciation and amortization of studio equipment and leasehold improvements used in production.
5. Rental of facilities on location.

Production costs are normally accumulated by individual films in four sequential steps:

1. Acquisition of story rights.

2. Preproduction activities, including script development, costume design, and construction.

3. Principal photography, which includes the actual filming of the movie.

4. Postproduction costs, including sound synchronization and editing.

The culmination of all these activities results in the completed master negative.

All production costs should be capitalized as film cost inventory and should be amortized using the individual-film-forecast-computation method. Another amortization method, the periodic-table-computation method, may be used if its results approximates the outcome that would have been achieved using the individual-film-forecast-computation method. The over-all objective of the amortization of film cost inventory is to relate the cost of the film to the gross revenues being reported and to generate a constant rate of gross profit before all period costs. The amortization of film cost should commence when a film is released and revenues are recognized. A discussion of the two amortization methods follows.

Individual-Film-Forecast-Computation Method   This method amortizes film costs in the same ratio as current gross revenues bears to anticipated total gross revenue. That is, a fraction is computed, with the numerator consisting of gross revenues from the film for the current period and the denominator being the anticipated total gross revenues from the film during its useful life, including future estimated total gross revenues derived from all markets in which the film will be seen. It should be noted that the amount recognized as revenue related to the sale of long-term, non-interest-bearing television exhibition rights should be included in an amount equal to the total estimated present value of those revenues as of the date they are expected to be recognized. Thus, the present value rather than the gross proceeds of the revenues from television exhibition rights should be included in both the numerator and denominator. The resulting fraction is then applied to production and other capitalized costs to determine the amortization for each period.

In computing the ratio, the estimates of anticipated total gross revenues should be periodically revised, when necessary, to reflect current information. When, in fact, anticipated total gross revenues are revised, a new fraction should be created where the numerator consists of actual gross revenue for the current period and the denominator includes only the anticipated total gross revenues from the beginning of the current year. The fraction that results should then be applied to unrecovered production and other capitalized costs as of the beginning of the current year to determine the annual amortization.

The Periodic-Table-Computation Method   This method amortizes film costs using tables that were prepared from the historic revenue patterns of a large group of films. It is predicated on the assumption that past experience will provide a reasonable guide for future groups of films. In general, this method should only be used to amortize the portion of film costs relating to film rights licensed to movie theaters. In addition, as was previously noted, it should only be used when the results of its use would approximate that which would be derived from the use of the individual-film-forecast-computation method. If the periodic-table-computation method is used, the periodic tables upon which it is based should be revised regularly whenever revenue patterns significantly change. In general, the periodic-table-computation method should not be used for a film whose distribution pattern differs significantly from those films used in compiling the table upon which its amortization is based.

Participations

A common procedure is for persons involved in the production of a motion picture to be compensated, in part or in full, with a participation in the income of the film. The amount of compensation that is payable to the participant is usually based on percentages of revenues or profits from the film from some or all sources. Television residuals owed to production people, for example, are comparable to participations. If it is expected that compensation will be owed under a participation agreement, the total expected participations should be charged to expense in the same ratio as current gross revenues bear to anticipated total gross revenues.

Exploitation Costs

Exploitation costs are costs incurred during the final production phase and during the release periods of films in both primary and secondary markets. These costs include film prints, advertising, rents, salaries, and other distribution expenses. Those costs that clearly will benefit future periods, such as film prints, prerelease, and early release advertising, should be capitalized as film cost inventory and amortized using the ratio of current gross revenues to anticipated total revenues. On the other hand, rent, salaries, and local advertising that are not clearly expected to benefit the film in future markets should be charged in the period incurred.

Inventory Valuation

The inventory cost of a motion picture consists of its unamortized production and exploitation costs. These collective amounts should be compared with the film's net realizable value each reporting period on a film-by-film basis. Net realizable value in the motion picture industry is defined as the film's estimated rental value less any estimated costs needed to complete and exploit the film. If the estimated future gross revenues from a film are not great enough to recover the unamortized film costs, other direct distribution costs, and participations, the unamortized film costs should be written down to net realizable value. If film costs are written down to net realizable value in a given fiscal period, they may be written back up in the same period (in an amount not to exceed the amount of write-down) if estimates of future gross revenues increase. However, film costs that are reduced to net realizable value at the end of a fiscal period should not be written up in subsequent fiscal periods. Special circumstances, such as a change in the overall popularity of certain types of films or actual costs being substantially in excess of budgeted costs, may require a write-down to net realizable value before the film is released.

Costs of Film Inventory— Story Costs and Scenarios

Film inventories include costs for film rights to books, stage plays, original screenplays, etc. Additional costs must be expended for the adaptation of the work to the production techniques of motion picture films. Story costs and scenarios owned by the motion picture enterprise should be reviewed and periodically evaluated to determine if they will be used in the production of a film. If it is ascertained that they will not be used, then the costs should be charged to production overhead in the current period. SFAS Statement Number 53 states that there is a presumption that story costs will be charged to production overhead if they have been held for three years and have not been set for production. Once charged off, GAAP precludes reinstatement of story costs if they are subsequently set for production.

Investments in Films and Guarantee of Loans to Independent Producers

Motion picture entities frequently make cash advances or guarantee loans to independent producers. Cash advances should be included as part of the motion picture entity's film inventory cost. Loans to independent producers that are guaranteed by the motion picture enterprise should also be accounted for as part of the film cost inventory and as a liability as well when the funds are disbursed.

Balance Sheet Classification

A motion picture enterprise has the option of presenting a classified or unclassified balance sheet. If a classified balance sheet is presented, then the motion picture enterprise must segregate its film costs as current or noncurrent assets. The following (film costs) should be included as current assets:

- Unamortized costs of film inventory released and allocated to the primary market

- Completed films not released (reduced by the portion allocated to secondary markets)

- Television films in production that are under contract of sale

All other capitalized film costs should be classified as noncurrent assets.

The portion of film costs expected to be realized from secondary television or other exploitation should be reported as noncurrent assets and amortized as revenues are recorded.

SFAS Statement Number 53 requires that a license agreement for the sale of film rights for television exhibition should not be reported on the balance sheet until the time of revenue recognition. Any amounts received by a motion picture entity on such agreements prior to recognition of revenue should be reported as an advance payment and should be included as a current liability. If, on the other hand, those advance payments relate to film cost inventory, then they should be classified as current assets.

Home Viewing Market

Motion picture entities frequently earn additional revenues by licensing film to the home viewing market. The home viewing market includes films that are sold or made available to residential viewers for a fee. They include, for example, video cassettes and disks and all forms of pay television, including cable and over-the-air transmissions. Programs licensed to the home viewing market should be reported utilizing the same guidelines noted in the previous paragraphs.

Disclosure

The components of film inventories of a motion picture enterprise should be disclosed. These include the following:

- Films released
- Films completed but not released
- Films in process
- Story rights and scenarios

RECORD AND MUSIC INDUSTRY

Primary Sources of Authoritative GAAP

The primary source of authoritative GAAP relating to guidance in the record and music industry is

- SFAS Statement Number 50 (*Financial Reporting in the Record and Music Industry*)

GAAP Abstract and Introduction

SFAS Statement Number 50 discusses the standards of financial accounting and reporting for licensors and licensees in the record and music industry. A licensor of a music copyright or the owner of a record master should recognize license fees as revenue if a license agreement is, in substance, an outright sale and collectibility of the licensing fees is reasonably assured. A licensee, paying minimum guarantees to a licensor, should record them as assets and charge them to expense in accordance with the terms of the license agreement. Compensation paid to artists in the form of royalties should be adjusted for anticipated returns and charged to expense in the period in which the sale of the recording takes place.

Primary GAAP

Accounting for Licensors

An entity may generate a significant amount of revenue by licensing the rights of ownership in a record master or music copyright. A record master is the master tape of the performance of an artist. It is used to produce the molds used for commercial record production and other tapes for use in making cartridges, cassettes, and reel tapes. In a licensing agreement, the licensor (owner of a record master or music copyright) grants the licensee the right to sell or distribute records or music for a fixed fee (paid to the licensor) or for a fee based on the sales of records or music. In many instances, a license agreement is, in substance, an outright sale. SFAS Statement Number 50 requires the earnings process regarding licensing fees relating to such agreements (licensor agreements) to be considered complete and reported as revenue if collectibility of the full fee is reasonably assured and the following criteria relating to the licensor has been met. The licensor must have

- Signed a noncancelable contract
- Agreed to a fixed fee
- Delivered the rights to the licensee who is free to exercise them
- In addition, there must be no remaining significant obligations to furnish music or records.

A minimum guarantee is commonly paid by a licensee. The licensor should report such a payment as a liability initially and recognize the guarantee as revenue as the license fee is earned. If the amount of license fee earned cannot be ascertained, then the guarantee should be recognized equally over the remaining period of the license agreement. Other fees (such as free records distributed by a record club in excess of a predetermined amount) that are required by a license agreement and are not fixed in amount prior to the expiration date of the agreement should be recognized as revenue only when reasonable estimates of such amounts can be made or when the agreement has expired.

Compensation to Artists

Royalties earned by recording artists should be adjusted for anticipated returns and should be charged to expense in the period in which the sale of the recording takes place. If an advance royalty is paid to an artist, it should be reported as an asset if the artist's current popularity and past performance provide a valid basis for estimating the amount of the advance that will be recoverable from future royalties to be earned by the artist. Advances should be charged to expense as subsequent royalties are earned by the artist. If it appears that a portion of future royalties is not recoverable from future royalties to be earned by the artist, such portion should be charged to expense in the period in which the loss becomes apparent. Advance royalties should be classified as either current or noncurrent assets.

Cost of Record Masters

Costs for record masters incurred by a record company should be reported as an asset if the current popularity and past performance of the artist indicate a sound basis for estimating the recovery of cost from future sales. Otherwise, the cost should be charged to expense. Costs that are recognized as assets should be amortized over the estimated life of the recorded performance using a method that reasonably matches the amount of net revenue to be realized.

The part of the cost of record masters (incurred by the record company) that is recoverable from the royalties of an artist should be accounted for as an advance royalty, as discussed in the previous section on compensation to artists.

Accounting by Licensees

Minimum guarantees are commonly paid in advance by a licensee. This amount should be reported by a licensee as an asset and subsequently charged to expense. If all or a portion of the recorded guarantee appears not to be recoverable through the future use of rights derived from the license, then that amount deemed unrecoverable should be charged to expense. Any other fees that must be paid (e.g., free records distributed by a record club in excess of a predetermined amount) that are not fixed in amount prior to the expiration date of the license agreement should be estimated and accrued by the licensee on a license-by-license basis.

Disclosure

SFAS Statement Number 50 requires that the following should be disclosed by a record entity:

1. Commitments for artist advances that are payable in future years and future royalty guarantees.

2. The recorded cost of record masters incurred by the record company that are recorded as assets.

GOVERNMENT CONTRACTS

Primary Sources of Authoritative GAAP

The primary source of authoritative GAAP relating to guidance in government contracts is

- Accounting Research Bulletin Number 43 (*Restatement and Revision of Accounting Research Bulletins*), Chapter 11, "Government Contracts"

GAAP Abstract and Introduction

Chapter 11 of ARB Bulletin Number 43 deals with the accounting problems arising under cost-plus-fixed-fee contracts (CPFF contracts). Fees received under government CPFF contracts should be credited to income on the basis of partial performance assuming reasonable assurance that realization has taken place. Billable fees may also be accrued as income unless the accrual is not reasonably related to the proportionate performance of the total work or services.

Contractor profit in a fixed-price supply contract that is unilaterally terminated by the government accrues as of the effective date of the termination. That is, the contractor in such a situation is entitled to reimbursement for all costs plus a fair portion of the fixed contractual fee.

Primary GAAP

Government contracts are generally prepared on a CPFF structure, which allows for possible renegotiation if the government believes that the contract has been generating excess profits. In addition, the government usually reserves the right in these agreements to terminate the contract at its convenience.

CPFF contracts allows the contractor to collect a fixed fee from the government as well as all costs incurred required to satisfy the contract. The government in contracting for the construction of some product or the performance of services may choose at its discretion to withhold a certain percentage of payments due on the contract while the work is being performed. If the government should choose to terminate the contract for a given reason, then the contractor is entitled to be repaid for all costs incurred as well as a proportionate part of the contracted fixed fee.

From the point of view of the contractor, the primary accounting problem is when profits on CPFF contracts with the government should be recognized. A contractor should not recognize any profits on CPFF contracts until the services have been fully performed and accepted unconditionally by the government or the product that has been manufactured has been deemed to meet the government's contractual standards. However, if a government contract is expected to last over an extended number of years, then the contractor should use the percentage-of-completion method.

When accounting for CPFF contracts, the following general rules prevail:

1. When the contract calls for only the performance of services by the contractor, then all fees charged should be included in the contractor's revenue account.

2. When the contract involves the manufacture of goods and products, then contractor's sales and revenue accounts should include the fees generated on the project as well as all reimbursable costs.

Renegotiating Government Contracts

As was previously noted, most government CPFF contracts allow the government to make adjustments of the original sales price of the contract when it is deemed that excessive profits are being generated by the contractor. Generally an estimate is made and an adjustment provision is accounted for. The basis for the estimate is predicated on the government's past experiences in the industry as well as the contractor's past experiences. If a reasonable estimate cannot be made and a renegotiation of sales revenue cannot be reached, that fact should be fully disclosed in the footnotes of the contractor's financial statements. The estimate of the reduction of sales revenue should be shown in the (contractor's) income statement as either contra-sales or contra-income. The adjustment provision should be shown as a current liability on the balance sheet, assuming it will be satisfied in one year or in the operating cycle, whichever is longer. In the next accounting period if it is determined that the estimate that was accounted for in the prior period was incorrect relative to the final adjustment, the change that is required should be shown in the income statement in the period in which final resolution is determined.

A contractor should account for revenue on CPFF contracts using the installment method or the cost recovery method, if it is deemed that collections from the government will not be reasonably assured. However, this situation is generally very unusual.

Government Contract Disclosures

When a material portion of an enterprise's revenue is derived from government contracts, that fact must be disclosed in the financial statements or in the notes of the contractor. Specifically, disclosure is required if at least 10% of the entity's revenue is generated from contracts with the federal, state, local, or foreign government. In addition, the following disclosures should be made:

1. Uncertainty exists that the provision that was made for renegotiation of the contract by the government is not sufficient and additional charges may be required.

2. The basis for ascertaining the provision for renegotiation should be disclosed (i.e., past experience, industry experience, etc.).

Terminated War and Defense Contracts

War and defense contracts have generally been made on both a CPFF and fixed-price basis. If the government terminates a war or defense contract, the determination of the extent of profit that should be accounted for should be made as of the effective date of the termination. The contractor, on this date, has the right to accrue any amount due from the government on that part of the contract that has been canceled. The amount of profit that should be accrued is the difference between all allowable costs that have been incurred by the contractor and the amount of the termination claim. However, most of the contracts that are signed with the government provide a minimum profit percentage formula that should be used if an agreement regarding what should be paid by the government cannot be reached.

If a reasonable estimate of the termination claim cannot be made for reporting purposes, then this fact should be fully disclosed in the notes to the financial statements, including the uncertainty involved.

Termination claims on the accounting records of the contractor should be shown as current assets. Prior to receiving these notices, advances that are paid should be deducted from termination claims receivable. Correspondingly, any loans that are received by the contractor based on the termination claims or security of the governmental contract should be disclosed separately on the contractor's balance sheet as current debt.

Sometimes a contractor reacquires items that were included in the termination claim. These items, known as disposal credits, should be recorded as a new purchase and applied as a reduction of the termination claim.

Termination Claims Disclosure Requirements

Termination claims based on governmental contracts should be classified as receivables on the balance sheet of the contractor. However, if material in amount, they should be separately disclosed from other receivables in the financial statements.

Contractors should fairly estimate the amount of the termination claim by determining the amounts that are collectible. In addition, provision should be made for those amounts whose collectibility are questionable. Of course, these items should be fully disclosed in the financial statements.

OIL- AND GAS-PRODUCING ACTIVITIES

Primary Sources of Authoritative GAAP

The primary sources of authoritative GAAP relating to guidance in oil- and gas-producing enterprises include

- SFAS Statement Number 19 (*Financial Accounting and Reporting by Oil and Gas Producing Companies*)
- SFAS Statement Number 25 (*Suspension of Certain Accounting Requirements for Oil and Gas Producing Companies*)
- SFAS Statement Number 69 (*Disclosures about Oil and Gas Producing Activities*)
- SFAS Statement Number 95 (*Statement of Cash Flows*)
- SFAS Statement Number 109 (*Accounting for Income Taxes*)
- SFAS Statement Number 121 (*Accounting for the Impairment of Long-Lived Assets to Be Disposed Of*)
- FASB Interpretation (FASBI) Number 36 (*Accounting for Exploratory Wells in Progress at the End of a Period*)

GAAP Abstract and Introduction

GAAP has followed a circuitous path in the establishment of guidelines relating to oil- and gas-producing companies. SFAS Statement Number 19 required that oil and gas entities follow the successful efforts approach. After strong opposition from small oil and gas producers, the SEC examined both the successful efforts approach and the full cost approach as an alternative and found both methodologies to be lacking. In place of them, the SEC believed that an alternative method would be appropriate. This alternative, entitled Reserve Recognition Accounting (RRA), had not yet been fully developed. In response to the SEC's decisions, the FASB then issued SFAS Statement Number 25, which suspended the requirement that the successful efforts approach be used. However, because of many insurmountable estimation problems relating to the RRA method, the SEC abandoned its choice and established guidelines that allowed oil and gas companies to use either the successful efforts approach (SFAS Statement Number 19) or the full cost approach. However, because of the importance of value based disclosures relating to oil and gas reserves advocated by the RRA method, SFAS Statement Number 69 was passed, which requires current value disclosures relating to oil- and gas-producing activities.

SFAS 69 establishes comprehensive financial statement disclosures which supersede the disclosure requirements of SFAS 19 and SFAS 25. It also incorporates the SEC's disclosure requirements relating to oil- and gas-producing requirements. Comprehensive guidelines relating to the full cost approach are described in regulations published by the SEC. Although many required compliance provisions of SFAS 19 have been suspended, these standards have been issued by the FASB and still remain in existence. In addition, SFAS 19's requirements relating to reporting accounting changes and allocating income taxes have not been suspended.

When presenting a complete set of annual financial statements, publicly traded enterprises with significant oil and gas activities are required to disclose the following as supplementary information not part of the primary financial statements:

1. Proved oil and gas reserve quantities.
2. Capitalized costs relating to oil- and gas-producing activities.
3. Costs incurred in oil and gas property acquisition, exploration, and development activities.

4. Results of operations for oil- and gas-producing activities.

5. A standardized measure of discounted future net cash flows relating to proved oil and gas reserve quantities.

GAAP advocates but does not require the use of the successful efforts approach of accounting for oil- and gas-producing activities. Under this method, costs should be accounted for as follows:

1. Geological and geophysical costs and costs of carrying and retaining undeveloped properties should be charged to expense as incurred.

2. Costs of drilling exploratory wells and exploratory-type stratigraphic test wells that do not realize proved reserves should be charged to expense when the wells do not find proved reserves.

3. Costs of acquiring properties, costs of drilling development wells and development-type stratigraphic test wells, and costs of drilling successful exploratory wells and exploratory-type stratigraphic test wells should be capitalized.

4. The capitalized costs of wells and related equipment are amortized as related oil and gas reserves are produced.

5. Costs of unproved properties should be assessed periodically and a loss should be recognized if it is determined that the properties are impaired.

Primary GAAP

Types of Assets Utilized in Oil- and Gas-Producing Activities

An oil- and gas-producing entity is involved in activities that require special types of assets. The costs of these assets should be capitalized when they are incurred. The following are definitions of the special types of assets that are used in the oil- and gas-producing industry:

Mineral Interests in Properties   Generally referred to as *properties*, these include fee ownership or a lease, concession, or other interest that provides the right to extract oil or gas. Properties may also include royalty interests, production payments that are payable in oil or gas, and agreements with foreign governments under which an entity participates in the operation of the properties or serves as producer of the underlying reserves. Properties do not include other supply agreements or contracts that represent the right to purchase rather than extract oil and gas.

Properties are classified as being proved or unproved:

1. *Proved properties.* Proved reserves consist of proved oil and gas reserves, proved developed oil and gas reserves, and proved undeveloped reserves. That is, proved properties are properties with proved reserves. A discussion of these three components follows.

    Proved oil and gas reserves include estimated quantities of crude oil, natural gas, and natural gas liquids which geological and engineering data demonstrate with a substantial degree of certainty to be recoverable in future years from known reservoirs. The following characteristics relate to these properties:

    (a) Reservoirs are considered to be proved if economic producibility is supported by either actual production or conclusive formation tests.

    (b) Reserves that can be produced economically through the application of improved recovery techniques (e.g., fluid injection) are included in the proved classification if successful testing by a pilot project, or the operation of an installed program in the reservoir, provides support for the engineering analysis on which the program was based.

    (c) Estimates of proved reserves do not include the following:

      (i) oil that may become available from known reservoirs but is classified separately as indicated additional reserves

(ii) crude oil, natural gas, and natural gas liquids, the recovery of which is subject to reasonable doubt because of uncertainty as to geology, reservoir characteristics, or economic factors

(iii) crude oil, natural gas, and natural oil gas liquids that may occur in undrilled prospects, and

(iv) crude oil, natural gas, and natural gas liquids that may be recovered from oil shales, coal, and other such sources

Proved developed oil and gas reserves are reserves that can be expected to be recovered through existing wells with existing equipment and operating methods. Additional oil and gas expected to be obtained through the application of fluid injection or other improved recovery techniques for supplementing the natural forces of primary recovery should be included as proved developed reserves only after testing by a pilot project or after the operation of an installed program has confirmed, through production response, that increased recovery will in fact be accomplished.

Proved undeveloped reserves are reserves that are expected to be recovered from new wells on undrilled acreage, or from existing wells for which a relatively major expenditure is required for recompletion. Reserves on undrilled acreage should be limited to those drilling units offsetting production units that are reasonably certain of production when drilled. Proved reserves for other undrilled units can be claimed only if it can be demonstrated with certainty that there is continuity of production from the existing productive formation.

2. *Unproved properties.* These are properties with no proved reserves.

Wells and Related Equipment and Facilities   These include the costs of items incurred to

1. Drill and equip the exploratory wells and exploratory-type stratigraphic test wells that have found proved reserves. Stratigraphic test

wells are drilling projects that are geologically directed to obtain information pertaining to specific geological information.

2. Obtain access to proved reserves and provide facilities for extracting, treating, gathering, and storing the oil and gas, including the drilling and equipping of development wells (a productive well drilled within the proved area of an oil or gas reservoir drilled down to the stratigraphic horizon) and development-type stratigraphic test wells and service wells (a well drilled for the purpose of supporting production in an existing field).

Support Equipment and Facilities Used in Oil- and Gas-Producing Activities   These include such items as drilling equipment, construction and grading equipment, seismic equipment, vehicles, repair shops, warehouses, and supply points.

Uncompleted Wells, Equipment, and Facilities   The costs of these assets include those incurred to (1) drill and equip wells that are not yet completed and (2) acquire or construct equipment and facilities that are not yet completed and installed.

Accounting for Costs when They Are Incurred

Acquisition Costs of Properties   Costs incurred to purchase, lease, or otherwise acquire a property (whether unproved or proved) shall be capitalized when incurred. These costs include lease bonuses, options to purchase or lease properties, portion of costs applicable to minerals when land including mineral rights is purchased, brokers' fees, recording fees, legal costs, and other costs that would be incurred in purchasing properties.

Exploration   Exploration involves

1. Identifying those areas that warrant examination.
2. Examining those areas that have been determined to contain oil and gas reserves.

Exploration costs may be incurred both before acquiring a given property (prospecting costs) and after its acquisition.The principal types of exploration costs (including depreciation and operating costs of support equipment and facilities; see the subsequent section on support equipment and facilities) and other costs of exploration activities consist of the following:

- Geological and geophysical costs, such as topographical and geophysical studies, rights of access to properties to conduct these studies, and salaries of geologists
- Costs of carrying and retaining undeveloped properties
- Dry hole contributions and bottom hole contributions
- Costs of drilling and equipping exploratory wells
- Costs of drilling exploratory-type stratigraphic test wells

Other Exploration Costs   Geological and geophysical exploration costs and the costs of carrying and retaining undeveloped properties should be charged to expense when these costs are incurred.

The costs of drilling exploratory wells and the costs of drilling exploratory-type stratigraphic test wells should be capitalized as part of the entity's uncompleted wells, equipment, and facilities pending determination of whether the well has found proved reserves. Based on what is found, the following accounting procedures should be followed:

1. If proved reserves have been found by the well, then the capitalized costs of drilling the well should become part of the entity's wells and related equipment and facilities.

2. If proved reserves have not been found by the well, the capitalized costs of drilling the well, net of salvage value, should be charged to expense.

It is common for an oil- and gas-producing entity to perform exploration activities on a property owned by another in exchange for the contractual right to receive an interest in the property if proved reserves are found to exist. If, in fact, proved reserves are found, the costs should become part of the proved property acquired. Alternatively, if proved reserves are not found, the entity performing the exploration activities is due reimbursement for the costs incurred and should account for them as a receivable.

Development   Development costs are incurred by oil- and gas-producing companies to obtain access to proved reserves and to provide facilities for extracting, treating, gathering, and storing the oil and gas. Development costs are incurred to

1. Prepare and allow for access to well locations for drilling, including determining specific drilling sites, clearing ground, draining, road building, and relocating public roads, gas lines, and power lines, and other considerations necessary in the development of proved reserves.

2. Drill and equip development wells, development-type stratigraphic wells, and service wells, including the costs of platforms and well equipment such as casing, tubing, pumping equipment, and the wellhead assembly.

3. Acquire, construct, and install production facilities. These include lease flow lines, separators, treaters, heaters, manifolds, measuring devices, production storage tanks, natural gas cycling and processing plants, and utility and waste disposal systems.

4. Provide improved recovery systems.

SFAS Statement Number 19 notes that all costs incurred to drill and equip development wells, development-type test wells, and service wells are, in fact, development costs and should be capitalized whether or not the well is successful. All costs incurred in the drilling of those wells as well as the costs of constructing equipment and facilities should be included in the entity's uncompleted wells, equipment, and facilities until drilling or construction is completed. At completion, the costs become part of these assets costs.

Costs of Production   The production process involves bringing the oil and gas to the surface as well as gathering, treating, field processing, and storing them. Production costs include those costs needed to operate and maintain an entity's wells, related equipment, and facilities; depreciation; and other costs of operating support equipment and facilities. These costs become part of the oil and gas that is produced. The following are examples of production costs incurred in lifting gas and oil to the surface:

1. Costs of labor to operate the wells and related equipment and facilities.

2. Repairs and maintenance.

3. Materials, supplies, and fuel consumed, and services utilized in operating the wells and related equipment and facilities.

4. Property taxes and insurance applicable to proved properties and wells and related equipment and facilities.

5. Severance taxes.

In addition to the aforementioned production costs, depreciation, depletion, amortization of capitalized acquisition, exploration, and development costs also become part of the cost of oil and gas produced.

Support Equipment and Facilities   Support equipment and facilities include such items as seismic equipment, construction and grading equipment, vehicles, repair shops, warehouses, supply points, camps, and division, district, or field offices. SFAS Statement Number 19 requires that all costs of acquiring or constructing support equipment and facilities should be capitalized. Some support equipment or facilities may have been acquired or constructed for a single activity, including exploration, development, or production. Others may serve two or more of these activities and may also serve in the transportation, refining, and marketing activities of the enterprise. If support equipment and facilities are used in oil- and gas-producing activities, their depreciation and operating costs are considered exploration, development, or production costs based on the specific use.

Disposition of Acquisition Costs after Capitalization

Acquisition costs of proved properties and the costs of wells and related equipment and facilities should be amortized and become part of the cost of oil and gas that is produced. In general, if impairment of unproved properties is found to exist, then it should be recognized. In addition, the costs of exploratory wells or exploratory-type stratigraphic test wells should be charged to expense if it is ascertained that the wells have not realized proved reserves. The following discussion of GAAP augments these concepts related to the disposition of capitalized acquisition costs.

Assessment and Reclassification of Unproved Properties A periodic assessment of unproved properties should be made to ascertain whether impairment has occurred. Impairment would likely have occurred if, for example, a dry hole has been drilled on it and the entity has no plans to continue drilling in the future. In general, if drilling has not begun on the property or nearby properties, the probability of its partial or total impairment increases as the expiration of the lease term approaches. If, in fact, impairment is indicated in a periodic assessment, then a loss should be recognized through the use of a valuation allowance account.

A property should be reclassified from an unproved to a proved property when proved reserves are discovered on or are otherwise attributed to the property.

Depletion and Depreciation Considerations

Depletion of Proved Properties Capitalized acquisition cost of proved properties should be depleted (amortized) by the unit-of-production method. By doing so each unit-of-production is assigned a pro rata portion of the unamortized acquisition costs. The unit-of-production method may be applied on a property-by-property basis or on the basis of some reasonable aggregation of properties with a common geological structural feature or stratigraphic condition, such as a reservoir or field. The unit cost should be computed on the basis of the total estimated units of proved oil and gas reserves. The total amount of depletion is then computed based on the number of units produced in the current period. Unit-of-production depletion rates should be reevaluated whenever it appears that there is a need for such reevaluation but at least once a year. All such revisions should be accounted for prospectively as changes of accounting estimates.

Depreciation of Exploratory Drilling and Development Costs   Capitalized costs of exploratory wells and exploratory-type stratigraphic test wells that have found proved reserves and capitalized development costs should also be depreciated by the unit-of-production method. Similar to proved properties, the depreciation should be computed either on a property-by-property basis or on the basis of some reasonable aggregation of properties with a common geological or stratigraphic condition, such as a reservoir or field. The unit cost should be computed on the basis of total estimated units of proved developed reserves rather than on the basis of all proved reserves, which is the basis of depleting acquisition costs of proved properties. As with proved properties, unit-of-production depreciation rates should be revised whenever there appears to be a need for such a revision. However, the revision must occur at least once a year. Such revisions should be accounted for as changes in accounting estimates.

Depreciation of Support Equipment and Facilities   Depreciation of support equipment and facilities should be accounted for as either exploration cost, development cost, or production cost based on the assets' specific use.

Dismantlement, Restoration, and Abandonment Costs and Salvage Values   In all depletion or depreciation calculations, estimated dismantlement, restoration, and abandonment costs and estimated residual values should be taken into account in computing applicable amortization and depreciation rates.

Amortization of Oil and Gas Reserve Costs That Are Produced Jointly

Many properties contain a combination of oil and gas reserves. This presents a problem for amortizing capitalized costs using the unit-of-production method, which requires that the number of current units of oil or gas produced be determined and be compared to the total units of gas or oil reserves in a property or group of properties to be estimated. In those cases where a combination of oil and gas resources is present, the gas and oil produced should be converted to a common unit of measure on the basis of their approximate relative energy content without considering their relative sales value.

If, on the other hand, the relative proportion of gas and oil extracted in the current period is expected to be the same throughout the remaining life of the property, the unit-of-production methodology may be computed on the basis of only one of the minerals. In addition, if either oil or gas dominates both the reserves and current production (evaluated on the basis of relative energy content), then the unit-of-production process should be computed on the basis of the dominant mineral only.

Information that Surfaces after the Balance Sheet Date Any information that becomes known after the balance sheet date but before the financial statements are issued should be considered as having existed at the balance sheet date. For example, information that may be ascertained regarding the assessment of an unproved property during the period subsequent to year-end but prior to the financial statements issuance should be considered to have existed at the balance sheet date and should be disclosed. In addition, if an exploratory well is in progress at the end of a financial period and is determined not to have any proved reserves before the financial statements are issued, then the costs incurred up until the end of the period, net of any salvage, should be charged to expense for this period. However, previously issued financial statements should not be retroactively restated for this new information.

Surrender or Abandonment of Properties SFAS Statement Number 19 requires that when an unproved property is surrendered, abandoned, or determined to be worthless, then all capitalized acquisition costs should be charged off against the related allowance that has been provided for impairment. If the allowance is insufficient, then a loss should be recognized.

If only a single well or piece of equipment is abandoned or retired as part of an individual property or group of proved properties (constituting an overall amortization base), and the remainder (of the property or group) continues to produce oil or gas, then no gain or loss should be recognized on the abandonment or retirement. Instead, the assets being abandoned or retired should be considered to be fully amortized and their cost should be charged to accumulated depreciation, depletion, or amortization. When the last well on an individual property or group of properties (on which amortization is aggregately computed) ceases to produce and the entire property or group is abandoned, a gain or loss should be recognized. A loss should also be recognized if a partial abandonment or retirement of a proved property or group of proved properties or group or the abandonment or retirement of wells or related equipment results from a catastrophic event or other major abnormality.

Mineral Property Conveyances   Mineral interests in properties are commonly conveyed to others. This may be due to a desire to obtain financing, spread risks, improve operating efficiency, and achieve tax benefits. Conveyances may involve the transfer of all or part of the rights and responsibilities of operating a property. Similarly, the transfer may be of a nonoperating interest to another party with full retention of the property's operation.

SFAS Statement Number 19 requires that a gain or loss should not be recognized at the time of conveyance in the following situations:

1. Assets used in oil- and gas-producing activities (including both proved and unproved properties) are transferred in exchange for other assets also used in oil and gas production.

2. Assets in a joint undertaking are jointly pooled with the intention of finding, developing, or producing oil or gas from a particular property or group of properties.

SFAS 19 also requires that a gain should not be recognized at the time of conveyance in the following situations:

1. A part of an interest owned is sold and substantial uncertainty exists about the recovery of costs applicable to the retained interests.

2. A part of an interest owned is sold and the seller has a substantial obligation for future performance (e.g., obligation to drill a well or operate the property without reimbursement for the portion of drilling or costs to the interest that was sold).

If a conveyance is not classified as one of the transactions described in the aforementioned sections, then a gain or loss would ordinarily be recognized unless there are other aspects of the transaction that would prohibit such recognition under GAAP.

Accounting for Income Taxes   Oil- and gas-producing companies are required to follow SFAS Statement Number 109 (*Accounting for Income Taxes*). These entities incur many transactions (e.g., intangible drilling and development costs that are deductible in determining taxable income when incurred but are capitalized and amortized for financial accounting purposes for successful exploratory wells and development wells) that enter into the determination of taxable income and pretax accounting income in different periods. These transactions generate temporary differences that result in deferred income taxes consequences. In applying SFAS 109 to the gas and oil industry, the possibility that statutory depletion in future periods will reduce or eliminate taxable income in future years should be considered. This is important in determining whether or not it is likely that the tax benefits of deferred tax assets will be realized. However, the tax benefit of the excess of statutory depletion over cost depletion for tax purposes should not be recognized until the period in which the excess is deducted for income tax purposes.

Capitalizing Interest Costs under the Full Cost Method   For oil- and gas-producing operations accounted for by the full cost method, assets that are in use in the earnings process of the entity are assets that do not qualify for capitalization of interest cost. Unusually significant investments in unproved properties and major development projects that are not currently being used (and as a result are not being depreciated, depleted, or amortized) and on which exploration or development activities are in progress are assets that qualify for capitalization of interest costs. In addition, in a cost center with no production, significant properties, and projects on which exploration or development activities are in progress represents assets qualifying for capitalization of interest costs.

Disclosures   All oil- and gas-producing enterprises must disclose in their financial statements the method of accounting for costs incurred in their oil- and gas-producing activities and the manner of disposing of capitalized costs relating to those activities.

For purposes of this section, an entity is considered to have *significant* oil- and gas-producing activities if it satisfies one or more of the following criteria: [This determination should be applied separately for each year for which a complete set of annual financial statements are presented (e.g., a statement of financial position, an income statement, and statement of cash flows including necessary footnotes).]

1. Revenues from oil- and gas-producing activities are 10% or more of the combined revenues of all of the entity's industry segments.

2. The results of operations for oil and gas activities, excluding income taxes, are 10% or more of the greater of

    (a) The combined operating profit of all industry segments that did not incur an operating loss

    (b) The combined operating loss of all industry segments that did incur an operating loss

3. The identifiable assets relating to oil and gas activities are 10% or more of the combined identifiable assets of all industry segments.

The aforementioned disclosures are only required for complete sets of annual financial statements. They are not required in interim financial reports. Interim financial reports should, however, include information about a major discovery or other favorable or adverse events that cause a significant change from the information relating to oil and gas reserve quantities presented in the most recent annual financial report issued.

Publicly traded entities that have significant oil- and gas-producing activities are required to disclose with their complete sets of annual financial statements the following information, which is considered to be of a supplementary nature:

1. Proved oil and gas reserve quantities.

2. Capitalized costs relating to oil- and gas-producing activities.

3. Costs incurred for property acquisition, exploration, and development activities.

4. Results of operations for oil- and gas-producing activities.

5. A standardized measure of discounted future net cash flows relating proved oil and gas reserve quantities.

Details relating to these categories are discussed next.

Disclosures Relating to Proved Oil and Gas Reserve Quantities   The following information relating to proved oil and gas quantities are required supplemental disclosures of publicly traded entities that have significant oil and gas production activities:

1. Net quantities of the entity's interests in proved reserves and proved developed reserves of (a) crude oil (including condensate and natural gas liquids and (b) natural gas. Net quantities should include reserves relating to royalty interests owned if the necessary information is available to the entity. If this information is unavailable, that fact and the entity's share of oil and gas produced for those royalty interests should be disclosed for the year. Net quantities should not include interests of others in properties owned by the entity.

2. Changes in net quantities or an entity's proved reserves of oil and gas. The following should be disclosed with an explanation:

   (a) Revisions of previous estimates either upward or downward resulting from new information derived from development drilling

   (b) Changes in reserve estimates resulting from the application of improved recovery techniques

   (c) Purchases of minerals in place

   (d) Additions to proved reserves that result from (1) extension of proved acreage through additional drilling in periods subsequent to discovery and (2) discovery of new fields with proved reserves

   (e) Production

   (f) Sales of minerals in place

3. Disclosure should be made of the fact that an entity's proved reserves of oil and gas are located entirely within its home country. If some or all of its reserves are located in foreign countries, appropriate disclosures relating to the net quantities of reserves of oil and gas and their changes should be made for the home country as well as for each foreign geographic area in which material reserves are located.

4. Quantities of oil and natural gas liquid reserves and any changes in them should be disclosed in barrels and cubic feet, respectively.

5. Important economic consideration or significant uncertainties affecting an entity's proved reserves should be disclosed. Examples are unusually expensive development or lifting costs, and the necessity of building major pipeline or other major facilities before reserve production could begin.

6. If a government restricts disclosure of estimated reserves for properties under its authority or of amounts under long-term supply or purchase agreements, or if the government requires the disclosure of reserves other than proved, then the entity should represent that the reserves estimates or amounts do not include figures for that government or that estimates of proved reserves that are disclosed include reserves other than proved.

Disclosures Relating to Capitalized Costs of Oil- and Gas-Producing Activities An entity must disclose the aggregate capitalized cost relating to its oil- and gas-producing activities as well as the aggregate related accumulated depreciation, depletion, amortization, and valuation allowances at the end of the year. In general, APB Opinion Number 12 (*Omnibus Opinion—1967*) requires that there be disclosure of balances of major classes of depreciable assets, by nature or function. Thus, there should be separate disclosure of capitalized costs for mineral interests in properties, wells and related equipment and facilities, support equipment and facilities used in oil- and gas-producing activities, and uncompleted wells, equipment, and facilities. In addition, combinations of these categories may be appropriate.

If material, capitalized costs of unproved properties should also be disclosed. If the entity's financial statements include investments that are accounted for by the equity method, the entity's share of the investees' net capitalized costs relating to oil- and gas-producing activities as of the end of the year should be shown separately.

Disclosures Relating to Costs Incurred in Oil and Gas Property Acquisition, Exploration, and Development Activities Information relating to property acquisition costs, exploration costs, and development costs (whether those costs are capitalized or charged to expense at the time they are incurred) are required supplemental disclosures of publicly traded entities that have significant oil and gas production activities.

If some or all of those costs are incurred in foreign countries, the amounts disclosed should be separately shown for each of the geographic areas for which reserve quantities are shown. If significant costs have been incurred to acquire mineral interests containing proved reserves, these costs should be separately disclosed from the costs of acquiring unproved properties.

If the entity accounts for investments using the equity method, the entity's share of the investees's property acquisition, exploration, and development costs should be separately disclosed for the year, in the aggregate, and for each geographical area for which reserve quantities are disclosed.

Disclosures of Results of Operations for Oil- and Gas-Producing Activities Information relating to the results of operations for oil- and gas-producing activities of an entity should be disclosed for the year as part of the supplemental disclosures requirement for publicly traded entities that have significant oil and gas production activities. This information should be shown in the aggregate and for each geographic area for which reserve quantities are disclosed. Information relating to the following areas should be presented:

1. Revenues
2. Production (lifting) costs

3. Exploration expenses

4. Depreciation, depletion, and amortization

5. Income tax expense

6. Results of operations for oil- and gas-producing activities (excluding corporate overhead and interest costs)

7. Valuations

Disclosure of a Standardized Measure of Discounted Future Net Cash Flows Related to Proved Oil and Gas Reserve Quantities   Information relating to a standardized measure of discounted future net cash flows regarding an entity's interest's in (1) proved oil and gas reserves and (2) oil and gas subject to purchase under long-term supply, purchase, or similar agreements and contracts in which the entity participates in the operation of the properties should be disclosed at the end of the period as part of the supplemental disclosures requirement for publicly traded entities that have significant oil and gas production activities. The following information should be shown in the aggregate and for each geographic area for which quantities are disclosed:

1. *Future cash inflows*—Future cash inflows should be computed by applying year-end prices of oil and gas relating the entity's proved reserves to the year-end quantities of those reserves. Future price changes should only be considered to the extent provided by contractual arrangements in existence at year-end.

2. *Future development and production costs*—Future development and production costs should be computed by estimating the expenditures to be incurred in developing and producing the proved oil and gas reserves at the end of the period based on year-end costs and assuming the continuation of existing economic conditions. If estimated development expenditures are significant, they should be disclosed separately from estimated production costs.

3. *Future income taxes*—Future income taxes are derived by applying the appropriate year-end statutory tax rates to the future pretax net cash flows relating to the entity's proved oil and gas reserves less the tax basis of the properties involved.

4. *Future net cash flows*—Future net cash flows are determined by subtracting future development production costs and future income tax expense from future cash inflows.

5. *Discount*—The discount amount is derived by using a discount rate of 10% a year to reflect the timing of future net cash flows relating to proved oil and gas reserves.

6. *Standardized measure of discounted future net cash flows*—This measure is determined by subtracting future net cash flows less the computed discount.

7. *The aggregate change in the standardized measure of discounted cash flow*—The following sources of change relating to this measure should be disclosed separately if individually significant:

   (a) Net change in sales and transfer prices and in production (lifting) costs related to future production

   (b) Changes in estimated future development costs

   (c) Sales and transfers of oil and gas produced during the period

   (d) Net change due to extensions, discoveries, and improved recovery

   (e) Net change due to purchases and sales of minerals in place

   (f) Net change to revisions in quantity estimates

   (g) Previously estimated development costs incurred during the period

   (h) Accretion of discount

   (i) Net change in income taxes

In computing the aforementioned nine amounts, the following guidelines should be followed:

1. The effects of changes in prices and costs should be computed before the effects of changes in quantities. As a result, changes in quantities should be stated at year-end prices and costs.

2. The change in computed income taxes should reflect the effect of income taxes incurred during the period as well as the change in future income tax expenses.

3. All changes except income taxes should be reported on a pretax basis.

8. Any additional information that must be provided in preventing the disclosure of the standardized discounted cash flow from being misleading should be included.

REAL ESTATE TRANSACTIONS

Primary Sources of Authoritative GAAP

The primary sources of authoritative GAAP relating to real estate transactions include

- SFAS Statement Number 66 (*Accounting for Sales of Real Estate*)
- SFAS Statement Number 98 (*Accounting for Leases*)
- SFAS Statement Number 121 (*Accounting for the Impairment of Long-Lived Assets to be Disposed Of*)

GAAP Abstract and Introduction

In retail land sales, full accrual accounting under GAAP requires the following be satisfied before profits may be recognized:

1. The seller's receivables from the land sales must be collectible.

2. The seller must have no significant remaining obligations for construction or development.

Other sales in retail land sales projects may be accounted and reported under either the percentage-of-completion or the installment method. The criteria for their applicability are based on the collectibility of the seller's receivable from the land sales and the seller's remaining obligations.

Profit recognition for other sales of real estate by the full accrual and several other methods is all delineated in the subsequent discussions. This recognition is dependent on whether a sale has been consummated, the extent of the buyer's investment in the property being sold, whether the sellers' receivable is subject to future subordination, and the degree of the seller's continuing involvement with the property after the sale.

Primary GAAP

This section distinguishes between retail land sales and other sales of real estate. The former are sales, on a volume basis, of lots that are subdivisions of large tracts of land. They are characterized by the following: (1) very small down payments; (2) the inability of the seller to enforce the sales contract or the buyer's note against the buyer's general credit; (3) return of the buyer's down payment if the cancellation is made within an established cancellation period; and (4) defaults by the buyer after the cancellation, resulting in recovery of the land by the seller and forfeiture of at least some of the principal payments by the buyer. Amounts retained by the seller are determined by federal and state laws.

Examples of real estate sales transactions that are not retail land sales are

- Sales of lots to builders
- Sales of homes, buildings, and parcels of land to builder of land and others
- Sales of corporate stock of enterprises with substantial real estate
- Sales of a partnership interest that is in substance a sale of real estate (for example, an enterprise that forms a partnership, arranging for the partnership to acquire the property directly from third parties,

and selling an interest in the partnership to investors, who then become limited partners)

■ Sales of time-sharing interests if the sales are in-substance sales of real estate (Time sharing real estate interests represent the right to occupy a dwelling for a designated period each year.)

Real Estate Sales Other Than Retail Land Sales

Sales of real estate other than retail land sales may be accounted for in one of several of the following ways:

■ The full accrual method—Profit is recognized when the real estate is sold.

■ Cost recovery method—Profit recognition is deferred until cash received exceed the seller's cost of the property sold.

■ Deposit method—No recognition of profit at consummation of the sale.

■ Reduced profit method—Profit is deferred until payments are made.

■ Percentage of completion—The amount of profit recognition is predicated on the relationship of costs incurred to the total costs to be incurred.

■ Installment method.

A discussion of these methodologies follows.

Use of the Full Accrual Method

The full accrual method should be used if

1. The sale has been fully consummated. A sale has been fully consummated when

   (a) All consideration specified in the contract has been exchanged.

   (b) The parties to the contract are fully bound by the contract.

(c) All requirements that had to be satisfied to close the sale of property have been satisfied (i.e., inspections, land surveys, title policies, etc.)

(d) Any permanent financing that is required of the seller has been arranged.

2. The buyer's initial and continuing investments in the property are considered sufficient commitments to pay for the property. A purchaser's initial investment should include

(a) Any cash that was paid as a down payment

(b) The purchaser's notes payable to the seller together with irrevocable letters of credit from established lending institutions

(c) Any payments by the buyer to third parties to reduce any existing debt that may remain on the property

(d) Additional cash proceeds that were paid by the buyer as a required part of the sales contract (i.e., points, prepaid interest, etc.)

(e) Any other payments or considerations that have been sold or converted to cash to the seller

The initial investment in the property is considered to be met by FASB Statement Number 66 for purposes of sufficiency if it is at least equivalent to that which an independent lending institution would require for a loan on the same type of property at the same price. For example, the following are some examples of the minimum initial investments expressed as a percentage of sales value that would have to paid in to satisfy FASB 66:

Property	*Percentage of Sales to be Paid in*
Land—Held for commercial, industrial, or	
residential development to commence within two years after sale	20
Held for commercial, industrial, residential, development to commence after two years	25
Multifamily residence:	
Primary residence:	
Cash flow currently sufficient to service all indebtedness	10

Startup situations or current deficiencies in cash flow	15
Secondary or recreational residence:	
Cash flow currently sufficient to service all indebtedness	15
Startup situations or current deficiencies in cash flow	25
Single-family residential property (including condominium or cooperative housing)	
Primary residence of the buyer	5
Secondary or recreational residence	10

Note: Minimum initial investments for other types of property are specified in paragraph 54 of FASB Statement Number 66.

Frequently, sales contracts relating to land sales contain certain provisions that require a seller to release a lien on a portion of property after receiving certain amounts of payments from the seller. The seller will release the lien only if it has obtained a sufficient amount of money that it believes places an acceptable level of risk on the remaining financing. In this situation, the initial investment of the buyer is considered to be sufficient for the property overall if (1) it is an adequate initial investment on the property not released and (2) it is considered adequate to cover the the property released at the date of sale. If the amounts applied to the unreleased portions do not satisfy the initial (and continuing) investment requirements, then each release should be viewed as a separate and individual sale.

3. The sale is not subject to future subordination. The seller's receivable should have a lien that is not subordinate to all other debt in the property except (1) a first mortgage loan existing at the date of sale or (2) a future loan provided for in the sales agreement assuming that any proceeds for loan repayment will be applied first to the receivable of the seller.

4. The sale of the property fully constitutes a transfer of all the risks and rewards of property ownership without any future seller involvement in the property. The fact that the seller has some sort of involvement may be indicative of the fact that the risks and rewards of property ownership have not, in fact, been transferred and a bona fide sale has not been made. For example, the seller may guarantee

the buyer some purchase price rebate if a minimum return is not generated for the new buyer.

Additional requirements must also be met in order for a retail land sale to be accounted for under the full accrual method. FASB Statement Number 66 requires that the following must also be met:

1. Development of the lots that have been sold must be complete.

2. The refund period has expired.

3. Cumulative payments are sufficient.

4. Receivables are subordinate to any debt on the property and are deemed to be fully collectible.

If these criteria are not met, then revenue should be recognized under the percentage-of-completion method, installment method, or deposit method.

EXAMPLE: FULL ACCRUAL METHOD

Assume that a company that develops land lots enters into a sales agreement with a contractor to purchase the land lots for $600,000. The agreement calls for the contractor to pay the development company $150,000 cash and a note for $450,000. The note is due in four equal installments, pays interest at the rate of 8%, is not subordinate to any new loans on the property, and is backed by an irrevocable letters of credit from an independent established lending institution. Land and development costs on the part of the development company equal $400,000. The land development company would make the following entry on the sale of the developed lots:

Cash	150,000	
Note receivable	450,000	
Sales from lots		600,000
Cost of lots	400,000	
Land and development capitalized costs		400,000

The full accrual method should be used when the aforementioned noted criteria have been met. If they have not been met, then the method of accounting that should be used depends on the criteria that has not been met. The following is a discussion of the method(s) that should be used when certain of the criteria have not been met.

Nonconsummation of the Sale

If the real estate sale has not been consummated, the seller should use the deposit method of accounting. However, when office buildings, apartments, condominiums, shopping centers, and similar structures are being built, the percentage-of-completion method may be used because of the relatively long construction period.

Buyer's Initial Investment Is Not Sufficient and Does Not Qualify

If the buyer's initial investment is not sufficient but recovery of the cost of the property is reasonably assured in the contingency of a default by the buyer, the sale should be accounted for using the installment method. However, if the recovery of the property's cost is not certain (the receipt of the full sales price of the property is uncertain), then the cost recovery method should be used.

It is possible for the seller of the property that has accounted for the sale under the installment method or cost recovery method to subsequently change to the full accrual method if the requirements for the full accrual method are satisfied. The accounting for the change consists of recognizing in income the remaining profit that had not been recognized under the installment or cost recovery method.

Buyer's Continuing Investment Is Not Sufficient for the Full Accrual Method and Does Not Qualify

If the purchaser's initial investment is sufficient to satisfy the full accrual method, but is not sufficient to recognize profit under that method because the continuing investment is not sufficient, then the seller should use the reduced profit method, installment method, or cost recovery method. The reduced profit method should be used if the purchaser's annual payments made to the seller are large enough to cover (1) principal and interest on the maximum first mortgage loan that could be obtained on the property and (2) interest, at the market rates, on the excess of the actual total debt on the property over such a maximum first mortgage loan. If these criteria are not both met, the seller should recognize profit by the either the installment method or the cost recovery method.

Receivable Accepted by the Seller Subject to Future Subordination

If the seller receivable is subject to future subordination, its recoverability is not assured since the seller would not have an unequivocal right to the property if the buyer defaults. In this situation, the seller should use the cost recovery method when its receivable is subject to future subordination except when (1) a first mortgage loan exists on the date of the sale or (2) a future loan provided for in the sales agreement if the loan proceed will be applied first to pay the seller's receivable.

Seller's Continuing Involvement Exists after It Is Sold

If the transfer of the risks and rewards of ownership to the purchaser has not occurred because the seller still maintains a continuing involvement with the property, the full accrual method of accounting should not be used. If the sellers' loss of profit because of his or her continuing involvement with the property is limited by the terms of the sales contract, profit may be recognized but should be reduced by the seller's maximum exposure to loss. In all other situations, if the seller has some other form of continuing involvement with the property, then the transaction should be accounted for in accordance with the extent and nature of the seller's involvement rather than as a sale (e.g., profit sharing, financing, leasing, etc.).

The following is a brief discussion of different forms of continuing involvement with the property and the accounting methods that should be used.

■ The seller has partially sold the property. Partial sales consist of those in which the seller maintains an ownership interest in the property or has an ownership interest in the buyer. In this situation, profit should be recognized only if

1. The buyer and seller are independent of each other. If the seller has a noncontrolling interest in the buyer, the seller should recognize profit in proportion to the outside ownership of the purchaser. However, if the seller has a controlling interest in the buyer, no profit should be recorded until it is realized by a (a) sale to an independent party or (b) profits from continuing operations.

2. The sales price is reasonably assured of being collectible. If the sale is not reasonably assured, then the installment method or cost recovery method should be used.

3. The seller is not obligated to support the operations of the property or its obligations to an extent greater than its ownership interest. If, in fact, the seller has to support the operations of the property or its obligations and the transaction is in substance a sale, then the seller should record profit to the extent that the proceeds from the sale exceed all the costs related to the property that are the responsibility of the seller.

■ The seller is required to repurchase the property or the contract contains an option that may be exercised by the buyer requiring that the seller repurchase the property. In substance, therefore, this transaction should be accounted for as a financing, leasing, or profit-sharing contract rather than a sale of real property.

■ The seller is required to support the operations of the property. If the degree of support provided by the seller is only for a limited amount of time, then profit on the sale should be recognized on the basis of the services performed. This assumes, however, that profit should not be recognized until there is reasonable assurance that future receipts will exceed operating expenses, debt payments, and other contractual obligations. On the other hand, if the seller is required to support operations for an extended period of time, the transaction should be accounted for as a financing, leasing, or profit-sharing agreement rather than a sale. If the support period is not specified in the sales contract, it is presumed for at least two years beyond the date that rental operations begin. Revenue should be recognized on the degree of performance of the seller in this situation. If actual rental proceeds exceed operating expenses, debt service, and other contractual payments before the two-year period ends, profit may be recognized at an earlier date. If the sales agreement requires that the seller manage the property without any compensation at all or less than the going rates that one would expect for such services, then compensation should be estimated as income as the services are performed over the contract term when the sale is recognized.

■ The seller is a general partner in a limited partnership which has acquired an interest in the property and the seller holds a receivable from the buyer for a material portion of the sales price. In this situation, the transaction should be accounted for as a financing, leasing, or profit-sharing agreement rather than a sale of property.

■ The seller leases back all or a part of the property for the remaining life of the property. This transaction should be accounted for as a financing, leasing, or profit-sharing arrangement rather than a sale.

■ The seller contractually guarantees a return of the buyer's investment in the property or guarantees some return on the investment for an extended period of time. The transaction is a financing, leasing, or profit-sharing arrangement rather than a sale. **Note:** If the guarantee of investment return is for a limited period of time, the deposit method of accounting should be used until operations of the property cover the operating expenses, debt service, and contractual payments. Profit should only be recognized subsequently when required services are performed.

■ On sales of condominiums or time-sharing interests, profits should be recognized based on the percentage-of-completion method. The percentage-of-completion method should be used on the sale of individual units (of condominium units or time sharing interests) if the following criteria are met:

1. The buyer can no longer require a refund (except for nondelivery of the unit or interest).

2. Construction is beyond the preliminary stage.

3. Sales prices are deemed to be collectible.

4. Enough units of the building project have been sold so that it may be assumed that the project will not become a rental property.

5. Total sales revenues and costs can be reasonably estimated.

If any of the aforementioned criterion were not met, then the deposit method should be used. When all are met, then the percentage-of-completion method should be used.

■ Although the form of the agreement appears to be a sale, the purchaser of the property has an option to buy the property. In this situation generally, the buyer makes a down payment and is not required to make any more payments on the property until certain conditions are resolved, such as obtaining a building permit or zoning modification. These transactions should be accounted for using the deposit method, and the funds from the sale should be accounted for as a liability and recognized as income when the purchaser exercises the option or allows it to expire.

■ The seller sells building improvements and leases the land underlying the improvements to the buyer. In this situation, the entire transaction should be accounted for as a lease if the land lease does not cover the entire economic life of the improvements or is not for a substantial period. If both of those criteria are met, then profit should be recognized on the sale of the improvements at the time of the sale and should be measured by (a) the present value of the lease rental payments (not in excess of the cost of the land) plus (b) the sales value of the improvements less (c) the carrying value of the improvements and the land. The seller should record profit on the buyer's rent payments that are made if they exceed the land's cost and the rent is received after the primary debt on the improvements is paid off. The profits should be recognized when

a. The land is sold or

b. The rents in excess of the seller's cost of the land are earned under the lease

■ The sales contract requires that the seller is obligated to develop the property in the future. In this case, if such obligation exists, or the seller is required to extend the facilities in any way, then the percentage-of-completion method is commonly used to account for the sale.

■ The sales agreement calls for the seller to partake in the future profits of the property without the risk of any loss. In general, if this transaction qualifies for the full accrual method of accounting and the seller partakes in future profits in the property without risk of loss, then the risks and rewards of ownership and the lack of continuing involvement are considered to be met. Future profit is recorded in the accounting period when the profits are in fact realized. All costs of the sale are recognized at the time of the sale. Specifically, no costs are deferred to periods when contingent profits are realized.

Retail Land Sales

Introduction

Retail land sales consist of large amounts of residential lots sales of subdivisions of large tracts of land. The developer of the land attempts to provide the buyer with financing terms that require a lower down payment than would be possible if the buyer would attempt to obtain the financing from outside financial institutions. In the latter situation, for example, financial institutions would require that buyer's note be purchased only at a significant discount. In general, the land developer is also required to provide the buyer with a refund period in which a full refund would be received and the sales contract would be considered null and void.

Accounting for Retail Land Sales

The following is a discussion of the methods used to account for profits from retail land sales.

Full Accrual Method   The full accrual method should be utilized when the following criteria are met:

1. Before the refund period has expired, the purchaser has made the required down payment and all other payments required by the contract.

2. The payments that are made cumulatively (principal and interest) must equal no less than 10% of the full contract price.

3. The seller's collection experience should be at least 90% of the contracts from the land sale project if they are not canceled with six months following the sales contract date. The criteria may be met if a down payment of at least 20% on the contract price is received.

4. The receivable from the sale of the land sale must not be subordinate to any new loans on the property.

5. The seller has satisfied all its legal obligations to make improvements of the lots sold or to build any other required facilities to lots that have been sold.

In accounting for the full accrual method, sales must be recognized at the amount contracted for, an allowance of doubtful collectibles must be provided for, the cost of the lots that are sold must be transferred from the seller's inventory account, and an allowance for discounts (contra contracts receivable account) must be recorded to reduce the receivable account to the presents value of all required payments. If the seller has initiated programs that are designed to accelerate the collection of receivables, any profit on the sale should be reduced by the charges for anticipated discounts being offered as a result of incentives. If sales discounts as a result of incentives are offered infrequently, they should be debited against income in the period in which they are granted.

Percentage-of-Completion Method   If a retail land sale satisfies all the conditions for the accrual method except that the seller has not met its obligation to complete all improvements or construction on the lots that are sold, then the percentage-of-completion method should be used if the two following conditions are met:

1. It is believed that the land can be developed for the purposes expected and that the properties can be used for these purposes at the end of the expected payment period.

2. The improvements and construction that are required on the property have been initiated and are in progress. There is every reason to believe based on the work that has already been performed that all improvements and construction will be completed according to the agreed upon plan. There do not appear to be any extenuating circumstances, such as delays or additional costs, that would mean the project will not be completed as expected.

Accounting for the percentage-of-completion method is as one would expect. Revenue should be recorded by computing the ratio of costs incurred to date to the total estimated costs expected to be incurred. This fraction is then multiplied by the net sales number. Costs incurred and total cost to be incurred include the following: land cost, interest and project carrying costs incurred prior to the sale (previously charged to expense), and selling costs associated with the project. Estimates for future improvement costs should be based on amounts that are expected in the construction industry in the area. Estimates of future improvements should be reviewed yearly and the percentage-of-completion should be recalculated when cost estimates are revised.

Installment Method   If a retail land sale has gone beyond its refund period, has had its cumulative payments equal no less than 10% of the full contract price, and does not meet any of the other criteria for the full accrual method or percentage-of-completion methods, then it should be accounted for under the installment method if the following two conditions are met regarding the financial condition of the seller:

1. The seller is able to provide both land improvement and any off-site construction that was committed to in the contract.

2. The seller is satisfying all other commitments made in the contract, including insuring the completion of the improvements of the project.

A seller originally accounting for a retail land sale by the installment method may adopt the percentage-of-completion method if the land sale subsequently satisfies all the conditions required of this method. In this situation, the seller may utilize the percentage-of-completion method for the whole project (both prior and current sales) and account for the change in methodology as a change in accounting estimate.

Deposit Method A retail land sale that fails to satisfy the conditions required for the full accrual method, percentage-of-completion method, and the installment method should be accounted for under the deposit method.

Disclosure Requirements

Real Estate Transactions—Other Than Retail Land Sales

The following are the disclosure requirements for some of the methods of accounting for real estate transactions as prescribed by FASB Statement Number 66:

> *Installment method*—Under this method, the income statement (or notes) in the period of the sale should disclose the sales value, the deferred gross profit, and the total cost of the sale. Revenue and the cost of the sales should be shown as separate items on the income statement or should be shown in the notes when the profit is recognized.

> *Cost recovery method*—Under this method, the income statement for the period including the sales date should disclose the sales value, the deferred gross profit, and the total cost of the sale. The gross profit that has not yet been recognized should be offset against the related receivable on the balance sheet. Gross profit should be pre-

sented as a separate revenue item on the income statement when it is recognized.

Deposit Method—Under this method the nonrecourse debt that has been assumed by the purchaser should be disclosed as a liability in the balance sheet of the seller. It should not be offset against the related asset.

Retail Land Sales

The following are the disclosure requirements for enterprises involved in retail land sales prescribed by FASB Statement Number 66:

1. Accounts receivable which mature for each of the five years following the date of the financial statements.

2. The weighted average of stated interest rates and range of receivables.

3. The balance of delinquent accounts receivable as well as the method used by the seller for determining the delinquency.

4. An estimate of the total costs and estimated dates of expenditures for contractual improvements for major areas from which sales are being generated for each of the five years after the date of the balance sheet.

5. Recorded debts for contractual improvements that must be made.

Supplemental and Related Guidance on These Topics from the Emerging Issue Task Force

REVENUE RECOGNITION

> EITF Issue Number 84–17 (*Profit Recognition on Sales of Real Estate with Graduated Payment Mortgages or Insured Mortgages*)
>
> EITF Issue Number 86–6 (*Antispeculation Clauses in Real Estate Sales Contracts*)
>
> EITF Issue Number 86–7 (*Recognition by Homebuilders of Profit from Sales of Land and Related Construction Contracts*)

EITF Issue Number 87–9 (*Profit Recognition on Sales of Real Estate with Insured Mortgages or Surety Bonds*)

EITF Issue Number 88–12 (*Transfer of Ownership Interest as Part of Down Payment under FASB Statement Number 66*)

SALE-LEASEBACK TRANSACTIONS

EITF Issue Number 84–37 (*Sale-Leaseback Transaction with Repurchase Option*)

EITF Issue Number 85–27, (*Recognition of Receipts from Made-up Rental Shortfalls*)

EITF Issue Number 86–17 (*Deferred Profit on Sale-Leaseback Transaction with Lessee Guarantee of Residual Value*)

EITF Issue Number 88–21 (*Accounting for the Sale of Property Subject to the Seller's Preexisting Lease*)

OTHER

EITF Issue Number 87–29 (*Exchange of Real Estate Involving Boot*)

EITF Issue Number 88–14 (*Settlement of Fees with Extra Units to a General Partner in a Master Limited Partnership*)

EITF Issue Number 88–24 (*Effect of Various Forms of Financing under FASB Statement Number 66*)

EITF Issue Number 89–14 (*Valuation of Repossessed Real Estate*)

EITF Issue Number 96–21 (*Implementation Issues in Accounting for Leasing Transactions Involving Special-Purpose Entities*)

EITF Issue Number 97–1 (*Implementation Issues in Accounting for Lease Transactions, Including Those Involving Special-Purpose Entities*)

HEALTH CARE INDUSTRY

Primary Sources of Authoritative GAAP

The primary sources of authoritative GAAP relating to guidance in the health care industry are

- SFAS Statement Number 105 (*Disclosure of Information about Financial Instruments with Off-Balance-Sheet Risk and Financial Instruments with Concentrations of Credit Risk*)

- SFAS Statement Number 107 (*Disclosure about Fair Value of Financial Instruments*)

- SFAS Statement Number 116 (*Accounting for Contributions Received and Contributions Made*)

- SFAS Statement Number 117 (*Financial Statements for Not-for-Profit Organizations*)

- SFAS Statement Number 124 (*Accounting for Certain Investments Held by Not-for-Profit Organizations*)

- SFAS Statement Number 125 (*Accounting for Transfers and Servicing of Financial Assets and Extinguishment of Liabilities*)

- FASB Interpretation Number 42 (*Accounting for Transfers of Assets in Which a Not-for-Profit Organization Is Granted Variance Power*)

- AICPA Audit and Accounting Guide (*Health Care Organizations*)

GAAP Abstract and Introduction

Accounting in the health care industry consists of reporting on the financial statements of enterprises whose primary functions consist of providing health care services to individuals. Financial statements of health care entities should be prepared in conformity with GAAP. Governmental health care entities should prepare their financial statements in accordance with Governmental Accounting Standards Board (GASB) statements and their interpretations as well as in accordance with FASB, APB, and other related pronouncements required by the GASB. In general, health care service organizations are classified in the following manner:

1. Investor-owned health care entities

2. Not-for-profit, business entities

3. Governmental health care entities

4. Not-for-profit, nonbusiness entities (voluntary health care and welfare organizations (not covered)

Primary GAAP

Required Financial Statements

Investor-owned health care enterprises are required to prepare the same financial statements as those of any investor-owned enterprise. Not-for-profit and governmental health care entities, on the other hand, are required to prepare the following financial statements:

1. Statement of operations

2. Statement of financial position

3. Statement of changes in equity (or net assets/fund balance)

4. Statement of cash flows

5. Notes to the financial statements

FASB Statement Number 95 (*Statement of Cash Flows*), and GASB Statement Number 9 (*Reporting Cash Flows of Proprietary and Nonexpendable Trust Funds and Governmental Entities*), establish the required guidelines for reporting cash flows for investor owned entities as well as governmental health care enterprises. In both groups, the direct method is considered the preferable method; however, the indirect method of reporting for cash flows is allowed. The statement of cash flows should always be reported in cash and cash equivalents. In addition, entities' balance sheets must disclose (1) total assets, (2) total liabilities, and (3) net assets. The last category should, in turn, be subdivided into the following groups:

1. Unrestricted

2. Temporarily restricted

3. Permanently restricted

These categories should also be used to report changes in equity in the statement of changes in equity.

Organizations that are not for profit require all the information of GAAP as well as other specialized requirements. For example, not-for-profit entities must fully disclose the information relating to the following items and areas:

1. Financial instruments

2. Contingencies

3. Extraordinary items

4. Cumulative effect of a change in accounting principle

For all of the aforementioned areas and in general, presentation and order in the financial statements should parallel that of profit-generating entities.

Health care entities should record all revenue on an accrual basis. This often requires that certain adjustments be accounted for and then deducted from gross revenue to derive what is termed net service revenue. The amount that should be recorded is the amount that the health service enterprise is contractually entitled to. Revenue payments to providers generally come from health insurance companies, Medicare, and Medicaid. Although not included in revenue, a health care provider should fully disclose the level of charity care it provides.

Contributions Made to Not-for-Profit Health Care Entities

The following are some general guidelines that should be followed in accounting for contributions made to not-for-profit health care entities.

Contributions made should be disclosed as resulting in increases in net assets from amounts that are

1. permanently restricted

2. temporarily restricted or

3. unrestricted

Contributed collections consisting of historical works, art, etc., that are held for education, research, or public exhibition are not required to be capitalized and recognized as revenue in the financial statements.

Contributions in service should not be recognized in the financial statements unless the following conditions are met:

1. Individuals providing the service contribution are qualified to do so with unique, specialized skills.

2. The service contribution resulted in the production or enhancement of nonfinancial assets.

Some not-for-profit health care entities are charitable enterprises that must conform with donor and grantor fiduciary responsibilities and guidelines. Therefore, these entities must use fund accounting in preparing their financial statements.

FINANCE INDUSTRY

Primary Sources of Authoritative GAAP

The primary sources of authoritative GAAP relating to guidance in the finance industry are

- SFAS Statement Number 91 (*Accounting for Nonrefundable Fees and Costs Associated with Originating or Acquiring Loans and Initial Direct Costs of Leases*)

- SFAS Statement Number 115 (*Accounting for Certain Investments in Debt and Equity Securities*)

- SFAS Statement Number 124 (*Accounting for Certain Investments Held by Not-for-Profit Organizations*)

■ SFAS Statement Number 125 (*Accounting for Transfers and Servicing of Financial Assets and Extinguishment of Liabilities*)

GAAP Abstract and Introduction

Accounting in the finance industry relates to accounting for nonrefundable fees associated with lending or purchasing a loan or a group of loans. The concepts enumerated here apply to all types of loans or lenders. Overall, the following are the salient matters of the area:

1. Loan origination fees should be recognized over the term of the related loan as an adjustment of yield.

2. Some direct loan origination costs should be recognized over the term of the related loan as a reduction of its yield.

3. In general, all loan commitment fees should be deferred except for certain retrospectively determined fees. Specifically, commitment fees that meet certain conditions, should be recognized over the loan commitment period. All other commitment fees should be recognized as an adjustment of the yield over the related loan life. If the commitment expires and is not exercised by the lender, then the loan commitment fee should be recognized in income at the date of the commitment's expiration.

4. The following should be recognized as an adjustment of yield by the interest method based on the contractual terms of the loan: loan fees; certain direct loan origination costs, and purchase premiums and discounts on loans.

Primary GAAP

Loan Origination Fees and Related Costs

An entity may acquire a loan by lending or by purchasing. The former situation is termed originating a loan. The latter is known as acquiring the loan from a party or other borrower. Loan origination fees should be deferred and recognized over the life of the loan as an adjustment of its yield resulting in an adjustment of interest income. Direct loan origination costs should also be deferred and recognized as a reduction in the yield of the loan. Direct loan origination costs should include only the following:

1. Incremental direct costs of the loan origination incurred in transactions with independent third parties for that loan.

2. Certain costs directly related to the loan performed by the lender (for example, these activities include evaluating the potential buyer's borrower's financial condition, evaluating and recording guarantees, collateral, and other security arrangements, etc.

All other lending-related costs include costs related to activities performed by the lender for such activities as advertising, soliciting potential borrowers, servicing existing loans, and other activities related to establishing and monitoring credit policies, supervision, and administration. These costs should be charged to expense as incurred.

Commitment Fees and Costs

In general, fees received for a commitment to originate or purchase a loan or group of loans should be deferred, and if the commitment is exercised, recognized over the life of the loan as an adjustment of the related loan's yield. If the commitment expires, unused, then the fee should be recognized in income at the date of the expiration of the commitment. There are two exceptions to this general rule. A brief explanation of these follows.

1. If the amount of the commitment fee is determined retrospectively as a percentage of the line of credit available but unused in a previous period, if that percentage is nominal in percentage in relation to the stated interest rate on any related borrowing, and if that borrowing will bear a market interest rate at the date the loan is made, the commitment should be recognized as service fee income as of the determination date.

2. If it is determined by the lending entity that the likelihood of commitment exercise is remote, the commitment fee should be recognized over the commitment period on a straight-line basis as service

fee income. If the commitment is subsequently exercised, in fact, over the commitment period, the remaining unamortized commitment fee at the time of exercise should be recognized over the term of the loan as an adjustment of its yield.

Direct loan origination costs incurred to make a commitment to originate a loan should be offset against any related commitment fee and the net amount recognized as a commitment fee, described previously.

Purchase of a Loan or Group of Loans

If a loan or group of loans are purchased, the initial investment should include the amount paid to the seller plus any fees paid or less any fees received. The initial investment frequently differs from the related loan's principal amount at the date of the purchase. The amount (difference) should be recognized as an adjustment of the yield over the life of the loan. All other costs incurred in connection with acquiring a purchased loan or committing to purchase loans should be charged to expense as incurred. If loans are purchased as a group, the purchaser may either allocate the initial investment to the individual loans making up the group or may account for the initial investment in the aggregate. Deferred net fees or costs should not be amortized during the periods in which interest income on a loan is not being recognized because of concerns about the realization of loan principal or interest.

Measurement of Loans Subject to Prepayment

Interest-only strips, loans, other receivables, or retained interests in securitizations that can be contractually prepaid or otherwise settled in such a way that the holder would not recover substantially all of its recorded investment should be subsequently measured in debt securities and classified as available-for-sale securities or as trading securities under FASB Statement Number 115.

Income Statement Classification

FASB Statement Number 91 requires that the loan origination, commitment, and other fees and costs that are recognized as an adjustment of loan yield should be reported as interest income. Amortization fees, such as commitment fees that are being amortized on a straight-line basis over the commitment period or included in income when the commitment expires should be reported as service fee income.

Balance Sheet Classification

FASB Statement Number 91 requires that the unamortized balance of loan origination, commitment, and other fees and costs and purchase premiums and discounts that are being recognized as an adjustment of yield should be reported on the balance sheet of the enterprise as part of the loan balance that it relates to.

INVESTMENT INDUSTRY

Primary Sources of Authoritative GAAP

The primary source of authoritative GAAP relating to guidance in the Investment Industry is:

- SFAS Statement Number 102 (*Statement of Cash Flows—Exemption of Certain Enterprises and Classification of Cash Flows from Certain Securities Acquired for Resale*)

GAAP Abstract and Introduction

An investment company aggregates shareholders' funds to provide shareholders with overall professional management expertise. Investment companies provide their shareholders with the following functions: selling shares, investing share proceeds in investment securities, and distributing net income and net realized gains to shareholders.

Liquid investment companies that meet certain criteria are exempt from the general GAAP requirement that a statement of cash flows be provided as part of a full set of financial statements.

Primary GAAP

Investment companies should report all of their investment securities at market value or fair value determined by management if market value is unavailable. Investment companies are exempt from FASB Statement Number 115 (*Accounting for Certain Investments in Debt and Equity Securities*), and as such have their own guidelines regarding securities disclosures.

Purchases and sales of investment securities should be at cost and recorded in the accounting records of the investment company at the trade date. This allows the company to include all securities purchased or exclude all securities sold in (from) its financial statement as of the balance sheet date. In addition, dividend income should be accounted for on the ex-dividend date rather than the date of payment so that the market prices of the securities on which the dividend was declared will not be affected by the dividend. Because mutual fund shares are purchased and redeemed at net asset value, it is necessary for the investment company to record its dividends payable liabilities on the ex-dividend date. As would be expected, if an individual purchases mutual fund shares between the date of declaration of the dividend and the ex-dividend date, the investor is entitled to receive the dividends. On the other hand, if shares are purchased after the ex-dividend date, then the acquirer is not entitled to receive them.

An open-end investment company is one that sells its shares to the public on an ongoing basis and is always willing to buy back its shares from investors who tender them for redemption. In accounting for an open-end company, a method known as equalization is utilized. This process precludes dilution of shareholders' per share equity in undistributed net investment income that results from the ongoing sales and redemption of mutual fund shares. The investment company makes the assumption that the net asset value of each share sold or redeemed is made up of the par value of the stock, additional paid-in-capital, any undistributed income, and any retained earnings that exist. As shares are bought and sold, the investment company continually determines the magnitude of undistributed earnings that are available for its shareholders to receive. Based on the number of shares that are outstanding, this amount is added to an equalization account when the shares are sold and subtracted when the shares are redeemed.

Under current Internal Revenue Code regulations, investment companies do not have to account for federal income taxes on their taxable income or taxable realized gains resulting from its investments. This occurs as a result of the requirement that an investment company must distribute all of its taxable income and taxable realized gains to its shareholders. Thus, for tax purposes the investment entity acts as a conduit or funnel with respect to its shareholders. If, on the other hand, all taxable income and taxable realized gains for a given tax period are not distributed, then the investment company must record a tax liability at the end of the last day of tax period. Thus, in this situation, shareholders of the investment company are entitled to a credit for taxes paid.

Exemption from Statement of Cash Flow Requirement

FASB Statement Number 102 provides that an investment company is exempt from including a statement of cash flows as part of its required financial statements if the following conditions are met:

1. The company's investments are all highly liquid.
2. The company includes a statement of changes in net assets with its financial statements.
3. The company had an immaterial amount of debt relative to its average total assets based on its average debt outstanding during the accounting period.
4. The company's investments were carried at market value in the accounting records and financial statements.

MORTGAGE BANKING INDUSTRY

Primary Sources of Authoritative GAAP

The primary sources of authoritative GAAP relating to guidance in the mortgage banking industry are

- SFAS Statement Number 65 (*Accounting for Certain Mortgage Banking Activities*)

- SFAS Statement Number 91 (*Accounting for Nonrefundable Fees and Costs Associated with Originating or Acquiring Loans and Initial Direct Costs of Leases*)

- SFAS Statement Number 115 (*Accounting for Certain Investments in Debt and Equity Securities*)

- SFAS Statement Number 124 (*Accounting for Certain Investments Held by Not-for-Profit Organizations*)

- SFAS Statement Number 125 (*Accounting for Transfers and Servicing of Financial Assets and Extinguishments of Liabilities*)

- SFAS Statement Number 127 (*Deferral of the Effective Date of Certain Provisions of FASB Statement 125*)

- SFAS Statement Number 134 (*Accounting for Mortgage-Backed Securities Retained After the Securitization of Mortgage Loan Held for Sale by a Mortgage Banking Enterprise—an Amendment of FASB Statement Number 65*)

- FASB Technical Bulletin Number 87–3 (*Accounting for Mortgage Servicing Fees and Rights*)

GAAP Abstract and Introduction

This area applies to certain activities of a mortgage banking entity and to mortgage banking operations of other enterprises, such as thrifts and commercial banks.

Mortgage loans that are held for sale should be presented at the lower of cost or market. Loan origination fees and related direct loan origination costs for loans held for sale should be capitalized as part of the carrying amount of the related loan and should not be amortized.

Loan origination fees and related direct loan origination costs for loans that are held for investments should be deferred and recognized as an adjustment to yield. Loan commitment fees should also be deferred and recognized over the life of the loan or until the loan is sold. Fees paid to permanent investors should be recognized as expenses when the loans are sold. Fees for services performed by third parties and loan placement fees should be recognized when all significant services have been performed.

Primary GAAP

Mortgage Loans and Mortgage-Backed Securities

Mortgage loans held for sale should be reported at the lower of cost or market value as of the balance sheet date. The amount by which cost exceeds market value should be accounted for with a valuation account. Any change in the valuation allowance account should be included in net income for the period. Mortgage-backed securities are securities that are issued by a governmental agency or corporation (e.g., Governmental National Mortgage Association [GNMA] or Federal National Mortgage Association [FNMA] or by private issuers. These are securities that are referred to as mortgage participation certificates or pass-through certificates (PCs). These certificates represent an undivided interest in a pool of specific mortgage loans. In general, after securitization, mortgage-backed securities held for sale by an entity engaged in mortgage banking activities should be classified based on its (the entity's) intent to sell or hold these investments. Purchase discounts on mortgage loans should not be amortized as interest revenue during the period the loans or securities are held for sale.

A mortgage loan transferred to a long-term classification should be transferred at the lower cost or market on the transfer date. SFAS 134 requires that after the securitization of mortgage loans held for sale, an entity engaged in mortgage banking activities should classify the resulting mortgage-backed securities or other retained interests in conformity on the provisions of SFAS 115, Accounting for Certain Investments in Debt and Equity Securities. However, a mortgage banking entity must classify as trading securities any retained mortgage-backed securities that it commits to sell before or during the securitization process. Any difference between the carrying amount of the loan and its outstanding principal should be recognized as an adjustment to yield by the interest method. A mortgage loan should be accounted for as a long-term investment if the mortgage banking entity has the intent and ability to hold the loan for the long-term future or until maturity. If the recovery of a mortgage loan held as a long-term investment is doubtful and the impairment is considered to be other than temporary, the book value of the loan should be reduced to its expected collectible amount, which will become its new basis. The amount of the write-down should be recognized as a loss. A recovery from the new cost basis should be reported as a gain only at the sale, maturity, or any other disposition of the loan.

The market value of mortgage loan and mortgage-backed securities held for sale should be determined by the type of loan. Separate determinations of market value for residential (one- to four-family homes) and commercial mortgage loans should be made. Either the aggregate or individual loan basis may be used in determining the lower of cost or market for each type of loan. Market value for loans subject to investor purchase commitments (committed loans) and loans held on a speculative basis (uncommitted loans) should be determined separately as follows:

1. *Committed loans and mortgage-backed securities* Market value for mortgage loans covered by investor commitments should be based on commitment prices. If the fair value of a mortgage-backed security subject to an investor purchase commitment exceeds the commitment price, the loss on the commitment should be fully recognized.

2. *Uncommitted loans* Market value for uncommitted loans should be based on the market in which the mortgage bank operates in. The following should be considered in this situation:

(a) Commitment prices representing market conditions at the balance sheet date

(b) Market prices and yields determined in the mortgage banker's normal market outlets

(c) Quoted GNMA prices or other public market quotations for long-term mortgage loan rates

(d) Federal Home Loan Mortgage Corporation (FHLMC) and FNMA current delivery prices

3. *Uncommitted mortgage-backed securities* Fair value for uncommitted mortgage-backed securities that are collateralized by a mortgage bank's own loans ordinarily should be based on the market value of the securities. If the trust association holding the loans may be readily terminated and the loans sold directly, fair value for the securities should be based on the fair value of the loans or the securities, depending on the mortgage banking entity's intent from a sales perspective. Fair value for other uncommitted mortgage-backed securities should be based on the published mortgage-backed securities yields.

In general, capitalized costs of acquiring rights to service mortgage loans associated with the purchase or origination of mortgage loans should be excluded from the cost of mortgage loans for the purpose of determining lower of cost or market value.

Loan and Commitment Fees

Mortgage banks may receive or pay nonrefundable loan or commitment fees representing various sources of compensation. These fees may include, for example, an adjustment of the interest yield on the loan, a fee for designating funds for the borrower, or an offset of loan origination costs. Loan and commitment fees should be accounted for in the following manner:

1. *Loan origination fees and costs* If the loan is held for resale, loan origination costs should be deferred until the related loan is sold. If the

loan is held for investment, such fees and costs should be deferred and recognized as an adjustment of yield.

2. *Fees for services rendered* Fees for the reimbursement for the costs of specific services performed by third parties with respect to originating a loan, such as appraisal fees, should be recognized as revenue when the services have been performed.

3. *Fees relating to loans held for sale* In general, fees received for guaranteeing the funding of mortgage loans to borrowers, builders, or developers should be deferred and recognized over the life of the loan as an adjustment of yield. Fees paid to permanent investors to ensure the sale of loans (residential or commercial loan commitment fees) should be recognized as expense when the loans are sold to permanent investors or when it appears that the commitment will not be used. In general, residential loan commitment fees relate to blocks of loans; therefore, fees recognized as revenue or expense as a result of individual loans transactions should be based on the ratio of the individual loan amount to the total commitment amount.

Loan placement fees—that is, fees generated for arranging a commitment directly between a permanent investor and a borrower—should be recognized as revenue when all significant services have been performed. In another situation, if a mortgage banking entity obtains a commitment from a permanent investor before or at the time a related commitment is made to a borrower and if the commitment to the borrower requires that the following conditions occur, then the related fees should also be accounted for as loan placement fees. The two conditions that must be satisfied are

- Simultaneous assignment of the commitment to the investor
- Simultaneous transfer to the borrower of the amount received from the investor

4. *Expired commitments and prepayments of loans* If a loan commitment expires without the loan being made or if a loan is repaid before the estimated repayment date, any unrelated unrecognized fees should be recorded as revenue or expense at that time.

Balance Sheet Classification and Disclosures

Mortgage banks' balance sheet presentation must distinguish between (1) mortgage loans held for sale and (2) mortgage loans held as long-term investments.

The method that the mortgage bank entity used in determining the lower of cost or market value of mortgage loans (either in the aggregate or on an individual loans basis) should be disclosed.

Self-Study CPE Program

THE CPE COURSE

Thank you for selecting our course. The course is based on the *GAAP Handbook of Policies and Procedures 2001.*

- *Prerequisites:* None
- *Recommended CPE Credits:* 8 hours per section. Since there are 5 sections, the total credit hours available are 40.
- *Level of Knowledge:* Basic
- *Field of Study:* Accounting

The recommended credit hours are in conformity with the American Institute of CPAs' guidelines for CPE programs. The CPE mandates for each state are established by them, so please check with your particular State Board of Accountancy.

The programs are accepted for CPE credit in the following states where we have entered into Program Sponsor agreements with the State Board of Accountancy:

Hawaii (99002)
New York (E-1126)
Texas (08058)
Virginia (0306 000621)
Washington (00156)

Our programs are also accepted for CPE credit in the following states:

Alabama	Illinois	Mississippi	Oklahoma
Alaska	Iowa	Missouri	Pennsylvania
Arizona	Kansas	Montana	Rhode Island
Arkansas	Kentucky	Nebraska	South Carolina
California	Louisiana	Nevada	South Dakota
Colorado	Maine	New Hampshire	Utah
Connecticut	Maryland	New Mexico	Vermont
Delaware	Massachusetts	North Carolina	Washington, D.C.
Georgia	Michigan	North Dakota	West Virginia
Idaho	Minnesota	Ohio	Wisconsin
			Wyoming

You may take as many of the sections as you wish for CPE credit. If you take and pass all 5 sections, you will receive 40 credit hours.

If you would like to take this course, follow the guidelines on the next page. The cost per section is $50.00. Payment arrangements are on the answer sheets. Your answer sheet must be postmarked no later than December 31, 2001.

Each CPE exam is scored within two weeks after receipt. A passing grade of 70% is required. Upon successful completion of the course, you will receive from Prentice Hall a certificate of achievement.

DIRECTIONS

Each course section refers to the chapters that should have been read, learning objectives, review questions and answers, and Prentice Hall's graded examination consisting of true/false and multiple-choice questions. For each section you would like graded, do the following steps:

1. Review the learning objectives for each chapter.
2. Read and study each chapter in the book.

3. Answer the review questions and then check your answers.

4. Redo any areas of deficiency.

5. Take our examination for each section you wish to receive CPE credit for. Enter your answers as true or false or as a letter answer on the line for that question on the answer sheet. Also complete the course evaluation form.

6. After you complete the exam, mail the answer sheet to the following address:

> Luis Gonzalez
> CPE Coordinator
> Prentice Hall
> 240 Frisch Court
> Paramus, NJ 07652

SECTION A (CHAPTERS 1-4)

Learning Objectives

A knowledge of Chapter 1 will allow you to:

- Prepare the proper format of the income statement.
- Distinguish between extraordinary, nonrecurring, and ordinary items.
- Report discontinued operations.
- Record and present research and development costs.
- Account for deferred compensation arrangements.
- Account for compensation under stock option plans.
- Compute earnings per share.
   Read Chapter 1 and answer review questions 1-4.

   A knowledge of Chapter 2 will allow you to:

- Account for revenue under the accrual and cash bases.
- Account, report, and disclose revenue recognition aspects associated with the sale of products or rendering of services.
- Account for long-term construction contracts under the percentage of completion and completed contract methods.
- Account for contract costs.
- Record revenue for warranty and maintenance contracts.
- Account for contributions received.

Read Chapter 2 and answer review questions 5-8.

An understanding of Chapter 3 permits you to:
- Account for cash.
- Report accounts and loans receivable.
- Account and present inventory.
- Record prepaid expenses.
- Account for fixed assets including exchange of assets.
- Respond to capitalized interest rules.
- Account for the impairment of assets.
- Treat involuntary conversion.
- Record intangible assets.
- Handle transfers of financial assets.

Read Chapter 3 and answer review questions 9-12.

A familiarity with Chapter 4 will allow you to:
- Account and report for liabilities.
- Record loss contingencies.
- Accrue compensated absences.
- Handle termination benefits.
- Deal with troubled debt restructuring.
- Provide for the refinancing of short-term debt to long-term debt.
- Handle callable obligations by creditors.
- Deal with debt issuance and retirement.
- Impute interest on noninterest notes.
- Account for environmental liabilities.
- Deal with the offsetting of assets and liabilities.

Read Chapter 4 and answer review questions 13-15.

SECTION A (CHAPTERS 1-4) Review Questions

1. What six conditions must be met for revenue to be recognized when there is a right of return?

2. Show the form of the income statement starting with income from continuing operations.

3. What is comprehensive income and what are its components?

4. What is the definition of an extraordinary item, and what are examples of them?

5. What are the four methods to recognize revenue from service transactions?

6. What conditions must all be met for revenue to be recognized at the completion of production?

7. What are the exceptions when the cash basis method rather than the accrual method to revenue recognition may be used for a business manufacturing or selling inventory?

8. What disclosures are required for long-term construction contracts?

9. A transfer of financial assets in which the seller surrenders control should be accounted for as a sale. Control is deemed surrendered if which conditions are satisfied?

10. What footnote disclosures are provided for accounts receivable?

11. What should be disclosed about impaired loans?

12. What should be disclosed about inventory?

13. What disclosures are required for debt?

14. If a loss amount for an estimated liability is within a range, how much should be accrued?

15. Compensated absences should be accrued if which conditions are met?

SECTION A (CHAPTERS 1-4) Answers to Review Questions

1. The six conditions are:

   A reasonable estimate can be made of future returns.

   The buyer's duty to pay the seller is not contingent on resale of the product.

   The price is determinable or fixed.

   The buyer must still pay the seller even if the product is stolen or damaged.

   The seller is not materially obligated to assist the buyer in selling the product.

   The product has economic substance to the buyer.

2. Income from continuing operations before tax

   Less: Taxes

   Income from continuing operations after tax

   Discontinued operations:

      Income from discontinued operations (net of tax)

      Loss or gain on disposal of division (net of tax)

   Income before extraordinary items and cumulative effect

   Extraordinary items (net of tax)

   Cumulative effect of a change in principle (net of tax)

   Net income

3. Comprehensive income is the change in equity (net assets) occurring from either transactions or other occurrences with nonowners. Comprehensive income has two components: net income and other comprehensive income. Other comprehensive income includes foreign currency translation gains and losses, unrealized gains or losses on available-for-sale securities, excess of additional pension liability over unamortized prior service cost, and changes in market value of a futures contract that is a hedge of an asset reported at fair value.

4. An extraordinary item is unusual in nature and infrequent in occurrence. Examples are gain or loss on the early extinguishment of debt, loss from government expropriation of property, gain on troubled debt restructuring, and catastrophe and casualty losses.

5. Revenue from service transactions may be recognized using the following methods: specific performance, proportional performance, completed performance, and collection.

6. The following conditions have to be satisfied for revenue to be recognized when production is completed:

   Absence of significant marketing costs.

   Stable selling price.

   Interchangeable units.

7. A company producing or selling inventory may use the cash basis revenue recognition method if one of the following exceptions exists:

   Inability to reliably determine the selling price at the time of sale.

   Risk of noncollection.

   Failure to reliably estimate expenses at the time of sale.

8. The disclosures required for long-term construction contracts are:

   Changes in estimate.

   Commitments.

   Claims.

   Accounting method used and any changes therein.

   Basis to determine estimate of completion.

9. The conditions implying control over transferred assets has been surrendered are:

   The transferred assets have been isolated from the seller.

   The seller does not maintain effective control over the transferred assets.

   The buyer may pledge or exchange the transferred assets.

10. The footnote disclosures provided for accounts receivable are receivables by major source, receivables that have been billed or unbilled, loss contingencies on receivables, subsequent event losses, collateral requirements, related party receivables, and concentrations of credit risk.

11. Disclosure for impaired loans include:

    Amount of investments for which no valuation allowance account exists.

    Creditor's policy for recognizing interest income on impaired loans.

    Total investment in impaired loans.

12. Inventory disclosures include inventory valuation basis, inventory method, classification or categorization, nature of accounting changes, risk exposure such as for health and safety concerns, and unusual inventory losses.

13. The debt disclosures are type of debt, amounts due to officers or related parties, categorization, maturity value, maturity date, restrictions, collateral or pledging requirements, conversion options, sinking fund requirements, open lines of credit, and unused letters of credit.

14. If a loss amount for an estimated liability is within a range, the accrual should be based on the best estimate within that range. If no amount within the range is better than any other amount, the minimum amount (not maximum amount) of the range should be accrued. A disclosure should be made of the maximum loss.

15. An estimated liability for loss contingencies should be accrued if all of the following criteria are satisfied: employee services have been performed, probable payment exists, employee rights have vested, and the amount of estimated liability is reasonably determinable.

PUBLISHER GRADED EXAMINATION: SECTION A (CHAPTERS 1-4)

1. (T or F) Revenues, expenses, gains and losses are the four major components of an income statement, according to Statement of Financial Accounting Concepts (SFAC) No. 6.

2. (T or F) Gain or loss on disposal of a division includes the income or loss from activities before the measurement date.

3. (T or F) Loss or gain on sale of a division includes the costs associated with the disposal decision.

4. (T or F) Research and development costs should usually be expensed as incurred.

5. (T or F) After technological feasibility, R&D costs are immediately expensed.

6. (T or F) After a working model, R&D manufacturing software costs are capitalized to an asset and shown at the greater of net realizable value or book value.

7. (T or F) In computing earnings per share, a stock split during the year is presumed to have been issued at the middle of the year.

8. (T or F) In comparative financial statements, the issuance of a stock dividend mandates the retroactive adjustment of each previous year's earnings per share.

9. (T or F) In deriving earnings per share, the if-converted method is used for convertible securities.

10. (T or F) In deriving earnings per share, the treasury method is used to account for dilutive stock options, stock warrants, or their equivalent.

11. (T or F) A loss on a construction contract is deferred under the completed contract method.

12. (T or F) The completed contract method is preferred over the percentage-of-completion method.

13. (T or F) Progress billings on construction-in-progress is recorded as a liability.

14. (T or F) As per AICPA Statement of Position 97-2, the total selling price of a software transaction is allocated to the contractual components using fair value.

15. (T or F) Contributions received are recorded at fair value and are credited to paid-in-capital.

16. (T or F) An installment note receivable should be offset against a related bank debt in a note amortization situation.

17. (T or F) Consigned merchandise is included in the consignor's inventory.

18. (T or F) Net realizable value equals selling price.

19. (T or F) Under LIFO, you cannot use the lower of cost or market value method.

20. (T or F) Under the retail inventory method, markups but not markdowns are part of the calculation of the cost to retail ratio.

21. Trade names have a legal life of how many years?
    a. 20
    b. 10
    c. 50
    d. 30

22. The maximum period to amortize intangible assets is over how many years?
    a. 17
    b. 40
    c. 50
    d. 10

23. Copyrights are granted for the life of the creator plus how many years?
    a. 20
    b. 30
    c. 40
    d. 50

24. (T or F) Direct costs paid by a debtor in an equity transfer lowers the fair market value of the equity interest.

25. (T or F) A current debt is reclassified as a noncurrent debt after year-end but before the audit report date that the current debt is transferred into stock.

26. (T or F) The effective interest method to amortize bond discount is not acceptable.

27. (T or F) Using the straight-line method, interest expense equals yield times carrying value of the bond.

28. (T or F) To recognize revenue if there is a right of return requires that the amount of returns be reasonably estimated.

29. (T or F) In the profit and loss statement, extraordinary items are shown before discontinued operations.

30. Which one of the following is a component of "other comprehensive income"?

   a. Cumulative effect of a change in accounting principle.

   b. Extraordinary items.

   c. Unrealized gains on available-for-sale securities.

   d. Nonrecurring loss.

31. (T or F) Comprehensive income equals net income plus "other comprehensive income."

32. (T or F) Comprehensive income must be shown in interim financial statements.

33. (T or F) A product available for sale has duplication costs of software charged to inventory.

34. (T or F) Using the intrinsic method, deferred compensation equals the difference between the option price of the shares and the par value.

35. (T or F) Restructuring costs are deferred to an asset.

36. (T or F) In presenting earnings per share, only diluted earnings per share is computed.

37. (T or F) Basic earnings per share includes the assumed conversion of convertible bonds having a dilutive impact.

38. (T or F) In computing earnings per share, when there is a pooling-of-interests, the weighted-average shares outstanding are from the middle of the year.

39. (T or F) The value of initiation fees related to service transactions which are not objectively determined should initially be deemed deferred revenue.

40. (T or F) Assuming a stable selling price, revenue can be recorded when production is completed.

41. (T or F) A firm selling inventory may use the accrual basis.

42. (T or F) Under the cost recovery method, profit is recognized after all costs have been recouped.

43. (T or F) The retail LIFO inventory method includes the initial inventory in deriving the cost to retail ratio.

44. (T or F) Dollar value LIFO groups dollars.

45. (T or F) With dollar value LIFO, inventory is not restated into base dollars.

46. (T or F) If idle capacity exists, self-constructed assets are recorded at the incremental construction costs.

47. (T or F) A donated machine is recorded at its book value to the donor.

48. (T or F) It is possible for land to be presented as inventory for a retail land sale company.

49. (T or F) Interest on borrowed funds to self-construct an asset is immediately expensed.

50. (T or F) In a similar exchange of fixed assets, the new asset is recorded at the fair market value of the old asset plus the cash paid.

51. (T or F) Construction-in-progress is an inventory account classified as a noncurrent asset.

52. (T or F) With the completed contract method, construction-in-progress includes profit.

53. (T or F) Extraordinary items are unusual or infrequent.

54. (T or F) Extraordinary items must be shown net of tax.

55. (T or F) Depreciation on an R&D building is shown in the income statement as research and development expense.

56. (T or F) Amortizing an R&D asset is based on the lower of the straight-line method or revenue generation.

57. (T or F) Revenue from separately priced long-term product maintenance contracts should be recognized in earnings immediately.

58. (T or F) Noncurrent liabilities include bank overdrafts.

59. (T or F) We deduct unearned discounts from gross receivables to get net receivables.

60. (T or F) An assignment of accounts receivable represents its sale to a bank.

61. (T or F) If financial assets are transferred and the seller relinquishes control, it represents a sale.

62. (T or F) Derivatives should be recorded at fair market value.

63. (T or F) If there is a range of loss for a contingency, the maximum amount should be accrued.

64. (T or F) A loss contingency is accrued if the loss is probable.

65. (T or F) Disclosure is made for a remote contingency.

66. (T or F) Gain contingencies are only disclosed.

67. (T or F) An estimated liability for compensated sickness is accrued.

68. (T or F) If a bond is issued at a discount, yield will be more than the coupon interest rate.

69. (T or F) In general, if a debtor violates the long-term debt contract making the debt callable, the debt should be shown as a noncurrent liability.

70. (T or F) If convertible debt is converted to stock because of an inducement offer where the debtor alters the conversion rights, the debtor presents a deferred asset.

71. (T or F) The gain on a troubled debt restructuring is an ordinary item.

72. Which one of the below is not a research and development activity?

   a. Design of a new product.

   b. Repairs during commercial production.

   c. Developing a prototype.

   d. Cost of a model.

SECTION B (CHAPTERS 5-8)

Learning Objectives

A knowledge of Chapter 5 will allow you to:

- Account for the issuance of stock.
- Treat the reacquisition of stock.
- Account for dividends.
- Deal with conversion of stock.
- Account for the costs associated with stock.
- Deal with stock splits.
- Handle appropriation of retained earnings.
- Record stock warrants and stock rights.
- Take into account a quasireorganization.
- Provide disclosures of stockholders' equity.
   Read Chapter 5 and answer review questions 1-4.

   An understanding of Chapter 6 will permit you to:

- Prepare the statement of cash flows including the operating, investing, and financing sections.
- Provide proper disclosures of cash flows.
- Assess cash inflows and cash outflows of the entity.
   Read Chapter 6 and answer review questions 5-8.

A knowledge of Chapter 7 will allow you to:

- Prepare interim financial statements.
- Formulate personal financial statements.
- Record the incorporation of a business.
- Account for divestitures.

Read Chapter 7 and answer review questions 9-12.

A comprehension of Chapter 8 benefits you to:

- Prepare accounting policy disclosures.
- Provide segmental information.
- Report on related party transactions.
- Record contingencies.
- Provide data on long-term purchase contract obligations.
- Provide information concerning derivatives.
- Report on development stage companies.

Read Chapter 8 and answer review questions 13-15.

SECTION B (CHAPTERS 5-8) Review Questions

1. What are the types of preferred stock?
2. What should be disclosed regarding a company's stock?
3. What are the major types of dividends?
4. Discuss what happens in a quasireorganization.
5. What are the components of reconciling net income to cash flow from operations?
6. What are included in the investing section of the statement of cash flows?
7. What are included in the financing section of the statement of cash flows?
8. What supplementary disclosure is made in the statement of cash flows?
9. What are some major provisions in preparing interim (quarterly, monthly) financial statements?
10. What disclosures are required in interim reports?
11. What are the major requirements in preparing personal financial statements?
12. What should be disclosed in personal financial statements?
13. When should segments be reported on?
14. What should be disclosed for each reportable segment?

15. List the major accounting, reporting, and disclosure requirements for development stage companies.

SECTION B (CHAPTERS 5-8) Answers to Review Questions

1. The types of preferred stock are participating, nonparticipating, cumulative, noncumulative, convertible, and callable.

2. Disclosures for stock include par value, shares authorized, shares issued, dividend rate, dividends in arrears, liquidation value, call features, conversion terms, participation rights, and restrictions.

3. The major types of dividends are cash, stock, scrip (liability), and property.

4. In a quasireorganization, the following occurs:

    Retained earnings will become a zero balance and bear the date of the quasireorganization.

    Paid-in-capital is charged to reduce any deficit in retained earnings.

    Net assets are adjusted to market value.

    Creditors and stockholders must agree to it.

5. Net income, plus noncurrent expenses, less noncurrent revenue, plus decrease in current assets other than cash, less increase in current assets other than cash, plus increase in current liabilities, less decrease in current liabilities.

6. The investing section includes buying or selling available-for-sale or held-to-maturity securities in other companies, buying or selling fixed assets, and making and collecting loans.

7. The financing section includes issuing or repurchasing the company's stock, issuing or paying back short-term or long-term debt, and paying cash dividends.

8. Supplemental disclosures in the statement of cash flows is presenting investing and financing activities that affect assets and liabilities but do not impact cash flow. Examples are the conversion of a bond payable to common stock, and the purchase of a fixed asset with long-term debt.

9. The major accounting aspects to interim financial statements are:

    Sales or service revenue should be recorded as earned in the interim period.

    Expenses are recorded in the interim period as incurred.

    Yearly expenses (e.g., pension) should be proportionally allocated.

    In estimating inventory, the gross profit method may be used.

A temporary liquidation of the LIFO base inventory should charge cost of sales at replacement cost.

Permanent losses should be recorded in the interim period they occur but the gain from a price recovery should be recognized in a later interim period. However, the gain cannot exceed the previously recorded loss.

10. Disclosures in interim reports include:

    Seasonal revenue and costs including seasonal factors influencing interim results.

    Earnings per share.

    Significant changes in tax expense.

    Information on disposal of a business segment.

    Contingencies and commitments.

    Significant changes in financial position.

    Material adjustments to the fourth quarter if such quarter is not presented in the annual report.

    Changes in the expected effective tax rate.

11. In preparing personal financial statements, the major requirements are:

    Do not segregate between current and noncurrent classifications.

    Present assets at current value and list in the order of liquidity.

    Report liabilities at current value and list in the order of maturity.

    Present estimated taxes payable as a liability including unpaid taxes of prior years.

12. Disclosures in personal financial statements include the individuals covered, method used to arrive at current values, method and assumptions used in determining income taxes, nature of joint ownership, face amount of life insurance, leasing arrangements, and nonforfeitable rights (e.g., pension rights).

13. Segments are reported on if any one of the following exist:

    Revenue is 10% or more of total revenue of all operating segments.

    Operating profit or loss is 10% or more of the greater of the combined operating profit or loss.

    Identifiable assets are 10% or more of the total assets of all operating segments.

14. The following information should be disclosed for each reportable segment: nature and identification of products or services, geographic areas of operation, tax effects, capital expenditures, cost allocation method, transfer price method, and aggregate depreciation and depletion.

15. The major requirements for development stage companies are:

    Follow the same GAAP as established companies.

    Head the financial statements as development stage company.

    Footnote the development stage activities.

    Show current year and cumulative amounts for financial statement categories (e.g., sales).

    In the first year the company is out of the development stage, disclose that in prior years it was in the development stage.

PUBLISHER GRADED EXAMINATION: SECTION B (CHAPTERS 5-8)

1. (T or F) Treasury stock participates in dividends paid.

2. (T or F) An aggregation of similar operating segments is not allowed.

3. (T or F) No entry is made upon the issuance of stock rights.

4. (T or F) Segmental information is required for unconsolidated subsidiaries.

5. (T or F) Common stock can usually be converted into preferred stock.

6. (T or F) Preferred stockholders have the most to gain if a company is successful.

7. (T or F) Interim financial reports may not contain earnings per share information.

8. (T or F) Legal capital usually includes common and preferred stock.

9. (T or F) Amounts held in bank accounts that are unavailable for immediate withdrawal should be considered cash for the purposes of preparing the statement of cash flows.

10. (T or F) Segmental information is not required in annual financial statements.

11. (T or F) Related party transactions are always assumed not to be at arm's length.

12. (T or F) Activities between a parent and its subsidiary are considered related party transactions.

13. (T or F) Demand deposits, such as checking accounts, should not be treated as cash when preparing the statement of cash flows.

14. (T or F) Cash flow per share should always be provided.

15. (T or F) A statement of cash flows shows an organization's ability to generate recurring cash earnings.

16. (T or F) Segmental information may be provided in the body of the financial statements, in separate schedules, or in footnotes.

17. (T or F) Treasury stock is stock issued by the federal government.

18. (T or F) A business is considered in the development stage for its first three years.

19. (T or F) Treasury stock may be kept on a FIFO or LIFO basis.

20. (T or F) If more than one accounting method is used (e.g., different depreciation methods), the one disclosed in the footnote should be the primary method.

21. (T or F) It is optional whether to disclose the amount of imputed interest required to reduce the unconditional purchase obligation to present value.

22. (T or F) The indirect method of preparing the cash flow statement is preferred by FASB Statement No. 95.

23. (T or F) A change in the anticipated effective tax rate should be disclosed in interim reporting.

24. (T or F) The cost to issue stock should be expensed immediately.

25. (T or F) Nonprofit entities are not required to disclose their significant accounting policies.

26. (T or F) If an unincorporated business incorporates and issues equity in exchange for the assets of the unincorporated entity, the stock issued is recorded at par value.

27. (T or F) In measuring a segment's earnings or assets, the measurement or valuation basis should be disclosed for explanatory purposes.

28. (T or F) The operating section is identical under the direct and indirect method of preparing the statement of cash flows.

29. (T or F) Stock warrants may be used to buy additional shares.

30. (T or F) Treasury stock does not have any voting rights.

31. (T or F) A statement of cash flows is required.

32. (T or F) Disclosure for common stock should include unusual voting rights and dividend rates.

33. (T or F) A development stage company may not use the same GAAP as an established company.

34. (T or F) The tax rate should take into account annual earnings, tax rates, and alternative tax treatments based on continuing operations.

35. (T or F) Interim financial reports must be certified by a CPA.

36. (T or F) The direct method of preparing the statement of cash flows is preferred by companies because of its simplicity.

37. (T or F) Activities between a company and employee trusts established and managed by the company, such as a pension plan, are considered related party transactions.

38. (T or F) If a segment does not generate significant revenue, it is not an operating segment to be reported.

39. (T or F) Unconditional purchase obligations with a term less than one year does not require disclosure.

40. (T or F) The financial statements of a development stage enterprise must be headed "Development Stage Enterprise."

41. (T or F) Preferred stockholders usually do not have voting rights.

42. (T or F) Tax expense must be based on the anticipated annual marginal tax rate.

43. (T or F) Purchase of treasury stock should be included in the investing activities section of the statement of cash flows.

44. (T or F) An interim cash flow statement should not be prepared.

45. (T or F) Preferred stock must always be participative.

46. (T or F) Stockholder's equity consists of common stock, preferred stock and bonds.

47. (T or F) Filing consolidated tax returns is an example of related party transactions.

48. (T or F) A management approach should be used in identifying segments.

49. (T or F) If an unincorporated business incorporates and issues equity in exchange for the assets of the unincorporated entity, the assets are brought forth at book value.

50. (T or F) Capital stock includes stock options and warrants.

51. (T or F) The investing and financing sections are identical under the direct and indirect method of preparing the statement of cash flows.

52. (T or F) Operating segments that are not reportable should be combined and disclosed in the "all other" category.

53. (T or F) Material accounting policies may be disclosed in the first footnote.

54. (T or F) Convertible preferred stock may be exchanged for common stock.

55. (T or F) Interim financial reports cannot be issued on a monthly basis.

56. (T or F) A fractional share warrant may be used to purchase a single common stock.

57. (T or F) If interim information is presented for comparative reasons, data should always be restated to conform with the new accounting policy.

58. (T or F) Gifts received by the corporation are part of additional paid in capital.

59. (T or F) A gain or loss should be deferred to a later interim period unless the deferral is allowable for annual reporting.

60. (T or F) If a change in accounting method takes place in a quarter other than the first, it is presumed that the change occurred at the start of the first quarter, showing the cumulative effect in the first quarter.

61. (T or F) A cash equivalent is a short-term liquid investment with a maturity of six months or less.

62. (T or F) When disclosing for derivatives, a distinction should be made with regard to the accounting for derivatives used for trading versus non-trading purposes.

63. (T or F) Legal capital is typically defined by federal law.

64. (T or F) Tax disputes is an example of contingencies requiring disclosure.

65. (T or F) A two for one stock split doubles the number of shares outstanding.

SECTION C (CHAPTERS 9-13)

Learning Objectives

An understanding of Chapter 9 will permit you to:

- Account for a change in principle.
- Report a change in estimate.
- Reflect a change in reporting entity.
  Read Chapter 9 and answer review questions 1-3.

  A familiarity with Chapter 10 enables you to:
- Account under the equity method for investments.
- Report under the market value method for investments.
- Record trading, available-for-sale, and held-to-maturity securities.

- Provide disclosures of the company's investing policy.

    Read Chapter 10 and answer review questions 4-6.

    A comprehension of Chapter 11 allows you to:

- Account for a business combination under the pooling-of-interests method.
- Record a business combination under the purchase method.
- Provide disclosure of business combinations.
- Apply the 12 criteria to use pooling of interests accounting.

    Read Chapter 11 and answer review questions 7-9.

    An understanding of Chapter 12 permits you to:

- Prepare consolidated financial statements.
- Make elimination entries between parent and subsidiaries.
- Handle joint ventures.
- Determine when control exists.

    Read Chapter 12 and answer review questions 10-12.

    An understanding of Chapter 13 has the following benefits to you:

- Account for an operating lease to lessee.
- Record a capital lease to lessee.
- Account for an operating lease to lessor.
- Present a direct financing lease to lessor.
- Show a sales type lease to lessor.
- Record sale-leaseback arrangements.
- Account for subleases.
- Treat lease renewals and extensions.
- Handle leveraged leases.

    Read Chapter 13 and answer review questions 13-15.

SECTION C (CHAPTERS 9-13)

Review Questions

1. What is in Level 1 of the hierarchy of GAAP?

2. What are the three exceptions to the cumulative effect rule for a change in accounting principle that requires the restatement of prior years' financial statements?

3. A change in reporting entity requires the restatement of prior years' financial statements as if previously separate companies were always combined. Provide three examples.

4. How are trading securities accounted for and reported?

5. How are held-to-maturity securities accounted for and reported?

6. What affects the "investment in investee" account under the equity method?

7. Discuss the accounting under the pooling-of-interests method.

8. How is a business combination recorded under the purchase method?

9. What are the disclosures under the purchase method?

10. When is a consolidation negated even though the parent owns more than 50% of the voting common stock of the subsidiary?

11. If the purchase method is used when preparing consolidated financial statements, what should be done in the process of eliminating the investment account?

12. What disclosures should be provided in consolidated financial statements?

13. What are the four criteria applicable to a capital lease to the lessee?

14. What footnote disclosures should be made by the lessee?

15. What two criteria must the lessor satisfy to account under the direct financing method?

SECTION C (CHAPTERS 9-13)

Answers to Review Questions

1. Level 1 consists of FASB Statements and Interpretations, APB Opinions, and AICPA Accounting Research Bulletins.

2. The three exceptions are:

   Change in accounting for construction contracts.

   Change to or from the full cost method used in the extractive industry.

   Change from LIFO to another inventory method.

3. Three examples are:

   Presenting consolidated or combining statements instead of individual company statements.

   A business combination treated as a pooling of interests.

   Change in subsidiaries making up consolidated financial statements.

4. Trading securities are listed in the balance sheet under current assets at their fair market value. Unrealized losses or gains on trading securities are presented separately in the income statement.

5. Held-to-maturity securities are presented in the balance sheet under noncurrent assets at amortized cost.

6. Under the equity method, the "investment in investee" account is increased for investment cost, ordinary profit, and extraordinary gains. It is reduced for investee dividends, permanent decline in market price of stocks, amortization of goodwill, and depreciation on the excess of market value less book value of specific assets.

7. Under the pooling-of-interests method, the accounting follows:

   Net income of the acquired company is brought forth for the whole year irrespective of acquisition date.

   Expenses of the pooling are charged against earnings.

   Net assets of the acquired business is brought forth at book value.

   Retained earnings and paid-in capital of the acquired company are brought forth at book value.

   A deficit in retained earnings for a combining company is retained in the combined entity.

8. The accounting under the purchase method follows:

   Net income of the acquired business is recognized from the acquisition date to year-end.

   Direct costs of the acquisition are charged to the investment in subsidiary account. Indirect costs are expensed as incurred.

   Net assets of the acquired company are brought forth at fair market value.

   The excess of cost over the fair market value of net assets is recorded as goodwill.

   The excess of the fair market value of net assets over cost reduces proportionately the noncurrent assets acquired except for long-term investments.

   Goodwill of the acquired business is not brought forth.

9. The disclosures under the purchase method include the name and a brief description of the combined entities, the fact that the purchase method is being used, the period for which operating results of the acquired entities are included, the cost of the acquired company, the number of shares issued and amount assigned, the amortization period for goodwill, contingencies, and commitments.

10. Consolidation is negated when:

    The parent is not in actual control of the subsidiary such as when the subsidiary is in receivership.

    The parent has sold or contracted to sell the subsidiary shortly after year-end.

11. In eliminating the investment account, do the following:

    Eliminate preacquisition retained earnings.

    Eliminate the subsidiary's equity accounts.

    Make fair value adjustments.

    Provide for the minority interest.

12. The disclosures in consolidated financial statements include:

    Consolidation policy.

    Composition of companies consolidated.

    Differences arising from different year-ends between parent and subsidiary.

    Tax effects.

    Intercompany transactions eliminated.

    Cost allocation methods.

13. A capital lease to the lessee exists if any one of the following four criteria are present:

    The lessee gets ownership of the property at the end of the lease.

    A bargain purchase option exists.

    The lease term is 75% or more of the property's life.

    The discounted value of minimum lease payments equals or exceeds 90% of the fair market value of the property.

14. The lessee should footnote:

    Nature and extent of leasing activity.

    Description of the lease agreement.

    Future minimum rental payments in total and for each of the next five years.

    Contingent rentals.

    Property under lease.

    Sublease rentals.

15. The two criteria are:

    No material uncertainties exist with regard to future costs to be incurred.

    Assurance of lease payments being collected.

PUBLISHER GRADED EXAMINATION: SECTION C (CHAPTERS 9-13)

1. (T or F) In the preparation of the statement of cash flows, available-for-sale securities are a part of the Operating section.

2. (T or F) The fiscal year-ends of the parent and subsidiary may be at most three months apart.

3. (T or F) Disclosure for debt securities classified as available for sale or held to maturity should include contractual maturity dates.

4. (T or F) A change in reporting entity requires the restatement of previous years' financial statements for a period of five years or more.

5. (T or F) If comparative financial statements are presented, there should be a retroactive adjustment for errors.

6. (T or F) In a direct financing lease, the lessor does not have to be a manufacturer of the leased item.

7. (T or F) The accounting for sublease transactions depends upon whether the original lessee is or is not relieved of primary liability.

8. (T or F) A change in accounting principle should not be presented using pro forma disclosure.

9. (T or F) In a related party lease where significant influence is involved, the lease should be accounted for according to its legal form.

10. (T or F) References to the AICPA statements of position and industry audit guides should not be made in determining the preferred accounting principle.

11. (T or F) Seven criteria must be satisfied for a pooling of interests to occur.

12. (T or F) If any of the 12 criteria for the pooling of interests method is not met, the purchase method must be used.

13. (T or F) The tax benefit of an unrecognized net operating loss carry forward arising from a purchase business combination may be used to restate prior years' earnings.

14. (T or F) Available for sale securities are presented in the balance sheet at fair market value.

15. (T or F) Earnings per share should be provided for the cumulative effect account.

16. (T or F) A temporary tax difference may arise when the equity method is used.

17. (T or F) A change in classification is considered a change in principle and should be shown net of tax.

18. (T or F) In cases where a change in estimate is coupled with a change in principle and the effects cannot be distinguished, the change should be accounted for as a change in estimate.

19. (T or F) The differentiation between a sales-type lease and a direct financing lease are only of concern to the lessor.

20. (T or F) If two or more stocks are bought for one price, the cost is allocated to the securities equally.

21. (T or F) Held-to-maturity securities may consist of debt and equity securities.

22. (T or F) FASB Implementation Guides are at the highest level in the hierarchy of GAAP.

23. (T or F) The SEC requires that the independent CPA state in writing that the newly selected accounting procedure is preferred in management's judgment.

24. (T or F) In accounting for a purchase, the net income of the acquired business is recognized from the acquisition date to year-end.

25. (T or F) The cumulative effect of a change in accounting principle equals the difference between beginning retained earnings using the old method, and the beginning retained earnings if the new method had been used in prior years.

26. (T or F) One exception to the cumulative effect of change in accounting principle is when an entity changes from LIFO to another inventory valuation method.

27. (T or F) Consolidation is permitted even when the parent is not in actual control of the subsidiary.

28. (T or F) An issuing company may impact a pooling by distributing treasury stock bought at least two years before combination.

29. (T or F) A permanent loss on an asset is not a change in accounting estimate, but rather a current period loss.

30. (T or F) A principle adopted for the first time on new events is considered a change in accounting principle for reporting purposes.

31. (T or F) In accounting for a purchase, the excess of the fair market value of net tangible assets over costs is considered negative goodwill.

32. (T or F) Trading securities are typically held till maturity by a company.

33. (T or F) In accounting for a purchase, goodwill of the acquired business is not brought forth.

34. (T or F) Trading securities are recorded in the balance sheet under long-term assets.

35. (T or F) A business combination accounted for under the pooling-of-interests method is considered a change in reporting entity.

36. (T or F) A change in accounting estimate should be shown net of tax.

37. (T or F) Held-to-maturity securities are always recorded at fair market value.

38. (T or F) Held-to-maturity classification of securities should be done only if the company intends to hold the securities to maturity.

39. (T or F) The cumulative effect of a change in accounting principle should be presented "net of tax."

40. (T or F) Unrealized gains and losses on trading securities are presented separately in the income statement.

41. (T or F) Bond discount or premium should preferably be amortized using the effective interest method on securities held to maturity.

42. (T or F) The cumulative effect account appears as the last item in the retained earnings statement.

43. (T or F) In a retroactive restatement, the effect of the change in accounting principle is adjusted directly to the ending balance of retained earnings in the year of change.

44. (T or F) In accounting for a pooling of interests, the retained earnings and paid-in-capital of the acquired business are brought forth at fair market value.

45. (T or F) In the preparation of the statement of cash flows, trading securities are a part of the Investing section.

46. (T or F) Real estate is classified as a sales-type lease only if the title to the leased property is transferred to the lessee at or shortly after the end of the lease term.

47. (T or F) The tax benefit of an unrecognized net operating loss carry forward arising from a purchase business combination may be used prospectively to reduce goodwill to zero.

48. (T or F) An acquiring company may record deferred income taxes on the acquired company's books before the business combination.

49. (T or F) In accounting for a pooling of interests, a deficit in retained earnings for a combining company is retained in the combined entity.

50. (T or F) In a pooling of interests, combining companies are considered independent if the percentage is greater than 10%.

51. (T or F) Footnote disclosure about the nature and justification for a change in principle is not required if the CPA concurs with the change.

52. (T or F) A change in the legal structure of a business, such as incorporating a partnership, is considered a change in reporting entity.

53. (T or F) Banks are not legally allowed to invest in junk bonds due to high risk.

54. (T or F) If a defined benefit pension plan is acquired in connection with a business combination using the purchase method, the amount by which the projected benefit obligation exceeds the plan assets is reported as a liability.

55. (T or F) A change in estimate requires only disclosure and prior years should not be adjusted.

56. (T or F) The acquirer must acquire at least 80% of the voting common stock for a pooling of interests.

57. (T or F) Available-for-sale securities bought when exercising an option are recorded at the option strike price plus the fair value of the option at the exercise date.

58. (T or F) Minority interests in net income are deducted to determine consolidated net income.

59. (T or F) A parent must own at least 90% of the voting common stock for the subsidiary to prepare consolidated statements.

60. (T or F) A footnote is required on the nature of and reason for the change in reporting entity.

61. (T or F) Retroactive application is required for a change in principle arising from an initial public offering of equity or debt securities by a closely held business.

62. (T or F) In accounting for a purchase, the excess of cost over the book value of net tangible assets is assigned to goodwill.

63. (T or F) If the option is worthless and the same security is bought in the market, the security is recorded at the market value plus the remaining carrying amount of the option premium.

64. (T or F) The purchase method is used when cash or other assets are given or liabilities are incurred for the other company.

65. (T or F) Real estate leases are of four types.

SECTION D (CHAPTERS 14–17)

Learning Objectives

A knowledge of Chapter 14 will enable you to:

- Account for pension plans.
- Compute pension expense.
- Determine pension liabilities.
- Record postretirement benefits other than pensions.
- Prepare pension information to interested parties.
  Read Chapter 14 and answer review questions 1-4.

  The benefits of learning Chapter 15 are to:
- Account for temporary differences between book income and taxable income.
- Treat permanent differences between book income and taxable income.
- Present intraperiod tax allocation.
- Account for changes in tax rate.
- Handle different tax rates in future years.
- Account for tax loss carrybacks and carryforwards.
  Read Chapter 15 and answer review questions 5-8.

  An understanding of Chapter 16 will permit you to:
- Translate the financial statements from the foreign currency into U.S. dollars.
- Account for foreign currency transactions.
- Record forward exchange contracts.
- Determine translation gains or losses.

- Understand key foreign currency terms.

  Read Chapter 16 and answer review questions 9-12.

  A comprehension of Chapter 17 will allow you to:

- Account and report for financial instruments and derivative products.
- Recognize accounting losses due to credit and market risks.
- Provide disclosures of information about financial instruments.
- Present disclosures regarding fair value.
- Know when to offset assets and liabilities.
- Determine what is included as derivative financial instruments.

  Read Chapter 17 and answer review questions 13-15.

SECTION D (CHAPTERS 14-17)

Review Questions

1. What should be disclosed for defined contribution pension plans?
2. What are the components of pension expense for defined benefit pension plans?
3. How are actuarial gains or losses on pension plans accounted for?
4. How is the additional pension liability determined?
5. Discuss the liability method to account for income tax allocation.
6. Explain and give examples of permanent tax differences.
7. What is intraperiod tax allocation?
8. How do we account for a change in tax rate?
9. In determining the functional currency of a foreign activity, what should be considered?
10. Explain the translation process if the foreign currency is the functional currency.
11. If the U.S. dollar is used directly as the functional currency because of high inflation, explain the conversion process.
12. How do we account for the gain or loss on a forward exchange contract that is intended to hedge a foreign currency commitment?
13. What should be disclosed if a financial instrument has off-balance sheet credit or market risk?
14. When is the offsetting of assets and liabilities permissible?
15. What are examples of derivative instruments?

SECTION D (CHAPTERS 14-17)

Answers to Review Questions

1. Disclosure for defined contribution pension plans include:

   Cost recorded for the year.

   Method and basis to compute contributions.

   Description of the terms.

   Categorization of covered employees.

   Discussion of items impacting comparability over the years.

2. The components of pension expense for defined benefit plans are service cost, amortization expense on prior service cost, return on pension plan assets, interest on projected benefit obligation, and actuarial losses or gains.

3. Actuarial gains or losses are deferred and amortized as an adjustment to pension expense over current and future years. The corridor method is used. Under that method, recognition is given to gain or loss exceeding 10% of the greater of the beginning of year balances of the projected benefit obligation or the market-related value of plan assets. The excess over the corridor is amortized over the average remaining service life of active employees.

4. The additional pension liability equals:

   Accumulated benefit obligation—12/31

   Less: Fair value of plan assets—12/31

   Minimum pension liability

   Less: Deferred pension liability

   Additional pension liability

5. Interperiod tax allocation must be accounted for under the liability method. Under that method, we use the tax rate that will arise when the temporary difference reverses. The deferred tax liability or asset must be adjusted for changes in tax rate.

6. Permanent differences do not reverse in later years and hence do not require tax allocation. They either impact book income or taxable income, but not both. Examples of expenses that are not tax deductible are fines and penalties. An example of tax-free income is interest on a municipal bond.

7. Intraperiod tax allocation is when tax expense is presented in different parts of the financial statements for the current year. It includes showing prior period adjustments net of tax in the retained earnings section.

8. A change in tax rate must be reflected in the accounts immediately by adjusting tax expense and the deferred tax liability. For example, a decrease in tax rate will reduce both accounts.

9. In determining the functional currency, consideration should be given to the local sales market for products or services, how the foreign activity is being financed, selling prices of goods, foreign operation's manufacturing costs, intercompany transactions, and cash flows.

10. If the foreign currency is the functional currency, balance sheet items should be translated at the current exchange rate at the balance sheet date. Capital accounts are translated using the historical exchange rate in effect when the foreign entity's stock was issued. Income statement accounts are translated at the weighted-average exchange rate for the year.

11. If the U.S. dollar is used directly as the functional currency because of high inflation, the conversion process is as follows. In the balance sheet, cash, receivables, and payables are converted at the foreign exchange rate in effect at the balance sheet date. Other assets and liabilities are converted at historical rates. In general, income statement accounts are translated at the weighted-average rate. However, revenue and expenses that relate to assets and liabilities translated at historical rates should be translated at such historical rates.

12. The gain or loss on a forward exchange contract intended to hedge a foreign currency commitment should be deferred and included in the measurement of the related foreign currency transaction (i.e., the purchase or sale).

13. The following must be disclosed for a financial instrument with off-balance-sheet credit or market risk:

    Amount of risk.

    Nature and terms of the instrument, including the type of credit and market risk, its cash requirements, and the accounting policy followed.

    Collateral policy.

    Liquidity and value of collateral.

14. The offsetting of assets and liabilities is allowed only if all of the following conditions are satisfied: There is an intent to set off; a setoff right exists; the setoff is legal; and each party owes the other a specified amount.

15. Derivative financial instruments include option contracts, futures, forward contracts, fixed-rate loan commitments, interest rate floors or caps, interest rate collars, forward interest rate agreements, swaps, and letters of credit.

PUBLISHER GRADED EXAMINATION: SECTION D (CHAPTERS 14-17)

1. (T or F) A statement of cash flows is not required to be disclosed in defined benefit plans.

2. (T or F) The spot rate is defined as the exchange rate for immediate delivery of currencies.

3. (T or F) The functional currency is the currency of the primary economic environment in which an entity operates.

4. (T or F) An example of a temporary difference that requires interperiod tax allocation is unrealized losses on trading securities.

5. (T or F) Real and property taxes may be combined with income taxes for financial statement purposes.

6. (T or F) An option with a longer maturity period will sell for an amount greater than one whose maturity period is shorter, all other considerations being equal.

7. (T or F) A multiemployer pension plan is one that includes the participation of two or more unrelated employers.

8. (T or F) Under SFAS 109, deferred tax assets are required to be offset against deferred tax liabilities and must be classified on the balance sheet as being either net current or net noncurrent.

9. (T or F) Actuarial calculations are required to ascertain the amount of postretirement benefit expense for a given period.

10. (T or F) The stockholders' equity section of the balance sheet is the section of the financial statements in which foreign currency translation gains or losses are usually presented.

11. (T or F) Postretirement benefits should be accrued under generally accepted accounting principles.

12. (T or F) Profit sharing plans may be categorized as being either discretionary or nondiscretionary.

13. (T or F) Foreign currency transaction gains or losses are required to be disclosed in the income statement in accordance with generally accepted accounting principles.

14. Of what degree should the US dollar be used as the functional currency when a country experiences a three-year inflation:

    a. 100% or more.

    b. 75% or more.

    c. 50% or more.

    d. Between 10% to 20%.

15. (T or F) A net operating loss may be carried back 2 years and forward up to 20 years.

16. (T or F) If it is determined that it is more likely than not that the tax benefits of deferred tax assets may not be fully realized in the future, SFAS 109 requires the use of a valuation account (contra account).

17. (T or F) The act of selling an option is called writing.

18. (T or F) Deferred taxes are recorded at the amount of settlement when a temporary difference reverses.

19. (T or F) The accrued pension liability is added to the minimum pension liability in determining the amount of the additional pension liability that must be recognized by an entity in a defined benefit pension plan.

20. (T or F) The fair values of cash, cash equivalents, accounts receivable, and accounts payable approximate cost because of their short-term maturity.

21. (T or F) Intercompany profits should be eliminated preferably through the use of the exchange rate at the date of the intercompany transaction in accounting for a consolidated entity.

22. (T or F) The amount derived in a forced or liquidation sale is the best evidence of the fair value of financial instruments.

23. (T or F) If the current price of stock is below the strike (or exercise) price of a call option and the instrument has much time before expiration, it can be priced at a premium.

24. (T or F) The term used to describe the partial or full discharge of an employer's pension obligation is called a curtailment.

25. Which of the following statements is most correct?

    a. An advantage of forward contracts is that they are default-free.

    b. Futures contracts usually trade on an organized exchange and are marked to market daily.

    c. Goods are almost always delivered under futures contracts but never under forward contracts.

    d. All of the above are correct.

    e. None of the above are correct.

26. (T or F) Foreign exchange contracts gains and losses are generally not recognized in net income in the year the exchange rate changes.

27. (T or F) By definition, an annuity contract is an irrevocable agreement in which the insurer has the unconditional obligation to pay employees either specific periodic benefits or a lump-sum payment to another party.

28. Which of the following is not an example of a permanent difference?

    a. Interest on state and municipal obligations.

    b. Difference in accounting for bad debts utilizing the direct write-off method and allowance for doubtful accounts method.

    c. Compensation expense associated with employee stock option plans.

    d. Fines.

29. Which of the following statements is not true?

    a. By definition, the fair value of a financial instrument is the amount at which the instrument could be exchanged in a transaction between two arm's length parties other than in a forced liquidation or sale.

    b. A financial instruments's fair value should be disclosed when it is practicable to estimate that value.

    c. When a price for a particular financial instrument is based on a number of markets, the price in the most active markets should be used.

    d. When fair value cannot be obtained, it should be estimated based on either: (1) the quoted market value of a financial instrument with similar characteristics or (2) best judgment.

    e. None of the above.

30. (T or F) The name of the instrument that gives the holder the right to sell a specific good at a given price at any time before it expires is called a put option.

31. (T or F) The use of the asset–liability method in accounting for interperiod tax allocation and deferred income taxes is required by present GAAP.

32. (T or F) A deferred tax asset is created when expenses are deducted on the tax return before being deducted on the financial accounting records.

33. (T or F) The payment of a fixed amount of debt is required for nonmonetary obligations.

34. (T or F) Pension costs in a defined benefit pension plan are not required to be accrued each period under generally accepted accounting principles.

35. Paying or receiving in the same foreign currency is best described by the term:

    a. Currency swap.

    b. Measurement.

    c. Conversion.

    d. Denominate.

36. (T or F) Deferred taxes will not be decreased if a change in tax law results in less taxes being owed in the future.

37. (T or F) Deferred tax assets should not be reduced by a valuation allowance account when there is a probability of more than 50% that some portion of the tax benefit will not be realized.

38. (T or F) When the income taxes for a period is allocated to the special sections of the income statement, the process is known as interperiod tax allocation.

39. (T or F) The American Institute of Certified Public Accountants does not recommend the use of the unit credit actuarial cost method.

40. (T or F) Which of the following represents an actuarial assumption?

    a. Salary levels.

    b. Turnover rate.

    c. Return rate.

    d. None of the above are actuarial assumptions.

    e. All of the above are actuarial assumptions.

41. When derivative financial instruments are held or issued for trading purposes, GAAP requires that disclosure must be made of the net trading gains or losses as well as average fair values.

42. Which of the following is excluded by the FASB as being classified as a derivative instrument:

    a. All on-balance-sheet receivables and payables.

    b. Options.

    c. Swaps.

    d. Forward contracts.

    e. All of the above.

43. (T or F) The tax rate that will arise when a temporary difference reverses determines the balance sheet recognition value for the related deferred tax liability or asset.

44. (T or F) Property taxes are recognized on the date that they are assessed by the taxing authorities.

45. (T or F) An example of a pension plan based on future salaries is career-average-pay.

46. (T or F) When a foreign country experiences a three-year inflation rate of 100% or more, the translation gains or losses are disclosed in the income statement.

47. (T or F) When deferred taxes are related to specific assets or liabilities, they are classified as being current or noncurrent based on the expected reversal dates of the temporary differences themselves.

48. (T or F) A foreign exchange contract that hedges a foreign currency commitment and results in gain or loss should be deferred and included in the measurement of the related foreign currency transaction.

49. (T or F) In determining the actual return on pension plan assets at the end of the year in a defined benefit pension plan, benefit payments must be subtracted.

50. (T or F) Net operating loss carrybacks require that the tax effects that are associated not be allocated to the current loss period.

51. (T or F) Deferred tax assets or liabilities should be classified as classification of the current or noncurrent items on the balance sheet based on the related asset or liability to which they relate.

52. (T or F) The current ratio represents the amount of shares of common stock that a convertible bond can be converted into at the date of conversion.

53. (T or F) An option contract gives the holder the right to buy or sell an asset at a predetermined price within a given period of time.

54. (T or F) Property taxes assessed on property that will be sold to customers or under construction for a company's own use are generally immediately expensed.

55. (T or F) An adjustment to deferred taxes is never made when the entity experiences a change in tax status.

56. (T or F) Under Generally Accepted Accounting Principles, disclosures regarding credit and market risks associated with financial instruments are required to be made.

57. (T or F) The spot price is the price of a good for delivery in the future.

58. (T or F) In the termination of a pension plan, the discounted value of future employer payments less the down payment equals the expense accrued.

59. (T or F) The use of purchased annuity contracts is used to transfer the risk of providing employee benefits from the employer to the insurance company.

60. (T or F) The pension assets of one plan may not be used to offset the minimum pension liability of another, when an employer has more than one defined benefit pension plan.

61. (T or F) A deferred tax liability will occur if revenue is included on the tax return after being presented on the financial records of an entity.

62. (T or F) Speculative risks offer the chance of a gain as well as the possibility of a loss while pure risks lead only to losses.

63. (T or F) The term describing the ratio of one unit of a currency to that of another at a particular date is called the quick ratio.

64. (T or F) The name of the contract that provides for the exchange of different currencies at a given future date at a specified (forward) rate is called a forward exchange contract.

SECTION E (CHAPTER 18)

Learning Objectives

Broadcasting Industry

Reading about the broadcasting industry will help you understand:

- A program license agreement.
- Components and details of license agreements to broadcast program details.
- Accounting for program rights by the licensee.
- Barter transaction by broadcasters.

Banking and Thrift Industry

Reading about the banking and thrift industry will help you understand:

- Accounting for the acquisition of a bank and thrift institution.
- Determination of goodwill and the valuation of other assets as a result of a business combination.
- How to account for financial assistance granted by a regulatory agency to an entity that has acquired a bank or thrift institution.

Cable Television

Reading about the cable television industry will help you understand:

- Establishment of the prematurity period and accounting for its costs.
- Capitalization of interest costs during the prematurity period.
- Recognition of hookup revenue and amortization of capitalized costs.
- Recoverability of capitalized costs.

Computer Software Development

Reading about computer software development will help you understand:

- Accounting for research and development costs relating to software development.

- Capitalization of computer software subsequent to the establishment of technological feasibility.
- Purchasing computer software with no alternative future uses.
- Amortization of software costs.
- Duplication of costs charged to inventory.
- End-of-period inventory and disclosures on the financial statements.

Franchising Industry: Accounting by Franchisors

Reading about the franchising industry: accounting by franchisors will help you understand:

- Initial individual franchise sales.
- Area franchise sales.
- Contractual arrangements between franchisor and franchisee.
- Allocation of initial franchise fee.
- Continuing franchisee fees.
- Product sales made to a franchisee on a continuing basis.
- Agency sales.
- Franchising costs.
- Repossessed franchises.
- Business combinations.
- Required disclosures relating to franchisors.

Insurance Industry

Reading about the insurance industry will help you understand:

- Classification of insurance contracts.
- Premium revenue recognition for short-duration and long-duration.
- Recognition of claim costs.
- Catastrophe losses of property and liability insurance enterprises.
- Liability for universal life-type contracts.
- Acquisition costs.
- Premium deficiency.
- Internal replacement transaction.
- Policyholder dividends.
- Contingent commission arrangements.
- Investments of an insurance entity.

- Real estate used in the business.
- Income taxes.
- Reinsurance.
- Indemnification against loss or liability relating to insurance risk.
- Recognition of revenues and costs.
- Disclosure requirements.

Motion Picture Industry

Reading about the motion picture industry will help you understand:

- Recognizing revenue by licensing films to movie theaters.
- Films licensed to television.
- Participations.
- Exploitation costs.
- Inventory valuation.
- Costs of films, inventory—story costs and scenarios.
- Home viewing market.
- Disclosure requirements.

Record and Music Industry

Reading about the record and music industry will help you understand:

- Accounting for records and music.
- Accounting for licensors.
- Financial reporting and disclosure.
- Cost determination for records.
- Accounting by licensees.

Government Contracts

Reading about government contracts will help you understand:

- Cost-plus-fixed-fee contracts.
- Renegotiating government contracts.
- Government contract disclosures.
- Terminated war and defense contracts.
- Termination claims disclosure requirements.

Oil and Gas Industry

Reading about the oil and gas industry will help you understand:

- Types of assets utilized in oil and gas producing activities.
- Acquisition costs of properties.
- Exploration and related costs.
- Development.
- Costs of production.
- Support equipment and facilities.
- Assessment and reclassification of unproved properties.
- Depletion of proved properties.
- Depreciation of exploratory drilling and development costs.
- Depreciation of support, equipment, and facilities.
- Dismantlement, restoration, and abandonment costs and salvage values.
- Amortization of oil and gas reserve costs that are produced jointly.
- Information that surfaces after the balance sheet date.
- Surrender and abandonment of properties.
- Mineral property conveyances.
- Accounting for income taxes in the oil and gas industry.
- Capitalizing interest cost under the full cost method.
- Disclosure requirements.

Real Estate Industry

Reading about the real estate industry will help you understand:

- Differences between retail land sales and other sales of real estate.
- Use of the full accrual method.
- Non-consummation of a sale.
- Buyer's initial and continuing investment is not sufficient and as a result doesn't qualify for recognition of profit by the full accrual method.
- Receivable accepted by the seller subject to future subordination.
- Accounting for retail land sales—Use of the full accrual method, percentage of completion method, installment method, deposit method, and disclosure requirements.

Health Care Industry

Reading about the health care industry will help you understand:

- The financial statements of the health care industry.
- Contributions made to not-for-profit health care entities.

Finance Industry

Reading about the finance industry will help you understand:

- Loan origination fees and related costs.
- Commitment fees and costs.
- Purchase of a loan or group of loans.
- Measurement of loans subject to prepayment.
- Income statement and balance sheet classification.

Investment Industry

Reading about the investment industry will help you understand:

- Reporting investment securities at fair value.
- Internal Revenue Code regulations relating to investment companies.
- Exemption from statement of cash flows requirement.

Mortgage Banking Industry

Reading about the mortgage banking industry will help you understand:

- Mortgage loans and mortgage-backed securities.
- Loan and commitment fees.
- Balance sheet classification and disclosures.

SECTION E (CHAPTER 18) Review Questions

Broadcasting Industry

1. What conditions must be satisfied in order for a broadcaster's acquisition of a license agreement for program material to be reported as an asset purchased and liability incurred when the license period commences?

2. What are barter transactions between broadcasters, and how are they accounted for?

Banking and Thrift Industry

3. In general, describe how the acquisition of a bank or thrift institution is accounted for under the purchase method?

4. What are the considerations one should be aware of when regulatory financial assistance is provided in the acquisition of a bank or thrift institution?

Cable Television Industry

5. What is the prematurity period?

6. How are costs accounted for during the prematurity period?

Computer Software Development

7. In creating computer software to be sold, leased or otherwise marketed, how should costs be accounted for?

8. What are product master production costs, and how should they be accounted for?

Franchising Industry: Accounting by Franchisors

9. When should franchise fee revenue from individual franchise sales be recognized by a franchisor? How should individual franchise fees be accounted for? What does "substantial performance" mean?

10. How should continuing franchise fees that the franchisee must pay to the franchisor be accounted for and reported by the latter?

Insurance Industry

11. In general, insurance contracts are classified as short-duration or long-duration. Discuss the characteristics of each of these categories of contracts.

12. How should an insurance entity account for its investments?

Motion Picture Industry

13. What are the accounting and reporting parameters relating to the recognition of revenue by producers and distributors of motion picture films relating to licensing films to movie theaters and to licensing agreements for television program material?

14. What are some typical production costs incurred to produce a film? How are they accounted for?

Record and Music Industry

15. How is compensation to artists accounted for?

16. How are the costs of record masters accounted for?

Government Contracts

17. Government contracts are generally prepared on a cost-plus-fixed-fee (CPFF). Explain this arrangement.

18. When should profits on CPFF contracts with the government be recognized by the contractor?

Oil and Gas Industry

19. How should costs be accounted for in the oil and gas industry under the successful efforts approach?

20. What are the production costs incurred in lifting gas and oil to the surface in the oil and gas industry? Give examples of some of these costs.

Real Estate Industry

21. Distinguish between retail land sales and other sales of real estate. Give examples.

22. What are various ways sales of real estate other than retail land sales may be accounted for?

Health Care Industry

23. What are the required financial statements in the health care industry? Discuss those required of investor-owned health care enterprises and not-for-profit and governmental entities.

24. What are some general guidelines that should be followed in accounting for contributions made to not-for-profit health care entities?

Finance Industry

25. What is the distinction between acquiring a loan by lending or by purchasing? What are direct loan origination costs, and how should they be accounted for? How should other lending-related costs, such as activities performed by the lender for advertising, solicitation of potential borrowers, servicing existing loans, etc., be accounted for?

26. How should fees received for a commitment to originate or purchase a loan or group of loans be accounted for? How should direct loan origination costs incurred to make a commitment to originate a loan be accounted for?

Investment Industry

27. What is an open-end investment company? Describe the equalization accounting method utilized by such companies.

28. What are the conditions that must be met under FASB Statement No. 102 for an investment company to be exempt from including a statement of cash flows as part of its required financial statements?

Mortgage Banking Industry

29. What are mortgage-backed securities, and how are they classified and reported on the financial statements?

30. Mortgage banks may receive or pay nonrefundable loan or commitment fees representing various sources of compensation. What are these fees? Give several examples. How are they accounted for?

SECTION E (CHAPTER 18) Answers to Review Questions

Broadcasting Industry

1. SFAS 63 requires that a broadcaster's acquisition of a license agreement for program material should be reported as an asset purchased and liability incurred when the license period commences and all of the following conditions have been satisfied:

   a. The program material has been accepted by the licensee in accordance with the conditions of the license agreement.

   b. The cost of each program constituting the program package is known or is reasonably determinable.

   c. The program is available for its first showing or telecast. This condition is not met when a conflicting license prevents program broadcasting. However, any restriction under this license or another license with the same licensor regarding programming should not be construed as causing this condition to fail.

   Any program license agreement that has been executed but did not meet the aforementioned three criteria and were not reported as an asset and liability should be fully disclosed in the notes to the financial statements.

2. Broadcasters commonly exchange unsold advertising time for products or services. That is, they frequently engage in barter transactions in which no material amounts of cash exchange hands between the parties involved. All barter transactions (with the exception of trading advertising time for network programming) should be accounted for at the estimated fair value of the products or services received or advertising time given up, whichever is more clearly determinable. The accounting parameters that must be followed in these transactions may be found in APB Opinion Number 29, *Accounting for Nonmonetary Transactions.* Barter revenue should be recognized when commercials are broadcast, and merchandise or services received should be reported when received or used. Thus, if advertising time is broadcast before the products or services are compensatorily received, then a receivable should be recorded at the same time that the advertising revenue is reported. Correspondingly, if merchandise or services are received prior to the broadcast of an advertising commercial, a liability should be recorded.

Banking and Thrift Industry

3. When a banking or thrift institution (including commercial banks, savings and loan associations, mutual savings banks, credit banks, etc.,) is acquired using the purchase method, each asset acquired and liability assumed is allocated a portion of the purchase price based on their fair value at the date of acquisition. That is, each item is separately valued at the date of acquisition. This technique, known as the separate valuation technique, is used to value all the tangible and identifiable intangible assets that are acquired. In general, the difference between the fair value of the tangible and identified intangible assets acquired and liabilities assumed using this method is viewed as goodwill.

4. A regulatory agency may grant financial assistance in the course of an entity acquiring a particular bank or thrift institution. For example, a regulatory agency may agree to pay the extent (the amount) by which future interest received or receivable on the interest-bearing assets acquired is less than the interest cost of carrying those assets for a period by a stated margin. The projected assistance (computed at the date of acquisition) should be considered additional interest on the interest-bearing assets acquired in determining their fair values for the purpose of applying the purchase method in accounting for the combination. Actual assistance should be reported as income in the period in which it accrues. Other forms of assistance may also be granted to either party by a regulatory authority in a combination accounted for by the purchase method. If the assistance is (1) probable and (2) the amount that is expected to be received is reasonably estimable, then the assistance should be accounted for as part of the combination. If either of these two criteria is not met, then any assistance subsequently recognized in the financial statements should be reported as a reduction of the unidentifiable intangible asset, i.e., the goodwill previously described. Subsequent amortization of the goodwill should also be adjusted. Any assistance recognized in excess of that intangible asset should be reported as income of the period. In general, any assets and liabilities that have been or will be transferred to or assumed by a regulatory authority should not be recognized in the acquisition. When financial assistance is granted in connection with the acquisition of a banking or thrift institution, the combined entity may agree to repay all or a part of the assistance that was provided if certain levels of operations are met. Such a repayment obligation should be met by recognizing a liability and charge to income when the repayment contingency is probable and the amount of repayment can be reasonably estimated. The nature and amount of any financial assistance granted to an entity during a given period by a regulatory agency in connection with the acquisition of a bank or thrift institution should be fully disclosed.

Cable Television

5. SFAS 51 presents the standards of financial reporting and disclosure for certain revenues and expenses related to cable television systems. The emphasis of the SFAS is on special accounting rules applicable to the prematurity period. During this period a cablevision television system is partly in use and partly under construction. The prematurity period generally begins with the first earned subscriber revenue and ends when the first major construction period has been completed or the achievement of a specified predetermined subscriber level has been reached. Prematurity status is very common in this industry. For example, over time it is usual for cable companies to expand throughout the geographical area that they have franchised. For large and medium-sized entities, this effort results in many parts of their system being "energized" while construction progresses in others. Thus, except for the smallest systems, programming is delivered to parts of the area being serviced (with revenues being earned) before construction of the entire system is complete. Thus, virtually every medium-sized and large franchise cable television system experiences a prematurity period during which it receives some revenue while continuing to incur substantial costs related to its completion. During the prematurity period, costs incurred that relate to both current and future operations shall be partially capitalized and partially expensed.

6. In general, costs incurred by the system should be charged to the portion of the cable television system in the prematurity period only if they are specifically identified with the operations of that portion. Separate projections for the portion shall be developed and the portion's capitalized costs should be evaluated separately during the prematurity period for recoverability. Other guidance related to accounting in the prematurity period includes the following:

   a. Subscriber-related costs and general and administrative expenses shall be expensed as period costs. Subscriber-related costs are incurred for obtaining and retaining subscribers to the cable television system. They include:

      1. Cost of billing and collection.
      2. Bad debts.
      3. Mailings.
      4. Repairs and maintenance of subscriber connections.
      5. Franchise fees related to revenue or the number of subscribers.
      6. Salary of the system manager and office rent.

7. Programming cost for additional channels used in the marketing effort or costs related to revenues from, or the number of subscribers to, channels or program services.

8. Direct selling costs.

b. Costs of the cable television plant should be capitalized in full, including materials, direct labor, and construction overhead.

c. Programming and other systems costs that are incurred in anticipation of servicing a fully operating system should be allocated between current and future operations. These costs do not change based on the number of subscribers. They include such items as property taxes based on valuation of the cable entity as a fully operating system; pole, underground duct, antenna site, and microwave rental based on rental costs for a fully operating system; and local origination programming to satisfy franchise requirements.

The proportion attributable to current operations shall be expensed currently and the remainder of the expenditures should be capitalized. The amount that should be expensed in the current period is derived by multiplying the total expenditures for the month by the following fraction:

The greatest of:

	a. The average number of subscribers expected that month as estimated at the beginning of the prematurity period.
Amount to be expensed = currently	**b.** The average number of subscribers that would be attained using at least equal (straight-line) monthly progress in adding new subscribers towards the estimate of subscribers that would be attained at the end of the prematurity period.
	c. The average number of actual subscribers divided by the Total number of subscribers that are expected at the end of the prematurity period

This fraction should be determined each month of the prematurity period.

In addition, depreciation and amortization expense should be determined by multiplying the monthly depreciation and amortization based on total capitalized costs expected on completion of the prematurity period by the fraction using the depreciation that will be applied by the entity after the prematurity period.

Computer Software Development

7. GAAP in the area of computer software to be sold, leased, or otherwise marketed relates to computer software developed internally and to software purchased. In creating a computer software product, costs incurred internally should be expensed when incurred to research and development costs until technological feasibility for the product has been established. Technological feasibility is deemed established when a detailed program design or working model for the product is completed. Thereafter, all software production costs should be capitalized and amortized to current and future periods.

8. Product master production cost incurred subsequent to the establishment of technological feasibility should be capitalized. These costs generally include the performance of coding and testing. SFAS 86 indicates that no software production costs shall be capitalized until technological feasibility has been established for the software and all R&D activities for the other components of the product or process has been completed. The capitalization process should be discontinued when the product is ready and available for general release to customers. Maintenance and customer support costs should be charged to expense when these costs are incurred or the related revenue is recognized from the product's sale.

Franchising Industry: Accounting by Franchisors

9. Franchise fee revenue from individual franchise sales should be recognized when the franchisor has substantially performed and satisfied all material services or conditions relating to the sale. SFAS 45 indicates that substantial performance on the part of the franchisor means:

   a. There is no obligation or intent to refund any cash received or forgive any unpaid notes or receivables.

   b. All initial services that the franchisor was contractually required to do by the signed franchise agreement has been completed.

   c. No significant responsibilities related to substantial performance by the franchisor remain.

   In addition, a provision for estimated uncollectible initial franchise fees should be recorded to insure a proper matching of revenues and costs. In exceptional cases, when franchise fee revenue is collected over an extended period, and no reasonable basis exists for estimating collectibility, it may be necessary to use the installment or cost recovery methods to account for revenue recognition. Unless there are unusual circumstances, substantial performance cannot take place before the franchisee starts his operation. Oftentimes, a franchise agreement calls for a large initial franchise fee and relatively small continuing franchise fees providing for future services that the franchiser agrees to perform throughout the term of the franchise agreement. If it is determined that the continuing fee will not cover the cost of the continuing services performed by the franchisor as well as earning a reasonable profit, then a portion of the initial franchise fee should be deferred and subsequently amortized over the life of the franchise. That is, the portion of the initial franchise fee that is deferred should be sufficient to cover the estimated cost in excess of continuing franchise fees and the earning of a reasonable profit on the continuing services themselves.

10. A franchisee may be contractually required to pay continuing franchise fees to a franchisor for the continued use of the franchised rights as well as for services performed by the franchisor. These fees should be reported by the franchisor as revenue as the fees are earned and become a receivable to the franchisor. In addition, any costs incurred by the franchisor related to the franchise fees should be expensed as incurred. The earnings process must be honored even though a portion of the continuing fee is designated for a particular purpose such as an advertising program. It should not be recognized as revenue until the fee is earned and becomes receivable from the franchisee. An exception exists when a franchise arrangement is an agency arrangement under which a portion of the continuing fee is required to be segregated and used for a special purpose. In this situation, the segregated amount should be recorded as a liability by the franchisor against which costs incurred by the franchisee would be charged.

Insurance Industry

11. *Classification of insurance contracts:* In general, insurance contracts are classified as short-duration or long-duration. SFAS 60 discusses each category in the following way:

   - *Short-duration contracts:* Most property and liability insurance contracts are considered short-duration. These contracts cover expected claim costs resulting from insured events that occur during a fixed period of short duration. The insurance company, in this situation, has the right to cancel the contract or revise the premium at the beginning of each contract period covering insured events. This enables the insurer to adjust the amount of the premiums charged or coverage provided at the end of each period. As was noted, short-duration contracts include most property and liability insurance contracts. It also includes certain term life insurance contracts such as credit life insurance. (Credit life insurance is decreasing term insurance issued on the lives of borrowers to cover the payment of debt of the insured.) Accident and health insurance contracts, for example, may be short-duration or long-duration based on whether the contract is expected to remain in force for an extended period. *Premiums from short-duration contracts are earned and recognized as revenue even as the insurance protection is consumed.*

- *Long-duration contracts:* Long-duration contracts include those insurance contracts that are expected to remain in force for an extended period such as whole-life, universal life, guaranteed renewable term life, endowment, annuity, title insurance, and participating life insurance contracts. These types of contracts are generally not subject to unilateral changes in their provisions. For example, policies that are of long-duration may be noncancellable or may be a guaranteed renewable contract. Premiums from long-duration insurance contracts are generally level even though the policy benefits and services provided do not occur evenly over the contract periods. They are recognized as revenue throughout the pay periods of the contract. Since this premium revenue generally exceeds the policy benefits that will be derived in the early years of the contract, the insurer is required to accrue a liability for the costs that are expected to be paid in the later years of the contract. Thus, for most types of long-duration contracts, a liability is accrued for current and expected renewal contract periods. The amount of the liability is equal to the present value of estimated future policy benefits to be paid policyholders, less the present value of estimated future net premiums to be collected from policyholders. These estimates are based on several assumptions such as investment yields, mortality, morbidity (the incidence of disability due to disease or physical impairment), terminations, and other expenses.

12. An insurance enterprise should account for its investments in debt and equity securities that have readily determinable fair values in accordance with SFAS 115, *Accounting for Certain Investments in Debt and Equity Securities.* Investments that are not addressed by SFAS 115 because they do not have a readily determinable fair value should also be reported at fair value with changes in such values accounted for as unrealized gains and losses and reported net of taxes in a separate component of equity.

Mortgage loans should be reported at their outstanding principal balance if acquired at par value. If they were purchased at a discount or premium, they should be reported at amortized cost with an allowance for estimated uncollectible amounts. Amortization of the discount or premium and related charges or credits should be charged or credited to investment income.

Investments in assets in which the holder would not recover substantially its recorded investment (such as interest-only strips, loans, other receivables, retained interests in securitizations, etc.) should be classified as investments in debt securities and reported in the available-for-sale or trading portfolio.

Real estate investments should be reported at its cost less any accumulated depreciation. Depreciation and related charges or credits should be charged or credited to investment income.

Motion Picture Industry

13. Exhibition rights to motion pictures are sold through the process of licensure based on either a flat fee or a percentage of the box office receipts. The entities licensing the motion picture may be motion picture production companies, independent producers, or distributors. Distributors own the rights to distribute films to movie theaters, individual television station, groups of stations, networks, etc. The licensing entities may require a nonrefundable guarantee against a percentage of the box office receipts. The guarantee in some markets, such as foreign markets, constitute the amount that the motion picture exhibition rights are sold for because the licensors have no means of controlling the distribution of the movie and ascertaining the actual percentage of box office receipts due with any degree of accuracy.

Motion picture revenues should be recognized on a percentage of box office receipts or flat fee basis when the film is actually shown. Thus, the date of exhibition is the date on which revenue is realized and accordingly recognized. If a nonrefundable guarantee is prepaid, it should be deferred and recognized as revenue on the date that the motion picture is run. SFAS 53 notes that guarantees received by licensors that are in substance outright sales due to the circumstances previously noted (e.g., foreign markets) should be considered revenue if all of the following conditions are met when the license period begins:

a. The license fee for each film is known.

b. The cost of each film is known or reasonably determinable.

c. Collectibility of the full license fee is reasonably assured.

d. The film has been accepted by the licensee in accordance with the conditions of the license agreement.

e. The film is available for its first showing or telecast. Restrictions under the same license agreement or another license agreement with the same licensee preventing usage should not affect this condition.

However, a conflicting license that prevents usage by the licensee does represent a bona fide obstacle to satisfying this condition.

A license agreement for television program material is granted by either motion picture producers, independent producers, or distributors (licensors) granting a broadcaster (licensee) the right to telecast either a specified or unlimited number of showings over a specified maximum period of time for a specified fee. A license agreement typically covers several films and contains a separate license for each film in the package covered by the overall license agreement. The licensee must pay the contracted fee whether or not exhibition rights are exercised and the rights revert to the licensor with no refund if they are not exercised.

SFAS 53 notes that revenue is to be recognized for television programming licensure when the license period begins and all of the following conditions have been met:

a. The license fee for each film is known.

b. The cost of each film is known or reasonably determinable.

c. Collectibility of the full license fee is reasonably assured.

d. The film has been accepted by the licensee in accordance with the conditions of the license agreement.

e. The film is available for its first showing or telecast. Restrictions under the same license agreement or another license agreement with the same licensee preventing usage should not affect this condition. However, a conflicting license that prevents usage by the licensee shall represent a bona fide obstacle to satisfying this condition.

When these conditions have been satisfied, the licensor and licensee are contractually bound and are required to comply with all the terms of the license agreement. If considerations arise that indicate doubt regarding one or both of the parties' ability to contractually perform, then revenue recognition should be deferred until these considerations no longer exist.

Revenues derived from licensing a film should be recognized in the same order as the market-by-market utilization of the film and at the time the licensee is able to exercise rights under the contractual agreement. That time would be the later of (1) the beginning of the license period or (2) the expiration of a conflicting license making the licensor able to then deliver the right to the licensee. The amount of sales revenue that should be recognized should be accounted for at the present value of the license fee specified in the contract.

14. Costs incurred to produce a film are known as production costs. They include the cost of the story and scenario to be used for the film and other costs typically consisting of :

a. Salaries of cast, directors, producers, extras, and miscellaneous staff.

b. Cost of set construction and operations, wardrobe, and accessories.

c. Cost of sound synchronization.

d. Production overhead including depreciation and amortization of studio equipment and leasehold improvements used in production.

e. Rental of facilities on location.

Production costs are normally accumulated by individual films in four sequential steps:

a. Acquisition of story rights.

b. Preproduction activities including script development, costume design, and construction.

c. Principal photography, which includes the actual filming of the movie.

d. Postproduction costs including sound synchronization and editing.

The culmination of all these activities results in the completed master negative.

All production costs should be capitalized as film cost inventory and should be amortized using the individual-film-forecast-computation method. Another amortization method, the periodic-table-computation method may be used if its results approximates the outcome that would have been achieved using the individual-film-forecast-computation method. The overall objective of the amortization of film cost inventory is to reasonably relate the cost of the film to the gross revenues being reported and to generate a constant rate of gross profit before all period costs. The amortization of film cost should commence when a film is released and revenues are recognized. A discussion of the two amortization methods follow:

- *Individual-film-forecast-computation method:* This method amortizes film costs in the same ratio as current gross revenues bears to anticipated total gross revenue. That is, a fraction is computed with the numerator consisting of gross revenues from the film for the current period and the denominator being the anticipated total gross revenues from the film during its useful life including future estimated total gross revenues derived from all markets in which the film will be seen. **Note:** The amount recognized as revenue related to the sale of long-term, noninterest-bearing television exhibition rights should be included in an amount equal to the total estimated present value of those revenues as of the date they are expected to be recognized. Thus, the present value rather than the gross proceeds of the revenues from television exhibition rights should be included in both the numerator and denominator. The resulting fraction is then applied to production and other capitalized costs to determine the amortization for each period.

In computing the ratio, the estimates of anticipated total gross revenues should be periodically revised when necessary to reflect current information. When, in fact, anticipated total gross revenues are revised, a new fraction should be created where the numerator consists of actual gross revenue for the current period and the denominator includes only the anticipated total gross revenues from the beginning of the current year. The fraction that results should then be applied to unrecovered production and other capitalized costs as of the beginning of the current year to determine the annual amortization.

- *The periodic-table-computation method:* This method amortizes film costs using tables that were prepared from the historic revenue patterns of a large group of films. It is predicated on the assumption that past experience will provide a reasonable guide for future groups of films. In general, this method should be used only to amortize the portion of film costs relating to film rights licensed to movie theaters. In addition, as previously noted, it should only be used when the results of its use would approximate that which would be derived from the use of the individual-film-forecast-computation method. If the periodic-table-computation method is used, the periodic tables upon which it is based should be revised regularly whenever revenue patterns significantly change. In general, the periodic-table-computation method should not be used for a film whose distribution pattern differs significantly from those films used in compiling the table upon which its amortization is based.

Record and Music Industry

15. Royalties earned by recording artists should be adjusted for anticipated returns and should be charged to expense in the period in which the sale of the recording takes place. If an advance royalty is paid to an artist, it should be reported as an asset if the artist's current popularity and past performance provide a valid basis for estimating the amount of the advance that will be recoverable from future royalties to be earned by the artist. Advances should be charged to expense as subsequent royalties are earned by the artist. If it appears that a portion of future royalties are not recoverable from future royalties to be earned by the artist, they should

be charged to expense in the period in which the loss becomes apparent. Advance royalties should be classified as either current or noncurrent assets.

16. Costs for record masters incurred by a record company should be reported as an asset if the current popularity and past performance of the artist indicates a sound basis for estimating the recovery of cost from future sales. Otherwise the cost should be charged to expense. Costs that are recognized as assets should be amortized over the estimated life of the recorded performance using a method that reasonably matches the amount of net revenue to be realized.

   The part of the cost of record masters (incurred by the record company) that are recoverable from the royalties of an artist should be accounted for as an advance royalty as discussed in the previous section on compensation to artists.

Government Contracts

17. Government contracts are generally prepared on a cost-plus-fixed-fee (CPFF) structure, which allows for possible renegotiation if the government believes that the contract has been generating excess profits. In addition, the government usually reserves the right in these agreements to terminate the contract at its convenience.

   CPFF contracts allows the contractor to collect a fixed fee from the government as well as all costs incurred required to satisfy the contract. The government, in contracting for the construction of some product or the performance of services, may choose at its discretion to withhold a certain percentage of payments due on the contract while the work is being performed. If the government should choose to terminate the contract for a given reason, then the contractor is entitled to be repaid for all costs incurred as well as a proportionate part of the contracted fixed fee.

18. A contractor should not recognize any profits on CPFF contracts until the services have been fully performed and accepted unconditionally by the government or the product that has been manufactured has been deemed to meet the government's contractual standards. However, if a government contract is expected to last over an extended number of years, then the contractor should use the percentage-of-completion method.

   When accounting for CPFF contracts, the following general rules prevail:

   a. When the contract calls for only the performance of services by the contractor, then all fees charged should be included in the contractor's revenue account.

    b. When the contract involves the manufacture of goods and products, then contractor's sales and revenue accounts should include the fees generated on the project as well as all reimbursable costs.

Oil and Gas Industry

19. GAAP advocates but does not require the use of the successful efforts approach of accounting for oil- and gas-producing activities. Under this method, costs should be accounted for as follows:

    a. Geological and geophysical costs and costs of carrying and retaining undeveloped properties should be charged to expense as incurred.

    b. Costs of drilling exploratory wells and exploratory-type stratigraphic test wells that do not realize proved reserves should be charged to expense when the wells do not find proved reserves.

    c. Costs of acquiring properties, costs of drilling development wells and development-type stratigraphic test wells, and costs of drilling successful exploratory wells and exploratory-type stratigraphic test wells should be capitalized.

    d. The capitalized costs of wells and related equipment are amortized as related oil and gas reserves are produced.

    e. Costs of unproved properties should be assessed periodically and a loss should be recognized if it is determined that the properties are impaired.

20. The production process involves bringing the oil and gas to the surface as well as gathering, treating, field processing, and storing them. Production costs include those costs needed to operate and maintain an entity's wells, related equipment and facilities, depreciation and other costs of operating support equipment and facilities. These costs become part of the oil and gas that is produced. The following are examples of production costs incurred in lifting gas and oil to the surface:

    a. Costs of labor to operate the wells and related equipment and facilities.

    b. Repairs and maintenance.

    c. Materials, supplies, and fuel consumed, and services utilized in operating the wells and related equipment and facilities.

    d. Property taxes and insurance applicable to proved properties and wells and related equipment and facilities.

    e. Severance taxes.

In addition to the aforementioned production costs, depreciation, depletion, amortization of capitalized acquisition, exploration and development costs also become part of the cost of oil and gas produced.

Real Estate Industry

21. Retail land sales are sales, on a volume basis, of lots that are subdivisions of large tracts of land. They are characterized by the following: very small down payments; the inability of the seller to enforce the sales contract or the buyer's note against the buyer's general credit; return of the buyer's down payment if the cancellation is made within an established cancellation period; defaults by the buyer after the cancellation resulting in recovery of the land by the seller and forfeiture of at least some of the principal payments by the buyer. Amounts retained by the seller are determined by federal and state laws.

    Examples of real estate sales transactions that are not retail land sales are:

    - Sales of lots to builders.
    - Sales of homes, buildings, and parcels of land to builder of land and others.
    - Sales of corporate stock of enterprises with substantial real estate.
    - Sales of a partnership interest that is in substance a sale of real estate. For example, an enterprise that forms a partnership arranging for the partnership to acquire the property directly from third parties, and selling an interest in the partnership to investors who then become limited partners.
    - Sales of time-sharing interests if the sales are in substance sales of real estate. Timesharing real estate interests represent the right to occupy a dwelling for a designated period each year.

22. Sales of real estate other than retail land sales may be accounted for in one of several of the following ways:

    - *The full accrual method*—Profit is recognized when the real estate is sold.
    - *Cost recovery method*—Profit recognition is deferred until cash received exceeds the seller's cost of the property sold.
    - *Deposit method*—No recognition of profit at consummation of the sale.
    - *Reduced profit method*—Profit is deferred until payments are made.
    - *Percentage-of–completion*—The amount of profit recognition is predicated on the relationship of costs incurred to the total costs to be incurred.
    - *Installment method*

Health Care Industry

23. Investor-owned health care enterprises are required to prepare the same financial statements as those of any investor-owned enterprise. Not-for-

profit and governmental health care entities, on the other hand, are required to prepare the following financial statements:

   a. Statement of Operations

   b. Statement of Financial Position

   c. Statement of Changes in Equity (or Net Assets/Fund balance)

   d. Statement of Cash Flows

   e. Notes to the Financial Statements

24. The following are some general guidelines that should be followed in accounting for contributions made to not-for-profit health care entities:

   a. Contributions made should be disclosed as resulting in increases in net assets from amounts that are:

   1. Permanently restricted,

   2. Temporarily restricted, or

   3. Unrestricted.

   b. Contributed collections consisting of historical works, art, etc., that are held for education, research, or public exhibition are not required to be capitalized and recognized as revenue in the financial statements.

   c. Contributions in service should not be recognized in the financial statements unless the following conditions are met:

   1. Individuals providing the service contribution are qualified to do so with unique, specialized skills.

   2. The service contribution resulted in the production or enhancement of nonfinancial assets.

   Some not-for-profit health care entities are charitable enterprises that must conform with donor and grantor fiduciary responsibilities and guidelines. Therefore, these entities must use fund accounting in preparing their financial statements.

Finance Industry

25. An entity may acquire a loan by lending or by purchasing. The former situation is termed *originating a loan*, which is known as acquiring the loan from a party or other borrower. Direct loan origination costs should be deferred and recognized as a reduction in the yield of the loan. Direct loan origination costs should include only the following:

   a. Incremental direct costs of the loan origination incurred in transactions with independent third parties for that loan, and

   b. Certain costs directly related to the loan performed by the lender. For example, these activities include evaluating the potential buyer's borrower's financial condition, evaluating and recording guarantees, collateral, and other security arrangements, etc.

All other lending-related costs include costs related to activities performed by the lender for such activities as advertising, soliciting potential borrowers, servicing existing loans, and other activities related to establishing and monitoring credit policies, supervision, and administration. These costs should be charged to expense as incurred.

26. In general, fees received for a commitment to originate or purchase a loan or group of loans should be deferred, and if the commitment is exercised, recognized over the life of the loan as an adjustment of the related loan's yield. If the commitment expires, unused, then the fee should be recognized in income at the date of the expiration of the commitment. There are two exceptions to this general rule. A brief explanation of these follow:

   a. If the amount of the commitment fee is determined retrospectively as a percentage of the line of credit available but unused in a previous period, if that percentage is nominal in percentage in relation to the stated interest rate on any related borrowing, and if that borrowing will bear a market interest rate at the date the loan is made, the commitment should be recognized as service fee income as of the determination date.

   b. If it is determined by the lending entity that the likelihood of commitment exercise is remote, the commitment fee should be recognized over the commitment period on a straight-line basis as service fee income. If the commitment is subsequently exercised in fact, over the commitment period, the remaining unamortized commitment fee at the time of exercise should be recognized over the term of the loan as an adjustment of its yield.

   Direct loan origination costs incurred to make a commitment to originate a loan should be offset against any related commitment fee and the net amount recognized as a commitment fee described above.

Investment Industry

27. An *open-end investment company* is one that sells its shares to the public on an ongoing basis and is always willing to buy back its shares from investors who tender them for redemption. In accounting for an open-end company, a method known as equalization is utilized. This process precludes dilution of shareholders' per share equity in undistributed net investment income that results from the ongoing sales and redemption of mutual fund shares. The investment company makes the assumption that the net asset value of each share sold or redeemed is made up of the par value of the stock, additional paid in capital, any undistributed income,

and any retained earnings that exist. As shares are bought and sold, the investment company continually determines the magnitude of undistributed earnings that are available for its shareholders to receive. Based on the number of shares outstanding, this amount is added to an equalization account when the shares are sold and subtracted when the shares are redeemed.

28. FASB Statement Number 102 provides that an investment company is exempt from including a statement of cash flows as part of its required financial statements if the following conditions are met:

   a. The company's investments are all highly liquid.

   b. The company includes a statement of changes in net assets with its financial statements.

   c. The company had an immaterial amount of debt relative to its average total assets based on its average debt outstanding during the accounting period.

   d. The company's investments were carried at market value in the accounting records and financial statements.

Mortgage Banking Industry

29. Mortgage-backed securities are securities that are issued by a governmental agency or corporation [e.g., Governmental National Mortgage Association (GNMA) or Federal National Mortgage Association (FNMA)] or by private issuers. These are securities that are referred to as mortgage participation certificates or pass-through certificates (PCS). These certificates represent an undivided interest in a pool of specific mortgage loans. In general, mortgage-backed securities held for sale with respect to mortgage banking activities should be classified as trading securities and reported at fair value.

30. Mortgage banks may receive or pay nonrefundable loan or commitment fees representing various sources of compensation. These fees may include, for example, an adjustment of the interest yield on the loan, a fee for designating funds for the borrower, or an offset of loan origination costs. Loan and commitment fees should be accounted for in the following manner:

   a. *Loan origination fees and costs*: If the loan is held for resale, loan origination costs should be deferred until the related loan is sold. If the loan is held for investment, such fees and costs should be deferred and recognized as an adjustment of yield.

   b. *Fees for services rendered*: Fees for the reimbursement for the costs of specific services performed by third parties with respect to originating a loan, such as appraisal fees, should be recognized as revenue when the services have been performed.

c. *Fees relating to loans held for sale:* In general, fees received for guaranteeing the funding of mortgage loans to borrowers, builders, or developers should be deferred and recognized over the life of the loan as an adjustment of yield. Fees paid to permanent investors to ensure the sale of loans (residential or commercial loan commitment fees) should be recognized as expense when the loans are sold to permanent investors or when it appears that the commitment will not be used. In general, residential loan commitment fees relate to blocks of loans, therefore fees recognized as revenue or expense as a result of individual loans transactions should be based on the ratio of the individual loan amount to the total commitment amount.

Loan placement fees, that is, fees generated for arranging a commitment directly between a permanent investor and a borrower should be recognized as revenue when all significant services have been performed. In another situation, if a mortgage banking entity obtains a commitment from a permanent investor before or at the time a related commitment is made to a borrower and if the commitment to the borrower requires that the following conditions occur, then the related fees should also be accounted for as loan placement fees. The two conditions that must be satisfied are:

1. Simultaneous assignment of the commitment to the investor.

2. Simultaneous transfer to the borrower of the amount received from the investor.

d. *Expired commitments and prepayments of loans:* If a loan commitment expires without the loan being made or if a loan is repaid before the estimated repayment date, any unrelated unrecognized fees should be recorded as revenue or expense at that time.

PUBLISHER GRADED EXAMINATION: SECTION E (CHAPTER 18)

1. (T or F) Franchise fee revenue should be recognized when the franchiser has provided substantial performance.

2. (T or F) Movie production costs that have been capitalized as film cost inventory should not be amortized using the individual-film-forecast computation method.

3. (T or F) In the insurance industry, investment contracts are insurance agreements not involving significant insurance risks accounted for as interest-bearing financial instruments.

4. (T or F) In the mortgage industry, accounting for mortgage loans requires that a distinction be made between those held for sale and those held as long-term investments.

5. (T or F) Loan origination fees for loans held for sale should be capitalized as part of the book value of the related loan and then amortized.

6. (T or F) A license agreement for the sale of film rights for television may be reported before revenue is recognized.

7. (T or F) In accounting for recording artists' revenue, earned royalties should be adjusted for expected returns and should be charged to a liability account in the year of the sale of the recording.

8. (T or F) Story costs in the motion picture industry that have been held and unused for more than three years should be charged to production overhead in the current year.

9. (T or F) Mortgage-backed securities held for sale in the mortgage banking industry should be classified as trading securities and presented at fair value.

10. (T or F) Premiums should be recognized as revenue over the insurance contract period in proportion to the amount of insurance protection provided in accounting for short-duration insurance contracts.

11. (T or F) Development costs should be capitalized by oil companies as part of the cost of an enterprise's wells and related equipment and facilities whether or not the well is successful or unsuccessful.

12. (T or F) The costs to acquire or construct support equipment in the oil and gas industry should be capitalized.

13. (T or F) In the motion picture industry, movie exhibition rights are sold through licensure and may be based on either a flat fee or a percentage of box office receipts.

14. (T or F) Under GAAP, costs incurred internally in the development of computer software should be capitalized as research and development expenditures until technological feasibility occurs.

15. (T or F) The unit-of-production method should be used in amortizing the acquisition costs of proved properties that are capitalized.

16. (T or F) Production costs become part of the oil and gas that is produced in the oil and gas industry.

17. (T or F) Dividend income should be recognized as revenue by the recipient on the ex-dividend date.

18. (T or F) When franchiser efforts related to the initial services are significantly impacted by the number of outlets opened in an area, franchise fees should be recognized based on the proportion of number of outlets opened.

19. (T or F) An insurance company should not account for its investment portfolio of debt and equity securities at cost.

20. (T or F) In the cable television industry, hookup revenue should be recognized as income to the extent to which direct selling costs are incurred.

21. (T or F) In the cable television industry, direct selling costs do not include supervisory and administrative expenses.

22. (T or F) Dividends on an insurance policy should not be accrued by the policy holder.

23. (T or F) In the cable television industry, GAAP provides that the prematurity period should not exceed more than ten years.

24. (T or F) Loan origination fees should be deferred and recognized as an adjustment to yield for loans held for investment.

25. (T or F) In accounting for computer software development costs, GAAP requires that balance sheet disclosure be presented at the lower of amortized cost or net realizable value.

26. (T or F) An investment company's purchase or sale of investment securities should be recorded at the settlement date.

27. (T or F) In accordance with GAAP, the appropriate disclosure of a capitalized program license agreement on the balance sheet of the licensee is lower of amortized cost or net realizable value.

28. (T or F) Health care entities should not use the accrual basis of accounting in the recording of revenue.

29. (T or F) Disclosure of mortgage loans held for sale should be presented on the balance sheet at the lower of cost or market.

30. (T or F) The costs incurred when computer software are duplicated from product masters should be recorded on a unit-specific inventory basis.

31. (T or F) A statement of changes in equity is not required to be prepared by not-for-profit and governmental health care entities.

32. (T or F) The premature period begins with the receipt of the first earned subscriber income in the cable television industry.

33. (T or F) In the insurance industry, estimated reinsurance receivables should always be presented separately.

34. (T or F) In accounting for franchisers, when a franchiser repurchases a franchise, the initial fee should never be deferred and considered a reduction of the repurchase price when the option is exercised.

35. (T or F) In the franchising industry, direct deferred franchising costs should not exceed the anticipated revenue less additional estimated costs.

36. (T or F) The equalization method is used to account for transactions in an open-end investment company.

37. (T or F) In the broadcasting industry, a broadcaster's network affiliation contract is accounted for as an intangible asset.

38. (T or F) In the motion picture industry, the inventory costs of a motion picture includes the unamortized production and exploitation costs of the movie.

39. (T or F) New and renewal insurance contract acquisition costs should not be expensed as incurred.

40. (T or F) In the gas and oil industry, the capitalized costs of drilling the well should become part of the company's wells and related equipment and facilities if proved reserves have been found by the well.

41. (T or F) Except for certain retrospectively determined fees, loan commitment fees should be deferred.

42. (T or F) In the real estate industry, if a sale has not yet been consummated, the deposit method of accounting should be used.

43. (T or F) Finance companies in accounting for a loan origination fee should defer and recognize this amount over the term of the related loan as an adjustment of yield and as an adjustment of interest income.

44. (T or F) Unpaid claim costs should not be accrued when an insured event occurs.

45. (T or F) An investment company is not required to distribute all of its taxable income and taxable realized gains to its stockholders in accordance with GAAP.

46. (T or F) Investment companies are required to disclose their investment securities at market value.

47. (T or F) Fees paid to permanent investors should be recognized as expenses when loans are sold.

48. (T or F) In the motion picture industry, accounting for film inventories requires that the components of the films be disclosed.

49. (T or F) Barter transaction revenue resulting from commercials should be recognized when the commercials are in fact broadcasted.

50. (T or F) The cost recovery method may never be used in accounting for sales of real estate other than retail land sales.

51. (T or F) During the prematurity period, subscriber-related costs should not be deferred and recorded as an asset.

52. (T or F) The amortization of a film, under generally accepted accounting principles, should begin when the film is released and revenue is recognized.

53. (T or F) Acquired broadcasting rights should not be expensed immediately.

54. (T or F) Capitalized software computer costs should not be amortized on a product-by-product basis.

55. (T or F) A highly liquid investment company may be exempt from including a statement of cash flows in its required financial statements if certain conditions are satisfied.

56. (T or F) The sale of lots to builders is not considered a retail land sale.

57. (T or F) Amortization expense of deferred software costs in accounting for computer software development costs is based on the lower of the percentage of current revenues to current and expected revenues or straight-line amortization.

58. (T or F) Financial aid received from a regulatory agency resulting when a business acquires a troubled bank should be reported as a reduction of goodwill recorded in the acquisition.

59. (T or F) The cost of sales discounts that arise from infrequent incentives to sell retail land should not be deferred as an asset.

60. (T or F) Commitment (loan) fees should be deferred and recognized over the life of the loan or until the loan is sold.

61. (T or F) Indirect franchising costs that are of a continuing nature should be expensed.

62. (T or F) In the broadcasting industry, the licensing agreement of a broadcaster that conveys the rights to televise a program is accounted for as a group of rights.

63. (T or F) The recognition of revenue by producers when movie film rights are licensed to movie theaters occurs when the films are shown.

GAAP Handbook of Policies and Procedures, 2001
Self-Study CPE Program
Answer Sheet

Please photocopy this form and the form on the facing page for as many tests as you intend to take (sections A-E). Indicate section A, B, C, D or E and record your answers below. Also complete the evaluation. Return answer sheet and evaluation form to:

> Luis Gonzalez
> CPE Coordinator
> Prentice Hall
> 240 Frisch Court
> Paramus, NJ 07652

Each section is $50.00. Make checks or money orders payable to Prentice Hall/CPE Program.

Name _____

Address Line 1 _____

Address Line 2 _____

City/State/Zip code _____

CPA License # _____

SECTION: _____ (Please indicate A, B, C, D, or E)

1.___	2.___	3.___	4.___	5.___	6.___	7.___	8.___	9.___	10.___
11.___	12.___	13.___	14.___	15.___	16.___	17.___	18.___	19.___	20.___
21.___	22.___	23.___	24.___	25.___	26.___	27.___	28.___	29.___	30.___
31.___	32.___	33.___	34.___	35.___	36.___	37.___	38.___	39.___	40.___
41.___	42.___	43.___	44.___	45.___	46.___	47.___	48.___	49.___	50.___
51.___	52.___	53.___	54.___	55.___	56.___	57.___	58.___	59.___	60.___
61.___	62.___	63.___	64.___	65.___	66.___	67.___	68.___	69.___	70.___
71.___	72.___								

GAAP Handbook of Policies and Procedures, 2001
Self-Study CPE Program
Evaluation Form

SECTION _____ (Please indicate A, B, C, D, or E)

1. Were you informed in advance of the:

—Course objectives? Y _____ N _____

—Requisite level of experience? Y _____ N _____

—Program content? Y _____ N _____

—Type and degree of preparation necessary? Y _____ N _____

—Method of instruction? Y _____ N _____

—Number of CPE credit hours? Y _____ N _____

2. Do you agree with our assessment of:

—Course objectives? Y _____ N _____

—Level of experience needed to complete the course? Y _____ N _____

—Program content? Y _____ N _____

—Type and degree of preparation necessary? Y _____ N _____

—Teaching method? Y _____ N _____

—Number of CPE credit hours? Y _____ N _____

3. Was the material relevant? Y _____ N _____

4. Was the content displayed effectively? Y _____ N _____

5. Did the course enhance your professional competence? Y _____ N _____

6. Was the course content timely and effective? Y _____ N _____

Index